Jerry
I am grateful f
& I hope you us
ad.

Wilson

SURVIVING ANARCHY

History, Challenges and Prospects for Regional Integration in Southern Africa

WILSON KHEMBO

SURVIVING ANARCHY

ISBN 978-99908-0-984-8

Cover design by
Wanthaza Mdu Mughogho

Editing and typesetting at
Skillsway Books

Published in Malawi by

Skillsway Books
Email: info@skillsway.org
Website: www.skillsway.org
Phone: +265 995 199 600
Lilongwe, Malawi

Table of Contents

FOREWORD

For the people of Southern Africa, the dream of the future looks different from the present and realising this dream requires action. While regional integration schemes have profound significance, a comprehensive review of the quality and impact of Southern African Development Cooperation (SADC) has long been neglected until now. With the lacklustre performance of SADC in the last three decades, we know from evidence that institutions have a significant impact on the success or failure of the regional integration agenda. This book presents and analyses SADC's issues in a holistic and unprecedented manner. SADC's history has shaped regional politics and economics and resulted in complex dynamics in a region that espouses sustainable and deeper integration, a lot more in theory than it does in practice. This book also presents historical facts, some of which have likely been introduced for the first time in the public domain which, have influenced the tide of politics in the region. Like the proverbial chameleon, the author looks backwards while presenting an insightful analysis of the present situation and the foreseeable future. There could have never been a better title that captures the resilience of the population of Southern Africa in defeating potential dictators through the ballot while surviving human security challenges such as drought, natural disasters and pandemics.

As far as regional governance is concerned, with no threat of inter-state armed conflict, the militaries of the SADC have regularly engaged in confidence-building measures via defence diplomacy. While the boldness manifested by the region in the formation of the Force Intervention Brigade (FIB) to support the United Nations Stabilisation Mission in the Democratic Republic of the Congo (MONUSCO) is commended, their stifling of the SADC Tribunal is condemned for crippling mechanisms to deal with governance challenges in the region effectively.

Although significant strides have been taken on economic integration showing a trend of a bottom-up integration agenda, intra-region trade remains below par as exports are still limited to few minerals and agricultural commodities destined for markets outside the region. The book identifies are as needing improvement that could drive the dream to prosperity and resilient Southern Africa. The book has benefitted from classical knowledge and new findings in the regional integration literature to re-imagine integration in Southern Africa.

This book challenges the SADC member states to unlearn old behaviours, closely-held prejudices, and embrace new thinking and redefine how nation-states relate to each other to successfully forge ahead with transforming the regional security, political, governance, and economic environment. I hope this book will assist individual citizens and policymakers in the SADC region and beyond to set an agenda for change in a chaotic but hopeful region. Just like SADC leaders and citizens have always endeavoured to bring lasting peace and prosperity to the region, the book sets the tone for the actualisation of that dream. Both the political and economic dimensions of regional integration in Southern Africa should operate as engines to effectively cope with regional poverty, xenophobia, corruption, inequality and unemployment.

Dan Kuwali
Extraordinary Professor of International Law, University of Pretoria; Adjunct Professor of Strategic Studies, Malawi University of Science and Technology; Fellow, Center for Human Rights, Harvard Kennedy School of Government

PREFACE

Now that this book project is complete, I can now perfectly appreciate the burning desire that kept me pushing forward. Some explanation must be given why Southern Africa deserves another book on regional integration. One important reason is the limited scope of the existing literature on regional integration in Southern Africa. Most books on regional integration in Southern Africa neglect to acknowledge the region's history, whose influence defines the integration model adopted. Many scholars are adopting an ahistorical perspective on integration that overlooks the underlying factors that shape integration agendas.

My first objective was to pay attention to the historical context by demonstrating the development and evolution of the Southern African Community. My interest in tracing the integration history was not to periodise the Southern African history per se. Instead, I intended to contextualise many of the current controversies and debates surrounding regional integration in Southern Africa. It is this history that has shaped the character of the Southern African Community.

Another objective was simply to show readers how the Southern Africa regional Community came to be. I have explained in detail how the community evolved and under which circumstances it did so. It is the failure to recognise the significant implications of history that regional leaders have failed to adjust the integration agenda, resulting in disastrous results. The post-colonial/Apartheid economic and political forces that have shaped the Southern African Community must be examined to understand the community's past, present, and trajectory into the future. This is of great significance if we are to identify some of the factors and actors coming in the way of an integrated Southern African economic, political, and security regime. Critical contemporary issues brought Southern African states together to establish the Southern

African Development Community (SADC) in 1992. The issues are enshrined in the SADC Treaty, which recognised the importance of promoting democratic governance, political stability, and stimulating economic growth.

The creation of SADC was interpreted as a success in terms of its early progressive goals of eradicating poverty, enhancing market integration, and promoting democratic norms. Yet, the challenges SADC continues to face are rooted in the very foundation and history of the community and continue to be central to its evolution. The failure of regional integration in Southern Africa continues to be conditioned by these regional historical factors. However, regional factors alone do not offer a complete explanation of how integration has evolved. Some factors were also influenced by global events like the Cold War, which turned Southern Africa into a battleground for Capitalist and Socialist ideologies. There is a need to bring together these historical perspectives to draw an accurate picture of the true character of regional integration in Southern Africa.

The institutional framework of SADC, which has created a balance between regional objectives and the different interests of member states informed by their domestic politics, also conditioned other factors that have presented constraints for regional integration. In this book, I have shown how various Southern African Community space factors have advanced to an extent whereby they have impeded the integration agenda in many respects. The 1992 treaty was about deepening integration; however, the member states' diverse political and economic characteristics have made the region even more fragmented. Furthermore, the regional decision-making processes are still founded on serving national-centric objectives rather than community-inspired objectives.

An unprecedented decline in political, economic, social and security conditions has suddenly prompted a flood of reforms across the region to prepare the region for the contemporary global challenges of globalisation. In many respects, the political and economic transformation of Southern Africa may not be completed within a short period. Nevertheless, remarkable changes adopted would necessitate a paradigm shift of what constitutes an effective regional integration agenda. Depending on how SADC will be reformed, the nature of the institutional framework will have different implications for the progress of the regional integration scheme. Further, it is essential to acknowledge that SADC has somehow failed to live up to expectations within its present institutional framework. The analysis points out the necessity of a robust regional body with instruments to foster political, socio-economic, and security development. Most of the existing defects are political factors that are critical to the evolution and the operationalisation of the Southern African integration agenda. The book concludes that only a robust supranational regional institution would neutralise the political and ideological aspects of the integration processes that domestic politics and the economic circumstances of member states have shaped.

Wilson Khembo

Acknowledgements

To Pam, Jaden and Mia, thank you for your encouragement and support as the book project kept me away from family activities.

As most of you understand, ideas make it to print due to valuable feedback and encouragement from colleagues and friends. Thank goodness for some brilliant, dedicated colleagues who reviewed and commented on my project. Although they are many people who provided their support, I cannot go without thanking Hon Atupele Muluzi, Professor Dan Kuwali, Dr Ken Lipenga, Dr Andrew Thomson, Dr Thoko Kaime, Dr Anna West, Dr Alan Msosa, Bright Mando, Captain Bright Mijiga for the feedback, guidance and encouragement.

It would also be unjust not to acknowledge the work of Tionge Msiska and Mzati Nkolokosa, who helped me edit the work. A special thank you also goes to Wanthaza Mdu Mughogo, who designed the cover for this book. The pleasant personalities and strong work ethic of these great people made the experience enjoyable.

LIST OF ABBREVIATIONS AND ACRONYMS

ADFLC	Alliance of Democratic Forces for the Liberation of Congo
AfDB	African Development Bank
AMGF	African Mineral Governance Framework
AMV	African Mining Vision
ANC	African National Congress
APRM	African Peer Review Mechanism
APSA	African Peace and Security Architecture
ASEAN	Association of the Southeast Asian Nations
ASF	African Standby Force
ASM	Artisanal and small scale mining
AU	African Union
BSAC	British South African Company
CAAU	Constitutive Act of the AU
CAF	Central African Federation
CCM	Chama Cha Mapinduzi
CEECs	Central Eastern European Countries
CFA	Central Franc Afrique
CIA	Central Intelligence Agency
CIO	Central Intelligence Office
COMESA	Common Market for Eastern and Southern Africa
CPI	International's Corruption Perception Index
CSOs	Civil Society Organizations
DRC	Democratic Republic of Congo
EAC	East African Community
EC	European Commission
ECJ	European Court of Justice
ECOWARN	ECOWAS Warning and Response Network
ECOWAS	Economic Community of West African States
ECSC	European Coal and Steel Community
EFP	European Peace Facility
ESCWA	UN Economic and Social Commission for Western Asia
EEC	European Economic Community

EITI	Extractive Industries Transparency Initiative
EPG	Eminent Persons Group (Commonwealth)
EPZ	Export processing zone
EU	European Union
EWS	Early Warning System
FDI	Foreign Direct Investments
FIP	Finance and Investment Protocol
FNI	Nationalist and Integrationist Front
FTA	Free Trade Agreement
FRELIMO	Frente de Libertação de Moçambique
FNLA	Frente Nacional de Libertaçao de Angola
FLS	Front Line States
GATT	General Agreement on Tariffs and Trade
GDP	Gross Domestic Product
GNU	Government of National Unity
GPA	Global Political Agreement
HRW	Human Rights Watch
HCB	Hidroelectrica de Cahora Bassa
ICG	International Crisis Group
ICRG	International Country Risk Guide
IGAD	Intergovernmental Authority on Development
IMF	International Monetary Fund
ISI	Import-substitution industrialisation
ISIS	Islamic State of Iraq and Syria
JOMIC	Joint Monitoring and Implementation Committee
LDCs	Least-Developed Countries
LESOMA	Socialist League of Malawi
LIE	Low-income economies
LNG	Liquified Natural Gas
LRA	L ord's Resistance Army
LSDVC	Least Squares Dummy Variables Correction
MAFREMO	Malawi Freedom Movement
MCP	Malawi Congress Party
MDC	Movement for Democratic Change
MERCOSUR	Mercado Comuin del Sur
MICs	Middle-Income Countries
SIDs	Small Island Developing States
MICs	Middle-Income Countries
MNCs	Multi-National Corporations

MNEs	Multi-National Enterprises
MONUSCO	United Nations Organisation Stabilisation Mission in the Democratic Republic of Congo
MOU	Memorandum of Understanding
MPLA	Movimento Popular de Libertação de Angola
MPR	Mouvement Populaire de la Révolution
MTEFs	Mid-term Expenditure Frameworks
NEPAD	New Economic Partnership for African Development
OAU	Organization of African Unity
OECD	Organization for Economic Co-operation and Development
OOI	Outward-oriented industrialisation
OPDSC	Organ for Politics, Defence and Security Cooperation
PAFMECA	Pan-African Movement for East and Central Africa
PDC	Political Democratic Convergence
PLAN	People's Liberation Army of Namibia
PLO	Palestine Liberation Organization
PMCs	Private Military Companies
PSAs	Production Sharing Agreements
RAM	Rational Actor Model
RECs	Regional Economic Communities
RENAMO	Resistência Nacional Moçambicana
RPF	Rwandan Patriotic Front
SAARC	South Asia Association of Regional Cooperation
SACU	South African Customs Union
SADCBRIG	SADC Brigade
SADC	Southern African Development Community
SADCC	Southern African Development Co-ordination Conference
SADF	South African Defence Force
SIDS	Small Island Developing States
SALW	Small Arms and Light Weapons
SIPO	Strategic Indicative Plan for the Organ
SWAPO	South West Africa People's Organization
UDI	Unilateral declaration of independence
UPDF	Uganda People's Defence Force
UN	United Nations
UNDP	United Nations Development Programme
UNECA	United Nations Economic Commission for Africa
UNCTAD	UN Conference on Trade and Development

UNITA	National Union for the Total Independence of Angola
UNSC	United Nations Security Council
USA	United States of America
USSR	Union of Soviet Socialist Republics
VECM	Vector Error Collection Model
WB	World Bank
WGI	World Governance Indicators
WTO	World Trade Organization
ZANU-PF	Zimbabwe African National Union (Patriotic Front)
2-TS	Two-track strategy

1

Southern African Regional Integration: An Overview

"The idea of African brotherhood is often just a cover-up for laziness. We must see what is achievable in our circumstances and evaluate all decisions. In terms of regional economic integration, sentimentality is not enough. We have to be frank and honest." – Benjamin Mkapa

Over the past six decades, regional integration has risen to prominence. The regional integration process does not just encompass economic and trade issues but also political, social, cultural and security. Nation-states have embraced the notion to build multilateral institutions for socio-economic development and political stability through regional cooperation. Regional institutions have mushroomed in different regions of the globe, with virtually all governments belonging to an economic bloc. In many respects, regional integration, also commonly known as regionalism, has become a fundamental strategy that allows countries to accelerate economic growth, increase their market base, and widen their economic space. Regionalism is a much broader concept that includes the political, institutional, economic, social, cultural, and security dimensions of integration. In this context, regional integration refers to efforts by neighbouring countries to address challenges relating to trade, security, infrastructure, foreign policy, public services, human rights, and natural resource management. In the belief that liberalizing trade and making collective decisions would promote cohesion and faster integration, countries build regional blocs.

There is no consensus on the independence of regional institutions and how states interact within the regional setting in international relations literature. Pentland (1976) distinguishes between 'high political' institutions that deal with sovereignty and security of member states and 'low political' institutions dealing with daily business such as economic, social, cultural and technical issues. Though there is this distinction between high political institutions and low political institutions, one must remember that institutions are constantly updating their objectives, thus blurring the high and low political objectives.

The challenges associated with inter-state cooperation in the international system have become subject to debate in two central theories of international relations: realism and liberalism. These two schools are also described as the power schools and liberal institutionalist schools. Genna and Tieko (2015) claim that the power school, which encompasses realism, views regional institutions as mere instruments established to benefit the most powerful states. From this perspective, regional institutions have no impact on the domestic affairs of member states, as they are only extensions of powerful states to exert more influence.

For realists, there is an assumption that the state exists in a condition of anarchy. Several writers have attempted to explain the state of anarchy in the international system. In their work titled "Realism", Dunne and Schmidt (2008) describe the international environment as anarchic since there is no overarching government that enforces the rules and regulates the activities of individual states. Consequently, the international arena resembles a unique environment than the environment within which sovereign states operate, where state machinery has exclusive rights to use force. Axelrod and Keohane (1985) have a more optimistic view of anarchy as they argue that saying world politics is anarchic does not imply that it entirely lacks organisation. In their perspective, "relationships among state actors can be carefully crafted in some areas while remaining loose in others." Mearsheimer (1995) agrees, seeing anarchy more as an ordering principle than as a chaotic environment.

Neo-realism advocates believe that surviving in such a competitive international environment is all about serving national interests. Neorealists believe states can cooperate, and Mearsheimer (1995) identifies two conditions for cooperation. First, they need reassurances that the state stands to gain more from this collaboration. Second, there would be no cheating during the process of cooperation. Cooperation is, however, inherently tricky because of the lack of trust among member states.

Liberal institutionalists view regional institutions differently. One example is the argument by Keohane (1984) that regional institutions have an independent effect on interstate relations. In the view of liberal institutionalists, regional institutions assist states in coping with challenges they cannot handle individually. According to Axelrod and Keohane (1985), international institutions increase trust in international commitments by increasing transparency, enforcing agreements, and making member states predictable. For liberal institutionalists, the rules, norms and values institutionalised by states guide the interaction between them.

From a liberalist perspective, there is more optimism about the outcome of inter-state cooperation. Dunne (2008) argues that liberalism is based on democracy, individual liberties, and equality, which are the tenets of a peaceful and secure society. For neo-liberalists, there is increased recognition of the fundamental significance of the state when they argue states should not interfere in the activities of their citizens. In this context, economic liberalism and democracy become the preferred systems of governance.

As a result, Dunne (2008) concludes that liberals perceive peace and security cooperation among states as the norm, whereas war is regarded as an anomaly. Kacowicz (1998) argues that with a harmony of interest among states, "war and other types of violence and threats of war are no longer acceptable rational or legitimate means to settle domestic and international conflicts." As for Keohane (1989), trade engagement with other states creates an environment of peaceful co-existence, a fundamental component for socioeconomic development and sustainable societies. The reason for this is that any war between two states would cause both parties to lose. In Keohane's view, a peaceful international economic environment is characterised by opportunities for mutually beneficial exchanges within orderly rules that provide incentives for peaceful behaviour, but not necessarily one that necessitates and ensures it. To Keohane (1989), cooperation cannot just happen; it must be planned and negotiated. At the same time, Axelrod and Keohane (1985) argue that cooperation is not equivalent to harmony. Axelrod and Keohane separated cooperation and harmony by advancing that: "harmony requires the complete identity of interests, while cooperation can only take place in situations that contain a mixture of conflicting and complementary interests. In such situations, cooperation occurs when actors adjust their behaviour to the actual or anticipated preference of others."

In Africa, the concept of regional integration is not so much a new phenomenon. From the dawn of independence, the politically and economically fragmented African states required a degree of political and economic order. This paved the way for regional integration. Ndomo (2009) observes that regional integration on the African continent became a priority to expand the cooperation between independent African states. There was a consensus among African leaders that integration could improve the African population's living standards. It was clear from the beginning that African states' unity would determine Africa's economic development and future. It was this pursuit of unity that inspired African nationalism and the ideology of Pan-Africanism. Early African leaders had a fundamental conviction that African countries had to regroup to fight the impact of neo-colonialism. It was through their determination and solidarity that African leaders coordinated their struggle against colonialism and Apartheid. For African states, regionalism presented an opportunity for nation-states within a specific geographic territory to cooperate in ways that would help them enhance their political, social, and economic integration. The commitment to continental integration formed part of the broader aspiration and vision that created the Organisation for Africa Unity (OAU).

A call for integrating African economies shared at the onset of independence gained traction again in the early 1990s. Africa's integration processes took place against the backdrop of significant changes in the global economy, whose implications could not be ignored. A comprehensive approach to development and political stability was clearly needed to address the magnitude of these challenges. Institutions at the regional level were to be responsible for taking charge of most of these discussions. Hence, regional bodies needed to be revamped and strengthened to meet the challenges of a more dynamic world. Developing regional consensuses that could be defended in major international forums became increasingly important because of this complex global agenda. Thus, it was yet another powerful reason for pushing forward with regional integration. This time, integration of states was suggested to begin from the regional level and ultimately end with the integration of all African countries.

O'Connell (1997) indicates that the pathway of contemporary regional integration in Africa is based on the signing of the Abuja Treaty of 1991, also referred to as African Economic Community (AEC), which committed African countries towards economic integration by creating a more effective mechanism to achieve an African Economic Community within 40 years. The treaty obliges member states to cooperate in harmonising laws and policies in the gradual pursuit of the AU objective. A key element of the integration strategy adopted by the Abuja Treaty is the use of Regional Economic Communities (RECs) as 'building blocks' for a free trade zone on the continental scale. AEC Treaty (1991) Article 5(1) provides that: "Member States undertake to create favourable conditions for the development of the community and the attainment of its objectives, particularly by harmonising their strategies and policies. They shall refrain from any unilateral action that may hinder the attainment of the said objectives." According to Panusheff (2003), removing various barriers to trade between countries could help promote efficient use of factors of production, which would build the continent's capacity to achieve economic prosperity, security, peace, democracy, and human rights.

Although the model of interstate integration through formal institutional frameworks has been dominant in African integration analysis for many years, Clapham (1999) argues that the state's declining control over its territory has increasingly challenged the model. According to Bach (2013), the revival of regional integration in Africa appears to have been caused by the endorsement of ambitious projects to constitutionalize integration and mutualize sovereignties retrospectively. For African countries, the proliferation of informal networks and their incorporation into the emerging global order on a lightly subordinate basis have also become a source of concern.

The concept of regional integration pursued in Africa has evolved since the late 1980s and often followed an uneven and troubled course. Geopolitical changes drove the evolution after the Cold War, leading to the unintended but unavoidable restructuring of the old bipolar international system into a multipolar one. Southern Africa pursued regional integration to address some of these challenges, creating SADC, a regional body established to provide mechanisms to enhance regional stability, development and stimulate economic growth. Over the past three decades, SADC has developed tools for promoting democracy, conflict prevention and regional economic integration. While SADC has achieved some progress in regional integration in areas such as the free trade area, critics have expressed frustration at the limited progress on political integration and conflict prevention, which have impacted the speed of economic integration. Beckfield (2006) describes political integration as transferring political responsibility from the national government to the regional authority. Beckfield believes that political integration limits the autonomy of national economies, which may lead to sovereignty concerns.

The existing instruments of SADC and their relevance have raised some pertinent issues that call for further examination. Therefore, this book aims to answer the following questions: What are the political, social and economic factors and actors guiding how SADC sets and implements its integration agenda? What are the root causes of instability and continued economic decline? Why has the SADC agenda failed despite having mechanisms to address the persistent political, economic and social challenges? The book focuses on crucial within-country and between-country historical, political, institutional and economic factors that have shaped how SADC functions. All these factors are mutually connected and critical to the SADC integration agenda. This analysis also raises questions about the potential significance of SADC and who should guide its agenda.

There is consensus among scholars and policy makers that regional integration offers small and isolated economies the opportunity to reap the benefits of economies of scale by pooling together regional resources. Schiff & Winters (2003) identified some factors behind the increased demand for regional integration, and among the objectives identified are:

(i) Governments' wish to bind themselves to better policies, including democracy and to signal to foreign and domestic investors that such policies are binding;

(ii) A desire to obtain more secure access to major markets;

(iii) The pressures of globalisation, forcing firms and countries to seek efficiency through larger markets, increased competition, and access to foreign technologies and investment;

(iv) Government's desire to maintain sovereignty by pooling it with others in areas of economic management where most nation-states are too small to act alone;

(v) A willingness to jog the multilateral system into faster and deeper action in selected areas by showing that the General Agreement on Tariff and Trader (GATT) as not the only game in town and by creating more powerful blocs that would operate within the GATT system;

(vi) A desire to help neighbouring countries stabilise and prosper, both for altruistic reasons and to avoid spillovers of unrest and population; and

(vii) The fear of being left out while the rest of the world swept into regionalism, either because this would be actually harmful to excluded countries or just because "if everyone else is doing it, shouldn't we?

Collier and Venables (2008) highlighted three problems associated with the current political fragmentation of African states, namely: "increasing inequality in the distribution of natural advantage; costs due to the loss of scale economies in production; and loss of public goods as the scale of political cooperation is reduced." In response to the changing global political economy, there is demand for African countries to adjust and rethink their choices for action, including adopting new, comprehensive approaches to regional integration. African countries are now set with the task of working towards the economic, political and social union. With all sovereign units interacting under conditions of anarchy, states pursue integration as this is one way of determining their survival in the anarchical international arena. Rugumamu (2004) argues that political and economic integration in Africa through Regional Economic Communities (RECs) is necessary for the continent's survival and is the only way Africa can respond to the processes of globalisation. However, the conceptual sharpening of these integration approaches has become a significant challenge, especially in Southern Africa, due to the state and sovereignty conceptualisation differences.

This book aims to define the complex challenges and enormous opportunities for the regional integration schemes in Southern Africa in clear terms. Its focus is to explore regional integration with particular reference to the Southern African Development Community (SADC). Over the past three decades, regional integration has become a significant phenomenon in the modern global political, security and economic system, characterised by two extreme spectrums of nationalism on one end and internationalism on the opposite end. In recent years, African governments have opened their economies to international trade through regional integration schemes as the concept of regional integration gained prominence. With global conditions becoming more favourable for integrated economies, countries recognise the benefits of integrated economies, resulting in trade integration and trade creation. Due to these contemporary global political and economic dynamics, African governments have a solid case to come together and create regional institutions. Southern Africa's definition varies from case to case, but for the sake of this book, Simon's (1998) definition is adopted where Southern Africa refers to SADC member states. In this case, SADC and Southern Africa will be used interchangeably.

In discussions relating to the modern state's future, there have been arguments regarding the state's diminishing stature as we know it due to globalisation, which requires economic, social, and political interdependence. The global economy is now transforming into what Ohmae (1990) identifies as a 'borderless world'. The internationalist philosophy of interdependence between sovereign nation-states challenges the realist school of thought, which is based on the assumption that state sovereignty and power are the primary factors in the international system. The interdependence school of thought implies that political, institutional and regulatory barriers between countries are reduced, and joint structures are developed to manage the inter-state engagements. Despite the difference in schools of thought, the significance of integrated communities as tools for overcoming the national, regional, and international challenges cannot be ignored even by those proponents of realism.

Evidence demonstrates that the regional arrangements have failed to positively impact Southern Africa's economic and political stability as aspired by regional leaders during SADC's inception, leading to many questions being raised. Different factors have inhibited economic, social and political integration in the SADC region, with the failure being overwhelmingly attributed to leadership and governance deficit. Undoubtedly, the concerns also relate to the level of commitment of SADC leaders to the regional integration scheme. The Abuja Treaty set the preamble for the SADC Treaty, which expressed the belief of Southern African countries that there is a need for closer cooperation which has also been supported by political, economic, and technological forces that have pushed for the new regionalism wave. Globalisation in principle has presented a critical paradigm shift for policy makers in Southern Africa to respond to the new international political economy.

Vickers and Yarrow (1991) point out that regional integration leads to greater trade openness, increased competition in the domestic market, increased efficiency in production and economic growth. For African countries, according to Bøås (2001), the common wisdom is that African states are already some of the most marginalised countries in the world trading system and cannot afford to be half-hearted in their pursuit of economic cooperation. From Bøås' (2001) perspective, Africa can only become more marginalised if the countries are not regionalised. Kouassi (2002) adds to the debate by suggesting that with growing global interdependence, regional integration is crucial for Africa since economic and political integration could enhance Africa's chances of becoming a substantial actor in the international political economy.

Furthermore, it is evident that the African continent is failing to compete globally in many critical economic sectors, especially those involving exports of manufactured products and services. As of 1976, Africa accounted for approximately 6% of the global exports, yet, by the year 2000, this export share had declined to just under 2%. This gives credence to Rugumamu (2004) view that: "The emergence and development of regional integration on a global scale indicate that individual states outside the major economic and security blocs will find themselves slowly but inexorably cast aside. If Europe needs economic and political integration for strength and prosperity, Africa needs it for survival." The emerging global political and economic system has shaped the evolution of international trade; this book suggests more progressive regional responses, which can drive the evolution of the region's manufacturing and market policies and respond to these economic difficulties. According to Rugumamu (2004), "only through integration can the continent collectively and effectively respond to the multi-faceted challenges posed by the processes of globalisation." In a competitive global arena where only the strongest survive, Southern African countries must unite to face globalisation's challenges from a united and strong front. More significantly, awareness of the competitive weakness of SADC within the global economic system should provide significant input to any economic and political policy reforms. A broader case should be made for integration in terms of Africa's position in the global economy.

However, regional integration has been conceptualised differently by different scholars. For instance, Thonke and Spliid (2012) perceive regional integration as an economic project involving preferential regional trade arrangements. In contrast, Mansfield and Solingen (2010) describe regional integration as political and security projects. One of the most commonly used definitions for regional integration was coined by Balassa (1962), where he defines economic integration as "a process and as a state of affairs. Regarding as a process, it encompasses measures designed to abolish discrimination between economic units belonging to different national states; viewed as a state of affairs, it can be represented by the absence of various forms of discrimination between national economies."

Two issues were particularly important in the background when Southern African states committed to the new Southern African integration agenda. Firstly, there was a desire to reintegrate South Africa, a country that had destabilised the region for over two decades. Secondly, there was also an argument for bringing together resources that could help accelerate regional economic growth and human development. However, the re-emergence of traditional debates on sovereignty promoted by nationalists in Africa and other parts of the world has posed challenges to regional integration efforts, in some instances, reversed the strides achieved over the past three decades. Despite these drawbacks, there is a consensus among scholars that African countries need to integrate to survive what realists perceive as 'anarchy' in the international arena. This book conceptualises regional integration as an inter-state interaction involving economic, political, institutional, and security regimes.

Tenacious anxiety appears to haunt contemporary discourse in the scholarship of regional integration, with concerns relating to the diverse and mostly contradicting regional projects' outcomes in the global south and the global north. According to Mattli (1999), regional integration efforts in Africa have had different results, unlike in other regions where regional integration projects have successfully transformed their economies and promoted stability. For Africa, RECs have had an immensely different impact on socio-economic development and regional stability. In the context of SADC, Adolfo (2009) argues that the institution has become a political battleground rather than an institution striving to achieve common objectives of economic development and political integration. This hostile environment has impeded the pursuit of a common agenda on economic, political, security, and foreign policy. Ayuk and Kabore (2013) also opine that trade liberalisation in developing countries has failed to yield the expected returns. In general terms, most African governments remain weak, and historical factors have worked against closer regional integration efforts. This disappointing outcome becomes more defined in intra-continental trade output in Africa, which remains dismal.

Several studies have examined Regional Economic Communities (RECs) performance in Africa (see Foroutan & Pritchett, 1993; Elbadawi, 1997; Longo & Sekkat, 2000). Although results varied, there was a general conclusion that the experience of regional integration in Africa is characterised by failure to achieve enhanced intra-regional trade and shared policy coordination. In general terms, the concept conveys an idea that although independent nation-states in a specific geographical region express a common desire for a shared identity and aim to pursue shared objectives in a structured arrangement, the outcomes are different depending on the nature of agreements in place. In Europe, according to Ayuk and Kabore (2013), political determination and a robust institutional organisation led to huge markets and the free circulation of goods and services. As for Latin America, Pavia and Gazel (2003) point out that Mercado Común Del Sur (MERCOSUR) experienced increased intra-regional trade, capital investment flow and created a standard external tariff structure. MERCOSUR also formed a negotiation bloc and promoted the consolidation of the democratic process and harmonisation of macroeconomic policies.

A common practice in regionalism scholarship equates regional integration to economic integration. Some scholars-very few, in fact-have emphasised political integration despite being a fundamental component for regional integration projects to succeed. Such notable exceptions include Olson (1992), who reports that political integration is characterised by jurisdiction integration in which "there is a shift to a new institution of the right to take at least some important decisions in economic policy." According to Buchanan (1990), "the European difference here lies, of course, in the juxtaposition of the historically familiar exercise of rent-seeking pressures within nation-states and the prospect for a constitution of a federal union that will ensure competition among producers and consumers of goods and resources across the territory that encompasses several nation-states." Incomplete appreciation of regional integration has gained credence in regional integration discourse due to economic terms like common markets, trade liberalisation, and free trade area that have dominated regional integration debates. This book highlights the significance of political factors as they provide an environment conducive to market integration and other macro-economic mechanisms necessary for regional integration to succeed. The book adopts the view that economic and political integration complement each other. The political rationale for regional integration focuses on security and political convergence, where states embrace democracy and create democratic instruments that can improve national and regional stability.

With regard to democracy, different studies have been carried out examining the relationship between regional institutions and democracy. For instance, Pevehouse (2005), in his book, *Democracy from Above: Regional Organisations and Democratisation*, utilised statistical analysis and case study evidence. The study found that the more democratic the composition of the membership of a regional institution, the greater the pressure on autocratic governments to adopt democracy. This analysis provides a persuasive explanation of regional institutions' vital role in transitioning to and maintaining democracy in their member states. The question remains as to what extent this applies to Southern Africa and, if not, the reasons for such.

Gleditsch and Ward (2002), in their publication titled *Diffusion and the International Context of Democratization*, also examine the link between regional institutions and democratization. The study argues that democracy does not evolve sui generis since international factors play a prominent role in influencing their durability. In this regard, the study maintains that the likelihood of a country's successful transition to democracy is more significant if there are many democratic countries within geographic proximity while maintaining that the diffusion of democracy increases political stability. From Gleditsch's perspective, diffusion of democracy, political stability, and economic interdependence are interlinked and influenced by outside forces.

In the context of Europe, Timmermans (2008) argues that the creation of the 1951 European Coal and Steel Community (ECSC) deviated from the character of the Westphalian system of absolute sovereignty, with member states agreeing to share their sovereignty to prevent a new outbreak of war between European countries. The European Union provides an excellent example where nation-states with limited democratic history and traditions like the Central, Eastern and Southern European countries embraced democracy by participating in the European integration scheme. The EU adopted the Single European Act in the late 1980s to formalise European democratic commitment as newly democratized Greece, Portugal, and Spain joined the union. Hoeksma (2021) describes the EU as a democratic regional institution shaped by democratic principles in its current form. The pursuit of the institution's closer union, according to Hoeksma, was given a new impetus at the 1973 Copenhagen Summit, which identified the European Community as a 'Union of democratic States' which had to be governed democratically.

The book maintains an argument that without democratic or political convergence, economic integration cannot succeed. In the context of Africa, the ruling elites have demonstrated a lack of total commitment to integration, often manifested in their failure to domesticate regional integration agreements and policies. This behaviour has undermined the effectiveness of regional agreements and protocols that could have improved trade and harmonised policies and regulations. Abraham (2000) argues that political elites' dominance in regional integration's implementation process had negated grassroots support. In most cases, African leaders have failed to explain the importance of regional integration to their people.

While the SADC region has faced widespread poverty, massive social injustices, and sheer relentless violence, the current regional conditions have become familiar and acceptable. Southern Africa is currently experiencing continued socio-economic decline and failure to face challenges due to changing global and political environments that require cooperation and integration. One might wonder why (or how) the SADC region has become synonymous with high levels of poverty, insecurity, proneness to conflict, and rampant corruption despite being one of the wealthiest regions in terms of natural and mineral resources. As scholars and students of regional integration, we might also question why so much academic work on regional integration in Southern Africa impart a sense of certainty of the current situation.

Since independence, Southern African states have experienced low capacity economic development and stability challenges due to their nature and character. The low production flows and the anarchical international Capitalist system require the region's small and fragmented economies to come together and confront the challenges as one bloc.

Southern Africa currently ranks last in the Human Development Indices despite having enormous natural resources. UNECA (2016) notes that the more profound and more extensive the regional community, the greater the member states' potential benefits. According to Machlup (1976), the most challenging question comes down to the definition of integration. What are we integrating? Is it the people, territories, markets, production, goods, resources, security, politics, policies, or something else? The book offers a robust and structured engaging framework that appreciates the current situation through a basic appreciation of historical and contemporary factors by pursuing a critical approach. As Adotevi (1997) so brilliantly put it: "we should start by contemplating our failures, not simply as a way of doing penance for them, but to find in our past some still-live embers capable of throwing some light, however diffuse and weak, to point the way." From Adotevi's viewpoint, ignoring the past would give us "false solutions that have paralysed our thinking and crippled our actions in terms of African integration."

This book's primary objective is to explain regional integration in Southern Africa and its relevance in realising socio-economic growth and political stability. The book focuses on two opposing and mutually exclusive ideological movements, nationalism and internationalism. These two concepts have played a significant role in international politics since the end of the 2nd World War. Holbraad (2003) distinguishes the two alternative approaches by defining internationalism as the "ideology of international bonding" with the purpose to "maintain or develop the existing order of international society, or to change order and transform international society in some way or another." While nationalism, according to Holbraad (2003), is "the ideology of opposition to international bonding." Although nationalism also recognises the existence of an international society and acknowledges its state-centric nature, it focuses on the nation unit rather than the international unit.

Nevertheless, there is recognition across all ideological spectrums of the growing global economic interdependence, a characteristic of the globalised international system. In the context of SADC, the current trends in politics and economics have continued to polarise the debate on regional institutions' role in achieving stability and economic prosperity. Most of the current discussions on challenges SADC is facing have ignored history. Some scholars argue that regional bodies in Africa can play a limited role, and even if they had an impact, it would be in pursuit of self-interests. Other scholars argue that regional bodies would succeed if a viable institutional framework ensured that all member states adhered to regional agreements and protocols. For this book, an optimistic view of regionalisation focused on overcoming the existing obstacles will be pursued.

The second objective is to provide critical analyses of the factors that have constrained regional integration efforts in Southern Africa. The book expands on the historical and contemporary aspects surrounding regional integration and convergence debates. With most African countries in a state of decline due to political and economic challenges, some scholars have argued that anarchy and collapse prevail on the continent. Some observers have spelt doom for Africa, saying the continent cannot overcome its challenges. For example, Chabal and Daloz (1999), in their publication *Africa Works: Disorder as Political Instrument,* describe Africa's condition as an "instrumentalisation of disorder." This refers to the seemingly inevitable nature of patron-client relationships central to African social and political life.

The most pessimistic viewpoint on Africa's current situation comes from Adotevi (1997), who observes that: "Africa today presents a sorry spectacle of disintegrating social structures in nation-states that are themselves breaking apart. Our euphoric faith in Pan-Africanism in the early years after independence has been sadly disappointed. Africa today is divided and torn from within and increasingly marginalised from the rest of the world-the impact of the slave trade, Islam, colonialism, and Christianity. Uprooted, partitioned, and divided, Africa today is on the verge of collapse. Africans everywhere recognise this because the threat is increasing daily that Africans will once again be the unwitting victims of their own history and accessories to the history of others." While Adotevi's perception of Africa may sound overly pessimistic, his tone has optimism in Africa's destiny on the condition that the continent becomes politically and economically united.

It would, however, be misleading to link all the African challenges to colonialism and slavery. To a large degree, some of the problems can be attributed to governance and leadership. Jackson and Roseberg (1986) argue that "when we speak of the state in Africa today, we are up to create an illusion... Many so-called African states are seriously lacking in the essentials of nationhood. They are ramshackle regimes of highly personal rule that are severely deficient in institutional authority and organisational capability." African states need to be rebuilt, if not to say reinvented. They must be politically united, on the basis of sound economic underpinnings, as part of a process firmly rooted in their own history.

Although some of the Afro-pessimism pieces of literature' dire conclusions can sometimes be viewed as profoundly exaggerated and troubling, there is a shared recognition that some of the assumptions are based on observable realities. From genocide in Rwanda, famine in Ethiopia, embedded corruption in Nigeria, xenophobia in South Africa, Jihadism in Mozambique, and collapsed state in Somalia, negative headlines continue to dominate international media coverage, which paints a grim picture about the continent. With all the challenges, regional integration has been touted as a vehicle for overcoming poverty and instability across the African continent. Enloe (2000) argues that a book about international politics should leave one with a sense that "I can do something." Unfortunately, much work on regional integration in the SADC area has failed to do that.

This book, therefore, sets out to contribute to the ongoing debate on the factors that have affected regional integration progress. The book discusses how Southern African countries have dealt with its challenges to identify new, comprehensive avenues for regional integration. Specifically, the book aims to answer the following question: How can regional integration contribute to economic growth and stability in Southern Africa? This question is critical since SADC has been around for three decades, yet the regional body has failed to achieve most of its objectives. In order to answer this question, an overview is given of the underlying problems SADC has been facing since its inception. At the same time, the SADC instruments and policy strategies are examined in-depth. In this way, the book aims to fill the information and academic lacuna regarding the regional integration literature for Southern Africa.

The book suggests that SADC member states should embrace new thinking and redefine governance and how nation-states relate to each other. This will help the region successfully forge ahead and transform the regional security, political, governance, and economic environment. With the persistent economic, political and security challenges that the SADC region faces, integration provides an opportunity for improvement. The political leadership in Southern Africa has not yet adjusted to this new reality or appreciated the urgency of regional integration. Thus, it is vital to investigate the constraints affecting regional integration and harness its potential. With this objective, the book provides theoretical, historical, economic, political, and security perspectives of regional integration in

Southern Africa by examining the complex factors that have shaped regionalisation. The debate offers a sustained reflection on the common factors contributing to the SADC region's downward spiral. The factors are the main variables that will determine Southern Africa's capacity to confront and respond to the regional political, economic, social, and security challenges. The book lays down the groundwork for a comprehensive analytical framework to contribute to the understanding of country-specific and regional-specific factors that affect integration while proposing solutions to mitigate the underlying challenges. The biggest challenge for SADC member states has been facilitating an influential regional institution to promote all member states' collective interests. That crucially requires a reflection on the process of how best to achieve policy convergence, considering the existing gap between regional treaty agreements and implementation of those agreements at the national level.

The book is organized into 12 Chapters. Chapter 1 is the introduction. Chapter 2 analyses regional integration's theoretical approaches that link regional integration theories and emphasise intersections of sovereignty and interdependence. This analysis will benefit from the extensive scholarly literature on regional integration, which analyses the history and theoretical approaches relevant to the African setting. Analysis of the past and examining theoretical approaches is necessary for understanding the present. Appreciation of the theoretical framework driving regional integration will also help us understand and problematise general trends and explain particular decisions taken by states. Chapter 2 also reflects on the evolution of regional integration theories and approaches that have guided Africa's integration scheme and lays the groundwork for exploring why some regional members are reluctant to forge ahead with regional cooperation. In an attempt to build bridges across theoretical divides, the chapter concentrates on the linkages between the theories. The central role of the theoretical analysis is to highlight the political character, motivation and intent driving states' perception of sovereignty and integration.

In Chapter 3, a historical background is provided on the emergence of new African states and the emergence of white nationalism in Southern Africa. It deals with the different aspects of the processes that led to the independence of African countries. In a broad and daring account, this chapter contends that Southern African countries were facing three significant challenges as they sought statehood:

(i) The political challenge caused by colonial powers' reluctance to grant independence to African countries due to the economic benefit of the African territories for the Europeans.

(ii) White nationalism was a problem because white settlers immigrated to colonial territories and occupied the lands, deliberately establishing race-based social, economic, and political structures.

(iii) Integration Institutional challenge due to African countries with weakened economies and political systems disagreeing on the type of integration they are going to pursue.

Chapter 4 traces the complex and context of historical inter-state relations and the relationship between the independent states and the liberation movements across Southern Africa. Though a sizeable scholarly literature exists on the liberation struggle in Southern Africa, there has been little work on analysing the intrinsic relationships between Southern African states and the liberation movements. Therefore, it is essential to highlight the social and historical context of SADC regional politics and appreciate the actors involved in the integration scheme. The chapter navigates through the historical landscape of interstate relations in Southern Africa. In addition, the chapter explores how regional relations were used to tackle security and economic challenges as soon as African countries gained independence. For African countries, the long history of regional cooperation schemes rooted in the notions of Pan-Africanism promoted the means of collective self-reliance, interdependency and solidarity as African countries attempted to create their identity detached from colonial manipulation.

The historical assessment of regional cooperation allows a critical debate on the extent of the shared objectives providing different periods in which there was momentum towards shared objectives and the disruptions that occurred along the way. This analysis is crucial as it illuminates the prospects, tensions and constraints that impact any regional objective or planned intervention. The chapter shows that the lack of in-depth analysis of this historical dimension gives us a limited understanding of contemporary regional relations. Addressing the gap in these relationships' history helps us appreciate SADC member states' behaviours and their willingness or unwillingness to fully participate in a coordinated response against white minority regimes in Southern Africa. The chapter traces the history of regional cooperation in Southern Africa, including the security-oriented ad hoc regional structures that emerged in Southern Africa during and after the liberation struggle. The chapter explores the roles played by South Africa and Malawi against the efforts of Tanzania, Zimbabwe, Zambia, Botswana, Namibia, Angola, and Mozambique. The chapter shows that bringing a historical dimension to the forefront of integration debate helps us appreciate the intrinsic relationships that existed and continue to guide the nature of inter-state relationships today. This chapter will also highlight the complex relationships between African leaders and leaders of the liberation struggle that have become the ruling elite in countries like Angola, Mozambique, Namibia, South Africa and Zimbabwe. Elements that defined relations between Southern African countries during Apartheid and colonial struggle have continued to define SADC member states' interactions. The analysis provides SADC member states with a platform to help them overcome historical differences and forge ahead with collective objectives by employing effective measures that address persistent challenges impeding the regional integration agenda. By pursuing an in-depth analysis of the colonial legacy and liberation struggle, the book also provides insights into the colonial governments' silent features that have shaped the contemporary nation-states' institutions in the SADC region.

Chapter 5 of the book looks at how SADC, from its inception in 1992, has pursued its objectives to realise economic and infrastructure development. The analysis focuses on regional policies and implementation of the SADC Treaty, protocols, agreements, and decisions. The socio-economic challenges in Southern Africa have impacted the well-being of citizens from the perspective of human security, trade, and infrastructure. Policymakers must understand the social and economic factors that have hindered progress on regional integration in the region. Any analysis of regional integration cannot be complete without understanding the factors affecting regional integration and their relevance to the feasibility of the integration scheme. The analysis in this chapter involves identifying constraints in the SADC institutional landscape, impeding the institution from addressing long-term economic and social problems. This analysis exposes each constraint and reviews existing limitations and persistent challenges that have impeded regional integration. In the context of SADC's institutional failure, the chapter investigates how SADC has performed over the past three decades in relation to shared objectives and how these objectives have been translated into practice. Unlike its predecessor Southern African Development Coordination Conference (SADCC), SADC has developed a firm policy script to address regional challenges. Unfortunately, these policies have faced some implementation limitations. Throughout the chapter, we argue that, in order to understand why countries worldwide are having different experiences of globalisation, one has to understand how the microeconomic forces and globalization context differ within each country.

Chapter 6 looks at how SADC has pursued governance, security and democracy issues that are enshrined in the SADC Treaty. Building on the previous chapter, the chapter also examines how SADC has developed some regional integration policies relating to democracy, governance, human rights, security, member states obligations and how individual nation-states have implemented them. The chapter identifies a dominant practice of *'à la carte'* cooperation where governments can adhere to or ignore regional agreements, protocols, or even the SADC Treaty without facing any penalties. The lack of coherent strategies among member states and lack of political commitment among the regional leaders demonstrate why SADC remains at the bottom of every global socio-economic indicator. The discussion in Chapter 6 adopts the view that by ignoring the complexity of the factors that affect regional integration efforts, SADC cannot overcome the existing challenges the bloc is facing. Considering the current state of the conditions in the region, the chapter argues that SADC needs to create durable institutional structures agreed upon by all member states to help the regional body overcome the existing constraints. In order to overcome the regional challenges, there is a need to recognise our failures and avoid false solutions that mask the problems. We need our past failures to help us build a solid foundation for a proper integration agenda.

Chapter 7 builds on the notion of regional instability, which is one of the constraints for integration discussed in 6. Chapter 7 is divided into four sections. Section one examines the development-security nexus, which assumes that economic development influences political stability and that political stability provides necessary conditions for economic growth. The section also explores Collier et al. (2003) conflict trap theory. The second section explores the significance of foreign direct investment on socio-economic development. The third section discusses political and market risk factors that influence investors' choice of their capital investment location. The fourth section is a discussion of the impact of regional integration on foreign direct investment. The section uses the EU to provide evidence supporting the notion that robust regional integration increases the chances of the quantity and quality of FDI. The section also advances the notion that integrated economies are needed to buffer against the adverse effects of globalization and enhance participating states' credibility.

In summary, the chapter argues that the rising regional instability and governance deficit in Southern Africa have impacted foreign direct investment (FDI) quality. The discussion provides an in-depth understanding of the hostile business environment in Southern Africa, which effectively creates undesirable conditions for investment in the region, conditions that have created unintended consequences. The understanding is achieved by investigating factors affecting the building blocks of regional economic prosperity. The chapter examines the causal relationship between integration, foreign direct investment, political stability, and the region's economic landscape.

Chapter 8 discusses the persistent rise of insecurity that informs the region's high-risk profile, affecting its desirability to quality FDI. The chapter examines whether regionalism contributes to peace, prosperity, and security in the member states of regional groupings. It considers the prospect of collective security for the SADC region utilizing the existing peace, security and governance instruments of the AU and SADC. The chapter also looks at the financial constraints of the peace and security operations and possible solutions for overcoming the resource deficit. The chapter argues that regional security and stability cannot be sustained without a regional collective response to challenges.

Chapter 9 pays detailed attention to the main political disputes and armed conflicts causing instability in the region. With some of the insecurity being traced to limited or no governance, unequal distribution of state resources, and democratic deficit, responding to emerging economic, political and security issues becomes urgent. The challenges have also been exacerbated by Jihadism, corruption, and leaders desperate to hang on to power. Focusing on the significant conflict hot spots of Mozambique, the DRC, and Zimbabwe, the chapter suggests military and political interventions emphasising the human security approach, whose objective is to address threats and insecurities that affect individuals and communities across Southern Africa. The demand for states to establish human security conditions has become urgent now as the cost of inaction or late action among member states can potentially be tremendous and devastating across the region. There is a potential risk that economic and political instability in one country can impact all member states. The discussion emphasizes on the significance of utilising the existing mandates to mitigate the region's peace and security challenges. The chapter maintains that the SADC peace and security architecture can effectively be deployed for conflict prevention, mediation, peacebuilding, and the enforcement of democracy across the region.

Apart from the conflict affecting the DRC, Mozambique, and Zimbabwe, this chapter recognises that these conflicts have also adversely affected the regional political risk profile. While acknowledging some of the SADC institutional framework's weaknesses, the chapter reinforces the argument that SADC leaders need the political will to deal with some of the region's immediate political and security challenges. In the long term, conflict resolution could help bring about a regional community that protects citizens from adverse actions perpetrated by state and non-state actors by emphasising human development and human rights. Since regional integration is at the core of regional stability and economic growth, SADC needs to overcome the existing challenges at the national or regional level and, most importantly, engage in innovative actions to respond to challenges.

Chapter 10 provides an in-depth analysis of the SADC institutional framework. It analyses how enhanced regional integration can help address most of the socio-economic and security challenges the region is facing. Unlike their counterparts in Europe, the chapter argues that regional integration schemes in Africa are characterised by inadequacies in institutional framework and coordination. Taking into account the institutional, political, security and social aspects of regionalisation, the chapter provides a comprehensive view of regionalization. By analysing the existing institutional structure of SADC, the chapter makes a plea for strengthening the regional institution that takes the form of revising the structure of SADC. Due to failures that have characterised the regional body in the last three decades, there is a demand for a change of attitude among regional leaders. For the past three decades, we have heard Southern African leaders repeat the same litany of solidarity and brotherhood as if it is a sine qua non for regional development and stability. In reality, SADC leaders have been building castles in the air with their vision remaining disconnected from practice. The regional body continues to face challenges in implementing its protocols, agreements, and the treaty. The chapter argues that the inevitable obstacles have come from SADC's institutional weaknesses due to systematic contradictions in the institutional framework. While SADC has attempted to mimic the institutional structure of the EU, which has supranational instruments promoting the integration agenda, the absence of supporting instruments has weakened SADC. The chapter recognises that SADC lacks the necessary instruments robust enough to accomplish its objectives since decision-making authority lies with the Summit of Heads of State. The chapter suggests that SADC member states must develop a practical and pragmatic new framework that will help SADC overcome past failures and create supranational instruments to implement all the fundamental objectives agreed by all member states. These changes would initiate a speedy take-off of the SADC regional integration project and create a new look and effective regional body capable of providing incentives for an environment conducive to economic growth, human development, and stability as aspired when SADC was launched.

Chapter 11 looks at the opportunities for socio-economic integration in the SADC region. With the SADC member states finding it challenging to deal with the many economic and infrastructure challenges they are facing. The chapter recognizes that regional integration is linked to a new role for private investment from abroad as well as the establishment of mechanisms for attracting both private and public capital flows from the rest of the world. Harmonizing macro-economic policies within the SADC region is likely more important than trade reform. By integrating markets and production structures, the region can attract private capital to develop infrastructure and diversify its exports. Regional integration in this chapter is primarily a response to globalisation's market-driven processes and its social consequences.

Finally, Chapter 12, which is also the conclusion, provides an overall assessment and summary. The chapter suggests the lessons we can learn from history to initiate a new journey towards shared regional prosperity. The chapter goes through the lessons learnt and patterns we can draw from the institutional failure of SADC. Observers have grappled with how historical relations between states, liberation movement legacy, domestic politics, regional stability, and economic environment have impacted regional integration in the SADC region. The questions are about how

SADC member states' domestic circumstances have affected the regional project's structure and outcomes. The debate on the future of SADC has also dwelt around the autonomy and sovereignty of regional members as they pursue their shared objectives. Forecasting future results has always been a challenge, and understandably, most scholars of regionalism are more comfortable analysing the past and the present from a pessimistic perspective. Notwithstanding the norm, the book believes that by identifying the factors that have inhibited regional integration and identifying the means of mitigating them, the SADC region will achieve its shared objectives, leading to economic development and stability.

The book advances the argument that both conceptually and practically, the onus is on SADC member states to get things right for today and tomorrow. Darwin (1845) is best known for his advice: "If the misery of our poor be caused not by the laws of nature, but by our institutions, great is our sin." For Darwin, it is the responsibility of the leaders to set out institutions that can uplift the wellbeing of the citizens, which has not been the case in the SADC area, a region endowed in natural resources and a young population. This book sets out an optimistic tone to setting out fundamental rules and codes of conduct that will set Southern Africa on the path to prosperity.

The central theme in the regional integration discourse in Southern Africa is to create a new form of organisation with the capacity to deal with the challenges facing the region. In order to overcome these challenges, there is a need to initiate social, political, and economic reconfiguration. Two issues are significant for any reconstruction of SADC. Firstly, we need to pay attention to the international strategic factors that necessitate regional integration. These factors can be globalisation, economic interdependence as well as market pressures. Secondly, we need to analyse the specific features like domestic political systems, governance systems, financial disparities, development levels, poverty, and interest groups. The potential to exploit the benefits of regional integration has made the concept a prerequisite feature of foreign policies across Southern Africa and beyond.

This book affirms the view that regionalism can significantly transform Southern Africa's fortunes if SADC member states embark on a process of achieving uniformity on essential issues like democratic governance, economic policies, and making commitments to resolving regional conflicts. Therefore, a new SADC framework should have the capacity to respond to international political and economic challenges presenting a burden to integration. Providing a stable regional environment may also help the SADC region become attractive for foreign direct investment (FDI) due to minimised political risk carried by investors and the investors benefiting from what Krugman (1991) refers to as economies of scale. Mansfield and Reinhardt (2003) comment that regionalism also has geopolitical significance. In some respects, this observation is accurate since robust regional institutions enable the participating states to improve their profile and become influential actors in global and interregional trade negotiations. This new status allows them to facilitate access to other regional markets.

It is imperative to recognise that SADC member states have focused on adopting protocols and signing agreements while failing to domesticate these protocols and agreements. By identifying failures, SADC member states will learn new ways of cooperating, alternative ways of thinking, formulating and implementing policies that acknowledge the sensitivities and challenges of integration. In turn, this will provide policymakers with the necessary resources for making informed decisions and predicting the realistic range of possibilities for regional integration. There are requirements for regional integration, and there are sufficient requirements for a successful regional integration agenda. There is a global consensus that enhanced regional integration is closely associated with promoting a culture of peace, security, and economic growth. The combination of high poverty levels and regional instability has increased the need and urgency for closer regional cooperation. It has become necessary for the SADC member states to deal with complex matters in the international political and economic arena. Thus far, there are few indications that most of the SADC leaders appreciate the seismic nature of the shift in the international political economy that has triggered the region's continued decline and the region's urgent need to overcome this reality. More fundamentally, Southern Africa's discourse is sometimes defined by a worrying degree of ambivalence between the democratic and authoritarian states in the region. SADC continues to send conflicting signals about how best to deal with governance and human rights issues. SADC has struggled to reconcile treaty obligations of promoting democracy, human rights, and good governance against member states' deeply ingrained authoritarian tendencies.

Several structural factors predating SADC have contributed to some of these challenges. The book exposes Southern Africa's central concepts such as liberation legacy, colonial legacy, solidarity principle, rent-seeking, the principle of non-interference, and sovereignty. Regional leaders need to relinquish their outdated and dangerously self-sustaining methods to protect their interests that usually contradict the collective objectives of the SADC Community. The book highlights the importance of moving on from confronting the challenges from a vacuum and abandoning the flag-waving mentality. This book seeks to demonstrate why SADC leaders need to adopt and advocate progressive ideas without any delay. SADC already possesses a progressive treaty, protocols and agreements regarding good governance, democracy, collective security and human rights. This book provides a comprehensive and thought-provoking analysis highlighting the limited success of regional integration projects and how this disarray led Southern Africa to fail to eradicate poverty, initiate peace, and speed up socio-economic development.

From the existing literature, not enough work has been done to provide a detailed analysis of SADC's institutional design and how this affects progress in the regional integration scheme. This book is structured to provide a comprehensive contribution to the ongoing debate and add to a body of regional integration literature, providing a holistic approach to understanding regional integration challenges. The book is broad and unique as it aims to appreciate regional cooperation in Southern Africa from what it was, what it is and what it can become. The book adopts a multi-dimensional coverage of regional integration issues to provide a complete picture of the argument. It acknowledges the significance of recognising historical, security, political, trade, and development factors critical to any regional integration scheme's success. The objective is to instigate a paradigm shift in the regional integration discourse in Southern Africa, narrowly focused on market integration while ignoring the other factors, which provides an environment conducive for market integration to succeed.

2

History and Theoretical Approaches to Regionalism in Africa

Introduction

Regional integration is essentially characterised by creating regional cooperation groups of countries with liberalised markets and production bases. Since the Treaty of Rome (1957) established the European Economic Community (EEC), the concept of regional integration has gained traction across all corners of the globe. Chapter 2 explores the historical account, theories, and foreign policy approaches to ascertain regional integration's relevant explanation and shortcomings. The desire for the political and economic reconstruction of Europe after the two devastating World Wars required the reconciliation of primary wartime opponents, the Federal Republic of Germany and France. However, the first effort to European integration can be traced back to 1948 when Belgium, Netherlands, and Luxemburg, commonly referred to as Benelux, created a Customs Union. In 1951, the European Coal and Steel Community (ECSC) was created, with France, the Federal Republic of Germany, and Italy joining the Benelux Customs Union member states. Winters (1997) points out that ECSC was formed to revive the coal and steel industries ravaged during World War II and link them across Europe to make war "not only unthinkable but materially impossible." Managing resource competition between the French and Germans was viewed as a primary element to avoid another devastating conflict. In 1957, the ECSE created a common market that led to the EEC formation. It was clear right from the beginning that security was an essential motive in regional integration.

Over the past six decades, we have observed an increase in the internalization of almost every aspect of our daily lives. A growing number of Africans are aware of the challenges their continent faces in terms of development, security, and governance. The notion of regionalism has ushered in a paradigm shift among scholars and foreign policymakers in recent years. As opposed to the traditional idea of sovereignty and the self-interest of states, regionalism places regional goals at the centre of national goals. The first step towards achieving regional stability and economic growth is creating an economic and political bloc that will replace the weak and isolated African economies susceptible to manipulation by the powerful and dominant economies in the global north. The book's primary focus is on regionalism, which has become the cornerstone of foreign policy decisions. This is the active pursuit of strategies that develop regional systems within a particular region, regardless of whether that region is particular or general in nature, geographically confined or not.

Regarding the relationship between regionalisation and globalisation, according to Bøås (2001), the point of departure is that regionalisation is a response to globalisation. According to Cox (1981), the nation-state has now been internationalised. The testimony of Mittelman (1994) adds weight to Cox's argument by arguing that nation-states are no longer effective barriers against the global political economy. State-led regionalisation attempts to regain control over a globalized international political economy through regional cooperation. Bøås (2001) defines globalisation as a "process of change which creates worldwide linkages, diffusion of ideas and identities, and interdependence between production locations and infrastructure at the subnational level, the national level, and international level, in particular, organised in transnational corporation (TNCs)." To Bøås, globalisation "turns national financial markets into subparts of an emerging global financial market, and it entails a trans-nationalisation of technology and innovation through knowledge structure largely under the control of TNCs but to some degree also in coordination with state power and interests."

Regional integration in different parts of the world, Africa included, was sparked by the rise and integration of Europe since the 1950s. The European Economic Community (EEC) success inspired a new wave of economic regionalism in Africa. The fear of marginalization has driven increased interest in regionalism among African countries. Since most African economies are too small and isolated to negotiate trade deals with more powerful trading blocs, regional bodies are needed. As Europeans and Asians have shown, states benefit more from cooperating than those working in isolation. As soon as World War II ended, regional integration became a fundamental component of regional economic development. As a result of regional cooperation, there was economic growth and stability in Europe and Asia.

This chapter analyses the history and theories of regional integration and their relationships to integration in Africa. It contextualizes the histories of regional integration and the guiding theories that have shaped it. Bringing the past to light and identifying integration approaches that have been guided by it is the central theme. The background to any integration scheme must consider two critical factors, national interests and collective regional interests. Managing these factors determines the progress of regional integration and the character that the regional bloc adopts. It is clear that global conditions demand deepening cooperation between states. However, states' willingness to cede some of their sovereignty is the most crucial factor in determining the progress of the integration processes.

The first section provides a general historical overview of regional integration in Africa and how these integration efforts affected domestic and foreign policy as African states became independent. Growing global economic interdependence was the dominant characteristic of post-colonial Africa. The focus is on the vulnerability of newly independent African states in the anarchical international political and economic environment. The historical analysis provides a perspective that underlines individual African states' political and economic weaknesses on the global stage and the necessity to foster a Pan-Africanist approach.

The second section introduces the history and rationale of theories of regional integration relevant to Southern Africa. This section aims to situate Southern Africa's regional integration scheme and explore its vertical linkages to the general integration theories. This section benefits from theoretical approaches interconnected with the factors that shape regional integration and state actors' behaviour in that integration scheme. These theoretical inclinations define the nature of the regional bodies they belong to and their willingness to participate in interventionist approaches. The key factors are why and under what circumstances states will cooperate with other states and how that cooperation affects the sovereignty of the states. At the same time, the historical approach sheds more light on the behaviours of state actors and the patterns for such behaviour. The historical approach is significant because of a demand for reconfiguration of inter-state relations, as in African states, where the threat of neo-colonialism still guides the political discourse and narrative. It is this history and theoretical inclinations that guide the foreign policy decision-making process of African nation-states.

The third section looks at the emergence of regional blocs as foreign policy actors. Drawing insights from European integration, the section explores how the EU has evolved into a powerful international actor without becoming a superstate. The section illustrates how the EU has affected the rest of the world through a well-defined foreign policy strategy. With the EU being able to speak with one voice and act as an economic powerhouse, the EU has used foreign policy to domesticate policies outside the EU. The EU governments have delegated authority on foreign policy to the European institution, which has allowed the institution to bargain for favourable outcomes from a unified, powerful position. The section also discusses how the EU has encouraged inter-regional cooperation with other regional institutions.

The fourth and final section discusses the foreign policy decision-making process, drawing insights from Graham Allison's decision-making models. From a foreign policy perspective, the analysis framework dwells on the influences and rationale behind the decision-making process. These are the factors that influence or constrain the decisions made by state actors on matters of foreign policy and define the nature of their relationship with other state actors. Through a better understanding of past foreign policies, we can appreciate our current challenges and equip ourselves with the means to iron out past mistakes. We can also analyse issues clearly and grapple with foreign policy challenges we face in a more structured and rigorous way through our knowledge of past relations. To most foreign policy scholars, the concepts of state sovereignty and how countries relate to each other remains a contentious issue. While preservation of sovereignty has nationalistic connotations, we live in a world where nation-states have to relate to one another and work together. However, countries involved in regionalism schemes have also realised that the more they remove barriers to trade, governance, and security, the more they lose control of domestic politics.

Brands and Suri (2016) opine that "history helps foreign policy professionals understand the countries and peoples they interact with. History provides perspectives and analytical leverage of critical issues, and it gives policy-makers access to the wisdom that their predecessors gained at considerable expense. However, one cannot decide solely based on historical knowledge, of course, but only a fool would ignore what history has to offer." In simple terms, history provides us with an insight that illuminates the complexities of the puzzles we are trying to solve. In this case, policymakers consciously and subconsciously rely on their appreciation of the past to address contemporary challenges. History helps us appreciate the past, understand the present and predict the future.

This book follows a broad definition of foreign policy as the total official relations conducted by independent actors, usually a state or international organisation with another independent actor. Foreign policy has had different and competing approaches, including historians who referred to the scholarship as' international history.' Foreign policy decision-makers need to include the historical component as part of their decision-making process. Although history may not always provide us with all the solutions to the challenges we face today, our knowledge of the past can have significance in shading a context into how states behave. With such appreciation of history, we can understand the nation-states we are interacting with; it can also help us understand our past actions or decisions that have influenced other states to behave the way they behave towards us. This context will be crucial when analysing relations between member states in the SADC bloc.

History of Regionalism in Southern Africa

From a historical perspective, the lives of African people have been moulded by foreign dominance for the past four centuries. The period of slavery led to Africans being uprooted from their homes and being forcefully taken to work in Europe and America. Colonialism, where the European powers came to Africa and dominated African lives' economic and political spheres, followed this period. The Berlin Conference in 1884-

85 started a series of events that irreversibly shaped what we know to be Africa today. Pakenham (1992) opines that the scramble for colonial dominance of the continent, commonly known as the Scramble for Africa, defined its political and economic evolution. According to Mazower (1998), these events were followed by the chaos that influenced two catastrophic World Wars. However, World War II disrupted the global colonial order and opened up African states' opportunities for independence. A new world view emerged that promoted new social systems globally, leading to the emergence of new African states after gaining independence from the European colonial powers.

The first generation of regional integration occurred soon after the 2nd War when European nation-states became more concerned about the economies devastated by the war and fundamentally worried about peace and security both regionally and globally. Scholars identified the nation-state as the problem rather than the ultimate solution to the regional and global order to respond to conditions that led to the devastating war. Scholars' scepticism over the nation-state inspired the creation of a new state that could co-exist with others. Since the pioneering work of Karl W. Deutsch (1957) and Ernst B. Haas (1958), the literature on regional integration has continued to evolve through the years. Inter-state relations are no longer dominated by how states behave towards one another, as there is now more emphasis on the regional institutions' increased responsibility.

However, Europe was not the only continent that had contemplated integration; some regional economic communities (RECs) in Southern Africa have been around for over a century. Africa's pre-independence history of economic integration can be traced back to 1889, when the Southern African Customs Union (SACU) was created. The British Colony of Cape of Good Hope and Orange Free State Boer Republic proposed and agreed on Customs Union Convention. In 1910, the membership was increased to include the British Commission of Basutoland (Lesotho), Bechuanaland (Botswana and Swaziland). SACU had the objective to facilitate the free movement of manufactured products, a standard tariff on all imported goods, and a revenue-sharing formula for distributing revenue proceeds. This is remarkable because Southern Africa is one region with the longest surviving regional economic institution.

Further attempts to build supranational units in Southern Africa were pursued just before territories started gaining independence. The Federation of Rhodesia and Nyasaland, also called the Central African

Federation (CAF), was created in 1953 and included modern Malawi, Zambia, and Zimbabwe. Three British colonial territories that made up the Federation were considered a new economic initiative that would complement each other's comparative advantage. This effort failed to withstand the independence tides with aspiring African nationalists pursuing territorial sovereignty and integrity. The initiative received much resistance from black Africans in Malawi, as they feared Southern Rhodesia (Zimbabwe) would dominate such an arrangement. The breakup of the federation in 1963 led to an illegal Unilateral Declaration of Independence (UDI) by the Zimbabwean white minority-led of Ian Smith in 1965. Regional integration gathered more traction and became a fundamental aspect of foreign policy as African states' got their independence. The demand for regional bodies in Africa and other parts of the world intensified, with nation-states feeling the need to organise themselves into regional integration schemes. From the early years of independence, almost all African states embraced the idea of regional integration and continue to guide Africa's development approach until today.

The transfer of power from the colonial administration to indigenous Africans in some parts of Southern Africa was more complicated because of a substantial white-settler population that had settled in the region towards the end of the 19th century. The presence of a large white population led to challenges in how the colonial administration could transfer power, and that is why Southern African nation-states gained independence in three different phases: the first phase was the peaceful transfer of power, achieved until 1968 when Malawi, Zambia, Tanzania, Botswana, and Swaziland gained independence; the second phase turned out to be more violent as liberation movements in Zimbabwe, Angola, and Mozambique engaged in a bloody war against the colonial administration and regimes under the minority white settlers who had established autonomous governments in the former British Rhodesia and Lusophone Mozambique and Angola; and the third and final phase occurred in the early 1990s with the independence of Namibia and the 1994 first democratic election in South Africa.

This chapter suggests three broad phases in the regional integration projects in terms of regionalisation. The first phase was the post-independence period between the 1950 and 60s when newly independent African states formed the Organisation of African Unity (OAU), inspired by Pan-Africanist ideology and the principle of solidarity. Ghana's Kwame

Nkrumah was a proponent of the absolute unification of the African continent. In contrast, the rest of the new African leaders supported functional cooperation by pursuing free trade and a customs union to help build robust economies. Here, the OAU was a compromise of these conflicting schools of thought.

The second phase was the sub-regional groupings formed to pursue regional political and security interests. Southern African states came to challenge the Apartheid regime in South Africa and other white minority regimes in Angola, Mozambique, Namibia, and Rhodesia. This led to the formation of the Frontline States (FLS), an alliance whose founding leaders were Julius Nyerere (Tanzania), Kenneth Kaunda (Zambia) and Seretse Khama (Botswana). The FLS aimed to create a security regime that could support the liberation movements fighting to overthrow the white minority regimes in Angola, Mozambique, Namibia, South Africa, and Zimbabwe. The Dar-es-Salaam Declaration in 1975 led to the official launch of FLS with newly independent Angola and Mozambique joining the founding countries of Botswana, Tanzania and Zambia. This was also a phase influenced by the Cold War's global geopolitical phenomenon, which affected the decisions made by the international community and regional governments' decisions on how to respond to the liberation struggle. The South African government intensified its destabilisation efforts on member states supporting the South African liberation movements during this period.

The third and final phase was inspired by the fall of the Berlin Wall in 1989 and the subsequent collapse of the Apartheid regime in South Africa. These two occurrences provided an enabling environment for what is known as 'new regionalism.' There was now a demand for closer and more advanced cooperation as states became less polarised by economic and political ideologies. This phase presented an opportunity for Southern African countries to advance closer to regional economic and political cooperation. The expected stability in the region also offered optimism amongst Southern African states, which encouraged them to revitalise and expand regional agreements, hoping to achieve economic growth and political stability. Bøås (2001) opines that regionalism presented a potential governance layer in the international political economy that could protect participating states from the worst storms in the global political economy.

The immediate aftermath of the last white minority government in Southern Africa presented an opportunity to countries in the region that had gone through dramatic political changes, with new opportunities arising from the need to realign regional relations. A South African Apartheid regime that destabilised its regional neighbours through economic sabotage, military raids and sponsoring proxies like RENAMO in Mozambique and UNITA in Angola had just collapsed. A country that was antagonising its neighbours was about to become a democracy led by a liberation movement that Southern African states had sustained at a high economic and human cost. As a consequence of South Africa's destabilisation efforts, the region's countries faced dire economic, political and social uncertainty. However, the new development presented a new era where the Southern African countries had an opportunity to forge ahead with improved relations and create mutual objectives that could transform the region both economically and politically.

Regional Integration Theories and Foreign Policy Approaches

There is a vast body of literature on regional integration, and making sense of the notion in all its forms can be rather challenging. A large body of literature on regionalism acknowledges that economic, institutional and political integration across the globe, to which Africa is not an exception, is ever-evolving. The conceptual perspectives of regionalism focus on trade, economic interdependence and political collaboration. This section analyses the theoretic underpinnings of regional integration approaches in Africa, which has raised many debates in the regional integration discourse. This section does not aim to trace regional integration theories' historical development or deal with all theoretical issues associated with regional integration. Instead, this section seeks to clarify the integration theories while offering a brief description of the theories relevant to this book's discussion. According to Adetula (2004), integration in this context is a formal arrangement involving agreed political and economic commitments, concessions, and benefits, which guides states' participation in the international economy.

According to Adar (2005), it is crucial to recognize that, when conceptualizing integration, it needs to be considered as a process. As a process, integration portrays how states shift some of their activities and loyalties to a more prominent political centre. As a condition, integration refers to "the process of formation and development of institutional mechanisms through which values are authoritatively dispensed among political units in a geographical area." Integration in this regard refers to the political union between states. In order to understand theoretical approaches, it is important to acknowledge that regional integration is often perceived as a precursor or prelude to unification. The existence of homogenous norms and regulations shaping the behaviours of member states has historically made states uncomfortable towards the cause. Critical regional integration theories that guided regional integration efforts in Africa are analysed by examining the leading approaches that emerged as African states became independent and how these theories have guided the regional integration discourse. Analysing these concepts in the international environment will help us understand how regional integration in Southern Africa has developed through the years. Two opposite sets of political forces, internationalism and nationalism, shape the theories of integration. According to Milward (1992), defenders of nationalism argue that the nation-state is an "indispensable form of organisation, politically, economically, culturally, or even physiologically."

While nationalism emphasises the continuity of national sovereignty, internationalism supports alternative organisational solutions beyond the state. Milward (1992) argues that the word 'integration' implies that the nation-state's economies, societies, and administrations gradually merge into a larger entity. This notion of internationalism has become a challenge for a growing cast of nationalist and authoritarian regimes that strive for their monopoly of power and absolute sovereignty. The nationalism and internationalism dichotomy has brought more questions that have remained unanswered. Does the establishment of a Community entail the suppression of the nation-state and its eventual replacement? The balance between the sovereignty of member states and regional institutions is what defines the degree of interdependence from that membership. In the context of Africa, the extent to which nation-states are willing to limit their sovereignty in the international system has remained a contentious issue.

However, there is a consensus among scholars that the more democratic a nation-state is, the more willing the state is to integrate with other like-minded states. There is also an overwhelming consensus in the theoretical literature that regional integration stimulates economic growth, reduces poverty, and enhances peace and security among the partners involved. Nevertheless, many factors determine the extent of the benefits and the sacrifices individual governments are willing to make to achieve the common regional objective. In a world full of relatively closed economies, regional integration and trade liberalisation have become go-to options beneficial to the participating economies.

Regional integration theories first emerged to explain European integration soon after World War II. The term "integration" has its roots in the Latin word "integer," which means "whole." Integration entails creating a union or new integrity of separate entities that act independently. There is no universal definition of regional integration. However, the discussion in this chapter will adopt Haas' (1958) definition, where regional integration was conceptualised as "the process whereby state actors from distinct national settings are persuaded to shift their loyalties, expectations and political activities toward a new centre, whose institutions have jurisdiction over actions in national-states." The eventual result is the creation of a new political and economic community superimposed over pre-existing ones. Ruggie (1992) contributed to the debate by suggesting that regional integration refers to an institutional body that coordinates relations of three or more states based on generalised principles of conduct. These common principles are shared values, unified objectives, shared responsibility for trade, economic growth, political stability, security, and democratic governance. In simple terms, regional integration exists when different units aspire to achieve common objectives that could not have been achieved if states remained isolated. Regional integration gives states opportunities for cooperation or competition. In Africa's context, Ademann (2003) viewed regional cooperation as the best (and sometimes only) way out of Africa's marginalised position.

Regional integration processes in Southern Africa present an excellent example highlighting the conceptualisation of regional integration. The concept is fundamentally different from Europe's, primarily because of nation-states' historical context and character. Haas (1961) and Hettne (2003) advocated the European Community as a perfect approach for regional integration and perceived other approaches as fragile and failed. The notion of Eurocentric integration grew traction as there were limited examples of other successful approaches. From a Eurocentric perspective, other integration approaches are perceived as loose and informal as in Asia or as failed as in African integration schemes. However, there is a growing resistance among some scholars concerning one of the most contentious issues in the regional integration debates, namely Eurocentrism. Scholars like Söderbaum (2014) have argued that to treat European integration as the foundation for conceptual development elsewhere is rather simplistic. He argues that this perspective is 'Eurocentric' and creates a 'false universalism' where European integration becomes a marker for integration for other regions worldwide. Although primary debates on regional integration are built around European integration, another smaller cohort of scholars has attempted to challenge Eurocentrism by focusing on non-Eurocentric economic integration. Given the historical context linking the integration theories to European integration, scholars have argued that the grand theories of integration have limited resemblance to regional integration in other parts of the world. Proponents of this notion, such as Lewis (1954) and Prebisch (1960), attempt to develop integration theories by appreciating integration from the structuralist perspective of economic development. Integration among developing economies, in this case, can be identified within the limited economic changes in existing economic structures. Africa's unique setting makes it challenging to pin down a single theoretical approach describing regional integration.

Since the 1950s, scholars have developed theories to explain regional integration, and these theories have continued to develop over the years. These integration theories were developed to explain nation-states' behaviours, while others came about to respond to historical occurrences. Nevertheless, there is a consensus among scholars that theories of regional integration can mainly be differentiated by what Hettne and Söderbaum (2000) refer to as the level of 'regionness.' The level of 'regionness' from this perspective is described as the degree to which a particular area constitutes a distinct entity and how less or more coherent the entity behaves. According to Hettne (2005), the higher degree of regionness refers to regional member states' capacity to act as one unit, also described as 'actorness'. Lower regionness implies regionness that is less coherent and is influenced by outside forces and national interests. It is essential to point out that this level of regionness can increase or decrease depending on different circumstances.

Commitments to regional integration nation-states are willing to make is the most critical determinant shaping the character of the regional institution to be set up and the choice of norms and values to be promoted. These institutions are supranational as with the EU or intergovernmental as with the Association of Southeast Asian ions (ASEAN). Permanent structures characterise the supranational institutions' core institutions, becoming responsible for initiating the integration agenda that would bind all parties concerned. The intergovernmental institutions adopt an ad hoc character where states remain the dominant actors shaping the integration agenda. This approach is flexible as states can change their commitment to any existing agreement without facing any repercussions.

Instead of rejecting mainstream theories to conceptualise regionalism in Southern Africa, it is vital to expose interesting insights concerning these theories' relevance to regional integration in the Southern African context. While the institutional structure might be similar, some historical elements have made the institutions adopt a completely different outlook. The critical point is that the regionally centred theories inspired institutional design in Africa's regional integration schemes. Abbot and Snidal (2000) pointed out that soft law institutions have been preferable in Africa in most circumstances. This has dictated the nature of collaboration, which has remained shallow and subject to the whims of political figures. This has also led to incoherencies in the appreciation of regional policies among member states, leading to shallow institutionalism of the integration schemes. Campos et al. (2015) described the distinction between shallow and deep integration. Shallow integration is identified by the free trade area model and is restricted to economic integration, while deep integration combines economic and political aspects of integration. Here, the EU is perceived as an excellent example of deep integration. The deeply entrenched perception of absolute sovereignty has made SADC member states poor integration partners. Reconciling and addressing sovereignty concerns could bring a more conceptual understanding of regionalism in the SADC region.

Regional integration in Southern Africa has also shown some determined efforts to forge closer economic cooperation, hoping to create a customs union, free trade agreements, common currency, and the creation of a Southern African political and security architecture. At the same time, states have failed to show interest in relinquishing some of their decision-making powers and have been reluctant to empower the progressive regional institutions already adopted. Failure to empower the regional institution has affected the cohesion between national and regional objectives. The institutional integration design has also brought a governance gap between policy formulation at the regional stage and policy implementation at the national level. For instance, the regional agreements have talked about democratic governance while being contradicted by member states showing authoritarian tendencies.

The following section will examine some of the most relevant theories of integration. The analysis of these theories has introductory information about how the theories came about and the theoretical self-definition. This background is vital because it allows us to understand theoretical approaches and their origins and evolution. It is also crucial to keep in a perspective that theories in themselves are not inspired by differentiating arguments or what Rosamond (2005) refers to as a reductionist picture of theoretical approaches. Theories in themselves do not claim completeness in themselves, and as explained earlier, most of the theories to be discussed have intellectual roots from European integration.

Conception of Integration from a Pan-African and Solidarity Perspective

African countries have held aspirations for the continent's political and economic integration for a long time. Like other regional integration theories, the Pan-Africanism movement also has its historical roots in Europe, where a Pan-African Congress organised a London Conference in 1900. The philosophy embodies the ideal of a united African people living in a continent that overcomes colonial boundaries. The movement remained popular among African academics, which inspired future African leaders of African states like Kwame Nkrumah, Julius Nyerere, and others, leading to the formation of the Pan-African Movement for East and Central Africa (PAFMECA) in Tanganyika (Tanzania) in 1958. Somalia and Ethiopia later joined the grouping. PAFMECA became a precursor for the Organisation of African Unity (OAU), formed in 1963.

According to the Pan-African philosophy, African states had an obligation through cultural conditioning to fight for an objective oriented towards their specific needs for positive collective development. At the same time, every African state was part of a more prominent African family of nation-states and their people. Although the early African leaders acknowledged the differences in the approaches to regional integration, they agreed that every struggle of African people was a struggle for every African. Pan-Africanism recognised that imperialism, neo-colonialism, and class exploitation were struggles experienced by all

Africans. As a family of African states, that struggle had to be confronted by all states in solidarity. During his address during the OAU launch in 1963, Haile Selassie argues: "Africa's victory, although proclaimed, is not yet total, and areas of resistance remain. Our liberty is meaningless unless all Africans are free. Our brothers in Rhodesia, in Mozambique, in Angola, in South Africa cry out in anguish for our support and assistance." This unity brought about the solidarity principle, which became the guiding principle during the liberation struggle.

Africa perceived the solidarity approach was in the context of social protection for all Africans. The solidarity principle in international relations was first introduced in the mid-1800s by a Swiss legal expert Emer de Vattel. Vattel (1958) argues that states have a duty to mutual assistance to improve their general situation and relations. According to Vattel, solidarity was an essential condition for the existence of a community of states and a compulsory natural norm that could not be altered, abolished, and negotiated. His understanding of solidarity was that the philosophy was a moral obligation rather than a legal obligation, thus making the solidarity principle challenging to enforce. In this regard, solidarity was considered essential and voluntary, fundamental to nations' law, yet practically unenforceable. The League of Nations enshrined the solidarity principle into Article 22 of the Covenant when the Organization of African Unity (OAU) also adopted the principle of solidarity and made it into the African Union (AU) Charter. The OAU's basic principles according to the OAU Charter were:

(i) Unity and solidarity amongst African states;
(ii) Coordination of intra-African and international cooperation;
(iii) Protection and defence of the sovereignty, territorial integrity, and independence of its member states;
(iv) Overcoming all forms of colonialism; and
(v) Promotion of international cooperation based on the United Nations Charter and the Universal Declaration of Human Rights.

Ghana's first president, Kwame Nkrumah, a passionate believer in African unity and a link with the historic Pan-African movement, promoted solidarity among African people across the continent in their fight against colonialism and racism. Until today, the solidarity principle remains the driving philosophy in African foreign relations and the

African Union. The focus of African solidarity moved outside of the AU into the general politics of sub-regional bodies. In Southern Africa, the regional institutions among member states became a virtual arena within which a sense of brotherhood was created among the regional political elites. The regional member-states built relations based on solidarity with the regime and non-interference on domestic issues. Any idea of intrusion continues to be perceived with contempt and likened to neo-colonialism. Most African states have found comfort in the regional forums as they seek refuge from domestic and foreign pressure. While most of these regimes have lacked the legitimacy to govern in their own countries and amidst facing international condemnation, regional bodies have served as a platform for their legitimacy. In turn, regional bodies have become part of the problem leading to a governance deficit across member states.

Interestingly, while nation-states have continued to embrace the concept of solidarity as a brother's keeper at the regional level, this solidarity does not go beyond the heads of governments and their regimes. As a result, this concept has encouraged undemocratic tendencies to flourish, mostly among states still governed by liberation movement political parties. Adolfo (2009) observes that liberation movements in Africa were only interested in decolonisation during the liberation struggle but not necessarily embracing democracy in newly independent states. However, these historical circumstances have continued to dictate the behaviours of Southern African states as we know them today.

Although Pan-Africanism has remained popular in understanding regional integration in Africa, the concept has been challenged in academic discourse as a regional integration theory. Odén (1996a) states that "while the Pan-African perspective and the idea of continental, regional integration can be seen at least as a rhetorical framework for some of the regional schemes in Southern Africa, the main factors behind the regionalisation efforts taking place are sub-regional." Regionalism based on Pan-Africanism also appears to be incompatible with contemporary challenges of globalisation.

Sovereignty in Regional Integration Discourse

The sticking point in theorising regional integration discourse is the concept of sovereignty and interests of the state. Regional integration is a process that impacts state sovereignty since regional institutions are made up of several members with diverse ideological and political inclinations. As a result, these differences in state character logically imply a multiplicity of interests. Since integration requires states to hand over part of their decision-making powers to the regional instrument, we can also argue that regional integration limits states sovereignty. With regional bodies comprising many different state actors unique in themselves, differing ideologies and governance systems have presented challenges to the regional integration scheme. In practice, how states manage the complication of their diversity entails the character the regional organization adopts.

Nevertheless, for more than three centuries, state sovereignty has remained the dominant principle of inter-state relations. Based on customary international law and the UN Charter, sovereignty is crucial for maintaining international peace and order. However, the concept of sovereignty is known for limiting consensus-building that is necessary for deepening integration through rational and negotiated. According to Hinsley (1966), the notion of sovereignty emerged in the 16th and 17th centuries as a double-headed notion. Brown and Ainley (2005) argue that the notion gained prominence after the Westphalia Peace Conference during the second half of the 17th century and has become the base upon which the structures of anarchy have been constructed. Morgenthau (1950) writes that "sovereignty is the supreme legal authority of the state to give and enforce the law within a certain territory and, in consequence, independence from the authority of any other state and equality with it under international law." The Legal Dictionary identifies sovereignty as a by-product of the Westphalia system that gives the nation-state the primary authority to govern itself without interference from other states. It is viewed as the state's international independence, combined with the right and power of regulating its internal affairs without foreign interference. Sovereign is the power of the state to do everything necessary to govern itself, such as making, executing, and applying laws, imposing and collecting taxes, making war and peace, and entering into treaties or engaging in commerce with foreign nations." Max Weber (1947) has a classical definition of sovereignty where the notion is described as "a state is a human community that (successfully) claims the monopoly of the legitimate use of physical force within a given territory." This concept appears to contradict the concept of regional integration to a great measure as states have used the concept to justify their refusal to surrender state sovereignty and decision-making powers to a supranational institution. Consequently, they find it challenging to engage in integration processes. Apart from sovereignty determining the state's role towards the society within the sovereign, sovereignty also determines the state's role towards the international system.

The study of regional integration focuses predominantly on sovereignty and the transfer of political power to the regional institution. Haas (1970) alludes that African leaders are reluctant to further undermine control at the national level through internationally binding commitments due to national political and economic challenges in their countries. Thus, unlike the European success story, there has been the failure to contain concerns relating to member states' sovereignty in Africa when deepening regional integration. Ideological differences among states have entailed a diversity of interests, which in most cases have led to non-convergence when it comes to agreeing on matters that concern the whole group. These differences have been more visible in Africa due to their differences in political and economic systems. With regional integration in Europe demonstrating the limit to which sovereignty impacts consensus building, the regional supranational structures have allowed a negotiated process of delegating powers to the EU. On the contrary, in Africa, the existing structures have failed to yield similar results. De Waal (2002) describes African leaders' commitment to African integration as only bordering on the rhetorical, emotional, and symbolic.

Mistry (2000) points out that the pursuit of regional integration in Africa has been influenced by two conflicting interests: the tendency to adhere to colonial borders and emphasise states' unity, although at arm's length. This contradiction was visible in the OAU Charter (1963), where there was an emphasis on cooperation and coordination as Africa's core integrative route. At the same time, the OAU Charter also emphasised territorial integrity and sovereignty. The OAU's non-interference approach to domestic affairs led to inaction in some extreme cases where catastrophic human rights abuses had been committed both by state and non-state actors. This non-interventionist approach led to gross human rights abuses committed by dictators like Idi Amin in Uganda and other parts of the continent, where regimes mercilessly killed citizens and assassinated political opponents without facing condemnation from their peers.

In the context of Africa, the notion of sovereignty has not yielded robust regional institutions, with De Waal (2002) describing African integration as bordering on rhetoric. The nationalist perspective and respect for national sovereignty remained the dominant perspective in African integration discourse until the late 1990s. After the Rwandan genocide, the OAU started devising new mechanisms for conflict prevention, which later led to the creation of the African Union. The new African Union (AU) concept was driven by the desire to secure democracy, human rights, and sustainable economic growth by ending conflicts on the continent, hence diluting the concept of sovereignty. Both the African Union and the regional bodies have created continental and regional peace and security and architecture with military capabilities to deal with security emergencies across Africa.

Sovereign states participate in regional integration for different self-interests, whether political, economic, or social reasons. Politically, a nation-state may participate in regionalism to improve its military capacity, improve its political status, and deter other hostile states' aggression. Economic motivation may be driven by the benefits of economies of scale, benefits from scarce resources available in another country, and the desire to speed up economic growth. Social interests may be motivated by efforts to control the influx of immigrants from poor neighbours. What is apparent is that the more advanced the integration scheme is, the more sovereign powers nation-states have to cede to the regional body.

Nevertheless, tensions have continued to exist between the nationalistic and interventionist approaches. The notion of sovereignty has presented challenges to the African regional integration agenda. Adotevi (1997) argues that "the creation of independent African states has had as a corollary the notion of national sovereignty as defined and managed by the state, which has sought to suppress all other sources of social identity." Driven by the fear of having an external actor like the regional body breaching a nation-state's sovereignty, some nation-states have demonstrated reluctance to become part of a robust regional institution despite acknowledging the importance of an influential and effective regional body. This contradiction has been visible when it comes to the African continental body's failure to enforce the principles of Article 4 of the AU's Constitutive Act, which provides a mandate for AU to intervene at certain levels of intra-state conflict. Whereas in Southern Africa, the member states are faced with a dilemma as to how far they are willing to sacrifice the control of their internal affairs in favour of international agreements and protocols. Sutherland et al. (2005) argue that sovereignty is one of the "most used and misused concepts of international relations and international law." Sutherland and his colleagues pointed out that: "acceptance of almost any treaty involves transferring a certain amount of decision-making authority away from states, and towards some international institution." Generally, this is precisely why "sovereign nations" agree to such treaties. For the states, "they realise that the benefits of cooperative action that a treaty enhances are greater than the circumstances that exist."

Realism and Neo-realism in a Community of States

Realism is perceived as one of the oldest theories of international relations. According to Haywood (1997), the theory can be traced back to Thucydides' conceptualisation of the Peloponnesian war (431-400 BC) and Sun Tzu's Art of War. In the European context, Milward (1992) opines that the state became the dominant form of political, economic and social organization in Europe from the sixteenth century when the territorial boundaries became more defined by European rulers and their armies. As states and their rulers attempted to strengthen their territorial claim, they used the powers of their armies to monopolise their use of power within their territories to collect taxes, enforce the territorial laws and, to a certain scale, use their power to fight for resources in territories outside their jurisdiction. Towards the end of the 1930s, some European states were no longer capable of protecting their citizens, let alone their territories, as they were occupied by more powerful hostile foreign powers during World War II and the Cold War that followed. It was during this post-war period that there was now increased recognition of state power and sovereignty. This period of war created the theoretical foundation and explanation for the theory of realism.

Goldstein and Pevehouse (2006) added to this debate by suggesting that a central assumption of the realist approach is that the international system is driven by anarchy; in this sense, anarchy is perceived as an absence of the central government to enforce rules and protect states from hostile powers. Waltz (1979), considered as one of the fathers of modern realism, linked this lack of a "world government" to violence among states. Lebow (2007) cited Mearsheimer's characterisation of this anarchical, self-help international system as "a brutal arena where states search for opportunities to take advantage of each other." This characterisation maintains the perception that international relations cannot escape from a state of anarchy and will continue to be dangerous because of anarchy's pre-existing environment. In simple terms, realists maintain a pessimistic view of the international arena.

It is crucial to understand the notion of anarchy to appreciate the international arena and understand how states behave the way they do. Hans Morgethau (1993) holds that realists understand the world as imperfect from the rational perspective, which results from forces inherent in human nature. The analytical foundation of realism is based on the balance-of-power logic where states compete to gain superior power, provoking other states to respond. With this backdrop, the states being a creation of men naturally resemble the character of the men who create them. For Classical realists, men are susceptible to vices like greed, mistrust, and envy, leading them to a struggle. In Morgenthau's view, the scarcity of resources with no one to serve as a referee could lead to competition over those resources and possibly war.

As observed by Baylis (2001), scholars like Thomas Hobbes and Machiavelli view the international system as a brutal arena in which nation-states are driven by the motive to achieve their security at their neighbours' expense. In this regard, inter-state relations come into play as states continuously attempt to take advantage of each other. Thucydides, Hobbes, and Machiavelli's pessimism were driven by the view that there was no genuine international order as states were always in the state of competition. Realists believe that the international system lacks a centralised authority to regulate relationships between states in the international arena. For this reason, states compete without established rules and norms except, what Hoffmann (1965) refers to as "the changing necessities of the game and the shallow conveniences of the players impose." Waltz (1979) observes that states depend on the "means they can generate and the arrangements they can make for themselves under these conditions." For realists, states are functionally similar, and their interests and interactions are shaped by their desire to safeguard their security and power. The practice of individual states' survival has long gone, and the concept of cooperating with other like-minded states to meet that collective survival has emerged. The political case for building closer cooperation in Africa was primarily motivated by economic, political and security considerations. This reference point originated from Europe, where states came together to manage their relations to avoid the inherently built pursuit of power by member-states. That led to what Gilpin (2001) labelled as "hegemonic stability", where states created alliances with a more powerful state to guarantee their survival.

Realism is both the best-known approach in international relations as well as being the most criticised. The theory assumes that power is the primary end of political action, whether in the domestic and international arena. Realism is an approach that emphasises the competitive nature of the global political arena as realists consider the states as the principal actors whose only concern is their security. In this regard, the states act to pursue their self-interests and are in an ongoing power struggle. Lebow (2007) identifies the survival of the nation-state as a critical principle of realist theory. According to Milward (1992), the growing incapacity of the state to carry out its primary function of protecting its territory and its citizens, the European Community became the vanguard of a more advanced stage of political organization. In domestic politics, governments have the authority to create and enforce laws that protect citizens, which reduces the prospect of conflict. However, the same cannot be said in international politics.

This approach became prominent in international relations scholarship after the failure of other moralistic approaches. The two bloody World Wars and the Cold War brought realism into the forefront of international discourse. Scholars provided evidence that states and military forces were the main features of the global system. However, the realist approach has been toned down over the years as discourse shifted away from state-centric approaches. For example, Waltz's (1992) neo-realism approach agrees with the notion of 'struggle for power with a different perspective on that struggle's motivation. Waltz argues that the struggle for power arises because people want resources and not necessarily because of the inherent evil in their desires.

Proponents of neo-realism like Grieco (1995) attempts to explain European states' behaviour during the negotiations of the Maastricht Treaty when he argues that "states share common interests and undertake negotiations on rules constituting a collaborative arrangement, then the weaker but still influential partners will seek to ensure that the rules so constructed will provide sufficient opportunities for them to voice their concerns and interests and thereby prevent or at least ameliorate their domination by stronger partners." Thus, in Grieco's view, the weaker states can become influential partners as they have a platform to have a voice.

In order to survive this anarchical environment, smaller African states must forge closer relations with other states to survive the political and economic anarchy. With the pursuit of power and global influence having brought Southern African states together, the regional market's competitive nature can also potentially drive the states apart as they attempt to protect their domestic industry. In complementing this argument, Yarbrough and Yarbrough (1987) argue that "nation-states are willing to abide by specific agreements under the rubric of *rebus sic stantibus* (so long as principal circumstances remain unchanged)". According to Emer de Vattel (1958), a key figure who promoted this view, "everybody bound himself for the future only on the stipulation of the presence of the actual conditions" and "with a change of the condition also the relations originating from the situation would undergo a change." This philosophy has been the guiding philosophy for African integration, where it is common practice for nation-states to try to break away from the agreement if they feel that honouring the agreements and commitments is undesirable. The realist blueprint must have predicted the failure of SADC, which has become the primary regional body in Southern Africa. In the context of SADC, regional integration policies, agreements, and protocols are being debated and accepted at the SADC Summit level. However, at the domestic level, where the effect of these decisions would be felt, most of the real-life obstacles for policy implementation are still existent.

From a neo-realist perspective, regional integration is perceived as a tool for satisfying specific national interests in the international arena. All agreements are driven by the desire to favour the interests of nation-states. Regional integration is perceived as a specific alliance among sovereign states that do not lead to any renunciation of decision-making power. Hurrell (1995) argues that: "for the neo-realist, the politics of regionalism and the emergence of regionalist alignments have much in common with the politics of alliance formation" This description suits the context of SADC, where member states' actions are determined by their interests to pursue policies that have maximum benefits and are framed by the political elites' thought process to maximise individual gains of their state. The economic environment in Southern Africa has failed to support regional integration efforts. With limited manufacturing capacity and infrastructure development, the member states have been unable to integrate the small and isolated economies, which have impacted exports due to the limited market and export base. With limited domestic capital resources and foreign capital investments, SADC has experienced little benefits from economies of scale than other regional bodies. Over the last three decades, SADC member states have neglected regional integration agreements, favouring nation-centric policies that have undermined the regional agreements despite outrightly showing interests and commitment at the regional level.

Functionalism, Neo-functionalism and Regional Integration

In contrast to realism, functionalism was viewed as an approach for peacebuilding that aspired to end the nation-state's aggressive nature and the conceptualisation of the international system as anarchical. Functionalism theory emerged after World War II with David Mitrany's publication, *A Working Peace System*. Mitrany's (1966) theory is based on a principle that "the problem of war could be solved and the war-prone system of nation-states escaped through international agreements in specific functional or technical areas such as health, postal services, and communications. Political integration of the world would thus result from economic and other forms of international cooperation." According to functionalists, functional cooperation is the only practical alternative for promoting peace. The idea is that states can initiate cooperation in sectors they are interested in cooperating. As Geddes (2004) argues, functionalists had hoped that the United States of Europe could shape post-war Europe as they felt the realist state system had led to the two devastating wars.

Dinan (2000) holds the view that the primary rationale for the existence of any community is welfare and security, and once a moderate sufficiency of what people want and ought to have is given to them, they will keep the peace. However, the system of global interdependence means that countries cannot escape its implications. Globally, RECs have to compete with other regional groupings in key strategic industries, where most regions have been growing their capacity. Hence, the need for countries to respond to these global market challenges. For Mitrany (1966), a peaceful international society is driven by states doing things together in a marketplace rather than signing agreements and treaties. In his view, states should transfer sovereignty to a new authority, mandated to carry out all those tasks. In this scenario, all the integrated arrangement members gain equally, and the benefits from the cooperation outweigh the incentives to be isolated. From this perspective, a more robust institutional arrangement was the only approach available for states to maximise welfare through functional spill over through their shared interests.

Neo-functionalism attempts to probe possibilities of an endpoint in regional integration. It is a gradualist approach to integration, developing from limited economic integration developing into a political unification. To functionalists, mutual trust and integration between states develop when states share public sector responsibilities through international agencies with limited but specific powers delegated to them and defined by the functions they perform. These functional agencies only have jurisdiction to operate in territories of governments that choose to join them, thereby not threatening the nation's sovereignty. David Mitrany considered functionalism to be the primary principle that should be guiding any social arrangement. At the same time, Rosamond (2000) believes that states are an obstacle to human interaction's functional organisation. For functionalists, the state-centric world view of the realists is challenged due to concerns about whether nation-states are competent enough to fulfil human needs. In this regard, supranational bodies are the preferred option if states are to enhance their integration agenda.

The federalist government system promoted by functionalists had failed to foster closer cooperation as nation-states restored their dominant nature. That prompted a new approach that could pursue closer cooperation without countries being forced to integrate too quickly. Neo-functionalism was perceived as the theory that guided the creation of the European Economic Community as it reflected in the early years of integration in Europe. The theory focused more on interdependence, increasing demand for nation-states' cooperation, and creating a more secure European community. The idea that states should lose their sovereignty to a supranational authority as promoted by Mitrany (1966) faced some resistance from some scholars leading to the birth of neo-functionalism. The father of neo-functionalism, Haas (1958), grappled with the idea of refining Mitrany's functionalism concept. Haas argues that: "Power and welfare are far from separable. Indeed, commitment to welfare activities arises only within the confines of political decisions, primarily based on power considerations." For Haas, the overall economic decisions must be made before any functional sector can be expected to show the kind of integrative evolution that the functionalist describes. Lessons learned in one functional context cannot be expected to be readily transferred to new contexts; success in one functional sphere does not set up a corresponding motion in other spheres: on the contrary, it may fail to develop and be forgotten.

Haas (1958) attempts to explain the integration process from the lower stages to the higher integration experience stages. Neo-functionalists acknowledged functionalism's primary argument that cooperation in one sector will inevitably spill over to other political and economic sectors. Spillover, according to Lindberg (1963), refers to "a situation in which a given action, related to a specific goal creates a situation in which the original goal can be assured only by taking further actions, which in turn create a further condition and a need for more action, and so forth." The spillover occurs because the agreements and policies made for an initial objective can succeed if the results expand to other sectors. Haas (1958) assumed that "once integration effort had been launched, there would be pressure for further integration as social and economic groups would demand additional economic integration, and that that would create new political actors interested in and ready to promote further integration. Political integration would be carried out by the actions of both domestic interest groups and international civil servants or entrepreneurs." In Haas' view, the EEC was created as a spillover effect of the ECSC.

However, neo-functionalists seem more concerned about the process that leads to political integration, whereas functionalists focus on the ultimate end of political integration. According to neo-functionalists, much emphasis was on the process, not the results. Thus, much focus was put on the interdependence of states and the increasing demand for closer cooperation. Nevertheless, neo-functionalism also faced criticism for being more of a historical description of European integration than a theory for regional integration, which could be applicable in other regional arrangements. Haas (1958) acknowledged that the spillover effect has limited success in integration schemes with a weak institutional framework. In the context of SADC, the current institutional framework for the organisation has no supranational mandate, unlike the EU, with all decisions being made by the Heads of State. It is clear from this background why SADC continues to experience challenges and limited the spillover effects across different sectors. This, in turn, has left an enormous gap between the institution's objectives and implementation of the agreed policies, agreements and procedures at the national level due to the plurality of state actors involved in the decision-making process.

The relevance of neo-functionalism in transforming SADC into a functional regional polity is attributed to the SADC Secretariat's failure to enforce regional agreements and protocols. The weakened SADC Secretariat inhibits the efficient and effective performance of the institution as it lacks the capacity to implement policies and enforce compliance. With SADC member states having diverse interests and diverse political systems, the process of creating an environment of shared values, norms, and aspirations has become a challenge. That has also affected the regional economic efforts to meet different timeframes for implementing trade, monetary, and customs protocols, which are meant to become part of the spillover process. The current institutional structure only suggests that member states are not willing to commit to regional integration fully.

(Liberal) Intergovernmentalism

Like neo-realism, intergovernmentalism also referred to as traditional intergovernmentalism, is a by-product of an international system characterised by anarchy and composed of functionally equal nation-states. Traditional intergovernmentalism is most commonly associated with Stanley Hoffmann (1964) in his publication '*The European Process at Atlantic Cross Purposes*', where he challenged neo-functionalism. According to McCormick (2008), the concept of intergovernmentalism was developed to explain European integration due to the perceived weakness of neo-functionalism. In this context, the international system was still based on state sovereignty, and the interests of individual states remained central to the discourse of any interaction between states. Hoffmann (1964) argues that states' integration had not replaced states' sovereignty and national interests.

The concept of intergovernmentalism aimed to reject the notion that the integration process could undermine states. The theory was influenced by neo-functionalism's failure to explain the early challenges European integration faced in mid-1960 as states became reluctant to surrender some of their sovereignty to the European body. The basic argument of intergovernmentalism is that European integration only succeeded in areas where all members benefitting from the outcome was guaranteed. The difference between traditional intergovernmentalism and liberal intergovernmentalism becomes more apparent when determining how states pursue integration as part of their national interest. From Hoffmann's (1966) perspective, there is a distinction between what he referred to as high and low politics. According to Hoffman (1964), European integration could not occur in areas of high politics where critical aspects of state sovereignty such as security and foreign policy were affected. However, integration was possible in low politics, which according to O'Neill (1996), refers to areas such as trade and agriculture.

Scientific innovation has allowed greater ease of interaction between states, leading to an increased number of sectors states can cooperate beyond agriculture and trade. However, intergovernmentalism was viewed as a more pessimistic interpretation of integration and faced some criticism as the European integration developed further, leading to the birth of liberal intergovernmentalism. A more developed notion of liberal intergovernmentalism rejected Hoffmann's distinction of high and low politics, which had faced criticism following the further development of European integration, which included some areas Hoffmann (1966) viewed as high politics. Hoffmann was correct to suggest that the EC was initially excluded from getting involved on issues of high politics, in this case, foreign policy and security. However, as the integration agenda progressed, according to Lodge (1989c), it became clear that "the successful pursuit of internal policies demands an expansion of the EC's external jurisdiction and concomitant lessening of member states' autonomy." For instance, trade and other economic related issues are often directly connected to diplomacy issues. At the 1969 Hague Summit, EC member states recognized and agreed that enhanced political cooperation was crucial if a unified Europe achieved its primary objective of becoming a significant global player. The European growth in confidence was inspired by a decade of collective economic growth and mutual trust. In challenging Hoffmann's traditional intergovernmentalism, Moravcsik (1998) argues that there is no hierarchy of interests as suggested by Hoffmann and perceived Hoffmann's viewpoint as simplistic.

Moravcsik (1991) conceptualised liberal intergovernmentalism as "a series of bargains between heads of governments of the leading states in the region." The signing of the Maastricht Treaty (1991) brought more questions in relation to the debate between high politics and low politics introduced by Hoffmann (1966). According to Rosamond (2000), creating a single European Monetary Union and establishing common foreign and security policies demonstrated that European states were willing to surrender their control on issues considered central to national sovereignty. Faced with this reality, Moravcsik (1991) tried to build on Hoffmann's notion as he attempted to develop a detailed account of European integration in his book '*The Choice for Europe*', where he devised the concept of liberal intergovernmentalism, which was different to traditional intergovernmentalism. Moravcsik (1998) argues that European integration had three elements:

(i) Liberal account of the development of national preferences;
(ii) An intergovernmental account of the intergovernmental bargaining and relative bargaining power of states; and
(iii) The institutional choice is underpinned by the desire to enhance the credibility of interstate commitments.

The basic assumption of liberal intergovernmentalism, according to Andrew Moravicsik (1991), is that "the primary source of integration lies in the interests of the states themselves and the relative power each brings to Brussels." Moravcsik was inspired by his realist and liberalist inclinations when he identified three conditions of regional integration. Traditional intergovernmentalism appears to be the integration framework adopted by the SADC, where member states have promoted the importance of national sovereignty and limit their cooperation on matters that can only be described as low politics. However, there is an acceptance that intergovernmentalism in the SADC region will gradually develop into liberal intergovernmentalism as demands for collective security and foreign policy become prominent. The SADC Tribunal and the SADC Protocol for Politics, Security and Defence Cooperation (SIPO) already recognise some elements that are considered high politics; however, in practice, SADC member states have avoided operationalizing the instruments in their original form and spirit.

Liberal intergovernmentalism has its roots in liberalism, a theory that offers a more optimistic view of the world and emphasises the well-being of individual citizens as a critical building block for any political system. Ensuring an individual's right to life, own property, and enjoy civil liberty is perceived as the supreme goal of a government. Therefore, the primary concern of the theory is to develop institutions that protect individuals' freedoms by mitigating the state's violent power. Liberalism challenges realism as it disagrees with a militaristic foreign policy, and liberal systems often limit military power. For liberalists, this state power can also be abused to oppress the citizens and fight other states if left unrestrained. Nonetheless, liberalism, according to Barry Buzan (2004), recognizes the notion of realism that the international system is composed of self-regarding nation-states even though, on itself, liberalism submits that international instruments are available to induce discrete episodes of international collaboration.

From a neo-functionalist perspective, integration was perceived as a process where the supranational institution weakened the nation-states. In contrast, according to Milward (1992), liberal integration was perceived as a state-centric choice aimed at strengthening or even rescuing the nation-state through more robust integration. Based on this background, liberal intergovernmentalism is preoccupied with creating an international community mutually beneficial to all states. Another underlying rationale for the concept is also based on the liberal peace hypothesis, which argues that closer economic integration binds all participating state actors from engaging in hostile acts against each other. Proponents of liberal peace theory believe that domestic and international peace results from a large majority of people in a society having influence over decisions on both economic and political matters.

Interdependence Theory and Integration

According to Robert Keohane and Joseph Nye (1977), dependence was defined as "a state of being determined or significantly affected by external forces. Interdependence, most simply defined, refers to mutual dependence." According to Keohane and Nye, "interdependence in world politics refers to situations characterized by reciprocal effects among countries or among actors in different countries." Keohane and Nye benefitted from Haas' (1958) contributions to challenge the realist theory by explaining international relations as an increasing interconnection between domestic and foreign policy. Interdependence in world politics refers to "situations characterised by reciprocal effects among countries or actors in different countries." Keohane and Nye took a modernist approach in their perception of international relations. Their argument leaned towards realising a global village, where the borders between states were becoming more blurred due to increased international air travel and international financial transactions. In their early observation, military power, although still significant, was diminishing in influencing international politics. Keohane and Nye's (1977) work is believed to have anticipated what we now call globalisation.

In a broader historical perspective, the tragic lessons of the devastating World Wars, global leaders had learned about the dangers of aggressive nationalism, which had resulted in catastrophic wars. Consequently, there was broad consensus within the Western world about the importance of multilateralism and liberalism in the international system. Keohane and Nye (1971) identified four primary areas of global interaction:

(i) Communication, the movement of information, including the transmission of beliefs;
(ii) Transportation, the movement of physical objects, including war material and personal property as well as merchandise;
(iii) Finance, the movement of money and instruments of credit; and
(iv) Travel, the movement of persons.

Keohane and Nye (1977) observed that states were becoming more interdependent in the interdependence era, especially in economics, leading to changes in the fabric of international relations. Due to interdependence, one actor's actions were perceived to impact other actors' policies and measures and vice versa. That led to what is now called complex interdependence. Genest (1996) defined complex interdependence as "an economic transnationalism concept that assumes that states are not the only important actors in international relations, with social welfare issues sharing centre stage with security issues on the global agenda, and cooperation being as dominant a characteristic of international politics as conflict." In complex interdependence, states cooperate with other states because it is in their common interest to establish prosperity and stability in the international system. According to Keohane and Nye (1977), "the politics of economic and ecological interdependence involve competition even when large net benefits can be expected from cooperation." Keohane and Nye's also acknowledged that interdependence must not be viewed as an "evenly balanced mutual dependence" when they stated: "It is asymmetrical independence that is most likely to provide sources of influence for actors in their dealings with one another. Less dependent actors can often use the interdependence relationship as a source of power in bargaining over an issue and perhaps to affect other issues." Complex interdependence provided the most significant challenge for realism as the proponents of interdependence argue the world has become intertwined, which has diminished the realist assumption relating to the state's dominance in international affairs with violence and military power as essential means of advancing the goals of the state. External pressure resulting from globalization has undermined the state's ability to remain independent, unlike in the past, where states could outmanoeuvre each other using military power.

As states became more interdependent due to globalisation, demand for supranational institutions similar to the European Union increased worldwide. This growing demand for interdependence inspired states to pursue what Keohane (1990) refers to as the "integration process", where there is a cosmopolitan society in which uniform norms and rules apply. This concept contradicts the realist approach, where states' rivalry is assumed to be the central concept of international interaction. Nevertheless, Keohane attributed the struggle for power and influence as characteristics of the Cold War. In his view, the fall of the Berlin War ushered in a new age of cooperation and mutual prosperity that required liberalisation of economies and a new era of regional and global governance. This move away from the traditional realist approach has been encouraged by the EU's success.

Despite nation-states' efforts to protect their sovereignty, states are expected to sacrifice certain aspects of their sovereignty for multilateralism to succeed. This willingness to sacrifice sovereignty is what strengthens multilateral institutions' ability to be effective. The creation of regional bodies demands establishing authority structures that transcend territorial boundaries, which inevitably undermine sovereignty, as has been the case with the EU. For instance, the European Commission has the authority to draft EU legislation, discharge monitoring tasks, and ensure that member states do not act or behave in such a way that contravenes EU law. The European Commission, which functions as the Secretariat, can hold member states accountable by taking any matters to the European Court of Justice (ECJ) whenever there is a dispute in interpreting the European Treaty. The ECJ itself plays a vital role in monitoring and enforcing EU laws and agreements. Walter Mattli (1999) suggests that the EU has limited all the member states' sovereignty, which has empowered the organisation to coordinate and act on behalf of all members as a unit.

The Covid-19 mitigation scenario presents an excellent example of complex interdependence due to its impact on individuals, societies, and governments. With the pandemic affecting almost every country globally, all states paid more attention to the importance of international cooperation to protect the world population and the global economy. Scientists across the world worked together to develop a cure and possible vaccine. The Chinese provided the genetic sequence and composition of the coronavirus at the earliest possible state, which allowed scientists worldwide to begin working on vaccines before the pandemic hit their shores. The threat of Covid-19 had implications on the world population's health, which directly impacted economic and security matters.

However, interdependence theory also faces some criticism from some scholars. For example, Krapohl (2019) argues that interdependence theory is a Eurocentric theory that is not be applicable in developing economies in Africa. In Krapohl's view, interdependence implies that intra-regional economic interdependence is the primary driving factor for integration. Krapohl comments that the level of economic interdependence depends on how developed the economies involved are. From this perspective, less developed economies in the Southern hemisphere, in this case, SADC countries, are less likely to maximise the benefits of interdependence than the more developed economies in the northern hemisphere. Although this argument is valid in some sense, an export-driven and trade-driven integration could also benefit emerging economies.

For this reason, despite the success of multilateralism in Europe, regional integration has produced different outcomes in other parts of the world. While northern hemisphere regional blocs like the EU and the Association of Southeast Asian Nations (ASEAN) have exploited the comparative cost advantage and economies of scale through regional integration, the Southern hemisphere's experience has been less than flattering. While SADC has introduced policy initiatives where member states have expressed commitments to regional integration, member states' self-serving interests undermine the regional frameworks that operationalise these agreements. With varying degrees of implementation of treaties, protocols, and agreements, the status of closer cooperation has been challenged by inadequate progress.

THE NEW REGIONALISM

New regionalism is a concept which began with the observation that the fall of the iron curtain in early 1989 contributed to a new wave of regional integration. As the Soviet Union collapsed, there was a considerable change in international trade and international political economy attitudes. The emergence of globalisation led to a new wave of regionalism, with the concept drawing insights from diverse regional integration approaches and attempting to balance different development and security factors. The new regionalism approach linked the concepts of globalisation and regional integration. Due to increased globalisation, as the Cold War structures collapsed, the antagonism between the Western bloc and the Eastern bloc had ceased to define the international order. The deepening integration in the European Union (EU) and its success presented other regions' opportunities to emulate. Mittelman and Falk (2000) argue that "regionalism only functioned as a part of the containment policy in a militaristic and strategic sense during the Cold War." While the old regionalism is characterised in the context of the Cold War's bipolarity due to the ideological contest between Capitalism and Communism, the new regionalism is a complex change of processes taking place in a multipolar global order. New regionalism spread in response to economic, political, and technological advancements, which significantly impacted the global economy than ever before. These developments made the world economy's governance a more demanding and fundamental issue where agreements were to be made on managing the world economy. Driven by the concept of new regionalism, there has been a sharp increase in regional preferential trade agreements to respond to other regions' preferential trade agreements.

The increased significance of interregional relations is also characteristic of new regionalism. Under old regionalism, regional cooperation was confined to specific cooperation sectors and was considered more introverted and driven by nation-states' self-interests. In sharp contrast to the old regionalism, which was inward-oriented, Axline (1994) and Palmer (1991) argue that the new regionalism has multi-sectoral linkages driven by globalisation. With globalisation becoming dominant as the structural barriers that created territorial borders become thinner, new regional alliances are created to forge closer economic and political cooperation to navigate the new world order. This recent phenomenon has led to the phenomenal growth in the number of international economic integration agreements across the globe to create a vast network of interconnected trading nations. New regionalism is perceived as a theory-building strategy that transcends the state-centric notion adopted by traditional regionalism. It is more applicable to states outside Europe, and according to Hettne (2005), the regional bodies on the African continent belong to new regionalism. SADC was formed to respond to the demands of new regionalism as the global market became more competitive. The new concept requires regional bodies to become actors in their own right with institutionalised mechanisms for dealing with different regional interaction sectors. Hettne and Söderbaum (2009) argue that the new regionalism transforms regional bodies from objects to subjects.

As states compete for market access on the global market, new regionalism presents states' opportunity to improve their access to extra-regional export markets. With developing regions coming together to speak with one voice in international trade negotiations, they can negotiate more favourable trade agreements with other regional bodies. Mansfield and Reinhardt (2003) suggest that countries can use regional trade agreements to increase their bargaining power in World Trade Organization (WTO) negotiations. By negotiating as a group bound by trade agreements, the countries become significant actors in these multilateral negotiations as they increase their chances of obtaining favourable trade deals. With most third-world countries having small and isolated economies, creating an economic bloc benefits them. This perspective has become relevant in the African context, with regional bodies like SADC being modelled on the EU framework. As a result, more attention is being paid to economic and political integration.

Regional Integration as a Foreign Policy Tool

From a foreign policy perspective, states can exert change to their environment based on the objectives they have set for themselves, which also impacts their behaviour in the international system. It is the character of the state or regime that determines the nature of diplomacy.

In this case, the exercise of influence is a primary way states relate to each other in actual practice in the absence of an international government. Regional integration is perceived as a possible step for breaking structural barriers between member states and building a new political community that can act on behalf of the states. Integration is not viewed as an end in itself but rather as a tool for reaching national interests in a context of an integrated political and economic front. During the early years of the European Community (EC), the institution had limited influence on international politics, as it was most concerned with the international dynamics of Europe. That has changed over the years as European countries became more integrated since adopting the Maastricht Treaty in 1993. As a result, the EU has become an active and influential player in the international arena. With the emergence of the EU as a prominent regional and international actor in international relations, there is evidence on how regional institutions can be utilised as a foreign policy tool. At the beginning of European integration, the European Community did not influence the international arena and was more streamlined towards facilitating international trade.

Over time, the institution matured into a robust international instrument, becoming a major global actor. A unified foreign and security policy allows the European institution to stamp its identity in the international arena. Title V of the EU's Maastricht Treaty sets out provisions on a common foreign and security policy which have become the second pillar of the EU. According to Charles Bidwell (1993), the provisions have six key objectives, which include:

(i) Safeguarding the shared values, interests and independence of the Union;
(ii) Strengthening the security of both the Union and its member states;
(iii) Preserving peace and strengthening international security;
(iv) Promoting international cooperation;
(v) Developing democracy and the rule of law; and
(vi) Respecting human rights and fundamental freedoms.

The EU's impact as a global player cannot be underestimated. The institution is associated with spreading its values and imposing its vision over other global actors like the UN and other RECs. The EU's economic power and growing international image have turned the institution into a key international player. The EU's efforts to assert its weight on global political, social, and security has grown over the past two decades. The EU now has its presence in almost all countries globally as it pursues its foreign policy objectives and builds new external relations. The evolution of the EU has led to changes in classical diplomacy of state-to-state interaction. The EU is now replacing the member states by aggregating their interests in foreign policy. With 27 member states delegating more power to the EU, the EU has become more robust and influential.

The EU's success has also illustrated that the best possible way to overcome ancient inter-state differences and foster economic and social growth is through robust regional institutions. The EEC brought together sworn enemies during the two devastating wars, France and Germany. Franco-German cooperation became critical for furthering the ideals of a united Europe, and the two countries have been described as the 'twin engine' of Europe. The European agenda strengthened the relations between the two countries and reduced any likelihood of future wars between EU member states. The success of European integration has inspired other regional integration schemes across the globe. Michael Reiterer (2006) postulated that "for better or worse, the EU model has become the yardstick to measure regionalism and consequently integration elsewhere."

The EU has become the ultimate reference point for other regional institutions in Africa and other parts of the world. The EU's status has allowed the European body to shape global governance. Some commentators argue that the EU assumed global leadership after the United States adopted nationalist policies under the Trump administration. The EU has not only portrayed itself as a model for regional integration, but it has also spent enormous financial resources and diplomatic efforts to promote regional integration. The EU has championed the regional integration processes and has inspired some institutions to mimic its institutional framework. The EU has also provided financial and technical support to such initiatives.

The EU has also pursued the concept of interregionalism to conduct effective interregional relations. Hanggi et al. (2003) define interregionalism as "a process of widening and deepening political, economic, and societal interactions between international regions." For Julie Gilson (2005), the interregionalism concept is described as "a double region project, responding to the need to pool an even greater percentage of resources in recognition of other interregional and global dynamics."

This concept demands regional institutions to project their regional identities, critical in harmonising foreign policy prerogatives and establishing trust. Söderbaum et al. (2005) opine that "regional integration could enhance peace, prevent conflict and promote cross-border problem solving and the better use and management of natural resources." As such, the EU has given special attention to the development of regional institutions in Africa and other parts of the globe. Söderbaum et al. (2005) identified the AU and SADC as some of the regional institutions the EU is focused on. Through this process, the EU has promoted democratic values, human rights, and governance issues.

In Africa's context, regional institutions in Africa had much influence in raising awareness about Apartheid in South Africa. The Organization of African Unity (OAU) and the Frontline States (FLS) consolidated their voice and built a coalition that pressured the global community to isolate the Apartheid regime. However, global influence enjoyed by these groups has waned out over the years due to regional disintegration resulting from African states' reluctance to surrender some power to the regional institutions. Unlike the EU, which enjoys a significant degree of independence from the member states, in Africa, the RECs are controlled by the member states. However, the EU has made an effort to promote regional integration on the African continent, with both the AU and SADC benefitting from budgetary support from the EU.

Graham Allison's Foreign Policy Approaches

The discourse on foreign policy-making approaches is still developing and relatively new. One of the main arguments raised by critics of foreign policy approaches is that despite the recognition of the transformation in international politics, foreign policy approaches are still driven by state-centric realism with the governments shaping the international system. The existing approaches are inspired by Western-centric experiences to provide explanations for other global phenomena. The development of foreign policy analysis is perceived as a response to this criticism. The significance of accurately understanding foreign policy dynamics as part of achieving international stability cannot be underemphasised. Pertinent questions concerning approaches have been debated in international relations scholarship as foreign policy has grown in popularity. There have been disagreements in foreign policy discourse about whether Western-centric foreign policy approaches are relevant in explaining the phenomena in Africa and other parts of the world.

To respond to this criticism, Allison et al. (1971) developed a substantial body of knowledge concerning how foreign policy processes occur. They argued that that "if a nation performs an action of a certain type today, its organisational components must yesterday have been (or have had established routines for performing) an action only marginally different from that action." From the context of the quotation and as also observed by Tanter (1972), foreign policy analysis seeks to explain foreign policy behaviour as "an output of subnational organisations following standard operating procedures or engaging in a problem-solving search." For scholars and professionals in foreign policy, foreign policy analysis is a crucial component of the field. Foreign policy analysis helps unpack the decision and logic at play concerning how international actors conduct foreign policy, diplomatic manoeuvres, and international relations.

Graham Allison et al. (1971), in a publication titled *The Essence of Decision*, aimed at explaining the 1962 Cuban missile crisis. The analysis developed three models that guide foreign policy: the Rational Choice Theory, commonly known as the Rational Actor Model (RAM), the bureaucratic politics model, and the organisational process model. The rational actor model is the most widely used model that drives foreign policy. RAM assumes that the actors in foreign policy are rational beings who can be relied upon to make calculated, informed, and sound decisions that are both ethical and beneficial to the states. Marijke Breuning (2007) argues that rationality is simply the requirement for foreign policy choices to be logically connected to the goals of the state actor. In this case, assessing the other actor's capabilities might influence the decision being made. Whereas Oppenheimer (2012) provides that RAM "presumes decisions to be the result of a conscious choice made by individuals to further the realization of their preferences." The idea of cost-benefit analysis also comes into play when determining a desirable foreign policy decision.

There is always an expectation that foreign policy driven by the rational model remains consistent and coherent throughout. For foreign policy decision making to occur, a problem has to be identified, desired outcomes defined, and consequences of the policy evaluated. As a result of this analysis, the most rational decision is chosen based on how the decision maximises the benefits. In this case, foreign policy decisions are conceived as rational solutions that can solve strategic problems with minimal negative consequences. Allison viewed this approach through the lenses of the United States' naval blockade of Cuba in 1962, driven by the threats posed to the US's strategic objectives when the Soviet Union stockpiled nuclear capabilities in Cuba. This approach gives us a better understanding of the US's foreign policy goals and intentions and how they were made.

While the rational actor approach has remained the most critical foreign policy model, critics of the approach have argued that the approach assumes that all actors are rational, which is not always the case. Moreover, some instances may limit any rationality from taking place, for instance, a response to foreign aggression, which requires an instant response. Although this appears to be a valid argument, it is also essential that any response would also require a calculated response considering the adversary's capabilities, the consequences of that response, and the level of attack faced. In contemporary terms, a a clear illustration is that of the Iranian military response to the assassination of the head of the Iranian Revolutionary Guard Corps, Qasem Soleimani, by the United States military drones in January 2020. While the Iranians were determined to retaliate and strongly respond to the assassination, they also calculated such a response's repercussions. In turn, the Iranians decided to fire missiles targeting US military bases in Iraq in such a manner that limited the number of casualties suffered by the US despite having the capacity to inflict more damage to US military installations in the region.

Despite all the differences in the objectives driving foreign policy, the rational actor approach comes into play as every decision is evaluated based on the cost-benefit analysis and long-term repercussions. International support of the foreign policy decision is also critical to legitimise any form of action taken. That is why the US always goes to the UN Security Council or the General Assembly to seek support on an adversary's military action despite having the capacity to go alone. From the rational actor proponents' perspective, there is an assumption that all foreign policy decisions made will lead to the best outcome for their countries. These rational actions are also supposed to consider past actions and how actors are expected to avoid making similar mistakes. In turn, the lessons from history help rational actors adjust their behaviours and decisions accordingly, which may sometimes lead to abandoning their favourite objective favouring a more realistic and practical second or third option.

Graham Allison's et al. (1971) second model is the bureaucratic politics model. This model views the state as a unitary actor. Unlike the rational actor approach, proponents of the bureaucratic politics model evaluate foreign policy decisions based on the premise that actions taken are driven by competing entities representing several independent and competing groups within a state. These competing groups exist at different state levels: businesses, religious groups; interest groups; international allies; and individual donors for political parties. All these competing entities bring value to the decision-making process, and the final decision is reached after a consensus has been agreed upon and satisfies all competing entities. The degrees of importance of each entity also play a part in every decision. According to Cleaves (1974), bureaucracies are driven by resources, goals, and the environment, which helps states formulate policies.

One good example that illustrates this is the US's response to Iraq's invasion of Kuwait. While there was overwhelming support for a military response in both the US Congress and the United Nations, the scope of that response differed. For the UN to support the coalition forces, it was agreed that the coalition forces could only drive out Iraqi forces from Kuwait without marching on to Baghdad and toppling Saddam Hussein. The US's strategic objective was to maintain the coalition that included Arab states as it was vital politically, militarily and diplomatically. The coalition partners, especially the Arabs, feared that removing Saddam Hussein would result in something far worse, like the rise of Islamic fundamentalism that could potentially spread throughout the region. These fears were later realised two decades later with the rise of Islamic fundamentalism and the creation of the Islamic State of Iraq and Syria (ISIS).

The third model is the organisational processes model. This model views the government as a mix of influential organisations working together rather than groups of partisan entities competing to influence the final decision. The central premise of this approach is that foreign policy decisions result from bureaucracies, processes, capacities, limitations and people rather than rational processes and outcomes. The foreign policy process is viewed as the decision-making process originating from rigid bureaucratic structures where actions are taken following the chain of command and standard operating procedures and laid-out protocols. Carlsnaes (2002) observes that the approach's primary focus is on "decision-making in general, and on the role of the decision-making units – particularly small groups – in this process." In this case, standard protocols are established on how to respond to different scenarios and occurrences. In this scenario, every response is choreographed and predictable irrespective of who is occupying the office. Critics of this approach have argued that this model underestimates people's ability to act differently on issues based on their personal beliefs and influences. This approach also reduces any prospect for flexibility due to the existing laid-out procedures that have to be followed at all times. According to Allison et al. (1971), foreign policy decisions made by US presidents are shaped by deliberations and thorough consultations. Nevertheless, Donald Trump's presidency was characterised by decisions based on his impulses and personal relationships with individuals affected, which challenges the assumption of the organisational processes model.

Africa's post-colonial foreign policy was shaped by colonial experiences and the liberation struggle against residual white minority governments. This experience gave the political elites inspiration for crafting foreign policy. In the aftermath of independence, Pan-Africanism was the guiding principle. This experience and history the expectation of African countries was premised on the assumption that every African government supported the liberation movements, which was perceived as the most rational choice. However, the momentum of this rational consensus of Pan-Africanism, as a foreign policy principle in Africa, faced some obstacles. Magu (2021) argues that: "Pan-African goals were swept up in personality disagreements and regional vendettas." A clash of national interests spearheaded by African leaders desperate to cling on to power has become a burden to African integration, an area that will be discussed in more detail in later chapters.

There has also been acknowledgement on how poor governance and high levels of corruption can impact foreign policy formulation in Africa. With many foreign actors using financial incentives to influence foreign policy decisions, the efficacy of African governments to formulate their policies has been called into question. Due to these complex influences, some of the decisions made by African governments may defy logic and rationality. For instance, 10 of the 15 seats on the UN Security Council rotate after every two years. Kuziemko and Werker (2006), in a publication titled *How Much is a Seat on the Security Council Worth? Foreign Aid and Bribery at the United Nations* found that politically and economically powerful countries strategically use their economic power to influence voting patterns of weaker states. Dreher et al. (2014) also found that payment of bribes achieves positive outcomes in Africa and Latin America. Dark money has been used to influence voting on other UN platforms like the UN Security Council, the General Assembly and the Human Rights Council. In most cases, the bribes given to government officials to influence decisions may have unintended consequences which may outweigh the cost and benefit.

3

AFRICAN REVOLUTION: PAN-AFRICANISM AND THE BIRTH OF WHITE NATIONALISM IN SOUTHERN AFRICA

INTRODUCTION

Chapter 3 provides a more detailed chronological description of the factors that led to the independence of Southern African states and the subsequent liberation struggle that followed in the countries that remained under the white minority rule. With much of the regional integration theoretical framework referring to the European experience, this chapter explains the unique conditions in Southern Africa that influenced states to come together during a period of protracted conflict in the region. This discussion presents the historical transition from the early security cooperation and economic arrangements; and the consolidation of freedom across the region, bringing a new environment for collaboration. This discussion does not seek to provide a detailed history of regional integration over time and place. Instead, the discussion is more concerned with examining the nature of relations and the institutional responses to the challenges posed by the remaining white minority governments in Southern Africa. It is also important to point out that while this debate is motivated to illuminate the drivers and effects of these relationships that developed, the chapter also hopes to engage the adjacent problems and issues resulting from those relationships.

The Southern African region's background has been transitive, beginning from the period the first black-led governments emerged in the 1960s until the early 1990s when the last white-led government in the region collapsed. The region was characterised by the armed struggle for freedom between African liberation movements and the white minority regimes during that period. Inspired by the changes relating to both global and domestic circumstances, the discussion analyzes the conditions that led to the three phases of independence in Southern Africa: the first phase being relatively peaceful and was achieved until 1968 as most of the territories were under British rule (Malawi, Swaziland, Zambia, Lesotho, and Botswana) attained independence; the second phase, was characterized by a bloody struggle for independence which occurred in the two Lusophone colonies (Mozambique and Angola) and Southern Rhodesia (Zimbabwe); the third and final phase characterizes the liberation of South West Africa (Namibia) in 1990 and the transfer of power to the South African black majority after the 1994 elections.

Most Southern African states share a unique feature due to their colonial and postcolonial history. Most of these territories were colonized by the British except for the Lusophone countries Angola and Mozambique, which were colonised by the Portuguese, and Namibia, occupied by the Germans and later South Africa. The region is also unique because some states remained under colonial or white minority governments much longer than any other region on the continent. The existence of white minority governments in the region led to a liberation struggle that pitted the liberation movements with support from the newly independent African-led governments rising against the white minority governments in Angola, Mozambique, Namibia, South Africa, and Zimbabwe. That led to a period of extended conflict in the region and an emergence of a diplomatic alliance of some black-led governments in the region called the Frontline States (FLS) to express their opposition to the white minority governments and support the liberation movements.

This chapter examines the evolution of each specific phase of independence and the roles played by regional neighbours and the liberation movement. In the post-World War II years, the establishment of independent Southern African states was substantially driven by two critical regional settings: the number of white settlers in the colonial territories and the colonial powers' economic interests in those territories. These two factors had an enormous effect on how and when Southern African states gained independence. The emergence of white minority regimes in Southern Africa brought about a cobweb of complex relationships. Southern African states had to navigate their national interest against the liberation movements' interests inspired by the solidarity principle that the OAU was promoting.

South Africa's economic dominance in the region created an awkward environment of co-dependence between Southern Africa governments and the Apartheid regime. Navigating this balance presented challenges to most Southern African governments as they were all relied upon by South Africa in one way or another. South Africa presented many opportunities for its regional neighbours from the transport system, trade, employment, financial support, and tertiary education. Unlike Mozambique, Angola and Tanzania, South Africa's significance was more significant for landlocked countries like Botswana, Zimbabwe, Zambia and Malawi. The four countries heavily relied on South African transport corridors to access the sea.

These complex relationships impacted foreign policies adopted by the Southern African states between the 1960s and the early 1990s. The implications of the theories like realism, solidarity approach and Pan-Africanism will also become more pronounced in this chapter as states attempt to protect their national interests while at the same time protecting the interests of the liberation movements. Understanding this history helps us appreciate the delicate relationships and behaviours of Southern African countries today that remain influenced by the past. This background also helps appreciate why some countries in the region are comfortable working with some while reluctant to work with others, thereby affecting regional cooperation and cohesion in infrastructure development, security, and market liberalization, which are essential factors of regional integration.

Early White Settlers In Southern Africa And The Rise Of White Nationalism

The birth of white nationalism in Southern Africa was a by-product of war, religion and an ideology of white superiority. To appreciate the complex dynamics of domestic, regional, and international rivalries in Southern Africa, we need to understand the origins of white nationalism that led to the birth of oppressive white minority governments in the region and the liberation struggle orchestrated by the black majority. The emergence of a racially divided society in the region is significant to appreciate the evolution of Southern Africa's relations. Issues of colonial land, labour policies, segregated communities, and deprivation of fundamental human rights became the genesis of African nationalism in Southern Africa, leading to decades of a liberation struggle.

The Dutch East India Company established the first European settlement in Southern Africa in 1652 at Table Bay (Cape Town). Dutch nationals, known as Boers (Dutch for farmers), supported themselves through farming and herding animals. The Dutch colony named Cape of Good Hope grew rapidly, providing fresh produce, fresh water and other necessities to passing ships crossing between Europe and Asia. Upon establishing the colony, slaves were imported from East Africa, Madagascar, and the East Indies. The white settlers brought with them ideas of superiority and the ability to act in ways that were not allowed at home. Early Cape of Good Hope officials were corrupted by the colonial concept of racial slavery even before slaves existed. While the Cape of Good Hope allowed white men to wed non-European women, racially mixed couples were not permitted. Since European settlers at the Cape of Good Hope began seeing themselves as citizens of countries far away, they tried to imitate home traditions as much as possible in overseas colonial settings.

Over time, the Boers pushed farther inland and up the coast, which led to a great deal of conflict with indigenous Africans. The European occupation of South Africa is better understood as colonial conquest than a peaceful process as white South Africans have historically portrayed the settlement. During the European invasion of the Eastern Cape, the Xhosa people put up a formidable fight against the Europeans. However, the Boers possessed superior weaponry, which they used to subdue the Xhosa and drive them off their land. The African inhabitants of the region were dispossessed of their land and forced into servitude as workers on the farms of the European settlers by the beginning of the eighteenth century. Boers exploited African locals while importing slaves from Indonesia, Sri Lanka, and Madagascar who, together with people of mixed descent, were called Cape Malays. The Boers ruled the region through exploitative economic practices until the British slowly took over.

After many English speakers arrived in the colony, they quickly took over manufacturing, trade, finance, and government, whereas Boer farmers remained largely rural. A constant conflict between the Boers and the local black populations in South Africa was prompted by stolen cattle and crops. In addition to African tribes fighting amongst themselves and the Boers, they also fought against the British settlers, ultimately unsuccessfully. As a result of the divisions within the region, the British often benefited from it.

As pioneer farmers who had lived independently for decades, the Boers disliked British rule. Boers were outraged when the new South African rulers abolished slavery in 1834. The Boer farmers moved north looking for new land outside of British control to maintain their way of life. During the "Great Trek" (*die Groot Trek*), thousands of Boer families migrated in groups called Trekboers to Southern Africa. The Zulu wars pushed many tribes out of their lands while other lands were already populated. By the 1860s, the Trekboers had occupied large land areas in South Africa, particularly along a fertile plateau known as the Highveld. Among those they moved were the Ndebele, a local black population. South Africa's black population, which had lived in some of these areas, was forced to move into more distant and less fertile regions. Consequently, the Trekboers created three independent states: Natalia, Transvaal, and Orange Free State. In 1843, the British occupied Natalia, a strategically located coast town, and changed its name to Natal.

Due to the location of Transvaal and the Orange Free State being farther away from the coast and the small value of the states, the British let Boers keep their new occupied territories for a short while as independent states. Eventually, gold and diamonds were found on lands claimed by the Voortrekkers. While the Boers were presented with an extraordinary opportunity to enrich themselves, they chose to maintain their rural lifestyle, allowing outside interests to exploit the resources - particularly British miners. Diamonds were discovered in 1869 in the Orange Free State, and gold was discovered in 1886 in the Transvaal. The diamond and gold fields-all owned and operated by English entrepreneurs-became extremely productive.

While many British considered the Boers as being backward farmers, the Boers referred to the new British settlers using a derogatory term referencing their sunburned necks. Boers, descendants of earlier European settlers in the region, saw the British as having one foot in England and Africa and viewed themselves as the rightful owners of the land that is now South Africa. In South Africa, the interrelationship of war, religion, and racial identity played a significant role in shaping group identity. Du Toit (1994) cites the following excerpt from a sermon preached by a Dutch Reformed Minister illustrates how Afrikaners viewed war as a consecration ritual during the Anglo-Boer War (1899-1902). From the sermon, a minister said: "God led us into war; it is to chastise us, but he has His sacred goal... He will not let us perish but will confirm us through this baptism of fire. The Lord Himself planted us in South Africa and let us flourish... [Like Israel] we are going through the Red Sea, but it will make us into a separate people." The Boers regarded their group identity as closely tied to God's intentions. As a people, the Boers regarded themselves as being chosen for something, whether it is a "high and holy mission" or to be distinct from others. It seems that religious and cultural boundaries, and perhaps even more significantly, those between religion and ethnicity, were blurred entirely. Afrikaner Christianity was, therefore, in essence, a religion that was confined to a particular ethnic group. These attitudes dated back to the frontier lifestyle of the Voortrekkers.

Boers became increasingly known as Afrikaners after the War. In contrast to the term Boer, which specifically related to the descendants of those who took part in the Great Trek, the term Afrikaner included all Dutch-speaking South Africans. As different colonies joined forces, this expansion of group identity became a powerful political strategy.

When we discuss Afrikaners, we need to remember that they did not only consider themselves separate from African populations but also other European ethnicities, including the British immigrants. It was increasingly accepted among the Afrikaner population in South Africa that they were distinct from other white South Africans. Protestant churches, within this context, played an essential role in creating and interpreting these cultural myths. Due to their strong Dutch Reformed faith, a rigorous form of Protestantism based on John Calvin's teachings, the Dutch inherited a passion for rural life, sensing they were pioneers against British oppression and the primitive black South African. As Boers believed God had chosen them as His chosen people, they often referred to this land as a new promised land.

With a sense of simultaneity as both victim and victor, Afrikaner nationalism quickly stepped up to the plate. The same could be said for the language we now call Afrikaans. When the Bible was translated into Afrikaans, Afrikaans achieved a higher status despite being a simplified version of Dutch. This linguistic endeavour was primarily the work of young Calvinist theologian J D du Toit (Totius). In addition to teaching theology at the Seminary of the Reformed Church in Potchefstroom, he was a famous poet and leader of the First Language Movement. The creation of the national mythology was due to him more than to anyone else. Hexham (1981) writes that Du Toit and his contemporaries "simultaneously created their myth and the written language (Afrikaans) in which that myth was enshrined."

Additionally, Totius drew many comparisons between Israel and Afrikaner culture using his biblical knowledge. He describes the Afrikaners in his poetry as God's suffering servants. According to Hexham, Potgieter's Trek is a Toitus poem that portrays the Great Trek as a hardship-filled pilgrimage, making the connection to Israel's exodus from Egypt. Here is what Hexham (1981) states about this poem that cuts to the heart of Afrikaner religious self-understanding: "Like Israel, and following the example of Christ Himself, the Afrikaner People achieve salvation through suffering. Totius' poem is, therefore, a psalm to national deliverance, an interpretation of history that makes the past bearable. The irrational pattern of past events fits into a divine scheme, which removes their arbitrary appearance and eternally legitimates them."

Boers and the British both sought to control the region, and Britain reassured some black South Africans who were threatened by the Boer republics that they would be protected. By the end of the 1880s, these protectorates had become British colonies, and their leaders lost control over their lands. The British also used physical force to suppress other groups, such as the Xhosas, whom they attacked in the 1800s, and the Zulus, in 1879.

It is pretty absurd that the Afrikaners, who considered themselves the suffering servants of God and innocent victims of British injustices, could conveniently forget that as they became the real oppressors, causing a tremendous amount of suffering from non-white South Africans. In order to understand how this could occur, one must recognize the pivotal role religion played in forming Afrikaner identity. The Judeo-Christian tradition creates a sacred history that may lead to a strong identification with biblical Israel, significantly when they recognize themselves to have suffered for a good cause. During the Great Trek and the Anglo-Boer War, the Afrikaners suffered hardships analogous to those experienced by Israel during their forty years wandering through the wilderness following the Exodus. Muller (2004) contends that this chastisement was necessary for entering "Canaan." With the establishment of Apartheid, the "heathen" black tribes were finally forced to leave their "homeland" areas, paving the way for the creation of Afrikaner Canaan.

It is also fair to say the Boers pictured themselves as pioneers fighting successfully in an uninhabited, vast land, while the British imagined themselves as enlightened, liberal rulers. Both groups thought of themselves as superior to the local black populations of South Africa, whom they considered unproductive, violent, and uncivilized. Thus, these attitudes shaped European interactions with the black population and justified the oppression of most of the population in the territory.

After the Berlin Conference in 1884–1885 brought about the "scramble for Africa" in which European powers vied for control over the continent, the British pushed farther into southern Africa, creating the current countries of Malawi, Zimbabwe, and Zambia. Even though the British claimed to have enlightened attitudes towards black South Africans, they were just as interested in colonial conquest and dominance as the Boers.

In 1833, after the British abolished slavery across their empire, people from the British colony of India began arriving in South Africa in large numbers, forcing settlers to look for new forms of cheap labour. Despite coming from territories now known as India, Pakistan, and Bangladesh, these people were collectively known as "Indians" in Southern Africa. As indentured servants, Indians often endured harsh working conditions, particularly on sugar plantations. In return for providing them with a living, the workers agreed to work for five or more years before they were allowed to immigrate and begin a new life. However, once their contracts expired, they were offered the choice of renewing their obligations or returning to their home countries. The majority stayed. Then there were the "passenger Indians" who paid for their travel to find better economic opportunities. Due to their commercial backgrounds and efforts to open retail shops, many European shop owners discriminated against them.

During a bloody conflict known by the British as the Second Boer War and the Afrikaners as the Second Freedom War (1899-1902), the British seized control of Transvaal and Orange Free State. It was a bloody war for both sides, but the Afrikaners perceived the British as particularly brutal. As the British set fire to the Boer farms in Transvaal and Orange Free State, 26,000 Boer families were forced to live in concentration camps to die of famine and disease. In a manner that will be ingrained in the collective memory of the Afrikaners for a long time, "the chosen people" were effectively displaced from their land, humiliated, and massacred.

In order to seize control of the gold mines, the British started the second war after a railway line through Mozambique threatened to cut off the British from the gold mines. Having been occupied multiple times by the British and eventually defeated by the British, the Afrikaners viewed themselves as persecuted people encroached on by the British and denied the right to govern their promised land. Afrikaner nationalist movements grew during the next century as the Boers asserted their rights while denying the rights of black South Africans. Afrikaners felt increasingly marginalized as Britain consolidated its grip on the region and local industry developed. As a self-governing British dominion, the Union of South Africa was dominated by an English-speaking urban population, which consolidated the Cape Colony, Natal, the Orange Free State, and Transvaal into one. Due to British tactics in the Second Boer War, the farmer's lifestyle, which was at the core of Afrikaner identity, declined. The majority of them moved to the cities, clamouring for industrial jobs alongside numerous immigrants. Among the migrants, some sought jobs in the mines, competing with blacks from South Africa.

England-linked mine owners grew concerned about the labour situation with the workers whose employment they depended on being perceived as threats. Though defeated by the British in the war, the Afrikaners continued to be resentful, and it was possible that they could turn to violence again. Owners of these mines employed large numbers of blacks across Southern Africa, encouraging them to migrate there. Nevertheless, they were also concerned that blacks were outnumbering whites in the region. It was feared that the Boers and blacks would join forces in order to win concessions in the wage and working conditions.

A compromise was worked out in which the British capitalists granted managerial and skilled labour positions to whites while low-paid heavy labour and low-skilled labour positions were assigned to the Afrikaner miners. In the process, whites' wages grew, while black South Africans' wages diminished, thus allowing a pay scale to develop that favoured whites. Following independence in 1910, the Union of South Africa enacted far-reaching legislation that reinforced this racial differentiation of labour, an idea of English-speaking whites. As a result, black South African labourers faced restrictions on mobility, such as being required to live in designated areas and not bringing their families along with them; these laws became the precursors to Apartheid.

With the gold rush, the gold industry entered a new phase of technology that demanded highly skilled labour. 1922 was marked by the bloody Rand Revolt, which mine owners and 20,000 white labourers started. In order to restore order, the government imposed martial law and used military force, but the white strikers prevailed: they won concessions that strengthened the two-tiered pay system. As noted in the book Mines in South Africa, work in mines was back-breaking, challenging, and treated as subhuman.

An English-speaking population in South Africa often mentioned Cornwall or Cardiff as home and identified themselves as British. Moreover, the cult of individualism prevalent in England hindered the development of a single group identity. German miners and other Europeans became integrated into English-speaking communities by learning English. Despite their commitment to local concerns, British immigrants and their descendants did not develop a uniform identity as independent and distinct as the Afrikaners.

Even though the Boers lost wars to the British, they did not lose power as a result. Fredrickson (1981) points out that: "For practical purposes, the Union of South Africa that emerged from a constitutional convention in 1910 was an independent nation. Although they had lost the war, the Afrikaners had in effect won the peace; for they remained a majority of the total white population and had the potential capacity if they could mobilize themselves politically, to establish their ethnic hegemony." Consequently, the Afrikaner war experience actually played a significant role in the formation of their cultural identity. The Afrikaner national identity developed further in the 1920s and 1930s due to the memories of defeat to the British. In the early 20th century, Afrikaners rallied around a nationalist movement due to feelings of economic and political marginalization. The leaders claimed that Europeans were racially superior and Afrikaners were cultural superior due to their self-reliance and strict Christianity over the British. The Afrikaner grassroots embraced a dogma that was very much in line with the working-class white men and women who thought the British oppressed them.

Identifying oneself as an Afrikaner means speaking Afrikaans, a dialect of Dutch with terminology borrowed from the local languages of South Africa - English, German, Portuguese, Malay, and Khoi Khoi. There were also individuals of non-European descent who spoke Afrikaans in Cape Town, such as the Cape Malays and mixed races. White elites sought to standardize Afrikaans by erasing its non-Dutch influence in strengthening Afrikaner nationalism. In the 1920s, nationalists replaced the Dutch language with Afrikaans as the official language of the country.

Efforts were made the following decade to rebuild Afrikaner self-confidence shattered by the Boer War. Reenactment of the Great Trek in 1938 culminated with the setting of the foundation for the Voortrekker Monument outside of Pretoria as part of the 100th anniversary commemorating the Afrikaner victory over the Zulu. Afrikaners highlighted their own superiority in reminiscing about military victories over black South Africans. Hamerton-Kelly (1993) makes the following insightful observation regarding the impact of pre-Boer War history on the mythological institutions of Afrikaner religion: "Afrikaner group identity was forged between the hammer of British imperialism and the anvil of black resistance. It contains two powerful motivating forces: the sense of being a victim of injustice and arrogance – in this case at the hands of the British – and the exhilaration of being the victor over unfavourable odds – in this instance over the superior numbers of the blacks in battle."

Afrikaners and Anglophones of South Africa found themselves at odds during both the First and Second world wars. Despite being led by an Afrikaner, Prime Minister Jan Smuts, a group within the Afrikaner community, felt strongly that South Africa should not enter the war on the side of Britain. As Afrikaner nationalism developed in the 1930s, many admirers acknowledged that the Nazi Germany policy of "racial purity" was an achievement. Many, however, wished to keep South Africa neutral in the conflict between Germany and Great Britain as they disagreed with South Africa's decision to enter World War II.

South African policy had already been shaped by segregation and white supremacy before Apartheid began. Three years after South Africa gained its independence, the controversial 1913 Land Act was passed in Parliament, prohibiting blacks from working as share croppers, marking territorial segregation. In opposition to the Land Act, blacks formed South Africa's National Native Congress, later becoming the African National Congress (ANC).

As South Africa suffered from the Great Depression and World War II, its policies of racial segregation became stronger. The pro-Afrikaner National Party (NP) came to power in April 1948 with a policy of Apartheid that was even more rigorous and authoritarian than previous segregationist measures. "Apartheid", which means "apartness", was a slogan of the Afrikaner National Party when it won the general election.

Among their goals was to divide South Africa's white minority from its non-white majority, as well as division between non-whites and to reduce the political influence of black South Africans.

A ban was imposed by the government in 1950 on marriages between whites and other races and prohibited black and white sexual relations in South Africa. It was in the 1950s that South Africans were divided by race, based on their race. They could be Bantu (African), Colored (mixed race), or white. The fourth category added later was Asian (meaning Indians and Pakistanis). In some cases, the legislation separated families: one's parents could be categorized as white and children as coloured. Over 80% of the country's land was set aside for the white minority, and the "pass laws" required non-whites to be accompanied by papers authorizing their presence in areas restricted to whites only.

Separate public facilities were built for whites and non-whites, and union participation was limited, thereby limiting contact between the races. As the white government of South Africa expanded its power, so did the black opposition. A young, more committed political movement was born in 1943 with the establishment of the ANC Youth League that would be responsible for nurturing leaders like Nelson Mandela, Oliver Tambo, and Walter Sisulu. Prime Minister Hendrik Verwoerd formulated a policy of "separate development" after becoming prime minister in 1958. This regulation created 10 Bantu homelands referred to as “Bantustans”. Through this system, the government was able to claim that there was no black majority in South Africa by separating black South Africans from each other, thereby reducing the likelihood that they would unify into one nationalist party. In South Africa, every black person became a Bantustan citizen, which provided them with full political rights while also excluding them from participating in the nation's political process. In 1961, Verwoerd, the prime minister, declared South Africa a republic after winning a whites-only referendum.

One of the most devastating aspects of Apartheid were the forced removals of black South Africans from rural areas designated as reserved for white people, and their lands were sold at low prices to white farmers. Approximately 3.5 million people were forcibly moved from their homes and thrown into poverty in the Bantustans between 1961 and 1994. Apartheid resistance in South Africa encompassed many forms throughout the anti-Apartheid struggle, from protests, strikes, and non-violent demonstrations to armed struggle. On April 17, 1952, the ANC and the South Indian National Congress organized a mass meeting, during which the passbooks were burned. Congress of the People adopted a Freedom Charter in 1955 that declared "South Africa belongs to all its people, white or black." One hundred fifty people were arrested and charged with high treason after the Apartheid government broke up these meetings.

As more African countries gained independence from the Europeans, resistance against Apartheid gained momentum. Blacks associated with the Pan-African Congress (PAC), an offshoot of the ANC, were shot and killed by the police in 1960 in the black township of Sharpesville. As a form of resistance, the group deliberately invited arrests by visiting a police station without passes. Approximately 67 blacks were killed and more than 180 injured. In the aftermath of Sharpesville, it became apparent to many anti-Apartheid activists that they were not likely to succeed through peaceful protests. Both the ANC and PAC established military wings, but neither posed any serious threat to the state. Most of the resistance leaders had been jailed, executed or exiled by 1961. Nelson Mandela, the ANC's founder of the military wing Umkhonto we Sizwe, was imprisoned between 1963 and 1990. His imprisonment led to more global condemnation of Apartheid.

Decolonization Of Africa And The Rise Of White Minority Governments

In the aftermath of World War II, European powers faced profound political and economic challenges. This was due to political and economic power realignments across the globe. These geopolitical changes later pushed the major powers into what is commonly known as the Cold War. The Cold War was an era of geopolitical tension that began in 1947 between the Soviet bloc and the Western alliance led by the United States and Western European countries. The political and economic consequences of the war impacted the world economy, as the ideologically different Soviet Union emerged at the heart of Europe. The Cold War's high politics defined foreign policy on economic, political, and economic spheres, and colonialism was part of that international agenda. The new conditions disrupted the colonial order and provided opportunities for independence, with India leading the way.

Except for the Lusophone countries (Mozambique and Angola), South Africa, Namibia, and Rhodesia, which went through a long and violent conflict, most Southern African states gained independence orderly with limited violence. The importance of Southern Africa to the Europeans cannot be over-emphasized. European colonization of Southern Africa occurred later as compared to South America and East Asia. Giliomee and Mbenga (2007) believe that the region initially lacked strategic value to Europeans. However, as trade between Asia and Europe grew, Southern Africa became a region of strategic importance. European powers like Germany, Portugal, Belgium, and Great Britain viewed Southern Africa as a strategic location where ships heading to India and other parts of Asia could utilize the Southern and East African Coasts as stopover ports.

However, mineral deposits discovered in Southern Africa exacerbated Europeans' interest in Southern Africa in the mid-1800s. Koponen (1993) argues that gold and diamonds' presence intensified the scramble for control of the continent as a strategic location leading to the Berlin Conference in 1884, which defined Africa's future and what is popularly known as the 'Scramble for Africa'. Horvath (1972) describes colonialism as a form of temporarily extended domination by one group of people over another group and, as such, part of the historical universe of forms of intergroup domination, subjugation, oppression, and exploitation. The weaker group becomes a periphery in this arrangement as all its economic and political spheres are dominated by the stronger group.

Colonialism on the African continent altered the history of Africa forever. The objective of creating African colonies was to exploit the continent's human and economic resources. The economic goals of Europeans were simple: to maximise economic benefits at the lowest possible cost. As a result, the Berlin Conference created the rules for managing these colonies. In Southern Africa, Mozambique and Angola became Portuguese overseas territories; Belgium occupied Zaire, now the Democratic Republic of Congo (DRC); and Germany colonized Tanganyika and South-West Africa (Namibia). At the same time, Great Britain became the dominant player in the region by colonizing areas that are now known as Botswana, Lesotho, Swaziland, South Africa, Malawi, Zambia, and Zimbabwe. This colonization led to Africans being stripped of their agricultural and ancestral land, leaving them with no alternative apart from providing cheap labour to the Europeans. The process expanded the European Capitalist economy, where the Europeans embarked on farming and extraction of mineral wealth while exploiting the cheap African labour.

Söderbaum (2016) argues that "the scramble for Africa and an attempt to gain control over mineral resources had strong regional implications, which has continued to influence the integration theory as well as the practice of African regionalism." While colonialism brought some form of infrastructure development on the African continent, these developments were explicitly modelled on maximising the economic benefits of the Europeans. For Europeans, opening up significant African landmasses required accessible road, rail and communication infrastructure, which required significant capital investment. This infrastructure was also used to portray European control of the territories; in his famous publication titled *How Europe Underdeveloped Africa*, Walter Rodney talks about developing the capital-intensive colonial infrastructure during colonialism. Rodney (1972) puts it: "All roads and railways led down to the sea. They were built to extract gold, manganese or coffee, or cotton. They were built to make business possible for timber companies, trading companies, agricultural concession firms, and white settlers. Any catering to African interests was purely coincidental." The colonial pursuit for exploiting minerals also implied the birth of the first regional groupings. Southern African Customs Union (SACU) is one of those initial regional institutions and remains the oldest customs union globally, dating back to 1889.

World War II had weakened colonial powers in both Asia and Africa. The colonial powers had recruited soldiers from their colonial territories to fight in the war. Britain and France had recruited hundreds of thousands of African troops to fight the Nazi Germans. During the brutal battle, 374,000 Africans from British territories served in the British military, while France recruited 80,000 from its colonial territories in Africa. Regiments made up of African soldiers were sent to Burma and India, where they fought brilliantly. As African soldiers fought on the Indian sub-continent, they learned from their Indian counterparts that they had been promised independence as a condition for their participation in the war.

While decolonisation appeared to be a voluntary decision for the Europeans, it is essential to point out that by 1942, Japanese forces had pushed out the British from Southeast Asian colonies of Burma, Malaya, Singapore, and others was a strategic blow for the British during World War II. Jeffrey (1999) argues that "the cataclysmic blows struck by the triumphant Japanese in Hong Kong, Malaya, Singapore, and Burma grievously undermined the myth of European invincibility." Europeans had relied upon the prestige of European invincibility crumbled in front of the African soldiers that the Europeans had recruited.

Despite the collapse of the foundations of European colonialism, Europeans remained determined to retain control of the remaining colonial territories. The economic benefits of these territories were of particular importance due to the presence of strategic mineral and natural resources in those territories. While Europeans were determined to preserve their strategic assets, the United States of America became strategically important. Any hope of defeating the Axis powers was dependent on American involvement in the war.

Figure 3.1: Prime Minister Winston Churchill (seated second from left) and President Franklin Roosevelt (seated third from left)

Source: UN Historical Photo

With European countries weakened during the war, power shifted from Europeans towards the new Super Powers, the United States of America (USA) and the Union of Soviet Socialist Republic (USSR). These two emerging powers had entrenched negative views of colonialism. The most significant development occurred in August 1941, as the United Kingdom pursuaded the US to provide military support to the Western Alliance. As a result, the Atlantic Charter was signed and a joint declaration issued on August 14, 1941, by US President Franklin Roosevelt and British Prime minister Winston Churchill at a secret conference held at sea. This agreement was not a Treaty but rather an affirmation of certain common principles in their respective country's national policies on which they based their hopes for a better future of the world. One of the outstanding tenets of the Atlantic Charter (1941) was the affirmation of the basic principles of justice, which included:

(i) No aggrandizement;
(ii) No territorial changes without the freely-expressed wishes of the peoples concerned;
(iii) The right of every people to choose their form of government; and
(v) Equal access to raw materials for all nations.

For the Americans, the colonial system allowed European powers to monopolize the vast wealth in Africa and Asia, which went against US interests. However, the British believed that the basic rules of justice only applied to occupied European territories, while the Americans believed that the agreement applied to all colonial territories. The impact of World War II and the anti-colonial attitudes of the US was inevitably disruptive to the European control of the colonial territories, which accelerated the activities of African freedom fighters. The African elites were encouraged to pursue independence soon after the war, and the Atlantic Charter was used as the source of legitimacy for demanding freedom.

In Southern Africa, the transfer of power to an African majority became complicated due to a large influx of white settlers in some of those territories. As African soldiers returned home, they had high expectations about the future of their homeland. With the new skills and ideas acquired during the war, they believed that they had gained the right competencies to assume self-governance, and participating in the war had earned them the right to do so. However, their ambitions met resistance from the colonial powers and, in other countries, the white settlers, who were not willing to grant them independence. With India and Pakistan gaining independence in 1947, Africans were hopeful that similar arrangements could be made on the African continent.

Notwithstanding the changing international opinion on colonialism, there was a rise in African nationalism on the continent. A growing number of indigenous political movements emerged, which stimulated increased demand for African participation in government. As the colonial powers delayed granting independence to the indigenous

Africans, the political movements became overly aggressive in their pursuit of early independence.

Southern Africa is mainly composed of Anglophone and Lusophone states, which had different characteristics in their colonial governance systems. Bollen and Jackman (1985) argue that the British transfer to the Africans was more orderly than in other colonies. In the context of Southern Africa, while the British showed a willingness to grant independence to their overseas territories after the war, the Portuguese were reluctant to give their overseas territories freedom. The Portuguese government (under the dictatorship of Dr Antonio de Oliveira Salazar) was critical of the Western powers' policy regarding Africa's decolonization. In a speech delivered to the Chairman of the National Union District Committees on May 23, 1959, quoted in Comte (1962), Dr Salazar argues: "The present and immediate needs are to save Africa...and to avoid its destruction by formulas that we know would be fatal to it." In his view, Portugal was a composite nation of African and European territories, and granting independence was like surrendering Portuguese sovereignty.

While the US supported the concept of self-determination during and soon after World War II, following the emergence of the Cold War, there was a growing concern in the US Government that the Soviet-supported regimes might achieve power in the new African states. The new Soviet influence in Africa could have geopolitical implications due to the rise of Communist-led governments while at the same time removing access to strategic economic resources from European powers that were part of the Western bloc fighting the rise of Communism. There was a growing concern that the Soviet Union would take the European's place as a significant power on the African continent, giving the Soviet Republics access to vast natural resources.

This ideological struggle also motivated white-minority governments to tighten their grip on power as they were determined to hold on to the vast wealth in the region. Meredith (2011) argues that the notion of African rule spelt disaster for the white minority in South Africa, Rhodesia, South West Africa, and the Lusophone territories of Angola and Mozambique. The white-minority governments in these countries were fearful of Communists using Africans to help the Soviets capture the mineral riches of Southern Africa.

As Botswana, Lesotho, Malawi, Swaziland, Tanzania, and Zambia gained independence orderly, the circumstances differed for South

Africa, Zimbabwe, Namibia, Angola, and Mozambique. The white-minority governments in those countries consolidated their power and used coercive force to counter any form of resistance. This inspired a new wave of prolonged liberation wars in the region heightened by the Cold War's ideological battles. For the white minority governments, their existence in the region was necessary to defeating Socialism in the region that gained popularity. As a strategy to contain socialism, African-led political movements were not allowed to operate in South Africa, Rhodesia, South West Africa, Angola, and Mozambique. African freedom fighters were arrested or exiled as the crackdown on political dissent grew. In Meredith's (2011) view, the South Africans used the fear of socialism to justify constructing an elaborate racial divide called Apartheid. From employment, residence, education, public amenities, and politics, the blacks were given a subordinate role in South Africa. In addition, the system removed millions of people from their ancestral land to ensure that blacks lived outside the territories strictly reserved for the whites.

Figure 3.2: An Apartheid Era Sign Depicting Racial Segregation in South Africa

Source: Getty Images

The South African government went further to extend this system of Apartheid to the newly occupied territory of South West Africa (Namibia). The white settlers withheld the right to vote from the native Africans and were deprived of all other rights to maintain their authority over the Africans. As a form of resistance to this oppressive governance system in South Africa, Southwest Africa, Rhodesia, and the Lusophone states (Angola and Mozambique), prominent liberation movements emerged in these countries. African National Congress (ANC) in South Africa; The South West Africa People's Organization (SWAPO) in Namibia; The Mozambique Liberation Front (FRELIMO); Angola's People's Movement for the Liberation of Angola (MPLA); and The Zimbabwe African National Union (ZANU), to name a few. With the white minority government surrounded by hostile member states that supported these liberation movements, South Africa embarked on a mission to destabilize its neighbours.

In Rhodesia, white nationalists embarked on a self-governance path following South Africa's footsteps, which had declared independence half a century before 1910. With most colonial territories rich in mineral and natural resources, the white settlers in some territories started demanding political autonomy. Unlike West Africa, where independence was less complex, some white settlers in Southern African territories believed that they had a right to claim political power in those territories. After the war, the European settlers' population had soared in the region as many white soldiers returning from the war were offered farming land in Southern Africa to venture on a new lease of life.

As the ideological war between Communism and Capitalism broke out around the same period, Southern Africa presented a new battleground for the ideological confrontation between the US-led Western bloc and the Eastern bloc, led by the USSR as more Southern African states gained independence. As a result of these new emerging concerns, both the US and its European allies became proactive in managing who was to gain power in the African territories. Some scholars have made arguments that colonial rule committed African countries to fragile authoritarian governments. As the Europeans attempted to retain control of the African resources after independence, they left behind weakened democratic structures with limited conditions for democratic politics. The Europeans even attempted to manipulate the elections to ensure that their preferred political parties won in a few countries. These conditions led to the emergence of fragile but repressive regimes as the post-colonial leaders faced multifaceted challenges to govern.

Cheeseman and Fisher (2019), in their book *Authoritarian Africa: Repression, Resistance, and the Power of Ideas*, argue that "the first rigged elections held on the continent were those organised by Britain and France." The Cold War competition with the Soviet Union later developed into the dominant feature of US foreign policy, which also distorted the USA's views on self-determination and human rights.

However, alternative colonial legacies have also left behind very distinctive administrative and bureaucratic traditions. There is a solid linguistic connection between francophone countries in Africa, a common legal system, and in some cases, monetary union, such as the CFA in West Africa. The same can be said for the current geopolitical tension in the Great Lakes region, stemming from the legacy of Belgian occupation. These histories have left African countries with a wide range of legal systems, linguistics, and geopolitical perspectives regarding regional integration. Furthermore, these histories have contributed to the emergence of a Pan-African spirit underpinning integration efforts.

Colonizing Africa came at a high price for Europeans. Political and strategic considerations were at play in addition to economic ones. A cash economy was needed in African colonies to pay for the administration costs of colonialism, which meant changing African production structures for European markets. Infrastructural and investment efforts were concentrated where a high return on investment was possible for European powers. Morrison et al. (1989) note that around £1,222,000,000 was invested in sub-Saharan Africa between 1870 and 1936. A combination of public and private capital was used to make these investments. Mineral exploitation accounted for only a quarter of the money invested in this area. In fact, the economies of African countries continue to be heavily reliant on foreign trade and financial support, as it was intended.

African national institutions are the result of colonization. According to Hydén (1983), the new political elite deemed existing macro-economic structures as being the main instruments of the exploitative imperialist rule when independence arrived. Despite being positive on a political and social level, the choice was detrimental to economic development.

After decolonization and the dawn of independence in Southern Africa, many integration schemes were adopted. Many countries in the regional grouping had ties to the same colonial power, so their official languages and institutions shared many similarities, except for the

Lusophone countries. There was another unique impetus for integration in Southern Africa. As a result of South Africa's political and economic dominance, Lesotho, Malawi, Namibia, Swaziland, Zambia, and Zimbabwe created SADCC, which has evolved into today's Southern African Development Conference (SADC), which also includes South Africa. Odén et al. (1993) note that SADCC was a positive measure for encouraging change in the region, in contrast to economic sanctions. As a result, the organization received a lot of outside aid. The organization received almost 90% of its budget for projects from foreign development agencies.

Pan-Africanism and Solidarity Approach of Organization of African Unity

As discussed in Chapter 2, since independence, almost all African countries embraced regionalism. A sense of Pan-Africanism, which calls for unity among African peoples, contributed to regional cooperation as well, according to Odén et al. (1993). During the liberation struggle, unity among African states was essential for overcoming foreign political and economic domination. The decolonization process and liberation struggles are common experiences in Southern Africa that facilitate integration. In turn, these enabled a sense of unity and belonging, which are reflected in Pan-African ideology. As the precursor to the African Union (AU), the Organization of African Unity (OAU) established its stated purpose in 1963 to serve both as a way to bring African countries together for unity and solidarity and stamp out all forms of colonialism throughout Africa. From creating the OAU, newly independent African states joined the grouping with the aspiration of continental integration and liberation of other African states under white minority rule. Influenced by Pan-Africanism, African leaders had a consensus on promoting and committing to continental unity. Tanyanyiwa and Hakuna (2014) argue that the post-independence era saw African states embracing regional integration, initially mainly for political reasons and later as an economic and development strategy. For the states to successfully rise above the challenges of small markets, landlocked territories and to benefit from economies of scale in production and trade, integrating their economies became a popular option. That led to a growing consensus among leaders that newly independent African states would struggle to survive in the anarchical international system if they remained isolated.

The Pan-Africanist movement had emerged in the US in the 19th Century amongst African American intellectuals. The philosophy focused on the belief that Africans could only achieve black civilization if the blacks established their own serf governed nations and wanted to do away with colonialism. Pan-Africanism philosophy centred on scholars like Du Bois and Marcus Garvey, who argue that colonialism was the genesis of Africa's economic, political and social problems. The idea of a united Africa appeared for the first time in 1924 in a Marcus Garvey poem titled '*Hail, United States of Africa*'. The poem symbolised African unity, which inspired black Africans to return to their continent and liberate their home countries from colonialism. These early events set up the motion for the direction of African integration. The early African leaders believed colonial self-interests inspired the boundaries drawn during the 1884-85 Berlin Conference; thus, they wanted to do away with them. Englebert et al. (2002) argue that there is "little disagreement that the boundaries of contemporary African states are unusually arbitrary as a result of their largely colonial origins." The Pan-Africanist desire for collective self-reliance, solidarity, development, peace and African unity led to the OAU establishment.

During this period, there was a discussion about the whole African continent's unification through regional blocs and democratic ideologies. Leaders of newly liberated African countries like Kwame Nkrumah in Ghana viewed Ghana's independence as the beginning of liberating other African countries. Centuries of exploitation of African resources and Africans' depersonalization had motivated educated Africans to challenge the status quo. Pan-Africanism introduced what Jinadu (2009) refers to as a new brand of nationalism that promoted African societies' integration, unification, and Africanization by establishing a federal-type governance system above the smaller African states. In Jinadu's (2009) view, Pan-Africanism promotes disparate people's integration, under a union government, as the only logical route to consolidating the independent African states into a formidable economic force. This conviction motivated Kwame Nkrumah to host the African conferences between 1958 and 1960 to speed up other African countries' liberation from colonial powers. When attempting to integrate newly independent African nations, the founding fathers acknowledged the existence of different approaches and differed on how they should proceed. A federal approach was proposed by Nkrumah, with a vertical central authority and supranational control.

The OAU was formed when most African leaders were experiencing self-rule for the first time and were more focused on consolidating their power. Cervenl (1977) argue that: "the newly-independent African States were sensitive about their sovereign rights and resented outside interference - hence their refusal to enter into obligations which would be enforceable by a supranational authority." Other African leaders viewed Kwame Nkrumah's ambition for a complete unification as a threat to the territorial sovereignty of newly liberated African states that had just come out of colonialism. While there was consensus among early African leaders on the importance of integrating African states, there were competing visions concerning the nature of unification. The ideological differences drove these different visions, and sometimes these differences got in the way of negotiations on the future of an independent African continent. These differences led to three competing approaches for integration emerging.

According to Van Walraven (2010), the Casablanca group championed by Kwame Nkrumah advocated for full continental integration. The group advocated a centralized model of government and was supported by Ghana, Guinea, Mali, Libya, Egypt, Morocco, and Algeria. The Monrovia group endorsed the sub-regional approach based on "state nationalism." The Monrovia group had the backing of Nigeria, Togo, Sudan, Liberia, Tunisia, Ethiopia, and Somalia. The group lobbied for a moderate unification approach, encouraging incremental steps instead of a more radical immediate integration. Finally, the Brazzaville group had the majority of Francophone states led by Senegal and Ivory Coast. This group wanted unification, which allowed these countries to maintain ties with France. Due to these differences, a gradualist compromise and decentralized unification model prevailed in the form of the Organization of African Unity (OAU), established on 25 May 1963.

The OAU was more intergovernmental in terms of decision-making, as its Charter failed to assign any sovereignty to supranational institutions. The OAU Charter also shows that states signing it were primarily concerned with decolonization, preserving the independence of already free states, and respecting sovereign boundaries. According to Murithi (2005), the main principle of the OAU was non-interference in internal affairs. African nations oppressed their citizens with impunity and did little to stop massive human rights violations in neighbouring countries. Therefore, according to Michel (2012), the OAU became a forum for discussion primarily without any actual competence. However, it was able to influence member states to lessen conflicts on the continent. It was evident that the member countries did not have the political will to give OAU power and responsibility.

Upon examining the founding fathers' ideas, it becomes clear that unity among African nations was their goal. Founders, however, failed to provide a specific definition of unity. There is an ambiguity regarding what unity actually is or ought to be. As a result of a lack of conceptual clarity in the OAU's formative years, "unity" has been used both as an expression of solidarity and as an expression of integration. "Unity," "solidarity," and "cooperation" were all used interchangeably in the OAU Charter without any attempt at providing any definition. In the process of transforming the OAU into the African Union (AU), the ambiguity of the term "unity" persisted, and it still exists today.

Efforts to integrate the continent on a sub-regional basis also demonstrate unity's dual meaning. The Southern African Development Community ("SADC") and its member states uphold principles such as solidarity, democracy, and the rule of law. Upon these principles, SADC Member States orient themselves in fostering integration by focusing on forging ties between member states. Nevertheless, there exist no mechanisms or guidelines for interpreting the principles of the SADC.

Although Southern African states enjoyed some harmony in their ideas and actions, especially when it comes to Pan-Africanism during the 1960s and the 1970s, disunity has created multiple nonviable organizations in the political, economic, and socio-cultural domains. Consequently, imperialism and neo-colonialism spread throughout the region and beyond. It resulted instead in the division of the region's socio-political and cultural development. Thus, we can define Pan-Africanism as the collective aspiration of blacks in Africa and in the Diaspora who identify themselves as being part of an African and black civilization that has been built out of the black struggle for victory against slavery, colonialism, and Apartheid. This regional and continental political unity aspiration was rooted in regional integration initiatives with the rest of the African continent. The current Southern African countries had considered joining forces to stand up to the past of slavery and colonialism as well as to the imperialism and neocolonialism that dominated markets and society in a globalized world.

By studying the history of the countries of Southern Africa as a group, especially considering the conditions in which they began these integration processes, one may be able to piece together a possible explanation for this situation. One can identify the origin of the first Southern African regional integration projects in the context of British colonialism, which led to the creation of the Southern African Customs Union (SACU) and Central African Federation, which established a standard and a shared management structure for the region's political entities. In order to solve the varying and enormous security, economic, social and cultural difficulties that existed at the beginning of independence, there were a number of uniting initiatives between the different states. As elsewhere in the newly independent and liberated world, Southern African countries faced the challenge of working to overcome developmental barriers generated by limitations in socioeconomic space, causing the new rulers to seek to expand political and geographical borders.

4

Complex Inter-State Relations and Liberation Struggle in Southern Africa

Introduction

It would be remiss to conceptualise the history of regional cooperation in Southern Africa without paying attention to the complex relations and tensions between countries during the liberation struggle that have continued to guide regional relations today. This chapter reflects and examines the neglected history of Southern Africa by contextualising the sophisticated and challenging environment in Southern Africa. The chapter aims to provide a valuable insight that can help shine a spotlight on relationships between states in Southern Africa. The chapter will go through complex and sometimes provocative debates that informed regional relations and provide lessons that should be learned.

With a rising number of regional institutions across the globe and their influence in the international political and economic arena, interest in Southern Africa's regional bodies grew significantly for different reasons. This section is primarily concerned with the intrinsic and most complex relationships between Southern African states during the liberation struggle and how these relationships shaped regional relations. This section will highlight various foreign policy objectives behind strategic decisions adopted by nation-states in the region soon after independence so as to understand their behaviours better. While the circumstances that drove those historic foreign policy decisions have now changed, we can best understand the current relationships between member states if we consider the historical context. Consequently, this chapter will examine the strategic context in which nation-states utilized diplomacy in the region, including the economic interdependency of states, Apartheid in South Africa, political leadership, and their relationship with the region's liberation movement.

This period was dominated by a struggle between the colonial/Apartheid ad hoc alliances pitted against the anti-colonial/Apartheid alliance that supported the liberation movements. This section provides a brief history of relationships between states and the liberation movements in Southern Africa while highlighting complex and critical events during this period. This analysis will benefit from Graham Allison models to understand the decision-making processes of Southern African states. The most commonly used model, in this case, is the rational actor model, where nation-states are perceived as rational actors and intrinsically good when making foreign policy decisions. In this context, the OAU promoted Pan-Africanism and the solidarity principle enshrined as fundamental principles of the OAU charter. This section will examine how Southern African countries fulfilled their obligations to support fellow Africans as demanded by the OAU. This chapter will analyze their behaviour based on their support to the liberation movements and their relationships with white minority-led governments in the region. There is a broad consensus and recognition concerning the decisive role played by Southern African states in supporting the liberation movements, although the support provided was diverse.

Ne-orealism, solidarity principle, Pan-Africanism and interdependence theories will also be utilised to explain some of the decisions made by member states. An argument will be maintained throughout the section highlighting that the decisions made by Southern African states were motivated by their desire to survive under an intense and hostile environment while also providing support to the liberation movements. In managing these complicated relationships with the liberation movements, states pursued diverse and sometimes conflicting approaches. South Africa's coercive policy of destabilizing states supporting the African National Congress (ANC) and rewarding those who had not supported the liberation movement influenced these diverse approaches. In addition, using counterinsurgency military operations, the South African Government carried out military strikes, raids and sponsored proxies in Mozambique and Angola. The Apartheid regime also adopted deliberate manoeuvres aimed at crippling the economies of Southern African states. In scrutinizing the underlying rationale for the different approaches adopted by nation-states, the book highlights the impact of the different approaches on each nation-state.

Balancing Solidarity Against National Interest(s)

Since Southern African states started gaining independence from the Europeans, liberation movements became a prominent feature in countries still in the hands of European settlers who had shown no willingness to give up power to the black majority. Inevitably, this led to the new liberation struggle where isolated white minority governments in South Africa, Angola, Rhodesia, South West Africa, and Mozambique were determined to hold on to power while surrounded by neighbouring hostile states that opposed their legitimacy. It is beyond dispute that the Southern African states suffered a great deal during the liberation struggle. The only issue subject to debate is the magnitude or the extent of that suffering. It is also evident that different states took different measures to mitigate the threat of white minority regimes due to the awkward interdependency between the Apartheid regime and Southern African states.

As more African states gained independence, the OAU demanded states to pursue a unified foreign policy that supported the liberation movements and isolated the white minority regimes. From this perspective, most African states adopted the principle of solidarity, which encouraged and supported nationalist movements fighting for freedom in Angola, Mozambique, Zimbabwe, Namibia, and South Africa. As promoted by the OAU, Pan-Africanism and solidarity were the primary guiding principles for foreign policy decisions adopted by the newly independent African states. By adopting these principles, African states were obligated to share the responsibility that promoted fundamental values of solidarity and brotherhood. Thus, from promoting boycotts and sanctions on white minority governments, providing support to liberation movements, and granting them diplomatic recognition, the

African governments were relentless in their effort to challenge the white minority governments. Any country diverting from that common standpoint of solidarity was treated with contempt by its peers and the OAU.

Several cross-border arrangements in Africa's different sub-regions also emerged to enhance regional integration as more countries became independent. In Southern Africa, the diplomatic coalition of independent Southern African Front-line States (FLS) emerged in 1975. FLS was about the geographical proximity of the states to the locations of the liberation struggle. In response, South Africa took a leading role in destabilizing the countries supporting the South African freedom fighters, African National Congress (ANC). The extended colonial conflicts in the region left a lasting effect on the region's economic, political, and social fabric. FLS' initial objective was to manage the Rhodesia-Zimbabwe civil war. They provided invaluable support to the nationalist movements in Zimbabwe, South Africa, and Namibia as South West Africa. Under pressure from military and economic destabilization from South Africa, frontline states established the Southern African Development Coordination Conference (SADCC) after what came to be known as the Lusaka Declaration in 1980. SADC was a new economic cooperation structure with important decisions at the senior political level. Adopting the Lusaka Declaration, member states agreed to achieve economic liberation by adopting regional infrastructure development that would necessitate regional integration and commitment to economic independence from Apartheid South Africa.

One fundamental reason that led to the formation of SADCC was Southern Africa's slow economic growth, high levels of poverty, together with the acceptance of globalization. Southern African states also realized that they could not survive independently in an environment characterized by South Africa's economic dominance and destabilization efforts. According to Evans (1984), South Africa's destabilisation policy had a primary objective of "smashing the stability of the FLS and blunting the development of SADCC while simultaneously striking at the ANC and its host nations." For Evans, the counterinsurgency efforts were part of "a tactical escalation, economic bludgeoning, and utilization of proxy forces like RENAMO in Mozambique and UNITA Angola." This destabilisation inflicted enormous damage to Southern African states' economic and political fabric, which according to Green (1992), includes the deaths of 1.6 million people and $65 billion worth of infrastructural damage.

Nevertheless, most Southern African economies continued to rely on South Africa for trade, employment, higher education, transport, and communication. Against the backdrop of South Africa's decision to cripple the economies of Southern Africa that had been dependent on Pretoria, SADCC was created to reduce their dependence on South Africa. However, under SADCC's flexible structure, most SADCC members failed to live up to the group's objective of lessening dependence on the Apartheid regime. SADCC member states maintained their relationship with South Africa, which directly contradicted SADCC's interests. During that period, South Africa's exports to African countries increased from $300 million in 1970 to $1.3 billion in 1980. Malawi also maintained its diplomatic ties with South Africa and remained the only African country with diplomatic relations with the Apartheid regime. Such an extreme decision within Southern Africa inevitably brought about conflicts and weakened the unity amongst regional neighbours. Even within relatively closed circles like the OAU Summit, the tensions between African states were also visible. Such divergent foreign policies underscored the pressure Southern African countries experienced as they mitigated the thin line between the solidarity principle and national interests.

With Zimbabwe joining FLS after her independence in 1980, FLS became a dominant grouping in Southern Africa and adopted an anti-Apartheid stance. Furthermore, according to Jenkins (1981), the stance taken by FLS member states was problematic to the South African Apartheid government. While countering the Apartheid regime's destabilization efforts remained the main objective of the FLS. The grouping also got caught up in the Cold War as some member states like Tanzania, Angola, and Mozambique adopted Marxist ideologies. South Africa viewed the Marxist-inspired states surrounding it as a threat to its political ideology of Apartheid and its Capitalist economic system. In addition, having Cuban and Soviet Union's influence across its border was a threat to the Apartheid regime.

When discussing the liberation struggle in Southern Africa, the politics of solidarity in Africa cannot be ignored. From the greater politics at the OAU to Southern Africa's sub-region, the politics of solidarity was driven by Pan-Africanism philosophy, which defined the relations between the black-led Southern African states and the liberation movements. The solidarity principle was influenced by Africa's colonial history, as earlier discussed. The North-South rivalry also influenced the concept of solidarity. Countries of the southern hemisphere felt threatened by any form of domination from the more superior powers from the global north. In this regard, the African states believed that they had to protect their territorial sovereignty and interests.

The struggle against Apartheid in South Africa and other white minority regimes in the region was a complex process that required a collective effort from African countries and the international economic and social isolation of the South Africa Apartheid regime. Southern African states stood firm despite South Africa and its partners' determination to destabilize the states through military raids and sponsoring anti-government movements in Mozambique (RENAMO) and Angola (UNITA). The Apartheid regime's support of the two proxies in Mozambique and Angola led to full-blown civil wars in the two countries. South Africa provided military, logistical, training, and financial support to the two rebel groups. Despite these challenges, the two countries continued to provide the ANC operatives with a safe sanctuary, while Tanzania and Zambia provided administrative offices in Dar es Salaam and Lusaka.

The smaller and poorer Southern African states underwent an excruciating shared history that led to the loss of lives and economic livelihood. These countries could not match the economic and military might of the Apartheid regime. Liberation movements from different countries fought wars together, which were bloody and had economic consequences on the whole region. This history continues to have significance in regional politics until today. Between the 1960s and the early 1990s, Southern African states' posturing towards the liberation movements led to instability in these states due to the counterinsurgency operations and economic response from the Apartheid South African regime. This response caused profound devastation across the region; thus, no nation-state could openly provide space for insurgency operations against South Africa. South Africa's regional policy was characterized by what can be referred to as a "carrot and stick" approach to deal with the Southern African states. The regime provided economic support to the nation-states hostile to the ANC while destabilizing those that supported the ANC. With all the Southern African countries being economically dependent on South Africa, it was easy for the South African Government to hurt Southern African states economically. To appreciate the white nationalist regimes' destabilization efforts in Southern Africa, we must understand how those actions impacted Southern African states. These actions were crucial to how the Southern African states responded to the white nationalist governments. The following section will offer a perspective on South Africa's destabilization efforts in Southern Africa by providing a brief background on significant events that transpired. Tracing the interactions between the liberation movements and the independent nation-states in Southern Africa will reveal some exciting legacies usually forgotten.

***

Tanzania

Tanganyika was a German colony of German East Africa, whereas Zanzibar and Pemba were British colonies. In the aftermath of World War I, German East Africa was granted to Britain under the League of Nations Mandate and renamed Tanganyika. As stipulated in the mandate, 'until the native populations are able to withstand the strenuous conditions of the modern world, the material and moral well-being and the social progress of the inhabitants form a sacred trust of civilisation'. The natives' readiness to self-rule was unclear from the terms set out in the mandate. Britain retained control over Tanganyika under the UN Trusteeship Scheme in the wake of World War I. On December 9, 1961, Tanganyika gained independence and became a republic a year later. The two islands of Zanzibar and Pemba gained independence in 1963, paving the way for a unification of the two islands to the mainland, Tanganyika. Tanganyika, Pemba and Zanzibar merged on April 26, 1964 to form the United Republic of Tanganyika and Zanzibar.

Julius Nyerere, Tanzania's first president, believed that the country's freedom would be meaningless if other African nations remained under colonial rule. An African socialist, Julius Nyerere was committed to Pan-Africanism and African liberation beyond the borders of Tanzania. Those beliefs shaped Tanzania's foreign policy and a period of uncompromising support for liberation movements throughout Africa and beyond. The country played a leading role in transforming liberation movements into ruling parties. Liberation fighters from Mozambique, Angola, Zimbabwe, Namibia, and South Africa received enormous assistance from Tanzania before becoming leaders in their countries. In addition to liberation movements from Africa, Tanzania also hosted movements from abroad, including Tupamaros from Uruguay. Nyerere was also the first African leader to recognize the Palestine Liberation Organization (PLO) under Yasser Arafat, with the first PLO African embassy opening in Tanzania.

Nyerere fully embraced the solidarity principle and was not afraid to risk everything to pursue solidarity and support liberation movements. Nyerere believed that Tanzania was responsible for actively assisting other nations in achieving independence from foreign and white minority rule. As a result, he made this a defining feature of Tanzania's foreign policy. The Arusha Declaration of 1967 gave the Tanzanian government an obligation to cooperate with liberation movements across Africa. Tanzania's support of the liberation movements wasn't just rhetoric; the liberation movements and their paramilitary wings trained and planned their operations on Tanzanian territory. Oliver Tambo, ANC's president, established anti-Apartheid missions across Africa; after going into exile, with Tanzania becoming the ANC's headquarters. The ANC's paramilitary wing, Umkhonto we Sizwe, was also trained in Tanzania.

Figure 4.3: Julius Nyerere

Source: Wikimedia Commons

Besides hosting the ANC, Tanzania also welcomed FRELIMO, ZANU, MPLA, and SWAPO from Mozambique, Angola, Zimbabwe, and Namibia respectively. Tanzania used its well-positioned geographical position to provide extensive support to the liberation movements. Tanzania's distance from South Africa played to its advantage as it avoided South Africa's destabilization efforts. Nyerere's philosophy allowed Tanzania to provide military training camps and serve as an entry point for firearms and ammunition used by the liberation movements. Unlike other Southern African states, which were still dependent on South Africa economically, Tanzania was one of the least dependent countries in the region, primarily due to historical and geographical reasons.

Despite Tanzania being an East African country, its role during the liberation struggle turned the country into a Southern African country more than an East African one. His conviction that Africa could be united was inspired by a broader belief in Pan-Africanism. Nyerere believed that racist white minority governments were obstacles to African unity and posed an existential threat to Tanzania. Nyerere was also a founding member of the African Liberation Committee, a subdivision of the OAU with its headquarters in Dar es Salaam. Mandela (1994), in his autobiography, *Long Walk to Freedom*, talks about his experiences after visiting Tanzania: 'I then truly realized I was in a country ruled by Africans. For the first time in my life, I was a free man. Though I was a fugitive and wanted in my own land, I felt the burden of oppression lifting from my shoulders. Everywhere I went in Tanganyika, my skin colour was automatically accepted rather than instantly reviled. I was being judged for the first time not by the colour of my skin but by the measure of my mind and character. Although I was often homesick during my travels, I nevertheless felt as though I were truly home for the first time."

Apart from chairing the OAU Liberation Committee, Tanzania hosted the headquarters of the Committee. Nyerere was one of the early leaders of the Pan-African Freedom Movement for East and Central Africa (PAFMECA), formed in Mwanza, Tanganyika, in 1958 and became its first chairman. PAFMECA was responsible for coordinating the independence struggle for Tanganyika, Kenya, Uganda, Northern Rhodesia, Southern Rhodesia, Nyasaland and Zanzibar. Liberation movements and the ruling parties in the region were heavily influenced by the socialist and Pan-Africanist philosophy of Julius Nyerere. The ideology was influenced significantly by the Chinese liberation approach of Maoism fueled by China's politically-driven support to newly independent and liberation movements in Africa. As African country's gained independence, their dislike of the colonial powers led to China becoming the leading Third World nation. With China's sustained supply of weapons, technical assistance, and training, Nyerere and the liberation movements remained solid and resilient.

Zambia

In 1890, Zambia became a British colony and was named Northern Rhodesia. The country became part of the Central African Federation in 1953, comprising present-day Malawi and Zimbabwe. On 24 October 1964, Kenneth Kaunda became the country's first President after Zambia gained independence. Kaunda was born to a Malawian father, a Church of Scotland minister who migrated to Zambia. Kaunda's academic ability won him a scholarship to study at Northern Rhodesia's first secondary school during his early years. Later, he became a teacher in the Copperbelt region of the country and later in Southern Rhodesia. His first political move was becoming a vegetarian in protest of a segregationist colonial policy that forced Africans to buy meat from a separate window at the butcher shop from whites.

In 1953, Kaunda became Secretary-General of the Northern Rhodesian African National Congress, a liberation movement that attempted to mobilize blacks against the newly formed Federation of Rhodesia and Nyasaland. The colonial administration arrested and imprisoned Kaunda in 1955 for distributing revolutionary leaflets that were deemed illegal. Following his release from prison after two months, Kaunda founded a new party, the Zambian African National Congress, which was banned one year later, resulting in Kaunda's rearrest and making him a national hero. In 1960, Kaunda founded a new political party, the United National Independence Party (UNIP). Inspired by the civil rights movements after visiting the United States, where he met Martin Luther King Jr, Kaunda galvanised blacks to pursue civil disobedience, which involved burning buildings and blocking roads. The public pressure paved the way for the 1962 election, which UNIP won after forming a coalition with the African National Congress. The Central African Federation was later dissolved in 1963, paving the way for independence in 1964.

Being a country liberated by rebellion, the Zambian government developed an interest in supporting other liberation movements within the region after independence. Zambia's efforts to support liberation movements were, however, a highly contentious issue in domestic politics. Several opposition parties expressed concerns about the retaliatory response from the South African government following the decision to support liberation movements in the region. Since Zambia, like Botswana and Malawi, are landlocked countries, these concerns were driven by its economic survival primarily relied on transport corridors controlled by white minority governments in Rhodesia, Mozambique, Namibia, and South Africa. Since the Portuguese ruled Angola and Mozambique, Ian Smith governed Rhodesia, and Apartheid Afrikaners ruled South Africa and Namibia; the Zambian economy was at the mercy of these regimes. In that situation, the Government of Zambia was left in a difficult situation; as th lose face with its peers if it remained neutral. While looking to balance an economy to ensure Zambia's survival, President Kenneth Kaunda backed liberation movements.

As chairman of the Frontline States, Kaunda was one of the leading opponents of the Ian Smith regime in Rhodesia and the Apartheid regime in South Africa. Kaunda built a coalition that brought UN sanctions against the two white minority regimes. Nevertheless, Zambia's support of UN sanctions against Rhodesia on the international stage came at a high cost. For these efforts, Zambia experienced military and economic retaliation. Due to the sanctions Zambia supported, the country's main trade route through Rhodesia was closed. The Zambian government later established alternative routes for trade, but the added costs negatively affected the Zambian economy.

When the country was experiencing financial challenges, providing financial and material resources to the liberation movements presented a heavy burden to the state resources during the early years after independence. The economic challenges facing Zambia forced her to make controversial decisions as she attempted to reopen the trade routes through Southern Rhodesia that had been closed since 1973. There was a scarcity of essential commodities in the country, and long lines of people waited to acquire crucial goods became common in the 1970s. Food riots became widespread in the Copperbelt, while civil servants and security forces suffered from low wages and a lack of essential equipment.

As a result, Zambia sought to work in a multi-faceted manner in Zimbabwe's liberation struggle. The Zambian government began to pursue diplomacy rather than supporting the armed struggle to resolve the Rhodesian conflict. In the course of his meetings with the South African and Rhodesian leaders, Kaunda adopted a moderate position as he hoped for peaceful relations that would accommodate both whites and blacks in the region. DeRoche (2016) argues that reopening the trade route through Rhodesia could ease economic pressure with the Zambian government benefitting from the Smith regime - an apparently difficult decision for Kaunda. Other Frontline States partners, including Nyerere and Machel, were upset by the decision.

Figure 3.4: Kenneth Kaunda with John Volster (South African Prime Minister second from left in 1975

Source: Getty Images

The peaceful settlement in Rhodesia became Kaunda's highest priority. The Zambian's support was only limited to coercing the Rhodesian Government to the negotiating table. These mediation attempts turned the relationship between the Zambian Government with the Zimbabwean freedom fighters rocky for different reasons. Liberation fighters from Zimbabwe even accused the Zambian government of sabotaging their cause. While Kaunda attempted to negotiate a South African-backed peaceful settlement with the Ian Smith regime, the Zambian Government also negotiated to unify Zimbabwean liberation movements. However, discord among the Zimbabwean freedom fighters posed obstacles to these mediation efforts. In that period, there were divisions within the ZANU ranks that provoked rebellions sparked by ethnic rifts.

While the Zambian Government was pursuing this unification effort, the head of ZANU's War Council, Herbert Chitepo, who was exiled in Lusaka, was implicated in the death of 250 ZANU rebels handed over to him by the Zambian Government on condition of their guaranteed safety. Eventually, the rebels were killed, and Chitepo was accused of breaking the agreement. In response, the Zambian police rounded up some ZANU members in Lusaka. Chitepo had also opposed the mediation exercise pursued by Kenneth Kaunda and his South African counterpart, John Vorster. Considering that Zambia had lost so much due to its support of the liberation movements since independence, Kaunda was angered to see Chitepo's lack of cooperation with the Zambian effort. Chitepo, however, insisted that only a military rebellion could bring freedom to Southern Rhodesia.

Muzorewa, Chitepo and others attended a meeting of liberation leaders hosted by Kenneth Kaunda at the state residence in March 1975 to salvage the mediation process. Chitepo is believed to have refused a security detail offered by the Zambian government after the meeting. He was later killed in a car bomb outside his house in Lusaka the same night. Some have claimed that South Rhodesian intelligence officers assassinated him, while others claim that a Karanga faction in ZANU carried out the killing with Robert Mugabe's approval.

Consequently, a refusal by Zimbabwean liberation movements to cooperate with Zambian mediation efforts and ongoing disagreements within the movements led to the movements being banned from Zambia. In 1978, the ban was lifted. The ban coincided with changes in Angola and Mozambique dynamics after the coup in Portugal, which enabled ZANU to shift some of its activities from Zambia to Mozambique due to close ties between ZANU and the FRELIMO government in Mozambique.

The economic hardships Zambia was still experiencing made its diplomatic efforts more critical. Working alongside the US Government, the Geneva Conference was organised to create a transitional government structure in Rhodesia. Zambia's initiatives did not meet the approval of the Zimbabwean freedom fighters. Kaunda attempted to unite Zimbabwean freedom fighters under Bishop Muzorewa's leadership. He believed that a united liberation movement could thrash out a negotiated settlement with the Ian Smith government under the Salisbury Plan. In March 1978, Ian Smith announced that he had reached an agreement with Muzorewa and NdabaningiSithole. The arrangement provided for a transitional government and an election within 12 months of a transition government. According to DeRoche (2016), the deal was overwhelmingly denounced by Mugabe and other freedom fighters since it implied the white minority controlled the police and the military. The Salisbury Plan was declared illegal and unacceptable by the UN Security Council on 14 March 1978.

Amidst the economic hardship, Kaunda continued to support liberation movements across the region despite these challenges. For example, the Liberation Center in Lusaka was established with help from the OAU Liberation Committee to accommodate liberation movements recognized by the OAU. At this Liberation Centre, the liberation groups could process refugees, provide transit through Zambia to other countries, and hold office space and distribute propaganda materials. It must also be emphasized that the Zambian government's decision to provide transit facilities and offices for the liberation movements was significant as it allowed the groups to recruit and transport new members for military training in Tanzania and parts of the world.

As part of its assistance to the liberation movements, Zambia provided diplomatic recognition, broadcast facilities, and financial and material resources. The country also hosted the ANC's headquarters after ANC was banned in 1969. The ANC's headquarters in Lusaka also coordinated Umkhonto we Sizwe, the paramilitary wing of ANC. After leaving South Africa, recruits were allowed to come to Lusaka before proceeding to Tanzania and socialist countries like China, Soviet Union, and North Korea. The unrestricted transit facilities and financial support were crucial for the day-to-day operations of freedom fighters, and the financial support catered for their living expenses. Zambia also hosted the ANC's underground radio station, broadcasting the ANC's propaganda on South African airwaves. A radio station was one of the factors Hortst (1986) believes helped ANC attract recruits. In response to ANC operations in Zambia, the South African government carried out air raids on ANC facilities to destroy those purportedly used by the organization. These raids jeopardized Commonwealth's Eminent Persons Group (EPG) efforts to negotiate a settlement between the South African Apartheid regime and the ANC. In addition to diplomatic support and facilities for the ANC's operations, the Zambian military also protected the party's conference in 1985 from South African attacks.

Zambia also supported FRELIMO from Mozambique and the MPLA from Angola. This support led to devastating cross-border raids by Portuguese forces pursuing insurgents operating in Zambia. The MPLA had offices in the Liberation Centre, and its fighters operated in western Zambia, which borders Angola. FRELIMO, Mozambique's most significant liberation movement, was allowed to operate in the Liberation Centre.

The Zambian territory also served as a logistical hub for the liberation movements. A large amount of ammunition, weapons, and other essential equipment was transported or stored in Zambia. Even though Zambia provided support to these liberation movements, their presence in Zambia required strict management due to their threat to the country's internal security. Counterinsurgency operations conducted by South Africa in the region were the main threat to security. Zambian authorities, therefore, strictly regulated these organizations' operations by formulating rules and regulations. Despite Zambia's agreement to accept shipments of military equipment belonging to the liberation movements, the government handled the equipment very carefully. Morris (1974) reports that the Zambian police confiscated a vehicle carrying arms and ammunition for a FRELIMO depot in Lusaka because it had no security escort. The consignment was released once the police confirmed the destination of the arms. It was always feared that the uncontrolled arms movement could allow unauthorized citizens to access weapons in Zambia.

In 1975, Mozambique and Angola became independent, bringing new challenges to Zambia. With the Apartheid government in South Africa and the Ian Smith regime in Southern Rhodesia feeling more vulnerable to insurgent attacks, they intensified destabilisation efforts. In response to this new phenomenon, FLS was formed, with Zambia becoming one of the original members to counter destabilisation efforts by white minority regimes. FLS emerged due to collaboration between Tanzania, Zambia, and Botswana to support liberation movements in Angola, Mozambique, Rhodesia, South Africa and Namibia. The two Lusophone countries joined FLS in 1975, following their independence.

Through its efforts to persuade the international community to engage the liberation leaders and extend recognition to the liberation movements, the Zambian government played a significant role in legitimizing the liberation movements. Zambian diplomats urged world leaders to support resolutions seeking to promote black majority rule in Southern Africa on international platforms such as the United Nations, the OAU, and the Commonwealth. Additionally, they supported economic sanctions and encouraged the Western governments to apply diplomatic pressure on white minority regimes. Thus, the Zambian government's efforts helped garner international support for the liberation movements and brought attention to the problems associated with white minority governments in the region.

Zambia also actively facilitated the independence of Namibia. Zambia hosted Namibian exiled freedom fighters from SWAPO led by Sam Nujoma shortly after independence. Although most SWAPO operations moved to Angola after the country gained independence in 1975, Zambians continued hosting UN-funded Namibian students at the University of Zambia. In 1978, the UN Security Council adopted Resolution 435, which created a roadmap for Namibian independence, resulting from Dr Kaunda's collaboration with the Carter Administration in the USA. According to DeRoche (2016), Kaunda also pressured the Carter Administration at this time to stop supporting UNITA in Angola. The efforts of Kenneth Kaunda in providing support to the liberation movements had a long term impact on the country's economy as Zambia failed to develop sustainable economic fundamentals that could uplift the wellbeing of ordinary Zambians. Zambia's location also made the country vulnerable as its critical economic supply lines were controlled by the white-minority regimes he opposed.

Botswana

The British Protectorate of Botswana (Bechuanaland) was established in 1885. Although there were attempts to merge Botswana with the South African Union, these attempts met resistance from the traditional leaders. They wanted Botswana to remain under British administration until the country's independence on 30 September 1966. As Richard Stevens (1972) points out, South Africa questioned Botswana's existence until 1959, when Prime Minister Verwoerd demanded Botswana's integration into the union. Apparently, Botswana was little more than a hostage to South Africa, according to Halpern (1965). Botswana became a member of the Southern African Customs Union (SACU) in 1910, whose benefits were significant for the country's economic survival.

Furthermore, the country's transport and communication systems were integrated with those of South Africa and Rhodesia. Botswana's location meant that the country was surrounded by white minority regimes, South Rhodesia in the East, Namibia in the West, and South

Africa on the southern border. Its complex relationship with South Rhodesia and South Africa made it impossible to end its relationship with these more powerful white neighbours. Botswana's situation was a perfect example of deliberate mechanisation that limited Botswana's ability to stand independently.

Despite its commitment to supporting the ANC and other liberation movements, Botswana was handicapped by its economic vulnerability. Tseretse Khama, the president of Botswana from the outset of independence, was evident in his opposition to the Apartheid regime while recognizing the country's vulnerabilities. Supporting the liberation movements could destabilize Botswana and undermine the country's trade and communication links, Botswana knew from the beginning. President Seretse Khama of Botswana acknowledged the challenges and was quoted in Niemann (1993) stating: “As a consequence of Botswana’s geographical situation, we face unusual and onerous handicaps. Whilst Botswana accepts that we are part of the Southern African economic complex and that the harsh fact of history and geography cannot be obliterated, for obvious reasons, we have to maintain normal friendly relations with South Africa.” While Tanzania, Angola, and Mozambique provided military and training bases for the liberation movements, Botswana could not afford to play a similar role as its economy was tied to the South African economy. However, Botswana stopped short of establishing diplomatic relations and continued to support liberation efforts with restraint. Keeping the relationship between Southern Rhodesia and South Africa and supporting liberation movements was a delicate and challenging process.

Botswana continued to provide diplomatic cover to liberation movements on the international front. In 1973, the country supported a UN resolution that included armed struggle as part of a legitimate liberation struggle against colonialism and racism. However, Botswana opted to oppose an OAU resolution calling for Arab countries to impose an oil embargo on South Africa, Rhodesia, and Mozambique because it relied on oil from South Africa.

Although the country's economic dependence on SACU became less significant as diamond production increased, Botswana could not make significant changes to its support of the liberation movements. Like Zambia, Botswana did not allow freedom fighters to use its territory for military operations. Botswana refused to allow ANC to carry out offensive military activities on its territory while allowing refugees from South

Africa, with estimates putting the number of refugees at about 30,000 between 1976 and 1978. Botswana also accepted Angolan and South Rhodesian refugees who had fled from the Portuguese in Angola and Ian Smith's regime in Rhodesia. The country also became a preferred transit destination for ANC freedom fighters heading to Europe, Tanzania and Zambia.

However, the refugees deemed a risk to Botswana's security were processed and deported to Zambia. These conditions sometimes prompted Botswana to play devil's advocate for the white minority regimes while also assisting the liberation movements. The Apartheid regime pressured the Botswana government into taking measures detrimental to the liberation movement at times. Botswana's strategy created numerous tensions, contradictions, and discomforts on several occasions. For instance, the detention of ANC operatives at Francistown in 1967 led to a diplomatic spat with the Zambian authorities. The ANC militias were arrested by a military unit under the command of a British commander and were charged with entering Botswana illegally and in possession of firearms. Chris Hani, the group's leader, was sentenced to six years imprisonment, only to be released and deported to Zambia after pressure from the OAU. After this incident, Botswana clarified its policy on allowing refugees at the Dukwi refugee camp while restricting any militants from operating on its soil.

Despite treading carefully on how the country managed its affairs with the liberation movement, Botswana could not escape South Africa's counterinsurgency operations on its soil. The country experienced South Africa's counterinsurgency operations, with kidnappings and assassinations carried out by the South African military and security agents on several occasions. For instance, in June 1985, the South African Defence Forces carried out military raids in Botswana in Operation Plecksy. A Gaborone raid resulted in the deaths of twelve people and the destruction of property. Nine of the dead were South Africans, two Botswana citizens, and one Somali. The attack was condemned worldwide, with the United Nations passing a resolution requiring South Africa to pay reparations. Several other raids occurred between 1986 and 1988. In addition to military raids, South Africa's intelligence operatives used bribes to gather information about the location of ANC operatives in the country. Despite the risks associated with aiding liberation movements, Botswana continued to host ANC liberation fighters.

Angola

Portuguese colonial governments in Angola and Mozambique were relatively weak compared to white minority regimes in South Africa and Southern Rhodesia. The colonial wars' unpopularity orchestrated this weakness in Portugal due to the war's sheer costs on the economy. The declaration of war by Portugal against the liberation movements in their territories resulted in over 70,000 Portuguese soldiers fighting in Mozambique and Angola. Because of this commitment, the Portuguese economy suffered, and the government in Portugal struggled to provide essential public services. As the Portuguese administration disintegrated after the fall of the Marcelo Caetano's dictatorship in Portugal, the transition from Portuguese control to African control became more complicated.

The development also weakened the coalition of white minority governments in Southern Africa. During the Carnation Revolution, a coup d'etat led by Antonio de Spinola overthrew the right-wing regime, ending the Estado Novo (New State) dictatorship that had ruled from 1932 to 1974. Before the coup, the deputy chief of the military, Spinola, had acknowledged that the colonial wars Portugal was engaged in were unwinnable. Immediately following the coup, the Portuguese colonial administration disintegrated. However, the three rival nationalist liberation factions in Angola were too weak and divided to agree on a peaceful settlement. Rather than negotiating a peaceful settlement, the liberation groups began asking foreign governments for assistance as they prepared for prolonged war. As the coup in Portugal occurred in April 1974, the National Front for the Liberation of Angola (FNLA) was the most potent liberation movement. The FNLA was led by Holden Alvaro Roberto, who received support from Mobutu's regime in Zaire. Mobutu, a proxy for the Americans, and Roberto were married into the same family, which enabled FNLA to operate its base in Zaire. Northern Angola was a stronghold for the FNLA.

Agostinho Neto led the Popular Movement for the Liberation of Angola (MPLA) with support from the Soviet Union. The group had widespread support in the Kimbundu region near the capital Luanda. The third faction was the National Union for the Total Independence of Angola or Portuguese União Nacional para an Independência Total de Angola (UNITA), led by Jonas Savimbi. Savimbi was Roberto's former associate and received support from the Ovimbundu people, the largest tribe in Angola's central highlands. In January 1975, after 14 years of armed struggle against the Portuguese colonial administration, the Alvor Agreement paved the way for independence. The Organization of African Unity pressured the three competing groups to form an interim coalition government with the Portuguese, and a November 1975 election was set. However, as the interim government took office on 31 January 1975, clashes between FNLA and MPLA continued in Luanda and surrounding areas. There were fears that a civil war was imminent, which caused the remaining Portuguese administration officials who had been part of the transitional government to flee the country, causing it to fall. In an attempt to install a pro-Zaire regime in independent Angola, Mobutu, with the help of the CIA, deployed armoured military units, airborne units and three infantry battalions in Angola to assist his brother in marriage. Cuban military units stationed in Luanda in support of the MPLA stymied Mobutu's military campaign, pushing FNLA and Mobutu troops back into Zaire. As a result of FNLA's retreat, MPLA seized power, and an all-out civil war ensued. In response to MPLA's growing strength, FNLA and UNITA regrouped to form a single fighting force under UNITA's banner.

Initially a liberation war, an all-out civil war was now raging over control of the government and its natural resources with the support of two Cold War powers. UNITA was able to recapture five provinces with help from South African forces and the CIA, which led to a long civil war that only ended in 2002. In support of UNITA, the South African government sent about 2,000 soldiers from Namibia. Due to Cuban soldiers' presence in Mozambique, South Africa's support of UNITA failed to impact Angola as it did Mozambique.

As newly independent Angola was engulfed in a deadly civil war, the Angolan Government began to accommodate refugees and freedom fighters from South Africa, Southern Rhodesia and Namibia, increasing tensions between white minority governments and Angola. ANC training and transit camps were set up in Quibaxe, Fazenda, and other sites to train Umkhonto we Sizwe recruits. Furthermore, the ANC operated a radio station, a printing press, and a vast warehouse to store clothing and food items for freedom fighters. In Luanda, the capital city, residential blocks were earmarked specifically for the ANC. In addition to the ANC, ZAPU from Southern Rhodesia and SWAPO from Namibia also operated camps in Angola. Due to the growing prominence of Angola as a safe haven for the ANC, the Apartheid regime intensified its support for

UNITA, provoking a retaliatory response from the South African government.

However, the presence of ANC in Angola did not go swiftly without controversy. The camps in Angola were characterized by discipline problems, discontent, and vulnerability to infiltration by South African security agents. There are reports of recruits committing serious crimes such as rape and murder. For instance, an ANC freedom fighter Thabo Makhubethe was executed by an ANC firing squad after being found guilty of rape. Also, other ANC recruits were found guilty of murder and sentenced to death.

In addition to the criminal activities, there was a mutiny at one of the camps in Pango. Mutineers stormed an ANC arms store killing one of the men guarding the armoury. This led to an all-out gun battle that resulted in some deaths. The mutiny was triggered by reported mistreatment of recruits at the training camp and recruits being drafted to fight alongside the Angolan government against South Africa-backed UNITA forces. This led to a mutiny among the rank-and-file members of the paramilitary wing, who argued that they had joined the liberation struggle to fight in South Africa, not Angola. The incident exposed ANC's leadership struggles and their failure to maintain order amongst the rank-and-file.

The Apartheid regime successfully infiltrated ANC training camps in Angola with government agents. On one occasion, all the members of the Novo Catengue camp were poisoned in September 1977 by suspected South African Government agents. In March 1979, South African Defence Force (SADF) bombed the Novo Catengue camp with accuracy, which led to the death of 14 ANC operatives and one Cuban soldier. The precision of the strike suggested that the camp had been infiltrated. Other targeted assassinations of senior ANC operatives were also carried out, which led to the camp being abandoned after its security was compromised. As a result of security concerns, other ANC camps were also closed. A suspicion of infiltration was confirmed in 1981 when some of the ANC's operatives were exposed as government agents.

As the war intensified in 1987, more Cuban troops were deployed in Angola, and the South Africans came into confrontation with the Cuban troops. Cuban assault fighter jets launched attacks on SADF positions 11 km north of the Namibian border in 1988. To prevent a Cuban advance into Namibia, the SADF destroyed a bridge near Namibia's border. The increasing involvement of Cuban forces in the Angolan civil war forced the South African Government to agree to a settlement that led to the withdrawal of the SADF from Angola. In December 1988, the South African government adopted UN Resolution 435, which it had shunned since 1978. This was an agreement wherein Angola was to close all camps belonging to the ANC and SWAPO within its borders, and it also served as a precursor to Namibia's independence.

Namibia

South West Africa (Namibia) became a German colony in 1884 and was named German South-West Africa. The League of Nations was established as World War I ended in 1918, which led to Germany losing all its colonial territories, including East Africa (Tanganyika). As a result of South Africa's victory over German soldiers stationed in South West Africa in 1915, the League of Nations granted South Africa administrative control of the territory in 1918, under Article 22 of the League of Nations Covenant.

However, after World War II ended, the League of Nations was dissolved, leading to a new international body, the United Nations (UN). In 1946, the UN instituted a Trusteeship Scheme to bring together all former German colonies under UN control. The South African government rejected the plan, and South-West Africa was declared a de facto fifth province in 1949. Longmire (1990) stated that South Africa contended that the League of Nations dissolution also meant that the mandate system had ceased to exist, rendering South Africa's claim to sovereignty over Namibia unrestricted. In 1966, the United Nations declared South Africa's presence in Namibia illegal under international law after 20 years of legal arguments about Namibia's status.

South West Africa provided South Africa with an extension of the Apartheid regime, resulting in its resistance to withdraw from the territory. The territory was vital to South Africa's economic and security strategy. Despite the change in colonial masters from Germany to South Africa, the circumstances for the ordinary black population did not improve. Namibian traditional leaders continued with their effort to petition the United Nations against South African rule. Namibians recruited to fight in World War II also began demanding independence, just like in other parts of Africa.

In addition to the mineral resources, Namibia provided strategic security cover to South Africa against the ravaging civil war in Angola and

ANC insurgents who had set up bases in Angola. The South African government believed that holding on to Namibia would limit the guerrilla warfare originating from Angola. Many white South Africans moved to South West Africa; due to this, the South African government established an Apartheid system identical to South Africa. This led to the black population being forcefully pushed further away from their ancestral settlements to pave the way for white settlements. When the indigenous population lost their ancestral land, there was increased discontent, which led to the Windhoek Massacre of 1959 (11 indigenous people died and 44 were injured) as the Apartheid regime employed repressive tactics. Apartheid regime police opened fire on protestors opposing their forced removal from their homes which was part of the Apartheid regime's initiative to isolate ethnic Black groups from living in close proximity to whites in Namibia's capital Windhoek.

As most residents did not want to move, a newly established liberation movement, the South West African National Union (SWANU), organized mass action, which led to a mass boycott of municipal services. Namibia's founding president, Sam Nujoma, discussed the Windhoek Massacre in his autobiography *Where Others Wavered*, published in 2001. In his autobiography, Nujoma (2001) recalls his lifetime of political struggle and mentions how thousands of people fled their homes following the massacre. The massacre location later became a symbol of Namibia's struggle for independence. After these events, the South West African People's Organization (SWAPO) and its military wing, the People's Liberation Army of Namibia (PLAN), were founded. Freedom fighters fled to newly independent Tanzania, Zambia and later Angola after the Lusophone countries gained independence in 1975.

According to Muller (2012), the SWAPO military wing was modelled after the ANC's Umkhonto we Sizwe. SWAPO benefited from the safe shelter provided by neighbouring countries in the 1960s after most countries in Southern Africa gained independence. The group started launching attacks into Namibia from its camps in Zambia. In 1975, Angola gained independence, and SWAPO moved its camps to the southern part of the country. In its South West African Territorial Force, the South African government enlisted Black Namibians. This effort pitted black Namibian soldiers against their countrymen at times, and on one occasion, one of the units revolted in protest.

In 1978, the UN Security Council drafted a roadmap for the country's independence while the civil war intensified in Angola and Namibia. The roadmap was approved under UN Security Council Resolution 435. Despite the UN's efforts, the South African government refused to cooperate with UN authorities. The enforcement of the plan was delayed by the US and UK governments, which opposed any effective sanctions against South Africa. The Namibian independence struggle was beset by Cold War politics, with South Africa presenting itself as a Western ally while the Soviets and Cubans supported the Angolan government. As a result, the Americans and British were unable to penalize South Africa.

As the war in Angola intensified, the South African government deployed more troops to support UNITA. The South Africans now faced a confrontation with Cuba, which had been sending troops to Angola. It was a situation that benefited SWAPO since the South African military did not intend to conduct major attacks across the Angolan border, providing a safe haven for liberation fighters. Consequently, the SWAPO guerillas grew in strength. They mounted attacks on the South African military positions on the Angolan southern border and the Namibian northern border without fear of retaliation from the South African forces. International support for Namibia's independence and opposition to the Apartheid regime gained traction during the second half of the 1980s. In 1986, the US Congress passed the Comprehensive Anti-Apartheid Act, which imposed sanctions on the Apartheid regime. Despite the sanctions not being enforced during the Reagan administration, they were eventually enforced by the Bush administration in January 1988. The change of US foreign policy inflicted significant pressure on the Apartheid government.

The Apartheid regime became isolated and weakened as international and domestic pressure intensified. Towards the end of the 1980s, the Apartheid regime could no longer sustain its war in Namibia and Angola. As international pressure intensified, it became apparent that South Africa's control of Namibia was on its last legs. In the face of international sanctions and economic pressure, the South African government succumbed to the pressure. Public opinion for the continued Apartheid system was also waning out, and South Africa's control of Namibia made no sense. Thus, on August 8, 1988, a cease-fire was announced in Geneva, Switzerland. In December 1988, all parties involved in the Angolan civil war reached an agreement under UN Resolution 435, which the Security Council had drafted in 1978. A timetable was drawn that set the tone for Namibia's independence and announced an election date. First democratic elections were held in

Namibia in 1989, which SWAPO won. In March 1990, Namibia gained its independence from South Africa, with South African Prime Minister F.W de Klerk and Russian Foreign Minister Eduard Ambrosis dze Shevardnadze in attendance.

Zimbabwe

Cecil John Rhodes and his British South African Company (BSAC) established Fort Salisbury in Mashonaland, and in 1898, Southern Rhodesia was named in Rhodes' honour. As white settlers increased in the new British colony, the locals were forced from their ancestral lands. Mines were established, which increased the demand for labour from the locals and other parts of the region. By 1923, the colony operated independently after the UK government gained control and took control of BSAC. Southern Rhodesia could draft its constitution and elect its legislature; however, all legislation had to be approved by the British Government.

It was not until 1965 that the Southern Rhodesian government, led by Ian Smith, unilaterally declared independence from the British. The collapse of the Central African Federation (CAF) in 1962 and the subsequent election of Ian Smith in 1964 presented an opportunity for the settler government to declare independence. Ian Smith had claimed that his government had a right to independence, just like other federation partners in Malawi and Zambia. This declaration of independence was deemed illegal by the British Government and failed to gain recognition from the international community.

During Ian Smith's repressive regime, African nationalist movements were banned, and their leaders were either arrested or exiled, leading to the liberation war. Rhodesian territory provided South Africa with a buffer zone against ANC freedom fighter attacks, resulting in an ad hoc political and economic alliance between Southern Rhodesia and South Africa. South Africa and Rhodesia, together with the other two Portuguese colonies, the white minority regimes coordinated their counter-insurgency operations.

Zimbabwe's liberation movements can be traced back to the early 1960s, when Joshua Nkomo, Ndabaningi Sithole, and Robert Mugabe formed the National Democratic Party (NDP) and its successor, the Zimbabwe African People's Union (ZAPU). Eventually, Mugabe and Sithole founded the Zimbabwe African National Union (ZANU), with Sithole as president and Mugabe as Secretary-General.

Figure 3.5: Southern Rhodesia's Prime Minister Ian Smith

Source: Britannica.com

In 1975, when the liberation movements failed to unite under one platform, Joshua Nkomo unilaterally attempted to negotiate a settlement with the Ian Smith government in a deal orchestrated by the South African and Zambian governments. Kadiagala (1994) reports that the Zambian government initiated negotiations with the South African government in 1974 to reach a negotiated settlement that would lead to majority rule in Zimbabwe. This initiative was rejected by ZANU, which considered it a tool for the Zambian government to secure access to export routes.

Mozambique, South Africa and Southern Rhodesia hare more than just borders; they also share a long history of freedom struggles against colonialism and Apartheid. The liberation movements in Southern Rhodesia were also closely attached in ideology and practice to the liberation movements in neighbouring Mozambique and South Africa. As well as the unity among liberation fighters from the three countries, the white minority governments also fostered close cooperation in their counterinsurgency efforts against the liberation movements through top-secret security alliance codenamed ALCORA. The coup d'etat in Portugal and the subsequent collapse of the Portuguese colonial administration in Mozambique presented a new challenge for the white minority government in Southern Rhodesia. The Ian Smith government had benefitted from support coming from the Portuguese in Mozambique and the Apartheid regime in South Africa. The coup in Lisbon changed Southern Rhodesia's fortunes as the already isolated Ian Smith regime was denied a crucial long-standing and reliable ally. The 760-mile long border shared with Mozambique presented a security challenge to the Southern Rhodesian government when FRELIMO successfully gained Mozambique independence in 1975. FRELIMO and Zimbabwean freedom fighters formed a close relationship, capitalising on their leaders' friendshipbuilt over years together sprnt in Tanzania and Zambia. According to Ian Smith, it was inevitable that the FRELIMO government would support the liberation movements fighting his government.

As Ian Smith had feared, the Mozambican territory quickly became a safe haven for Zimbabwean freedom fighters, leaving Southern Rhodesia vulnerable to guerilla attacks. Additionally, Mozambique imposed sanctions on Ian Smith's regime, which relied upon Mozambican transport corridors. The intelligence chief of Ian Smith's regime, Ken Flower, created the Resistencia Nacional Moçambicana (RENAMO) as a counter-measure against the Mozambican threat. At first, the group's goal was to gather information about ZANU operations in Mozambique and protect the Mozambique/Rhodesia border. The objectives, however, escalated into insurgency operations aimed at destabilizing the country. The Southern Rhodesian government provided training and material support to RENAMO between 1977 and 1980 while allowing the group to operate freely.

Zimbabwe joined the Frontline States grouping soon after independence in 1980 to show its commitment to supporting liberation movements in the region. As a result, Zimbabwe played an important role in providing an area of operation for ANC operatives. ANC formally established its presence in Zimbabwe under Joe Gqabi, who coordinated the movement of freedom fighters and provided support to refugees from South Africa.

Apart from hosting ANC freedom fighters, South Africa also believed that ANC attacks were coordinated and launched from Zimbabwe. In retaliation, South African Defence Force (SADF) carried out attacks on ANC targets in Zimbabwe on numerous occasions. Many Zimbabweans and South Africans were killed and injured by booby-trapped TVs, car bombs, and rocket attacks. Additionally, the Zimbabwean government had its air force and new military equipment destroyed during South African air raids. Gqabi was assassinated in Zimbabwe by South African security agents on 31 July 1981, after surviving an attempted car bomb attack in February of that year. Apart from supporting the ANC after independence, Zimbabwe also supported the Mozambican government's fight against the RENAMO rebels that the Apartheid government was now backing.

Zimbabwe's efforts to assist the ANC were sometimes compromised by intelligence operatives loyal to Ian Smith, still part of the government's security apparatus. The remnants of Ian Smith's security operatives in Zimbabwe cooperated with South African security services, leading to the exposure of ANC operatives' locations. In 1988, three Zimbabwean intelligence officers were arrested in Zimbabwe on suspicion of participating in a bombing that killed a Zimbabwean driver and injured six ANC operatives. The Zimbabwean government intensified its support for the African National Congress' attacks on the South African soil in response to these hostile attacks on Zimbabwean soil, which often led to casualties.

Newly independent Zimbabwe facilitated the movement of weapons and fighters arriving from Zambia. In his eulogy for Robert Mugabe, Thabo Mbeki stated that Edson Mnangagwa, the then State Security Minister of Zimbabwe and now the Zimbabwean president, helped move ANC fighters to South Africa's Limpopo River in the late 1970s. According to Mbeki, Zimbabwean military trucks transported weapons from the

Zambian border to the South African border. South African freedom fighters would then come and collect these weapons to use for attacks inside South Africa.

The relationship between the ANC, FRELIMO and ZANU stemmed from the liberation struggle when the groups operated side by side in Zambia and Tanzania. The groups shared the same socialist ideology and came to rely on Soviet and Chinese support. Soon after Mozambique gained independence from Portugal in 1975, the ANC and Zimbabwean freedom fighters operated together in Mozambique to plan their military operations against the Apartheid government in South Africa, the Rhodesian Government. In light of these early relations and familiarity, it was inevitable that the Zimbabwean government would support both the ANC and the Mozambican government. ANC operatives were also provided with Zimbabwean passports, allowing them to attend sensitive meetings worldwide without being detected.

In the aftermath of geopolitical changes that led to the weakening of Apartheid, Zimbabwe played a significant role in the negotiated settlement between the ANC and Apartheid. On August 21, 1989, South Africa's government, the ANC, the FLS, the OAU and the UN adopted the Harare Declaration at a conference in Harare, which laid the groundwork for the end of Apartheid in South Africa.

Mozambique

Mozambique provides a perfect picture in regards to the political crisis orchestrated by regional neighbours. Upon independence, the country was plunged into a bloody civil war as white minority governments in Southern Rhodesia, and South Africa feared it would harbour liberation movements. To understand the status of Mozambique as a Portuguese colony, we need to go back to the formation of the colonial system in the country that dates back to 500 years. According to Newitt (1995), the Portuguese presence in Mozambique was initially restricted to trading posts, coastal enclaves, and later foreign concessionaires. Portugal thus maintained an ad hoc colonial system with limited integration of all parts of the country into the colonial political and economic system. When Dr António de Oliveira Salazar took over power in Portugal in 1932, he established a semi-fascist dictatorship called Estado Novo (The New State). According to Newitt (1981), the new system embarked on turning all Portuguese colonies into Portuguese overseas provinces. Hedges (1999) argues that the new Portuguese policy increased white migration to African colonies. Unlike the highly skilled white British who migrated to the British colonies, most Portuguese immigrants were unskilled labourers competing with locals for work. Therefore, indigenous Mozambicans were pushed out of basic jobs in Mozambique.

Frente da Libertação de Moçambique (FRELIMO) was formed in 1962 by Mozambican exiled freedom fighters in Tanzania. Tordoff (2002) asserts that FRELIMO brought together three nationalist parties and different classes (workers, peasants, and petty bourgeoisie) to oppose colonialism and demand independence. Fauvet (1984) cites the Makonde African National Union, the Mozambican National Democratic Union (UDENAMO) and the Mozambique National Independence Union (UNAMI) as the three organizations that created FRELIMO in June 1962. FRELIMO began its armed struggle in 1964 when it launched offensive attacks against colonial settlements in Northern Mozambique out of bases in Tanzania. These military victories allowed FRELIMO to establish its administration in northern Mozambique. Despite these successes, FRELIMO unity was fragile as cracks persisted due to two opposing conceptions of nationalist struggle that emerged within the movement. In 1969, Eduardo Mondlane was assassinated and later replaced by Samora Machel.

The collapse of Marcelo Caetano's right-wing regime in Portugal led to the collapse of the whole Portuguese colonial empire and impacted colonial administrations in Mozambique, Angola and Guinea Bissau in West Africa. Caetano was overthrown by a bloodless coup orchestrated by left-wing military officers who had fought in the Portuguese colonial wars in Africa. The Portuguese military had been deployed to fight in Angola and Mozambique as the Portuguese government struggled to control its 500-year-old African empire. The wars had become very expensive for the Portuguese, and public opinion had changed in Portugal. The Portuguese government's management of the economy and the never-ending colonial war led to resentment and disillusionment among the soldiers and general population. The military hierarchy believed that the military actions were not sustainable and could not be won. The colonial authority of Portugal was dissolved following the coup, which led to the disintegration of the Portuguese colonial empire.

The withdrawal of Portuguese troops from offensive positions allowed FRELIMO to negotiate a power transfer from the Portuguese without holding an election. Meredith (2011) points out that FRELIMO demanded the Portuguese recognize FRELIMO as the "sole legitimate representatives of Mozambicans." In September 1974, Portugal agreed to transfer power to FRELIMO after nine months of transition. Mozambique gained its independence in June 1975.

FRELIMO's history and the liberation struggle in Mozambique are intertwined with the ANC and ZANU. The relationship between the three organisations is reflected in the personal lives of their leaders. Both Angola, Mozambique played a critical and direct role in the ANC's military efforts against the Apartheid South African regime. Consequently, the country faced the harshest retaliation from the South African Government while also being attacked by Ian Smith's government through its proxy paramilitary wing Resistencia Nacional Mocambicana or Mozambique National Resistance (RENAMO). Ken Flower, the Rhodesian head of the Central Intelligence Office (CIO), established RENAMO in 1976 with the sole objective of destabilising Mozambique as its territory had become a safe haven for Rhodesian and ANC freedom fighters. RENAMO's insurgent operations eventually led to a bitter civil war.

Following the collapse of the Ian Smith regime in Rhodesia, which led to Zimbabwe's independence, the South African Government filled the vacuum by supporting RENAMO. The civil war in Mozambique exposed the divisions in the region among its neighbours inspired by South Africa's destabilization efforts. Besides relying on Rhodesia and later South Africa, according to Vines (1996), RENAMO also benefited from logistical support from Dr Banda's regime in Malawi. South Africa's increased support to RENAMO, which was channelled through Malawi, exposed Malawi's involvement in the war. Through Lilongwe, the new Capital City of Malawi, the South Africans would supply weapons and equipment to Dr Banda's paramilitary wing, the Malawi Young Pioneers (MYP). In Phiri's (2000) account, "MYP delivered equipment and weaponry to RENAMO agents for transmission and distribution to the districts of Angonia and Tete in the west, Milanje and Niassa in the east."

The FRELIMO government responded kindly by supporting opponents of Dr Hastings Kamuzu Banda of Malawi. For Cabrita (2000), Mozambique considered its support to Dr Banda's opponents as part of the struggle against Western imperialism. Also, Mozambique provided this support to steer Malawi away from Apartheid South Africa and Ian Smith's Rhodesia. We must also recognise that Mozambique made efforts to destabilise Malawi, although the outcome of these efforts had a limited impact on Malawi's political stability. Samora Machel provided a safe refuge to opponents of Dr Banda who wanted to infiltrate Malawi through Tanzania and the Mozambican provinces of Niassa, Tete, and Zambezia. Dr Attati Mpakati, leader of the League of Socialist Malawi (LESOMA), was one of those who received support. Mpakati had lived in exile in Maputo following his escape from Malawi.

The Apartheid regime took more aggressive measures against the countries assisting the ANC in the 1980s, particularly those that allowed ANC bases. The impact of South Africa's support for RENAMO marked a turning point in the organisation's operations. RENAMO was now able to escalate its operation and quickly expanded its operations from central Mozambique to Gaza, Manica, Tete, Zambezia Province and Inhambane Province. With the aid of the South Africans, RENAMO increased its operations by disrupting rail networks, destroying the Cahora Bassa dam's electricity grid, and cutting critical connections to harbours. Besides attacking infrastructure, RENAMO perpetrated some of the most heinous human rights violations in African history. The group gained a reputation for mutilating civilians and recruiting children as soldiers. Dolan and Schafer (1997) conducted a study on RENAMO ex-combatants; the study results showed that 87% of RENAMO soldiers had been forcefully recruited.

In addition to aiding RENAMO, South Africa also carried out air raids across the border into Mozambique as part of its destabilization efforts. The counter-insurgency led to catastrophic consequences for Mozambique in the early 1980s as the war intensified. For instance, in January 1981, the South African military launched an attack on Matola that led to the killing of 23 people. In retaliation, the Soviet Union, an ally of the Mozambicans, sent two warships to Maputo to demonstrate the Soviet's commitment and support. A pact between Mozambique and the Soviet Union had been signed in 1977, making the country the third black African nation to establish formal ties with the Soviet Union after Angola and Somalia. This arrangement was a threat to Western Capitalism as Western powers feared Soviet influence in the region.

Hanlon (2010), citing UNICEF figures, observes that the civil war cost Mozambique half of its potential Gross Domestic Product (GDP). He states that "the number of health posts had been increased from 326 at independence to 1195 in 1985. Apart from attacking health posts, more than 60% of all primary schools were destroyed or closed, and more than

3,000 rural shops were also destroyed or closed." South Africa used these military efforts to force Southern African states to enter into a special relationship with the Apartheid regime. As a result of this distraction, the Mozambican government was pressured to sign a non-aggression pact with the South African Government, commonly known as the Nkomati Accord, on 16 March 1984. This was a non-aggression pact meant to stop South Africa's support to RENAMO and the Mozambican government, eliminating the ANC's military bases.

In essence, the Nkomati Accord was an agreement portraying Mozambique's surrender to the Apartheid regime. The country could no longer cope with the destruction caused by South Africa's destabilization efforts. As the country faced a catastrophic humanitarian crisis and lacked resources to continue fighting the South African-backed RENAMO, the agreement was the only viable option. Although Mozambique honoured its side of the agreement by limiting ANC's military operations, South Africa continued its support for RENAMO. The Apartheid regime strengthened the rebel group further by airlifting significant supplies for RENAMO. The South African government also continued its efforts to cripple the Mozambican economy by demolishing infrastructure and damaging rail and road networks. On 19 October 1986, Mozambican President Samora Machel was killed in a plane crash, rumoured to be an assassination carried out by the South Africans. He was flying back home from a summit in Zambia where a strategy had been devised to pressure Malawi to end its support for RENAMO.

Malawi

Malawi's relatively small size in the region did not prevent it from adopting one of Africa's most pragmatic and contentious foreign policies. Malawi's foreign policy stood in contrast to that of its neighbours and the rest of the continent. As a result of the Pan-African and solidarity principle of the OAU, African countries had an obligation to assist liberation movements and facilitate their independence collectively. The foreign policy of Malawi, since independence in 1964, differed significantly from its newly independent neighbours, such as Tanzania and Zambia. Under the solidarity principle, the two countries had offered to become Frontline States (FLS) for the OAU's effort to end Apartheid and residual white minority governments. The OAU's Liberation Committee had called for the total independence of all African territories still governed by white minority governments and demanded all African states support the continent's liberation movements.

Contrary to that call, Malawi's first president, Dr Hastings Kamuzu Banda, developed close relationships with the remaining white majority regimes of South Africa, Southern Rhodesia, and Mozambique. The country was pitted against its neighbours due to this, and the unique relations it had with white minority regimes turned it into a pariah state. Dr Banda's foreign policy also contradicted the objectives of other senior cabinet officials who wanted Malawi to forge closer ties with its neighbours. Banda demonstrated his dislike of the radical anti-colonial regimes and their support of socialism. As soon as Dr Banda came to power, his regime imposed strict restrictions on FRELIMO and other liberation movements in Malawi. Malawi's strategic location could have been essential for FRELIMO; however, the country decided not to offer refuge to the liberation movement.

Despite being hostile to FRELIMO, Dr Banda enjoyed a cosy relationship with Mozambican colonial authorities. The Portuguese intelligence services coordinated with South African agents in training Malawi's security forces, including the Malawi Young Pioneers, starting in 1965. As an added insult, Dr Banda was also openly sympathetic to the Portuguese. In the hope of gaining control of Northern Mozambique, Dr Banda backed the Portuguese colonial government. In his address to parliament on 23 March, 1969, Dr Banda made these remarks: "You do not hear any more harsh treatment...Even their methods of administration are becoming more liberal...We Africans, North of Zambezi, have no right to speak for all Africans now under colonial rule. What do we know about what the Africans of Mozambique themselves want?" The soon-to-be Mozambique president, Samora Machel, was angry with this speech and condemned Dr Banda for undermining Mozambique's liberation struggle. Samora Machel contrasted the vital support he received from Tanzania with Dr Banda's hostile stance. Dr Banda's stance undermined the liberation struggle, and the FRELIMO took offence to this statement. Samora Machel argued that Dr Banda provided cover to the Portuguese colonial administration by arguing for its legitimacy.

A relationship between Dr Banda and the Portuguese colonial administration can be traced back to 1961. According to Robinson (2006), the Mozambican colonial administration contacted Dr Banda through Jorge Jardim to discuss future economic relations. Jardim served as

Secretary of State for the Portuguese colonial administration in Mozambique and later became very close to Dr Banda. Banda's relationship with the Portuguese colonial administration was motivated by his vision for a Greater Maravi, with Malawi gaining some Mozambican territory which the Portuguese administration promised. The Portuguese Foreign Minister in 1967 cited in Henderson (1977) spoke of relations with Malawi as "that kind of mutual respect which ensures good neighbourliness, cordial relations and constructive cooperation." Dr Banda's former Foreign minister, Kanyama Chiume, in his 1975 autobiography, stated that: "Both the (Portuguese president) Salazar and the Portuguese settlers had convinced Dr Banda that they would give him the northern portion of Mozambique in return for not allowing freedom fighters to pass through Malawi and for the recognition of Mozambique's independence after the death of Salazar." As part of this effort, as early as 1966, at the height of the Mozambican liberation struggle, according to Martin Rupiya (2005), a pro-Malawi proxy led by Amos Sumane was created. Sumane, a FRELIMO defector living in Malawi since 1965, helped create the National Union of Rombezia with assistance from the Portuguese colonial administration. Together with the MYP, they conducted a secret operation code-named 'Malawi II' to create a black-controlled state in Northern Mozambique adjacent to Malawi that could later integrate with Malawi. A year after Mozambique gained independence, Sumane established Partido Revolucionario de Moçambique with the support of other FRELIMO defectors freeing the Samora Machel regime.

Malawi's stance on the white-minority governments in the region was also a blow to the OAU, challenging its Pan-African ideology and solidarity principle. In accordance with the OAU's expectations, white minority governments were to be isolated in South Africa, Rhodesia, Angola, and Mozambique. However, its diplomatic relations with South Africa pitted it against its regional neighbours and the OAU. While the South African government intensified its counterinsurgency operations in the region, Malawi's relationship with its regional neighbours was further tested. According to Mayall (1970), the Prime Minister of South Africa's visit to Malawi and Rhodesia focused on Malawi's isolation from the rest of the black African countries and how the white minority governments could support Dr Banda. Dr Banda provided legitimacy to white minority governments as they attempted to convince the rest of the world that they could co-exist with other African countries.

Cervenl (1977) argues that Tanzania opposed Malawi's membership in the Liberation Committee at the 1965 OAU Summit in Accra due to Malawi's foreign policy stance. Tanzania opposed the admission of Malawi, alleging that Malawi colluded with the Portuguese colonial administration in Mozambique to sabotage the Committee's work and threatened to leave if Malawi was admitted. Malawi withdrew its candidature in response, and Somalia and Zambia were elected instead. Also, Malawi was excluded from receiving the OAU's regular military bulletins on liberation movements circulated to all member states since it had diplomatic relations with Portugal, South Africa, and the Ian Smith regime in Southern Rhodesia.

In 1966, the OAU suffered another setback in its anti-Apartheid policy during the UN General Assembly. The Malawi delegation was the only Afro-Asian delegation who heard the South African Foreign Minister speak at the UN General Assembly. All African, Asian and Arab delegations walked out in protest. This occurred when the UN attempted to wrestle South West Africa from the Apartheid government after declaring South Africa's official occupation of Namibia illegal under international law.

Even though Malawi was not geographically at the mercy of South Africa, unlike Botswana, Lesotho, and Swaziland, the relationship between South Africa and Malawi was difficult for most African countries to comprehend. In February 1967, Malawi established a diplomatic mission in South Africa, becoming the only country with an official diplomatic relationship with the Apartheid regime. Malawi's relationship with the Apartheid regime irritated liberation movements like ANC in South Africa, FRELIMO in Mozambique, and ZANU in Zimbabwe. For instance, during the commemoration of the ANC's 60th anniversary on 8 January 1972, ANC President Oliver Tambo said: "Already we have much cause for worry. A few examples will suffice; the seizure of Malawi, now the scene of busy comings-in and goings-out by top-ranking officials, cabinet ministers, and military personnel from the conquering fascists of the South. But the bloodsuckers of our country appear to be winning one or two new black co-suckers, the titanic struggle which the militant leaders of Africa are waging against colonialism and racialism in Africa." From the ANC leader's perspective, South Africa and Malawi's relationship was viewed as part of South Africa's attempt to subdue and re-colonize some independent African states, contradicting the OAU's efforts to unite African states.

Regarding Zimbabwe's liberation struggle, Dr Banda always abstained from voting on resolutions that called on Britain to use force against the illegal Rhodesian government at the United Nations and the Organisation of African Unity. He was just as opposed to Mozambique's liberation struggle as he was to Zimbabwe's. In 1976, Dr Nathan Shamuyarira, who later became Zimbabwe's Foreign Minister, was arrested at Chileka Airport in Malawi while flying from Tanzania to Mozambique. After spending two weeks in a Malawian prison. When his ZANU colleagues heard about his arrest in Malawi, they contacted the OAU Liberation Committee. To ensure Nathan's safe departure, the Secretary-General of the OAU called Malawi's Head of State Kamuzu Banda, demanding Shamuyarira 's immediate release. Shamuyarira was released and deported from the country.

Another senior freedom fighter from Zimbabwe, Dr Sakupwanya, was also arrested by Malawi's Special Branch in the 1970s after his plane landed at Chileka Airport in Blantyre on transit. Dent (1994) states that Sakupwanya was immediately taken off the plane by Malawian security agents upon being alerted by Ian Smith intelligence agents. Dr Sakupwanya recollected using his relationship with Mama Kadzamira, Dr Banda's official hostess, an influential figure he grew up with, in Harare. During his detention, he requested to speak Kadzamira. Kadzamira arranged Sakupwanya's release when she learned of Sakupwanya's arrest, saving him from being extradited to the Ian Smith regime.

As a consequence of its stance toward the liberation movements in the region, Malawi also faced hostile responses from its neighbours, particularly the government of Mozambique. Hedges (1989) contends that after Machel visited Japan in May 1986, he initiated a diplomatic campaign that emphasized Malawi's role as host and transit pathway for mercenaries from South Africa and its support for RENAMO participants. The RENAMO rebels were believed to operate out of Malawi, and Machel loathed Malawi's President, Dr Banda. During a meeting of Frontline States in Luanda, Angola, in August 1986, according to Hedges (1989), "the Mozambican government presented a dossier of information that showed proof of Malawi's support to the Mozambican rebel group. The dossier included copies of new Malawian passports issued to RENAMO operatives and letters written by RENAMO operatives to the Malawi Government officials." Machel's allegations are supported by Babrita (1983), who argues that: "RENAMO officials, foreign correspondents and an array of other individuals enjoyed transit facilities in Malawi whenever they wanted to visit the guerrillas' territory in Mozambique...and that South Africa's Air Force planes are known to have flown from Malawi to drop logistical supplies to RENAMO bases in northern Mozambique."

On 19 October 1986, Kenneth Kaunda hosted Frontline States leaders in Mbala to discuss how best to deal with Dr Banda and Mobutu Sese Seko of Zaire, two African leaders accused of supporting Apartheid-sponsored rebel groups in Mozambique and Angola, respectively. In a plane crash on 19 October 1986, Machel and 34 others died on their way back from Zambia. Conchiglia (2017) asserts that the plane crash on South African territory raised questions about a possible assassination. However, the Western governments agreed with South Africa's assessment that the crash occurred because of pilot error. Interestingly, this explanation contradicted the Soviet Union and Mozambique analysis who believed that the plane had been diverted by a VOR (Very high-frequency Omnidirectional Range) signal. The decoy beacon transmitted at the same frequency as Maputo airport, resulting in pilot error.

Dan Moyane, a South African-born journalist scheduled to fly with Machel, reported that Machel threatened to close the Mozambican border with Malawi and deploy missiles on both sides of the border if Dr Banda continued to support RENAMO. A City Press article published on October 15, 2015, written by Moyane, stated that Machel had just threatened Malawi at the Zambian summit and the plane crash sparked suspicion among Mozambicans. Closing the border could deprive Malawi's landlocked country of access to the Indian Ocean. According to Moyane, "the plane was believed to have been brought down to stop Machel from causing any harm to Malawi, South Africa's only African ally".

There are particular reasons why Malawi chose that foreign policy path. Did the benefits justify the means? Scholars of diplomacy and foreign relations are puzzled by that question. To better understand Malawi's motives, it is helpful to review Malawi's political and economic dynamics. Malawi's independence followed the usual trajectory of post-World War II political aspiration, which led to early political parties and trade unions being formed, civil disobedience, and a movement led by young and militant nationalists that called for decolonization. Nyasaland African Congress (NAC) was formed in 1944, which Dr Banda later joined in 1958. Dr Banda joined the liberation struggle late when the liberation movement had already begun challenging British colonialism. Following Dr Banda's arrest in Operation Sunrise on 3 March 1959 and his release a year later, a gradual process toward independence began between 1960 and 1963. In 1964, Dr Banda became prime minister.

Figure 3.6: President Dr Hastings Kamuzu Banda

Source: britannica.com

While Dr Banda's party, the Malawi Congress Party (MCP), opposed colonialism, it lacked a unified ideology. Three months after Malawi's independence, conflicts within the new government were caused by diverging perspectives on its direction. The differences centred on Dr Banda's role in the new independent Malawi and the new government's foreign and domestic policies. The young nationalists, whom one time Governor Roy Welensky (1964) described as 'immoderate', were more determined to follow the popular socialist policy that was being followed by Julius Nyerere in Tanzania and wanted to dismantle all colonial structures and were dissatisfied with the pace of Africanization. Dr Banda's political ideology was at odds with that of these young politicians.

A disagreement also arose on the two-China policy, with Dr Banda, a capitalist, supporting Taiwan, while his opponents favoured Mao's China.

Younger peers of Dr Banda such as Dunduzu Chisiza, Henry Chipembere, Orton Chirwa, and Yatuta Chisiza believed they were the true custodians of the Malawi liberation struggle and challenged his leadership. Additionally, they viewed Dr Banda as becoming increasingly autocratic on both domestic and foreign policy issues. In what is known as the 'Cabinet Crisis', on 26 August 1964, exactly seven weeks after independence, Dr Banda dismissed three ministers and a parliamentary secretary, with three others resigning in protest. That left Dr Banda with only one cabinet minister, although one minister rescinded his resignation. Instead of negotiating with his opponents, Dr Banda took advantage of the situation to consolidate his power. As a result, Dr Banda's opponents were arrested, and some of them fled into exile. Dr Banda's determination to suppress opposition was emphasised in his speech on 1 April 1965, as cited in Short (1974), when he stated: "If to maintain political stability and efficient administration I have to detain 10,000, 100,000, I will do it... I want nobody to misunderstand me. I will detain anyone who is interfering with the political stability of this country. When a country is building its political institutions, it is likely to do many nasty things. Well, we are building our political institutions here now."

Several of these exiled politicians sought refuge in neighbouring countries, including Mozambique, Tanzania, and Zambia. His inherent suspicions made him increasingly paranoid that Malawi's neighbours would help the exiled Malawians overthrow him. Among the organizations that Banda was concerned about were the Socialist League of Malawi (LESOMA), the Malawian Freedom Movement (MAFREMO), and the Congress for the Second Republic of Malawi. Some of the fired ministers orchestrated an armed insurrection in the country, thus justifying this suspicion. According to Baker (2006), Masauko Chipembere, a minister who had resigned, fled to the mountains in Malawi's Lake District, Mangochi, and organized guerrilla warfare against Dr Banda's regime. In February 1965, Chipembere's militias attempted to attack Malawi's capital, Zomba. The government security forces repelled the attack at Liwonde, and Dr Banda ordered Chipembere's arrest, alive or dead. Baker (2006) suggests that Chipembere was safely escorted out of Malawi with the assistance of Malawi's Governor-General, Sir Glyn Jones.

Being a landlocked country with limited resources and a multitude of tribal groups, the new government of Malawi faced many economic and political challenges. Due to high poverty levels and the risk of rebellion by exiled politicians, Dr Banda needed reliable partners who could provide economic and security support to his government. Plaut, Unterhalter, and Ward (1981) argue that to ensure his survival, Dr Banda moved the capital city from Zomba in the Southern Region to Lilongwe in the Central Region, where he had the most support from his ethnic group, the Chewa. The South African government provided financial assistance to Dr Banda in the form of soft loans for his Lilongwe project, which led to the construction of Kamuzu International Airport and Capitol Hill. In response to threats to his power, Dr Banda strengthened the Malawi Young Pioneers (MYP), a paramilitary wing of his party, the Malawi Congress Party (MCP). It has been noted that resources that should have gone to the Malawi Defence Force (MDF) were instead allocated to MYP.

The MDF was unique because it did not directly correspond with the ruling party, unlike other militaries across the region. That effectively enhanced the military's independence from direct political manipulation. Unlike other countries where freedom fighters became officers and generals soon after independence, the MDF maintained the British structures with most senior white officers remaining within the ranks for another decade or so, allowing a gradual and organised transfer of military authority. This military structure helped to create a disconnection between the ruling party and the military. It was against this background that Banda found comfort in using the MYP for his errands.

While the rest of Africa was removing all colonial structures, Dr Banda was reinforcing them. Malawi retained British bureaucratic structures, including its personnel. For instance, Malawi did not have a Malawian heading the army until 1972, and the first Malawian head of the police only came in 1973, nine years after independence. Kamuzu maintained the colonial security structures to maintain cohesion with the country's foreign policy, which aligned the country with British and American interests against Socialism. These structures allowed the security institutions to continue collaborating with colonial security institutions in Ian Smith's Zimbabwe, the colonial administration in Mozambique, and Apartheid South Africa. Malawi's complicated and complex foreign policy pitted the MYP against the MDF during the Mozambican civil war. While the MDF supported the FRELIMO government forces in securing the Beira-Nacala transport corridor, the MYP assisted RENAMO and facilitated their movements within Malawi. During Operation Bwezani, the MDF disarmed an estimated 6,000 armed MYP militias towards the end of Banda's rule in 1992.

Dr Banda's opposition to Communism made him a darling of Western governments and a villain to Pan-Africanists. Dr Banda's trust in the colonial structures went beyond security issues, as he also preferred neo-colonial administrative and educational structures. For instance, at his ambitious 'Eton of Africa' project, Kamuzu Academy, only white British teachers were recruited. Kamuzu Academy was an elite school where the brightest and most gifted children went. The school followed a classical education system where Latin and Greek were part of the curriculum. British senior executives also ran the government-owned corporations and his private companies. It was not a surprise that Dr Banda found comfort among the white minority leaders in Zimbabwe, Mozambique, and South Africa. It was not an anomaly because Dr Banda trusted white people, and the white people trusted him.

Despite debates about what motivated Dr Banda to adopt such extreme measures concerning the liberation movements and the white minority governments in the region, some scholars have been kind in their lauding of these policies. Mayall (1970) holds that the Malawi government's foreign policy was driven by political realism to respond to an anarchical international system, and Banda's remarks support these claims. Cockram (1970) quotes Dr Banda as saying: "Do you know what would happen if I detached Malawi from South Africa?" he asked. "There would be economic chaos and, after that, political chaos." A year later, he argued: "We cannot boycott South Africa; that would mean the breakdown of Malawi's economy." Dr Banda's second justification for maintaining diplomatic relations, according to Cockram (1970), was that he did not believe they could defeat the Apartheid regime when he remarked: "South Africa is here to stay." In Banda's view, his duty was to the people of Malawi. Quoted in Cockram (1970), Dr Banda argued: "If in order to look after my people I have to deal with the devil, I will do so." He suggested that Communist countries had maintained diplomatic relations with Capitalist countries despite having different ideologies and saw no reason he could not do the same with Apartheid South Africa. From Dr Banda's perspective, his government could not survive without South Africa. Power politics influenced his foreign policy both as a means to an end and in response to the anarchical international system, which provided hostile political and economic challenges for newly independent African states like Malawi.

South Africa

Ntloedibe (1977) argues that "the political concept we know as South Africa came into existence on 31 May 1910, when the South Africa Act of 1909 of the British Parliament merged into the Union of South Africa." This new coalition brought together former colonial administrations of the Cape, Transvaal, Natal, and Orange Free State. In South Africa, the new government was set up as a white government with blacks excluded from all political activities. However, South Africa was not recognized as a sovereign state by the United Kingdom in 1910. According to the Status Act of 1934, South Africa's parliament was declared a "sovereign legislative body" outside the British monarch's jurisdiction. Three years later, the 1937 Act passed in the South African Parliament guided the British monarch's status as head of state. This status remained the same until 1961, when South Africa became a republic.

The white minority regime in South Africa impacted all the territories in Southern Africa's post-independence years. The South African government supported the settler administrations in Angola, Mozambique, and Rhodesia, while causing havoc on the black majority governments that supported the liberation movements. With the majority, the black population was marginalised by elaborate racist philosophy called Apartheid; the racist South African regime took a hardline on political dissent, which led to the banning of African nationalist movements and black South Africans being stripped of their citizenship rights. Apartheid, an Afrikaans word meaning "apart-hood," was a set of legislation passed in 1948 to enforce strict racial separations of the South African society with the white population dominating political, economic, and social spheres. There was segregation in housing, employment, marriage, and government-orchestrated by the ruling white Nationalist Party. The black population revolted, leading Nelson Mandela and many others to be arrested while other key leaders such as Oliver Tambo, who fled exile.

Keohane and Nye (2001) argue in complex interdependence theory that countries with the superior military could yield their power through other means: "If there are no constraints on one's choice of instruments-the state with superior military force will prevail. If the security dilemma for all states were highly acute, military force, supported by economic and other resources, would be the dominant power source." With most Southern Africa states gaining independence in the 1960s, states that challenged their legitimacy surrounded the Apartheid regime. This posturing allowed liberation movements like ANC and SWAPO to benefit from safe sanctuaries provided by the Frontline States. These hostile neighbouring countries were perceived as a threat to the South African Apartheid regime and its survival. The regime started counterinsurgency operations in Southern Africa to respond to this new threat, destabilising these newly independent states. Apart from carrying out military attacks in Mozambique, Zimbabwe, Angola, Botswana, and Zambia, South Africa also armed dissidents in Angola and Mozambique, leading to prolonged civil wars in the two Lusophone countries. Davies (1999) pointed out the regional relations between Southern African states that took place between 1960 and 1990 and were driven by three main factors:

(i) Increased political instability between Apartheid South Africa and independent states in the region;
(ii) The economic effect of import restrictions caused by South Africa's import substitution policies;
(iii) The impact of South Africa's politico-military destabilization agenda in neighbouring states.

The third factor appears to have had the most significant impact on these relationships. As Ostergaard (2003) suggests, South Africa's destabilisation agenda might have cost the Southern African states more than $60 billion in the 1980s, measured in losses on the gross domestic product (GDP), more than a million people killed and millions more displaced as refugees. Angola and Mozambique were the most affected states because of the civil wars propagated by South Africa's support of proxies, such as RENAMO in Mozambique and UNITA in Angola. Robert Gersony, a US State Department official as cited in Ostergaard (2003), referred to South Africa's action as "a systematic and brutal war of terror against innocent civilians through forced labour, starvation, physical abuse and wanton killing and becoming one of the most brutal holocausts against ordinary human beings since World War II." The systematic destruction of transport routes between Beira and Nacala in Mozambique alone led to a net loss of $1.5 billion in Mozambique's transit traffic revenue.

THE END OF APARTHEID AND THE NEW DAWN IN SOUTHERN AFRICA

South Africa's destabilisation efforts in the region could only delay the end of the Apartheid regime but could not prevent the inevitable. Bombings in Mozambique, Zimbabwe, Zambia, and Botswana crippled the region's economies. However, Southern African countries were relentless in supporting the ANC and building an international coalition that put pressure on the Apartheid regime and leading to its isolation. South African white voters had just re-elected John Vorster's Nationalist Party on 24 April 1974, giving him an absolute majority in parliament. Simultaneously, Portugal's right-wing government, which had become South Africa's biggest Western ally in its fight against the liberation movements, had just collapsed. The Carnation Revolution in Portugal became a turning point and was a prelude to the disintegration of the remaining white minority governments in Angola, Mozambique, Namibia, Southern Rhodesia, and South Africa.

In southern Africa, the structures that had supported the remaining white-ruled governments were weakening. The coup d'état profoundly impacted the Apartheid regime, which had benefited from its friendly relations with the two Lusophone states (Mozambique and Angola). These two allies were about to disintegrate and be replaced by hostile regimes to the Apartheid government. It was feared that a FRELIMO-ruled Mozambique would provide a sanctuary for ANC liberation fighters, thereby exposing South Africa's industrial capital Transvaal to insurgent attacks. An independent Angola under a Black government also presented challenges, as the country could provide a sanctuary for both ANC and SWAPO. In Rhodesia, the civil war also intensified and weakened the white minority neighbour, leading to its inevitable collapse in 1980. Hostile powers, where the freedom fighters could launch insurgent attacks on the Apartheid regime, now surrounded the South African Apartheid regime.

High-ranking South African, Portuguese, and Southern Rhodesian military officials had been meeting regularly since the early 1970s as part of the ALCORA security structure to coordinate military planning, intelligence sharing, and counterinsurgency operations in the region. It surprised the South Africans that the Marcelo Caetano dictatorship had ended in Portugal during the Carnation Revolution. One of the driving forces behind the revolution was a desire to end Portuguese colonial rule in Africa, primarily due to the costlier colonial wars in Portuguese territories. It is believed that much of the planning for the military coup took place at military installations in the African colonies, and the military leaders behind the revolution had fought in Africa.

Figure 3.7: South Africa's Prime Minister John Vorster

Source: brittanica.com

The collapse of two friendly regimes in Angola and Mozambique was a significant setback to the South African government's security strategy. The weakening of the Soviet bloc led to new re-alignments in international relations and affected the survival of the Apartheid regime.

The relationship between the Soviets and some Southern African states had primarily sustained the region's balance of power. South Africa had remained a beacon of capitalism that was in line with the Western coalition's interests. From a global perspective, the weakening and subsequent collapse of the Soviet empire weakened international support for the Apartheid regime. Towards the second period of the 1980s, Soviet influence in Southern Africa and the rest of the world had waned out. Much of the Cold War's strategic tension had eased as the Soviet Union succumbed to pressure from the West.

While the Western countries were publicly against Apartheid in South Africa, the regime's existence in the region presented a reliable ally for countering Communist influence in the region. However, the end of the Cold War undermined South Africa's Apartheid regime's significance to U.S. foreign policy. The support the regime had enjoyed from the U.S. and its Western allies had vanished. President Harry Truman's foreign policy goal of limiting the expansion of the Soviet Union drove a U.S. foreign policy that had helped sustain the Apartheid regime. Here, maintaining an ally against the Soviet Union was necessary for the U.S. South Africa had provided a platform for future American presidents to continue providing subtle support to the Apartheid regime to limit the spread of Communism in Southern Africa. President Ronald Reagan, in his speech in 1981 quoted in Schraeder (1994), said: "can we abandon a country that has stood by us in every war we have ever fought, a country that strategically is essential to the free world in its production of minerals we all must have and so forth." Reagan defended the South African Apartheid regime by suggesting that the Apartheid in South Africa was similar to the racism in the United States. The Americans appeared to be more focused on the Cold War, and anyone who opposed Communism was an American ally. In this regard, the means justified the ends for the US government. When President Lyndon Johnson started enacting the civil rights and social equality laws, the administration also began listening to calls for support for the anti-Apartheid movements. However, the US support continued as the Central Intelligence Agency (CIA) was actively involved in the Angolan civil war.

The period of the liberation struggle was a period that tested the foreign policy of Western powers, especially the US and UK, as they provided support to the Apartheid regime. What is disturbing is how the special interests of Western powers undermined their credibility to serve the narrow interests of an ideology. Stiglitz (2002) rightly believes that

America's credentials were tainted by its "Manifest Destiny" of fighting the expansion of Communism across the world while compromising or ignoring democracy and human rights principles. The Soviet-bloc countries took advantage of the Western powers' absence of support to the liberation movements by aligning themselves to the liberation struggle and providing financial, material and diplomatic support. This provided the Soviet bloc with a moral ground to discredit the West's liberal agenda. This also undermined the US's efforts to win support from the global south. It was the Soviet bloc that was leading the calls for racial justice and equality. The Western support of the Apartheid regime had a corrosive effect on the underlying narrative and conviction of Western liberal democracies. It was the Soviets who benefitted from this fallout as Western political, legal and civil values were put into question.

At the start of the 1980s, it had become apparent that Western support for the Apartheid regime could no longer be sustained, as support of the liberation movement continued to gain momentum in the US Congress. In 1986, the US Congress enacted the Comprehensive Anti-Apartheid Act (CAAA), allowing the first substantial economic sanctions against South Africa. Among some of the provisions of the Act were:

(i) Outlawed the importation of many South African products such as steel, iron, uranium, coal, textiles, and agricultural commodities into the United States;
(ii) Prohibited the South African government from holding US bank accounts;
(iii) Banned South African Airways from landing at US airports;
(iv) Blocked any form of US. foreign aid or assistance to the then pro-Apartheid South African government; and
(v) Banned all new US investments and loans in South Africa.

President Ronald Reagan vetoed the Act. However, the House of Representatives, with the help of the US Senate, could override Reagan's veto. Although the Reagan administration continued to avoid the Act's enforcement, the George H.W. Bush administration that followed declared its total commitment to comply with the Act's enforcement. Defenders of the Apartheid regime outside South Africa had touted the regime as a necessary defence against Communism in Southern Africa; however, the Cold War's inevitable end rendered this argument irrelevant. Furthermore, the country's economic turmoil forced the regime to participate in an agreement that could lead to Namibia's independence, a country South Africa had occupied illegally since the end of World War II.

By the end of the 1980s, the South African government was experiencing intense pressure from economic and cultural sanctions, and with an economic recession looming, the Apartheid regime was weakened. The new generation of white South Africans saw no value in defending the archaic Apartheid system. The emerging political dynamics on the domestic scene made it difficult for the hardline politicians to maintain their grip on power and Apartheid support. This domestic resentment ushered in increased support of moderate politicians that rendered the far-right politics of P.W. Botha, the then Prime Minister, unpopular. F.W. de Klerk promised a reconciliatory approach, and in 1989, the moderates led by de Klerk won the elections.

The new South African Government immediately lifted the ban on the ANC and other liberation parties, restored press freedom, and released political prisoners, including Nelson Mandela, who had spent 27 years in prison. In 1993, de Klerk agreed to hold the first national elections, which allowed all races to participate, leading to the U.S. lifting all sanctions. After negotiating a new non-racial constitution in 1993, the first democratic elections took place in April 1994, with Mandela ascending to the presidency.

The emergence of an ANC government presented new opportunities for South Africa and the region is general to for a new direction due to the end of South Africa's destabilisation efforts that had weakened Southern states from an economic, political, social and security perspective.

5

SADC and the Renewed Hope for Economic Revolution

Introduction

From a historical perspective, the colonial/Apartheid struggle years had been a difficult period for Southern African states. South African counter-insurgency operations caused severe economic, social, and political disruption. Angola and Mozambique, for instance, were destabilized by bloody civil wars supported by the Apartheid regime. Zimbabwe, Botswana and Zambia were also affected by military raids by South African agents on their territory. These counter-insurgency attacks were compounded by economic maneuvres by the Apartheid regime surgically aimed at crippling the economies of Southern African states. Further economic disruptions awaited Southern Africa in the aftermath of Apartheid and the Cold War. Chapter four outlined the interconnections established between Southern African states and the liberation movements that later became ruling parties. The chapter also briefly considered the implications of these relationships to regional cohesion. These are conditions that will become more defined from chapter five and going forward.

The post-Cold War era also saw an increase in the pressures of globalization. The aid from Western countries came with many conditions for the aid-dependent states in Southern Africa. African governments were urged to pursue Stabilization and Structural Adjustment Programs (SAPS) with support from the International Monetary Fund (IMF) and the World Bank. SAPs emphasised macroeconomic adjustments, deregulations and market liberalization, which led to changes in the manufacturing industry and other sectors. However, the market reforms failed in the region since they missed specific structural factors like individual countries' institutional and historical contexts.

The anticipated harmonious development of relations between the Southern African states and soon to be democratic South Africa belied a more profound integration process in the region. The shared history between Southern African states provided a platform for cooperation in the region in the aftermath of the Apartheid regime. Regionalism takes different forms and is recognized as an instrument that can address multiple objectives. As espoused by early African leaders, closer economic and political cooperation among African states was recognized as the continent's bedrock for economic success and stability. After the Frontline States had finally achieved their quest in defeating colonialism and Apartheid across the region, the regional changes required a paradigm shift in regional relations and aspirations.

All forms of regional integration inevitably imply some form of constraint on member states' sovereignty, and SADC is not an exception. However, the extent to which integration affects member states' autonomy varies depending on the legal and institutional structure of the institutions created. With the inception of the Southern African Development Community (SADC) Treaty in 1992, Southern African integration, which started with the Lusaka Declaration in 1980, took a decisive step. The SADC Treaty was innovative in both political and economic terms. The treaty created an economic framework of regional integration, establishing a regional customs union, common market and regional infrastructure. The treaty also attempted to address political, social and security issues. The Southern African states' objectives had shifted entirely from survival focused on overcoming South Africa's destabilization efforts to closer economic cooperation that could stimulate economic growth and enhance regional stability.

The last chapter touched upon how Southern African states employed the concept of solidarity, clearly implying that all states in the region had an obligation to support the fellow African people still under white minority governments. The fall of the Apartheid regime in South Africa presented new opportunities for Southern African countries to forge new relations as they embarked on a project to recover from the effects of South Africa's destabilization efforts. However, there cannot be any economic success and development without a stable political environment and competent regional governance structures. The chapter traces the evolution of SADC from its inception in 1992 and attempts to identify existing constraints impeding regional integration efforts. It examines SADC through the lenses of the agreed objectives adopted at the regional. The analysis benefits from the SADC Treaty, protocols, and agreements, which provide a framework for common policies to be followed by all member states. While these protocols and agreements portray a very positive SADC image, there are a number of inherent contradictions that have posed obstacles to progress. One of those contradictions is the agreed system of governance in member states. While SADC has promoted democracy and good governance, member states' actions to pursue these objectives are characterized by failure. The chapter raises the argument that unsatisfactory progress in the regional integration scheme combines diverse and inherent factors in individual SADC member states' DNA.

According to the SADC Treaty (1992), the Southern African Development Community (SADC) is primarily an arrangement facilitating economic recovery and integration with the view to "improve the quality of life of the peoples of the region." The primary objective of SADC reflects the institution's priority and is reflected in the SADC vision driven by the desire to create "a shared future, a future within a regional community that will ensure economic well-being, improvement of the standards of living and quality of life, freedom and social justice and peace and security for the peoples of Southern Africa. The establishment of SADC was also motivated by the desire to strengthen member states' position in the global political arena and enable the region's economic progress. The revamped regional body had the vision to promote its equitable development, inclusive of new cooperation with South Africa. More significantly, awareness of the competitive weaknesses of Southern African states within the emerging global economic system has led to a paradigm shift in the conceptualisation of regional integration.

However, achieving the objectives outlined in the SADC vision is not an easy task. It requires objective preconditions. Development analysts and academics have reasoned that regional integration in Southern Africa should move beyond abstract visions and adopt pragmatic actions that include sustainable political and economic reforms. This gives credence to Andresen's et al. (2001) view that regional integration in Southern Africa provides a path towards liberalizing developing countries' trade and integrating them into the global economy. For the smaller African economies to survive, they must create an enlarged economic space with integrated regional markets and harmonise the regulatory, economic, political and social environment. Regional integration provides a framework for institutionalized regulations and regional governance that guide the international life of member states in a particular region. According to Mattli (1999), regional economic integration is viewed as a mechanism used by sovereign states to conduct economic integration in trade and links the government's national policies to a supranational entity. Regional integration proliferated on the African continent as soon as states started gaining independence. For African countries, Pan-Africanism was a driving force behind regional integration, an approach that promoted the creation of a supra-African government. However, integration efforts of the African continent and its sub-regional groups have failed to bring satisfactory outcomes. Some African countries have even experienced a political and economic decline due to a wrong set of priorities pursued by regional political elites and a lack of honest socio-economic development commitment. For example, according to the Economist dated 26 February 2005, the per capita income in Zimbabwe was about 50% in 2005 of what it was in 1980 when the country became independent.

Lee (2002) commented that the political stability of Southern Africa is a prerequisite for regional integration because of its implications on economic development. SADC member states' lack of commitment to the regional agenda is inspired by their reluctance to surrender some of their powers and authority to the regional body. The survival and apparent success of the EU bear strong testimony to the potential benefits of regional integration schemes. Thus, identifying and overcoming the constraints affecting the integration project has tremendous potential to harmonize regional political and economic instruments that could bring about an environment conducive to economic growth and political stability. This approach would also allow SADC member states to create a common front for promoting their interests from a stronger position in the global system.

However, the regional integration schemes in Africa have achieved limited economic development and, in most cases, have turned out to be ineffective. The continent lacks a regional integration agenda viable for economic growth, and market integration has not been translated to increased intra-regional trade. The current status of regional integration in Southern Africa has characteristics that include: overlapping membership schemes; competing for national interests and xenophobia; non-complementary trade and lack of export diversification; diverse economic status of member states; overambitious projects that lack planning; poor infrastructure and inefficient customs and logistics; diverse political systems and governance deficit; lack of collective measures for accountability; and most importantly regional instability. The mentioned factors suggest that the high risks of doing business in the SADC region come from conflicts, political instability, governance deficit, and the high costs associated with the infrastructure deficit and regulatory deficiencies.

Traditional arguments for integration are increasing productivity and efficiencies, economies of scale, a larger market, a more remarkable ability to complement the economy, and public goods. Integrating economies has also proven to reduce conflict and increase resilience to external shocks and joint exploitation of global economic opportunities. The same is true for collective action to address concerns relating to democracy, human rights, and shared governance natural resources.

SADC: New Political and Economic Arrangement in Southern Africa

Margaret Lee (2003) described regional integration as "the adoption of a regional project by a formal regional economic organisation designed to enhance the political, economic, social, cultural, and security integration and/or cooperation of member states". In Southern Africa's context, despite tremendous natural and mineral wealth and the shared history, Southern Africa remains politically unstable, with political and armed conflicts impeding stability and economic development. The addition of South Africa, Africa's largest economy, provided the basis for successful economic cooperation. With over 350 million people from 16 independent nation-states, the regional body presented an opportunity to transform the region based on the assumption that regional integration could create a more extensive economic space and allow the regional members to benefit from economies of scale.

The rationale for regional integration in Southern Africa from a global perspective is obvious. It is difficult for small and isolated African economies to survive the global market on their own. Schiff and Winters (2013) argue that regional integration could strengthen the voices of small nations that would generally face severe disadvantages in dealing with the rest of the world because of their minimal bargaining power. In this case, according to Hettne et al. (1999), developing countries need to integrate their national economic and political systems to overcome the effects of the hostile global political and economic systems.

Regional integration in Southern Africa manifested itself historically from the Pan-Africanism concept discussed in chapters 2 and 3. FLS member states formed the Southern African Development Cooperation Conference (SADCC) in 1980, soon after Zimbabwe's independence in 1980. SADCC had an explicit security function to insulate member states from disruptions orchestrated by the South African government. According to the Organization of Economic Cooperation and Development report (2005), SADCC's strategy was aimed "to reduce economic dependence on South Africa both as a trading partner, and as a conduit for the SADCC trade with the outside world." FLS had been formed in the 1970s as an informal collective security framework by Angola, Botswana, Mozambique, Tanzania, Zambia, and representatives of the liberation movements in Southern Africa. FLS was set up to facilitate assistance to the liberation movements in Zimbabwe, Namibia, and South Africa. The establishment of SADCC in 1980 was significant for the future creation of SADC in two ways. Firstly, despite the operational difficulties SADCC faced, the initiative demonstrated that economic integration in Southern Africa was feasible. Secondly, the unity shown among Southern African states eventually provided a model in which a more robust SADC could be established. The anti-colonial and anti-Apartheid struggle that had pitted the majority black population against minority white dominance provided an impetus for the original frontline states members to accommodate South Africa and Namibia in the new-look regional body. Against the backdrop of economic and political turmoil engineered by the Apartheid regime, the region had been overwhelmed by the refugee crisis, civil wars, and considerable economic destruction.

An Apartheid regime in South Africa and its destabilization efforts had undermined any efforts to enhance economic integration and regional stability. In the aftermath of Apartheid, conditions conducive for regional political and economic integration in Southern Africa were presented, leading to the birth of SADC. Gambiri (1991) noted that developing countries could not separate economies from politics and that the spillover of economic to political cooperation could not be a natural process. Nevertheless, the new regional body recognized the significance of political and economic convergence in the region. To usher in a new dawn in Southern Africa, the SADC Treaty recognized the importance of promoting democratic governance, stability, and stimulating economic growth. Following its formal inauguration in 1992, SADC embarked on an elaborate initiative to create an institutional framework that could address the lingering political, security and socio-economic challenges the region was facing. SADC presented an instrument for the Southern African states to overcome political and economic difficulties. Unlike SADCC, the SADC Treaty (1992) provides a critical institutional framework that binds member states. However, this legal obligation rests on member states. It is the member state-driven approach that has defined the institution's character and its slow progress.

For SADC member states to avoid the further decline of SADC as it is currently the case, member states must articulate the institution's objective and its mandate. According to SADC (2002), the main objective of SADC was to promote "economic and social development through cooperation and integration...the next logical step after independence." The regional body also embraced a more explicit common agenda in 2001 when SADC introduced market integration and development. The new common objective of SADC was to:

(i) Promote sustainable and equitable economic growth and socio-economic development that will ensure poverty eradication.
(ii) Promote common political values, systems, and other shared values transmitted through democratic, legitimate, and effective institutions.
(iii) Consolidate democracy, peace, and security. SADC has now adopted a more centralized approach. The 21 Coordinating Units

were grouped into four clusters: Trade, Industry, Finance and Investment; Food, Agriculture and Natural Resources; Infrastructure and Services; and Social and Human Development and Special Programmes.

SADC currently consists of sixteen member states: Angola, Botswana, Comoros, Eswatini, Lesotho, Madagascar, Malawi, Mauritius, Mozambique, Namibia, Seychelles, South Africa, Tanzania, Zambia, Zimbabwe, and the Democratic Republic of Congo. The Summit of Heads of State is the highest decision-making body of SADC and is responsible for:

(i) Adopting decisions regarding SADC;
(ii) Determining the organizational structure of SADC and any changes thereof;
(iii) Electing the annually rotating SADC Chairperson; and
(iv) Appointing the Executive Secretary of SADC.

Figure 4.1: SADC Institutional Framework

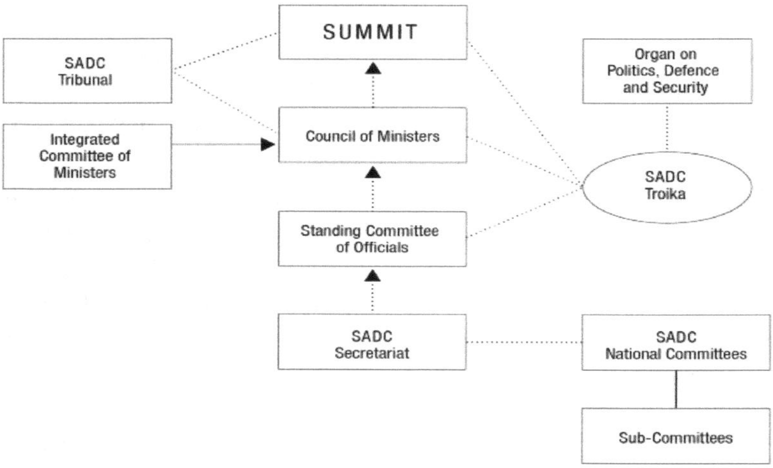

Source: Generated by Author

The Summit of Heads of State and Government is the ultimate decision-making body for SADC. The Summit meets once every year but can also be summoned to deal with emergencies. The SADC Summit's decision-making process follows the consensus principle, which has presented challenges in achieving mutual decisions due to the diversity in member states' interests. SADC also follows the Troika principle for its leadership, ensuring that the regional body's leadership is collective. The concept allows the former and future chairpersons to provide support to the current chairperson. That means SADC only elects the next chairperson instead of selecting the current chairperson.

Alemayehu Geda & Haile Kibret (2002) opine that any regional integration scheme's success or failure is measured in the context of the objectives it sets out to achieve and the political, economic, and institutional context under which it operates. In the case of SADC, the objectives were to achieve economic prosperity, promote and consolidate democracy, and enhance peace and stability across the region. Judging against these objectives, the regional body has failed to achieve the common objectives. SADC countries are still characterized by absolute poverty, authoritarian regimes and are facing political and armed conflicts. The capacity of SADC to respond to these challenges is conditioned by the need for all member states to follow their treaty obligations. In other words, while SADC remains a champion of democracy, good governance, and market liberalization, the scope of its success is dependent on how member states overcome the constraints of integration.

Figure 4.2: Map of SADC Member States

Source: SADC

The EU has acted as a model for RECs in Africa, and SADC is not an exception. Lenz (2012) argues that SADC followed the EU institutional model, yet the integration scheme's outcome in Southern Africa has differed from Europe's. The identity SADC has adopted is shaped by the political leadership in the region.

Robust regional integration is a critical component that allows countries to overcome divisions that impede the flow of goods, services, capital, people, innovation, and technology. To achieve this, SADC member states need to evolve policies that meet the requirements to overcome the existing challenges. Regarding SADC, the rationale is that a united Southern Africa could enhance development, stimulate economic growth and promote peace and security across the region. Unfortunately, the post-Apartheid years that had promised hope have become ended being a difficult period for SADC. Since the inception of the SADC, evidence suggests that the regional integration scheme has failed to guarantee peace and development. The priorities of member states have been divergent, and in most cases, do not take into account the interest of the SADC Community itself. Saurombe (2012) observes that the SADC Treaty covered each member state's obligations and provided its legal, institutional framework, organizational principles and objectives, cooperation with external international organizations, financial issues, and dispute settlements. However, the SADC area is still characterized by economic and political instability, social unrest, and political and armed conflicts that have impeded some of the desired collective regional objectives.

For SADC to overcome its challenges, member states need to overcome the challenges that continue to affect the creation of a robust economic, political, security, and social regime. The first dimension is the political and governance environment within the regional framework which has affected structural changes since political instability leads to limited integration while relative political stability increases regional integration. Political stability, in this case, can be measured from the lenses of democratic or authoritarian regimes and domestic political tensions. The second dimension is the security environment, which is another prerequisite for effective regional integration. Intra-state conflicts become a regional challenge through people seeking refuge in neighbouring states, economic migration, and disturbance of regional development initiatives. Without security, socio-economic development will continue to deteriorate. The third dimension is economic development which recognizes the significance of economic cooperation on production, markets, trade, regional infrastructure, and regional economic policies. Economic convergence is vital to establish commonality in economic performance, regulatory framework, institutions, infrastructure, administrative processes and a common approach to policy formulation. In summation, political, economic, and security integration and convergence come down to domestic and regional governance. It is assumed that a unified political, economic and security regime provides a necessary environment for deepening the regional integration process. Convergence also provides SADC countries with significantly diverse and different political and economic development levels to catch up with their peers and reduce disparities.

Regional integration can be perceived as a long-term attempt to solve economic and political challenges, while in the short term, integration can help tackle unemployment challenges and stimulate economic growth. A UNCTAD (2012) study identified five factors justifying regional integration schemes in emerging markets that could help exploit the region's development potential. These factors include:

(i) As a means which enables developing countries to achieve economies-of-scale;
(ii) As a means of taking advantage of location and specialization;
(iii) As a means which enhances efficiency in the industry;
(iv) As a means which reduces the external vulnerability of the developing economies; and
(v) As a means of increasing the bargaining power of the developing countries.

According to UNECA (2004), regional integration schemes benefit participating countries, especially when they are small in size and market. Under such conditions, regional cooperation between member states enables countries to combine their markets, thereby enabling businesses to expand and the market environment to become more competitive. This market environment attracts foreign direct investment, which stimulates economic growth. Although the idea of regional integration gained traction in the 1950s and 60s, it is crucial to recognize that assertions that nation-states can just come together and achieve sustainable regional integration are a far cry from reality.

Regional integration in Southern Africa is different from other sub-regional bodies in other parts of the world because of historical circumstances. Over the years, suitable frameworks and developmental approaches for enhancing regional integration in Southern Africa have been debated since SADC was established in 1992. Mutambara (2001) and McCrathy (1999) argue that these approaches aim at facilitating equitable distribution of costs and benefits of regional integration, enhancing equal development across the region and all states benefiting from economies of scale. According to UNDP (2011), the process of regional integration can, through regional economic activities, have significant consequences for economic activity at the community and household levels, mainly due to increased formal and informal employment opportunities. The employment created has an impact on household income and is a critical driver in expanding human development. However, despite establishing a new institutional framework and economic framework, economic growth and political stability have remained far-fetched. There are several reasons for this. First, SADC institutional framework has been weak to act as a regional instrument that guarantees regional peace and safeguards democracy. Secondly, the South African government has failed to provide leadership and shape the regional integration agenda, which is pivotal to the SADC economic and political stability. Finally, external actors and factors have contributed to the political and economic stability of the region.

With SADC also characterized by small agriculture-based economies, a limited manufacturing base, inadequate infrastructure, and political instability, the region has not attracted the necessary FDI to increase trade and bolster economic growth. Deeper integration among SADC member states is vital for the region to achieve socio-economic development and regional stability. However, the SADC region's economic development shows that the current trajectory has not met the expectations aspired during SADC's inception. The following section will examine the factors and actors impeding regional integration. This analysis will provide building blocks to help the subsequent parts identify the mechanisms and instruments to help the region address existing challenges.

FACTORS IMPEDING REGIONAL INTEGRATION IN SOUTHERN AFRICA

The viability and efficacy of any regional integration scheme are determined by the strengths and weaknesses of member states constituting the institution and their willingness to meet their obligations in the integration project. Winter, McCulloch & McKay (2004) observe that regional integration could help alleviate poverty through long-term economic growth. Their argument suggested that income levels are raised by faster economic growth resulting in the government having access to more tax revenue that can be used to deliver a robust public service system. However, the expectation that SADC member states would have the capacity and commitment to fulfil their regional obligations has fallen short of expectations, thereby contributing to the shortcomings of regional integration in Southern Africa. An overview of the region's economy over the last few decades confirms that SADC still faces constraints. The optimism shared at the dawn of SADC has been replaced with pessimism, and dynamism has been replaced with passivism.

Regionalism in Southern Africa has not fared well in the first three decades since SADC's inception. So far, SADC has failed to uplift citizens' socio-economic conditions, and member states are characterized by numerous peculiarities and constraints that present challenges for the regional integration processes. SADC has so far been affected by diverse challenges that have undermined the region's prosperity; hence, failing to address these challenges may lead to the region's economic potential remaining underexploited. The viability and effectiveness of regional bodies are determined by how they can achieve their objective. In the context of SADC, the performance of the regional body has fallen short of expectations despite adopting a range of ambitious institutional policies.

In the post-independence era, discourse on regional integration emphasized political cooperation as member states supported liberation movements in the region and opposed the oppressive white minority governments. In the post-Apartheid era, the SADC member states made efforts to use regional cooperation to stimulate economic growth, infrastructure development and enhance regional peace, security, and democracy. Thus, regional integration was recognized as a process where states came together to sign agreements and form common objectives from an early stage. However, the progress in the regional integration project in the SADC region has taken a different form due to member states' inherent differences.

The institutional framework and structure of SADC have also failed to match up to an effective regional body's demands and requirements. The coming together of mostly individual sovereign states with diverse political and economic circumstances and the nation-states' reluctance to relinquish some of their sovereignty willingly and become part of a functional and robust regional body have become a burden to effective integration. The fear of losing sovereignty remains one of the biggest impediments to SADC's success. The small, sparsely populated, and often isolated economies in the region make a compelling case for SADC member states to integrate for the economies to exploit economies of scale and reduce the restriction challenges. The more general arguments for reasons behind the failure of regional integration in Africa were succinctly listed by Mistry (2000), which includes:

(i) "The failure of African governments to translate their commitments in regional treaties and agreements into substantive changes in national policies, legislation, rules, and regulations. There was no follow-through in translating regional commitments into national actions;

(ii) The unwillingness of African governments to subordinate immediate national political interests to achieve long-term regional economic goals or to cede essential elements of sovereignty to regional institutions; and

(iii) An absence of monitoring and enforcement mechanisms to ensure adherence to agreed timetables on such matters as tariff and NTB reductions or in achieving more difficult objectives."

In pursuance of regional integration objectives in Southern Africa and enhanced socio-economic development, SADC has established regional instruments to advance market integration and commit to democratic principles. The nations of Southern Africa have shown their desire to give their people prosperity through the SADC Treaty, protocols, agreements and declarations. However, prosperity and social progress require necessary conditions like larger markets and creating a single economic unit, as with the EU. Nonetheless, the overall progress over the last three decades has been sluggish. The general assessment has shown that SADC member states have been unable to accelerate economic growth and sustain democracy across the region, despite a consensus among scholars that regional integration is essential for countries' economic, political, and social development. Irrespective of the challenges SADC is facing today, there is a collective recognition that regional integration remains a precondition for accelerated economic growth and regional development; hence the regional integration project cannot be abandoned. While the rhetoric and agreements have failed to match the desired objective, there is an urgent need to scrutinize the factors that have impeded progress.

Understanding the SADC regional dynamics is vital to identify and overcome the barriers to regional integration. For economic and political integration in Southern Africa to succeed, policymakers must understand and consider the fundamental factors and actors that have impeded regional integration. Discussion on regional integration in the SADC region cannot be fully complete without appreciating the acute political and economic structural imbalances among member states. While there was consensus that establishing SADC could enhance economic growth, eradicate poverty, and help build one prosperous shared economy that could compete with other regional blocs globally, these sharp differences continue to challenge the region's integration agenda.

Regional integration is achieved when countries develop formal agreements regarding how trade between member states should be conducted. Ernst Haas (1961) understood this as "the process whereby political actors in several distinct national settings are persuaded to shift their loyalties, expectations and political activities toward a new centre, whose institutions possess or demand jurisdiction over preexisting national states. The result of a process of political integration is a new political community, superimposed over the pre-existing ones." Establishing these regional blocs strengthens countries' influence on the global political arena and enables governments to achieve sustainable economic growth.

The steps the member states take would determine the outcome of the regional integration agenda. The questions that must be answered are: Given the reality that the integration agenda promoted by early African leaders failed to materialize, what changes have been made to ensure that the optimism of integration now meets the desired expectations? What went wrong when the unified Southern African Community vision was cast and how has that been rectified? As we go through the factors that have impeded regional integration, we will observe that conditions that could set the region on a socio-economic development trajectory are still non-existent. In contrast, the political elite seems to be focusing on the wrong priorities and have shown no real commitment to the regional integration agenda. Regional integration can only be effective if bold and pragmatic actions are taken at the domestic and regional levels to respond to the regional challenges.

While there is consensus that the establishment of SADC provides an environment for economic growth and development, these ambitions have been affected by factors that have prevented the organisation from achieving its objectives. Without a developed infrastructure, credible governance systems, effective regulatory systems and political stability, it is impossible to survive in the increasingly interdependent international system. These factors underscore the need for a new approach to regional integration if SADC is to overcome some of the existing challenges of persistent poverty and instability. The analysis of this section traces the evolution of regional integration in Southern Africa and identifies some of the factors that have impeded integration in the region. It argues that that the lack of progress in the regional integration scheme is due to a myriad of factors that include:

(i) Overlapping and multiple memberships;
(ii) Non-complementary trade, export diversification, and protectionist policies;
(iii) Poor infrastructure, Logistics, and unfavourable legal and regulatory environment;
(iv) Economic disparities of member states;
(v) Contradicting national interest and xenophobia;
(vi) Historical rivalries and animosity;
(vii) Failure of a collective mechanism for accountability;
(viii) Diverse political systems; and
(ix) Regional instability.

Overcoming these challenges could help the SADC bloc attain regional economic integration, economic prosperity, freedom and justice for all SADC citizens, which are fundamental tenets of SADC's shared values and principles. These shared values could usher in stability and sustainable development across the region. Global political and economic conditions are also pointing to the need for a more robust Southern Africa integration. The arguments for a new form of Southern Africa integration are as much political as economic. Making regional integration work in the SADC region requires a paradigm shift from the current approach to a form of integration based on a transformative strategy that ensures progress in structural and governance transformation. SADC must provide the cornerstone for the region's political and economic recovery and reconstruction. A broader case for integration needs to be made as Africa's export share to the global market in the 1970s was as high as 6%, yet, by 2020, this has declined to about 2%. It is apparent that the export share has fallen and might continue to fall behind other regions. The World Trade Organization (WTO) (2007) identified trade as a powerful tool for economic growth and development and for improving Southern Africa's global competitiveness. Dunning and Robson (1987) presented general economic arguments for integration which include:

(i) To overcome structural market distortions, such as tariff barriers, and to encourage competition;
(ii) To reduce imperfections in foreign exchange, capital and labour markets;
(iii) To facilitate product and process specialization by firms;
(iv) To develop economic and strategic strength by adopting common policies towards non-member states; and
(v) To increase the market size and improve the technological capacity of member states.

However, regional integration can take different forms depending on uncertain and dynamic factors. These factors create necessary conditions which will dictate the inevitable outcome of integration in Southern Africa. All these are benefits that motivated the birth of SADC, and the organisation is famous for signing spectacular agreements. At the moment, the organization has 26 active protocols for regional integration covering diverse socio-economic sectors. However, Cawthra and Nieuwkerk (2004) pointed out that "while protocols and treaties have been signed, there has been a limited history of common action and collective policy formulation." Although legal instruments empower SADC instruments, the SADC institutional and legal structures lack the mandate to enforce the collective pursuit of regional objectives. Vanheukelom et al. (2016) argue that there is a gap between the institutional forms of African regional institutions and the actual functions they perform. It now seems like an excellent opportunity to deeply examine the international standing of SADC's economies and how regional integration can play a role in this.

Overlapping and Multiple Membership to Similar Regional Bodies

Like other regions on the African continent, southern Africa has some of the most complex regional institutional structures. A fascinating aspect of regional economic agreements in Africa is the duplication of membership in similar bodies. African countries are usually members of more than one regional grouping with similar objectives. However, they belong to different economic communities for strategic and political reasons, with 47 out of 53 African countries belonging to two or more regional trade agreements. Jackobeit (2008) argues that holding multiple memberships and overlapping memberships are not a recent occurrence in Africa and date back to colonial times.

The increase in overlapping membership to similar RECs reflects what Bhagwati (1995) refers to as the "spaghetti bowl." This duplicity of membership has hindered progress in regional integration due to the complex entanglements of political and economic obligations. According to Malamud (2013), Southern African states belong to multiple regional bodies with competing objectives. Since the objective of each REC is to liberalize trade within the group, in effect, the duplicity of memberships undermines the goals of the agreements in one way or another. Efforts by African governments to have multiple memberships illustrate their desire to pick and choose what suits their interests, even if it means obstructing the general objectives of the REC. The same message has been preached by Viljoen (2007), who argues that African states' simultaneous membership to numerous regional economic communities presents a hurdle regarding the integration process. Among other things, the numerous memberships create confusion, competition, and duplication. It has also become a burden for taxpayers as poor nation-states continue making financial contributions to the groupings. Apart from SADC itself, other regional economic integration agreements and bilateral agreements occur within the global multilateral trading systems in Southern Africa. Among others, these institutions include:

(i) Common Market for East and Southern Africa (COMESA).

(ii) Southern African Customs Union (SACU)

(iii) Regional Integration Facilitation Forum (RIFF)
(iv) Common Monetary Area (CMA)
(v) Economic and Monetary Community of Central Africa (CEMAC)
(vi) East African Community (EAC)
(vii) Economic Community for East and Central African States (ECCAS).
(viii) Indian Ocean Commission (IOC)

Figure 4.3: African Regional and Sub-regional Economic Integration Groupings

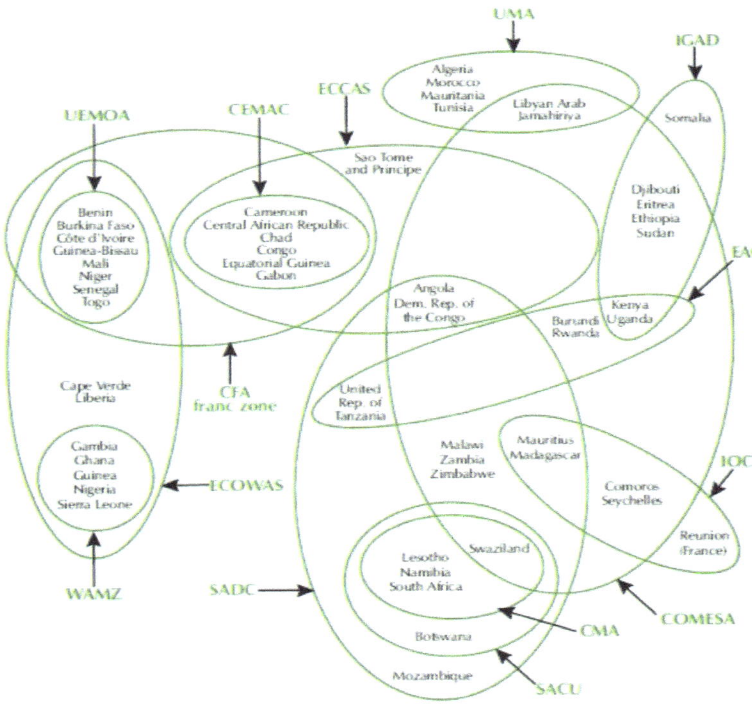

Source: UN Economic Commission for Africa (2010)

An illustration of the REC network in sub-Saharan Africa is shown in figure 4.3. Based on the figure, it is apparent that there is much overlap of membership in Southern Africa. Apart from being members of SADC, South Africa, Lesotho, Swaziland, and Botswana are also members of

SACU. Besides the Common Market of East and Southern Africa (COMESA), Namibia and Swaziland are also members of the Common Monetary Area (CMA). In addition, they are involved with the Regional Integration Forum (RIFF).

There are four regional groups in which Tanzania is a member: SADC, EAC, ECCAS, and COMESA. DRC, Africa's second-largest country, is a member of SADC, COMESA, EAC and ECCAS. Angola has membership in both SADC and ECCAS. Seychelles, Mauritius, and Madagascar are part of SADC, COMESA, and IOC. Among the members of SADC, only Mozambique does not belong to another grouping, though there has been discussion about joining SACU. In general terms, almost all SADC member states are members of two or more other economic integration groupings. For African countries, only three countries out of the 54 countries belong to one regional organisation. It is not problematic for SADC member states to have multiple financial agreements; however, overlapping membership between these groups presents a conflict of interest and an additional financial burden. As a result, the implementation of integration policies is burdened by a lack of coordination. These problems become more defined as the member states engage in closer trade and economic cooperation.

Simultaneous and multiple memberships to similar regional bodies impede regional integration for various reasons. Aryeetey and Oduro (1996) cited McCarthy as arguing that: "It is difficult to envisage how SADC and COMESA, given their convergence to both sectoral cooperation and trade integration, can live and prosper with the overlapping membership of the Southern African countries." These problems and sometimes conflicting objectives have in the past led to member states being caught up in a predicament. Ndongko (1985) suggests that: "the multiplicity of regional groupings, coupled with dual memberships, give rise to numerous commercial problems because of the trade obligations member states have either individually or collectively, under the different treaties and protocol agreements establishing the groupings which they are members...To be sure, some touchy commercial problems are bound to arise in the course of fulfilling these obligations." For instance, under the SADC protocol, Zambia was obligated to remove tariffs for South African goods altogether. Zambia, however, is required under the COMESA agreement to adopt a standard tariff regime for states that are not members of COMESA, in this case, South Africa. These complex arrangements caused by multiple memberships have given rise to inefficiency. Integration cannot be achieved in an environment where state actors are pursuing different and sometimes conflicting objectives.

Due to the duplicity of membership, operationalizing regional peace and security tools like the SADC Standby Force (SADCBRIG) poses challenges, and subsequent parts will shed light on its impact. For instance, due to Angola's membership in SADC and ECCAS, the country is expected to contribute troops to the ECCAS Standby Force. Because of the divided allegiances and lack of institutional cohesion, this duplicity has had severe negative consequences for regional member states. In a scenario where all the existing regional groupings decide to form their own customs union, the current form of regional integration becomes unsustainable. In Sharer's (2001) opinion, the current integration process is characterized by overlapping memberships, conflicting obligations, different strategies and objectives, and conflicting procedures and rules. As part of regional integration politics, the regional body symbolizes unity and commitment to one cause. Multiple memberships represent weakness and division among member states, weakening the regional institution's position and undermining its goals. A regional grouping's size and stability send a positive message to other regional bodies and increase their credibility in their commitment to trade liberalization. The more competing regional agreements are established, the less persuasive these regional bodies become to extra-regional partners. This could lead to legal uncertainty due to conflicting state obligations.

Thus, as the number of regional agreements increases, the value of each agreement declines faster. The duplication of memberships also reveals African states' inability to genuinely commit to a single regional integration scheme. The duplicity of membership increases the likelihood of non-commitment to regional objectives. Fully integrated regional communities play an essential role in integrating the African community. The spaghetti bowl scenario does not serve the integration agenda as there is no commonality of objectives. According to UNECA (2008), progress in the integration process would ultimately lead to African economic unity. Achieving this goal would provide an impetus for harmonising all African RECs under the Abuja Treaty agenda, creating the African FTA and customs union. This becomes a prelude to the Africa-wide economic integration that can overcome the artificial state boundaries that are part of the colonial legacy and promote African unity.

It is clear that structural constraints of African RECs constrained progress on African integration. The integration agenda will continue lagging if African countries cannot address and surmount the constraints of integration; the multiplicity of membership is one of them. SADC member states should push forward in making a real commitment to one economic community and allow the institution to serve as the only building block to the African economic integration.

Non-complimentary Trade and Inadequate Export Diversification

Although regional integration has dominated African countries' economic and political relations over the past three decades, based on UNECA (2014) data, manufacturing in Africa has continued to decline from 12.8% in 1990 to 9.8% in 2014 despite the expectation of enlarged markets. According to the same report, the share of manufactured exports from Africa declined from 25.6% in 1995 to 18.9% in 2014. According to UNECA (2010), intra-regional trade in Africa is negatively affected by the decline of the manufacturing industry on the continent. Intra-regional trade has also consistently remained low compared to other regions. Why has manufacturing in Africa declined despite all the economic integration agreements African governments are signed to? Why are regional integration agreements not translating into manufacturing growth? Evidence suggests that the region is experiencing what Rodrik (2016) calls "premature deindustrialization," which poses a challenge to inclusive growth and formal job creation. Rodrik defines premature deindustrialization as the process by which an economy's manufacturing sector begins to slow down prematurely as it develops. Economic development is a process where labour and other resources gradually move from agriculture to the manufacturing sector before navigating to the services sector, which is the highest stage of development. Therefore, any slowdown or disruption of that process is considered a threat to the entire industrialization process. An assumption is that increased trade between member states is a central feature of industrialisation and enhanced regional integration. Africa's exports, however, are not complementary, which has negatively impacted the development of regional integration schemes.

Despite the long history of integration in the region, SADC has suffered from the artificial economic borders between the Southern African economies. Economies in the region depend on limited primary export commodities that are vulnerable to external market shocks and price fluctuations. In a globalised economic arena, the country's and region's trade performance is determined by export sophistication and diversification of exports which are fundamental drivers of export competitiveness. The constrained business environment in the SADC area is mainly due to differences in the composition of commodities destined for the SADC market and those exported to other parts of the world. SADC's role is to foster intra-SADC trade, and trade integration does not happen in a vacuum. It requires removing trade barriers, and Machlup (1977) refers to it as the "utilization of all potential opportunities of an efficient division of labour."

Southern Africa would be a region of enormous potential if more profound integration policies were vigorously implemented. Market integration has been identified as an essential building block for growing international trade, and strengthened trade among member states is the primary feature of regional integration. Most of the trade challenges the region is facing can be linked to weak production systems and poor trade facilitation. These challenges can be identified at both domestic and regional levels making intra-regional trade expensive and time-consuming. Beginning with weaknesses in the production sector that constrain trade, the macro-economic environment in most SADC member states also creates significant difficulties. The small fragmented and isolated economies in Southern Africa make a compelling case for Southern African countries to pursue integration and exploit the economies of scale and efficiency gains. Trade can be developed through a multilateral trading system, increased regional cooperation, or domestic reform programs. SADC opted for regional market integration as the driving force behind the regional integration project from the earliest stage. The SADC Treaty (1992) and the Trade protocol identified trade integration as a period when "product flows between countries are on the same terms and conditions as within countries. In an integrated market, prices of identical products are the same across countries' geographical jurisdictions."

Although the stimulation of intra-regional trade was the primary objective of SADC, there has been limited strategic thinking on enhancing regional trade. The SADC region has a wide range of opportunities that can be exploited to stimulate trade. For SADC to enhance market integration, there must be an increase in goods and services produced and traded within the regional bloc. These goods and services are divided into three categories: The primary sector, which comprises the agricultural and mining activities; the secondary sector includes manufacturing activities, construction, and production of power; and the tertiary industry comprising activities related to services like banking, real estate, insurance, hotel services, and communication services. However, that is only achievable if there are policy reforms, increased investment and initiatives to promote non-traditional exports. Langhammer & Hiemenz (1990) argue that the challenge of African countries is not the limited scope for inter-industry specialization, nor do the countries have the option of inter-industry specialization. Integration projects are effective if a market-driven integration focuses on mutual trade to increase mutual market penetration. In this case, regional integration alone is not enough to improve the manufacturing industry and intra-regional trade. Despite the disappointing manufacturing results in Africa, regional integration remains an effective vehicle for promoting manufacturing and trade. Integration needs to be accompanied by robust manufacturing policies capable of stimulating momentum for manufacturing.

International trade remains one of the most critical factors behind the fastest-growing economies globally, and this begins from growing intra-regional business. In SADC, trade among regional member states remains one of the lowest globally, and this low SADC intra-regional trade contrasts sharply with the circumstances in the EU and ASEAN. According to the African Economic Outlook (2017), a report for the African Development Bank (AfDB), trade among African countries has tremendous potential for building sustainable economic development and integration. The report cited data where trade expanded from 10% in 2000 to approximately 16% in 2016, which is still the lowest compared to other global regions.

According to Hummels (2007), a quarter of world trade occurs between neighbouring countries, and half of the world trade occurs between countries less than 3,000 kilometres apart. However, in Africa, 88% of Africa's trade is with partners located several thousand kilometres away. The limited range of traded products in the SADC region and Africa reduces the opportunity for intra-regional trade. Low regional trade is also due to non-complementary trade, export diversification deficit, and protectionist policies that have inhibited intra-regional trade. The non-complementary nature of intra-regional trade continues to undermine regional trade's colossal potential if SADC member states diversified their export commodities. Regional cooperation and diversification of production can allow individual countries to benefit from enormous cost savings compared with a parallel in protected domestic markets. However, the performance of intra-regional trade in Southern Africa demonstrates that it has failed to develop fully. Intra-regional trade is a precursor for the region's competitiveness in the global market. In this regard, SADC needs to develop its intra-regional market before pursuing a more competitive global market. Given that intraregional trade in the SADC area is underdeveloped, trade among SADC member states holds great potential.

SADC member states would increase their export range if there were improvements in regional physical and institutional trade infrastructure. SADC can play a critical role in enhancing intra-SADC trade growth, bargaining power with other trading blocs, and enhancing the region's credibility as a reliable trading partner. However, market integration does not develop in a vacuum. There is a requirement for creating conditions that can support and reinforce production, trade and capital investment. Sophisticated market and trade policies could kickstart a new wave of a more robust integration process in the region. With the SADC region trading in large volumes with markets beyond Africa, there is potential to develop intra-regional trade if suitable trade measures are implemented and trade obstacles are eliminated. For intra-regional trade that benefits all member states to be enhanced, the member states' production structures must be diversified and complementary products introduced. Yeats (1998) noted that most Southern Africa countries have highly concentrated exports on a limited number of products; most of those products are not even attractive to the regional market since they also produce similar commodities or products.

Similar export products have led to undesirable competition among regional neighbours in the SADC bloc over export markets on most occasions. Mattli (1999) argues that the more developed and diversified the economies are, the more they profit from integration trade and investment. Ricardo's 1871(1971) theory of comparative advantage from a liberal perspective presents opportunities for a liberal international economic order. Ricardo's objective was to provide a logically sound answer to one of the critical challenges posed by international trade and the significance of states producing complementary products for trade. From this perspective, similar countries with efficient production structures can produce different products that can be traded within a specific multilateral setting. In instances where countries produce the same products, Ricardian theory (1971) proposes that one country may be more efficient at minimizing the comparative production costs. With this argument, Ricardo provided liberals with a powerful argument supporting the liberal international economic order.

Diversification of production is critical as economies can produce different products by utilizing their comparative cost advantage. The comparative advantage may be in the form of cheap labour, cheap raw materials, and technology. Wage rates are a significant incentive for foreign investors to outsource the production of labour-intensive commodities in countries with lower labour costs. For instance, with average wages in the US at $15 an hour, MNCs are more inclined to outsource production in India, where hourly labour costs can be as low as $1 an hour.

Regional integration projects with less diversified products are likely to be weak even if trade barriers are removed, and this is the scenario present in the SADC area. Southern Africa's global trade role has primarily involved producing and exporting undiversified primary commodities susceptible to price volatility. There is a consensus among trade experts that countries with a more diversified export base benefit from comprehensive FTA, which is not the case with SADC. A profound factor influencing investors is access to a single market with very low or no tariff barriers. However, many factors determine FDI, and it is almost impossible to isolate individual factors and the nature of the industry in question and the source of FDI. SADC member states export a limited range of products to neighbouring countries despite an FTA in place. Southern Africa can only grow its economy if there is a shift from being an exporter of primary commodities to an exporter of diversified commodities. In this case, FDI can significantly transform SADC exports from raw material dependent exports to diversified commodity exports. Countries with diversified exports are likely to produce a wide range of products that can be attractive and consumed by the regional market. With more diversified export commodities, SADC member states could produce a wide range of products that could be exchanged with regional partners, limiting the import of products from a third-party country.

A broader market through market integration presents a necessary condition for industrialisation in the SADC region. Winters (2005) raises a compelling question of whether political independence is the fundamental problem for small and fragmented countries. Another critical economic argument on the integration of fragmented economies comes from Green and Seidman (1967). They advance that "there is no point in producing manufactured goods if there are not enough people or do not have enough cash income to buy them." Trading off some form of sovereignty for prosperity is a price worth paying and one which SADC leaders must consider seriously. To a greater extent, Southern African countries have a choice to make on whether they sink in isolation due to acute limitations or swim together to prosperity.

Manufacturing is critical for regional economic growth as different studies have shown that economies exporting a high share of manufactured commodities grow faster than countries exporting unprocessed products. Fusi (1990) explores the different effects of primary and manufacturing products on economic growth in developing countries. The study finds that manufactured exports have a more significant effect on economic growth. In contrast, exports of primary raw materials did not have a significant impact on economic growth. Hausmann et al. (2007) share the same observation when they suggest that the type of exports a country specializes in has a significant impact on its economic performance. The study results demonstrated that economies with exports associated with manufacturing grew faster than countries exporting primary raw materials. Sachs and Warner (1995) put it in a broader context when they argue that countries with a high ratio of raw material exports to GDP are prone to low economic growth.

Improving the manufacturing and processing capacity could help enhance trade among African countries, requiring capital investment. The private sector's involvement could help the regional manufacturing industry avoid duplication of products manufactured across the region, thereby allowing each member state's private sector to benefit from the large market base. Thomsen (1994) argues that host country market size is one of the strongest determinants for FDI. Hence, through the reduction of trade barriers, prospective investors are offered large markets. Investors are also likely to invest in larger markets formed under the regional integration project than investing in a single and isolated market due to increased credibility associated with integrated markets. According to Fernandez (1997), regional integration increases reciprocal trust due to stable domestic and regional institutions. Export diversification is vital as it allows countries to build resilience to market fluctuations due to movements in demand and economic downturns of importing countries. On the part of the exporting countries, diversification allows countries to shift from their over-dependence on primary raw materials to higher-value-added commodities. The value addition processes allow other small and medium-sized businesses to be involved, thereby enhancing innovation, expanding markets and providing new employment opportunities.

Diversification could also help stimulate demand for intra-regional imports and the sophistication of export products. Landlocked countries find regional integration particularly attractive. Land-locked countries benefit from regional transportation investments and transit corridors, which facilitate trade with the outside world. With almost half of the SADC member states being landlocked, manufacturing for the regional market is more profitable while regional transit corridors reduce export costs for extra-regional markets.

Nevertheless, for the limited number of exports among SADC member states, trade is predominantly unprocessed agricultural and mineral products susceptible to low prices and market fluctuations. In 2014, SADC adopted the Industrialization Strategy and Roadmap 2015-2063 to enhance intra-regional trade to address SADC's manufacturing capacity deficit. However, the set target date is too far for the member states to urgently address some persistent challenges inhibiting regional trade requiring immediate attention. In most cases, there is no urgency at all as target dates are usually moved with ease.

The deficit in manufacturing in the SADC area can be traced back to the region's colonial legacy. The European colonial powers viewed their territories in Southern Africa as a source for primary raw materials that could satisfy the manufacturing industries' demands in Europe to exchange finished manufactured European products. During that period, the colonialists made no effort to add value to the coffee, tea, tobacco, rubber, and various minerals extracted from the region. Manufacturing industries were only established by the Europeans if there was a need to reduce transport costs. Green and Seidman (1967) argue that: "Colonial economic policy geared the cash economies of dependent territories to the export-'import trade with Europe. Investment-flows, transportation networks, tariff rates, commercial and government purchasing policies, and provision of infrastructure and services were shaped in terms of this pattern and served to reinforce it." This problem continues to form part of the colonial legacy, and SADC member states have failed to explore and exploit a new range of export products and initiatives that could help them break the current trading cycle.

With trade liberalized in the SADC area, there has been a gradual but limited increase in intra-regional trade. However, SADC has been facing challenges in exploiting its full potential of intra-regional trade. Based on FTAs from other parts of the world, evidence shows that FTAs are a catalyst for boosting intra-regional trade. For SADC, the current FTA has increased trade by 62% as it moved from 10% to 16%. However, that only demonstrates the enormous potential for growth if more aggressive production and trade-driven measures are adopted. The most significant advantage for SADC member states is the shorter distance between states and limited language barriers.

Figure 4.4: Global market share by continent from 1948 to 2016

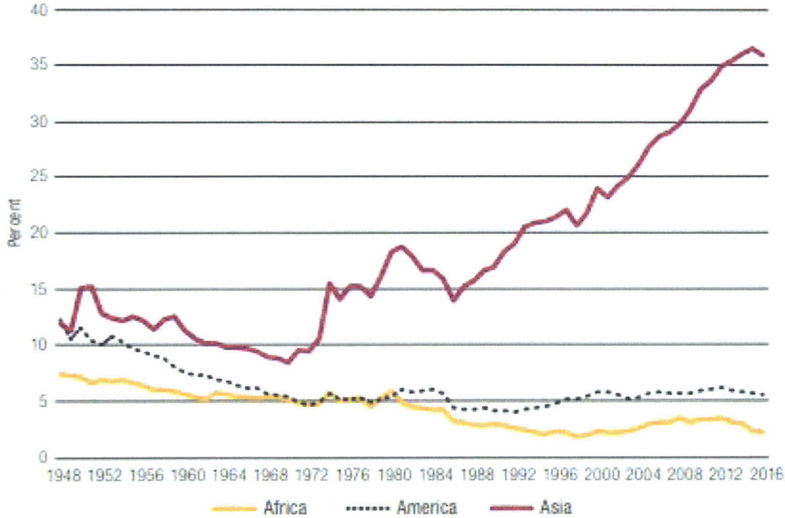

Source: UNCTAD Statistics database (2019)

According to UNCTAD (2018), export diversification reflects the degree to which a country's exports are spread across many products and trading partners. That contrasts with an export concentration where a greater trade focus is on a small number of commodities and/or trading partners. Diversification is achieved by increasingly changing the exported items or improving the existing exports by adding value or enhancing them through technology and innovation. Regional trade integration is an essential factor that can enhance this process due to increased foreign direct investment and technology transfers enhanced by the broader regional market. Although some studies have shown that intra-regional trade in the SADC region has been growing since SADC was established in 1992, in reality, the growth has failed to meet the expectations. Simultaneously, the global share of exports from the SADC market to the world market has also been low at an average of 1% over the past two decades. The majority of the SADC countries are still relying on the export of primary raw materials as the primary source of foreign currency due to their limited manufacturing capacity. With most SADC exports having a lower level of diversification than other developing regions of Asia and South America, evidence has shown that diversification has remained the same since the 1990s. At the same time, evidence shows a downward trend in manufacturing in the SADC region, as explained earlier. Lack of diversification of exports has impacted employment as there are limited manufacturing activities to stimulate job creation and investment.

Figure 4.4 illustrates the declining global market share of African exports on the global market. In the 1970s, Africa had 6% of the global market share, dropping to 3% in the 1980s and further declining to around 2% in 2016. Exports from the SADC region have also replicated this decline. The SADC region's manufacturing value has also dropped from 18.2% to 12.6% of GDP between 2000 and 2015. With the SADC region's export performance against the global market remaining relatively flat for a very long time, SADC countries have failed to benefit from globalisation; instead, it is fair to say SADC has become a victim of globalisation. As a result, the share of global exports for the SADC region remains the lowest amongst other developing regions.

In contrast, as illustrated in the above figure, Asia's global export market share increased from 8% in the 1970s to 36% in 2016. SADC's and Africa's export share decline has been attributed to SADC's limited range of export products and lack of export diversification, as widely discussed earlier. At the same time, Africa imports 80 to 90% of its goods from outside the continent despite most of the primary raw materials used to manufacture these imports originating from Africa.

While the EU's integration has always allowed the EU to perform well in terms of global trade share, European countries continue to enhance regional integration. According to UNCTAD (2019), intra-European trade lies at 69% in Europe, 59% in Asia, 55% in America, while intra-Africa trade lies at 16%. Some of these outcomes have fuelled growing opposition to globalization and increasing support of economic populism. Over the past two decades, the EU has continued to expand its market base, which has led to the EU becoming the largest trading bloc in the world as a single economic unit. Based on the EU's capacity to grant and withhold market access to the region, the EU has become a significant trade negotiation player. The bloc continues perfecting its bargaining abilities during trade negotiations and has used its hegemonic power to go beyond its market and economic interests. The EU can now dictate the terms of any new trade agreements, and the trade policy pursued has also embedded foreign, security and social policies. The EU can now demand changes in its trading partners' domestic policies, like labour laws, human rights issues and environmental policies.

Looking at the EU and other prosperous regional blocs, it is clear that all these institutions possess highly competitive market structures. In the context of SADC, structural transformation strategies are required, which will address challenges of diversification and overreliance on a small number of export products. SADC member states need to expand exports within the regional market by utilizing the different mechanisms and adopting new structural mechanisms discussed in detail in Chapter 10. This will ensure intra-regional trade growth and product specializations to replace some import products with regionally manufactured products. In a nutshell, SADC needs to develop a manufacturing industry that is more targeted towards strengthening the industrial capacity and diversified production. An effort to expand the regional market and improve the SADC region's production capacity remains a critical priority for regional leaders towards achieving the SADC economic aspirations. According to Signe (2019), sound trade initiatives in Southern Africa could spur rewarding negations and stimulate economic growth. Integration would also offer opportunities for foreign capital investment, production capacity, and value chain creation. Production fragmentation has led to a greater need for human capital in production coordination. As value chains have grown in the global economy, the region market space has become a more critical factor. Contemporary production networks are largely shaped around specific regions, which can be explained by the importance of geographical proximity when creating fragmented production processes between many countries. In order to achieve this goal, common legal frameworks need to be established that encourage firms from different countries to link up their operations with others. When these factors do not exist, productive integration becomes an aspiration rather than a reality.

There is consensus in the scholarship of regionalism that good governance is a prerequisite in creating an enabling environment for economic diversification. Good governance is crucial both at the national and regional levels. To nurture vibrant and fledgling production sectors, designing and implementing enabling policies is required if states are to develop an environment that allows diversification to flourish. From reform of customs procedures to stimulate manufacturing, removing administrative burdens that slow down the import of essential materials, and government interventions are essential in cutting the red tape. Botswana presents a great example of government intervention in diversification when the government swiftly responded to reductions in diamond sales. With a $1.5 billion loan from the African Development Bank (AfDB), Botswana diversified its economy away from diamonds by creating a new economic area. In addition, an economic diversification project was launched in February 2020 to strengthen small stock, tourism, and horticulture industries by improving business linkages between small and medium enterprises (SMEs).

Poor Infrastructure, Logistics, and Unfavourable Regulatory Environment

In addition to trade, a robust regional infrastructure is equally important for achieving market integration and sustainable economic growth. According to Kim et al. (2020), higher infrastructure capital is strongly correlated with higher income. It is, therefore, crucial to ensure sustainable regional development that infrastructure is in place. Infrastructure improvements in transport, energy, and communication facilitate production and trade, critical to successful regional integration initiatives. A sound infrastructure enables mobility (labour, goods, and finance) within an integrated market, thereby enhancing productivity while at the same time reducing production and trade costs, which are vital to enhancing competitiveness.

The historical pattern of the African infrastructure always tended to be outward-looking because production was primarily focused on primary raw materials for Europe's manufacturing industry. Africa's infrastructure network was developed from crucial production zones to seaports, and only a limited amount of inward-looking infrastructure was developed. Despite independence, the trend of inward-looking infrastructure continued. As a result, the African economies remain fragmented and markets uncoordinated. Limited infrastructure links have impacted Africa's integration into one market.

Regional economic development, market integration, and intra-regional trade are all dependent on reliable regional infrastructure. International trade is becoming increasingly dependent on "Global Production Sharing," according to the World Bank. Global Production Sharing refers to the practice of industries spreading their manufacturing across multiple countries to maximize efficiency. Production sharing can, however, only take place if adequate infrastructure is in place. In Africa, the lack of infrastructure has therefore hindered the potential for production sharing.

In other parts of the world, infrastructure development in transport and communication has allowed emerging economies to establish a fledgling industrial base, expand and diversify production. Manufacturing industries have exploited comparative advantage by concentrating labour-intensive products in countries with cheap labour by breaking up the production chain into different countries. In the SADC region, limited infrastructure and weak regulatory frameworks have made the delivery of goods difficult, hindering potential production sharing.

Due to high transport costs, inefficient and inadequate infrastructure in Southern Africa presents one of the biggest obstacles to business and trading. It is well known that there is a lack of adequate infrastructure in the SADC region to support intra-regional and export-oriented trade. It has been noted by Van Niekerk and Moreira (2002) that the cost of transport alone accounts for 40% of the business cost, which contrasts with 12% in developed countries. These disparities in transport costs make export products from SADC less competitive on both regional and global markets. The SADC region's investment attractiveness has also been affected by poor infrastructure conditions. The investment climate is more favourable in countries with better infrastructure, possibly forcing investors to abandon countries with poor infrastructure. While the SADC region has a comparative advantage in low-cost labour, labour costs alone do not determine FDI. Despite the availability of low-cost labour in sub-Saharan Africa, investors may be hesitant to invest due to other factors such as inadequate infrastructure and political risks.

It is well documented that the SADC region faces infrastructure challenges, and these challenges continue to thwart deeper regional integration. Its potential to stimulate economic growth and development has been dampened by the absence of well-functioning regional infrastructures like transport networks, telecommunications, and electricity. Regulatory deficiencies and corruption, in addition to inadequate infrastructure, have been significant hindrances to intra-African trade, according to Iqbar and Khan (1997). Limão and Venables (2001) argue that institutional and regulatory burdens impede the flow of goods across borders by creating unnecessary delays, which raise the cost of moving goods and manufacturing. Furthermore, Raballand (2008) and Johnson et al. (2007) argue that market regulations, institutional weaknesses, customs environment, and port inefficiency hinder African trade more than tariff barriers.

The biggest challenge for developing regional infrastructure has been financing the projects due to the lack of financial resources and political commitment of SADC leaders. The neo-functional integration approach emphasizes the importance of regional infrastructure projects in addressing production and logistical deficiencies. There is a direct correlation between infrastructure, structural, and logistical deficiencies in the SADC region and the cost of doing business. Having an adequate legal and regulatory framework in place is crucial to business operations and regional trade.

In Africa and the SADC region, there is a growing realization that the implementation and attainment of economic targets are dependent on effective and efficient infrastructure. In the areas of energy, transport, and communication, there is a demand for addressing the challenges of inadequate infrastructure in the region and highlighting the potential impacts and economic losses resulting from underdevelopment. The African Union established the New African Partnership for Africa's Development (NEPAD) to channel development funds into regional projects. The SADC region has yet to achieve enhanced regional infrastructure initiatives, as individual countries champion national-focused infrastructure development. Considering infrastructure development from a regional perspective could help leverage economies of scale in infrastructure funding.

Eustance and Fay (2007) allude that good infrastructure stimulates growth; conversely, increased growth leads to a growing demand for more infrastructure. According to Eustance and Fay, there is a symbiotic relationship between infrastructure development and economic growth. According to scholars of regional integration, in both intermediate and final product processing, infrastructure plays a vital role in economic development. The ease of mobility of labour, goods, and finance facilitates the production of intermediate products, thus improving productivity and reducing costs. Sound Infrastructure ensures easy access to energy for the manufacturing industry and reliable ICT for coordinating production structures in different locations. AfDB (2006) outlined a detailed status of infrastructure deficiencies:

(i) 30% of the population has access to electricity, compared with rates at 70% to 90% in other major geographical zones of the developing world (Asia, Central America, the Caribbean, the Middle East, and Latin America). Africa, with 13% of the world's population, consumes only 3% of the world's commercial energy, although its share of the world's energy production is 7%;
(ii) 65% of the population has access to safe water and sanitation, compared with rates of 80% to 90 % in other developing countries;
(iii) Africa has a telecommunications penetration rate of about 3%, compared with an average of 40% in other parts of the world, and it has a very low penetration rate for broadband services;
(iv) Africa's road access rate is 34% compared with 50% in other geographical zones. Roads are the dominant mode of transportation, accounting for more than 90% of passenger and freight transport in Africa, compared with around 50% of freight in Europe;
(v) The continent's rail network coverage is sparse, with low interconnectivity;
(vi) African maritime ports and inland waterways are not exploited for travel; and
(vii) Continental transport costs are among the highest in the world, with those of land-locked countries accounting for up to 70% of the value of exports

The current situation in Africa illustrates why infrastructure development is an essential sector that requires close attention. Southern Africa will always be left in the shadows of its ambitions without the necessary physical infrastructure like roads, power, water, and telecommunication systems. Logistics present a significant challenge for producers and exporters in the SADC region when moving goods within or outside the region. According to the African Union Commission (2015b), Africa's infrastructure deficits can cost the continent up to 2 percentage points of its annual economic growth. Thus, infrastructure investment is essential for enhancing trade and economic growth. In the context of developing infrastructure, regional cooperation is strongly justified under neo-functional principles. Since transport and communication go hand in hand, cooperation in infrastructure development may spill over into other sectors, such as information technology. According to Balassa and Stoutjesdyk (1975), regionally coordinated infrastructure projects can yield economic benefits if production on a regional scale results in lower production costs than production on a national scale, even when distribution and production costs are taken into account.

Table 4.1: Cost of Trading across the borders

	Documents to export (number)	Time to export (days)	Cost to export (US$ per container)	Documents to import (number)	Time to import (days)	Cost to import (US$ per container)
OECD	4.4	10.9	1,058.70	4.9	11.4	1,106.30
East Asia & Pacific	6.4	22.7	889.8	6.9	24.1	934.7
Eastern Europe & Central Asia	6.4	26.7	1,651.70	7.6	28.1	1,845.40
Latin America & Caribbean	6.6	18	1,228.30	7.1	20.1	1,487.90
South Asia	8.5	32.3	1,511.60	9	32.5	1,744.50
Middle East & North Africa	6.4	20.4	1,048.90	7.5	24.2	1,229.30
Sub-Saharan Africa	7.7	32.3	1,961.50	8.7	38.2	2,491.80

Source: World Bank Trading Across Borders 2010

As you can see from table 4.1, the cost of trade varies from one region to another. In some SADC countries, shipping routes are very far away from the areas of production, which affects the cost of shipping a container. In sub-Saharan Africa, exporting a container costs $1961; $890 in East Asia, and Latin America, $1,228. Sub-Saharan Africa has even higher importing costs, costing $2,471 to import a container. SADC's high shipping costs adversely affect its competitiveness and ability to benefit from global value chains. In a global economy where 60% of trade involves global value chains, industrialization and infrastructure development would help African countries move away from economies dependent on raw materials to a diversified economy with increased exports of manufactured products and services. The African Development Bank (AfDB) believes regional infrastructure projects are critical to integrating smaller economies like Malawi and Zambia.

To decide where to invest, investors examine infrastructure availability, cost, and reliability. It is vital for investors that the host country they are investing in has reliable and efficient power, transport and telecommunication systems. Therefore, inadequate infrastructure affects foreign direct investment. Africa's relative competitiveness in relation to freight costs was examined in a World Bank study. The study concluded that "freight costs are therefore a far more restrictive barrier to African exports than tariffs." The study report found that net freight payments for landlocked countries like Botswana, Lesotho, Malawi, Swaziland, Zambia and Zimbabwe accounted for 42% of the trade costs. The availability of an adequate infrastructure reduces production costs, but the predictability of the infrastructure is also crucial for businesses. Businesses can become less concerned about the cost of using the infrastructure if the infrastructure is predictable and reliable. Here, the security and safety of the cargo take precedence over monetary costs. The transport service that guarantees the timely movement of commodities and the safe return of the commodities would be worth more to an African farmer exporting flowers to Europe. In the same way, a poultry farmer would invest in a diesel-powered generator to ensure that there is a reliable power supply, limiting the risk of power outages that could destroy the business.

There can be no doubt that improvements must be made to the infrastructure of SADC to make the countries competitive. According to Simuyemba (2000), infrastructure improvements will enhance competitiveness and lower production and consumer costs. The region must focus on enhancing regional integration and taking advantage of available opportunities with the emergence of a new generation of leaders. Thus, SADC member states need to realize the benefits of working together to overcome their challenges. Various geographic, political, economic and social factors in Southern Africa contribute to its separation from international markets, thereby reducing export competitiveness. According to the Malawi Growth and Development Strategy (MGDS), transport adds 55% to the price of Malawian exports compared to 17% for other developing countries. As a result of transport challenges, the cost of doing business in Malawi and the region has also increased, thus affecting FDI.

The primary element in integrating nation-states' economic and territorial systems is the logistics infrastructure and services, making transactions within regional geographic and economic space possible. For SADC member states to connect national economies with the rest of the global trade network, value chains need these networks. In this way, this infrastructure plays a crucial role in ensuring sustainable and inclusive development in SADC. Good infrastructure also facilitates intra-regional trade and developing a value chain approach to manufacturing. As a result, private sector development and modernization occur, resulting in job creation and increased participation of countries in regional and global economies. The World Bank Doing Business report (2019) contains an overview of key indicators of regional business climates. According to the report, inadequacies in infrastructure and the lack of regional policies promoting exports and consumption hamper foreign direct investment in the SADC region. In addition to increasing intra-regional trade, integration may also help integrate regional markets with the global market by improving trade infrastructure, which is harming the SADC exports' competitiveness on the global market due to high transport costs.

Improving infrastructure is essential in the SADC area, where the manufacturing sector contributes less than 9% of the GDP. Improved regional infrastructure could facilitate the movement of people, goods, services, and capital between member states. A reliable cross-border transport infrastructure, operational communication infrastructure, and dependable energy infrastructure enable investors to penetrate markets in neighbouring countries. Furthermore, regional infrastructure could spur the SADC region's economy to grow and increase the purchasing power of its citizens as a result of improved economic fundamentals. Considering that the SADC region is at the height of its potential, addressing the infrastructure deficit is an essential step forward. As a result of infrastructure deficiencies and regulatory restrictions, producers in the region cannot fully utilize market access opportunities in regional and international markets.

Poor road infrastructure, delays at border crossings and ports, and a range of formal and informal checkpoints have also hindered the flow of goods while simultaneously increasing transport costs. The docks have been disadvantaged by inadequate equipment for loading and unloading large ships, while exorbitant port charges have added an extra layer of costs to the transportation of goods. Although regional economic integration presents a compelling opportunity for regional economic growth, gaps in the region's infrastructure development have limited the SADC bloc's ability to fully engage in advanced trade-driven development. A skills deficit and inadequate technological advancements have resulted in delays in cross-border trade, which have increased cross-border trade costs.

Balassa and Stoutjesdyk (1975) stated that regional infrastructure projects could have a positive economic impact due to their ripple effects on production and distribution. The SADC region urgently needs institutional and structural reforms to mitigate the logistical challenges associated with cross-border trade. These reforms could facilitate the speedy transportation of imports and exports. According to NEPAD (2020), the efficiency of border crossings is a factor to consider in assessing a transport corridor's potential performance and appeal. To boost intraregional trade, eliminating border impediments and delays is essential in reducing trade costs and easing the burdens associated with the movement of goods, services and people. There is more to easing these constraints than just physical infrastructure. It also calls for the reform of the overall legal framework governing customs and immigration procedures. Newman et al. (2016) indicate that a 3,000 km journey between Kolwezi (DRC) and Johannesburg (South Africa) may take up to 20 days. These delays are caused by inefficient customs systems, with 70% of the time spent at border crossings.

The SADC can reduce these unwanted delays by implementing a one-stop border facility, efficient customs and logistics. Beitbridge, a border crossing between Zimbabwe and South Africa, is Africa's busiest land border, with over 500 trucks and 25,000 people crossing daily. The World Bank (2005) reports that Beitbridge, which should be one of the most sophisticated border crossings in the region, experienced delays of up to six days in 2003, which resulted in expected earnings losses of $1750 per vehicle. This costs the same amount of money to ship a container from Durban in South Africa to a port in the US.

There are plans for the One-Stop Border Post (OSBP) to be operational at Beitbridge in 2024. This will help boost the speed of trade between countries using this border crossing. Having a one-stop border would streamline customs clearance procedures and help reduce congestion. Charalambides (2010) states that a South African grocery retailer named Shoprite, which operates across the SADC region reported that every day that one of its trucks is delayed at a border crossing, it costs the company $500. As part of the COMESA agreement, Zimbabwe and Zambia already have a one-stop border crossing at the Chirundu border. According to Mo Ibrahim Foundation (2014), trucks spent less than two hours at the border instead of two or three days, as was the case before the one-stop border post.

There is a need for SADC to pay more attention to regulatory issues, such as the ease or difficulty of going through all the bureaucratic procedures. Regulatory inadequacies and sometimes excess regulations have been blamed for delaying goods, people, and capital movement. Several of these border crossing delays can be attributed to high levels of corruption among customs officials, immigration officials, and security officials. Travellers between Southern African countries often face harassment, extortion, and threats, which causes delays in the movement of goods within the region. A large number of extra check-points are usually created by corrupt law enforcement or border personnel for the purposes of extortion, resulting in bribes being paid at each check-point to facilitate their movement, and this practice occurs throughout the region. It has even been reported that some traders consider these bribes as routine costs associated with cross-border transactions. To address corruption issues, SADC needs to implement institutional reforms that streamline border regulations. This will require harmonizing national and regional policies and regulations to eliminate the customs and regulatory obstacles exploited by corrupt security and border officials. There is also a challenge related to international payment systems and customs guarantees, both of which are obstacles to a more effective logistics process. For example, in East Asia and the Pacific, it takes 24 days to import a container; in Zimbabwe, it takes 73 days; in Zambia, it takes 64 days; in the Democratic Republic of the Congo, 63 days. The delays and costs involved in exports and imports have contributed to the region's poor economic performance, with very high tariffs imposed and different policies and regulations restricting trade. The liberalized trading system in SADC can only be successful if the intra-SADC trading costs are reduced so that regional producers can compete on a regional and international scale. If trade costs are not lowered, the region will not attract the foreign capital needed to improve production. While there are disparities in the economic development of state members of SADC, these differences should not inhibit regional integration. However, they should instead accelerate it to realise economies of scale and economic growth stimulated by broader export markets. This integration process will also provide a more robust bargaining platform to negotiate better trade terms with other trading regions.

Infrastructure investments are critical to the viability of investments since they impact transportation costs. A country may have a competitive advantage due to its low-cost labour force; however, if transportation costs are high to transport the goods to regional and world markets, the comparative advantage of cheap labour becomes insignificant. In recognition of the importance of cooperation in mitigating transport and logistics challenges, the SADC adopted the Protocol on Transport, Communications and Meteorology on 24 August 1996 as a tool for member states to address all transport and communication constraints. As a result of the protocol, inter-state transportation corridors have been constructed and rehabilitated since 1998. So far, ten Development Corridors have been established or being developed, which include:

(i) Limpopo linking Mozambique, South Africa, Botswana, and Zambia;
(ii) Beira and Zambezi Development Corridor linking Malawi, Mozambique, Zambia, and Zimbabwe;
(iii) Lobito Development Corridor linking DRC, Zambia, and Angola;
(iv) Maputo Development Corridor Mozambique and South Africa;
(v) Mtwara Development Corridor linking Malawi, Mozambique, Tanzania, and Zambia;
(vi) Nacala Development Corridor linking Malawi and Mozambique;
(vii) Tazara Development Corridor Tanzania, South Africa, Zambia, and Zimbabwe;
(viii) North-South Development Corridor (Durban Corridor), which links to other regional corridors like Beira and Maputo;

(ix) Swaziland-South Africa Tourism and Biodiversity Corridor, which links South Africa and Swaziland; and

(x) Walvis Bay Development Corridor links Botswana, Namibia, South Africa, Zambia, the DRC, and Angola.

Through NEPAD, SADC countries are also undertaking efforts to enhance their railway network, which will allow them to connect with the rest of Africa. In the NEPAD (2020) Infrastructure Master Plan, there is a recommendation to enhance passenger and freight rail transport to complement existing road transport initiatives. Ultimately, this would facilitate economic and physical integration of the region and enable people, resources and capital to move freely within the region.

The limited access to trade infrastructure goes beyond transport costs; this also entails high production costs due to limited access to production infrastructures like electricity, credit facilities, and skilled labour. Almost all SADC member states face difficulties with their energy infrastructure, with many of them experiencing power outages due to load-shedding that hinder economic development. The intermittent electricity supply has also contributed to increased production costs in the region. Globally, of the 1.4 billion people without access to energy, 40% are in sub-Saharan Africa, according to the UN's Africa Renewal (2012). In many cases, manufacturers have to rely on generators to deal with power outages, and the power backup measures cost three to five times as much as the regular grid supply. As a result of the failure to introduce new power generation capacity, power shortages and regular electricity supply interruptions have occurred.

Energy security is a long-term problem that SADC member states are struggling to solve. With an ever-growing population, rapid urbanisation, and accelerated economic growth, the SADC region's energy demand keeps rising. For SADC to overcome the electrical energy deficit, member states must invest in the energy sector to increase their electricity generation capacity for long-term economic benefits. SADC member states have already initiated new mechanisms for enhancing energy supply to meet the growing energy demand. The initiative to link the hydroelectric power plants together in a regional grid through the Southern African Power Pool (SAPP) is welcome. SAPP is an intergovernmental Memorandum of Understanding (MOU) composed of 12 member states represented by their respective electric power utility companies from the region. To meet this objective, the member states of

SAPP created a common market for electricity in the SADC region, which allows their customers to benefit from the shared energy market. Foster et al. (2010) pointed out that the SADC region's energy sector has immense unmet needs. The current quality and quantity of energy infrastructure in the region remain the worst in the World, which is affecting industrialisation.

The regional trade market remains fragmented and characterised by low manufacturing industry capacity with limited regional value chains. To mitigate these infrastructure challenges, SADC adopted the SADC Regional Development Fund (RDF) in 2016 to finance the ambitious industrialisation plan despite the concept being on the cards since signing the SADC Treaty in 1992. However, as the RDF was being launched in 2017, there was no consideration of potential costs, sustainability, and member states' ability to contribute to the fund. While the proposed funding structure of RDF recognises disparities in regional economies and provides for different contribution requirements for member states, it is difficult to ensure that all member states adhere to their obligations even within the flexible terms.

In 2012, according to Wentworth (2013), the RIDMP earmarked an estimated $500 billion for regional infrastructure projects in 15 years. Although there have been some financing challenges for these ambitious projects, evidence suggests that some bankable projects with identified financing have failed due to a lack of project preparation and delivery. According to the Development Bank of Southern Africa (DBSA), $55 billion was available between 2009 and 2010 but was not disbursed due to inadequate project preparation and execution. The challenges and delays associated with project development and preparation are related to how projects are introduced. The majority of these projects are conceived as ideas and not as fully developed projects. This inadequacy is related to a lack of capacity and coordination problems at the project definition stage. There have been challenges in selecting projects that support SADC's industrialization agenda and what constitutes 'regional' projects as the term is not clearly defined. In addition, the private sector offers an opportunity to finance these regional infrastructure projects and close the funding gap. That can only be achieved if members of the region harmonize their regulatory and domestic frameworks. Besides adopting standard criteria for bid selection and evaluation, there is also a need to establish a common oversight process and adopt procurement transparency. Due to the limited availability of capital at the regional level, significant investments require foreign direct investment.

As a result of the high level of political risk attributed to instability in the region, foreign private capital has also been held back from investing in infrastructure development. In addition, attracting investment in financing for regional infrastructure will enable other region members, rather than South Africa, to increase their manufacturing capabilities.

Regional infrastructure projects must also consider the sensitivities associated with some of the projects or member states involved. In terms of sharing natural resources such as water bodies for energy infrastructure, Cahora Bassa offers both a good and a poor example. Built on the Zambezi River in the early 1970s by the Portuguese colonial administration in Mozambique, the dam provided Mozambique and neighbouring South Africa with an improved electricity supply. The project became the largest hydroelectric project in the nation designed exclusively to export cheap energy. Walker (2017) argues that the project's legacy has not been viewed favourably because of an agreement signed in 1969 between the colonial administration in Mozambique and their South African counterparts. Considering the dam's capacity of generating more than 2,075 megawatts, 82% of the electricity produced would be sold to South Africa under the terms of the deal. To put it bluntly, this arrangement was both disproportional and opportunistic by any standard. According to Isaacman and Sneddon (2000), the hydroelectric project symbolised the security alliance between the Portuguese colonial administration and the Apartheid regime of South Africa.

The sale of electricity could provide foreign currency to Mozambique; however, the ownership agreement of the dam made the whole deal less desirable to the Mozambican government. Hydroelectrica de Cahora Bassa (HCB) was established to operate the dam and supply electricity to Mozambique and South Africa. At the time of independence, Mozambique had limited access to capital and therefore agreed to minority ownership of HCB. According to the agreement, the Portuguese government retained 82% of the dam, compared to Mozambique's 18%. In 2007, the Mozambican government renegotiated the agreement after agreeing to pay US$950 million to the Portuguese government. Mozambique's stake in the company was increased by 85% under the new contract. An increase to 92.5% was made to the Mozambican shareholding in 2012. While the Mozambican government owns the majority stake in HCB, the electricity generated at Cahora Bassa has yet to be mobilized in a meaningful manner to benefit the domestic market in Mozambique. The South African government continues to export 70% of the electricity under a long-term agreement at below-market prices until 2029.

The construction of the Cahora Bassa dam also had short-term and long-term consequences that affected the livelihoods of the displaced population and the economic well-being of the people who resided on the Zambezi River. The Tawara community, whose ancestral homes and farmlands were flooded to create the vast lake behind the dam, lost its livelihood, identity, and dignity. The colonial administration strategically repositioned the population into areas devoid of basic amenities, according to Jungnanian (1974). As part of Portugal's broader counterinsurgency efforts, these specific locations were targeted to cut off the rural support base of FRELIMO. The colonial administration also moved people with the assistance of the police or military without offering them alternative options or compensation. The colonial administration had moved more than 42,000 people by the end of 1973. The project Cahora Bassa has also been associated with disruptions in the ecosystem. The Zambezi prawn fishing industry, which contributed 15% of the country's exports, declined by as much as 50% since the dam was built. This was a colossal trade-off for Mozambique, considering that the government could only utilize 18% of the dam's electrical capacity.

According to the New Partnership for Africa's Development (NEPAD), political will plays a significant role in achieving the goals of regional infrastructure cooperation. There is a need for the regional leadership to carefully examine all concerns raised by host countries regarding the project's infrastructure. A consideration of this nature is necessary because member states respond differently to different projects, and their history and past experiences primarily affect their cooperation. Mozambique's raw deal with the Cahora Bassa project may impact the perception of future regional infrastructure projects by the country in the future. McCarty (1996) argues that regional infrastructure development must precede regional integration efforts since most integration efforts are undermined without sufficient infrastructure. Mistry (1995) advocates a broader integration approach that encompasses sectoral investment cooperation and institutional capacity development. It is evident that in SADC, infrastructure gaps, bureaucratic delays, and customs formalities have all contributed to high trade transaction costs, which have impacted the competitiveness of SADC products.

According to Hancock (2010), SADC members have set targets with a reasonable degree of success but have barely made a dent in achieving those goals with some missed targets. The SADC has some development agendas that are overly ambitious and unrealistic with regard to objectives, targets, timetables, schedules, and funding. The SADC sets numerous targets over a specific period, and most of them have failed to materialize. In addition to failing to achieve the agreed target, the projects have been hampered by a lack of planning and a slow implementation process. For economic integration to fulfil its role as an instrument supporting the development of member states in the SADC region, all states must have a clear understanding of their development ambitions and strategies before making commitments to regional goals. Plans and strategies for domestic development should be incorporated into regional development strategies. These national strategies must reinforce and promote the virtues of regional integration strategies and a better understanding of how regional goals contribute to national development objectives. SADC can learn a lot from ASEAN regional integration projects. ASEAN regional projects have demonstrated a more realistic approach and a transparent implementation process.

As soon as SADC was established, it was driven by a desire to link regional economies through regional infrastructure development. For any infrastructure project to reach the preliminary phase, part of the decision-making process must involve analysing the project's viability. During the planning phase of the project, it is important to include this element. Starting with the pre-feasibility stage, SADC should establish relationships between stakeholders to ensure that all members are aligned on the same objective. In the long run, undergoing this initial phase eliminates any possibility of initiating a project that will fail at a later stage. While SADC member states have shown interest in regional infrastructure development, the biggest challenge has been the micro or what we can refer to as the projects' human-level management.

A lack of political will has hampered the implementation of critical regional infrastructure projects in Africa. In order to ensure effective implementation of regional infrastructure projects, all regional infrastructure development efforts must be incorporated into national development plans, including budgetary requirements. In this case, the regional development projects are incorporated into the national project implementation framework. There is, however, a problem for SADC member states because most governments only think regionally while acting nationally. Allen Hagerman (2012) identified that a major challenge is gaining long-term assurances that the politicians who have signed agreements with financiers or a neighbouring country to develop regional infrastructure projects will stand by and demonstrate their commitment. To achieve this, political stability is necessary, and before investors commit their capital to infrastructure investment, they want to feel comfortable with the political situation.

Regularly, regional projects are also advanced to the implementation phase without adequate time devoted to consensus-building and dialogue. The Walvis Bay transport corridor CEO recalled the amount of time spent at the preliminary stage establishing relationships with relevant government representatives in the DRC and Zambia. Due to the adequate investment in building a good relationship with project stakeholders, the project implementation overcame inevitable problems. Hagerman (2012) calls human issues like self-interest, distrust, and concerns about ceding power to an external entity are the reasons for the failure to plan and implement regional infrastructure projects. There is no better example of overambitious projects characterized by inadequate planning than the Shire - Zambezi Waterway, a transport project championed by Malawi. Specifically, this project aimed to open up the Shire-Zambezi route for navigation into the Indian Ocean to enable commercial shipping, with benefits for Malawi, Zambia, and Mozambique. However, this project did not succeed for several reasons, including the strained historical relations between Malawi and Mozambique. In addition to the diplomatic failures, the project's success could affect the revenue of Mozambique from Malawi imports, which posed another difficulty. A waterway was not in the interest of the Mozambican government as alternative modes of transport used by Malawi to reach Mozambican ports were more financially beneficial to Mozambique.

In this regard, Malawi required a strategy that would provide leverage over the Mozambican government. Considering that Mozambique benefited from Malawi's port fees via alternative means of transportation, Malawi needed to design a financial structure that would entice the Mozambican government. Malawi did not develop a sophisticated plan to gain the Mozambicans' cooperation. In the negotiations with Mozambique, Malawi used low-level officials from the Ministry of Foreign Affairs with little expertise in foreign policy, led by a minister of transport who was an inexperienced engineer with little experience in diplomatic matters. As a result, Malawi's ambitious infrastructure project failed at a crucial time when adequate planning could have allowed Malawi to mitigate some of the challenges the Mozambicans were raising.

Economic Disparities of Member States

In a logical sense, economic integration increases trade benefits, enhances foreign direct investment by reducing risk for investors, and lowers production costs by utilizing the movement of resources to maximize efficiency. These optimistic views of integration omit to examine the structural arrangements of the regional institutions established. There is no doubt that regional economic convergence provides a path forward for growth; however, this growth cannot be achieved if regional institutions fail to evolve into effective instruments that can contribute to convergence among all participating states. Convergence on a regional level involves the erosion of state structures and adopting incremental community identity by creating cooperative equilibrium in the market environment. Due to these new conditions, state structures can only remain relevant if they provide an environment that will benefit entrepreneurs in their pursuit of new market opportunities and provide a safety net for those negatively affected by liberalization and increased market competition. There is a need for state institutions to adapt quickly to changes resulting from liberalization and potential imbalances.

It is evident that there are gross economic imbalances between SADC member states. Lewis (2001) also reports that there is a significant disparity in their economies and population distribution between SADC countries. Blizkovsky et al. (2018) opine that SADC accounts for 29.1% of Africa's GDP. The region is not only home to South Africa, one of Africa's largest economies, but it is also home to some of Africa's poorest countries. There are high-income countries in the SADC region, such as Seychelles with GDP per capita of $17,000 and middle-income countries such as Botswana, South Africa, and Mauritius with GDP per capita ranging from $11,000 for Mauritius to $6,000 for South Africa. In contrast, it is relatively homogeneous in low-income countries, such as Malawi and Mozambique, with GDP per capita between $250 and $350.

The region is comprised of agriculture-dependent countries like Tanzania and Malawi, where agriculture accounts for 34% and 45% of their

GDP, respectively, to South Africa and Botswana, where the sector contributes 1.7% to 2.8%. Furthermore, the region includes South Africa, a country with an advanced infrastructure instead of infrastructure-constrained Malawi. There have been few attempts in the region to address the very pronounced economic inequalities in the region. Since independence, the poverty levels in some SADC countries have increased due to economic decline in member countries like Zimbabwe, where 60% of the population lacks access to clean water. Not only are there disparities between countries, but the region also has one of the highest rates of economic disparity among its different demographic groups. White South Africans constitute 5% of the South African population, but they own 80% of the land and control the capital. The economic growth within the SADC framework has failed to reduce the overall economic disparities over the last three decades.

In practice, studies on income inequality and regional integration are rare, and most of the empirical research focuses on European integration. Social development in the region remains uncertain as a result of economic integration. Inequality and poverty in the region may have been influenced by intra-regional trade. In the context of Africa, To address plausible issues of endogeneity, Ametoglo et al. (2018) employed a least squares dummy variables correction (LSDVC) method and panel estimation methods with a dynamic specification in their analysis of economic disparities in the ECOWAS integration scheme. First, the ECOWAS political integration decreased income inequality by a significant amount. Secondly, as evidenced by intraregional export ratios or international goods trade (percentages of ECOWAS trade), economic integration strongly correlates with income inequality. Lastly, the increase in the Gini coefficient was better explained by the unification of intraregional trade (as a percentage of total ECOWAS trade) than by individual intraregional exports (as a percentage of total exports of a country).

For this logic of regional market integration to have its desired consequences, its implementation must be pure. As a matter of theory, market liberalization generates a net benefit for participating states over a long period. However, new exposure to trade competition results in winners and losers in the regional community. It has been argued that the more profound the integration, the greater the risk of economic vulnerability, with some of the results not meeting the expectations of member states. According to Fielding (1996), larger economies are more likely to benefit from integration than smaller economies if the economic shocks suffered by smaller economies are not mitigated. Narsey (2004) states that new free trade agreements will result in unacceptable job losses and reduced public revenues.

This explains early expectations in integration among SADC states. As a result of the economic disparities in the region, citizens from poorer countries have migrated to South Africa and Botswana in search of employment opportunities. Low-income countries are often regarded as vulnerable to economic shocks and as having low levels of human development. One of the major obstacles to regional integration efforts in Southern Africa has been some member states' poor economic state. In some countries, severe economic challenges have forced some member states to abandon or delay fundamental regional integration protocols to meet short-term economic needs. In response to the growing economic disparities, some politicians have manipulated the sense of injustice across the region to gain political leverage, in turn undermining regional integration efforts.

Some of the economic conditions in the SADC region are shaped by regional factors. In contrast, other factors, such as globalization, have had a widespread impact on the economic and social environment. Scholars like Rodrik (2011) and Wallerstein (1976) describe the process of globalization as a stance led by core countries, who believe the free movement of goods, services, capital and labour is a prerequisite for peripheral countries to also benefit from it. Even though the concept of globalization has transformed the economic fortunes of most East Asian countries, Africa has had a completely different experience. A major component of globalization was opening countries to international trade, resulting in economic growth based on increased exports. The Bretton Woods institutions (World Bank, IMF) became the cheerleaders for globalization. A World Bank study (2002) confirms that globalization has increased the quality of life of millions of Asian countries. The study found that countries such as China, Malaysia, Thailand, and Singapore achieved per capita growth rates four per cent higher than countries that liberalized slowly. Srinivasan and Bhagwati (1999) demonstrate that promoting liberalization and ensuring sound domestic policies can expedite economic growth. East Asian economies have grown faster than the rest of the world, which has opened up new opportunities for trade and investment within the region. Trade and investment growth has created jobs, spurred economic growth, and enhanced poverty reduction as significant production relocated to the region. As a result of market liberalization, major MNCs like Nike took advantage of the new phenomena by exploiting access to cheap labour in East Asia.

However, globalisation has not been without controversy in other parts of the world, despite its positive economic effects. Some of the economic and market reforms promoted by the World Bank and IMF have failed to meet expectations. In many cases, it has worsened the economic situation among the general population. Apart from economic concerns, other non-economic challenges have also emerged, exacerbating anti-globalisation sentiments in different parts of the world.

Joseph Stiglitz, the winner of the 2001 Nobel Prize in Economics, agrees with this observation in his 2002 book Globalization and its Discontents. Stiglitz (2002) gives a rare glimpse behind the closed doors of monetary institutions in this book. The IMF, according to Stiglitz, prescribed: "standard solutions without considering the effects on the people of the countries that follow these policies." He continues. "Rarely did I see forecasts about what the policies would do to poverty. Rarely did I see thoughtful discussions and analyses of the consequences of alternative policies. There was a single prescription. Alternative opinions were not sought. Open frank discussion was discouraged-there was no room for it. In terms of ideology and policy prescription, countries were expected to follow the IMF guidelines without debate." The IMF completely ignored the risks of exacerbating economic conditions in African countries, which in turn exacerbated the existing economic conditions. In this regard, well-intentioned inflexible conditions attached to IMF support detracted the country's capacity to address the critical pressing issues. These conditions by the IMF engendered resentment among the African population. The institution's narrow ideological perspective of pursuing rapid privatization led to problems arising from failures of the privatization initiatives that had no sensitivity to the social implications. Under these IMF programs, market liberalization led to the restructuring of production and companies pursuing cost-effective mechanisms. This meant moving resources from low productivity areas to promote efficiency. As a result, inefficient industries closed down under pressure from international competition. This new phenomenon led to massive deindustrialization for most African countries, with domestic production replaced by cheaper imports. As a result, the labour market was disrupted, with many people losing their employment as the manufacturing industry disappeared.

According to the IMF's theoretical perspective, new jobs would be created due to economic restructuring; however, jobs were destroyed in Africa, and no alternatives were created. In Malawi, for example, the once vibrant textile and retail industries have collapsed, resulting in a loss of jobs. Although employment layoffs are covered by safety nets such as unemployment insurance and statutory unemployment benefits in developed economies, rising unemployment has negative social consequences in developing economies. Due to the worsening economic conditions, IMF policies are viewed with suspicion in most African countries, which has resulted in social unrest in some cases. The austerity measures imposed on African countries have resulted in a decline in the quality of public services due to the removal of subsidies to the once vibrant public sector. Szentes (2003) argues that the development gap between the centre and the periphery is reflected in the asymmetrical interdependencies in which the centre exploits the periphery. Taking into account the disintegrated internal structure of the economy, Szentes states it is necessary to study the manifestations and consequences of unequal international conditions. According to Stiglitz (2002), the advanced industrial countries are hypocritical in pushing globalization to maximize their benefits while refusing to open up their markets to the goods of the developing countries.

The creation of new businesses and employment opportunities requires a great deal of capital investment and entrepreneurship. As a result of a shortage of capital revenue streams and a shortage of educated individuals, opportunities for establishing new businesses were limited. In this manner, the IMF initiatives resulted in many African countries finding themselves in worse economic circumstances. The industrialised countries took advantage of Africa's struggling manufacturing industry by expanding exports and flooding the African market with cheap products, with China being the biggest culprit. Africa has become a primary exporter of raw materials in the absence of a manufacturing sector, and Africa's share of global exports has declined.

While advanced economies had learned the harsh lessons of financial deregulation after the 1997 Asian financial crisis, which was a prelude to the global financial crisis in the late 1990s; the IMF was advancing unmitigated market deregulation to the developing countries that had no capacity of managing what had already proven to be a problematic initiative fraught with risks even under the best circumstances. Market liberalization was not pursued by advanced economies until the latter stages of their development. According to Blizkovsky et al. (2018), European countries overcame their economic difficulties after World War II by initiating financial aid to farmers and supporting the manufacturing industry for modernization. These policies were combined with border protection measures and export support.

In addition, the IMF SAPs required African governments to accelerate poorly executed monetary reforms based on the simplistic premise that countries cannot attract foreign direct investment without liberalization. It is interesting to note that China, a country that received a significant amount of FDI, did not follow any of the IMF strategies. The success of China demonstrated that capital market liberalization was not necessary to attract FDI.

In poor African countries, the reforms championed by the IMF frequently involved devaluing the domestic currency and increasing borrowing from high-interest lenders. The new measures resulted in people with savings in domestic banks losing their savings and experiencing very high inflation levels. As a result of these new economic shocks, the rich began holding foreign currencies in their homes, resulting in the depletion of banks' foreign reserves. Consequently, depleting foreign currency reserves in countries such as Malawi, essential commodities such as petroleum products, medicines, and other vital commodities were unavailable.

The resulting misery led globalization critics to accuse Western governments of sabotaging African economies to their advantage. Some MNCs have been criticized for supporting certain armed groups to maximize their profits. Globalization has also been credited with exacerbating political instability in Southern Africa. African countries tend to view the IMF from a rather negative perspective, as they perceive the institution to be a centre of broken promises. In general, the institution does not enjoy the trust of developing countries.

Globalization failed to live up to its promise of economic prosperity; instead, it damaged African countries' social and economic fabric, reinforcing hostility toward the concept. Although developed countries encouraged trade liberalization in sectors in which they had a comparative advantage, they introduced protectionist policies on sectors in which developing countries had a comparative advantage. There was widespread criticism of the developed countries' double standard, and the IMF was viewed as an instrument used by the developed countries to advance their special interests.

The IMF plays a unique role in reviewing each country's macroeconomic situation and ensuring that each country lives within its means. After the Bretton Woods institutions' failures, the SADC region is desperate to create an institutional and social foundation that can facilitate targeted human development of the marginalized population. Regional integration provides an opportunity for regional economic transformation. For the African population, mindsets cannot be changed overnight, with the two institutions still viewed as an extension of neo-colonialism. As was the case with colonial masters, these institutions continue to assert that they know what is best for Africa. On the other hand, these institutions can still do enormous good on the continent by promoting transparency and fiscal discipline without harming the social safety net. With the hope period over, new challenges arose that required an urgent regional response, including integration.

The SADC has sequenced several activities to move towards economic integration throughout the region. With initiatives such as the SADC Free Trade Area (FTA) and a common market, SADC has created an environment that facilitates economic integration, as outlined in the SADC Regional Indicative Strategic Development Plan (RISDP) macroeconomic convergence. However, the implementation of these initiatives across the region has faced some challenges due to the level of regional trade participation. The majority of intra-regional trade in the SADC region is highly concentrated. South Africa accounts for 60% of intra-regional trade in the SADC region, holds 70% of GDP, and has the most developed and diversified manufacturing sector.

Due to the vast economic disparities between South Africa and the rest of the member states, other states perceive South Africa as a hegemon superimposing its will upon its regional counterparts. As Krapohl (2010) noted: "Economic asymmetries within and between regions have various implications for regional integration in the South, leading to the fact that such integration projects differ fundamentally from those in the global North." The success and stability of regional integration in the south are much more dependent on the reaction of extra-regional actors, Rambo [going alone] situations occur more quickly due to intra-regional competition, implementation problems are consequently more severe, and regional institutions are less likely to solve these problems." SADC's experience illustrates some basic lessons on how economic asymmetries can challenge regional integration. This is yet another example of how an economic hegemony in South Africa has contributed to macroeconomic instability in some SADC member states, especially in the less developed economies.

Figure 4.5: Share of GDP (%) for the SADC Member States

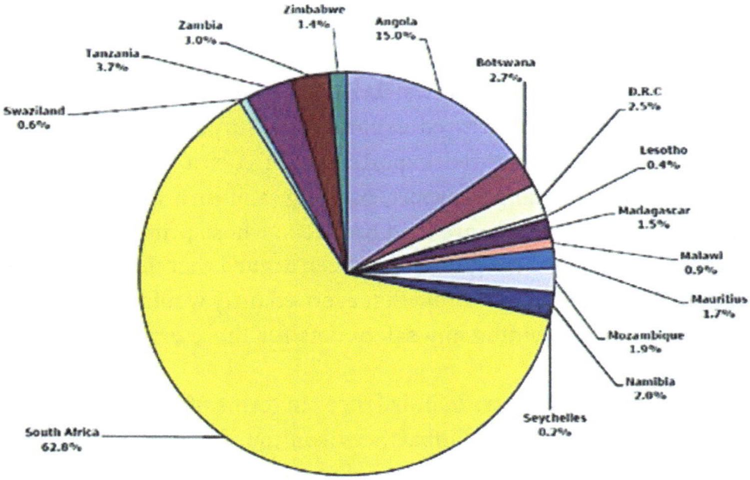

Source: SADC National Statistics Office, 2012

As shown in Figure 4.5, South Africa's economic power is overwhelming in Southern Africa as a whole. Angola, Tanzania, and Botswana are the other major economies in the region in addition to South Africa. The three countries with the least developed economies are Malawi, Lesotho, and Swaziland. A fundamental condition of regional integration is the membership of states of similar economic standing. In the case of SADC, this is not the case. One of the primary motivations for states to participate in regional integration schemes is the expectation of both short- and long-term economic benefits, which could inevitably improve citizens' welfare. A country losing out on economic benefits due to the integration project is more likely to undermine the initiative in an environment like this. As a significant portion of their revenue is derived from tariffs, the weaker and smaller economies are likely to lose out on the benefits of regional integration in the short term.

From the experience of SADC, countries with the most robust economies, such as South Africa, have benefited more from market liberalization than countries with smaller economies, such as Malawi, which have lost tax revenue generated from import tariffs. Having a developed economy and a sophisticated manufacturing industry, South Africa has a competitive advantage in manufacturing goods at a lower price that can be sold on the regional market, making it difficult for its regional partners to compete. While South Africa's exports to the region grew exponentially, exports from the smaller economies saw limited growth and were primarily focused on primary raw materials. Taking advantage of its advanced manufacturing base, South Africa has been exporting diversified manufactured goods to meet the growing demands of middle-class consumers. The SADC has become the top destination for South Africa's manufactured exports after surpassing Europe in 2010. Aside from manufactured exports, South Africa has also dominated sectors such as retail, transport, banking, and insurance. Interestingly, the top export products are food products, whose primary raw materials are sourced from the region. It has been argued that the failure of FTA is due to SADC simply assuming that every country would benefit from free trade without providing any safety nets for those experiencing adverse effects.

We can measure trade imbalances in terms of the diverse economic status levels, and these imbalances continue to present challenges to regional integration efforts. A fundamental weakness of SADC has not been a lack of ideas but rather the execution of those ideas, with most ideas failing to reach a logical conclusion. Other than the political motives that have led some member states to reluctance to implement agreed protocols, the economic imbalances of those member states have also posed an integration challenge. It appears that SADC member states have resisted any cooperation on protocols and agreements that they perceive to cost them more than benefit them or that the costs and benefits are not distributed equally. This relates to the fact that member states have experienced varying levels of economic development, resulting in disagreements. It is universally acknowledged that the success of any regional integration is determined by the ability of its member states to address their challenges.

Manirov (2015) argues that when a small country joins forces with a large one, the benefits are more remarkable because the demand for its exports increases. This can only be achieved when the small country is developing, and the large country is a developed country with a greater purchasing power. The smaller economies cannot benefit from this arrangement if they have a struggling manufacturing base, which is characteristic of most SADC members. SADC lacks the flexibility and capacity to respond to increasingly complex changes in regional and global economic conditions. The economic disparities have revealed some of the limitations of the current regional integration framework. It has proved difficult to agree on standard economic policies and positions that satisfy the different interests of the Southern African states as a result of these disparities. There has been an unequal increase in trade between member states, resulting from a lack of equality between member states. Foreign direct investment has indeed transformed the economies of China, Malaysia and Singapore. However, unmitigated foreign investment also experiences some real downturns. When foreign companies are introduced into economies with underdeveloped manufacturing bases, they destroy domestic competitors and destroy the prospects of small business development.

Several examples of this can be found in the context of the SADC. As a result of the entry of South African companies into the domestic market, the retail and manufacturing industry in Southern Africa has been severely disrupted. For SADC countries to compete with the developed manufacturing and retail sector of South Africa, domestic businesses have found it impossible. The SADC Free Trade Agreement has displaced manufacturing in member states, with South African products replacing domestic products. Even though the concerns of other SADC member states are valid, we must maintain a perspective as to why South African manufacturers and retailers are prospering. A significant factor is that South African manufacturers efficiently deliver their products and services at competitive prices.

Some have argued that South African companies have abused their financial monopoly to drive out domestic competitors with low prices while also benefiting from tax breaks and other sweeteners. However, in SADC member states, the benefits of low prices have been short-lived, as prices increased once the competition was eliminated. As a result of the imbalances, SADC should establish an environment where local businesses can develop and compete reasonably. In pursuing market liberalization, SADC must also be attentive to the broader social context before implementing safety nets.

In order to reduce poverty in Africa, Asakwe (2015) argues that an integrated approach that promotes and ensures development in terms of building productive capacity and achieving structural transformation is needed to move from trade reform-oriented integration. Kweka and Mboya (2004) study determined that regional integration within the

SADC and EAC enabled trade to improve. A higher anti-poverty impact was also attributed to regional trade because it directly provided employment and sales opportunities to the poor. While tinter-regional trade has increased in the SADC region since the inception of the FTA, an increase in trade volume alone is not the best measurement for the success of economic integration without looking at the conditions in each member state.

Frankel (1997) argues that economic integration should be measured by the percentage of an export's value that goes to all its collaborating countries in a regional community. In this case, the share of intra-regional trade over the volume of trade, in other words,intra-regional trade share. This describes the intensity and relative importance of intra-regional trade among trading partners within a particular trading bloc. It is crucial to make these specific measurements to ensure that every member state benefits from the integration process. If regional integration is not appropriately managed, there might be winners ad losers. Viner (1950) was one of the first to consider welfare in a theory of regional trade in general and in the theory of customs unions in particular. As a result of economic integration, he found two possible effects: trade creation and trade diversion.

Figure 4.6: South Africa's manufactured exports per region

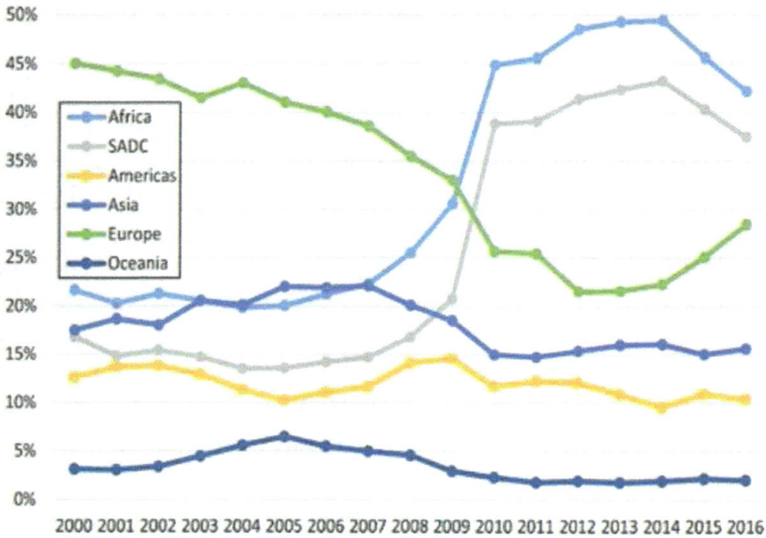

Source: Arndt & Robert (2018)

South Africa exports manufactured goods to different parts of the world, as illustrated in figure 4.6. Based on the export data between 2000 and 2016, South African manufactured product exports increased from 22% to 43%. The member states must understand the SADC bloc's regional economic dynamics to identify and mitigate some of the fundamental challenges that affect regional integration. Several member states, such as Malawi and Zambia, are landlocked and have small economies. Mauritius, Namibia, and South Africa are considered Middle-Income Countries (MICs) with entirely different challenges related to Small Island Developing States (SIDS). For the Least-Developed Countries (LDCs), the challenges primarily relate to securing financing for regional infrastructure projects and moving on with regional integration protocols that may have a short-term financial impact on their revenues. Without developing the production and logistical infrastructure across the region, smaller economies will continue to lose out from potential regional and global value chain approaches, limiting their production and trade potential. SADC must start focusing on industrial restructuring across different sectors in the region to ensure that no country is left behind.

Nevertheless, it is essential to acknowledge that in the longer term, the size of the large Southern African community may lead to a significant reorganization of trade in the region if adequate measures are implemented to improve production in countries experiencing a decline in manufacturing. Some of these measures will be discussed in Chapter 11. The free-market ideology is premised on Adam Smith, who is recognized as the founder of modern economics in his 1776 publication, *The Wealth of Nations*, Smith 1776(1976) argues that the profit motive drives the economy to efficient outcomes as if by an invisible hand. However, more recent economic theories have acknowledged that whenever there is inadequate information and the market is incomplete, which is the case in developing economies, the invisible hand works imperfectly. Ricardo 1871(1971) perfected Adam Smith's theory of comparative advantage which is premised on the labour theory of value, which recognises labour as the most significant factor of production.

Getting the larger, more influential countries on board is crucial for a free trade area's success. In most instances, regional powers have supported the creation of successful regional agreements around the world. A number of things will depend on the attitude and behaviour of these champions toward the FTA. It may be more advantageous for economies with larger populations to take advantage of trade liberalization. Furthermore, they may be nervous about opening up their own "backyard" to competition from other member states with more robust economies.

As part of the market integration agenda, a focus is placed on eliminating policy barriers to investment and trade. The SADC Protocol on Trade (2001) envisioned that; "the establishment of a free trade area (FTA) in the SADC region by 2008 and its objectives was to liberalise intra-regional trade in goods and services further; ensure efficient production; contribute towards the improvement of the climate for domestic, cross-border and foreign investment; and enhance economic development, diversification and industrialisation of the region." Despite the FTA facilitating free movement and trade, evidence suggests that SADC countries have deliberately introduced measures to violate the FTA indirectly. For instance, states have introduced or maintained non-tariff barriers (NTBs) for some products. NTBs are deliberate economic policies that aim to restrict international trade to benefit domestic producers. Non-tariff barriers include import quotas, customs delays, technical barriers, or other policies intended to restrict trade. Mozambique, for example, insisted on translating English origin certificates into Portuguese, and Zambia insisted that Zimbabwean milk could only enter its market if it were labelled in the Zambian language.

It is essential to distinguish between non-tariff barriers and non-tariff measures (NTMs). NTM is a policy measure adopted to ensure the quality of imported goods. Most NTMs apply to agriculture products, and member states may implement these policies to enforce food safety and standards. For example, fruits may carry insects, while meat may contain salmonella, hazardous to human health. While South Africa continues to campaign for opening markets in SADC member states, a study conducted by Tekele and Ndlela (2003) noted that South Africa had implemented controls on some agricultural and manufactured products, and frozen fish, dairy products, oats, and maize. The South African government insisted that some of the products comply with South African Bureau of Standards requirements, which presented a challenge to most SADC member states. There is no question that standards are necessary to protect consumer interests and limit exposure to toxic foods and products. However, in South Africa, the SADC member states believed South Africa was using the standards argument as a protectionist strategy.

In SADC, the imperfections of free trade can be corrected by ensuring inclusive prosperity where each country has a role to play in the regional market while taking advantage of its comparative advantages. This could help reduce intra-SADC trading costs to make regional producers competitive regionally and globally. Without lowering trading costs, the region will fail to attract desperately needed foreign capital investment that could help improve production in countries falling behind. Despite the disparities in economic development among SADC member states, these differences should not inhibit regional integration but rather promote integration to gain economies of scale and stimulate economic growth due to the broader market presented for exports. The integration process will also provide a better bargaining platform to negotiate better trade terms with other trading regions; however, better trading terms alone are insufficient. Consequently, although the SADC area could benefit from the free trade area, in the long run, there is also a possibility that some countries may lose out in the short term due to trade imbalances.

Heckscher-Ohlin-Samuelson theorem says the developing countries benefit from increasing global trade when they produce goods for which they are best suited. As such, low-skilled labour is likely to rise in demand, as well as low-skilled wages. Therefore, inequality may decrease. Rich countries could experience the reverse situation: They may face greater inequality by exporting more high-skilled goods. In the context of SADC, the smaller economies have a comparative advantage over South Africa regarding low-cost labour, but South Africa also has other advantages. A combination of these factors makes South Africa more desirable for investors. In the World Bank's (2020) Doing Business report, South Africa ranks 84th out of 190 countries, taking the number one spot in the SADC region and third in Africa. Some of the factors playing to South Africa's advantage include:

(i) Its demographic location (easy access to the sea);
(ii) A diversified economy;
(iii) Sophisticated economy;
(iv) Abundant natural resources;
(v) Developed infrastructure;
(vi) Higher labour skills; and
(vii) Developed governance institutions.

Figure 4.7 reveals that the smaller economies in the SADC are also prone to attracting lower levels of FDI. For example, Malawi, Lesotho and Swaziland are the smallest economies in the region, and they have received the smallest amount of FDI compared to the bigger economies. However, studies have likewise shown that FDI inflows and GDP growth in SADC countries have also followed the same trend. Hence, international capital flows appear to have a direct impact on the economic growth of SADC countries. According to De Mello (1999), FDI helps to promote the "incorporation of new inputs and foreign technologies in the production function of the recipient economy." However, the FDI asymmetries in the SADC region are associated with widening regional imbalances with regional inequality on the rise.

Figure 4.7: Share of Total FDI (1980-2011) in SADC Countries

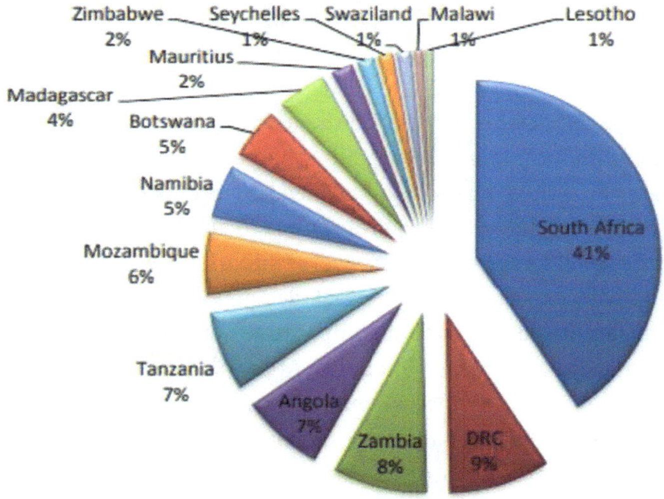

Source: UNCTAD (2013a) Database

The difficulties faced with maintaining fiscal discipline in the trade liberalisation era remain enormous. Burgess and Stern (1993) argue that most low-income countries rely on trade-related taxes for a larger share of their revenue due to tax administration capacity limitations and large informal sectors, which undermines the efficacy of other forms of taxation. With most SADC member states having limited income sources, replacing lost trade taxes is challenging and can create fiscal gaps, affecting public services delivery. For countries susceptible to losing potential tax revenue, political consequences resulting from this revenue loss can impede cooperation in some policy areas. Blizkovsky et al. (2018) argue that some African countries have shown reluctance to let go of taxes and duties on goods as they fear losing government revenue derived from these measures. For example, Zimbabwe and Malawi were reluctant to implement the SADC Trade and Investment Protocol to liberalise trade under the SADC FTA. The critical aspect of the protocol was the requirement for SADC member states to harmonise trade and economic policies. The table below illustrates why this is the case.

Table 4.2: Estimated impact of SADC FTA on revenue

	(a) % change in customs revenue	(b) Customs revenue as % of total revenue[2]	(a)*(b)=(c) Per cent change in total revenue	Tax revenue per cent of GDP	Total government revenue per cent of GDP
Angola	-1.8	4.3	-0.08	35.7	36.3
Botswana[1]	-3.0	15.4	-0.46	15.0	37.4
Lesotho[1]	-3.0	45.0	-1.35	47.1	69.3
Malawi	-23.9	22.0	-5.26	16.0	17.3
Mauritius	-17.0	33.5	-5.70	16.3	19.0
Mozambique	-5.8	22.2	-1.29	16.7	18.3
Namibia[1]	-3.0	29.8	-0.89	31.5	36.1
South Africa[1]	-3.0	1.8	-0.05	25.6	26.4
Swaziland[1]	-3.0	49.4	-1.48	33.1	34.7
Tanzania	-5.8	27.6	-1.60	18.1	20.0
Zambia	-28.7	11.6	-3.33	31.5	34.2
Zimbabwe	-32.2	17.2	-5.55	26.4	29.6

Source: Leape, J. (2000) Taxation and Fiscal Adjustment

Table 4.2 illustrates the percentage of revenue in some of the SADC member states. The short-term national interests in SADC member states have stood in the way of regional objectives when implementing regional protocols and agreements. Reducing trade costs by lowering tariffs can increase trade in the SADC region. However, SADC has failed to experience uniform trade gains across all member states. Member states with minimal regional exports have experienced minimal gains with the removal of trade barriers. That has been the case with Malawi, as illustrated above. Malawi has failed to benefit from the FTA because Malawi's major exports are tobacco and sugar, with the EU being the primary export market.

According to Nye (1970), the lower a country's income and industrialisation level, the lower its tolerance to both (domestic and regional) asymmetries. The more sensitive the problem of fair distribution of benefits, the more significant challenge remains in the structure of the economies and the character of intra-regional trade. The history of unsuccessful regional cooperation attempts in Africa shows the danger of such a process when expectations of member states become skewed by domestic factors, which affect the shared objectives that are significant for progress. That is why measures must be put in place to address the economic imbalances in the region. Robinson (1996) argues: "The requirements for making complete forms of regional integration work are demanding. Distribution of gains has to be carefully enumerated, compensation mechanisms established — to make the distribution equitable — and a degree of national sovereignty surrendered to achieve the necessary harmonisation at the regional level. By contrast, regional cooperation in infrastructure and natural resources is far less demanding. Typically, there are clear gains for all the countries involved in regional cooperation in infrastructure, irrespective of their size and level of economic development." SACU already has the Revenue Sharing Formula (RSF), and this formula should be extended to the rest of the SADC area. However, with Malawi and Zimbabwe relying on tariff revenue to a greater extent than others, removing tariffs has eroded the two countries' tax revenue base. With diversity in SADC member states' dependency on national income tariff revenues, creating an FTA was always a challenge for states with smaller economies. These short-term costs include output and potential job losses.

The nature of the resources found in these countries has contributed to the disparities in their economies. SADC (2003b) RISDP acknowledged this challenge when it stated: "The policies and strategies that are adopted for trade, industry, finance, and investment should take into consideration the special needs of less-developed member countries and ensure that a win-win situation prevails." Despite trade liberalisation presenting challenges to SADC member states, governments should not view the loss of customs revenue in isolation without considering the long-term benefits. SADC should attempt to mitigate the short-term effects by creating a safety cushion that could support the countries experiencing adverse effects, as with the SACU. SADC member states should also adopt domestic macro-and microeconomic adjustments that may help cushion this adverse impact. These adjustments may include fiscal discipline and adjustments to the government budget as a short-term solution.

While SADC member states' economic diversity presents an opportunity for mutually beneficial trade driven by each member state's comparative advantage, the region's economic and development gaps have impeded some countries from engaging in trade-driven economic growth. Some member states' poor economic health remains a significant obstacle to the regional integration agenda. Financial constraints have restricted most SADC member states' investments in transport, energy, ICT, and logistics infrastructure to reduce trade costs and make the region attractive to FDI. Establishing a more stable regional economy conducive to long-term investment and development must become one of SADC member states' preconditions. In the SADC region, the small economies and small capital markets have affected the competitiveness of the small emerging industries in these countries' export potential. Unlike in Asian countries' large domestic markets, which allow small industrial sectors to have access to significant economies of scale before pursuing the external export markets, the SADC member states have smaller populations with insignificant purchasing power. The small domestic markets limit the manufacturing industry's potential to grow before pursuing export markets.

From the European experience, sound policies allowed the countries to turn around their economic fortunes. This was achieved through a collective pursuit of shared prosperity. Blizkovsky et al. (2018) argue that the Common Agriculture Policy (CAP) can be a source of policy inspiration for African countries. The policy is relevant for SADC countries to realize their Treaty objectives; as for the Europeans, CAP enhanced the European food supply and improved the welfare of farmers. As a result, European countries could increase agricultural output and reach self-sufficiency by the turn of the 1970s. It wasn't until the 21st century that European countries have started discussing reducing financial support to farmers progressively. From this European experience, it is clear that African agricultural and manufacturing sectors need nurturing to bring them up to speed with the developed world and other emerging economies.

6

Regionalisation, Governance and Political Stability

Introduction

Regional integration occurs only when the states within a region desire it. A triggering political event can often be identified that sets the integration process in motion, whether it is a convergence of political regimes, economic policies, or security issues. African policymakers have long regarded regional integration as a highly desirable goal. Though this is the case, no meaningful steps have been taken in the direction of integration. The smallness of Southern African economies and the notion that numbers are comforting are two of the reasons for the intuitive appeal of regional integration. Thus regional integration institutions have traditionally been perceived as a way to make Southern African economies grow beyond the cons traints of their considerable size, which have hindered their ability to industrialize efficiently, particularly in light of the import-substitution industrialisation path they adopted before the 1980s and 1990s reforms.

For several decades, the appeal for integration has been strong; however, perceptions concerning integration should be pursued differ.

According to Jebuni (1997), macroeconomic reforms in various countries have not produced significant positive outcomes, and domestic policies have not changed despite pursuing preferential trade areas. In some cases, SADC Treaty provisions and agreed norms and values have been completely ignored. Thus, member states and regional institutions have experienced challenges in governance that have contributed to regional instability. As a result, countries will pursue their policy goals at varying paces, resulting in a widening of the economic and political disparities, making harmonisation more difficult.

Economic, social, and political difficulties have plagued the SADC region for some time. SADC governments suffer from a loss of credibility, affecting their ability to mobilise resources to address mounting problems. Integrating the Southern African countries should include more than just trade integration; it should include integrating production and macroeconomic policies and conflict resolution and coordination of policies to ensure democratic governance, human rights, and democratic representation. This chapter looks at the factors that are impeding governance and political convergence.

Contradicting National Interests and Xenophobia

In Waltz's (1979) view, a state's principal objective is to ensure its survival, which is deemed as a national interest. As nationalism grew across Africa, it fuelled calls for emancipation for African people and the subsequent creation of national identities. This legacy has led to the jealously guarded national sovereignty becoming the hallmark of African states. The regional integration process requires a certain degree of sharing of sovereignty. According to Lee (2002), a lack of understanding of national interests has been one of the main obstacles to regional integration. Integration efforts have resulted in greater hostility than unity among countries of the SADC region. In regional debates, the fear of one country dominating the other is always lurking in the shadows. Evidence suggests that SADC member states continue to pursue national interests at the expense of regional objectives.

For SADC to function effectively in its current form, its member states must develop and implement common policies applicable throughout the Southern Africa region. In this regard, the last three decades have been a disappointing period in the Community's history. The character of SADC clearly indicates that regional integration in Southern Africa has failed to coincide with national-focused economic strategies, and this has thwarted efforts to liberalize regional markets. In an effort to combat the import of competing goods into their markets, some member states have instituted national regulations that discriminate against market liberalization. For member states to circumvent existing regional trade agreements, additional barriers have been erected for imports. As a result of the fear of South Africa becoming the dominant state in the region, nations like Zimbabwe have shown resistance to South Africa's domination. A failure of SADC member states to transfer some decision-making powers to the regional body, according to Herbst (2000), means that member states can pursue their national interests without facing any institutional constraints. Often this comes at the cost of obstructing efforts toward regional integration.

Establishing strong regional cooperation is impossible without political cooperation and stability. Due to political and ideological divergences among regional leaders, regional integration has faced challenges. It is generally accepted that more significant regional trade and integration require national policies that support international trade; however, the policies implemented on the national level tend to counterbalance regional policies. From an ideological and political point of view, SADC governments have pursued divergent and sometimes contradictory national interests. Many countries worldwide have put aside their historical differences to negotiate a regional integration initiative that benefits all participants; however, the countries of Southern Africa have failed to overcome their historical disagreements, and trust issues remain a significant problem. Due to historical and ongoing regional tensions within the SADC region regarding foreign policy, security, leadership, and democracy, regional integration has been hampered. As a consequence of the principle of non-interference in the internal affairs of member states, some member states continue to challenge the governance of the regional bloc. The shared experience of liberation movement leaders and leaders of Frontline States has influenced the policies of SADC member states regarding intra-state conflicts.

The interests of national governments and outside influences have also undermined regional agreements. The implementation of regional initiatives occurs when they are coherent with fundamental national interests as they are perceived and defined by the decision-makers in the country and according to domestic political pressures. Integration is easy for leaders to advocate, but ensuring national decision-makers commitment that are operating on the basis of national interests is much more difficult. Although there was consensus across the region regarding tariff reductions, outside forces affected the pace at which member states could implement the trade protocol. As an example, Zambia suspended the implementation of the trade protocol in 2004. Specifically, the country was under a program monitored by the International Monetary Fund (IMF) before Zambia could meet its obligations as a High Indebted Poor Country (HIPC). Moreover, in countries such as Namibia, any proposed changes to tariffs must pass through the national legislative process before they are implemented.

According to Asante (1986), "unlike Europe, where public opinion is what facilitates European integration, integration systems in the SADC region tend to be highly vulnerable to regime changes because the actions of political elites are what sustain integration efforts." Governments earn legitimacy by solving critical social problems. Often, SADC regimes lack legitimacy, which leads to political elites taking more inward-looking policy decisions based on their whims, which undermines regional integration efforts. Furthermore, the leaders are more determined to maintain their power, which inevitably weakens their support for the regional agenda. Vale (2003) states that there is a lack of a real sense of community between states of Southern Africa. Vale argues: "That may again sound... well, mischievous: after all, the region's states claim to be joined in the Southern African Development Community (SADC), and a treaty, protocols, a sense of renewal, and even a few buildings attest to their commitment." While the ruling elites have espoused nationalism, the narrative of Pan-Africanism and solidarity principles has been undermined. Laporte (1995) argues that one of the integration challenges during the first wave of regional integration was that the integration process remained detached from the public's lives, promoting ignorance of regional integration benefits. Mistry (2000) suggests that regional integration has remained an enterprise of the top government officials. SADC leaders have failed to galvanise public support for the integration agenda. Integration initiatives have been confined to the political elite, with the general public excluded from the integration discourse. As a result, popular support for integration has been lacking.

Developing a coalition that supports the regional integration agenda can only be achieved through a bottom-up approach that brings together civil society, the private sector, and other interest groups. According to the Afrobarometer (2016) report, less than 30% of Africans understand the significance of their respective RECs. However, a majority of the citizens support the free movement of people, which could allow people to work and trade in their regional neighbours. This only demonstrates that African people enjoy the benefits of regional integration, although they lack proper knowledge about the integration processes. SADC National Committees should be strengthened and involve the active participation of all sectors of the society so that the regional objectives reflect the interests of the public, not just those of the state actors.

The historical legacy of the struggle against racial inequality and the rule of the white minority has contributed to the development of these distinct competing interests. For regional blocs that have integrated, people, goods, and services move freely across the borders. It is, however, important to note that even though protocols and agreements exist for unrestricted movement, the movement of people, goods, and services remains a challenge within the SADC region. For instance, on paper, the South African government appears to have undermined regional obligations by failing to support the regional industrialisation strategy due to domestic labour market pressures resulting from high unemployment. With the ANC government benefiting from union support, the South African government has been forced to protect its markets due to domestic political pressures. The political leadership of the SADC region has failed to promote regional integration among its citizens for many years. Several misconceptions about the regional project have undermined the efforts to create a collective regional identity and foster a sense of brotherhood among the people. Much ignorance exists amongst the regional population, and as a result, shared rules and norms are being undermined.

Several populist leaders within the ANC have tried to gain political support by promoting anti-immigrant rhetoric. Recent years have seen increased anti-immigrant sentiment among a broad cross-section of social, economic, and political groups. A restrictive and discriminatory immigration policy in South Africa has increased xenophobia. Limited employment opportunities, resources, and business opportunities have caused hostility towards migrants influenced by this toxic rhetoric. As a result of xenophobic violence in South Africa, hundreds of immigrants have been killed and their property destroyed. As long as the dangerously divisive rhetoric persists, there will be hostility among Africans in the region. According to Heleta (2019), South Africa's deputy police minister made unfounded allegations in 2017 when he suggested that foreigners had taken control of the country's biggest city Johannesburg and that the entire country "could be 80% dominated by foreign nationals and the future president of South Africa could be a foreign national." These xenophobic sentiments have exacerbated nationalist views growing across the SADC region, with xenophobic attacks in South Africa spurring reprisals across Africa. In December 2018, protesters in the DRC destroyed the window of a South African consulate in Lubumbashi. Nigeria went as far as recalling its High Commissioner from South Africa.

Economic and market integration involves overcoming this type of resistance to the integration scheme, which politicians sometimes amplify. A robust regional community that can improve citizen welfare depends on a robust regional integration process that provides opportunities for collective learning. In the past decade, xenophobia has displayed an inhumane disregard for human life and threatened to destroy the tradition of brotherhood in the SADC region and the continent in general. Among the goals of post-colonial Africa, Okem and Asuelime (2015) argue, is the integration of disparate countries across the continent. Among the attempts to achieve unification of the continent is the creation of the OAU, which has later become the AU and pertains to the sub-regional bodies. Nationalism and xenophobia are incompatible with the principles of economic integration since, without the free movement of people, goods, and services, the whole purpose of integration is defeated. A regional community is unlikely to succeed in an environment where nationalist and populist views are encouraged among citizens. Due to SADC's inability to deliver tangible results to the average citizen, politicians will continue to exploit the people's grievances in countries such as South Africa and Botswana as marginalized workers from the poorer African countries move to the richer countries.

Initially, the rise of nationalism in Africa led many Southern African people to seek independence from European colonial powers and white minority regimes. As a result, national identities were created, and every country exercised and protected its national sovereignty. At the same time, Southern Africa's longstanding vision has been for a united, peaceful, and integrated region. Sadly, the legacy of fiercely guarded national sovereignty is becoming a hindrance to regional integration.

Even though SADC leaders have actively promoted integration at the summit level, little emphasis has been placed on ensuring that citizens across the region understand the significance of cooperative efforts among member states. Despite Zimbabwe, South Africa, Namibia, Angola, and Mozambique benefitting from the support they received from their regional counterparts during the liberation movement, increased incidents of xenophobia against foreigners in the region have exposed the process' shortcomings.

Land concerns among the African population are legitimate; however, political leaders have taken advantage of these challenges and weaponized land issues that have resulted in the violent occupation of white-owned farms in Zimbabwe without following internationally accepted legal procedures. Even though SADC legal instruments attempted to address this issue through the SADC Tribunal, the regional body could not enforce the dispute resolutions, allowing the Zimbabwean regime to pursue actions deemed illegal by the SADC Tribunal. Therefore, Zimbabwe blocked the SADC Tribunal's functions even though the Tribunal was established to improve SADC processes in a rules-based manner (Erasmus,2012). Due to this, the Zimbabwean government has avoided legitimately redistributing land for almost 20 years, causing the economy to collapse.

In almost all SADC countries, just like in Zimbabwe, populist decisions have been implemented to excite the population and gain political support at the expense of preserving the unity of all of the people within the region. By failing to address xenophobia, regional integration efforts could be negatively affected, and leaders must take responsibility for taking advantage of people's anxieties and mistrust for political gain. SADC citizens have a diminished sense of belonging to the regional community because they lack information regarding some of member states' basic agreements and obligations. In the opinion of the SADC political elite, the question has never been whether the countries should pursue regional integration; there is broad consensus on this topic. Currently, the biggest challenge is effectively implementing the protocols, policies and adhering to the SADC Treaty to enhance trade, market, security, and political integration. Regional leaders must demonstrate political will, coherence, and commitment to effectively nurture regional integration in the SADC region and realise their long-held regional aspirations and vision for prosperity and stability. Such commitment should begin at the national level, where all aspects of integration are promoted, embraced, and citizen participation is encouraged to legitimize the process. In addition, there must also be a willingness to accommodate necessary compromises about national sovereignty, to surrender certain aspects of national sovereignty for the benefit of the regional community. Additionally, political will allow for predictability and consistency of decision-making processes committed to regional integration instead of nationalistic policies currently being implemented.

It is evident that SADC has failed to demonstrate an economic rationale and that member states have failed to sell the regional project to their citizens, which has hampered its acceptance. As a consequence of the lack of citizen engagement in the regional project and its aspirations, regional social cohesion has been undermined, resulting in regional instability. SADC member states must develop consensus on a people-to-people integration approach and promote free movement of people as part of the regional integration process. Therefore, governments, civil society organizations, policymakers, the private sector, and other stakeholders need to have serious policy conversations on the fundamentals of regionalism and how this can positively affect regional economic growth. Most xenophobic attacks occur in more impoverished areas, so community-based approaches to conflict management are needed, along with an early warning system that helps identify sources of potential conflicts at the earliest stage of their development and implement countermeasures to mitigate them. According to Okem and Asuelime (2015), SADC integration can only be realized if the issue of xenophobia is acknowledged and dealt with. If this is not done, the vision of the continent's integration could become just another intellectual and elitist fantasy.

Inter-State Rivalries and Animosity

In addition to the complex political and economic relationships among individual countries, other factors have also harmed regional integration. As a result of South Africa's efforts to destabilize the Frontline States, the region had suffered greatly. As a result of these historical factors discussed in detail in Chapters 3 and 4, it appears that tensions exist between member states and between member state interests. Some aspects of these complex relationships have remained dynamic, primarily regarding how the region's leadership views integration. After Apartheid ended, there was an opportunity for Southern African states to move away from the hostility that characterised relations between states, resulting in hostility between the Frontline States and Apartheid South Africa and its ally Malawi. When assessing the strategic objectives of SADC member states, the region faces inherent differences in its political and economic structures. Similarly, there have been mixed feelings regarding the liberation movement legacy and how it has affected closer cooperation. Finally, the historical foreign policies and ideological differences that pitted some of the SADC countries against each other in the past have resulted in inherent mistrust, which has hindered cooperation.

These differences have hindered any attempts to improve relations. Malawi's past relationship with Apartheid South Africa almost led to a military confrontation between the country and the Frontline States. Several days before Samora Machel's death, he threatened to launch ballistic missiles into Malawi if Malawi continued to support RENAMO rebels. In 1986, after the death of Samora Machel, demonstrators attacked Malawian embassies in Zimbabwe and Mozambique, accusing Malawi of assisting South Africa in the alleged assassination of the president of Mozambique. Significantly, these differences have continued to influence bilateral and multilateral discussions.

In SADC, divisions have affected the political and economic entity, impacting integration progress. As a result of serious internal divisions among member states that hardly reflect in their official communications, SADC has become a battleground for regional politics rather than a place for integration which could reshape regional economic and socio-political fortunes. As a result of disputes and bickering among member states, the establishment of SADC served to increase Southern African fragmentation. The liberation legacy and colonial history continue to influence regional relations for several complex reasons. Examining the relationship between the original Frontline States members and the relationship between their leaders, we can see how they have maintained a closer relationship. For instance, Zimbabwean, Mozambican, and South African leaders have had more intimate relations, while Mozambique harbours negative feelings towards Malawi. Resentment toward Malawi stems from its historical decision to strengthen ties with the Apartheid regime, examined extensively in Chapter 4.

As a result of its colourful history, Malawi is viewed with suspicion by its peers and has continued to fuel mistrust. It has been found that the failure to resolve historical differences among member states has negatively affected regional integration and relations. Despite the hypothesis that comprehensive regional integration may assist in resolving interstate and intrastate conflicts, such an assumption is simplistic if we ignore the complex unresolved historical factors that guide these relationships. The International Crisis Group (ICG) takes a more critical view by suggesting that "insistence on a regional approach ignores that the five states have taken very different political and economic routes since independence and have different needs and priorities...to approach regional cooperation issues without taking account of political realities would yield nothing." Despite the public display of elite solidarity among regional leaders, there are inherent differences in opinion regarding what SADC should look like. Despite the reduced hostilities among member states compared to the 1980s, there is still a lack of a shared identity, vision, and mutual trust resulting from the turbulent history, political divergence, and economic differences. There is a difference between regional cooperation and regional integration, and according to Schiff and Winters (2002), countries may be unwilling to cooperate due to national pride, political tensions and a lack of trust. According to Wendy (1999), when states interact with each other, they bring their needs into these interactions: security, autonomy, economic welfare, and collective self-esteem. Although none of these needs is inherently egoistic, actors will resist acquiring identities that conflict with their own.

During the past three decades, regional relations between SADC member states have fluctuated between warmer and cooler depending on the issue at hand. Generally speaking, disagreements have resulted from mistrust and resentment among member states and how some member states have responded to internal conflicts within their states. Additionally, these differences have become more pronounced as new leadership disassociated from the liberation legacy challenges the self-imposed statesmen in the region. The diverse governance systems of states in Southern Africa, ranging from democratic to authoritarian, obstruct efforts to bring the states together due to their self-serving interests. A group of so-called statesmen from the liberation struggle also seek to become the regional bloc's custodians. Currently, South Africa has failed to deal with the Zimbabwean crisis under the leadership of the ANC freedom fighters. A sense of debt exists between the South African leadership and the Zimbabwean government due to the Zimbabwean government's assistance provided to the ANC. Against this background, the Zimbabwean elites have assumed the position of custodians of the regional bloc.

There are now new rivalries between SADC members as a result of the admission of ANC-led South Africa. As the longest-serving leader in the region, Robert Mugabe attempted to challenge South Africa's influence. This resulted in hostile relations between Nelson Mandela and Mugabe. As a result of this discontent, mainly concerning regional security and foreign policy, further divisions developed between the two leaders. In discussions concerning creating the SADC Organ on Politics, Defence, and Security (OPDS), a progressively integrated security instrument, Mandela argued that it should fall under the Summit. At the same time, Mugabe wished that the Organ remain independent from the Summit and that he assume leadership of the Organ. Due to confusion and lack of unity in regional security matters, the SADC responded to the conflict in the DRC in a divided manner. Under the Mutual Defence Pact that the three countries had signed, Zimbabwe deployed troops to the DRC with support from Angola and Namibia.

In contrast, the new generation of leaders, especially in Botswana, have embraced a more democratic stance and challenged authoritarian regimes led by so-called liberation statesmen. In the past two decades, relations between Zimbabwe and Botswana have also deteriorated due to the influx of illegal immigrants and refugees from Zimbabwe into Botswana and the spread of foot and mouth disease. This led Botswana to construct a high fence across its border with Zimbabwe. Botswana has also taken a hardline stance towards the Zimbabwean regime, where Zimbabwe's leadership has been blamed for the country's political and economic instability. Former Botswanan President Ian Khama publicly criticized the 2008 Zimbabwe elections, denouncing the former Zimbabwean president Robert Mugabe for being repressive and calling for internationally supervised elections.

Furthermore, Zambia and Tanzania also expressed their opposition to the elections, despite the rest of SADC adopting the principle of solidarity and non-interference in a more subdued manner. The relationship between Botswana and Zimbabwe nearly divided SADC into two blocs, the countries led by the liberation parties on the one hand and the countries led by the post-liberation parties on the other. South Africa's lack of leadership in this dispute worsened the country's attempt to associate with both sides. Wendt (1999) argues that regional integration can only succeed when regional discourse is driven by a shared appreciation of regional challenges that require deeper regional integration, which has not been the case in the SADC region.

Nathan (2012) observes that the biggest problem associated with the absence of trust and shared values embedded in SADC member states is prioritising solidarity with the regimes. The collective response of SADC member states to conflicts and disputes within their member states has been characterised by solidarity and non-interference. However, states have taken a different direction, as in Botswana's case, they have been accused of conspiring with the West to overthrow Zimbabwe's government and undermine the liberation struggle. There is no doubt that critical issues concerning governance and development remain unresolved within the SADC region. These issues continue to impede the region's integration efforts. Regional efforts to achieve critical regional integration goals have been hampered by the absence of good governance and the pursuit of absolute sovereignty. This, in turn, has resulted in the SADC region maintaining a low level of integration and development among the world's major regional organizations.

Relationships between South Africa and its regional neighbours have also been affected by negative perceptions of the country's past. The signing of a trade agreement between South Africa and the European Union and its involvement in the BRICS group has undermined its relations with SADC member states. The near-permanent differences in infrastructure and economic power in the region have also led some regional members to be suspicious of South Africa. As South Africa contributes over 60% of the regional GDP and has a large and diverse manufacturing sector, there is concern that SADC would widen the economic gap between member states rather than narrow it.

In the 1960s, 1970s and 1980s, neighbourly hostilities occurred in the SADC region due to unaligned foreign policies, which resulted in regional governments adopting foreign policies that pitted neighbours against each other. It was evident how the Southern African governments handled the white minority governments and the liberation movements. For the region's member states to promote collective commitments to the continent and global community, they must establish common foreign policy guidelines. The SADC Organ for Politics, Defence and Security recognizes the need for member states to develop a common foreign policy and a joint international lobby on matters of common interest. Despite this, SADC member states have continued to pursue contradictory foreign policies, which have posed a challenge to regional relations. Malawi, for example, announced its intention to open a diplomatic mission in Jerusalem, Israel. This is contrary to SADC's continual support for a settlement based on internationally recognised boundaries that place Jerusalem and other surrounding areas under Corpus Separatum. According to the UN plan, Jerusalem is placed under an international regime until Israelis and Palestinians reach other agreements. The opening of an embassy in Jerusalem is prohibited by international law under this arrangement.

The member states of SADC must recognize that long-term factors support the logic of cooperation in the region. As a result of historical grievances and contemporary differences, the region faces challenging circumstances. The region will likely experience low economic growth and political instability as long as these constraints persist, which will pose a challenge to regional integration. Some regional challenges, such as fragmented markets, poverty, inadequate infrastructure and political instability in the SADC region, support the logic of deeper economic and political integration.

A great deal of the politics, security and economic dynamics in SADC are shaped by shared identities derived from colonial and liberation legacies. Based upon this shared history, a broader regional integration scheme can be established on a cross-border basis. At the same time, the shared history has also offered SADC political elites opportunities and challenges to build an integrated regional community. Political elites have instead created a new pact of loyalty that benefits only those in power at the expense of ordinary citizens. Despite the growing mistrust among member states of SADC, the neutrality of the SADC Secretariat must be seen as a vehicle serving the interests of all members.

FAILURE OF COLLECTIVE MECHANISMS FOR ACCOUNTABILITY AND COMPLIANCE

While SADC adopted institutional structures that resemble the European Union, in practice, SADC continues to function on an ad hoc basis, with frequent personal relations among the political elites. According to the 1992 treaty defining the SADC, the objectives are more comprehensive than just economic and market integration. Its purpose is to promote common political values, systems, and institutions throughout Southern Africa. SADC has an obligation and mandate to introduce positive changes to enhance good governance and socio-economic development through democratic consolidation and accountability. Making community laws legally enforceable across all member states has been one of the critical challenges of regional integration. The community laws include treaty agreements, protocols, principles, objectives, and regulations. The institution possesses limited powers delegated by the member states, and failure to enforce these community laws undermines the effectiveness of any regional integration agenda. SADC and other regional organizations have a vested interest in ensuring that all member states observe community laws. SADC's success is dependent on member states' willingness to adhere to regional protocols, treaties, and other regional agreements. In the SADC region, member states tend to be reluctant to delegate far-reaching decision-making authority to a regional institution. The member states intentionally enforce community laws less effectively, and the institutional framework has been silent on the matter.

The most striking thing is that many African states taking part in regional integration programs are concerned about a deeper regional agenda fearing losing sovereignty to a regional integration body. There has been some reticence on the part of SADC members to make the regional body supranational. Even when there are instruments for dispute settlement, these instruments are seldom used, and SADC decisions are sometimes ignored. Regional institutions can only be as effective as their members' commitment to respect and adhere to the organization's norms, rules, and regulations. An institution's decision-making mechanism demonstrates its ability to serve the interests of the region or individual members. SADC adheres to the principle of unanimity, which prevents member states from being forced to make decisions without their consent. According to Erasmus (2011), the SADC decision-making process prevents member states that violate the SADC Treaty from being penalized. Hence, every state has the right to veto any potential sanctions that could be imposed for their violations.

In contrast, European countries have enacted fundamental constitutional changes as part of the legal requirements for becoming members of the European Union. Deliberate efforts have been made to transfer certain powers to the EU as part of their accession to EU treaties. The European Parliament was directly elected in 1979, and over the years, has demonstrated its ability to act as a separate political institution, independent of national influences. It is critical for the successful functioning of the EU that the institutions of the EU demonstrate the European institution's status as an independent actor on the international stage. As a result, the EU can articulate and aggregate their member states' interests without falling foul of obstructionist interests with respect to individual states.

From a historical perspective, some African countries introduced constitutional provisions designed to reinforce the integration of their states after independence. Many African states' post-independence constitutions included legally binding provisions suggesting that national sovereignty may be ultimately surrendered to facilitate regional integration. For example, Article 13 of the Ghanaian Constitution (1960) stipulated that "the independence of Ghana should not be surrendered or diminished on any ground other than the furtherance of African unity." Similarly, Article 34 of the 1958 Constitution of the Republic of Guinea provided that "the Republic may conclude with any African State agreements providing for an association or establishing a community and involving partial or total relinquishment of Sovereignty with a view to the achievements of African unity." Schwelb (1960) documented similar provisions in other countries.

It is somewhat ironic that, against the backdrop of these early constitutional provisions in Africa, African states have become more protective of state sovereignty and the state's inalienable right to independent existence. Most of these provisions are no longer present in most African states' constitutions, including those of countries that advocated unification, such as Ghana. It speaks volumes about the national commitment to integration in Africa, as most African constitutions nowadays pay little attention to regional integration requirements and, sometimes, contradict community objectives.

SADC member states have acted opposite to the view held by some scholars that states are rational actors whose compliance with community laws is motivated by their shared objectives. Talberg (2002) argues that "states' interests may include signature, but not compliance." SADC's decision-making structure gives too much power to heads of governments that are more driven by their self-interests, which sometimes go against the SADC's shared values and objectives. According to Sundaram (2006), "SADC has successfully built inter-state and government-to-government solidarity. This solidarity has been spurred by the liberation struggle and has created a strong Southern African identity only among the governing elites, albeit not amongst the region's peoples." Looking at the performance of SADC over the past three decades, it is fair to conclude that the institution has failed to serve the citizens' interests and instead appears to favour the interests of the political elite. Therefore, it has become a challenge to discourage and tame non-compliance by member states. The Amended SADC Treaty, Article 6:1 states that "Member states undertake to adopt adequate measures to promote achieving the objectives of SADC." The Article also states that member states "shall refrain from taking any measure likely to jeopardize the sustenance of its principles, the achievement of its objectives and the implementation of the provisions of this Treaty." However, the treaty is silent on the actual powers and authority of SADC.

SADC's consensus-based decision-making process has been criticized as flawed and has proven difficult in dealing with contentious issues. A decision-making system based on absolute sovereignty is in place. No country should oppose any decision made, regardless of the country in question is responsible for any infringement of their treaty obligations. In general, African governments prefer consensus decisions because their interests are protected. Nonetheless, they have given authoritarian regimes an escape route from scrutiny or accountability. Those who support consensus decision-making argue that this process has prevented other states from imposing their decisions upon other member states. Laporte (1995) reinforces this argument by suggesting that fear of political leaders losing political sovereignty is one of the reasons often seen as limiting possibilities of successful regional integration. Therefore, they have viewed consensus as a means to guarantee those collective decisions are owned by all member states and prevent discomfort from majority decisions. Dirar (2014) argues that "consensus decision making is a manifestation of consensus of non-enforcement among SADC countries with a treaty obligation." This view is also shared by Nathan (2014), who argues that self-determination takes precedence over regional efforts.

Furthermore, Gathii (2011) added to the debate by arguing that African regional integration treaties are "flexible by design and practice." Dirar (2014) perceives non-enforcement of Southern African integration schemes as a deliberate effort to subterfuge treaty obligations through political relations. Due to this, consensus-based decision-making processes have also handed a great deal of power and influence to member states, undermining efforts to adopt fundamental changes. Furthermore, sovereign equality among states provides equal voting power to all SADC member states. Concurrent national demands result in a complex decision-making process that exposes the limits of its decision-making process.

Consequently, Rotich (2012) asserts, "decision making by consensus means that the slowest member dictates the pace of integration." This implies that SADC member states use consensus decision-making to protect their sovereignty, and authoritarian regimes remain unchallenged. It is not a mistake to suggest that consensus of non-enforcement is equivalent to the discourse of lack of political will in this situation.

Among the difficulties associated with regional integration are relationships formed during liberation struggles. During the Zimbabwe political crisis, Gevisser (2007) argued that the relationship between Thabo Mbeki and Robert Mugabe impacted South Africa's handling of the situation. Accountability has been absent among member states due to the existing solidarity norms. In the absence of accountability for human rights violations and poor governance, authoritarian leaders have remained unchallenged when they break regionally agreed norms. SADC member states have refused to pressure the Zimbabwean regime to institute tangible economic and political reforms under the pretext of respecting Zimbabwe's national sovereignty. SADC has endorsed flawed Zimbabwean elections for the past two decades, and its leaders have avoided enforcing the already adopted election code. As SADC has effectively lost its hold on regional norms and values, it cannot harmonize democratic governance, which is necessary for regional stability and economic development.

The SADC Tribunal presents an excellent example of SADC member states' reluctance to embrace regional accountability. As part of SADC's 1992 Treaty, the SADC Tribunal was established under Article 9 and became operational in 2005. This was seen as one of SADC's significant achievements because it provided an environment where law and jurisprudence could be developed and enforced. Article 18 of the SADC Protocol on the Tribunal's Rules of Procedure reads: "Subject to Article 14 of this Protocol, the Tribunal shall have exclusive jurisdiction over all disputes between natural or legal persons and the Community. Such disputes may be referred to the Tribunal, either by the natural or legal person concerned or by the Community's competent institution or organ."

In addition, Article 24(3) of the Protocol provides that the Tribunal's decisions and rulings are final and binding. Although the SADC Tribunal was initially welcomed as a viable instrument, its popularity began to wane as the mandate began to be tested. SADC governments felt threatened by the Tribunal and considered its mandate an affront to their jealously guarded sovereignty, which led to disagreements over its composition and functions among member states. An institution that initially seemed to unify the region and make strides towards regional integration exposed a set of protectionist challenges associated with accepting a jurisdiction outside member states' territories.

The Tribunal received its first cases in 2007, and one of the cases was related to the ongoing land reform and redistribution scheme in Zimbabwe. *Campbell vs the Republic of Zimbabwe*, a case concerning Zimbabwe commercial farmers, stood out. Member states were tested in the case on their willingness to surrender some form of sovereignty to an external body and be held accountable. Mike Campbell Limited, a Zimbabwean farming company, filed a lawsuit against the Zimbabwean government challenging its land seizure. According to the complainant, the Zimbabwean government's racially motivated land acquisition was illegal under SADC Treaty Article 4. Among other things, the article states that all SADC member states must adhere to human rights principles, democracy, the rule of law, equity, balance, mutual benefit, and a peaceful resolution of disputes. According to Article 6 (2) of the SADC Treaty, SADC member states shall not discriminate based on gender, religion, political views, race, ethnic origin, culture, or disability. As the SADC Tribunal evaluated this complaint, the Zimbabwean Supreme Court was also considering the case, with a final ruling pending.

Temporary relief was granted by the Tribunal to the complainants in December 2007, allowing the Campbell family to remain on his farm until the final ruling. An appeal filed by the plaintiff was dismissed by the Zimbabwean Supreme Court in January 2008, before the Tribunal's decision. The following day, the Zimbabwean government announced that it was seizing the farm, even though the final ruling of the Tribunal had not yet been delivered and was scheduled for July 2008. Campbell and his family members were attacked on their farm and forced to sign papers withdrawing the Tribunal's case. In an urgent application before the Tribunal, the Campbell family accused the Zimbabwean government of contempt of the Tribunal's orders. A few days later, the Tribunal ruled in favour of the farmers after finding the Zimbabwean government contemptuous. Thus, the Tribunal reported the matter to the SADC Summit so that the leaders could take appropriate action. The

Zimbabwean government contested the ruling and campaigned for the suspension of the Tribunal.

Zimbabwe's refusal to abide by the ruling on human rights violations and its subsequent withdrawal from the Tribunal challenged SADC's integration ambitions. It tested the independence and efficacy of the regional court. Zimbabwe's failure to comply with some of the institution's provisions proved that the regional bloc could not enforce its provisions. Having a member state get away with such violations exposed SADC's weaknesses. As mandated by SADC's Treaty, the SADC Tribunal is the regional body's court of law responsible for interpreting the SADC Treaty. The SADC Tribunal, which had presented itself as a regional instrument allowing citizens' recourse to justice against their repressive governments, was thus put to the test. As an incentive to protect their future individual interests, the judges' contracts making up the Tribunal were not renewed, leading to a de facto suspension of the Tribunal. As a result of the dissolution of SADC's tribunal, it was evident that SADC's instruments are not independent and can be bullied by Summit leaders.

The event also highlights how any potential loss of sovereignty to a supranational institution thwarts the integration agenda. The SADC Summit in 2014 stripped the Tribunal of its mandate on human rights and people's rights by repressive measures against the wishes of an array of civil society organizations and interest groups. Later, the Tribunal mandate was reviewed and amended to address only interstate disputes. The restructuring process of the Tribunal thus restricted the Tribunal's domain of interpretation to interpreting the SADC Treaty and Protocols relating to disputes between member states. The Tribunal could no longer receive complaints from individuals and organizations in this case.

The Tribunal debacle illustrates how SADC's ability to promote democratic values and governance standards has failed. As Zimbabwe was being subjected to diplomatic campaigns and sanctions for failing to adhere to international standards and human rights, its regional neighbours actively supported the country. According to Gray (2013), "it was not in the interest of any of the member states to override those objections, since such a court ruling would have potentially compromised them." Countries like South Africa and Namibia shared the same characteristics as Zimbabwe due to their large settler population. South Africa, for instance, retains 84% of its agricultural land under white ownership, despite its white population being only 5%. Fewer than 4,000 white commercial farmers own more than 80% of agricultural land in

Namibia. In this context, the land issue made some SADC member state countries uncomfortable since they were also experiencing similar resource distribution and land redistribution challenges. Across the region, populist politicians supported the land redistribution exercise in Zimbabwe due to socio-economic imbalances based on race.

Rather than strongly criticizing the Zimbabwean government for alleged violations of the SADC Treaty, the South African government and most of the SADC member states reacted with caution and, in most cases, appeared to support such violations by Zimbabwe. Schoeman and Alden (2003) observe that former South African President Thabo Mbeki advocated constructive engagement. He sought to encourage Mugabe privately to pursue reforms while publicly proclaiming support for his government's efforts. Except for Botswana, all the SADC members remained silent. Any challenge to the authority of the liberation leaders by any African leader is handled with sensitivity, and those responsible are accused of serving Western interests. The struggle against the white minority governments and colonialists has pushed Southern African leaders to defend one another. Due to insecurity and paranoia, SADC leaders are reluctant to cede control of their states to the regional body.

In addition to the SADC Tribunal controversy, SADC also has an excellent electoral instrument called the SADC Principles and Guidelines Governing Democratic Elections. This instrument was created to provide a space for free and fair elections across the SADC region. Although all SADC member states have committed to democratic elections, the countries have not consistently followed regional electoral norms. Thus, SADC member states continue to experience electoral disputes, whose outcomes are usually recognized as fair, credible, and free by the regional body. Since this instrument's inception, there have been electoral disputes in Zimbabwe, Malawi, Lesotho, Mozambique, Angola, and the DRC. SADC has failed to hold most of the perpetrators accountable, as expected.

As a result of SADC's sovereign equality and non-interference principle, there is a degree of disunity within the organization. Whether the decisions of the SADC Summit are binding and whether SADC can enforce these agreements is not addressed in the SADC Treaty. The silence regarding the treaty enforcement has left ambiguity regarding the authority of the regional body. In the revised SADC Treaty of 2001, sanctions are permitted as a means of enforcing compliance, although the mechanisms have rarely been used. As a result SADC has been left weakened and unable to enforce compliance.

Because of the region's recent colonial history, and since some of Africa's youngest nations are still governed by liberation parties, most SADC region leaders are reluctant to sacrifice their sovereignty and prerogative to an autonomous regional body. As a result, regional institutions have been transformed into fora where political leaders reinforce their sovereignty's external legitimacy, with most leaders losing their legitimacy to govern at home. SADC states are still hesitant to transfer sovereignty to other organizations as they seem to be sceptical, apprehensive, and feel threatened by external power structures, according to Franke (2008). As evidenced mainly by liberation movements that now rule in some SADC states, a fixation on national sovereignty has hampered progress on building democratic governance and accountability structures.

SADC's current governance environment has limited economic growth, increased socio-economic inequality, and created less transparency in its governance processes. Members of SADC have opted for a business-as-usual mentality, with little appetite to make effective changes. Additionally, globalization has led to a greater degree of competition on the global market, which has exacerbated the socio-economic decline in the region. As a result, less organized government systems have been slow to catch up with the rest of the world, and in some cases, Southern Africa has fallen far behind the development race. The current socio-political crisis will continue to impede economic progress unless a more ambitious approach is taken.

Diverse Political Systems, Leadership, Liberation Movement and Colonial Legacy

Democracy remains a principal prerequisite for development, peace, and stability. Similarly, it is impossible to achieve peace and development in a conflict environment. That is why political convergence is a fundamental feature for the success of any regional integration agenda. Over the past three decades, REC treaties have adopted democracy clauses, where democracy and political stability have been recognised as a necessary condition for enhancing regional integration. This new requirement has influenced RECs to adopt political objectives ranging from:

(i) Enhancing common political values and governance systems;
(ii) Strengthening democratic institutions; and
(iii) Consolidating peace, security, and stability across the region.

Genna and Hiroi (2015) argue that democracy clauses in RECs provide another layer of protection for promoting and defending democratic norms and good governance institutions across the regional bloc, which is beneficial for member states to enhance their transparency and credibility. A democratic institution is essential for establishing and consolidating a political leadership culture that is accountable, transparent, and unafraid to exercise its leadership functions instead of being motivated by safeguarding a few groups' interests. Bryson and Crosby (1992) defined leadership as the act of inspiring and mobilizing others to take collective action for the common good. From this perspective, political leadership in most African countries is rarely associated with the pursuit of the common good. In contrast, African political elites increasingly see democracy as a continuation of neo-colonialism, which they view as a threat. Crocker (2019) argues that in most African countries, "the rule of law is in competition with the rule of men." The Freedom House (2018) identified a pattern of democratic governance decline in Africa, with 7 out of 12 worst scores for political rights and civil liberties coming from Africa. The reasons for this decline varied from:

(i) Patrimonialism gone wrong (the 'big man's problem);
(ii) Extreme state fragility and endemic conflict risks; and
(iii) The perverse mobilization of ethnicity by weak or threatened leaders.

Consolidation of democratic values, good governance, the rule of law, and respect for human rights has become one area of focus for cooperation in the SADC political area. These norms and values are enshrined in the SADC Treaty agreements and protocols. Regional integration should strengthen political systems and improve the decision-making capacities of regional bodies under normal circumstances. Diverse political systems within the SADC bloc complicate national and regional structures and negatively impact regional integration. In terms of governance structures, SADC member states are at different stages of political development. At the rhetorical level, SADC member states have all endorsed integration narratives that promote democracy, good governance, respect for the rule of law, and human rights.

The reality is that some agreements and protocols have faced resistance, resulting in a governance deficit. As a result, some SADC member states are experiencing a decline in democracy, while authoritarian regimes and personal rule govern countries like Swaziland. Cawthra (2008) pointed out that SADC member states have kept authoritarian traditions where the ruling parties are supreme. This has been exacerbated in countries where liberation movements and ruling parties under a one-party system are still in power. This character of governance originates from the liberation struggle, where, according to Adolfo (2009), the internal practices of the liberation movements during the liberation struggle were undemocratic. As Dubell (1998) argues, the post-colonial liberation parties in power have adopted these undemocratic practices by showing intolerance to criticism in the public domain, where any criticism is construed as betrayal or disloyalty. Due to the inherent authoritarian tendencies of the liberation parties, some SADC regimes have taken steps to contribute to the continued decline of democracy in the region. For instance, the regimes have used the state's coercive instruments like the military and police to monopolise power and safeguard the regimes' survival, making any possible democratic transition difficult. These coercive instruments have also been used to promote the political elites' economic interests, with most SADC regimes using similar coercive governance techniques to consolidate power. Most SADC countries retain democratic structures, such as the legislature and judiciary, which provide checks and balances to the government executive arm. However, these government arms remain weak, with consequential power mostly concentrated in the executive arm.

Scholars of regional integration generally agree that integration can only succeed if the economies integrate and the political systems adopt a common identity, or what is referred to as political convergence. Peters (2010) defined political democratic convergence (PDC) as "the collective process within a regional integration body working towards the adoption and practice of higher degrees of democracy at the national level. PDC ensures that there are similar political and economic conditions in all member states, which leads to predictability across all member states. In Peters's (2010) view, the less democratic or autocratic a state is, the less predictable it is to apply the rule of law, stabilize its regime, and provide economic development impetus to the regional integration project.

Figure 4.8: Freedom House Survey 2019

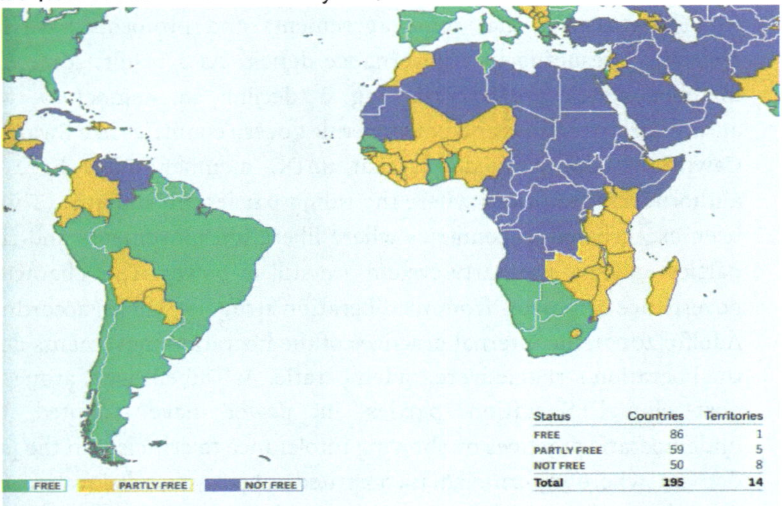

Source: Freedom House (2019)

Authoritarian governments are not interested in an effective regional institution based on democratic principles, Nathan (2002) argues. As a result, governments are reluctant to cede their political powers to SADC as the region has not yet reached political convergence. For Nathan, "SADC member states are not willing to be governed by an independent forum whose decisions are binding on all member states" That has led to political leaders being reluctant to turn their regional commitments into domestic policy. In Malamud and Schmitter (2006), they identified three factors that contribute to the success of regional integration:

(i) Only governments with strong legitimacy within their respective national societies can make credible commitments necessary for them to enter into agreements, ratify them conclusively, and monitor their eventual implementation.
(ii) The presence of a democratically accountable government within all members is a supplementary assurance that none

of them will resort to force in resolving disputes. Moreover, whatever temptations more powerful governments might have to extract concessions by threatening weaker recalcitrant members, it seems unlikely that its citizens would support this.

(iii) If the neo-functionalists are right, a key element driving the integration process forward will be the formation of transnational interest associations and social movements and their intervention in supranational policy-making. Only in national democracies will citizens have the freedoms needed to organize collective action forms and create links with others across national borders.

Historical factors contribute to these differences in political systems among SADC member states. As a result of regional cooperation forged during the liberation struggle, freedom fighters have attempted to claim the right to rule and go to extreme lengths to consolidate their power. As a result, the 2019 Freedom House Survey of political rights and civil liberties classified the SADC member states in three different categories: Botswana, Mauritius, Namibia, and South Africa were classified as "free"; Malawi, Mozambique, Tanzania, Seychelles, Zimbabwe, and Zambia as "partly free"; with Angola, the DRC, and Swaziland classified as "not free." Although some people might argue against how some of the member states were classified, we can all agree that there is a considerable difference between member states concerning people's enjoyment of political rights and civil liberties.

Institutional weaknesses in the Southern African region remain a cause for concern for governance in the region. By building effective governance systems within nation-states, effective regional bodies can be established. Good governance and democracy are vital for the regional integration agenda in SADC, and member states cannot ignore their importance. The regional integration process requires member states to adopt sound governance principles and democratic values to implement protocols, agreements, declarations, and policies. Habib et al. (2006) argue that: "These norms are critical to deepening integration further... Africa will unite faster if Africans embark on democratization drives and create democratic institutions based on the logic of the self-empowerment of the people on the foundation of an effective and engaged state-civil society nexus." The biggest challenge in Africa is that the citizens continue to be excluded on regional integration issues. The exclusion of citizens in integration processes has become more pronounced in discussions of nationalism and xenophobia that have become rampant over the past decade.

The integration of regional states must be based on democratic culture and practices that respect the highest democratic standards in its member states. Yet, governance deficits are a fundamental reason for instability and failure to develop both on the African continent and in the SADC region. In addition, corruption and rent-seeking have siphoned off resources that could have been diverted to education, health, and infrastructure development, which undermines governments' ability to provide public services. Diamond (2005) argues that corruption constitutes an egregious violation of human rights in the following ways by:

(i) Preventing the full realization of economic, social, and cultural rights as well as political and civil rights by sucking out public resources into private hands
(ii) Perpetuating discrimination against the most impoverished class of society.

Most Southern African nations have maintained a political life characterized by patrimonialism and clientelism, which means that all political and administrative activities are based on personal relationships. In this case, there exists no difference between public and private interaction. Ravenhill (1985) defines clientelism as a relationship between a patron and a client and the bargaining process between the two entities, where they exchange their resources reciprocally, and the client has some power over the patron. A separation between the institutions and the individuals is impossible in this scenario. Southern Africa's politics, economy, and governance structures were influenced dramatically by European colonial powers. Some scholars have argued that British colonialism left behind better political and economic institutions than French, Portuguese and Belgian colonialism. However, there is also compelling evidence that colonialism had a detrimental impact on political and economic institutions in all African countries. Okoyo (1977) argues that "colonial rule was, for all practical purposes, military rule and by a simple transference the new political class, which inherited the mantle of the colonial masters, also inherited the latter's concept of a leadership role that was structured in authoritarian terms." As such, the colonial regime machinery made no effort to prepare the Africans for self-rule.

Cheeseman and Fisher (2019) argue that "Colonialism reinforced authoritarian elements in African societies while undermining the inclusion and accountability that once balanced them." It is essential to point out that colonial governments did not have enough officials to run the territories they governed effectively and maintain control; they subordinated the existing leaders and power structures, like chiefs. The colonialists used highly repressive laws with limited freedom of speech, media censorship, banning public gatherings, and political leaders' detention to maintain stability. Intimidation was also used whenever the colonial regimes came under threat. It was sometimes necessary to arm local collaborators to exert power over their communities and prevent rebellions. According to Chabal and Daloz (1999), the colonial legacy created incentives for new African leaders to use "disorder and a political instrument" to stay in power. Due to the lack of strong institutions in place, the governments in Africa have been unable to achieve sustainable economic development.

The weakened capacity of governance systems, according to Chabal and Daloz, benefits the political elite whose primary objective is maintaining the big man's political authority. According to Chabal and Daloz, this often leads to short-term personal gains rather than long-term community benefits since "neopatrimonialism's logic focuses on the proximate: local and communal." Its legitimacy depends on the ability to deliver to those people linked with political elites through the micro-networks of patronage and clientelism. Chabal and Daloz continue to argue that "when patrons are expected to only work for their customers, it is harder for clients to accept sacrifices for more ambitious national goals. The claim by one Big Man that he must reduce expenditures on his clients because resources are needed for national development would not usually be credible or acceptable."

Colonial governments did little to help democracy thrive as African states attained independence. The colonial government refused to hold elections until the day before their departure in some cases. Several colonial governments manipulated election results in Africa to ensure that natives friendly to the colonial regime won, as in Nigeria and Kenya. A complex colonial system provided an environment characterized by weak democratic structures and fragile authoritarianism. The post-colonial African states maintained the colonial patrimonial culture as the new regimes aligned the new state with pre-existing authoritarian governance systems based on the distribution of resources by those in power and their patrons, as Macqueen (2002) argues.

Except for Lusophone colonies, South Africa, Namibia, and Southern Rhodesia, which experienced a long and violent conflict, the rest of the Southern African states experienced limited violence, which permitted peaceful transition of power as they gained independence. However, the transition failed to eliminate the damaging institutional colonial features of the colonial governments. Political elites of newly independent states adopted the same bureaucratic structures left behind by colonial powers. Herbst (2000) tried to explain the weaknesses in democratic institutions, pointing out that the colonial powers were not interested in creating these democratic institutions to protect their colonies. Instead, it was essential for them to create institutions that exploited natural resources and cheap African labour. Bayart (1993) argues: African politicians sharpened the "politics of the belly," which is the predatory pursuit of wealth, power, and spoils as a governance model. As a result of this predatory behaviour, leaders in the region were incentivized to "eat" from the resources of the state, a notion Bayart (1993) calls "eating from the state." This implied unproductive rent-seeking by the political elite and their cronies. The political elites created informal political networks in the broader spheres of economic activities, as observed in Mozambique, Zimbabwe, and other states across the region. In extreme cases, the elites used war and violence to consolidate political power and wealth. Most of the governments, led by the region's liberation movements, failed to transform into a democratic political organization. They were more concerned about consolidating their hold on power at the expense of empowering the masses. State institutions became instruments serving narrow partisan interests, with the police and the military being used to attack the opposition, civil society, and the media.

African elites learned the art of coercion from colonial masters to demobilize popular movements. The majority of repressive laws in these countries remained unchanged even after independence, and the ruling elites continued to repress any form of dissent. The centralization of all political powers in the executive is an identifiable feature in most Southern Africa leaders. Unlike in established democracies, where all heads of state leave office either before reaching their constitutional term limit or after losing an election, this is not the case in Africa. In some SADC member states, leaders have demonstrated a desire to hang on to power even after losing their legitimacy to govern after losing an election. Over the past two decades, the region has been marred by electoral disputes, regular fraudulent elections, and constitutional manipulation to disenfranchise some candidates who present a credible challenge. The leaders have also exploited the high levels of illiteracy to manipulate the electorate with unachievable promises.

Nieuwkerk (2011) argues that: "Few ordinary Southern Africans can identify with rulers and bureaucrats who romanticise the past, fear the future, and suffer from policy implementation paralysis." In some states, political elites have insisted on preserving the liberation movements to avoid foreign interference. It has allowed the ruling elites to monopolize power, and aspiring politicians can only access power through the ruling party. Having former leaders of liberation movements still in power has also been problematic for democratic governance in the SADC bloc. The undemocratic tendencies displayed by these leaders are being reflected in the governance of the regional body. The shared experiences between liberation movement leaders and the Frontline States leaders have continued to impede leaders from being held accountable. Clapham (2012) argues that it is difficult for freedom fighters to understand that anyone else could be equally entitled to rule. Their involvement in the struggle confers on their minds a virtually permanent claim on state power for the liberation movements. Individuals, who took no part in the freedom struggle, including those too young to contribute, were forced to abandon their ambitions to govern.

Liberation movements have become integral parts of the nation's identity, with the liberation struggle becoming the narrative on which patriotism is based. The liberation movement has also become the source of legitimacy for political parties like Chama Cha Mapinduzi (CCM) in Tanzania, Zanu-PF in Zimbabwe, MPLA in Angola, and FRELIMO in Mozambique. Having fought for liberation, these veterans believe that have a permanent and unconditional right to govern, and the state machinery suppresses any suggestion for alternative leadership. The ruling elites in these states have deliberately developed new political structures to extend their legitimacy and present a new constitution. There is a mythical status associated with African leaders, making them essentially demi godlike. As a result, the political sphere has become personal, dominated by figures with godfather-like qualities. Political figures with a vast patronage network emerged in the region in Malawi; according to Decalo (1992), Kamuzu Banda rejected the idea of having opposition political parties on quasi-theological grounds. Decalo cited Dr Banda as saying: "There is no opposition in Heaven. God himself does not want opposition-that is why he chased Satan away. Why should Dr Banda have opposition?"

Although all SADC member states have become multiparty democracies, the strong man syndrome has persisted in which power remains concentrated in the presidency and checks and balances have been weakened. The leaders in that region have been able to suppress or at least retard democratic institutions. The cult personality of the leadership has been entrenched in the society, where the presidents have encouraged their portraits to be displayed in people's houses and government offices and assuming folk titles. The objectives of independence and self-determination defined the parameters of the liberation movements in Southern Africa. The attainment of freedom and African rule would transform the repressive colonial institutions to serve the colonialists' interests. Overcoming and remodelling these repressive institutions would allow the Black population to attain socio-economic empowerment and social justice, which they had been deprived of for over five centuries since the beginning of slavery. However, when African states attained self-governance, the liberation ended with controlling political power instead of empowering the oppressed Black population. While the political elites were empowered, the masses remained underprivileged. Politicians created a new class to replace white minority rulers, while ordinary citizens continued to be deprived of human dignity and fundamental freedoms.

First-generation African leaders abandoned any sense of ideological values arising from their sincere desire to better their people's condition. In general, this desire had driven the independence struggle throughout the region and the rest of Africa. As a result, the leaders accumulate immense wealth for themselves and their cronies and are consumed with power. The region has a difficult socio-economic situation because of the high levels of corruption and looting of state resources for private consumption. Collier (2007) argues that countries with bad governance and poverty in the bottom billion are also likely to end up as what he termed "failed states." In Collier's view, in these countries, initiatives for reform are overwhelmed and undermined by those who benefit from the disorder, in what he termed "the bad governance trap." Collier added to his argument by suggesting that countries experiencing governance deficits usually have individuals benefiting from the failed system; hence they make every effort to undermine any reform efforts.

Collier's theory can describe many third-world countries, which is also a fundamental characteristic of some SADC members. Political elites in these countries have made every effort to undermine governance structures for accountability. These instruments are known to obstruct the political elites or their cronies from benefiting from state resources at the general population's expense. As a result, political elites have directly benefited from the governance deficit and are afraid of being held accountable if they lose political power. That is what Collier (2007) called "the natural resource trap," where resource rents make democracy malfunction by unleashing patronage politics in societies lacking sufficient restraints on such behaviour owing to pervasive institutional weaknesses.

Among SADC member states, only Botswana and Mauritius allowed democracy to flourish soon after independence. Thus, it is not surprising that the two countries have remained the most democratic states in the region. Although one-party governments have vanished from the SADC region, democracy has taken on different forms; most SADC member states are only democracies by name. Most of the SADC member states also have judicial systems that are not independent. Additionally, civil liberties such as freedom of speech the press are constantly violated. As a result, having monarchical dictatorships in the region like those in Eswatini creates additional difficulties. As part of the regional political reform in the last three decades, this political system goes against the norms of participatory democracy.

Eswatini operates a democratic system, which is commonly known as the *Tinkhundla* system of government. Tinkhundla is a unique parliamentary government system where members of parliament are not elected as political parties but as individuals. The Swaziland (Eswatini) monarch Sobhuza II established this system to protect and preserve his kingdom's traditions. In 1964, the King repealed the British constitution when he restored the traditional system, which allowed the monarch to retain absolute power. The only concession he made to modern democracy was a cabinet and prime minister selected by the king. The King, the primary head of state, is involved in the administration of the government, and there is no space for a vibrant civil society. Therefore, the Eswatini political system violates every tenet of democracy espoused by the regional bloc. Nathan (2003) argues: "In the absence of sufficient congruence, states are unable to resolve or transcend their major disputes, achieve cohesion and act with a common purpose in crises." That has made it impossible for the SADC bloc to reconcile their political and economic demands to achieve sustainable regional integration. Effective regional integration is only possible if there is a consensus on democracy and good governance in the SADC region. The regional integration aspirations in the SADC area will continue to be limited as long as the commitment to democratic and good governance remains only on paper, not in practice.

Ihonvbere (1989) argues that it is "impossible to build self-reliance, meet basic human needs and effectively replace dependence with interdependence without first dismantling all the oppressive and exploitative structures within the African state." Any prospect for collective prosperity and regional stability would be conditioned on improved governance, eliminating corruption, and ensuring equitable distribution of state resources. However, this is impossible for SADC because of structural constraints. Adedeji (2002) opines that "it is now clear that the economics of regional cooperation is principally responsible for the slow progress made during the past forty years. By focusing virtually exclusively on economic cooperation and integration while making – the heroic ceteris paribus assumption, as far as political and social factors are concerned, has contributed significantly to the lack of progress in the actualization of the vision." Prospects for success can only be fully actualised if the region pursues political convergence, democratization, good leadership, and overcoming the existing colonial structures through wholesale reforms across the region.

Political Instability

Regional blocs are unique in the globalised international community because they allow participating states to integrate faster and more deeply. However, deeper integration and interdependencies expose other states to each other's domestic issues. When seeking collective economic prosperity through regional integration, it is impossible to ignore political, security, and social underpinnings related to economic collaboration. In this regard, domestic political stability has implications for the regional integration agenda. Political instability in participating states has economic consequences and makes it difficult for states to pursue a long-term integration agenda. Morrison and Stevenson (1971) describe political instability as a condition in political arrangements in which the institutional structure of authority breaks down. In such circumstances, expected compliance with political authority is replaced by political violence and conflicts. Söderbaum and Tavares (2009) argue that the persistence of conflicts in Africa has significant regional implications, with impacts that extend far beyond the borders of a single nation-state. There has been widespread instability and poor governance in Southern Africa, which have hurt the region's appeal to foreign capital, critical for economic growth.

Aeby (2018) argues that some armed conflicts and political instability in the region can be traced to the post-colonial and violent colonial past. The SADC region has been grappling with the long-term damage caused by colonialism. Leão (2007) observes that Southern Africa's history is characterised by conflicts rooted in colonialism and Apartheid struggles. The effects of the Cold War and internal political rivalry and tension have impacted political instability. Moreover, the region was also ravaged by two violent civil wars fueled by international actors in Mozambique and Angola. Across Southern Africa, authoritarian regimes and less transparent governance systems have undermined political stability. Some governments have been unable to meet the expectations of their citizens, so political elites have been concentrating on retaining power for their selfish interests as their legitimacy declines. Political and economic pressures have ultimately resulted in social instability that sometimes culminates in violence and social disintegration. SADC is presently experiencing armed insurgencies, political unrest, authoritarian rule, and abuse of state resources. Although the violence has been intrastate in nature, some of these conflicts now pose a serious threat to neighbouring countries. The region is once again at a crossroads despite a commitment to peace and security by regional stakeholders. The persistent intra-state conflicts can be traced to bad governance resulting in massive human rights violations and, on some occasions, leading to the state's complete collapse.

In promoting integration, democracy, and good governance through the SADC Treaty, member states demonstrated a growing collective understanding of the persistent challenges they face. Despite the rhetoric of good governance and democracy being supported at the regional level, some SADC member states have actively resisted the wholesale implementation of democracy and good governance. This has resulted in the governance, peace, and security architectures failing to generate the support of SADC leaders. As a result of the absence of a functional political framework, democracy and the SADC Treaty agenda for good governance have declined. A secure and stable SADC region requires democracy, good governance, and transparency. It involves free and regular elections in which citizens can vote for their political leaders, an independent judiciary that adheres to the rule of law, a security apparatus that respects human rights, a robust civil society, and press freedom.

During the Extraordinary Summit of Heads of State and Government held in Addis Ababa on 25-26 May 2011, the former Chairperson of the AU Commission, Dr Jean Ping, stated that the uprisings in North Africa "should be used as an opportunity to further the democratic and governance agenda of the AU." As things stand, the SADC area remains engulfed in a conflict threatening the region's stability. Poser and Young (2007) claim that the "formal rules of the game are beginning to matter in ways they previously did not." This is due to a direct relationship between regional stability and economic decline. The Southern African region has suffered from many conflicts owing to electoral disputes, democratic deficits, and governance challenges. Kastler and Liepert (2008) assert that conflicts in Africa have had an enormous impact on the struggle against poverty, impairing the continent's prospects for long-term stability, economic growth, and sustainable development. As a result, maintaining peace and security in Southern Africa is the greatest challenge for the integration project. In Southern Africa, since Apartheid ended, conflicts have tended to be intrastate rather than interstate due to the decline of democracy and good governance. Based on a more in-depth examination of the Freedom House ratings of 2010 and 2005, 23 African countries were ranked worse in 2010 than in 2005 regarding political rights and civil liberties. With the decline of political rights and civil liberties in Southern Africa, some states are still experiencing violent internal conflicts caused by political, economic, and ethnic exclusion.

The destructive nature of these conflicts has had catastrophic consequences for the states and the entire region. Conflicts like these are marked by gross violations of human rights and brutality perpetrated by both state and non-state actors. According to Sharamo and Ayangafac (2011), "more than half of African countries are at risk of facing peace and security crises in the form of state collapse, weak states, civil wars, ethnic massacres, and social and political deprivations of its citizenry." Deng et al. (1996) took the position that some states have collapsed and that there is no government to take over essential aspects of sovereignty. Human security is compromised across the SADC region by low levels of human development, poor service delivery, and protracted intrastate conflicts. A culture of violence fueled by illegal firearms proliferation, international organized crime, and socio-economic challenges exacerbates these conflicts. In such an environment, weak and sometimes dysfunctional state institutions or collapsed states cannot deal with challenges and, as a result, are not in control of social, economic, political and humanitarian security. Despite having some of the worst governed countries in Africa, SADC also has four of the best-governed, with Mauritius, Namibia, Botswana, and South Africa ranking highly in governance indices.

Countries prone to conflict and political instability present a significant deterrent and discourage foreign direct investment. As the sub-Saharan African region is marked by conflict, poverty, corruption, and underdeveloped infrastructure, the region has been deemed the riskiest region for foreign direct investment. The alarming political uncertainty in the SADC area has sparked many debates about how the region can deal with these challenges. Even though most of the conflicts reported in the SADC region are intrastate, a few of them may have an external dimension due to the involvement of external actors and their potential to spill over into neighbouring countries. There are few regions on the African continent and in the entire world with as much natural resource wealth as the SADC region. The region is rich in mineral resources like oil, natural gas, and precious metals; the region has vast potential with a primarily young population.

Nevertheless, the region is also ranked at the bottom of most human development indices. As a result of economic imbalances among the population, poverty has made the region vulnerable to conflict and instability. As a result of increasing conflicts in different parts of the region, most states have become weaker and more unstable.

Most of the conflicts are nationally instigated rather than externally influenced. Except for the DRC, where external actors have used proxies to instigate conflict, most of the conflicts have been sparked by local grievances that have remained unresolved for far too long. The longstanding conflict in the Democratic Republic of the Congo, which has claimed more than one million lives, has no signs of slowing down. The problems in the country have a long history, dating back to colonial times. The Belgian colonial government set up a system of government that aimed to maximize mineral resource exploitation. In addition, the conflict in the DRC has become more complex over time due to factors related to politics, economics, institutions, and social issues. A total of more than 100 rebel groups have fought in the conflict in the past three decades. However, the main ones have been backed by the country's neighbours and used as proxies by their governments to advance their security, political and economic agendas.

Governance issues are commonly cited as the culprit in most recent regional conflicts--from electoral disputes to authoritarian rule to government non-accountability, which causes widespread mismanagement. Even though nearly all the nations in the region are democracies, regimes with authoritarian tendencies have undermined democratic institutions by using the military and other national security institutions to suppress dissent and civil liberties. Most of the SADC member states have a personal rule and a patronage system. From Zimbabwe, where the military and the police are used to suppress freedom of speech and expression, Swaziland remains an absolute monarchy with a severe governance deficit. Generally, the interest of the general public and civil society has not been reflected in the legitimacy of ruling elites. Like Zimbabwe, events in Lesotho and Malawi following elections have shown that instituting democratic processes in an undemocratic environment may not always reduce conflict in the region. In Madagascar, the country has experienced more civil unrest since the collapse of a socialist regime in 1989.

A critical litmus test for SADC's failure to deal with human security issues has been its response to the crisis in Zimbabwe. Zimbabwe's internal conflict has been unresolved for more than two decades, owing partly to the country's adverse political and economic conditions. Despite the consensus calling on the international community to lift the economic sanctions on Zimbabwe, regional leaders have said nothing about human rights abuses and suppression of civil liberties. Instead, the group has successfully deflected criticism by arguing that Zimbabweans must resolve their political ills. Apart from Zimbabwe, the Kingdom of Eswatini (Swaziland) has also been experiencing deteriorated governance, with protesters calling for democracy. Despite the protests in Eswatini, which at times have turned violent, King Mswati has not been subjected to much pressure to enact a new democratic constitution that ensures civil liberties and respect for the rule of law.

SADC countries are driven by a solidarity concept in which the regime's protection takes precedence over the protection of citizens. In that regard alone, SADC member states have demonstrated unity and cohesion. SADC has displayed a lack of foresight in achieving its sustainable regional security and peace ambitions in light of the ongoing political instability across the region. A historical and contemporary analysis of Southern Africa shows that it has had a prevalence of conflicts. Conflicts have been caused by liberation wars, authoritarian rule, uneven distribution of national resources, ethnopolitical movements, religious intolerance, economic crisis, and land disputes. The socio-economic development of the region has been adversely affected by this phenomenon. As a result, questions have been raised regarding whether regional institutions can maintain peace and security. Violent armed conflicts and political conflicts have had devastating consequences on the SADC region's development and security agenda. It remains imperative to create an environment of trust and confidence across the SADC region for a successful regional integration agenda. As a result, the SADC Organ on Politics, Defense and Security Cooperation was established in 2001. This Organ has the objective of promoting peace and security across Southern Africa and protecting the region's people from instability because of the breakdown of law and order, developing a common foreign policy throughout the region, and cooperating on security and defence matters.

In the SADC, a broad spectrum of shifting peace and security threats threatens regional integration and stability. The lack of a comprehensive, common approach to some security challenges has reduced security cooperation due to fragmented responses to the crisis. Member states have challenged the regional legal framework and jurisdiction, undermining legally binding tribunals and protocols with regional mandates. This behaviour has reversed some of the democratic strides achieved in the past, which could have guaranteed human security, people's rights, and regional stability. As a result of the liberation legacy, a culture of solidarity has been the biggest obstacle to these efforts. Welz (2013) identifies the link between countries, like Zimbabwe, Mozambique, and South Africa, that have fought bloody wars to defeat white minority rule and refuse to surrender sovereignty. All foreign intervention is viewed by leaders from these countries as an intrusion into their sovereignty. A culture like this stifles effective diplomacy, provides cover to oppressive regimes, and allows them to escape accountability for human rights abuses.

As a result of this instability, markets and regional value chains have been disrupted, leading to limited economic activity. A conflict in one country has negatively affected the performance of the region's economies as its economies have become more integrated and markets and value chains have become more interconnected. Further, the institution's failure to safeguard citizens' human security has caused the institution to lose credibility. SADC is now considered an institution that protects authoritarian regimes and safeguards the legacy of the liberation movement. Among member states, the only values shared are those of elite solidarity and cooperation. According to Marsh Political Risk Index (2020), SADC was expected to struggle to manage security risks as Islamist militants intensify their Cabo Delgado activities, leading to many deaths. There is also the possibility that Islamists in Mozambique might use the porous borders and weak regional institutions to carry out terrorist attacks in its neighbouring countries, as has already happened in Southern Tanzania. Concerns have also been raised about DRC and the political conflict in Zimbabwe. Nathan (2012) asserts that SADC has failed to achieve one of its main objectives: ensuring regional peace and security. As a result, the region's economic growth and development have not been successful due to a lack of peace and stability. There are distinct regional characteristics reflected in Freedom House, Marsh Political Risk Maps, and other political risk matrices that pronounce terms of governance and democratic indicators. Indicators such as these demonstrate that regional stability in the SADC region is based on flawed foundations.

Had the trend toward democratization, which began in the 1990s, been sustained in the SADC region, the region might have experienced open societies with stable democratic institutions. Thus, SADC countries' risk of sliding back to authoritarianism could have been decreased in that way. In the region, governments could have enjoyed legitimacy, and countries could have become solid and stable. Because of these factors, economic growth and development could have been enhanced. However, a few of the SADC countries refused to accept the democratic strides made in the 1990s, which resulted in the reversal of the semi-democratic path to authoritarianism. A holistic approach dedicated to the root causes of insecurity will be necessary for the SADC area to achieve sustainable peace and security.

A sustainable and enhanced regional integration project requires a secure environment in Southern Africa. SADC member states cannot ignore issues of peace and security, given their enormous importance. Currently, several SADC member states continue to experience political instability and armed conflicts. Even the most advanced country in the region has not been spared from this violence. From xenophobic attacks in South Africa and rioting, as a response to former President Jacob Zuma arrest in July 2021, suggests that every SADC member state is vulnerable to violence. There is an ongoing civil war in the Democratic Republic of Congo, an armed insurgency in the Mozambican Northern Province of Cabo Delgado, Zimbabwean political crisis, and other political challenges in Lesotho Swaziland and Angola. The conflicts' high-intensity and destructive nature have had far-reaching consequences to the regional integration project, as the violence has impacted economic growth and human development. As a result of the political and security crisis in the region, people have lost their lives, refugees have fled, infrastructure has been destroyed, and institutional capacity has been eroded. As such, SADC is now at crossroads to overcome regional instability.

7

Regional Integration, Foreign Direct Investment, Political Stability, and Economic Growth

Introduction

The discussion in Chapter 5 and 6 demonstrates that the pursuit of improved welfare, economic development and political stability has been a failure in the SADC region. The discussion in the two chapters traced the components of the factors impeding the regional integration agenda and the reasons for the rapid deterioration of the economic and political conditions. Although regional integration commonly assumes to signal the beginning of a new era, the conditions in Southern Africa has suggested otherwise. Three decades after the inception of SADC, the region is still characterized by governance failures, social and internal insecurities, unemployment, armed conflicts, poverty, and high levels of corruption. Scholars have argued that the challenges identified are symbiotic and feed off one another. Helliwell (1994) and Mauro (1995) suggest that the level of economic development impacts corruption levels and the extent of political instability. Less developed countries tend to be more corrupt and politically unstable than developed countries.

Political instability, in this case, distorts predictability of outcomes, complicates contracts negotiations, and impedes investment opportunities. Political stability or lack thereof has become a primary factor in making investment decisions since an unstable governance environment can increase market risks. Thus, political stability is necessary to achieve collective prosperity and improved integration within the political sphere. An attempt is made in this chapter to explain the effects of one member state's instability on the entire region. It is argued in this chapter that the national or domestic political climate in a member state affects the achievement of regional integration objectives. Regional institutions have a significant role in domestic political processes and outcomes in participating member states.

The chapter draws on some theoretical analysis and empirical research to show how interconnected factors manifest themselves. In Southern Africa, policymakers are motivated by the idea of regional integration and its potential for stimulating economic growth and stability. Foreign capital and Regional Economic Communities (RECs) have become increasingly important elements of international political economy discourse in light of globalization's effects. The slow pace of regional integration and economic growth was identified due to political instability and concerns about governance. Chapter 7 argues that countries prone to violence and fragility present a challenge to regional integration. The purpose of this chapter is to clarify the conceptual debate around stability, governance, and development. To accomplish this, we will review some pieces of literature explaining the causal relationship between conflict and development. The former United Nations Secretary-General Kofi Annan (2005) once made these memorable remarks: "We will not enjoy security without development, we will not enjoy development without security, and we will not enjoy either without respect for human rights."

Over the past two decades, the relationship between development and security has gained traction in Africa. The concept of development goes well beyond the increase in the gross domestic product of a country; it also encompasses improvements in the standard of living of people and the effectivene ss of governance-related authority structures. Integration has broadened its focus from economic integration to governance, political stability, and human rights. Toward the end of the Cold War, in the early 1990s, a more holistic view of development led to the rise of the concept of human security in development discourse, a people-centred concept built on the premise of safeguarding human rights and human development. The Human Development Report (1994) defines human security as a people's "safety from chronic threats and protection from sudden, hurtful disruptions in the patterns of daily life." Peace and security issues have played a significant role in African reforms initiated by the African Union (AU) and the subsidiary Regional Economic Communities (RECs) like SADC in this case. A number of these reforms have been aimed at establishing instruments for peace, security, and efficient governance. As a result of the paradigm shift, the principle of non-indifference has been elevated, giving regional authorities the responsibility of protecting citizens.

The New Partnership for Africa's Development (NEPAD) has attempted to address broader issues related to Africa's peace and security, governance, and economic development. By accepting security and development as interdependent factors of a better future for Africa, NEPAD has built a link between the two. In the last two decades, foreign direct investment (FDI) has been an important indicator of political and socio-economic stability in the SADC area. Iglésias (2009) described FDI as an "international loan" from countries with surplus capital to the countries offering profitable investment opportunities. FDI helps to stimulate economic growth for the recipients of the capital due to increased economic activities. FDI has become increasingly important due to the changing nature of the international economy. Haskel et al. (2007) note that trade is a fundamental component of global trade; while FDI plays a vital role in developing economies in the host country as a factor input, FDI generates significant spillover effects across an industry. According to Blomstrom and Kokko (1998), there are three forms of knowledge spillover caused by FDI:

(i) Local firms improve their productivity by copying some technology used by affiliates of foreign firms operating in the local market;
(ii) The entry of an affiliate leads to more severe competition in the host economy so that local firms are forced to use existing technology and resources more efficiently; and
(iii) Competition forces local firms to search for new, more efficient technologies.

As a result of the decline of democratic institutions in Southern Africa, the region has become less appealing to foreign direct investment. Busse (2003) supports this premise by arguing that the type of democratic and governance regime impacts FDI attraction. That is why it is essential to pay attention to the factors that make a country an attractive FDI destination. Ahmad and Ahmed (2014) argue that institutions are crucial to disciplining economic agents' behaviour, thus promoting a set of rules and preventing opportunism while also enhancing transactional trust which ultimately, increases investor confidence. Low FDI has resulted in low economic activity and increased poverty levels in the region, both of which have contributed to instabilities in the region. The current peace and security environment now demands the regional body to urgently play an active role in coordinating and harmonizing the peace and security environment in Southern Africa.

On a positive note, the chapter acknowledges that robust regional institutions can mitigate some of the negative perceptions of political risk and enhance the credibility of member states. To reinforce this position, the discussion in this chapter provides examples from the EU, where member states had experienced changes in quality, regulatory effectiveness, and governance, which positively impacted the direction of FDI inflow. In this case, a robust regional body in Europe enabled FDI, political stability, and economic growth. It aims to contribute to the body of literature on foreign investors, regional integration, and mitigation of political risks. The analysis also suggests that conflict harms FDI, thereby depressing economic growth in those countries involved in the conflict and having spill-over effects on their neighbours.

Furthermore, outliers are discussed regarding some individual investors' behaviours. The chapter acknowledges that some investors can mitigate some of the political risks; however, this is only applicable to a few types and qualities of FDI. Extractive and communication industries are regarded as unique industries insulated from the adverse factors that hinder FDI. In this case, the two industries are still attracting FDI, despite the availability of similar risk conditions and perceptions. This chapter seeks to understand the drivers of these different FDI characteristics and how investors mitigate these political risks. Despite these outliers' presence, the discussion maintains the argument that deterioration in the effectiveness and enforcement of investment regulations and political stability harms the quality of FDI the region can attract.

In Southern Africa, the political economy often presents an adverse environment for foreign capital due to multi-layered government structures, weaker institutions, government regulations, and undemocratic tendencies. In this context, the chapter recognizes the urgent need to set up minimum requirements to help all member states manage the political and economic environment to facilitate foreign investment and ensure human security. While conflicts are among the highest political risk factors, the chapter identifies other investment conditions, like adverse government interventions and regulatory changes, as significant risk factors investors are most worried about than war and risk of terrorism. Investors' decisions are influenced by their perception of political risks to their assets and property rights. The absence of institutional infrastructure to protect their interests is likely to lead them to walk away from potential business opportunities. Nevertheless, there is a consensus that reducing conflict and resumption of political stability improves governance and economic performance.

By analyzing the potential role of regional economic communities to overcome some of the challenges related to FDI, this chapter sheds some light on the role of FDI on economic development. The following sections summarise this chapter: after this introduction, the second section discusses Collier's (2003) conflict trap and the development-security nexus. Through analysis of the available body of literature, the relationship between development and security will be established. The third section explores the value of FDI to socio-economic development. From the theoretical perspective, neo-classical economic growth models provide the basis for most scientific studies on the relationship between FDI and economic growth. Chowdhury and Mavrotas (2005) suggest that there are four main channels explain the relationship between FDI and growth:

(i) Determinants of growth;
(ii) Determinants of FDI;
(iii) Role of MNCs in the host country; and
(iv) The direction of causality between the two variables.

FDI provides a sustainable capital source, complements domestic private investment, creates new jobs, and enhances the transfer of technologies, all vital factors for driving economic growth, according to Chowdhury and Mavrotas.

The fourth section will explore the impact of political risk and market risk on investors' decisions about where and when to invest their capital. The final section examines the causal relationship between regional integration and foreign direct investment. Chapter 7 argues that a robust regional integration agenda can reinforce regional investment policies and enhance member states' credibility. The perception of an investment environment is greatly affected by that, which influences investors' investment decisions. Furthermore, as regards regional policy integration, Schiff and Winters (2003) observe that it benefits trade agreements, reduces uncertainty regarding reform, and helps mitigate domestic opposition to reform. A regional institution's role, in this case, is to enforce the obligations and commitments of its members. Additionally, this prevents the government from using domestic policy mechanisms to replace regional policies, as all policies are declared illegal when they contradict regional policies. For instance, European law prevails whenever there is any inconsistency between European law and the norms of national law.

Conceptualizing The Development-Security Nexus And Conflict Trap

The purpose of this section is to provide a brief overview of the conceptual debate on the development and security nexus. Since the end of the Cold War, discussions about the relationship between security and development have gained traction. There is debate about the causal connection between development and security policies. It is inherently necessary for countries and development partners to adopt a more holistic approach to development and conflict. Without overcoming violence and political instability, those involved in development politics cannot eradicate poverty. There is a consensus that improving peoples' welfare can reduce conflict risks among those involved in security policy. In light of this, there is an increased awareness of the complementary nature of security and development initiatives.

According to Goodhand (2001), poverty and conflict are widely accepted to be closely linked; poverty makes a country more vulnerable to civil war, whereas armed conflict essentially undermines governance and economic development, increasing the likelihood of a relapse. Conflict cannot be detached from more comprehensive social, political, and economic processes. As such, according to Goodhand, "violent conflict is therefore not merely a 'side issue' that developmentalists can ignore." The continent of Africa makes a strong case for this premise. There is no surprise that more development organizations are getting involved in promoting peace and security in Africa. The scope of development partners has expanded since the turn of the century, from economic development to peace and security initiatives. Brock (2004) argues that the "securitisation" of development policies and "developmentisation" of security policies have gained ground since 9/11. One of the EU's foreign policy instruments is the European Peace Facility (EPF), which was introduced recently. Funding facilities such as this one highlight the growing importance of peace and security among donor partners, and Africa will likely benefit from this. The EPF will enable the AU and other African RECs to initiate targeted conflict prevention schemes to create political stability on the continent. Besides the new funding stream, the EU emphasizes providing technical and logistical assistance to peace and security initiatives across the globe.

The concept of political instability varies, and according to Alesina et al. (1992), political instability is perceived as the threat of a change in governments either by constitutional or unconstitutional means. Most of the work on the causal relationship between conflict and development has been influenced by the work of Collier, who linked higher per capita incomes with a diminished likelihood of conflict. Collier et al. (2003), in a World Bank report '*Breaking the Conflict Trap*,' argue that: "once a country stumbles into civil war, its risk of further conflict soars." In the report, Collier et al. (2003) observe that "conflict weakens the economy and leaves a legacy of atrocities as it creates leaders and organizations that have invested their skill and equipment that are only useful for violence."

Political instability has become the leading factor that retards development, and in a vicious circle, development retards the chances of conflict developing. It is not surprising that 90% of all conflicts and armed conflicts are in poverty-stricken countries. According to Collier (2000), of the 27 armed conflicts that occurred in 1999, only two were inter-state conflicts, with the rest being internal. Cliff and Luckham (2000) argue that once an armed conflict breaks out, it transforms itself and everything around it—the state, livelihoods, national economy and social relations. War disrupts production, consumption, investment, taxation, and the provision of public goods, according to Starr (2006). Once a violent conflict emerges, it compounds poverty as state resources are diverted to the war effort, and the citizens are deprived of public goods. For countries that are developed, the risk for war becomes reduced; hence they become safe. According to Collier et al. (2003), conflicts are perceived as "development in reverse." The notion implies that when a country becomes involved in a conflict, the poverty that results from this conflict increases the likelihood of further conflicts. Due to the persistent poverty in SADC member states, it is no surprise that political instability persists in the region. As a result of that reciprocal relationship, we are concerned that more attention should be paid to resolving the underlying causes of conflict in the region.

It is from this perspective that development and economic conditions have become an essential aspect of security studies. Thus, countries with three economic characteristics of low income, low growth, and dependency on natural resources are the most vulnerable to conflict. In this context, human security has become the cornerstone in tackling socio-economic problems and establishing security policies that affect individuals' well-being. Cilliers (2004) suggests that the common obstacle to Africa's stability is its severe development failure; poverty is the common cause of civil wars in Africa. Bad policies and poor governance cause a large part of that poverty.

Figure 5.1: GDP per capita before and after the civil war

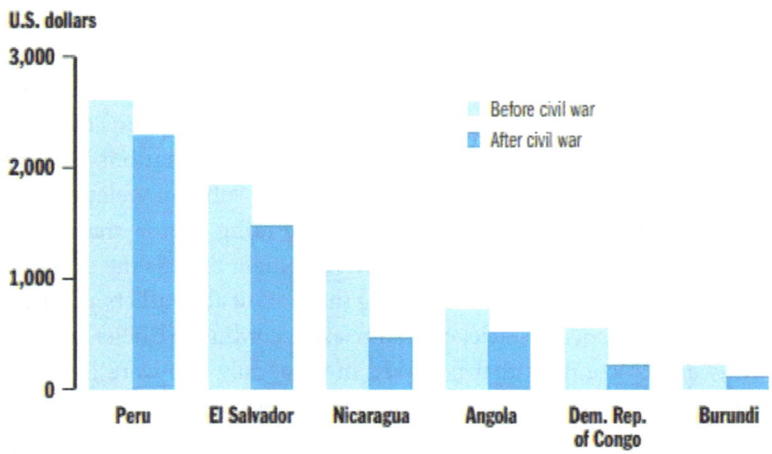

Source: Sambanis (2003)

Figure 5.1 illustrates the claim made by Collier (2003) that incomes drop by 15%, and the incidence of poverty increases by 30% after a violent conflict. Today, development policies are associated with resolving violent conflicts, given that violent conflicts hinder economic and human development. There is a consensus within the field of development scholarship that violence cannot be defeated without eradicating poverty. As stated by Collier (2003), "the security-development nexus is, therefore, significant for development cooperation." Tschirgi (2006) asserts that fragile states, civil wars, and poverty are seen as direct threats to the security and well-being of Western states. As a result, donors have been pressing for security strategies to be incorporated into their development agenda.

According to contemporary discourse, political elites' failure to manage the risk of political instability and armed conflict reflects a deficit in leadership and governance. Although this argument is valid, any country experiencing similar conditions could also experience such a risk environment. Bueno de Mesquita (2005) suggests that the survival of the political elite depends on their ability to distribute resources to key domestic constituencies that could help improve the welfare of their citizens. Abadie (2004) argues that political grievances conflict proneness is most likely to lead to different forms of violence—from terrorism to civil war. Good governance can, however, mitigate the link between poverty and conflict. Rose (2004) argues that good governance shapes a country's structural and economic vulnerability to conflict.

Thus, governments realize that attracting foreign direct investment is crucial to their economic development plans since their economic performance strongly influences their fortunes. Democracies rely on economic growth and employment to keep elected officials in office. Violence and political disorder may result from a lack of economic development in undemocratic countries. There is great awareness in security and development discourse regarding the potential overlaps between these two concepts. There is now demand for close collaboration between security and development policies, commonly known as "nexus management." Security and development are correlated; it is not surprising that RECs like SADC have created peace and security architectures with civilian components that provide a platform for building bridges between the military and non-military areas of conflict management.

Natural resource rents and patrimonialism raise the risk of violent conflict, as discussed in Chapter 6. Conflict risks are exacerbated by corruption and mismanagement of natural resources, assert Ballentine and Haufler (2009). In any society, these conditions lead to grievances in the short term, and in the long run, these grievances can become socialized. According to Aspinall (2007), the socialization of grievances becomes a strong justification for conflict once an "identity-based collective action frame" is created. Stewart (2002) and Cederman, Weidmann, and Gleditsch (2011) link grievances to ethnic groups when they argue that ethnic groups excluded from economic activities are more likely to engage in conflict. This is consistent with Marx and Engels' (2010/1848) argument that workers' ends can only be attained by overthrowing all existing social conditions. They have nothing to lose but their chains.

Furthermore, Davies (1962) lays out the theory of "relative deprivation," where he argues that a large gap between people's actual "need satisfaction" and what they expect might lead to frustration, a strong sense of injustice, and a revolutionary "mood." An excellent hypothetical example would be a presidential candidate in Mozambique promising Cabo Delgado residents (who hold grievances against the unequal distribution of wealth) that he would provide them with a fair share of the region's natural gas wealth during the campaign. As soon as he is elected, the new president fails to deliver his campaign promises to Cabo Delgado's residents. Using this illustration, it seems there is a disconnect between the people's expectations and what is delivered, resulting in additional frustration and amplification of grievances. Inequitable resource distribution and marginalization of some demographic populations contribute to ethnic rivalry, religious extremism, and political mobilization, leading to conflict. The failure to meet the expectations of some individuals may cross the threshold that they will resort to violence. A similar argument can be found in Sigmund Freud's (1950) frustration-aggression hypothesis, which suggests aggression is a natural reaction to frustration.

Of course, we also need to acknowledge that there are other pathways to aggression outside frustration. The lure of opportunity and greed can be driving factors for conflicts, claim some scholars. According to the "greed-hypothesis" coined by Collier and Hoeffler (2002), civil war is more closely related to the availability of lootable primary commodities. O'Gorman (2011) links greed to grievances by stating that grievances are a "by-product of conflict, manufactured by armed groups to maintain the popular bases of support and labour needed to ensure the continued looting." However, Collier, Hoeffler & Söderbom (2008) refined the "greed-hypothesis" by introducing what they called "feasibility-hypothesis," which predicts that "conditions that determine the feasibility of rebellion are more important than those that influence motivation." From this new argument, "greed" is extended by considering factors that allow armed groups to sustain the conflict. The factors may include environmental conditions or socio-demographic factors. Geographic factors such as mountainous terrain or dense forests in Cabo Delgado and Eastern DRC have allowed armed groups to establish secure and heavily fortified camps. Socio-demographic factors point to the existence of disgruntled and unemployed youth, providing a ready supply of recruits.

In our discussion so far, we have been able to identify a strong relationship between poverty, limited development, and an increased likelihood of conflict. However, since this book is about regional integration, the discussion will be incomplete without looking at the impact of conflict on neighbouring countries. Brown (1996) argues: "Civil wars should be considered an international problem, since they almost always affect and involve neighbouring states, thereby undermining regional stability." In Duffield's (2006) view, the war on terrorism has led Western governments to refocus aid and resources on geographies, groups, and issues threatening their homeland security. By addressing the underlying risks that fuel crises like poverty, corruption, and authoritarianism, the international community presents an opportunity to reduce violence.

A growing body of literature examines the spill-over effects of conflicts in one country on its neighbours. Buhaug and Gleditsch (2008) and Salehyan and Gleditsch (2006) analyze the spill-over effects of conflicts on neighbouring countries. Murdoch and Sandler (2002) demonstrate how spill-over effects of conflicts affect neighbouring countries' GDP. There has been an increased recognition that a conflict in one country can spill over and affect neighbouring countries and the international community at large, according to a World Bank report authored by Bannon and Collier (2003). Bannon and Collier argue that the costs suffered by neighbours can sometimes exceed those suffered by the country at war. A few of the negative spill-over factors identified by Murdoch and Sandler (2002) include trade disruptions, heightened fear of capital investors, and resources to assist refugees. All of these factors have an adverse economic impact on countries that are neighbouring the country experiencing conflict. Collier and Hoeffler (2001) argue that conflict is contagious because a rebellion in one country increases the risk of an internal rebellion in another. The Arab uprisings of the Middle East and North Africa are an excellent example of this phenomenon, as an uprising in one country triggered conflict in many other countries in the region as well.

Conflict environments can hinder FDI, but some businesses can also prosper in these environments. Keen (2009) argues that some influential businesses may be interested in continuing certain forms of violence even when peace has been achieved. Cooper (2002) asserts that the political economy of conflict trade influences the nature and effectiveness of post-conflict peace-building and reconstruction because proceeds from conflict trade promote a return to war and undermine peace initiatives. Cooper argues that warlords' influence over critical economic sectors during conflict may lead them to pursue war economies under non-war conditions in places where peace has prevailed. Collins (1999) explains that conflicts can affect development in four ways: destruction, disruption, diversion, and dis-saving. Over the course of history, conflicts have destroyed production lines, public services, infrastructure and resulted in unnecessary deaths.

In light of this, developing countries have succeeded by securing increased manufacturing and service production through foreign direct investment. Without FDI, countries have experienced limited economic growth. Many countries with limited economic growth depend on primary raw materials, such as agricultural products and extraction resources, leading to conflict if they are not appropriately managed. "Modern political violence (particularly organized violence) occurs in states where assets are immobile and unequally distributed," explains Boix (2008). In relatively equal societies, peaceful, democratic means of resolving conflict benefit all parties, and violence is rare. When wealth is mobile or hard to tax or confiscate, sustained political violence to nab it does not pay off, since its owners can either leave when threatened with confiscation or are indispensable to the optimal exploitation of assets." By diversifying their economies, countries with strong manufacturing capacities can expand their economies more rapidly. The widespread diversification allows states to trade with each other by specializing in commodities that can be traded.

Hegre (2003) and Rohner (2008) recognize the relationship between poverty and conflict as a characteristic of a country's political system. Hegre (2003) argues that economic growth and development only reduce the risk of conflict in a democratic environment since, in non-democracies, economic development does not change the risk of conflict. The Libyan uprising that forced Muammar Gaddafi to step down is an excellent example to support this point. Libya was one of the leading African countries with solid economic fundamentals, and most Libyan citizens enjoyed a certain level of prosperity despite being led by an authoritarian leader. The oil and gas industry employed the majority of the country's population. The people not employed received benefits from the government. Despite these favourable economic conditions, Gaddafi was overthrown due to the country's authoritarian government and limited political space. In light of the high level of repression in Libya, Hegre (2001) claims that regime type is one of the critical indicators for the outbreak of political violence. By suppressing opposition groups, restricting press freedoms, and using force to suppress civil disobedience, an authoritarian regime increases the likelihood of full-scale violence.

Economic activities are affected by violent conflict, which slows economic growth. It is, therefore, necessary to reduce conflict and improve governance to create stability, resulting in pro-growth economic policies. Countries become safer when development succeeds, which is why governments need to be sensitive to the political, economic, and social factors influencing conflicts. Countries already experiencing conflict must break the conflict trap by reducing long-term violence risks through human development, negotiation, or the use of military force. For countries to address the grievances that can turn into conflict, structural elements such as political, security, economics, and social needs must be implemented to address the critical stress points. Africa has experienced half of its conflicts because the underlying conditions of the conflicts have not been addressed. It is crucial to understand the factors contributing to the socialization of conflict, such as polarization and resentment against the government system. Eventually, this deep resentment creates fertile grounds for disgruntled populations to get involved in future armed conflicts.

VALUE OF FDI TO SOCIO-ECONOMIC TRANSFORMATION

The Organization for Economic Co-operation and Development (OECD) defines foreign direct investment as investments made by entities based in one economy pursuing business opportunities in another economy. A significant difference between FDI and international trade is that FDI requires a business entity to maintain its foreign economic presence by mitigating the challenges presented by different political and legal environments. According to Schiff & Winters (2003), "investment is a key component in economic development and has become one of the main objectives of countries pursuing regional economic integration."

Foreign direct investment has been recognized as one of the prime factors in the economic transformation of any country as it helps the country catch up with technology and access to capital. By setting up export links with the country where FDI originates, FDI is primarily intended to increase market access to larger and more developed markets. Another objective is to take advantage of local comparative advantages. These advantages include cheap labour and low-cost raw materials. Foreign companies based in the SADC region can thus benefit from cheaper labour and raw materials while at the same time having easy access to large developed markets in their home countries.

Figure 5.2: FDI to Sub-Saharan Africa: Volume and Share in World Inflows, (1970-2005)

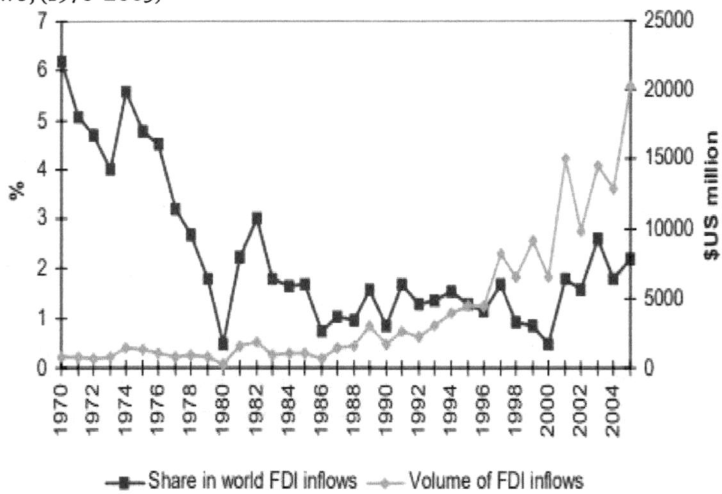

Source: UNCTAD, FDI online database.

Figure 5.2 shows the volume of FDI inflows in Sub-Saharan Africa which has experienced a decline from the investment levels in the 1970s. The SADC region is not an exception. The region has continued to attract limited investments in the extraction sector. Institutional quality and political risk factors obstructed FDI inflows while also hindering economic growth and socio-economic development. These negative investor perceptions have not been helped by political risk reports identifying sub-Saharan Africa as the riskiest place to investors due to political risks and the enormous infrastructure deficit, which keeps growing. In light of the capital deficiencies of SADC economies, initiatives that can reverse the investor perception scenario could increase the region's capital inflow.

Despite the slowing down of FDI, UNCTAD (2013) reported that FDI in Africa had surpassed foreign aid in recent years. Much of that money is directed to extractive industries that exploit the region's mineral wealth. However, Africa attracts low FDI compared to other developing regions. Global economic conditions remain unstable, exposing small economies in Southern Africa to adverse economic conditions. The declining global market share and reduced economic growth have prompted emerging economies to initiate economic reforms to attract foreign direct investment and reverse the unsustainable economic trends. FDI has become one of the most dynamic resources flowing to emerging economies because of its nature. The increasing importance of FDI has sparked competition among emerging markets to attract FDI because of the benefits like capital, technology transfers, and international networks associated with it. Thus, foreign direct investment has played a significant role in the economic development of emerging economies, and its importance as a source of financing has increased in the last four decades.

As demonstrated by the EU, regional economic communities (RECs) are an effective tool to improve member states' chances of attracting foreign direct investment. The effectiveness of the RECs has become a significant determinant for the location of FDI and quality. The way RECs supplement and complement FDI has been cited commonly as a reason for regional integration. Brenton et al. (1999)) support this assertion with observations that "recent evidence suggests that regional economic integration can provide an important stimulus to trade as well as foreign direct investment." Investment from foreign direct investment helps countries and regions improve their production efficiencies, improve their technological transfer, and attract financial resources. FDI also enhances export capabilities by facilitating access to new export markets. FDI can only be sustained by a stable and conducive investment climate in any country or region that wishes to attract it. There is evidence that countries that offer FDI opportunities with a high level of safety and profitability tend to win in the global competition. Economists generally agree that FDI is a form of capital flow that spills over into the rest of the economy. As such, a country's economic and development potential is enhanced by foreign direct investment. FDI positively impacted Asian emerging economies, where it boosted economic growth and created spillover effects.

As a result, attracting FDI has become an essential part of emerging economies' economic strategies. According to Mabey and McNally (1998), the focus on FDI has resulted in substantial public subsidies, diplomatic efforts, and promotion activities to attract capital investors. However, these efforts can also lead to what Justice Louis Brandeis cited in William W. Olney (2010) described as "a race to the bottom" if not properly managed. Olney (2010) explains that a "race to the bottom" refers to countries lowering their labour standards, environmental standards, or tax rates to attract foreign capital. More specifically, the race to the bottom hypothesis hinges on two critical predictions. First, multinational enterprises (MNE) choose to invest in countries with less restrictive standards. Second, countries competitively undercut each other's standards for the sake of attracting foreign direct investment (FDI).

According to Bhalla (1983), political risk changes due to elections, revolts, and recessions may affect tax regimes, local ownership requirements, and changes in FDI incentives. A change in these factors may impact the profitability of any investment and affect capital budgeting. Investors, therefore, need a stable political, legal, and regulatory environment to make their investment decisions. In a nutshell, the rule of law provides investors with comfort and confidence that their property rights and investments would be protected. An excellent example of investor fears is a possible nationalization of private businesses and governments failing to adhere to agreed contracts. From this background, the investor's confidence plays a critical role in deciding how to invest and where. Investors consider several other factors, including corruption, the security of personnel and assets, and the accessibility to a fair judicial system, to name a few.

Foreign direct investments can be in the form of expanding existing investments, mergers and acquisitions, build and lease infrastructure, joint ventures with host country entities, and establishment of local subsidiaries. FDI plays a critical role in global economics, as researchers agree and empirical studies support this conclusion. Through it, reliable and effective links between economic systems are established, providing businesses with expanded marketing channels and access to technology advancements through global value chains. These factors promote economic growth and provide employment opportunities in the country or region hosting the business entity.

Studies have attempted to explain the impact of foreign direct investment on economic growth from a theoretical standpoint. Conclusions have been drawn to illustrate the importance of FDI to economic growth and productivity. A large body of literature exists focusing on the FDI-growth nexus. For example, Schneider and Frey (1985) found an association between FDI and growth to be positive and statistically significant.

Using 1970-2003 data, Braithwaite and Greenidge (2005) also looked at the relationship between FDI and economic growth of the Barbadian economy. Braithwaite and Greenidge found that real FDI flows significantly impact real GDP based on cointegration analysis. Kida (2014) examined the models of economic growth and the dynamic interactions between them, from the Solow Model to the New Endogenous Models. The results of this study pointed to the fact that FDI affects economic growth in developing countries. Adeniyi et al. (2012) studied the relationship between FDI and economic growth in Côte d'Ivoire, Ghana, Nigeria, and Sierra Leone. The study examined financial data between 1970 and 2005 to determine how financial development has changed over time. The Vector Error Correction Model (VECM) results illustrated that financial sophistication affects FDI benefits and economic growth in small developing economies. These studies consistently show that theoretical consensus and empirical evidence support the hypothesis that foreign direct investment accelerates economic growth in host countries.

FDI has enabled emerging economies to build capital, create employment opportunities, and develop production capacity. This has led to rapid industrialization, which has managed to keep pace with domestic development needs. This has also allowed countries to respond to opportunities presented by regional and global economic integration. The general observation has been that FDI has helped promote long-term and sustainable economic growth for emerging economies by taking advantage of labour-intensive economic activities. With FDI, host countries have utilized their comparative advantage. Thus, the availability of low-cost, unskilled labour has become a critical, location-specific determinant of FDI in emerging economies.

Globalization, technological advancements, and competitive pressures have allowed MNCs to split their production structures across the globe, focusing on specialized activities. Thus, activities like production, customer service, information technology, training, and finance have been delegated to different affiliates in places best suited for each activity. For this reason, FDI is no longer just about expanding the market and building new production lines; it is also about gaining access to new technical production support systems that require highly skilled human resources rather than low-cost, unskilled labour. Foreign direct investment has served to boost the competitiveness of the country and secondary supporting industries.

As some SADC member states are trapped in a conflict trap due to high poverty levels, FDI can be instrumental in alleviating poverty through job creation and direct investment in social welfare. The study by Gohou and Soumare (2012) evaluated African countries from 1990 to 2007. Based on the results, FDI has a substantial impact on poverty alleviation, and the experiences of the fast-growing economies in East Asia support this assumption. Newly industrialized East Asian economies provide SADC member states with a blueprint for increasing foreign direct investment inflows. In light of many investors' adverse political risk perceptions, SADC must fix these perceptions by reworking regional macro-economic policies and establishing favourable market regimes that will attract foreign direct investments. There are different motives for an investor seeking to invest in another country in the FDI literature available. According to Basu and Srinivasan (2002), investors are motivated by the following factors:

(i) Resource-seeking investment, which aims to exploit the natural resource endowments of countries. Companies extracting natural gas (in Mozambique), gold (in South Africa), and diamond (in Botswana) belong to this category;
(ii) Market-seeking investment, which aims to access new markets that are attractive as a result of their size and/or growth;
(iii) Efficiency-seeking investments, which aim to take advantage of unique features in a certain area, such as the costs of labour, the skills of the labour force, and the quality and efficiency of infrastructure; and
(iv) Strategic-asset-seeking

Resource-seeking FDI refers to an investment made in a market to minimise cost by benefitting from resources and raw materials that are too expensive in the home country. This situation occurs when investors identify an offshore location to acquire raw materials, extractive resources, and low-cost labour that cannot be found in their home country. Businesses constantly look for cheaper alternatives to lower production costs to remain competitive. As Basu and Srinivasan (2002) cited, resource-seeking investment is one of the factors influencing investment in the SADC region. Due to the region's high-value mineral resources, food commodities, and energy resources, complemented by the low-cost labour, the region has a great deal of untapped manufacturing and investment potential.

For instance, the $60 billion investment in the Ruvuma Basin natural gas fields off the coast of Cabo Delgado, Mozambique, is an excellent example of major MNCs like Total, ExxonMobil, and others investing in the SADC region. The natural gas extracted has been earmarked for export into Europe, China, Japan, and America. Usually, existing national technological and technical capacity does not play a role in determining FDI inflows. In most cases, resource-seeking investment brings limited or zero technology transfers.

By capitalizing on existing gaps on different products in the host country or an integrated regional market, market-seeking foreign direct investment seeks new markets. Market size, market growth, and the market structure determine this type of foreign direct investment. FDI is generally targeted at selling products directly to markets where the investment has been attracted. Economic growth and population size are factors that affect the attractiveness of a market for potential foreign direct investment. Growing middle-class households would increase FDI even if the population remained the same. Mozambique's new natural gas find may also be a catalyst for economic growth, corresponding to income and human welfare.

Consequently, the high-paying skilled jobs will create a new middle class in the country with a greater appetite for luxury items that were not in demand before the economic boom was anticipated. Additionally, this growth can be spurred by regional integration, which combines small economies into one enormous market. Toyota, for example, opened a manufacturing plant in South Africa to reduce its supply costs. Toyota South Africa can now supply vehicles to the SADC region due to the FTA created in the SADC market. Investors are attracted to large, stable markets with a growing middle class with disposable income.

The concept of strategic asset-seeking FDI was introduced by Dunning (1993) and involved investing in countries to acquire assets that can promote long-term strategic objectives. An investor acquires assets overseas, in this case, to improve the performance of their portfolio. These are business interests that are strategically important to the investor. An investor locates a new firm to take advantage of new technological advancements and research and development. In this case, the objective is to exploit the new firm's resources, capabilities and innovation. For example, during the development phase of the Covid-19 vaccines, large pharmaceutical companies were searching for opportunities to acquire small pharmaceutical companies that showed promise of developing effective vaccines. Due to the increasing demand for an effective vaccine, pharmaceutical companies improved their research and development pipelines by pursuing small biotech companies and funding vaccine development's initial and riskiest stages. New acquisitions were made on the most promising companies at the early stage of clinical trials.

Efficiency–seeking FDI refers to investment to create the most cost-effective and competitive global production network. Investors capitalize on available research and development, technical capability, and costs associated with those activities. AstraZeneca's mass production of Covid-19-vaccines in India is an excellent example due to the country's significant manufacturing capacity to produce vaccines. With the world's largest vaccine production capacity, India has a proven track record on the scale at which vaccines are produced. Since India has developed a mass vaccine production capacity due to its large population, it was an attractive candidate for manufacturers of the Covid-19 vaccine, including AstraZeneca and Johnson and Johnson.

What is clear from the motives identified is that seeking natural resources, seeking new markets, and efficiency-seeking are primarily asset-exploiting in nature, where the investor is taking advantage of existing structures like raw materials, labour force, or the available market. In contrast, strategic asset-seeking refers to the process of purchasing a new asset that complements or improves an investor's existing holdings.

As Görg & Greenaway (2004) state, FDI is regarded as: "a key driver of economic growth and development. Therefore, attracting foreign direct investment is a priority for most governments, particularly in emerging and transition economies. It is given this emphasis not just because it boosts capital formation but also because it can enhance the quality of the capital stock." However, available evidence indicates that the countries in the SADC region, and Africa in general, have been receiving the least amount of global foreign direct investment, and the share has been declining over the years. This outcome is not surprising due to the market factors discussed earlier. For SADC countries to create a level playing field for all member states and businesses, the region must undertake comprehensive market integration initiatives to harmonize FDI incentives, policies, and norms. This could minimize fierce competition to lure investors between member states.

Because of the international community's pessimistic worldview about Africa, potential investors have often ignored Africa as a destination for their investment. Uncertainty is one major factor affecting the flow of foreign direct investment into Africa. This uncertainty is either supported by evidence or mere perceptions. Lehmann (1999) study found a negative relationship between uncertainty and FDI in developing countries. Lehman examined capital expenditures by US-owned investments in 29 emerging economies between 1985 and 1994. The study observed that economic and political risks discourage capital expenditure by foreign investors. Market reforms or liberalization are also ineffective when investors attach a small probability to their reversal. At the same time, Dixit (1989) identified delays in FDI inflows whenever there is uncertainty in the business environment. Nonetheless, empirical evidence indicates that the rate of return on investment in Africa is higher than in other emerging economies.

What is puzzling is why Africa is still lagging when it comes to receiving FDI? The answer always comes back to perception, built over a long period of media reports of negative publicity. Media reports have also damaged Africa's image as a favourable location for foreign direct investment. UNCTAD (1999) observes that: "For many people in other parts of the world, the mere mention of Africa evokes images of civil unrest, war, poverty, diseases, and mounting problems. Unfortunately, these images are not just fiction. They reflect the dire reality in some African countries – though certainly not in all." Africa's economies are complex and diverse, and the opportunities that exist are often hidden under negative publicity. Rogoff and Reinhart (2003) assert that African countries are more likely to experience conflict and unrest than other parts. As a result, these incidents harm the entire continent's investment potential and climate.

A high level of poverty and unemployment in the SADC region makes foreign direct investment critical for growth, and it provides the means to accelerate economic growth. According to Acemoglu and Robinson (2012), the existence of inclusive and trustworthy political institutions characterized by an open and pluralistic system with competition for political office, a widespread electorate, and openness to new political leaders conforms to the foundations of developing appropriate economic institutions, is a prerequisite to fostering sustainable economic growth. In this light, a country's business climate is determined by the political and governance systems that create the transactional environmental factors present. Transparency, regulatory regimes, and ethical norms comprise the transactional environment. Public trust in the political and governance systems is a critical factor that generates trust in government institutions and political institutions. Botswana stands out as an excellent success story for countries undergoing economic transformation and development due to credible governance institutions in the region. As soon as Botswana gained independence, it provided favourable conditions for FDI, beginning with massive investments in diamond mining. Botswana graduated from a per capita income of $100 in 1966 to about $8,000 in 2020, comparable to Costa Rica and Mexico. Botswana is one of the most prosperous countries in the SADC region and Africa as a whole today. Based on Ajayi's (2006) findings, Botswana is in a position to attract foreign direct investment due to the following factors:

(i) A stable political environment; and stable macroeconomic policy;
(ii) Competitive exchange rate relative to the South African Rand;
(iii) Low crime level;
(iv) Good human capital development;
(v) Good labour relations; and
(vi) Botswana producers have access to South African markets because of Botswana's membership in SACU and the Zimbabwe market because of the 1956 trade agreement.

In light of the factors outlined, Ajayi (2006) highlights Botswana's politically and economically stable institutions. From the onset of independence, Botswana established strong institutions to ensure political stability and economic growth. Today, the country is a consolidated democracy and is one of the few countries in Africa that has held free and fair elections since independence. Botswana is also ranked as one of the least corrupt countries in Africa on the corruption perception index. Only Mauritius is ranked higher on freedom indices than Botswana. The country is also ranked the most transparent country in Africa by Transparency International and has an A+ rating by Moody's for its creditworthiness, which is the highest in Africa. Political stability has created an environment conducive to business, driven by its export-led growth strategy and the credibility of its governance systems.

Political Risk and Market Factors Affecting Foreign Direct Investment

International business research involves analyzing differences between countries with respect to political, institutional, social, economic, infrastructure, and technological factors that influence investors' decisions to invest in a given country. As a result of political and market risk factors, the economic performance of Southern Africa states lags behind other emerging economies in other parts of the world. As Brüthers (2002) argues, foreign companies that enter foreign markets need to be aware of the political and institutional conditions of the country. It is no surprise that North (1990) came to the same conclusion when he argued that political risks are influenced and determined by institutional structures that facilitate or hinder business performance. Likewise, institutions are responsible for governing societal transactions on a political and economic level. Geopolitical risks and policy uncertainty influence global FDI.

According to Hamada et al. (2004), political risk refers to all decisions, conditions, or events resulting in financial losses or physical damage to an investment. This definition conveys the qualitative nature of the factors driving political risk. Ruprah and Sierra (2016) argue that creating a favourable business environment is necessary to attract foreign direct investment, entrepreneurship, and sustainable economic growth. A World Bank (2017) report noted that reducing risk in developing countries is crucial for spurring investment and economic growth. The World Bank survey examined the circumstances under which FDI is most likely to produce benefits and concluded that FDI benefits developing countries by bringing in technical know-how, enhancing workforce skills, raising productivity, generating business, and creating better-paying jobs. Apart from investors avoiding high political risk areas, a World Bank report (2019) observed that failing to address political and governance factors have caused 25% of foreign investors who have already invested in the region to withdraw or cancel their expansion plans every year.

Investment decisions depend on different dimensions of public institutions, corruption environment, a country's regulatory framework, stability of economic policies, intellectual and property rights protections, effective judicial systems, and law enforcement. They also use various instruments like expert reports, surveys, international credit rating agencies and other sources of information to ensure the accuracy of information. *Doing Business*, the World Bank's flagship publication provides a set of indicators for evaluating countries' business environment and competitiveness compared to others across 190 countries. In addition to the World Bank, other important instruments are also used to evaluate a country's business climate. World Governance Indicators (WGI), Transparency International's Corruption Perception Index (CPI), and other Political Risk profiles developed by the World Bank and other private risk institutions have become crucial indicators.

Compared to other developing markets, the business environment in Southern Africa is unfavourable, according to the World Bank Doing Business (2020) report. A Verisk Maplecroft report (2020) identified sub-Saharan Africa as a region with the highest investment risk, with seven of ten highest-risk countries located there. Risk factors in South Africa go beyond the security risks associated with the region. Government systems, democracy, and macroeconomic factors also impact the region's political risk profile. Institutions and regulations that permit and enhance FDI are incredibly relevant in shaping a country's risk profile, as Ruprah and Sierra (2016) point out. These political risk factors constitute a significant factor affecting FDI flows, significantly affecting foreign investors' decisions.

At the beginning of the 20th century, Marxism's collective economic theory gave rise to the concept of political risk in economic discourse as the risk of a political takeover of all means of production by the state increased. This was a period when states compensated for their capital deficiencies simply by taking over private companies. Chapter 5 discussed that the early independent states in Southern Africa were guided by socialist ideologies, making private businesses vulnerable to nationalization as governments sought to overcome neocolonialist economies. This resulted in private businesses becoming at risk of confiscation, which was a major concern for investors.

Since the fall of the Berlin Wall, the nature of political risks has changed, and the risk of nationalization has declined. Because of this, changes in the international political economy have impacted risk-generating events. In contrast to the 1960s and 1970s, when states often seized private businesses without compensation, contemporary political risks are centred on government measures that may affect profitability. These measures may be related to regulatory frameworks and macro-economic factors, which have become a new form of political risk in what is known in international practice as "creeping expropriation." The concept of "creeping expropriation" is defined by the United Nations Conference on Trade and Development (UNCTAD) as "a slow and incremental encroachment on one or more of the ownership rights of a foreign investor that diminishes the value of its investment."

This refers to the gradual removal of property rights from private or foreign investors through a series of government measures, including taxes, regulations, and changes in the law, to reduce investment value to the investor. Under international law, states have a sovereign right to take property held by nationals or foreigners through nationalisation or expropriation of economic, political, social or other reasons. However, for the process to be lawful, according to UNCTAD (2012), the following conditions have to be met:

(i) Property has to be taken for a public purpose;
(ii) On a non-discriminatory basis;
(iii) In accordance with due process of law;
(iv) Accompanied by compensation.

As a result of the inadequacies in savings necessary to finance domestic investment, Levine (2005) argues that developing countries rely on external sources of financing to meet their economic goals. However, Mallampally & Suvant (1999) state that investors analyze various factors influencing their investment decisions. Numerous economic and non-economic factors influence FDI inflows, according to the literature on FDI and economic development. Fourie & Burger (2017) identified political and economic environment expectations and rates of return on investment as some of the significant factors affecting capital inflows. Scott (1995) defined institutions as the physical, cognitive, and normative structures that affect social behaviour and ensure stability. North (1990) describes institutions as: "the rules of the game in a society or, more formally, the constraints that shape human interaction." Because of this, they influence human exchange, whether political, social, or economic. Institutions, in other words, are humanly conceived constraints that govern human interaction. According to Henisz & Swaminathan (2008), host country institutional characteristics include normative and regulatory components and cognitive domains that virtually impact investor behaviours. Furthermore, Peng et al. (2008) believe that institutional arrangements in emerging markets differ significantly from those in developed countries. Nevertheless, the political environment and the stability of host countries have become significant factors in influencing investment decisions.

Three main types of political risks impact investor decisions, according to Asiedu (2002). First and foremost, there is the issue of nationalization. The second factor is the risk of policy instabilities, affecting investment performance due to uncertainty in the investment environment. The third factor is armed conflicts, terrorist activities, and political violence, which may damage investors' assets. Investor surveys have also confirmed that political stability and macro-economic factors, including the host country's legal and regulatory environment, remain important factors influencing global investment decisions. Wilkin and Manor (2001) argue that: "Today's political risks are not the classic risks associated with Communist takeovers or post-colonial outbursts of anti-foreign sentiment. They are more subtle, arising from legal and regulatory changes, government transitions, environmental and human rights issues, currency crises and terrorism. Because these risks are subtle (often occurring simultaneously as the government is declaring the country open for business) they are often hard to manage." Because of the diversity of political risks to FDI, these risks are more complex and challenging to manage. Investors often estimate the probability of occurrence of every political risk factor to aggregate and contextualise the risk factors. The aggregate scores are compared to the profitability of the potential investment. Investors use Agmon's political dependence matrix to analyse the risk environment associated with any potential business into two components; vulnerability and costs.

As shown in Figure 5.3, the degree of vulnerability is measured against the probability that a political event may affect the business; in this case, each factor is considered separately. The investors may disregard some political risk factors in cases of high profitability and employ some mitigating measures, which may incur additional expenses. In emerging economies like those in Africa, institutions' weaknesses impact heightened political risks since political risks are institutional in nature. As such, investors attempt to make estimates relevant to their operations and evaluate the likelihood of risks presented against profitability.

Figure 5.3: The Agmon's Political Dependence Matrix

		Vulnerability	
		High	Low
Cost	High	Political risk is important	
	Low		Political risk can be ignored

Source: Agmon (1985)

The concept of vulnerability has seldom been examined independently, according to Simon Green (2007). Walklate (2011) explores how different perceptions of vulnerability and risk may lead to different outcomes regarding a company's resilience. Some scholars have even argued that stereotypes can sometimes shape these perceptions. Pain (2003) provides one example of the presumption of older people's vulnerability, although not all older people are weak. These stereotypes also extend to how African countries are perceived. While some African countries are experiencing unstable political environments, armed conflicts, mounting social problems, and economic depression, many other countries have also experienced positive developments facilitating foreign direct investment. Despite these positive developments, they are rarely reported since Africa is treated as a country rather than 53 countries with varying economic and political systems. In some African countries, reforms have been initiated which facilitate FDI, such as maintaining macro-economic stability and improving regulatory frameworks. Despite their efforts, these positive efforts are undermined by conflicts and instability in neighbouring countries due to oversimplification, common in African discourse.

Figure 5.4: Factors Affecting Investment Decision (% of Respondents)

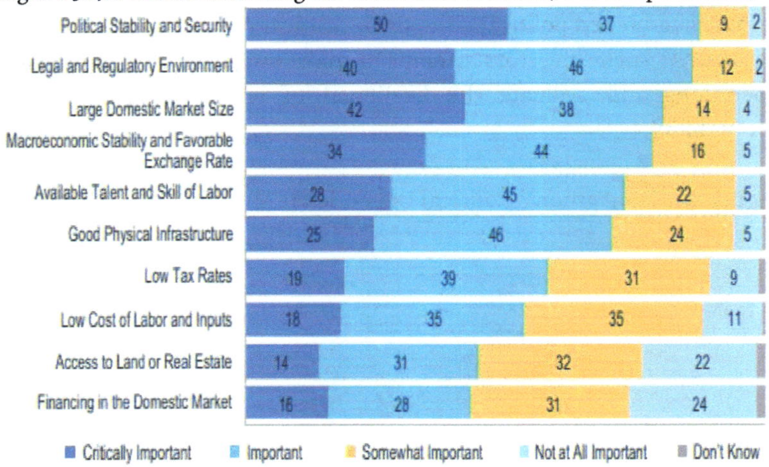

Source: World Bank 2017/18 Global Investment Competitiveness Report

In figure 5.4, it is shown that at least 96% of investors put a high priority on political and security stability, with 86% saying the variable is important or very important. 98% of respondents indicated that the legal and regulatory environment is important to some degree. As a result, almost all investors consider the regulatory and legal environments a critical variable, although political stability and security also rank very high. Rather than investing in countries where political and regulatory instability exists, many investors invest in countries where property rights and assets are protected.

Bloom (2009) argues that political and regulatory frameworks that can harm investments have a dampening effect that reduces investors' response to new investment opportunities. Investors who are already involved in this market may decide to delay or outsource operations when the risks are elevated. Ketemich and Schnitzer (2010) suggest that high political risks increase the likelihood of joint ventures in some circumstances, which could aid investors in mitigating political uncertainty. Political and economic reform can reduce political risks; however, attractive liberalized political and economic policies alone will not reduce political risk. For investors to believe those policies, there must also be credibility in the commitment and in cases where credibility is lacking, they may stay away. In simple terms, reforms lacking government credibility are just as bad as not having the reforms. To earn investors' trust, governments need to take away power from the politicians susceptible to public pressure and populist manipulation during reforms to convince them that they are serious about reforms.

Busse and Hefeker (2007) suggest that investors have concerns about political instability since it is most likely to impact business profitability and return on investment. In this context, countries with high conflict risks and weak institutional and structural foundations are unattractive. As a result, foreign direct investment volume and composition are affected. Having covered conflict and development in our previous discussion, it is widely agreed that FDI stimulates economic growth and development, which helps ease the fragility and risk of conflict in a country. According to Gringle (2004), political instability in a country harms the feasibility of a business project and the capacity of a country to service debt obligations and make infrastructure investments. Political risk, as a result, has a profound impact on social cohesion, which goes beyond enhanced economic activity. The political instability in the DRC, Zimbabwe and to some extent Mozambique provide excellent case studies in the discussion presented in Chapter 9..

A power shift has occurred between investors and governments as a result of the global economic revolution. SADC member states need capital investments for their economies to be vibrant, thus the need for policies that make the region attractive to investors. The region must open itself to the economic and trade flows of the global economy so that it can grow. The power to implement necessary reforms lies in the political arena where decisions are made.

Foreign direct investment has remained a key driver of economic growth. Foreign direct investment is essential for creating new employment opportunities, providing capital, and improving productivity. Furthermore, FDI strengthens the link between the host country's economy and the global economy, as MNCs engage in exports through their global sales and supply networks. For many developing countries that do not have sufficient capital accumulation to spur economic growth, FDI presents a reliable and less risky source of private capital that also comes with a positive cascade effect. As an initial condition for considering investment targets such as these, political stability is required. Because of a lack of political stability and high economic growth levels, foreign capital has not been able to flow into the SADC area. The region faces a turbulent political environment, including the Zimbabwean political crisis, violent conflict in the DRC, Islamic insurgency in Mozambique, riots and xenophobia in South Africa, and has faced rioting due to electoral disputes in Malawi, Madagascar and Lesotho. These political factors have disrupted commercial operations and have contributed to the rising political risks in the region. More risks developing in the region, the outlook in the region has impeded investment in the region.

In host countries, political risks are primarily determined by uncertainty over the actions of government and political institutions, as well as other groups in society, such as armed insurgents or rioters. These risks may also be caused by international sanctions directed at the investment destination, as with Zimbabwe's international sanctions. Other factors may include domestic policies that limit foreign investment, such as externalizing profits, breach of contract by the host government, and failure to honour sovereign financial obligations. In a nutshell, most of the factors highlighted in Chapters 4 and 5 can also be considered by investors as adverse country or regional political risk factors.

Figure 5.5: Marsh Political Risk Map 2020

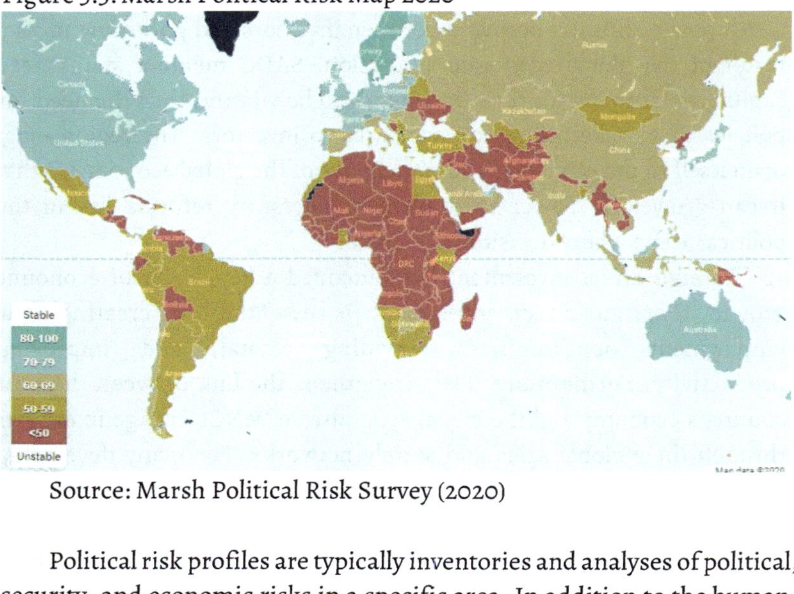

Source: Marsh Political Risk Survey (2020)

Political risk profiles are typically inventories and analyses of political, security, and economic risks in a specific area. In addition to the human costs of fragile states, the regional risk profile shapes foreign investors' perceptions of how the environment impacts private sector activities. Investors use risk maps to decide where to invest their capital based on the risk profile. A worsening economic environment due to insufficient capital investment may also result in a decline in political stability, creating a vicious circle. For SADC to succeed, attracting foreign direct investment must be a priority; the region must also ensure that it can grow, expand, and diversify economically. Singapore, Malaysia, and China have all presented evidence on the importance of maximizing foreign direct investment on growth and diversification of exports. Achieving this success would not have been possible without enabling policies that promote an enabling environment for investors, ensuring long-term certainty and an ability to expand their business.

A map of political risks in the SADC region is shown in Figure 5.4, which shows how businesses and investors perceive changing political risks. Political risk is measured globally on the map, and most SADC member states are ranked below 50, which is worse than North Africa and the Middle East. Investment decisions are made based on these indices and maps of political risk, and having a score below 50 is considered the lowest. It is more worrying for SADC that individual member states are still far from breaking out of the 50 scores except for Botswana, South Africa, Mauritius, and Namibia. Because of this, the region has become a very high-risk investment destination because of its political instability and regulatory environment. FDI attractability depends on a range of factors, one of which is the combined perception of political risk.

Investors can use the map to identify and track the different sources and magnitudes of risks, which will help them plan and protect their assets, contracts, and loans that may be adversely affected by economic and political changes in their operating countries. The political risk map highlights all areas of high political risk and explains all factors and sources of risk, such as political violence, institutional and regulatory risks, and economic conditions. In addition to having an impact on the business environment, these factors undermine the regional economic outlook. For foreign direct investment to flourish, policy continuity is essential. Without it, investment viability is impeded. Investors are typically frustrated by political interference from export restrictions, tax pressures, stringent regulations, contract reviews, and increased government involvement in the industry. Regulation changes that adversely affect foreign direct investment and contract breaches hinder the flow of FDI. DRC has been notorious for its interference in mining policies since implementing a new mining code in 2018 that includes:

(i) Raised royalties from 2% up to 10% for minerals deemed strategic
(ii) Reduced exploitation licenses from 30 to 25 years and allowed for only one renewal
(iii) Increased the state's non-dilutable equity stake from 5% to 10% and increased it by a further 5% upon renewal
(iv) Declared that Congolese citizens must hold 10% of shares in a mining company
(v) Declared that mining companies must work only with Congolese-majority-owned suppliers of goods and services
(vi) Created a special 50% tax on excess profits
(vii) Cancelled a 10-year stability clause that offered protection for existing mining projects.

According to Schiff and Winters (2003), potential investors may be sceptical of the government's stated intentions if they have been burned before by sudden tariff changes, tax hikes, or nationalization. Very few investors with specific objectives and plans will bear the risks of malfunctioning political, regulatory, and legislative systems. Based on the new mining code of the DRC, investors found it problematic to use Congolese suppliers in highly technical supply chain areas. Since the DRC introduced the new code, significant investments in the mining industry have been reduced, and production has slowed. Although the new populist regulatory policies appeared to have positive economic development implications, these policies' general outcomes had adverse effects. For instance, in the Katanga region of DRC, a Chinese copper mining company saw its monthly mining output drop from 18,000 tonnes to 10,000 tonnes. This is reminiscent of what is happening in other countries across the region. In most cases, fragile economic policies are driven by the desire of ruling elites to win an election. Having investors guess whether the investor-friendly regime will last is a factor that scares many investors.

Investing is more vulnerable to political risks generated by government instability than to those generated by terrorism and war, according to Roberto Echandi, World Bank's Global Lead for Investment Policy and Promotion. Since most investors borrow from banks for their investment, based on projected profits predetermined by contracts in place and projected market prices, any significant changes in contracts will likely affect loan repayments. For investors, the rule of thumb is to only invest in jurisdictions that are more welcoming of foreign capital and maintain policy continuity regardless of political changes. According to Benassy-Quéré et al. (2007), the quality of an institutional environment is one of the most important factors affecting FDI. Adding to this debate, Wei (2000) argues that institutions' quality is critical for macro-economic stability and the development of the private sector. Gani (2007) demonstrates that controlling corruption, improved regulatory quality, political stability, and government effectiveness positively impacted FDI inflows in Latin America. Poor institutions generate additional investment costs due to high levels of corruption. To ensure the institutional stability of an agreement, investors commonly seek agreements with strong contractual protections.

Figure 5.6: Variables used by FDI measure the quality of institutions in a country

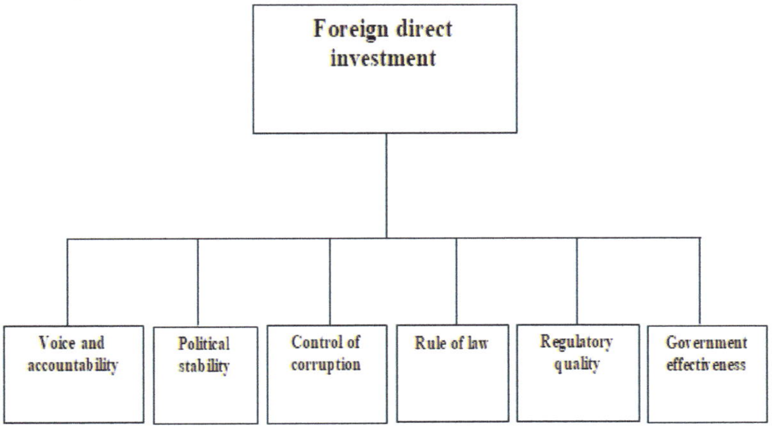

Source: Generated by author

Institutional stability heavily influences investment destinations, so investors must consider certain variables before committing to a destination. These variables allow investors to evaluate whether a market is attractive to FDI from an institutional stability perspective. This assessment will help investors plan and implement contingencies to mitigate these factors where required. Where risks are high, investors are likely to pull out of any prospective business interests and deals.

Voice and Accountability

Indicators of voice and accountability are captured by the World Governance Indicators (WGI), which capture the level of citizen participation in government and how the government is chosen. Currently, the WGI captures data on 213 countries and territories worldwide by rating their governance status. The factors examined include political process, civil rights, awareness of rights, empowerment, and institutions that enable government accountability. It also includes the involvement of trade unions and the free press in the governance discourse. Specifically, the focus is on the availability of an enabling environment that allows citizens to voice their interests and the government's response to public concerns. Jenkins (2003) argues that generating credibility with investors requires democratic governance institutions. As Li and Resnick (2003) argue, democratic rights are crucial to inducing property rights, which are crucial for investors.

Furthermore, having key transparency and accountability measures is critical to ensuring long-term sustainable economic growth. A direct link between democratic values and economic growth exists with a study by Acemoglu et al. (2019) titled "*Democracy Does Cause Growth*." The study concluded that countries adopting democracy see a 20% increase in GDP over 25 years compared to remaining authoritarian. Investors are attracted to emerging markets because of their prospects for economic growth.

Political Stability

Essentially, political stability refers to the likelihood of a government collapsing or being destabilized due to an outbreak of violence or any unconstitutional removal of power. Any abrupt change in government may result in changes to FDI policies. During Hugo Chavez's socialist presidency in Venezuela, the leftist government seized oil companies, steel companies, and food manufacturing companies. Furthermore, the local currency, Bolivar, was devalued, making savings in the local currency worthless. Recent reports suggest that Venezuela may reprivatize some of its nationalized oil companies. While large energy multinationals like BP, Total, and ExxonMobil would get a substantial return if they invested in Venezuela, political instability would dissuade them from investing due to persistent concerns about the future of the private sector under the socialist government. Past government actions have long term consequences for investors that extend beyond the duration of the event. Therefore, any potential policy shifts affecting African economies should be evaluated, taking future repercussions into account.

Control of Corruption

Control of corruption analyses perceptions of illegal activities of bureaucrats such as accepting bribes and corruption and protecting investors against illegal payments to public officials. According to Anyanwu (2006), corruption is one of the most significant barriers to doing business in Africa. The World Bank defines corruption as the abuse of power by public officials to obtain personal benefits and favours through bribes, embezzlement, irregular payments in public procurement, and influence peddling. Most SADC countries rank in the lower third of the global corruption perception index because of rampant corruption. As Kaufmann et al. (2003) note, corruption raises uncertainty and increases business costs. Corruption also causes deliberate delays in bureaucratic processes, which forces investors to resolve these issues informally, primarily through bribes.

Corruption decreases investor confidence and lowers the chances of future investments because government officials' overhead costs increase. Shileifer and Vishny (1993) contend that the secrecy of corruption is what makes it substantially more distortionary than paying taxes as it increases uncertainties. In his empirical study, Mauro (1995) found that corruption negatively affects the ratio of private investment to GDP in a country, thus hurting economic growth. Wei (2000) examined data on bilateral FDI stocks from the Organisation for Economic Cooperation and Development (OECD) countries. The study found that corruption has a significant impact on capital inflows.

The Rule of Law

The rule of law refers to the efficiency and predictability of judicial processes and the enforceability of agreements and contracts.

Dupasquier & Osakwe (2006) point out that foreign investors are attracted to countries with sophisticated and transparent legal and judicial systems that ensure the safety of their investment, property rights, and assets. An investor's decision can be affected if the judicial system lacks credibility due to its vulnerability to abuse and outside influence. Except for a few countries in the SADC region, the judicial systems in most states in the SADC regions are considered not to be independent. The judicial environment is susceptible to manipulation by the political elite and to bribery by the private sector. Alexander (2014), however, points out that investors have also relied on relationships with senior government officials to reduce uncertainty caused by the weakened rule of law. The quality of a country's judicial system is crucial in determining whether the country attracts quality investments. A robust judicial system and a strict rule of law facilitate long-term investments and reduce investors' anxieties.

Regulatory Quality

Regulatory quality refers to policies of the government that include trade policy, licensing laws, monetary policies, labour regulations, import and export procedures, taxation systems, and regulations governing foreign businesses. In order to minimize uncertainty, foreign investors are attracted to explicit and consistent regulatory procedures. The robust regulatory procedures ensure that investors' property rights and assets are also protected. An inadequate regulatory framework distorts investments and is susceptible to influences that may affect investor's interests. Stringent regulations are also known to restrict growth through FDI due to bureaucratic red tape that may also invite corruption. SADC countries must find a sweet spot in regulations to ensure that the private sector strives without impeding the socio-economic development agenda. The quality of the regulatory framework impacts FDI because investors feel more confident since it reduces unnecessary burdens for them.

Government Effectiveness

A significant amount of attention has been paid lately to the link between institutions and FDI flows. International investors place a great deal of importance on the institutional framework of a country, according to the OECD (2012). A democratic government tends to attract foreign direct investment more than an authoritarian government because it tends to reduce political risks associated with nationalization and expropriation and increase the credibility of the host country, as Jensen (2003) and Ahlquist (2006) claim. Democratic countries have good governance as a prerequisite to how the government structure, which enhances government effectiveness.

Kaufmann et al. (2003) defined government effectiveness as the quality of bureaucracy, competence of civil servants, the credibility of the civil service, the quality of public services, and the credibility of the government's commitment to policies and regulations. These policies govern acquisitions, mergers, taxes, pricing, and tax policies. Public policies have an impact on the business environment, which in turn affects foreign direct investment. African governments are notorious for unpredictable interventions in business matters, and politics heavily influence these interventions as politicians cheer populist initiatives in order to garner votes. In emerging markets, academic studies have unanimously concluded that improved government performance facilitates investments. Institutional quality has a significant impact on the performance of all social interactions. Daude and Stein (2007) studied the effects of governance quality on foreign investors' investment decisions. They found that unpredictable policies, excessive regulatory burdens, and lack of government commitment discourage foreign investment. According to different studies, there is a positive correlation between government effectiveness and foreign direct investment.

Behavioural Drivers of Foreign Direct Investment

Despite a consensus in the empirical analysis concerning the determinants of foreign direct investment, the results differ based on how these factors are managed. According to Frey and Eichenberger (2001), managers have other intrinsic motivational factors that shape their operational environment and may result in inconsistent decisions regarding a reasonable appreciation of political risk. It is relevant to consider the cognitive characteristics of decision-makers when evaluating the making process. Since most managers are evaluated based on their performance and how they compete with others, some may develop a thick skin towards moral, social and cultural values, an aspect of economic decision-making widely ignored in economic literature. Most often, these choices are shaped by their personal experiences and motivations. A manager's decision to invest in a particular location is influenced by how they view the values of these variables against the expected revenues and costs. Investing in business opportunities in areas other investors would not consider is not surprising because investors have different cognitive characteristics.

In the preceding section, variables discussed were likely measured by surveys and other evaluations collected from non-governmental organizations (NGOs), donors, think tanks, and corporations that operate in the countries. The six variables discussed are recognized as the key pillars that affect investment and development prospects. Despite the increasing competition for FDI and Africa's declining attractiveness to FDI, it must also be acknowledged that FDI also has a bad reputation in some emerging economies, especially in Africa. Africa's history, ideologies, and post-independence politics are all factors that contribute to the negative attitude towards FDI. Despite member states embracing liberal economies at the regional level, economic nationalist rhetoric continues to occupy political discourse where foreign investment in natural resources is perceived as another form of neo-colonialism. The negative public opinion does have an impact on FDI due to the anxieties of investors. Investors become sensitive to government interference in their business and possibly reneging on contracts.

While these investor anxieties are legitimate, it is also important to recognize that some investors have exacerbated the suspicions ofAfricans towards FDI. In corporate practice, there are accepted moral constraints that are supposed to influence decisions. While decision-makers are expected to follow the informal and formal socially accepted norms, others do not. In some quarters, investors have even resorted to unconventional techniques to maintain their investments; some of the adopted measures are unethical. FDI perceptions have been adversely impacted by some of the behaviours displayed by multinational corporations. As most African countries are still recovering from colonial experiences, exploitative foreign direct investment is perceived as an attempt by Western countries to exploit raw materials and cheap labour. There is also valid concern that some forms of foreign direct investment haven't impacted Africa's socioeconomic status and welfare. Images of collapsed factories and oil spills are usually associated with foreign direct investment in Africa. Many multinational corporations' actions have aggravated concerns rather than ease them. Any lack of social resilience in African countries, SADC countries included, signifies that social, political, and economic conditions will deteriorate further in the future.

Janeba (2002) and Okafor et al. (2011) argue that some environments with high political risk have brought in some form of FDI that has exacerbated the existing political violence and corruption. It has been postulated by Dar-Hsin et al. (2005) that some countries undervalue their assets excessively to attract foreign investments because they are considered high-risk areas. Moreover, Janeba (2002) argues that this undervaluation of assets has made most high-risk political areas even more attractive to FDI, potentially opening up more profit opportunities and high returns serving as acceptable risk trade-offs. This is not surprising, considering some investors actually find high-risk locations more attractive for investing. Okafor et al. (2011) reached a similar conclusion in a study that examined the impact of the democratic component of political risk on FDI inflow; the study concluded that observance of democratic norms and principles by developing countries discourages some investors from investing in the countries as a country moves toward a more robust democratic system, the volume of FDI declines. It is usually investors who exploit the absence of democratic institutions that are affected. Li and Resnick (2003) contend that some investors prefer developing countries governed by authoritarian governments.

Their preference for authoritarian governments is often inspired by their desire to avoid ethical and environmental scrutiny. Since an authoritarian government is not held accountable by its people, this operational environment protects the investors from labour unions and other civil society organizations that generally take issue with bad business practices in a democratic environment.

Figure 5.7 illustrates that a majority of investors, are willing to make investments in sometimes highly volatile environments when their investment benefits outweigh the security risks. If the return on investment is enormous, security risks are easier to mitigate for most of these investors. Thus, some investors have demonstrated a willingness to invest in violent hot spots, while others have gone so far as providing aid to armed groups. The Human Rights Watch (HRW) report in 2005, which exposed AngloGold Ashanti, a British mining company operating in the Democratic Republic of the Congo (DRC), provides a good example. It was alleged in the report that the company provided the militias that committed atrocities in the country with financial and logistical support. It was revealed in the HRW report that the company developed relations with the Nationalist and Integrationist Front (FNI) warlords in exchange for security assurances and access to the mining concession. In return, the mining company provided financial and logistical support to the militias, which directly fuelled further atrocities and violated international laws. As AngloGold Ashanti's actions demonstrate, investors can effectively protect their investments in such an environment using different means, including illegal ones.

Figure 5.7: Why political risk does not scare off some investors (%) of respondents

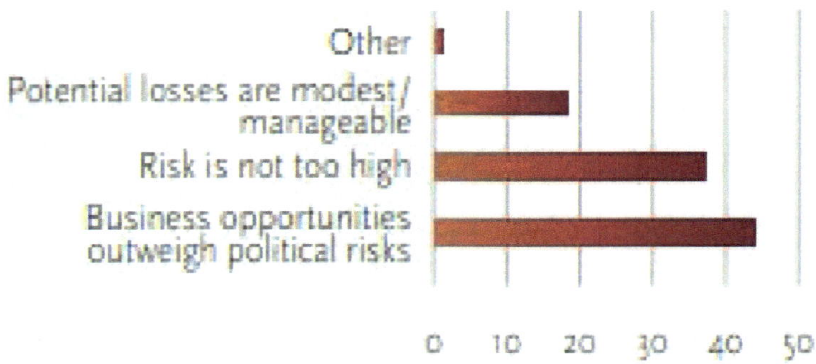

Source: MIGA-EIU (2010) Political Risk Investors Survey

In their study, Barta et al. (2003) concluded that corruption is the highest constraint to FDI in Sub-Saharan Africa. UNCTAD (2000) also pointed out that corruption and political outlook harm FDI inflows. There is a consensus that high political risk restrains FDI opportunities for most industries except exploitative industries like the extraction industry. MNCs are also known to exacerbate corruption and support armed groups, as demonstrated by AngloGold Ashanti. Some scholars like Kwok and Tadesse (2006) acknowledged that FDI could both enhance transparency and amplify corruption. In this regard, it is reasonable to conclude that quality FDI will move to countries with transparent business environments. At the same time, predatory FDI will profit from corrupt environments by creating additional incentives for corruption.

In addition to the extractive industry, the telecommunications industry has also experienced growth in Southern Africa, even in politically complex areas. An overwhelming majority of the investment has come from the Indian MNC Bharti Airtel Limited, commonly known as Airtel, and other Middle Eastern and African investors. According to Madichie (2011), mobile phone subscriptions in sub-Saharan Africa are growing at the highest rate in the world. The reason for the increase in investments in Africa, according to Ndikumana and Verick (2008), is partly due to the underdeveloped telecommunications sector, which offers investors substantial profit margins and greater access to an untapped market. Investment growth has also been noted in highly volatile countries like the DRC owing to poor fixed-line infrastructure conditions, allowing mobile operators to become the primary telecommunication companies.

Beyond the risk of political instability, the SADC market is also characterized by elevated currency risk. With the SADC region having small and isolated economies, the member states are prone to wide fluctuations in currency values, implying a lack of predictability of revenues and investors' costs. In an attempt to limit capital flight due to high currency fluctuation levels, host countries usually impose capital controls that inevitably diminish investment. In addition, foreign exchange remittance restrictions imposed by states due to foreign exchange shortages can impact dividends' payments to shareholders and loan payments.

An excellent example of successful regional currency cooperation in Africa was the now-defunct Franc des Colonies Françaises d'Afrique (CFA-Franc) in West Africa, which allowed the region to use a common currency. Because the member countries did not control the monetary policies of the former French colonies, the CFA made them more attractive to foreign capital. The French treasury had the responsibility of setting the policies since the CFA was established in 1946. Thus, foreign investors were assured that their currencies would be protected because there was no risk of currency manipulation in these Francophone countries. Former French colonies are moving toward a new regional currency called Eco, but using one currency across the region still helps the countries avoid the currency fluctuations that would result from each having its currency. However, a neo-colonial perception of the Franc Zone did not deter its success. According to Adotevi (1997), it was rooted in historical, social, and cultural realities supported by a common language and similar public administration and fiscal management traditions. The credibility of the business environment is a critical factor for investors.

Herbst (1998) argues that regional institutions in Africa can play a crucial role in promoting credibility because of the 'democratic deficit' often caused by attempts to place specific policies beyond the reach of politicians.

Regional Integration And Foreign Direct Investment

Regional integration schemes have become a fundamental feature of the modern international political economy. Africa's commitment to building institutional capacity for trade facilitation and regional integration is reaffirmed by establishing free trade areas across the continent. Despite all these economic integration initiatives, intra-regional trade in Africa is still limited compared to other regions. Within Africa, the intraregional trade hovers around 10 to 15%; in Europe, the trade between EU member states hits as high as 69%. In order to enhance trade between African countries, there is a need for trade diversification and value addition to exports, both factors requiring massive foreign direct investment. Although the task of overcoming these challenges may seem overwhelming, it is not impossible. There is nothing wrong with emulating what European countries have accomplished through integration.

Although regional integration studies have mainly focused on their positive effect on trade, they also impact FDI inflows. The increase in regional economic communities (RECs) has been attributed to African countries abandoning inward-looking strategies during the last three decades. Macroeconomic fundamentals provided by the RECs are viewed as valuable tools for attracting foreign direct investment. The premise that deeper regional integration stimulates foreign direct investment is strongly supported by empirical evidence. To attract FDI, RECs in emerging economies use both consensus and evidence relating to how FDI can boost economic growth. In particular, liberalized regional markets in ASEAN countries have positively impacted economic development and socio-economic welfare. MERCOSUR also experienced an increase in global FDI share from 1.8% to 4.4% between the mid-1980s to mid-1990s.

A steady and large inflow of FDI is necessary for countries to develop economically and sustainably. The only way to achieve this is if countries adopt robust national and regional regulatory policies and laws that protect investors' rights, improve political and social stability, reduce corruption incidents, and establish an effective judicial system for resolving disputes. The SADC member states can take actions that attract or repel investors, and reconciling national and regional interests is one way of attracting investment. Reforms within the context of the integration agenda provide opportunities for existing businesses to expand while allowing new businesses to explore new ventures. To attract foreign investors, host countries need to have strong economic fundamentals. A thriving regional integration initiative creates a larger market size, a robust production network, an effective trade policy, and political and macroeconomic stability. Investors view the regional market as one market when there is deep integration because of policy and market convergence. Blomström and Kokko (1997) argue that regional integration has a lasting positive effect on FDI inflows to the level of the integration scheme stimulating economic growth. Based on these observations, it is almost impossible to separate the effects of integration from FDI. Further, Blomström and Kokko (1997) suggest that the impact of regional integration on FDI in a particular member state is more likely to become positive if (i) integration is profound and (ii) the country in question benefits from a strong location advantage. From this perspective, removing trade barriers provides all members with a location advantage since they all are part of one extended economy.

FDI is drawn to regions with well-developed institutions, as many studies have shown. North (1990) argues that institutions influence economic activities, with good institutions lowering transaction and production costs. Most of these conditions indicate an increased potential for high returns for investors, which is the primary goal of any business. Dunning (1998) argues that investors prefer to invest in areas with the best economic and institutional infrastructures. Weerakoon (2004) reached a similar conclusion in a study on South Asia Association of Regional Cooperation (SAARC) economic integration, finding a high degree of positive correlation between regional trade liberalization and investment. Jensen (2008) also examined the relationship between transnational institutions and reduced political risks for foreign investors. In the study, transnational institutions were found to constrain "bad behaviour" from member states and mitigate political risk for investors.

However, Schiff and Winters (2003) argue that the link between regional integration institutions and foreign direct investment growth is unclear since other factors play a role. For the integration initiative to succeed, favourable investment conditions must be available at national and regional levels. Still, Schiff and Winters agree that regional integration agreements allow the country to gain investors' confidence since the agreements help lock in reforms made under the deal. A study conducted by Jaumotte (2004) also examines whether the market size of regional integration schemes affects the FDI received by the countries participating in the scheme. The study covered 71 developing countries taking part in regional integration schemes. The study results found that REC market size influenced foreign direct investment positively in participating countries and that the size of the population also mattered.

It takes various measures to mitigate obstacles impeding FDI, ranging from establishing stable political conditions that promote peace and security to establishing appropriate governance measures that improve regulations and policies that are a primary attraction for investors. Investing in good governance leads to sound macroeconomic policies that encourage investors, traders, and producers to expand their businesses. If SADC is to forge a path towards socio-economic development, enhanced regional integration and foreign direct investment are critical. Hettne et al. (1999) argue that integration of national political and economic systems is critical if developing countries are to counter the effects of an increasingly turbulent global political and economic system. It is beneficial to create mutual interdependence as it would create economic space that could increase efficiency, growth and generate economies of scale.

Even though Southern Africa has pursued integration schemes and is endowed with mineral wealth, it attracts limited foreign direct investment and continues to suffer from economic decline. In Africa, just as in other parts of the world, the governance system determines socio-economic development and stability. Expansion of the market and removal of trade barriers will only have a limited impact on attracting quality FDI if other macroeconomic fundamentals are not in harmony with the integration initiative. FDI inflows are significantly impacted by the reduced institutional quality, thereby undermining the advantages of increased market size. Indicators of global governance are positively correlated with economic growth, and at the moment, Southern Africa lags behind in almost all of those indicators. As a part of SADC's effort to attract foreign direct investment, it must create a robust macroeconomic and economic framework, along with an appropriate investment climate.

A growing number of countries are joining regional economic communities to benefit from integration, leading to economic growth and development. Europe offers a good example. Foreign direct investment (FDI) flows with the integrating regional community will determine the success or failure of these aspirations. However, it is important to note that the results will vary among different regional integration initiatives. The degree of integration and the reforms adopted have the most significant impact on any regional integration scheme's outcome and how complementary the economies are. Devlin and Ffrench-Davis (1999) argue that regional integration's effects depend on whether the regional agreements are fully adopted and enforced effectively. Deeply integrated economic structures lower investors' risks by harmonizing general policy frameworks for engaging with investors. A single, integrated structure and the institutional framework increases an integrated region's attractiveness as a location for FDI, thanks to significant efficiency benefits.

Prior work on the regional integration and FDI relationship focused mainly on European integration. Yannapoulos (1990) examined the period following the formation of the European Community, which coincided with a large influx of US FDI in the 1960s and 1970s. A study found that the common market in Europe attracted US investments that might have been allocated elsewhere in Europe. The results of this study are consistent with the theoretical hypothesis regarding the effects of RECs on inter-regional FDI. For instance, Molle and Morsink (1991) examined FDI flows between EC member states from 1975-1993. The study concluded intra-EC trade and intra-EC investment are complementary. In Europe, liberalized economies helped stimulate GDP growth and expand market size as fragmented economies integrated into a single market. Membership in the institution in itself was a positive factor, owing to its positive reputation, which enhanced the credibility of some countries that might otherwise have had difficulty attracting quality foreign direct investment.

Apart from improving the SADC region's investment climate, SADC needs to identify incentives (sweeteners) to attract the right investment type in the right sectors. Increased specialization and improved economic efficiency associated with integrated economies is a catalyst for FDI. FDI has also played a critical role in facilitating growth and economic transformation among the East Asian Tigers, which have attracted enormous FDI inflows over the past four decades. However, these incentives need to be managed as failure to manage incentives can be harmful in some cases because there is a risk of "racing to the bottom" as countries compete for FDI.

Recent research on the relationship between economic integration and foreign direct investment was conducted by Bruno et al. (2017). The study investigated how much additional FDI a country received after becoming an EU member state. Using a structural gravity modelling econometric technique, the study found that EU membership increased inflows of FDI by between 14% and 38%. Despite this, the study also found that countries leaving the EU can potentially suffer a reduction in FDI inflows in addition to trade disruptions. Therefore, it was concluded that a country leaving an economically deeply integrated regional bloc such as the EU could have significant adverse effects.

FDI, however, does not automatically lead to economic development unless it fulfils five other conditions linked to investment quality. The quality of investment must link the FDI to the country's economy and must have the following characteristics:

(i) Contributing towards the creation of decent high paying jobs;
(ii) Enhancing the skill base of host economies labour force through learning, development, and training;
(iii) Facilitating the transfer of technology, knowledge, and technical and organizational know-how;
(iv) Boosting competitiveness of domestic firms and enabling their access to markets; and
(v) Operating in a socially and environmentally responsible and ethical manner.

Particular types of FDI seem to be attracted to countries or regions with specific domestic and regional conditions. An investor's choice of FDI destination depends on a host of factors, including the country's political stability, economic policies, regulatory structures, governance structures, production, trade infrastructure, and human capital. Where there is political stability, robust regulatory framework, credible governance structures, and favourable macroeconomic policies, the chances of attracting quality FDI increases. It is clear that all these factors are linked to good governance and can only be achieved if SADC member states introduce regulatory regimes and a business environment that address the regional imperfections that are prohibiting quality FDI. In countries with political instability and high levels of corruption, predatory FDI, mainly linked to the extraction industry, is attracted.

Despite promising integration results in Europe, regional integration in Southern Africa has failed to meet the same efficiency and capacity standards. As a region, SADC remains threatened by chronic poverty and underdevelopment, as well as governance failure. Despite democratization and economic liberalization efforts, most SADC countries have seen their human development indicators decline in the last three decades. In countries where liberation movement operatives and political parties are still in power, they have profoundly entrenched authoritarianism and made the democratic transition difficult. A result of that has been political instability in the region, as well as security problems. Even though the SADC Treaty and the AU Constitutive Act emphasize the protection of people and development, the regional integration structures have continued to represent the interests of the ruling elite, which are often the perpetrators of human rights violations.

Regional integration is a critical intervention strategy that can break Collier's conflict trap. The conflict trap hypothesises that poverty-stricken communities are more prone to violent conflicts. In Africa's context, inadequate political and economic governance systems have impeded economic activities that expose the community to generate grievances against the government due to limited access to state services and public goods. Regional intervention and integration prevent further conflicts by eliminating factors that fuel conflict. Regional integration provides opportunities for market expansion, stimulating economic growth. At the same time, trade liberalization mitigates economic and income shocks that may cause grievances in the community and provide incentives for armed group recruitment. A booming economy also makes the business environment in the integrated markets more attractive for foreign direct investment (FDI). Polacheck et al. (2012) further suggest that trade and FDI complement each other by reducing conflict risk. Adding to this debate, Sweeney (2008) asserts that the conflict environment is marked by a combination of economic, political, security, and social and demographic factors, which brings challenges to the private sector. In his description of the characteristics, Sweeney listed:

(i) The political and security-related characteristics include low legitimacy and capacity of the state, residual violence, and a lack of functioning judicial system;
(ii) Social characteristics include the tension between groups, weak or disrupted social networks, fractured families and communities, low levels of trust, and psychological trauma in people affected by the conflict;
(iii) Demographic characteristics include a high number of female-headed households and more women in the workforce, high numbers of incapacitated and disabled people, population displacement, high numbers of unemployed youth, and low education levels.

Most SADC member states have become bogged down by patrimonialism. Undemocratic states have been hesitant to pursue closer regional cooperation because they perceive it as a challenge to their sovereignty and its attendant benefits. Thus, SADC's members have been reluctant to utilize SADC's instruments for economic prosperity and political stability in the region. An increase in patrimonialism and rent-seeking negatively impact FDI inflows in a country. The political and economic environment in SADC has also contributed to the quality and quantity of FDI flowing into the region. African countries must therefore start solving regional and continental problems through RECs and the AU.

African countries that could have attracted FDI have been affected by perceptions of political risk. RECS like SADC could introduce some regional policies to alleviate some of these challenges and drive investment into the region. Commonalities among countries must be taken seriously, and institutions play an essential role in enhancing convergence. In Europe, it was clear that democracy had to be deepened to spur good governance, which then created a favourable environment for investors by lowering the cost of doing business, reducing uncertainty, and increasing productivity. Portugal and Spain, for instance, were excluded during the founding of the European Community because they lacked democratic institutions. Central Eastern European Countries (CEECs) from the former Soviet Union that joined the EC also provide a valuable and excellent example of institutions' importance. Investor perceptions of these countries improved due to their association with a robust and credible regional organization whose norms and values were enforced. These countries were required to comply with EU membership criteria a decade before becoming members of the EU. These conditions included democracy, institutional stability, market economies, independent judiciaries, and adherence to EU policies.

Among CEEC members from Communist and authoritarian backgrounds, Grossmann (2006) argues that some conditions were hard to satisfy but desirable. The conditions symbolized economic prosperity, economic growth, security, prestige, and a clean break from the Soviet era. Asmus (2012) went further to suggest that the EU integrated the CEECs to "lock-in democracy and put an end to the geopolitical competition that had bedevilled the CEECs." EU membership ensured stability in Europe, but it also prevented future conflicts on the whole continent. Upon joining the EU, the countries experienced an increase in economic growth, foreign direct investment, trade, and export penetration into the large EU single market, which had four of the ten biggest economies globally.

To become a member of the EU, these conditions had to be met. A deeper integration cannot be achieved by ad hoc arrangements, as is currently the case with African RECs. According to Schiff & Winters (2003), regional integration expands markets, enhances policy credibility, and induces foreign direct investment. Therefore, deeper regional integration in the SADC region could improve and harmonise governance and regulatory system. That could become a suitable platform for accountability and transparency, which enhances state credibility. By locking in certain regional policies and regulatory frameworks through treaties and agreements, countries can overcome credibility challenges that have impacted the region's attractiveness to FDI. These credibility challenges impact location determinants of foreign investment driven by the perceptions of country risk. In most emerging economies, poor credibility originates from political pressures and interest groups influencing government policies. If investors lack faith in a new government, the prospect of wholesale macroeconomic and regulatory reforms will affect their interest.

Schiff and Winters (2003) argue that investors may not respond to regulatory and macroeconomic reforms if they anticipate that those reforms will be reversed. For Schiff and Winters, it is difficult for an individual country to raise its credibility by itself; hence, one way of achieving that is by initiating reforms through credible and binding commitments. However, initiating reforms through a robust regional institution provides an extra layer of credibility as investors are guaranteed that domestic politics and domestic interest groups would have a limited impact on adopted reforms. In most cases, regional institutions are known for adding incentives for sound policies.

Regional integration can lead to better governance and economic prosperity, given the success of regional integration in Europe and East Asia. An increase in cooperation in the region would alleviate some of the region's political and socio-economic challenges, reversing the region's FDI fortunes. Uncertainty about policies, political instability, weak infrastructure, and ease of doing business are essential factors that foreign investors analyze before committing to an investment. Some of these conditions can be improved with regional integration, and negative perceptions of the region might change. An increase in the market size and a liberalization of trade arrangements may also reduce the political risk associated with foreign capital investments in the region.

It takes more than institutional arrangements for regional integration to succeed. It takes political commitment and a sense of urgency to create an economic environment that allows growth and development in the region. Moreover, SADC's organizational culture could play a vital role in the effectiveness of the organization. The organizational culture that mainly emphasizes non-intervention continues to dominate despite the organization's shift to a non-indifference-oriented culture. Bogland et al. (2008) identified three factors that determine the level of commitment of the regional body in addressing persistent challenges that hinder an integration strategy. Among the factors are:

(i) The organization's objectives and culture;
(ii) The organization's capacity to intervene; and
(iii) The member states' will and ability to contribute towards political decisions, finances, and personnel.

In the short term, states may have difficulty making some decisions, but those decisions could transform the region over time. There will be a cost to some of these economic integration decisions, but the price is worth paying. Some states have kept their nationalistic economic policies due to the lack of an evaluation and monitoring mechanism, which has caused delays in implementing SADC trade protocols. An increase in market size resulting from market integration offers investors new investment opportunities. For example, companies that previously supplied the individual countries in the SADC region through imports may establish a production line within the SADC region to supply the whole SADC market and beyond. In a region where foreign direct investment is pivotal to supply chain creation and production networks, membership in a regional body makes investment more attractive. According to Jensen (2003), democratic regional institutions constrict individual governments' policy flexibility, which sends positive signals to foreign investors. According to Li and Resnik (2003), in a democratic setting, property rights are respected, enhancing investor confidence in the host country that their assets will remain protected. Investors would feel less anxious if robust regional regulatory frameworks were complementing the domestic policy framework. A thriving regional integration scheme is seen as a crucial factor in boosting FDI expectations.

There is a general consensus that development takes place when the economic environment is stable and predictable. Investors feel secure about their property rights, and every economic agent has recourse to an effective judiciary. Regional integration confers policy credibility on commitments made by democratic governments belonging to a robust regional institution. It assures investors that government commitment to respecting contracts and limiting contract breaches will be maintained.

In light of most Africa's economies being too small and isolated to attract significant foreign direct investment, regional integration provides a desperately needed boost to the continent by integrating small markets into one large one. These agreements allow countries to benefit from economies of scale and enhance their credibility as investors are protected under binding regional agreements. Increasing intra-regional and inter-regional trade would boost economic activities driven by trade, resulting in an increase in foreign exchange reserves and economic growth. As discussed in Chapter 5, improved production industries and diversified export products could reduce the region's susceptibility to a volatile global market of primary raw materials. The critical challenge for Southern African countries is adding value to their export products due to weak inflows of FDI and limited development of global value chains.

The increased economic activities would also lead to the establishment of more businesses due to the FDI availability, which would improve the citizens' welfare and increase government savings to invest in better public services and infrastructure. Additionally, with improvements in production, technological capacity, and human resource capacity, young entrepreneurs may have more chances to develop new ideas that expand the region's export base. Furthermore, these innovations can also attract further investments from major global investors seeking to expand their asset ownership, creating new African dollar billionaires.

8

Future of Regional Peace and Security Architecture in Southern Africa

With a youthful population, extensive agricultural lands, and abundant natural resources, the SADC region has immense potential to become one of the global centres of economic growth. With a strong cultural and social bond, the region's potential benefits for regional integration and stability are enormous. However, this potential has been burdened by persistent conflicts and under-development. The manifestation of conflict in every society, irrespective of its nature and form is disruptive, especially whenever it assumes a crisis dimension (Ibrahim, 2008). As a result of conflict, law and order break down, human rights are violated, property is destroyed, and lives are lost, creating big consequences for peace, security, and development at the national, regional, and global levels. As a result, countries form communities to protect themselves. Thomas (2010) argues that communities that require security and self-preservation merge into new regional communities. In general, nations that are geographically close together pool resources to benefit their citizens.

While external security threats have diminished since the end of Apartheid and the Cold War, SADC member states are still confronted with severe intra-state conflicts that have undermined national constitutional order and stability. Loss of lives and property, displacement of refugees, and grave violations of human rights have devastating effects on peace, security, and development at the national, regional, and global levels. Even though some of the region's challenges stem from political, social, institutional, and economic disruptions for centuries, the region must develop a holistic approach to address the consequences of these conflicts. Historical factors like slavery, colonialism, the Cold War and post-independence oppressive regimes have impacted regional stability; however, the current regional conflicts and instability are also symptoms of democratic and governance deficit.

Africa is a continent beset by a litany of political instability and armed conflicts. In order to realise human rights and human security, peace is an essential component. Several goals that form an essential part of the international community's actions are preserving peace, preventing conflicts from turning into violence, and strengthening international security. Human, economic, social, or even political development cannot happen in the absence of peace. A lack of human rights leads to a lack of peace, and any other human rights that are infringed will follow: rights to life, safety, dignity, and development. Society as a whole is affected, especially the most vulnerable. Violent conflict results in the death of people, human rights violations, displacement of people, economic decline, fragility of states, weak governance, and national and regional security compromised. However, Africa's history is blotted with conflicts and wars that go back centuries, spanning pre-colonial, colonial, and postcolonial periods. According to the Department for International Development (2001), Africa has accounted for more conflicts since the Cold War ended than any other continent. In light of this, African countries under regional cooperation have been pooling their resources to maintain security and self-preservation. Political instability and armed conflict in Southern Africa have transformed the regional cooperation agenda of Southern Africa to place issues of peace and security at the centre of regional integration. Collaboration between SADC member states on peace and security issues was one of the main objectives of the regional integration scheme during its inception in 1992.

Conflicts and political instability are major obstacles to implementing regional economic integration in many sub-Saharan African countries. The number and intensity of conflicts and the effects they have on societies are also growing. There is an increasing role for the

AU and the REC in the developing African Peace and Security Complex. The preceding chapter outlined the interconnection between stability, FDI, regional integration, and economic growth. Chapter 7 posited that the conflict environment in the SADC area had impacted the quality of FDI, which is a prerequisite for economic growth.

Furthermore, Chapter 7 demonstrates how the conflicts within one country affects neighbouring countries. If the leaders pursued sound regional policies, the region could overcome most of the region's challenges. Sound policy decisions can interfere with the conflict trap from the governance perspective. From the structural perspective, SADC has an ambitious mandate to steer the region into economic prosperity and political stability; however, the organization is still experiencing constraints and challenges to its functioning from a practical perspective. As a result, SADC is experiencing institutional challenges in fostering economic and political governance coordination among member states, slowing down integration. As such, the region is still experiencing long-standing unresolved conflicts that impact socio-economic development.

SADC member states are, however, increasingly concerned about the security risks resulting from a lack of good governance in their neighbours that could cause cross-border instability. Thus, Hammerstad (2005) suggests that regional governments, particularly in Africa, are more likely to replace "hard sovereignty," in which interference in other member states' affairs is explicitly forbidden, with regional regimes that allow for intervention in some instances. In this regard, regional security structures for managing complex security issues are needed.

From the backdrop of Southern Africa's instability, peace and security have become a priority issue for SADC and the international community. Concern over instability in the region has increased SADC member states' willingness to respond to these challenges. There is a growing demand for SADC member states to rethink their policies. The SADC member states have adopted normative, legal and institutional frameworks to reaffirm the institution's commitment to political stability, democracy and mitigating the risks of conflicts. According to Article 3 of the AU Constitutive Act, the AU and the RECs like SADC are viewed as guarantors of security, peace, good governance, political stability and democracy. Many critics have argued that despite SADC's efforts to enhance stability and safeguard democracy in the region as enshrined in the SADC Treaty, SADC's track record remains disappointing, especially on democracy, good governance and human security issues. As a result, the region is now engulfed in conflicts that have led to catastrophic socio-economic conditions.

Coser (1967) defined conflict as "the clash of interests and values, the tension between what is and what some groups feel ought to be." There is no doubt that the increasing demand for a resolution to the conflict in Southern Africa has become more pressing. An ailing economy, authoritarian regimes, and broad socio-economic challenges have contributed to the urgency. Internal political and armed conflicts are prevalent in developing countries, an area discussed in great detail in Chapter 7. The impact of poverty and the failure of governmental institutions have exacerbated the inequality and marginalization of some demographic communities. The high poverty levels in Southern Africa have sustained violence, terrorism, socio-economic tensions and uncontrolled migration of unskilled labour.

A political conflict that has plagued Zimbabwe, the once economic powerhouse and a beacon of stability in Southern Africa, is another critical issue that cannot be ignored. With democracy and governance eroding, violence in the country has risen as incumbents desperately attempt to hold on to power. The manipulation of elections has also fueled the instability in Zimbabwe. The Northern Province of Cabo Delagado in Mozambique has also been experiencing insurgency activities since 2017. Like many Southern African countries, the DRC has experienced persistent conflict throughout its history. However, the war that toppled Mobutu Sese Seko resulted in the former Belgian colony slipping into a civil conflict that still rages on today. The combination of the issues mentioned informs some of the region's complex challenges, including those relating to peace and security. Despite current challenges, SADC leaders lack the capacity and political will to address them.

Chapter 8 builds on the preceding chapter by examining regional conflict hotspots that have affected political stability in the region. It is becoming increasingly urgent to overcome political instability and armed conflicts due to a paradigm shift in understanding security, which now includes human security. In order to achieve human security, it is necessary to observe good governance, human rights, freedoms, the rule of law, and poverty reduction. Although most countries' constitutions and national policies recognize the attributes of human security mentioned, actualizing human security remains a distant dream. Bilder (1992) points out: "The time has come for the international community to undertake a contemporary reassessment of the implications of the world system of sovereignty... international security will be enhanced only when human security is enhanced. Both require democracy and popular participation, the rule of law and respect for human rights and fundamental freedoms." Towards achieving sustainable peace and prosperity in Southern Africa, good governance and human development must bridge the gap between present and collective visions. Governance deficit remains the primary cause of conflicts in the SADC region, despite democratic and governance norms enshrined in the regional treaties and protocols.

Cohen (1996) examined the violent conflicts in Africa, including the violence perpetrated by intolerant regimes that failed to deal with political problems that could have been resolved through a democratic political process without resorting to violence. Cohen identifies this trend as "blocked political systems that cannot resolve individual or group differences through nonviolent procedures." The Zimbabwe political crisis fits this description, as it involves disputes arising from an election dispute. Apart from Zimbabwe, other countries such as Malawi, Madagascar and Lesotho have also experienced electoral disputes with the incumbent government refusing to submit to the will of the people, which has resulted in protests, riots and protracted court battles.

According to the Human Security Report (2005), the decrease in violent conflict is not due to changes in underlying risk factors but rather to greater involvement of the international community and African RECs in conflict resolution and post-conflict reconstruction. For most African states, the costs of inaction can have devastating consequences in both economic losses and human suffering. The political conflict in one country may increase the risk of political conflict in the neighbouring countries, a premise acknowledged by Collier and Hoeffler (2001). For this reason, RECs have now assumed the primary responsibility for resolving regional conflicts.

International organizations and nation-states neutral to the conflict are typically viewed as being primarily responsible for conflict prevention. To resolve conflict, de Bono (1985) points out that a third party, in this case, a regional organization, plays a crucial role in facilitating communication. As he puts it: "In a conflict situation, the two parties are unable to stand outside their own perceptions. In order to move from the argument to the design mode, there is a need for a third party. The third party is not a go-between negotiator or mediator. The third-party acts as a mirror, an overview, a provider of provocation and creativity and a director of thinking." For SADC, an established normative framework is outlined in the SADC Treaty, which is supposed to serve as a mirror for those involved in the political dispute to reflect upon. Coercive interventions with military deployments or economic measures should be considered when mediation is not possible. Cohen (1996) argues that African intervention in intra-state conflicts has been outlined by three fundamental principles: respect for national sovereignty, non-interference in internal affairs of member states, and inviolability of frontiers inherited from colonization. The majority of conflicts in Africa have remained unresolved due to these barriers.

These conflict resolution mechanisms include short-term efforts such as mediation and peace support initiatives. In this case, regional integration is established for both economic and security purposes. With anocracies (hybrid regimes that are neither fully democratic nor fully autocratic), a common feature in many SADC member states, balancing the two systems has proven challenging. Abadie (2004) states that conflict is more likely in anocratic countries when poverty, unemployment, and inequality are coupled with a repressive government. The persistent instability in some countries has now started posing a threat to the region's economic and political stability. There is a consensus around the scholarship of regional integration, as noted in Chapter 7, that stability is a prerequisite to economic development. Political stability creates an environment that encourages economic development and attracts foreign direct investment (FDI). SADC member states must come together and face the regional challenges in order to sustain economic growth and stability in the region. Barwani (2005) identified rationales used to justify a regional collective response to security threats, including:

(i) The necessity for joint security as a result of instability at the regional/global level;
(ii) The existence of collective external threats;
(iii) Economic rationales;
(iv) Geographic proximity; and
(v) Political, institutional and cultural similarities.

SADC, however, has made some progress in adopting ambitious protocols to promote security cooperation between SADC member states and solve the region's significant challenges in the field of governance, democracy and security. For instance, the SADC Treaty (1992) focuses on future regional cooperation on security. According to Cilliers (1999), the section outlines "a framework of cooperation which provides for strengthening regional solidarity, peace and security, in order for the people of the region to live and work together in peace and harmony... Therefore, the region needs to establish a framework and mechanisms to strengthen regional solidarity and provide mutual peace and security." The SADC Treaty articulates a new vision of shared responsibility on matters of peace and security in a bid to secure favourable conditions for economic growth and development in the region. As a result of this framework, the Protocol for Politics, Defence and Security Cooperation was adopted.

This chapter provides a critical analysis of the main conflicts in Southern Africa by tracing the evolution of significant conflict hot spots in the region and identifying effective methods for resolving them. SADC has established these instruments to enhance security regionalization through the SADC peace and security framework. For the SADC to exercise its security mandate, its security mandate is derived from UN Charter Chapter VIII, recognising RECs' role in conflict management. The UN Security Council is tasked with authorizing force. As Haftel (2007) argues, regional institutions can enhance state-to-state interdependence while also creating dependable expectations that conflicts can be resolved and help establish institutional mechanisms to build confidence in the dispute settlement process based on a rules-based action.

In the past two decades, the United Nations has promoted the regionalization of peace and security as a fundamental paradigm for managing regional conflicts. Malan (1999) called it a "peace pyramid," with the RECs acting as first responders to armed and political conflicts. This part explores the critical role regional peace and security architecture can play in resolving regional conflicts. Conflict resolution efforts in Zimbabwe, the DRC, and Mozambique have been hindered by a lack of cooperation among SADC member states. This part examines how the principle of solidarity politics has undermined regional intervention efforts. There are recommendations provided on how to navigate and facilitate long-term peace in identified regional conflict hotspots.

Several important issues emerge from the SADC region that guides our understanding of the region's member states when dealing with conflict, peace, and human security. Chapter 4 touched on the nature of leadership, governance and intra-state conflicts. Other issues have also arisen due to this climate: corruption, patrimonialism, nepotism, and a leadership that is not interested in providing for the needs of the people. The convergence of such leadership to drive the SADC agenda has created challenges for progress in the region. There is now demand for SADC to take full responsibility in reversing these trends. Because most conflicts in Africa spill over into neighbouring countries, it becomes essential that member states and institutions in the region play an active role in mediation and intervention in intra-state conflict.

As part of the mission to promote and secure African democracy, human rights, and sustainable development, the African Union (AU) was founded in 2002. Five Regional Economic Communities (RECs), including SADC, have been entrusted with parts of these AU responsibilities. A majority of scholars have focused on the role of regional organizations in military peacekeeping. Chapter 8 examines the role of non-military peacemaking strategies in countries experiencing political conflicts and a decline in democracy and governance.

This chapter focuses on the peace and security architecture and how it can manage conflicts and improve democracy throughout the region. Likoti (2011) argues that democracy is a fundamental prerequisite for development, peace, and stability. Thus, development and peace cannot be achieved in conditions of conflict caused by poorly managed elections and marginalization of some communities. There is an increasing awareness that regional development and economic growth can only occur in a stable, peaceful, and secure environment at the regional and global levels. According to Hendrickson et al. (2013), unless the causes and underlying threats to security are addressed, Africa's economic, human and social development will continue to be stifled. The chapter provides a conceptual analysis of the outstanding conflicts in the SADC region, highlighting the need for a comprehensive regional approach to address the challenges to peace and security.

Background to the Peace and Security Challenges in Southern Africa

European integration's achievements remind us that regional organisations can only pursue intrusive institutional agendas if member states agree to reduce territorial authority and prerogatives. The first precondition for doing so is a capacity and willingness to do so, which involves the formulation and implementation of 'public' policies that do not represent the political elite's private interests. Because some states cannot design public policies and guarantee citizens' protection, the engagement of regional institutions in conflict prevention, peacekeeping initiatives, and post-conflict transitions has increased. Since the turn of the century, African regional institutions have taken an increasingly active role in reconstructing interactions between state and society.

The nature of governance is critical as it defines the relationship between the rulers and the ruled. The relationship determines whether the authority is based on coercion or democratic rules and norms in terms of legitimacy. It is important to note that some SADC member states are also engulfed in violent conflicts due to political, economic, and ethnic exclusion. The region performs poorly in all development indices due to high unemployment, low income, and poor production structures because of limited investment in the manufacturing industry, which has led to regional instability. Except for the DRC, the primary sources of conflicts are found within the state's borders, commonly referred to as intra-state conflicts. Even in the DRC itself, the primary source of the conflict is within its borders, with external actors taking advantage of existing instability. These destructive and protracted conflicts have had catastrophic consequences for the SADC region and the African continent. As a result of the conflicts, many people have been killed, thousands displaced, socio-economic infrastructure destroyed, and an environment of perpetual instability has been created. The domestic conflicts within SADC have threatened regional peace and security, and a regional response is now necessary.

There are certain deeper and more complex root causes of conflicts in Southern Africa, which are rooted in historical factors, socio-economic crises, legacies of dictatorships, political exclusion, and external influences. Conflicts in the region continue to be caused by numerous factors, including bad governance, corruption, human rights violations, poverty, economic decline, ethnic marginalization, and the proliferation of small arms and light weapons. Considering the diversity and range of conflicts in Southern Africa, it is clear that their causes are as varied and complex as their consequences. Okoyo (1977) argues that "political instability in Africa is rooted in the very structure of society and, for most new countries, in the colonial past." Okoyo adds that "Africa's colonial past has shaped Africa's postcolonial present." One of the legacies of colonialism is the arbitrary international boundaries largely shaped by colonial powers' resource exploitation and commercial interests, leading to the division of Africa into more sovereign states than the continent was capable of supporting. Furthermore, the multiple colonial regimes in

Africa left behind an unbalanced and inequitable economic, political, and social development pattern. Omeji (2005) stated that another appalling manifestation of this phenomenon was the privileging of members of a preferred ethnicity in education, employment in the public service and the military, which was prevalent in the colonial administrations.

Lewis (1996) states that some of these conflicts have roots in colonialism, while others are rooted in primitive tribalism, poverty and inequality in the region, and authoritarianism. Typical ethnic or religious diversity is not by itself a significant and direct cause of violence in civil war, according to Fearon and Laitin (2003). Nonetheless, Annan (2014) argues that for a diverse population in Africa, ethnicity has been a cause of violent conflicts among communities and states, destabilizing the peace in the sub-region. Most of the instability in Southern Africa has been caused by governments desperate to hold on to power as they lose legitimacy to govern. Some conflicts are also characterized by demographic divisions such as religion, ethnicity, and geography.

Consequently, some groups or communities have been marginalized, leading to disproportionate distribution of state resources favouring those who hold power. In the context of poor governance and corruption, throughout Southern Africa, since independence, some regimes have mismanaged state resources and undermined the institutions for governance, leading to economic decline, political disorder, and the breakdown of social peace. In the present day, violent conflicts are commonly caused by these twin factors.

Poor governance and corruption are notably at the root of conflicts in Zimbabwe, Mozambique, and the DRC. For example, in Mozambique, poor governance and corruption are deeply rooted in the social, political, judicial and economic realms, leading to bitter feelings that have been expressed through violence among certain sections of the population. The Cabo Delgado conflict has thus been attributed to corruption and bad governance as major contributing factors. We can draw similar conclusions regarding Zimbabwe and the DRC, where greed and patrimonialism have led to civil strife. Violent conflicts are more likely to occur when inequalities exist between groups rather than between individuals. The risk of conflict is higher in countries with high rates of youth unemployment. The effects of conflicts are short- and long-term, implying the absence of social stability and the threat to human, economic and institutional development. Biswaro (2013) notes that there are many costs and consequences associated with violent conflict. Attempts to estimate conflict costs often focus on discussing the political, economic, ecological, social, cultural, psychological, and spiritual dimensions.

There are few redeeming qualities to violent conflict, except for liberation wars. Omeje (2001) states that conflicts cause a heavy burden on society, the economy, and the environment, both directly and indirectly through deaths and injuries, sexual crimes, and population displacement within and across national borders. Conflicts cause damage and distortions to social networks, interpersonal associations, intergroup interaction, the destruction of ecosystems, lands, and wildlife, the destruction of infrastructure, and the increase of abnormal and self-destructive behaviours. According to Omeje (2001), conflict exacerbates poverty and food insecurity by destroying human and physical capital, economic disruption, and distortion of state expenditures. Collier (2000) notes that there is also a reduction in social expenditure due to increased military expenditures, which affects both education and health care.

Moreover, countries affected by war are also plagued by weak, fragmented, and volatile markets, contributing to hyperinflation and unstable currencies. Conflict also destroys basic infrastructure such as roads, rails, schools, health care facilities, and power supply. As a result of conflict, infrastructure is not maintained, and investment in new infrastructure is limited.

This discussion reveals that the development of Southern Africa has been negatively affected by conflict, which has become one of the most significant causes of poverty in the region. According to a UN (1999) report, this has resulted in the displacement of peoples and the destruction of communities. Violent conflict negatively impacts the affected area and damages regional infrastructure, markets, and investments in the region. The interconnected nature of African economies also means that the costs of conflict within one country generally affect its neighbours. Production losses are caused by reduced migration opportunities, trade losses, increased costs of policing, and refugees' support costs.

Established primarily as an economic union that could positively enhance the socio-economic development of SADC members, the unending conflicts in the region have had a debilitating effect on its economic, social, political, and national security fabric. SADC has expanded its mission to include security responsibilities in recognition that regional economic cooperation cannot be fully realized until peace, security, and stability are assured in all the Community member states. The organization's first initiative was adopting a Protocol for Defense,

Security and Security Cooperation in 2001. Later in 2003, a Mutual Defense Pact was adopted. SADC adopted these mechanisms as part of its commitment to promoting peace and security in the region through a collective security mechanism. One of the components of this undertaking is creating the SADC Standby Force, which is designed to meet the security requirements of the region. Although this is a laudable arrangement, it remains unclear if the SADC's collective security goals will be achieved. In Cawthra (2010)'s view, the SADC's response to regional political crises historically has been characterised by support for the incumbent regime while disregarding any violations of human rights or breaches of the rule of law. SADC has even ignored certain gross violations of the SADC Treaty and regional agreements. In order to prevent conflicts, accountable governance is essential since it gives citizens and groups access to effective processes to resolve the various conflicts and disputes within societies.

In terms of conflict management in Africa, both continental institutions and regional economic communities (RECs) were inspired by the principle of non-interference, which aimed to protect African countries from foreign influence in domestic affairs. Despite the objective of collective security being enshrined in the SADC Treaty, members of the organisation have previously shown unwillingness to pursue it because of their varying human rights and democratic records. The OAU Charter prioritizes territorial integrity and sovereignty, which resulted in the continental body failing to intervene in major conflicts. Because SADC has limited power over individual members, peace and security initiatives have been hampered by sovereignty arguments, unlike the EU, limiting the sovereignty of all members. However, African countries have made substantial progress initiating rapid peace, security, human rights, and democracy intervention mechanisms over the past two decades. With many African states facing a decline in democracy and more armed conflicts developing, new mediation and conflict resolution practices have emerged.

In its new role as the successor to the old Organization of African Unity (OAU), the new African Union (AU) has taken steps to change norms and to provide new normative frameworks. The African Union Charter on Democracy, Elections, and Governance is a binding normative instrument known as the Governance Charter. In addition to promoting democratic norms, respecting the rule of law, and fostering better political, economic, and social governance, this is a legally binding tool.

The organization also developed a Peace and Security Architecture (APSA). In these two instruments, the African Union (AU) expressed its determination to promote and protect human and people's rights, consolidate democratic institutions and culture, and ensure good governance and the rule of law. Adopting these two instruments has led to changes guiding the interventionist agenda of the AU and RECs like SADC. "African solutions to African problems" is the AU Constitutive Act's bold mantra. The African continent's conflicts require the regional bodies to take a proactive role in safeguarding peace and security.

Due to this, regional institutions such as SADC have been compelled to adopt better collective political and security regimes as part of the regional integration agenda. The expansion of regional bodies' roles to include peace and security has added a new dimension to conceptualising regional integration schemes and what Deutsch (1957) calls a security community. In his publication, *Political Community and the North Atlantic Area*, Deutsch defined a security community as an integrated grouping in which there is a "real assurance that the members of that community will not fight each other physically." The term 'integration' refers to creating institutions and practices that guarantee dependable expectations of "peaceful change" among its population by creating a "sense of security". The sense of community allows a belief that common social problems can be resolved through processes of "peaceful change." In this case, peace and development become intertwined as states eliminate conflicts and their root causes. Adler and Barnett (1998) work, Security Communities, agreed with Deutsch that a common external threat provides the incentive for nation-states to band together. Liberal democracies, according to Adler and Barnett, may be better suited to participate in a security community due to their ability to embrace shared norms. In an effort to embrace democracy and regional identity, members of RECs share norms that guide their cooperation in many areas, including security. Moreover, evidence suggests that the less democratic a member state is, the less interest it has in enhancing deeper regional integration, especially political integration.

Although the AU and SADC frameworks are impressive, many observers have remained sceptical about whether these instruments can fulfil their intended functions due to the region's political dynamics and record. African countries have a limited institutionalization of democratic values, which resonates with Adler and Barnett's (1998) argument that democratic states safeguard security more easily.

Kacowicz et al. (1998) argue in their book *Stable among Nations* that states develop shared expectations of peaceful change through cognitive learning. Kacowicz et al. claim: "Each side realizes that its security depends on the other," which leads to "a mutual interest in establishing and maintaining peace ... This change in perception of national interest has the effect of making war look unjust and immoral." A stable, predictable, consistent regime, in this case, creates the conditions for state cooperation and trust. Under a regional democratic environment, there is transformative potential that enables states to step away from mistrusts and rivalry and transition into a common security regime. Buzan (2004) states that members of a security community go beyond peaceful coexistence by developing the rules and institutions that govern their activities, resolving disputes peacefully, and preventing power imbalances from escalating.

Africa's sub-regional organizations have demonstrated unique dynamic differences in their ability to deal with peace and security challenges. The ability to establish effective regional bodies to promote peace and security initiatives is determined by the political will of regional leaders. As Kacowicz et al. (1998) and Adler and Barnett (1998) point out, liberal democracy provides a necessary condition for a shared security regime. Bellamy (2003) highlighted the difficulty in realizing humanitarian interventions in Africa because countries often disagree on what constitutes 'grave circumstances' and 'supreme humanitarian emergencies.

SADC has the SADC Protocol on Politics, Defence and Security Co-operation (SIPO), which was created to deal with the political and security challenges facing Southern Africa. The protocol established the framework for creating the Organ for Politics, Defence, and Security Cooperation. Van Nieuwkerk (2011) summarized the objectives, strategies and activities of SIPO as democracy building, peacekeeping training, police cooperation, particularly in the cross-border crime, disaster management, conflict management (with emphasis on conflict resolution), and food security. SIPO's long-term objectives are to promote institution-building, peace enforcement, and harmonisation of foreign policies. Even though SADC has a comprehensive peace and security architecture in place, it has been unable to resolve political conflicts in DRC,Mozambique, Swaziland, and Zimbabwe. As Van Nieuwkerk (2006) points out, the instrument is perceived as a tool for pursuing national interests by member states. SADC was supposed to act as a united democratic force; however, SIPO has demonstrated a preference for protecting regimes in power, not citizens. Africa's challenge is striking a balance between building the peace and security architecture and proactively responding to peace and security challenges.

Several references in the Protocol establishing the SADC Organ for Politics Defence and Security Cooperation (OPDSC) acknowledge the importance of a security approach that emphasizes the safety of people and non-military dimensions. Among other things, it affirms that peace security, and strong political ties are crucial to creating an enabling environment for regional cooperation and integration'; A commitment to the development of democratic institutions and practices on the territory of State Parties and to the observance of universal human rights which can be seen in Article 2, 2(g); and, Article 2, 2(i). Both Articles call for a community-based approach to regional security.

The SADC Protocol also contains certain ambiguities that may lead to disputes due to divergent views if they are not clarified through additional consultations and agreements and amendments to the Protocol, where necessary. It is worthwhile to mention the apparent omission to consider existing conflicts that do not fit either the traditional definition of an intra-state or an inter-state conflict but rather cross those lines. These issues will need to be clarified by the OPDSC in the regional context and decision-making procedures will have to be institutionalized.

Even though the SADC region has impressive peace and security structures, many obstacles stand in the way of their operationalisation, mainly due to the political dynamics among member states. Due to the lack of supreme power among SADC member states, the region cannot step up to the plate and intervene in regional conflicts due to a lack of political influence. Aside from providing troops and supporting the budget, South Africa has played only a peripheral role in SADC's peace and security initiatives, unlike Nigeria, which assumes military responsibilities within ECOWAS. According to Klingebiel et al. (2008), the presence of structures established for managing and resolving conflict in the SADC region has failed to function effectively due to rivalry and tension between member states. These rivalries and mistrust have thus made a formalized security mechanism impossible. Instead, conflict management activities have relied on ad hoc alliances and mediation efforts.

Diamond (1999) saw democracy as the ideal form of government, better than any other form. Most scholars regard democracy as rational, and Przeworski (1999) described democracy as a set of rules that provides solutions to conflicts without bloodshed. Political and armed conflicts have arisen in Southern Africa as a result of an absence of democratic governance. Conflicts like these cause catastrophic humanitarian challenges, leaving states vulnerable to more conflict and socio-economic decline. A democracy is a set of rules, and thus, all outcomes become binding on all participants; therefore, conflicts could be avoided if everyone followed the same rules. Similarly, lack of political convergence in regional bodies has been attributed as the primary constraint to the effectiveness of regional bodies.

In the past two decades, fundamental changes have taken place in the concept of governance, security, and peace in Africa. Persistent conflicts leading to catastrophic loss of life, such as the Rwandan genocide, have sparked this paradigm shift. In Africa, conflicts have hindered socio-economic and human development; the AU has acknowledged. With this in mind, the AU has undertaken ambitious initiative processes to build a practical peace and security apparatus that can address Africa's political and security challenges. Against this background, the OAU was transformed into the AU, which presented a paradigm shift from non-interference to interventionist principle. These new changes demonstrated a shift from regime-centric security to human-centric security, and this assumption resonates with King and Murry's (2001) argument that 'territorial security does not necessarily ensure the security of citizens within a state." The contemporary conceptualization of security is reflected in the norms and values that set political interaction in Africa. The norms and values include democratic principles, respect for human rights, the promotion of social justice, the rule of law, and the equitable benefit of state resources.

There are already mechanisms in place in the SADC that can deal with persistent political and security challenges. SADC needs to get its act together and resolve outstanding challenges affecting regional integration through the intervention of the regional body in tandem with top political decision-makers. As part of national and regional security, one of the main obstacles is facilitating and strengthening relationships between the human, regime, and state security. To achieve this, regional politics must be reconstructed in a way where the paradigm shifts from regime-centred security to people-centred security where there are improved relations between the rulers and the ruled. Furthermore, the current international political economy demands the adoption of regional integration approaches that address the challenges of globalization, regional stability, and human security.

Creating a security community in the Southern African region would make sense in light of these relationships between security and development. A common security concept is a step beyond recognising mutual security interests towards incorporating norms and values. Furthermore, it foretells the need to align every nation's domestic policy and behaviour with that of the community, thus implying a degree of disregard to sovereignty based on mutual trust within the community.

Southern Africa has never before felt the need for such an urgent security arrangement since the region's destabilisation during the height of Apartheid in the mid-1980s. The leaders of Southern Africa must realize these realities and create a safe and secure environment in which accelerated development can take place by renewing and transforming existing collective security arrangements amongst them and appointing further mechanisms to achieve this goal. In seeking a common sub-regional agenda for peace, human security, and conflict management, however, a number of obstacles have arisen, and there are still more to tackle. The concept of a security community in Southern Africa has been long recognized, and numerous agreements have been signed to this end; however, practically no such community exists in the region. Although the legal basis for these arrangements is in treaties and protocols, many argue that the political will to implement them lacks entirely. As things stand now, we can best define the region's current security regime as collaborative or cooperative, characterized by weak institutions that cannot identify shared security interests. SADC must address a number of institutional, conceptual, and other challenges systematically and sustainably as it moves toward a standard security system.

According to Ewusi and Nelson (2015), the quest for justice in Africa may be sustained by combining western justice systems, such as courts and institutional frameworks, with indigenous post-conflict justice systems to strengthen and build resilient African societies. The lack of resilient societies in Africa will lead to a perpetual cycle of bad governance, conflict resolution, and post-conflict peacebuilding associated with western-inspired approaches that will never be sustainable in the long run. In this context, Paul Collier's contention that sustainable peace in Africa depends on the priority of developing the economies of African countries, creating jobs, and building a clean government through the long-term engagement of the international community in conflict resolution, management, and peacebuilding after conflicts makes sense. Youth populations in Africa have grown exponentially over the last two decades, and due to this exponential growth, African youth are experiencing extreme difficulty finding employment. African Economic Outlook (2012) shows that Southern Africa has the highest unemployment rates, with 51% young women and 43% young men unemployed. Since millions of young people are unemployed, these communities and nations are not benefitting from their potential. This has also impacted economic growth in the region. This has fundamentally altered the long-term security and stability of the region. Achieving sustainable peace in Southern Africa will seem impossible so long as development programs in the continent do not create jobs for young people and harness their potential.

Financing Peace And Security Operations In Africa

Apart from political will, Africa's peace and security initiatives face another major challenge: funding. The SADC is funded by equal contributions from member states and donations from development partners. To function effectively, SADC's peace and security instruments need a sustainable revenue source. Already cash-strapped member states are unable to provide sufficient contributions for maintaining peacekeeping initiatives, and reservations over-relying on donor funding are raised. Considering that some of the financial resources supporting both the budgets of the AU and SADC are provided by donors, funding peace and security operations remain one of the significant challenges affecting peace and security initiatives in Africa. For European policymakers, the security problems in Africa, starting with the spread of Jihadism and the increase in undocumented migration into Europe, pose a threat to the stability of Europe. There is an increasing demand for some of these security issues to be addressed in Africa. As a result, the AU and SADC require significant financial resources to implement the peace and security initiatives and improve their capacity to predict, prevent, and manage conflicts across the region. As United Nations Organization Stabilization Mission in the DRC (MONUSCO's) peacekeeping mission winds down, SADC must up its engagement in DRC's peace and security operations and respond to the Islamic insurgency in Cabo Delgado and the political crisis in Zimbabwe.

African countries are among the poorest in the world, with limited national budgets, which donors largely support. In addition to the contributions assessed annually by member states, the AU receives financial assistance from donors, most notably the European Union. The peace and security in Africa and other parts of the world are resource-demanding. According to AU, the operational budget for 2020 was $647.3 million, which is a tiny amount when compared to the operational budget of the EU, which stands at $158 billion. Blizkovsky et al. (2018) stated that only 28% of the AU's operating budget is financed by AU member states, with the remainder being provided by the EU and other donors. Budgets for (MONUSCO) have averaged $1.1 billion per year between 2017 and 2020. Therefore, the UN's peacekeeping mission in the Democratic Republic of the Congo alone costs nearly twice what the AU spends. Baker (2007) contends that the lack of financial resources by the AU contributed to the organization's inability to respond quickly and effectively to the Ethiopian invasion of Somalia in 2006, which sparked a revolt. Due to insufficient resources, the AU only deployed a fraction of the 8,000 troops it initially planned to deploy. For peacekeeping operations, adequate funding is crucial because it allows the deployment of adequate personnel, equipment, and resources, which helps boost soldiers' morale. The AU's lack of resources exposed the gap between ambition and capability. Today, despite these financial constraints of African countries, there are a variety of financing strategies and aid modalities that can be used to finance peacekeeping operations.

Initially established in 1993, the AU Peace Fund has been revitalized since November 2018 to act as a principal financing mechanism for peace and security activities on the continent. The Peace Fund is one of the African Peace and Security Architecture (APSA) components. Article 22 of the Protocol on the Establishment of the Peace and Security Council lays out the legal basis for the Fund. As outlined by the Assembly of the AU, the Peace Fund is structured around three thematic windows:

(i) Window 1: Mediation and Preventive Diplomacy
(ii) Window 2: Institutional Capacity
(iii) Window 3: Peace Support Operations

As of January 2020, African states had contributed $141 million to the Peace Fund, and the fund was expected to increase to $400 million by 2021. A Board of Trustees manages the Peace Fund, which was created to ensure predictable and sustainable financing for peace and security operations in Africa. The Fund's Board of Trustees consists of five African member states representing the five AU regions and two international partners from the EU and UN. By overseeing the Fund's administration, the Board ensures cohesion and enhanced governance of the fund. Despite the AU's commitment to pursuing peace and security interventions across the continent, it also lacks sufficient resources to sustain its operations. A few of the AU's challenges are logistical capacity, administrative systems, and reliable funding sources. AU peace and security architecture is not an isolated peace and security scheme; it is part of a broader international framework for peace and security. That has prompted the AU to start negotiations with the UN Security Council to extend UN funding to AU peacekeeping missions.

A sustainable UN funding mechanism can help bring stability to Africa, as the AU and African RECs take the lead in counterterrorism and peace enforcement operations. The UN and the AU have worked on a formula based on percentages to determine the financial resources earmarked for peace and security operations in Africa. Funding is being discussed as a 25:75 split, with African states contributing 25% and the UN Security Council contributing 75% through UN assessed contributions. AU has so far succeeded in securing member states' mandatory contributions to its 25% and imposing sanctions against those states that default on their contributions. However, achieving a balance between African ownership of peace and security operations and external funding has been challenging, leading to a dispute over jurisdiction. When 75% of the funding comes from the United Nations, whose mandate should the operations fall? The UN Security Council has insisted that the authority to authorize the missions should remain with the UN. In its argument, the UN Security Council cites UN Charter (1945) Article 2, which gives the Council priority in deciding over the use of force.

The UN Security Council outlined conditions that must be met before funding is approved to ease these concerns. Besides the financial commitments, the UN demands better financial management, human rights compliance, accountability, and good governance. The UN Security Council has consistently demanded that the AU take human rights and humanitarian law concerns seriously to prevent and investigate human rights abuses and violations. There have also been disagreements over the AU's accountability and transparency standards, leading to the UN, especially the UK demanding these issues be resolved to their satisfaction before the arrangement is approved. In 2018, Côte d'Ivoire, Equatorial Guinea, and Ethiopia sponsored a draft resolution to address the concerns of UN Security Council members regarding any future operations. Maintaining international peace and security was acknowledged as a priority of the Security Council. AU-led operations authorised and funded by the UN remained under the Council's oversight, while the AU remained in charge of the troops.

It is also crucial for the UN to budget for the appropriate volume of predictable and manageable support. To prevent immediate access to UN resources, the UN insisted that all previously AU-authorized missions be placed outside the UN funding scope. Only future missions are provided with UN funds. Despite these safeguards in the resolution, the Trump administration showed reluctance to support the resolution on substantive grounds. Fearing a US veto on the resolution, South Africa started working on a new resolution in consultation with the US representatives in 2019. The new resolution clearly outlined contribution by capping UN contributions at 75% and the AU covering the remaining 25% of the overall cost of every mission. In addition, the resolution emphasized giving the UN Security Council the responsibility for the planning, oversight, accountability, formulating mandates and reporting for all missions. At the same time, the African Union retained control over operational matters. However, Egypt and Nigeria, among others, have demonstrated a reluctance to make further concessions since the AU assumes a diminished role in managing African conflicts. This has led to a further impasse on the scope of funding and oversight of operations.

Suppose a new resolution is to be agreed, accepted and approved; then the negotiators must be committed to getting a deal by resolving political questions first, and both sides must be willing to compromise and make concessions. The AU should acknowledge the UN Security Council's concerns and address the issue of oversight. Rather than focusing on the political aspects of the operation, a comprehensive response to outstanding conflicts in Africa must be the primary objective. As a result, the peace and security initiative's objectives must be achieved as soon as possible. As the UN finances 75% of the operation, the UN's oversight is justified considering the AU's track record. There is also renewed optimism in the international community with the new Biden administration in the United States, which has promised to reclaim US leadership in global security. It is hoped that the differences between the

AU and the UN Security Council will soon be resolved, unlike during the Trump administration, which promoted a nationalist agenda.

Along with the UN, other external international actors support the AU's peace and security activities through technical and budgetary assistance. In response to the growing recognition of the causal relationship between development and security, Western development partners have taken a more holistic approach in bringing development and security policies together. According to Tschirgi (2006), Western governments have adopted a comprehensive view of the relevance of security and development since 9/11. In the wake of the 9/11 attacks in New York and the 7/7 attacks in London, it was revealed that Western countries were exposed to terrorist attacks originating from unstable states and conflict zones. There is widespread consensus among Western countries that international peace cannot be achieved without international peace and development. The link between extreme poverty and conflicts has led to incorporating security issues into international development policy. Military defences alone are not sufficient for securing borders leading to peace and security playing a significant role in reform strategies adopted by Africa countries and the donor community.

For instance, the EU's restructuring of its foreign and security policy is an outstanding example of alignment of diplomacy, security policy and development. The EU has made efforts to streamline its funding model for peace and security by creating a European Peace Facility (EPF). The EPF will receive an increased budget of over $6 billion for six years starting in 2021. The new funding facility will support institutional capacity building and help create Early Response Mechanisms in regions prone to conflicts. The EPF has become a new tool for EU foreign policy that allows the organization to support coalitions designed to combat Islamic State (IS) expansion, including IS-inspired insurgency in Mozambique and the DRC. Therefore, the EU will directly supply military and defence-related assistance and equipment to African countries. Aiming to become a formidable foreign policy player globally, the EU launched this new initiative, which provides peace and security funding streams to the AU and SADC. An opportunity of this nature could not have come at a better time for African countries. West African states have already formed ad hoc military coalitions to combat Boko Haram's insurgency in the Lake Chad basin and the Sahel, and SADC member states have also committed to deploying troops to Cabo Delgado to fight IS-backed Ansar al-Sunna. These two coalition forces have already been earmarked for EU funding.

The result is that African countries can now commit to peacekeeping missions at the earliest possible stage without being burdened with concerns over funding.

9

Responding to Regional Political and Security Challenges

An attempt by states in a geographical area - an emerging area - to transform conflict-generating interstate relations into cooperative connections within a security community is known as security regionalism. A stable regional environment is important for neighbouring states whose credibility internationally depends on it and for those who may intervene when shenanigans break out in their state. For instance, Nigeria is keenly interested in the stabilisation of the West African region despite its own shaky status. Africa suffers the vast majority of conflicts within its own states, and if one of them is Hobbes-like, some replacement for the state authority vanishing must be found. The threat as such makes the region a major player regardless of whether it likes it or not. As such, a security community is created.

In chapter 8, peace and security frameworks created at both the continental and SADC levels were discussed as instruments for the regional security regime. Consequently, these instruments provide a permanent regional arrangement that can be used to direct an external intervention intended to reverse the disintegration that could grow into a regional security crisis. This chapter looks at how these instruments can be operationalized in the SADC region, especially in three conflict hotspots.

Regionalism In The SADC Area

Apart from Mauritius and Botswana, all countries in Southern Africa were either under dictatorships, one-party rule, or Apartheid until the early 1990s. Due to ideological differences inspired by the Cold War, democratic governance in Southern Africa hardly occupied the international community's attention and when it did, it was not seen to as worth requiring serious. As the region dealt with large-scale armed conflicts and unrest sparked by Apartheid and the Cold War, it became somewhat of an arena for global geopolitical rivalries. In the wake of the end of the Cold War and Apartheid, democracy has blossomed. The region adopted a democratic governance system with the exception of Swaziland, an absolute monarchy. It is important to note that whereas most SADC member states have adopted democracy, these efforts have not been successful in consolidating it. The majority of countries in this region have hybrid governance systems, also known as anocracies.

Consequently, the limited democratic system has failed to bring stability and development to this region, with HDI (Human Development Index) slipping since the 1990s. In the region, progress towards democracy has been slow, and some states have experienced democratic reversals. Armed insurgencies, political unrests, and governance deficits caused by eroded democratic structures and poor governance have become the region's most acute sources of instability.

In the post-Cold War era, changes have been observed in conflict and humanitarian crises and changes in conflict management strategies. There has been a shift from centralized collective security to decentralized peacekeeping, peace enforcement, and humanitarian operations undertaken by regional organizations in many countries worldwide. These organizations have developed new capabilities to combat threats to peace and security in their regions.

Currently, Southern Africa is overwhelmed by intrastate conflicts, and numerous SADC member states have had significant internal conflicts. A flawed institutional framework has hindered the SADC's ability to cope with these challenges. In the SADC region, the persistence of poverty and exposure to conflict environments has shaped the region's environmental dynamics and poses a long-term risk to socioeconomic development and stability. Political and security issues are beginning to receive prompt attention within SADC due to conflicts in Mozambique, DRC, and Zimbabwe. In the DRC, for example, there has been an armed conflict for more than 25 years. Over the past two decades, Zimbabwe has been ravaged by electoral disputes and economic decline. Islamic insurgents have been responsible for killings and displacements in the Northern Province of Cabo Delgado in Mozambique. As discussed in the preceding chapter, the conflict environment has hampered economic growth and development in the region. Therefore, SADC member states must embark on comprehensive initiatives for conflict resolution and safeguarding democracy, civil liberties, and human rights in the region. The initiatives should go beyond resolving the conflicts; they should also address the underlying causes of the conflicts attributed to leadership and poor governance.

Conflicts within the SADC region must not be ignored, and the member states must take appropriate steps to defuse and resolve them as soon as possible. Events in the DRC, Zimbabwe and Cabo Delgado demonstrate that any delayed action may result in a country becoming more vulnerable and prolonged conflict. Because instability in the region has had catastrophic effects, the cooperation of regional states is crucial in addressing the root causes of conflict. A consensus on good governance and democracy is fundamental to a collective response that tackles the structural causes of instability. Genna and Hiroi (2015) observe that RECs are increasingly adopting "democracy only" clauses in their treaties, demanding democracy and political stability for membership. According to Gena and Hiroi, uncertainty regarding economic exchange increases without political stability and undermining the integration process. Schiff and Winters (2003) use the European experience to argue that membership in regional bodies will likely support the achievement and maintenance of democratic norms, principally if the bloc contains large democratic hegemony. When democracy becomes a requirement for membership in the regional body, countries with less-developed democracies embrace democratic norms. Earlier efforts of Southern African integration have been regarded as integration attempts in a top-down manner, according to Schönerbaum (1998). Therefore, the general public could not appreciate the benefits of regional cooperation since there was no connection between regional integration and their everyday lives. As a consequence, regional integration efforts did not receive the support they deserved from the general public. Additionally, there have been concerns raised in regards to the introduction of electronic visas by the South African government for some citizens from SADC member states, even though SADC free movement was ratified by all member states.

As Gyandoh (1990) notes, the history of humanity, both ancient and contemporary, has taught us that individual states cannot be fully trusted to protect their citizens from arbitrary, discriminatory, or repressive actions or decisions of state officials acting on behalf of the regime. The demand to tackle the challenge posed by regional conflicts being a prerequisite to a thriving regional integration scheme has led to regional economic communities (RECs) becoming more complex. The biggest challenge for Southern African countries is a show of unity in silencing the guns and overcoming some of the political disputes that have delayed economic development in the region. There has been debate in the academic literature on why and how peace and security operations must be conducted. Due to the complexity of most conflicts in the region, there have been debates regarding the scope of peacekeeping initiatives, what events deserve international or regional intervention and RECs' role in conflict resolution and intervention. Academics have argued that RECs only serve a limited role, and even if they and when do, their purpose is to serve their interests. Other scholars maintain that RECs play a vital role in replacing the UN as the most viable and effective framework for regional peace and security. The Economic Community of West African States (ECOWAS) presents an excellent example of a peace and security framework that has intervened in conflicts across West Africa. ECOWAS is mainly recognized for its achievements in the political and security spheres than in the economic realm. The West African regional institution's peace and security efforts in Liberia and Sierra Leone is impressive.

On paper, both the African Union and SADC have created peace and security structures necessary to address some of the region's ongoing peace and security challenges. African Peace and Security Architecture (APSA) is a piece of the AU Constitutive Act adopted in 2001. APSA's tools include the AU Standby Force, an Early Warning System, and the Post-Conflict Reconstruction and Development Framework. Article 4(h) of the Constitutive Act authorizes the AU to "intervene in a member state in respect of grave circumstances like war crimes, genocide, and crimes against humanity." Simultaneously, the Constitutive Act also retained some OAU principles, such as the sovereign equality of states and the non-interference into member states' domestic affairs. While the principle might seem contradictory, appreciating the philosophy that led to the changes adopted allows us to understand the reasoning better. African conflicts are usually intra-state in nature, so the AU adopted the Responsibility to Protect (R2P) principle of the United Nations. The shift in international norms that emphasize the R2P principle has provided solid policy platforms for dealing with peace and security challenges in Southern Africa. A principal authorizes states to provide protection to citizens in other states if their governments are unwilling or unable to do so.

As African states commit themselves to safeguard human rights, democracy, and good governance and enshrining these norms in national policies, putting this commitment into practice requires collaboration among member states. While most regional conflicts may be resolved through the determined commitment of regional political leaders, as in Mozambique and Zimbabwe, the conflict in the DRC is more complex due to the involvement of external state and non-state actors.

It is now the responsibility of regional bodies to develop and implement peace and security mechanisms, tools, and strategies. In recognition of the fact that sustainable development cannot be achieved in an atmosphere devoid of peace, SADC member states committed themselves to promote lasting peace in the region through mechanisms for collective security and peace, which led to the negotiation of the Protocol for Political, Defence, and Security Cooperation (OPDS) was adopted in 2001, with the SADC Standby Brigade serving as the crucial tool for regional collective security responses. The OPDS is required, among other responsibilities, to prevent, manage and resolve intra-state conflicts. Clapham (2001) says building a regional peace and security architecture is crucial for defining a broader good governance agenda that supports economic growth. Although having the instruments is essential, it does not guarantee that SADC can address all its governance, political, and security challenges. SADC's capacity to anticipate, prevent, and deal with the region's political and security challenges is contingent on political will and a necessary readjustment on how the grouping operates. Article 2(a) and (g) of the OPDS includes objectives such as to "protect the people and safeguard the development of the region against instability arising from the breakdown of law and order" and "promote the development of democratic institutions and practices within the territories of State Parties and encourage the observance of universal human right." These objectives were inspired by the human security agenda, which recognizes individual people's safety primacy.

Baischoff (2012) argues that the coming together of African states as sub-regional bodies to promote cooperation and protect citizens in member states demonstrates an increased desire for collective security. Even though both the AU and SADC have adopted the necessary protocols and established the necessary instruments to safeguard democracy and stability, operationalizing these tools remains a challenge. There have been numerous occasions when SADC members have shown their lack of willingness to intervene in member states' domestic affairs, including political and armed conflicts. Despite adopting the principle of indifference, SADC member states have failed to uphold democratic governance and collective security ideals. In some cases, SADC has gone as far as shielding regimes that have deliberately violated democratic norms, the rule of law and committed human rights violations. As a result of their shared liberation struggles, regional leaders have developed a personalised relationship that has stopped governments from taking stern actions against regimes that violate regional agreements and protocols.

Zimbabwe's political crisis, Mozambique's Islamic insurgency, and DRC conflict remain SADC's top concerns. There is an urgent need for SADC member states to take a leading role in ensuring democracy, stability, and economic development in the region. Even though the SADC area already has a common political and security regime, the tools have been underutilized due to ideological differences among SADC leaders. This destabilization is not limited to the countries affected; neighbouring countries are also now feeling its effects. The Centre for Conflict Resolution (2012) reports that SADC economies lost $36 billion in potential investment between 2000 and 2008 due to Zimbabwe's economic crisis. Zimbabwe has also received financial assistance from SADC member states, with Botswana providing $76 million to support Zimbabwe's struggling private sector. As a result, SADC member states miss out on FDI and waste scarce resources supporting countries experiencing conflict. The region could have developed infrastructure if the region had political stability, hence the urgency to resolve the security and peace challenges.

SADC must deploy efforts and take holistic approaches to prevent, manage and resolve regional conflicts. Fundamental progress has been made at the normative level; however, in practice, the AU and SADC need to operationalize the existing structures and mandates to initiate measures to prevent, manage and resolve regional conflicts. A key element of the AU Constitutive Act was incorporating indifference as a virtue higher than non-interference. In addition to safety and socio-economic development, AU has broadened its responsibilities to activities related to democracy and intra-state conflicts, meaning the commitment of African RECs to develop mechanisms for resolving conflicts to ensure citizens' safety.

Among the African states who have repositioned regional institutions as tools for promoting democracy and regional stability, there is a growing consensus that the narrow conception of sovereignty that guided inter-state relations after independence is now a barrier to regional integration. In the current context, sovereignty in the SADC region continues to be a highly controversial topic, especially with the adoption of the R2P principle. With most member states struggling to provide essential public services, many political actors are vulnerable to either losing an election or being overthrown through different social unrest forms. This environment has led to most regimes adopting some coercive form of governance, leading to erosion in democratic norms, civil liberties and human rights in some SADC member states. With the region's violent past driven by the bloody liberation struggle and the destabilization efforts of South Africa, the region has a shared history that has allowed ruling elites to form silent ad hoc alliances that have allowed authoritarian regimes to thrive. Sundaram (2006) observes: "SADC has successfully built inter-state and government-to-government solidarity. The liberation struggle has spurred this solidarity and has created a strong Southern African identity amongst governing elites, albeit not amongst the region's peoples. There have also been efforts at harmonizing policies, laws, and programs aligning the region around common policy positions." The current environment has hindered the convergence of democracy and governance, which is essential for upward economic mobility and human advancement.

Regional peace and security tools have made good progress over the past fifteen years, but the initiative still faces a range of complex dynamics. According to Jackson and Rosberg (1982), African countries are weak states in many ways, and their vulnerability contributes significantly to the fragility of regional bodies. Fragile states are often overwhelmed by a lack of resources and face a range of challenges that affect the foundation of regional integration projects. SADC's inherent character has been shaped by its weaker members, whose inherent nature has been labelled weak. In recent years, some member states have become resistant to regional institutional frameworks that could strengthen the regional institution. Nation-states' reluctance to relinquish sovereignty via binding agreements and decisions has been strengthened by their fear of a more robust regional body. In this respect, collective regional efforts are considered foreign interference. The SADC Secretariat proposed in 1996 that the organization be mandated with monitoring member states' human rights policies and democratic advancements. This initiative was deemed foreign interference to domestic issues despite member states already being party to similar monitoring mechanisms by the UN and AU treaties. Interestingly, even monitoring treaties already ratified by the UN and AU was considered intrusive.

Because good governance and political stability are prerequisites for economic growth, the concept of non-interference, which has guided regional relations for many years, becomes redundant and counter-productive. Instead, a limited democratic environment has precipitated conditions allowing erosion of the rule of law, regime stability, and limited socioeconomic development. Therefore, SADC member states need to abandon the old thinking about peace and security cooperation and embrace a new vision for regional integration based on human security as the primary guiding principle.

Therefore, the region's economic integration objectives have expanded to include collective political and security interests, together with the need for greater bargaining power on the international market. The complex task of incorporating so many functions under the regional body's institutional framework is a significant challenge SADC should accept. It has gained credence that regional integration theory conceptualizes the process as a dialectical unit of social, economic, and political processes when it expands its roles and functions to include peace-building and conflict management. Scholars agree that economic development through regional integration projects is only possible in a peaceful and stable environment. There have been more violent conflicts in Africa since 1960 than on any other continent; these conflicts have stagnated economic growth and development. Due to delayed humanitarian intervention by the United Nations and regional bodies, most of these conflicts have worsened.

Due to the ongoing civil war in the DRC, its destructive nature has had devastating effects on one of the world's most resource-rich countries. With the destruction of socio-economic infrastructure, eroded institutional capacity, and loss of human lives, it has become increasingly difficult for the SADC region to achieve its economic and development potential. So for the SADC region to achieve its economic development goals, another conflict cannot be tolerated.

In the SADC region, threats to individuals and states manifest themselves in different forms. Criminal activities and corrupt practices committed by both state and non-state actors exacerbated the risk of political and armed conflicts. Clapham (1998) supports this argument when he suggests conflict is a symptom of bad governance practices, including corruption, autocratic leadership, nepotism, marginalization of segments of society, promotion of ethnic and religious differences, poor economic policies, and mismanagement of state resources. In this case, democratic governance is conceptualized as an essential prerequisite for peace, stability, and economic development. Despite this, the multidimensional and complex nature of intra-state conflicts in Southern Africa poses a challenge to conflict management and resolution. Some. SADC member states have inevitably fallen into or are falling into a "failed state" category due to conflicts in the region. With a large population displaced and a surge in refugees escaping to other areas within the country or neighbouring countries, large populations have become desperate for protection and sustainable livelihoods. Due to the complexity and multi-dimensional nature of the political and armed conflict in the SADC region, the regional collective response requires a committed and coordinated response by SADC member states.

Despite having the capacity and legal framework to intervene in regional conflicts effectively, SADC leaders lack the political will to carry out a robust intervention. The SADC leaders are reluctant to accept external power penetration, fearing a threat to their tightly guarded sovereignty. Nathan (2012) asserts authoritatively that the SADC has failed to achieve one of its main objectives: ensuring regional peace and security. What has become evident is the institutional design of SADC, which has had implications on what the regional body can and cannot do.

It is also important to note that SADC has been unable to fully develop its ability to offer economic and security assistance to its members due to insufficient financial support. The organization's financial capabilities fall far short of what it intends to achieve. Achieving the organization's collective security ambitions still depends heavily on optimism, hope, and goodwill from members, donors, and international organizations. However, blame for SADC's failures should first be placed at the feet of its constituent states, many of whom have never ceased to perform poorly since gaining independence.

According to Bilder (1997), various techniques have been identified and employed in conflict management efforts. The following are the most prominent: First, conflicting parties are brought together to establish a mutual agreement. Second, governments or third parties to the strife may directly intervene to introduce or impose a decision. Third, new initiatives, programs, or institutional structures, e.g. elections, are implemented to address the conflict in question. Fourth, contending parties are compelled or coerced to utilize previously established means of resolution or containment. Fifth, government or another third party may use coercion to eliminate or instil fear among one or all those engaged in a given conflict, leading to subsidence Even though diplomacy, mediation, fact-finding missions, and military intervention are effective initiators in addressing regional conflicts in the SADC region; operational prevention is needed in most cases. The primary goal of conflict prevention is to prevent escalation of violent conflict engagements, limit the occurrence of violent exchanges, or a combination of these elements. Conflict prevention is often used to resolve an active conflict or prevent its escalation or violent manifestation. These activities may be referred to as preventive diplomacy or crisis prevention. However, their fundamental purpose is to maintain the status quo as a safeguard against potential crises or the anticipated outcomes of a dispute. That implies early engagement with a deliberate intention of creating conditions for SADC member states to take the lead in resolving the conflicts. Wallesteen (1998) argues that preventive measures can be either operational or structural. The operational measures have short term objectives, including early warning, preventive diplomacy and economic sanctions. Conflict prevention also recognises that to avoid the tragedies associated with strife, especially violent unrest, change is often required, for example, through the emergence of new institutions or power-sharing agreements.

However, structural preventive measures have long-term strategies such as implementing peacemaking mechanisms, international legal instruments, and integrative arrangements. Simply put, conflict resolution and settlement require political and military approaches that deliberately address the prevention, containment, and integration of all conflict's political and military components. Within the past decade, the SADC has developed mechanisms that enable limited stabilization mandates to be established. The regional body has developed a comprehensive peace and security architecture that needs to be operationalized. Currently, Mozambique, Zimbabwe, and the DRC require such immediate operational measures, with the UN mandate in the DRC coming to an end.

Regional collective agreements that acknowledge the importance of peace and stability in the region require a collective regional identity for SADC, guided by a human security agenda. The integration of SADC member states' policies will help alleviate some of the security and political challenges that have affected regional peace and stability. A more practical approach requires SADC to develop strategies that could transform the region from a hostile security complex into a developing security community. With the upsurge in global terrorism and other human security challenges, leaving these problems unsolved poses a risk of undermining the region's collective potential. One of the biggest challenges in the region has been the control of borders against transnational organized crime. Currently, SADC is at a critical juncture in its socio-economic and political development. Several challenges have rendered the region fragile and vulnerable to political instability, economic crisis, and violent conflict. From terrorism, firearms proliferation, and transnational drug smuggling, the region is now vulnerable to Mozambique's Islamic insurgency, the civil war in DRC, and a two-decades-long political crisis in Zimbabwe.

Collectively, the cumulative effects of the Liberian conflict on West African countries, resulting in violence spilling over into Sierra Leone, large numbers of refugees, a proliferation of firearms, and drug smuggling, highlight the importance of immediate regional response to managing conflict in neighbouring countries. ECOWAS's response to the conflict can also be used as a model for SADC member states to deal with conflict in Mozambique and the DRC. Currently, transnational organized crime networks are operating in Mozambique, which has led to the country becoming the number one transit destination for illicit drugs. Mozambique has become a paradise for organized international criminal gangs due to its ideal conditions for trafficking contraband. It now serves as a top transit point for drugs from Afghanistan and East Pakistan, which are then smuggled into Europe through different countries across the region, making the whole region susceptible to becoming 'Latin America

2.0'. In addition to its strategic location, Mozambique has porous borders, weak governance, widespread poverty, and extensive corruption at all levels of government. Islamic insurgents in Mozambique have created an alliance of terror with Islamic insurgents in the DRC, posing a threat of radicalisation throughout the region.

SADC cannot achieve regional stability if the region does not overcome existing security challenges. In conjunction with an existing regional political and security architecture, the instruments provide the SADC with a platform for initiating joint military and humanitarian responses across the region. Furthermore, the current architecture provides a credible framework that can address the needs of states affected by political and armed conflicts, including the population's requirements and preventing the escalation of these conflicts. The immediate needs are humanitarian assistance, political governance, and transition, as well as socio-economic initiatives.

Regional integration refers to the voluntary process of bringing together resources for the purpose of protecting regional interests. The Arusha Conference Report (1998) points out that the OAU had tendencies to undertake "fire brigade" activities, which was reflected in the absence of long-term planning. A number of the tenets of the OAU Charter constrained the OAU's response because member states continued to hold sovereignty sacred. As a result, the OAU Charter left no room for African states to manoeuvre. Following this, the AU Constitutive Act was drafted, which granted the AU the right to intervene in a member state's intra-state conflict following the Assembly of Heads of State or whenever a member state requests assistance to restore peace and security. This authority has now been adopted by regional bodies such as SADC and ECOWAS. The AU Constitutive Act provides African states with a legal mandate to pursue collective action while considering the costs and consequences of inaction. In this context, a regional intervention must be viewed as a mechanism to assist member states in fulfilling their regional obligations.

The globalization process is flourishing and rewarding the fastest-growing industrial economies at the expense of those still struggling to emerge from the ravages of colonialism, socialism and conflict. Currently, the regional and international discourse on Africa is dominated by conflict issues at the expense of economic development. The peace and security discourse is stifling debates on economic integration and infrastructure development. Southern African Development Community

Summit debates have been dominated by the Cabo Delgado insurgency since the beginning of 2020, while the Covid-19 pandemic is causing havoc on Southern African economies. Despite the health and economic havoc caused by Covid-19, the pandemic also created new business opportunities as countries scrambled for protective equipment and vaccines. Amid the mass production of protective equipment in Asian countries, SADC member states acquired Covid-19 equipment from Asia, including essential items like masks and hospital gowns, despite having a comparative advantage over cheap labour. SADC member states have lost an opportunity to create new jobs and exploit new export avenues through the Covid-19 economic activities. Instead, member states have spent more time discussing regional conflicts. In no way does this argument diminish the importance of tackling the insurgency in Mozambique; instead, it highlights the urgency of resolving the regional conflicts so that SADC member states can focus on socio-economic development. The region must achieve market integration and stability to create an environment conducive to regional integration.

With this in mind and recognizing that the development of Southern Africa requires a secure and safe environment, the leaders are taking steps to resurrect and transform existing collective security arrangements among them and to agree on new mechanisms to facilitate this. Despite attempts to forge a common regional agenda for peace, human security, and conflict resolution, several obstacles have emerged that may jeopardize the prospects of achieving unified regional responses. Our argument in the following section is for the necessity of a clear and institutionalised policy framework that will ensure the SADC peace and security structure is free of political interference and advances the interests of all Southern African citizens.

Islamic Insurgency in Cabo Delgado-Mozambique

Rehn (2003) comments that "terrorism is always a provocation; the question is, how do we respond to a provocation? In the last two decades, terrorism and violent extremism have taken centre stage in Southern Africa's policy agenda. In 1994, Robert Kaplan authored a book titled "*The Coming Anarchy: How scarcity, crime, overpopulation, tribalism, and disease are rapidly destroying the social fabric of our planet.*" In this book, Kaplan described failed states in Africa and other developing parts of the world as the most alarming indicator of what he perceived then as the incoming global anarchy. Mozambique is a microcosm of what is happening throughout Southern Africa and much of the African continent: where the central governments have weakened, where the rise of tribal and religious-inspired militias has orchestrated violent armed conflict. Western Europe and Western America have seen a drop in terrorist activity, but Islamic State's global reach has grown with affiliate groups emerging in sub-Saharan Africa. As a result, the landscape of terrorist activities has shifted, and the SADC region has not been spared. According to the Global Terrorism Index (2020), IS-affiliated groups increased from two in 2013 to 27 in 2019. It is an unpleasant situation that is worsening quickly, with the insurgent's capacity growing at an alarming rate. Governments from within and outside Africa must respond to the new environment and the new threats presented. The new security challenges arise in different locations that threaten domestic, regional, and international peace.

We can trace the conflict source in Mozambique to more than three decades of a failed governance system since the end of the Mozambique Civil War in 1992. Long-standing socio-economic grievances have inspired the insurgency in Mozambique's natural gas-rich Cabo Delgado. As a result of economic and political conveniences, the Mozambican government failed to pay much attention to the region, which allowed Islamists to take advantage of the existing grievances. Located in Mozambique's northern region, Cabo Delgado Province borders Tanzania. The province has the highest Muslim population in a predominantly Christian country, allowing some people to take advantage of the province's unique demographic profile. The majority of the agricultural land in Cabo Delgado has been earmarked for mining and natural gas exploration, with the remaining land being controlled by political elites. Thousands of people have been thrown off their land, leaving the locals with no means of sustaining their livelihoods. Local grievances against the government increased due to the lack of employment, economic opportunities, health, and education facilities in Cabo Delgado. Residents in Cabo Delgado have witnessed profits from mining, natural gas discoveries, and other illegal trades leaving the region while the residents' livelihoods are deteriorating. There has been corruption at all levels of government for many years, which has left locals feeling betrayed by the government. Against this background, the Islamic State (IS) backed

Islamist militant group Ansur al-Sunna led by Abu Yasir Hassan, has thrived in the Cabo Delgado, taking advantage of the hostile environment.

Initially, the government of Mozambique attempted to play down Cabo Delgado's violence by silencing journalists and aggressively attacking political opponents in the region to establish order. When this effort failed, the Mozambican Defence Armed Forces (FADM) were deployed. However, the Mozambican government continued to deny reports that violence was escalating. Some reports suggest that the idea of a regional response was met with some resistance from the FRELIMO elite, who was concerned about the possibility of SADC troops operating beyond Mozambican control. It was driven by the country's political elites, who did not want local grievances driving the insurgency to be scrutinized. In response, the Mozambican government initiated a heavy-handed military operation, which led to allegations of gross human rights violations, arrests, and journalists' silence, further unpopularity for the government. Mozambique's response to the Islamic insurgents is not unique; just like other countries, counter-terrorism responses have often led to human rights abuses. When misused, the responses have exacerbated the problem.

As FADM operations failed to contain the insurgency, the Mozambican government began engaging foreign private military contractors (PMCs) to assist the Mozambican military in fighting the insurgents. The Kremlin-backed paramilitary contractor, Wagner Group, is one of the PMCs that was engaged. The Wagner Group, also popularly called 'Putin's private army,' has an operational presence in other conflict countries such as Syria, Ukraine, Libya, the Central African Republic, and Sudan.

In addition to matching Mozambican military might, insurgents also managed to force the retreat of well-equipped Wagner Group mercenaries who had infantry fighting vehicles, drones, and helicopter gunships at their disposal. The harsh terrain in Cabo Delgado challenged the PMC's military superiority, despite their air superiority and battle-hardened experience gained from counter-insurgency operations in other parts of the world. Wagner group mercenaries suffered many casualties and were forced to withdraw at the end of 2019. The Mozambican government also contracted Dyck Advisory Group, a South African company founded by retired Zimbabwean Colonel Lionel Dyck. Even though the Mozambican government has used PMCs, they have not been able to control the situation. The heavy-handedness of the

Mozambican military and the involvement of foreign mercenaries has worsened the plight of civilians and provided fertile ground for insurgent recruitment. In the absence of action, the insurgency is likely to grow and spread to neighbouring countries. The recent discovery of natural gas in Cabo Delgado has posed similar, if not worse, challenges for the SADC region. In Africa, where valuable natural resources are discovered, conflict is inevitable, a situation which Auty (1993) referred to as the "resource curse."

A number of existing instruments and protocols provide SADC with the necessary legal framework to enable a regional response to help combat the insurgency and prevent violence from spilling over into neighbouring countries. Being a SADC and AU member state, the Mozambican government has recourse to regional and continental support. As a ratifying country of 15 international conventions and protocols against terrorism and violent extremism, Mozambique is also entitled to country assistance under these circumstances. In addition, there are existing SADC instruments that oblige SADC member states to assist Mozambique. SADC Mutual Defence Pact Article 6(1) provides that "an armed attack against a state party shall be considered a threat to regional peace and security and as such shall be met with immediate collective action." Also, SADC developed a comprehensive counter-terrorism strategy (2015), which aligned with the United Nations global counter-terrorism strategy, to prevent youth radicalization, border security, humanitarian assistance, and tackling the root causes of terrorism.

Ansur al-Sunna has already carried out targeted assassinations and attacked security, transport, and energy infrastructure. SADC's regional response presents an opportunity for SADC's security regime to be effectively activated as the Mozambican government struggles to thwart the terror attacks. Because of similar demographic characteristics, the insurgency in Mozambique is a symptom of governance failure, and it should serve as a warning to other SADC member states. Extremists promote political, religious, and cultural measures beyond norms to alter social structures through violence. Insurgents have carried out offensive attacks that resulted in more than 3,000 deaths and the displacement of more than 800,000 people, including children. Northern towns like Muatide, Palma, Mueda, Ntushi, Pundanha, Nanjaba, and Mocimboa da Praia have been either captured or attacked, leading to abductions and beheadings. Ansar al-Sunna fighters originate from neighbouring countries, with reports of Tanzanians, Kenyans, Malawians, South Africans, and others joining the militant organization, thus exposing their home countries to terrorist attacks. The fact that fighters from across the region have joined the Islamic militias highlights that the Islamic militants and youths from other SADC regions share common grievances and belief systems. To contain any potentially armed insurgency in their territories, it is also imperative that SADC member states reevaluate their own countries' situations.

Postmodern terrorism, according to Peters (2004), is telegenic. For Peter's, postmodern terrorism is aware that wars and terrorism must use the media in all its forms to shape the subjectivities of the viewing people." With international terrorist organizations using diverse media networks, this environment has enabled terrorist groups to establish sympathizers' cross-continental networks. Violent, gruesome attacks and the transnational nature of terrorist groups have put states on edge in the fight against extremist messages that have benefited from modern technological advances that exceed government control. A free flow of information has facilitated the spread of extremist political, religious, and cultural values. The deployment of media technologies to facilitate extremist promotional campaigns must be a concern for SADC. It appears that Ansar al-Sunna has made strategic use of websites and social media to disseminate their values and have allowed the extremists to recruit and carry out attacks with ease.

Extremists have legitimized their violence by manipulating ideologies and taking advantage of people's discontent, mainly the youth. With the expansion of internet access, extremists are taking advantage of youth unemployment and poverty. Due to the massive amount of propaganda available on the Internet, destroying terrorist cells is nearly impossible. It is tough to eradicate the ideology and the threat posed by that ideology.

It is of critical concern for all SADC member states that insurgents have already attempted to operate outside Cabo Delgado. The vast borders Mozambique shares with Malawi and Tanzania are impossible to patrol and secure. As a result of the existing illegal cross-border trade and people smuggling, the locals have the capacity to assist the insurgents in smuggling weapons and communication equipment into and out of Mozambique. The US State Department in March 2021 designated Ansar al-Sunna as one component of the Islamic State of Central Africa, highlighting the group's threat to the region. Following its defeats in Syria and Iraq, the Islamic State is believed to be reestablishing itself in Central and Southern Africa. It is also believed that Ansar al-Sunna is linked to the Allied Democratic Forces (ADF) in the Democratic Republic of Congo (DRC), which is also part of the IS Central Africa Province network. During 2017, the ADF recruited in South Africa and Mozambique, and some of the commanders for the group are believed to have served in both groups. In April 2019, ISIS announced the Islamic State Central Africa Province (ISCAP) launch to promote its presence in the region. Islamic State funding and recognition have strengthened Ansua al-Sunna's capabilities, sophistication, and recruiting ease. Candland et al. (2021), in a study by the George Washington University Program on Extremism, found evidence of terrorism financing coming from South Africa, which suggests a regional funding and recruitment network.

Figure 6.1: Ansar al-Sunna Territorial Control in Mozambique and Tanzania

Source: IHS Markit (2020)

As shown in Figure 6.1, Ansar al-Sunna's influence has grown in the SADC region since 2017. Various shades depict the group's operational reach, territories under firm control, confirmed sleeper cells, and safe enclaves. With the areas of operational reach, the group has a strategic and operational advantage that allows free movement of fighters and weapons along the Indian Ocean territorial waters from Pemba in northern Mozambique to Tanga, towards the coast of Tanzania.

Additionally, the operational reach extends from the Indian Ocean in the east to Lake Malawi in the west. Ansar al-Sunna also has a safe enclave in Kigoma, a town bordering the DRC in the North-Western region. This suggests closer coordination between the Allied Defense Forces and Ansur al-Sunna. Given the region's porous borders, it is not surprising that radicalization and recruitment have been reported in the territories within the group's operational reach. This map presents the best illustration of the group's operations and potential areas of expansion. The group has also been able to recruit and continue to gain support from the locals in the highlighted areas.

Another concern about Ansar al-Sunna is their use of English to communicate their propaganda. Although English is the fourth or fifth commonly spoken language in Cabo Delgado, the group's communication medium has been English, indicating that the group targets a broader audience beyond Mozambican borders. Cabo Delgado shares many similarities with neighbouring SADC states regarding economic, cultural, political, and social dynamics. Pointing and Whyte (2012) note that the new form of terrorism sets up an image of an enemy that is both more apocalyptic and dangerous while, at the same time, being more resistant to traditional forms of tactical control. Ansar al-Sunna has demonstrated resilience and combat success by implementing both guerilla and conventional tactics.

While Ansar al-Sunna in Mozambique is of primary concern to SADC, the Allied Defense Forces (ADF) should also be examined. Among the ADF is a contingent of Tanzanian, South African and Mozambican nationals. According to Candland et al. (2021), some of those militants trained by the ADF are behind Ansar al-Sunna's establishment. Islamic groups aligned with the Islamic State have received thousands of dollars from South Africa since 2018. Abdul Rahman Faisal, a former sheikh of Kampala's Usafi mosque, was arrested in Mozambique with five other Ugandans. Faisal was a notorious religious leader in Uganda, whose audio-recorded teachings on Jihad were often shared among the youths in the Great Lakes region. After his arrest, the Mozambican security agencies named Abdul Rahman Faisal, one of Ansar al-Sunna's senior leaders. All this only shows how interconnected these extremists are across the region and that radicalization, extremism, and jihad are not border-bound. It is in the interest of SADC member states to combat the scourge, given the presence of two Islamic State-aligned groups in the region.

One of the recent insurgent attacks on Tanzanian territory occurred in October 2020, when 300 militants attacked the village of Kataya, located in the rural Mtwara Province bordering Mozambique. It was the first time the Tanzanian government acknowledged Ansar al-Sunna operations on its territory. Other reports indicate the government has covered up the number of civilian casualties in other insurgent attacks. A message released by ISIS on 15 October 2020 claimed responsibility for the attack in Tanzania, which stated that the group had attacked a military installation in the village of Kitaya a day earlier, killing some Tanzanian soldiers and capturing weapons and ammunition. Over the past few years, Ansar al-Sunna has evolved into a formidable fighting force capable of launching simultaneous attacks from multiple locations. In deploying violence, the group has resorted to new and sophisticated offensive methods and the use of what Hoffman (1999) calls "high-lethality" attacks.

Terrorist attacks perpetrated by al-Shabaab in East Africa and the violence linked to Boko Haram in Nigeria and nearby states provide SADC with two powerful case studies that can aid the institution in studying the regional risks of Islamic insurgencies. Both Boko Haram in Nigeria and al- Shabaab in Somalia started as local militia groups in the two countries, just as Ansar al-Sunna did in Mozambique. As a result of a delayed military response, the violence quickly spread across the region. These two groups developed the capabilities to attack neighbouring countries as a result. Boko Haram has carried out attacks of considerable magnitude in Cameroon, Chad, and Niger throughout the last decade, including the kidnapping of close to 300 school girls in Chibok, northeastern Nigeria.

On the other hand, Al Shabaab has carried out attacks in Tanzania, Uganda, and Kenya, killing hundreds of people. Al-Shabaab's first attack outside Somalia took place in June 2010 when coordinated bombings in Kampala, Uganda's capital, killed 74 people. A four-day siege in Nairobi's Westgate Mall followed, resulting in the death of 67 people by four gunmen. Al-Shabaab militants attacked the Garissa University campus in Kenya in 2015, killing 148 students. Al-Shabaab militants ambushed and killed eight police officers in Kibiti, Tanzania, in 2017. Most recently, in January 2019, Al-Shabaab militants stormed a luxury hotel in Nairobi, setting off explosions and shootings, resulting in the deaths of 15 people.

What plays to SADC member states' advantage is the member states' history when they created a united front against the Apartheid regime in South Africa. During the liberation struggle, the member states stood united, showing their willingness to confront a common enemy collectively. Mozambican freedom fighters also benefited from Tanzanian and Zambian assistance during the liberation struggle leading to independence in 1975. This organic link between SADC member states has continued to this day. The fact that Namibia, South Africa and Zimbabwe gained independence with the unwavering support of Mozambique would motivate many SADC member states to assist the government of Mozambique.

Any deployment of troops by SADC member states may also result in a retaliatory response from militants. The Kenyan intervention in Somalia led to subsequent al-Shabaab attacks on Kenyan soil. Besides, it is not surprising that the militants have already warned South Africa after the South African government expressed consideration for sending troops to Mozambique. An editorial in ISIS's "Al-Naba" newsletter dated 3 July 2020, read "Crusaders in Europe and America" are persuading the South African Government to deploy troops in Cabo Delgado. The editorial warned that the South African Government's involvement "will place it in a tremendous financial, security and military predicament, and may result in prompting the soldiers of ISIS to open a fighting front inside its borders." A threat from the Islamists should not be ignored, considering how the Ansar al-Sunna organization has evolved in the past three years.

Even though SADC has established all the necessary ambitious protocols, treaties, mechanisms, and instruments to deal with Mozambique's violence, deploying them has proved difficult. Van Nieuwkerk (2014) attributes this to the leadership of the member states, who control the foreign policy decision-making process. Sometimes it appears as if the leadership of these member states wants the integration to fail. Gibb (2009) identifies this as the most important factor determining the success of regional integration in practice and regional response to conflicts. Insurgency in Mozambique deserves urgent attention from SADC member states since Mozambique shares porous borders with Malawi, South Africa, Tanzania, Eswatini, Zimbabwe, and Zambia, making all these countries vulnerable. This geographic location presents the militants with an opportunity to spread to the entirety of SADC. Theattacks in Southern Tanzania should serve as a warning to the rest of the region and illustrate just how easy it is for insurgents to attack neighbouring countries. Foreign fighters returning to their home countries pose a risk of new fronts for insurgents. In light of the limited information provided by the Mozambican government and a media blackout, the SADC's deployment of troops provides it with a better understanding of the conflict.

Since Mozambique requested SADC to stem the violent Islamic insurgency in Cabo Delgado province in April 2020, SADC member states acknowledged this request as a priority due to deteriorating security conditions caused by Islamic extremist attacks. However, SADC leaders demonstrated the common tendency to procrastinate on such important matters. It took almost one year before SADC authorised a coordinated regional military response to the crisis. On 23 June 2021, SADC approved the deployment of the regional standby force to Cabo Delgado to help the Mozambican government combat an escalating Islamic State-linked insurgency that threatens the whole region's stability. As SADC member states struggled to contribute the required number of troops, Rwanda deployed more than one thousand soldiers in Mozambique, which came as a surprise and embarrassment to SADC.

Figure 6.2: SADC Standby Force Capabilities

Framework documents	✓
Memorandum of understanding	✓
PLANELM	✓
Brigade HQ	✗
Pledged Units	✓
Civilian components	**On-going**
Centres of excellence	✓
Stand-by roster	**On-going**

Source: AU 2009

These delays took place despite SADC member states already contributing troops to the SADC Standby Force, which has successfully conducted training in the past. To face some cross-cutting challenges related to maintaining the local population's livelihood, dignity, and survival, the SADC Brigade is designed to emphasise human security. Strategically, SADC Brigade has a civilian component, an outstanding component for any success of the regional military response. This civilian component would enable the SADC armed forces to win the hearts and minds of the locals, an essential element of intelligence gathering. Despite earlier communication that suggested deploying troops and civilian components to the Republic of Mozambique, it appears that SADC is only deploying combat troops at Mozambique's request.

Cabo Delgado's situation was declared a crisis requiring collective regional intervention, but that is only the beginning of the challenging path to planning, deploying, and sustaining regional military response. For Mozambique's peace enforcement operation to succeed, comprehensive, results-driven plans must be developed with achievable objectives. The functions also need to be given clearly defined and unambiguous mandates, which has not been the case in Cabo Delgado. The presence of Rwandan troops in the country outside SADC's mandate complicates things. SADC's military response will be successful if it draws lessons from previous missions. However, some of these operations took place when Rwanda was an antagonist. For example, Zimbabwean, Namibian and Angolan troops fought Rwandan troops and proxies in the DRC. In 2013, South African, Malawian and Tanzanian troops under the UN Force Intervention Brigade fought against Rwandan sponsored M23 rebels, and Rwandan operations in the DRC continue to conflict with the UN peacekeeping mission in the country.

There is also a need for planning at tactical, strategic, and operational levels beginning with an initial fact-finding and reconnaissance operation in Cabo Delgado, where Mozambique has not allowed any reconnaissance operations that the Mozambican government does not authorise. In May 2021, authorities in Mozambique arrested South African secret agents conducting drone surveillance in Cabo Delgado. What is also worrying is the reported infiltration of Ansar al-Sunna's operatives in the Mozambican military. It is feared that some soldiers have divulged information to the insurgents about potential military operations, which has compromised counter-insurgency operations. Despite all the Mozambican military's challenges, the government insists all regional troops come under its control.

SADC member states need to address the underlying factors fueling violent extremism in the vulnerable areas identified. To combat extremism, SADC will need to identify practical measures that are rooted in the underlying factors. Non-coercive approaches leverage public engagement to win the hearts and minds of vulnerable communities. Member states of SADC must realize that eliminating violent extremism can only be achieved by addressing the factors that inspire radicalization.

Due to the complexity of Cabo Delgado's conflict, it is difficult for SADC to initiate a quick-fix because the problems that led to the insurgency are ingrained. The military response alone is not sufficient, as the Government needs to address the socio-economic grievances. SADC military responses must include a civilian component that could help win local hearts and minds. For the SADC region to combat violent extremism in Mozambique and across the region, sovereign security and human security must share equal weight. Mozambique must build dialogue and initiate mediation between its government and communities to promote inclusive and sustainable development. In addition, SADC member states need to understand the enemy they face and the motivation behind the insurgency. As part of the mission planning phase, the SADC must acknowledge the context of social marginalization, absolute poverty, and inadequate development in the province.

Local conditions provide an environment conducive to extremism, so identifying and acknowledging its underlying causes is a great start. The government of Mozambique must also address the local dissatisfaction, which has shifted support away from the government's attempts to contain violence. Cabo Delgado ranks at the bottom of all social indicators, including illiteracy, unemployment, poor housing conditions, child marriage rates, large families, poor sanitation, inadequate clean water sources, and insufficient healthcare infrastructure. Apparently, the Mozambican government has acknowledged these grievances, which led to creating a new agency called the Integrated Development Agency for the North (ADIN). ADIN was launched on 20 August 2020. This initiative presents a good starting point that may help Cabo Delgado's disenfranchised and disillusioned population by providing them with much needed resources and development infrastructure.

An effective SADC Force needs to be equipped with the necessary mechanisms to detect and deter and deal with governance failures that have contributed to conflicts in countries such as Mozambique. Presently, violence in the country presents a fundamental threat to national and regional stability, which justifies a regional collective intervention. For Mozambique, the regional response must go beyond military intervention; the SADC Civilian component of SADCBRIG should encourage the Mozambican Government to engage in reconciliation efforts with Cabo Delgado's residents. It is possible to end the conflict by addressing the real challenges the locals face honestly and compassionately while isolating those who support violence. Winning hearts and minds can be achieved if the SADC response team implements mechanisms to gain local support, which the Mozambican government has so far failed to do. This includes enforcing regional norms associated with liberal democracy, governance and protection of human rights. As an instrument of peace, stability, and security across the region, SADC's regional institutions are responsible for mitigating the region's risk of falling into a security crisis.

Figure 6.3: Most significant increases in terrorism deaths, 2018-2019

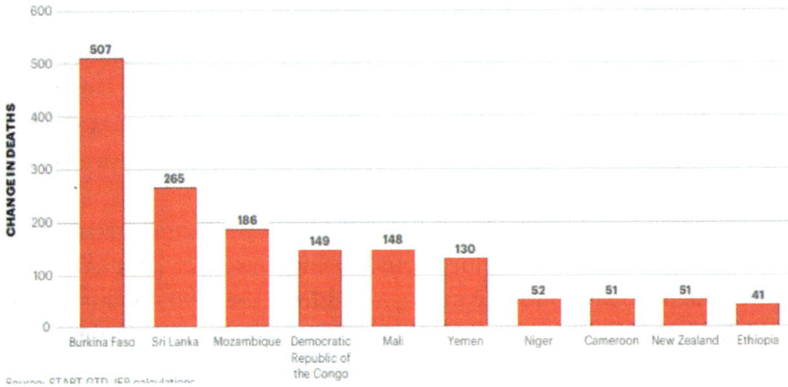

Source: Global Terrorism Tracker 2020

Figure 6.3 shows which countries have experienced the highest increases in terrorism fatalities in 2019. It is noteworthy that this graph showed data from 2018-19 when the insurgency in Mozambique was still in its infancy. Yet, the country was ranked third globally in terms of the largest increases in terrorism deaths with 186. This significant increase is attributable mainly to the Cabo Delgado terror attacks linked to Ansur al-Sunna. The DRC experienced the fourth most significant increase in 2019 with the deadly terror attacks linked to the ADF. As IS affiliate groups intensify activities in the region, Mozambique and the DRC are expected to see some of the most significant increases in terrorism deaths in 2021. Due to their horrific human rights violations, both the ADF in the DRC and Ansar al-Sunna in Mozambique are among the deadliest terrorist groups in the world today.

A fundamental challenge to ending the conflict in Mozambique is a lack of understanding of the fundamental causes of the conflict. By assuming the root cause of the current Cabo Delgado insurgency is the terrorist activities of IS affiliate Ansur al-Sunna, the international community has hindered the process of finding a lasting solution to the conflict. Consequently, the focus has shifted from the root cause: corruption, discrimination, ethnic marginalization, and an unstructured military governance structure to terrorist activities, which are a consequence of the conflict. In this instance, the failure to acquire a deep understanding of conflict challenges makes it difficult to formulate appropriate responses to the conflict.

SADC members' window of opportunity to avert the growing risk of insurgency within the region is getting smaller and smaller by the day. A counter-terrorism strategy needs to be drawn and implemented, and this strategy should include both a military component and a peacebuilding component that SADC member states are already familiar with. The regional bloc also can test the effectiveness of the regional counter-terrorism strategy adopted in 2015. However, the Mozambican military's heavy-handed approach can easily undermine this effort, and reports of human rights violations can drag any country involved into negative publicity. Thus, it is of utmost importance that SADC adopts robust engagement rules, which are still vague at present.

Since Mozambique requested SADC assistance, its response has been disappointing despite the urgency of the situation. Recently, the international community has questioned the role of SADC member states in dealing with a crisis that threatens regional stability after the Mozambican government sought assistance from the EU, Rwanda, Portugal, Russia, France, and others. The lack of resources, including financial, human, and material, hinders the resolution of conflicts in the region. For instance, most national security forces lack the requisite equipment and capacity to deploy troops in regional conflicts adequately. SADC members' unending dire financial condition has affected the capacity of those member states to support the organization to carry out its security and peacekeeping functions that need heavy expenditures. In the case of the insurgency in Cabo Delgado, lack of adequate resources from SADC member states delayed the deployment of regional troops.

The security situation in Cabo Delgado requires an urgent concerted effort towards combatting extremism and terrorism in the region. As an institution, SADC member states need to build trust because this is their best hope to resolve the significant regional challenges. In retrospect, however, the past differences between members have hampered trust-building. With what is at stake in Cabo Delgado, both the security threats and the economic potential, SADC should spare no effort to contain the insurgency and the root causes of the conflict. SADC leaders decided to deploy their peace and security instruments in Cabo Delgado in June 2021, contrary to norms where most instruments only existed as declarations. Despite reluctance from member states to operationalize existing peace and security tools, the SADC's deployment to Mozambique is unique and represents a big test for SADC.

Along with the challenges posed by the Islamic insurgency, Mozambique is a priority country for the UN Office on Drugs and Crime (UNODC). Mozambique has become a major transit hub for narcotics and other Class A drugs, such as heroin, coming from Afghanistan and Pakistan in recent years. The illicit drug trade in SADC, as in Latin America, is a major concern that requires a detailed response. As a result, cartels, traffickers, and drug lords are flourishing in the country. Criminal transnational networks have expanded their operations into neighbouring countries, where drug mules are being used to smuggle illicit drugs into Europe.

PMCs employed by the Mozambican government pose another challenge to regional stability. PMCs have been dubbed "soldiers of fortune" or "dogs of war" because they fight for financial gain in foreign wars. There is a serious concern regarding PMCs regarding their lack of accountability and lack of a regulatory framework for managing them. Evidence shows that PMCs have exploited the absence of a regulatory framework in Africa to unscrupulously broker illegal arms trades to supply small arms and light weapons (SALW). Often, PMCs provide weapons to opposing factions in a conflict to sustain their businesses. They have also been involved in criminal activity, such as illicit arms smuggling and mineral resource smuggling. As a result of their criminal activities, small arms proliferation has accelerated, and conflicts have escalated in many regions where they operate. Their services, including their participation in combat and training for combat, have usually increased the demand for their services even in countries not experiencing conflict. PMCs have a high risk of contributing to the militarization of communities that did not previously require military training and firearms and can provoke new conflicts to sustain their existence.

PMCs large surplus stockpiles of firearms have been offered to individuals at a low price or for free, hoping that they will be reimbursed through lucrative access to minerals and other natural resources. Their continued presence can threaten regional stability beyond Mozambique's borders. Additionally, mercenaries are the key players in the criminal networks that sustain the conflict since their interest is to maintain the conflict, not end it.

CONFLICT IN THE DEMOCRATIC REPUBLIC OF CONGO

As with other African countries that have struggled to create a stable state within arbitrarily drawn borders, the DRC also falls into that trap because of its people's splintered identities and colonial history. The common problems in the country are immense obscure differences among the different groups that are in the country. As a result, the conflict in the DRC continues to be one of the most complex wars on the continent, and international intervention efforts have produced ambiguous results. After independence in 1960, when the Congo war broke out, the political crisis became an international conflict that dragged the continent into Cold War politics.

DRC's conflict dates back to Belgium's rule under King Leopold II, who treated the colonial territory as his private business property. Kisangani (2012) argues that the Belgian colonial administration prioritized establishing a political system based on mineral exploration rather than addressing citizens' needs. Over the course of history, capitalism's evils have been best demonstrated through the turmoil it brought upon Africa through the Atlantic Slave Trade, the Scramble for Africa, colonialism, and economic exploitation. Arguably, there was no greater display of capitalism's arrogance, cruelty, hypocrisy, greed, and inhumanity in history than Belgium's involvement in the Congo.. For most factors considered, among this vast capitalist firestorm, none burned as hellishly as King Leopold's barbarities in his so-called Congo Free State. The best book to describe the havoc on the Congo is Hochschild's (1999) *King Leopold's Ghost: A Story of Greed, Terror, and Heroism in Colonial Africa*. The king, desperate to create a colony of his own and working with the ruthless American adventurer Henry Morton Stanley, ended up carving out vast swathes of land in Africa for himself, not for his country. In a moment of precision, Hochschild describes how Leopold accomplished his goal. Hochschild claims King Leopold II used mercenaries to kill thousands of Congolese while in power, triggering the cycles of violence that continue today. Hochschild proceeds to lay bare the king's corrosive greed and guiltlessly search for wealth, no matter the cost of human lives. The book describes the experience of living as an indigenous Congolese in a land where Leopold and his cruel and sadistic operatives established a brutal, unscrupulous system meant to exploit the country's natural resources for whatever purpose they see fit. Its indigenous male inhabitants were offered the choice of facing death either by completely devoting the little life left in them to fulfilling the unrealistic weekly quotas of labour he imposed. Instead of being shot and having their private parts or right hands chopped off as evidence of a kill for which Leopold's operatives were paid generous bounties or by any other callous and torturous method, which Leopold's operatives devised, africans had a choice to join forces with him. With little hope that Leopold's agents might miss them, their only chance of survival was to join the Force Publique, Leopold's powerful private army, and kill or burn their own people and villages.

Joseph Kasavubu, the first President of the Democratic Republic of Congo (DRC), led the country into independence from Belgium in June 1960 by forming a coalition with Patrice Lumumba, the first Prime Minister. At the time of the country's independence, Lumumba aimed to eliminate the chaos and secessionist moves supported by foreign mining interests that made governing the country nearly impossible. His efforts led to a mutiny in the military that led Lumumba to seek US assistance to suppress the Belgian-backed mutiny led by Moise Tshombe. When the United States refused to assist Lumumba, he approached the Soviet Union.

Because of DRC's vast natural resources and Lumumba's Pan-Africanist philosophy, which resents colonial influence, Belgium and the United States feared the country could fall out of their sphere of influence and fall into the hands of the Soviet Union. Eventually, Lumumba was assassinated by the US's Central Intelligence Agency (CIA) because he was considered a threat to Belgian and US interests in the region, according to Ludo de Witte (2001). The political instability nfluenced by domestic and foreign influence resulted to the rise of Joseph-Désiré Mobutu, the longest serving president of the DRC.

Mobutu, a former Sergeant Major in the Belgian Congolese Army, was initially appointed as the Secretary of State for National Defense by President Joseph Kasavubu and Prime Minister Lumumba. After independence, a power struggle developed between President Kasivubu and Premier Lumumba as Kasivubu attempted to dismiss Lumumba. Despite being Lumumba's ally, Mobutu quietly supported Kasavubu's efforts to remove him. Mobuto's soldiers captured Lumumba in February

1961, and he was handed over to Moise Tshombe, a Belgian-backed Katanga secessionist who assassinated him. Following Lumumba's elimination, Tshombe became prime minister, Kasabubu was restored to the presidency, and Mobutu was appointed commander-in-chief of the military. In his new role, Mobutu reorganized the military and appointed his loyalists to all-important military posts. When another power struggle erupted between Kasavubu and Tshombe, Mobutu Sese Seko removed Kasavubu from power and imposed himself as the supreme leader.

As President, Mobutu changed the name from Congo to Zaire as he attempted to Africanise the country. Before 1990, Zaire was a one-party state, with Mobutu's Mouvement Populaire de la Révolution (MPR) the only legal political party. During Mobutu's rule, exiled politicians who had served in previous governments and Angolan-backed Katanga successionist rebels operating from Angola attempted to overthrow Mobutu. Thanks to France and the US, Mobutu's government survived rebellions and coup attempts. However, the Western governments Mobutu had relied upon to sustain his grip of power no longer supported him as the country lost the strategic significance it enjoyed during the Cold War era. With the myriad of internal conflicts, Mobutu had to deal with them on his own. Therefore, opposition to Mobutu's oppressive rule grew, and his dictatorship, like others in the region, was challenged.

Biswaro (2013) argues that the second wave of violence in DRC was a continuation of the Rwandan civil war following three decades of oppression under the Mobutu's regime. Mobutu's regime enjoyed excellent relations with Juvenal Habyarimana's Hutu-led Rwandan government before the genocide there that led to the death of 800,000 Tutsis. While the Tutsi population was persecuted in Rwanda, the Tutsi community (Banyamulenge) in Eastern Zaire bordering Rwanda was marginalized and violently oppressed by the Mobuto regime. The fall of the Hutu regime in Rwanda led to an influx of Hutu refugees into Zaire. Refugee camps in Kivu and other parts of Eastern Zaire provided a safe haven for Hutu militias to rearm themselves to launch cross-border attacks on the newly formed Rwandan Patriotic Front (RPF) government. To repel Hutu attacks, Rwanda armed Banyamulenge militias in response to a Hutu threat. When Mobutu Sese Seko's regime in DRC became weak, the Rwandan government organized and provided equipment to some opposition groups, including the Banyamulenge, to help Laurent-Desire Kabila topple the Mobutu government. A friendly government in Zaire was of interest to Rwanda because the Mobutu regime would not disarm the Hutu militias destabilizing the country in Eastern Zaire.

Banyamulenge is a small Tutsi group in Eastern DRC, which makes up less than 1% of the Congolese population. They are believed to have migrated from Rwanda to Zaire in the seventeenth century. For many years, the Banyamulenge were denied political and economic rights in DRC. Based on a 1988 legislation initiated by the Mobutu regime, Banyamulenges could not own land due to structured discrimination. The Banyamulenge were deprived of their legal right to appropriate homes in 1995, which led to the uprising against Mobutu. Kabila's Alliance of Democratic Forces for the Liberation of Congo (ADFLC) overthrew Mobutu in May 1997 with the help of Banyamulenge militias, Rwanda, and Uganda, and the country adopted a new name, the Democratic Republic of Congo.

Almost immediately after assuming power, Kabila's authority was undermined by the presence of Rwandan and Ugandan troops in the country, some of whom held top positions in the new coalition government. In seeking to consolidate power, Kabila started distancing himself from the Rwandan government, a regime that had propelled him to power. Kabila also started removing some of the top government and military officials from Rwanda and the Banyamulenge ethnic group to limit Rwandan influence in Congolese politics. Kabila's actions caused divisions within the ruling coalition, and between the end of July and the beginning of August 1998, he demanded the deportation of Tutsi soldiers who had assisted him.

According to Nzongola-Ntalaja (2002), Kabila fired Rwandan commander James Kabarebe from his position as Chief of Staff of the DRC Army on 27 July 1998, as he preempted a coup d' d'état from the deposed military leaders. The expulsion led to other senior military leaders being removed, and some units defected in support of the expelled commanders. The expelled troops regrouped and launched an armed rebellion against Kabila in Goma and Kinshasa as a result.

Rwanda and Uganda took an active role in overthrowing Kabila as hostilities continued. As a result of a Hutu militia attack on Rwanda, Rwanda deployed troops into DRC, explaining that Kabila was responsible for Rwanda's incursion. The Ugandan government also sent its troops into the DRC, and, like Rwanda, the Ugandan government claimed that rebels were attacking Uganda from the DRC. The Ugandan government says the Uganda People's Defence Force (UPDF) made incursions into Eastern DRC to attack the Lord's Resistance Army (LRA), a militia group accused of widespread human rights violations in Northern Uganda. Nevertheless, Mamdani and Clark (2001) maintain that Uganda only deployed troops to assist its ally Rwanda. Rwanda and Uganda have continued to participate in the conflict, driven primarily by national security and economic interests. Burundi has also been involved in the war in the DRC to a lesser extent, with the Burundian army pursuing members of armed opposition groups, such as the National Forces for Liberation (FNL). As Birgit Hoffmann (1999) notes, foreign state actors have weakened the DRC and aggravated the conflict.

SADC's broad membership has posed challenges, having admitted the DRC in 1997 and being entangled in a Great Lakes conflict. For SADC, Rwanda and Uganda's involvement in the conflict, countries that are outside SADC's spheres of influence, poses a challenge. The two countries continue to play an influential role in the conflict and politics of the DRC due to their divergent geostrategic interests, which make the process of negotiating a peaceful settlement in the DRC difficult. Conflict in the DRC is an excellent example of a conflict with transnational dimensions. In the current state of affairs, the country faces one of the most severe state failures, resulting in a humanitarian catastrophe, rampant abuse of human rights, and sexual violence. Violence in the country has led to the displacement of more than five million people, mainly in the country's eastern provinces. As far as the region and the international community are concerned, the conflict in DRC remains a major obstacle to prosperity and stability in the region. Mineral-rich DRC has the potential to play an essential role in the transformation of SADC's economic fortunes. To create lasting peace in the region, the SADC needs to play a more significant role. SADC has already been involved in substantial military intervention through the United Nations Organization Mission in the DRC (MONUSCO).

In addition to the involvement of external state actors in the DRC conflict, SADC is also concerned about the rise of Islamic militants in the country. The Allied Democratic Forces (ADF), led by Seka Musa Baluku, active in North Kivu and Ituri, have pledged allegiance to the Islamic State. On 18 September 2020, Mujahideen TV released a video in which Seka Musa Baluku announced the group's loyalty to ISIS: "There is no longer an ADF. Allah willing, ADF ceased to exist a long time ago. Currently, we are a province, the Central Africa Province, one province among the numerous provinces that make up the Islamic State under the Caliph and

Leader of all Muslims, Abu Ibrahim al-Hashimi al-Quraishi." According to UN figures, the ADF killed 849 civilians in 2020 alone, and the DRC saw the fourth largest increase in terrorism-related deaths, according to the Global Terrorism Tracker (2020) report. The ADF is closely linked to Ansar al-Sunna, one of the most deadly Islamic militias currently operating in Mozambique. The two Islamic extremist groups operating in the SADC region under the ISIS banner are known as Islamic State Central Africa. In an Al Jazeera report of 20 October 2020, the group attacked Kangbayi central prison and freed 1,300 prisoners. In light of this new development, SADC faces a more urgent crisis because, according to Candland et al. (2021), the ADF may contain Tanzanians, South Africans and Mozambicans in its hierarchy. According to Candleland et al. (2021), South African financiers have been transferring thousands of dollars to the group since May 2018, demonstrating the expansion of the terrorist recruitment and financing network.

In the DRC, the scramble for illegal exploitation of the country's natural resources has caused a humanitarian catastrophe. Although the conflicts in the Democratic Republic of the Congo are mainly due to political and ethnic violence, the economic demand for resources has triggered a flare-up, with some multinational corporations (MNCs) abandoning their ethical obligations by backing rebel groups. AngloGold, for example, is known to have assisted rebel groups to obtain mining concessions and security which can only be guaranteed by warlords motivated to maintain political and economic influence through these natural resources. As a result of the enormous wealth that the country has obtained from mineral resources, some multinational companies have chosen to abandon their ethical responsibilities. In the DRC, the multinationals' operations have not improved local living conditions; instead, their activities have created socio-political challenges. Due to this exploitative behaviour, the Congolese people have been deprived of basic human needs. Their fragile government has failed to provide essential public services, including protecting them from physical harm. Because most mining companies are based in Western nations, their unregulated mining operations have remained a primary obstacle to long-term sustainable peace.

The DRC is not only rich in minerals such as gold, diamonds, coltan, tin, uranium, and oil but it is also a leading copper and cobalt producer in Africa. The DRC is also the world's largest producer of cobalt, a rare metal whose value keeps rising as electric cars and electronic devices gain popularity. It is also home to one of the world's largest rainforests, which act as a carbon sink for greenhouse gases. Rivers in the DRC also present untapped sources for generating hydroelectric power capable of powering the whole of Africa. The country has more than 80 million hectares of fertile arable land and favourable climatic conditions, offering vast agricultural production opportunities. In the DRC, there are volcanoes, wild animals, and stunning landscapes that could make it an attractive destination for tourists. Even with this immense economic potential, the DRC remains one of the world's poorest countries with one of the highest child mortality rates. In sum, the abundance of natural and mineral resources has made the DRC a battleground for controlling these resources, and the country fits perfectly with Richard Auty's (1993) resource curse hypothesis.

The involvement of Rwanda, Burundi, and Uganda in the DRC is more complicated and complex as their interests go beyond their security interests. In fact, the Rwandan army has been fighting the Democratic Forces for the Liberation of Rwanda (FDLR), a political-military movement active in the North and South Kivu provinces of the DRC since the Rwandan Patriotic Front (RPF) came into power in 1994.

The movement consists of ex-Rwandan Hutu Armed Forces, who fled to eastern DRC after the 1994 Rwandan genocide and have continued to recruit young Hutu soldiers directly from Rwanda. Coltan mining proceeds from Eastern DRC have also funded a significant part of the Rwandan military. Coltan mining proceeds also reportedly funded national development in Rwanda. Despite the region's richness in coltan, there is no functioning government in the DRC, permitting the federal government of Rwanda to oversee mining in the region. Resources derived from illegal exploitation have been used to support armed groups in Eastern DRC.

Nagar (2020), in her book *Politics and Pan-Africanism: Diplomacy, Regional Economies and Peace-building in Contemporary Africa*, observes: "Minerals originating from DRC are transported across borders to Uganda, Rwanda and Burundi. The three Great Lakes countries have been used to smuggle billions of dollars of minerals out of the DRC. Tantalum is primarily produced and sold in north Katanga, Rubaya in the Masisi territory of north Kivus, and Shabunda in South Kivus. The warlords in Shabunda control cassiterite mining and distribution." According to Nagar (2020), "DRC produced and traded 150.58 kg of gold in 2014 and 180.76 kg in 2013, less than 2% of total gold production. As for the remainder, it is estimated to have been smuggled, weighing between 10 tonnes and worth between $391 million and $418 million. The DRC produced 40 tons of gold in 2014, and illicit gold exports were estimated to be between $118 million and $11.8 billion. Burundi officially exported two tonnes of gold in 2008, of which one tonne originated in the DRC, and Rwanda exported nearly twice its production."

UN Security Council members seek new methods to stabilize the country so that the long-running peacekeeping operation can be wound down. SADC member states should rise to the occasion and pledge to suppress the armed groups in DRC's eastern provinces. With most of the diverse militia groups being used as proxies by neighbouring countries to control the mineral resources, SADC must take action against these countries through sanctions and UN and AU resolutions. The political links of armed groups need to be analyzed by SADC with the UN's help to identify sustainable solutions for resolving the local grievances being exploited by these groups. The MNCs using the conflict to exploit the country's resources need to be exposed and have international sanctions imposed on them.

The civil war in DRC, which has devastating implications for peace in East and Southern Africa, requires SADC, the AU, and UN to formulate a comprehensive roadmap to resolve the current crisis and enhance the conflict transformation process in DRC. Transnational institutions can play a crucial role by providing resources and leadership to assist the government and people of the DRC in developing and implementing a roadmap for lasting peace. SADC-led efforts succeeded in the DRC in 2013 when SADC member states operating under MONUSCO's Force Intervention Brigade (FIB) defeated the Rwandan-backed rebel group M23. The idea of FIB came about after MONUSCO faced criticism for failing to contain the violence projected by the M23 in Eastern DRC, leading to the capture of the region's major city, Goma. In response, the UN Security Council created the FIB, which consisted of three infantry ground battalions, one artillery battery, one Special Forces unit, and a reconnaissance company.

South African, Malawian, and Tanzanian troops formed the Force Intervention Brigade, illustrating the political will and commitment of the SADC to bring about stability in the DRC. A successful military operation was launched against M23 because the FIB deployed sophisticated technologies like South African attack helicopters to combat this armed group. Thus, the regional body raised the political stakes for the M23 and its enablers, especially Rwanda. Rwanda had to choose between waging an all-out war with SADC forces or allowing the defeat of M23 to proceed. Rwanda had no choice but to withdraw its forces, leading to signing a series of peace agreements.

Figure 6.4: United Nations Force Intervention Brigade in DRC (2013)

Source: UN photo

The UN Security Council first granted a one-year mandate for the FIB in 2013. The mandate fell under the UN Special Representative of the UN Secretary-General and the UN Security Council. As a result of the FIB structure, the military leadership could make quick decisions without going through traditional red tape. Based on the M23 operation, SADC needs to employ a similar strategy with other rebel groups receiving support from Rwanda, Uganda, Burundi, and exploitative multinational corporations. Furthermore, the SADC must gather support from the international community and deepen constructive engagement with the DRC's neighbours, particularly Angola, Rwanda, Burundi, and Uganda. As illustrated by the FIB operations, SADC member states have already proved that they can bear the burden by intervening in the DRC conflict. SADC can gain insight into the feasibility of a collective security system capable of dealing with complex security challenges across the region using the framework used for troop deployment. FIB demonstrated that SADC member states could effectively resolve political and security challenges by speaking with one voice.

Since the UN Security Council extended MONUSCO's mandate in DRC only until 20 December 2021, new arrangements are necessary for SADC to achieve sustainable peace and stability. According to a UN Security Council communique (SC/14395), the Security Council endorsed the Joint Strategy for the Progressive and Phased Drawdown of MONUSCO, including its withdrawal from Kasaï in 2021 and progressively from Tanganyika in 2022. Clearly, the UN is determined to wind down its activities in the DRC as soon as possible from the adopted resolution. In the event of the UN peacekeeping mission departure from DRC, a vacuum will exist that needs to be filled by SADC.

SADC has avoided getting involved in DRC's domestic politics, which has usually exacerbated the country's tensions, aside from its commendable military operations in the DRC under the UN. SADC, for instance, chose not to pressure Joseph Kabila, who remained in power illegally after postponing elections scheduled for 2016. Kabila delayed the elections for three years despite growing calls for him to hold the elections without facing any pushback from his SADC peers. In August 2017, SADC took an uninspiring stance on the political developments in DRC at the 37th Ordinary Summit of Heads of State. As expected, SADC commended Kabila while condemning international actors for the targeted sanctions imposed on Kabila for his failure to hold the elections. According to a communiqué released by the South African Department of International Relations and Cooperation, SADC invoked the principles of sovereignty, non-interference, and mutual respect. SADC's statements show that it prioritizes regime survival over democratic processes in the DRC, as has been the case with other conflicts in the region. Since some of the DRC violence has originated from electoral disputes, it is in SADC's interests to take a stronger stance and pursue more decisive action whenever governance fails.

As a whole, the country's conflict is one of the most complex conflicts on the continent, encompassing political, economic, social, security, and institutional dimensions. The last two decades have shown that solving these challenges in the DRC remains complex and ambiguous. SADC should do more to create an environment conducive to democracy and stability in the DRC and requires a multifaceted approach, which must include: international pressure on foreign state actors and business actors involved in the conflict; pressure on the DRC government to work closely with the opposition; and commitment and actions taken by SADC to protect the human rights and security of all citizens through the continued military deployment of FIB troops.

There is a range of peacebuilding approaches that must be integrated and guided by a hierarchy of priorities tailored to the specific needs and political dynamics of the DRC. Creating a hierarchy of this kind requires a comprehensive strategy covering politics, social, economic, security, and governance. SADC's ability to effectively press the DRC government to adopt necessary reforms in political and governance systems also depends on its assertiveness in collaborating with the opposition parties and civil society actors. It is essential to realize that military intervention can only offer relative stability in the short term, while democratic governance can provide long-term stability. SADC must assist the DRC in building legitimate political institutions that represent all citizens while harnessing ethnic unity in the face of ethnic tensions.

Civil society organizations and the Catholic Church are active in the Democratic Republic of the Congo. The Catholic Church and civil society organizations have played a central role in the country's political arena for many years. According to the Africa Center for Strategic Studies (2016), DRC's civil society was critical to establishing the Rassemblement, otherwise known as the rally. This initiative brought together four key opposition groups: the G7, La Dynamique de l'opposition, Alternative 2016 and Étienne Tshisekedi's Union for Democracy and Social Progress. Additionally, the Catholic Church continues to influence Congolese society and should be utilized in future negotiations.

In order to achieve peace in the DRC, the country must transform its past of ethnic division into a vision of the future via a politically reasonable settlement that unifies the interests of the large majority of the population. As a result, a constitutional compromise is needed to ensure that the new constitution reflects the historical, cultural, and socioeconomic reality in the DRC. With these changes, the DRC will be able to re-invent a new democracy while at the same time being able to run an independent and credible election. The time is suitable for a SADC intervention when the United Nations peacekeeping mission in the country is nearing the end of its mandate.

Political Instability in Zimbabwe

Zimbabwe has been slipping into decline over the past two decades. The country is characterized by a fragile political situation and a dysfunctional socio-economic environment. The political climate remains tense. The economy is in a state of collapse. Zimbabwe's political and socio-economic challenges are attributed to the ruling party, the Zimbabwe African National Union-Patriotic Front (ZANU PF). As ironic as it may seem, a country that once hailed as the breadbasket of Africa and was considered one of the top four industrialized countries in Sub-Saharan Africa is now thrown into two-decades-long political and economic crises. Zimbabwe's crisis can be traced back to 1980 when the country became independent. Mlambo and Raftopoulos (2010) claim that Zimbabwe's crisis has been long in the making; therefore, the current situation is merely a symptom of its history. In redressing historical policies that forced indigenous Zimbabweans from their lands, ZANU-PF veterans promoted a radical redistribution of white-owned land.

Cawthra (2010) traces Zimbabwe's current political and economic crisis back to February 2000, when President Mugabe lost a referendum on a new constitution. In the aftermath of this referendum loss, there was a perception that his authority and power were undermined. Despite the irregularities, the parliamentary elections that followed the referendum were also closely contested. According to Cawthra, this was the first time ZANU-PFs electoral dominance had been shattered which came as a shock. It is clear from this that the crisis resulted from blocked democratic transitions at the turn of the century, which is crucial for the region. Zimbabwe's situation is unique and more about a lack of political stability than an open conflict like in the Democratic Republic of the Congo and Cabo Delgado conflicts.

After the political and economic crisis led to the loss of legitimacy of the ZANU-PF regime in Zimbabwe, the government used the state's security apparatus to unleash terror on people who opposed it and from then onwards, manipulated election results. SADC has been unable to apply its normative institutional framework during this crisis, despite a decline in democracy and poor economic governance that has resulted in a political, economic, social, and humanitarian crisis over the last two decades. The political conflict has also worsened due to economic hardships driven by international economic sanctions and economic mismanagement of the ruling elites. Thanks to the economic crisis, a virtual standstill in industrial production and a decline in agricultural output have caused severe shortages of goods and inadequate public services. The AU, SADC, and the international community must play a crucial role in normalizing Zimbabwe's political and socio-economic climate in order to set Zimbabwe on a path to political stability and economic recovery.

Although the colonial legacy impacted the post-colonial African states, African leaders' contributions should also not be overlooked. The entitlement to rule demonstrated by the liberation movement leaders from ZANU-PF has become a burden on democratic transition. As a result of SADC leaders' misconstrued principle of solidarity, Zimbabwe's authoritarian leadership has escaped regional isolation despite international condemnation for alleged human rights abuses and economic mismanagement. SADC's reluctance to entertain constant international calls for the organization to take a stronger stance against Zimbabwe represents a perfect example of this solidarity principle's failure. This stance is motivated by the historic ties formed between freedom fighters from different countries during the liberation struggle, where they fought together and supported each other. The ideals of solidarity had even discouraged some SADC leaders from breaking ranks with their regional peers even when, in private, they disagreed with the repressive regime in Zimbabwe.

As a result of Zimbabwe's political crisis, SADC has been negatively affected, and regional cooperation has been hindered. In light of differences in how the SADC countries are categorized on the governance spectrum, disagreements have emerged among member states regarding dealing with Zimbabwe's crisis due to internal politics. Even though SADC members have committed to democratic governance, peace, and human rights, the SADC member states have often been slow to condemn gross human rights violations in other countries. Some of the SADC countries, such as Zimbabwe, South Africa, Namibia, Angola, and Mozambique, are still governed by liberation parties whose relationships date back to the liberation struggle to retain a spirit of solidarity with the current regimes. Adolfo (2009) argues that liberation parties in the SADC region have consolidated their relationships following Zimbabwe's economic and political crisis. In 2001, a senior member of the ANC formed a regional network of liberation movements in Southern Africa due to the Zimbabwean crisis. The objective was to strengthen their solidarity and generate support for Zanu-PF. According to Nathan (2006), SADC member states have continuously demonstrated that the principle of solidarity only pertains to regime security and not to individual security. Governments controlled by liberation movement parties in the region have hampered the prospects of a robust regional integration based on democracy, good governance, and human security. Adolfo (2009) argues that SADC liberation leaders are sensitive to insecurity from within, which presents a threat to their regimes' security. Most South African leaders' support for the government in Zimbabwe appears to be motivated by their interest in preserving their legitimacy to stay in power, which is also directly tied to the liberation struggle.

As an excuse for their lack of intervention, SADC has argued that the political crisis can only be resolved by Zimbabweans while ignoring the governance system's deterioration and human rights violations. The argument that the regional bloc protects political elites at the expense of citizens and exhibits insensitivity to human suffering is not misplaced. The lack of political commonality among the member states has led to some members disregarding rules and policies, which in many cases has led to member states adopting divergent approaches. SADC's continued support for Zimbabwe's oppressive regime risks lowering the bar for democracy and human rights in the region. Instead, SADC has blamed international economic sanctions for Zimbabwe's economic and political decline while ignoring the Zimbabwean government's repressive tactics and policy failures.

For many years, SADC's position concerning the Zimbabwe crisis has been passive or what Thabo Mbeki referred to as 'silent diplomacy.' While the regional body has remained silent on human rights violations, it has issued Summit statements congratulating the Zimbabwe government on the success of its land redistribution process, despite the process being declared illegal by the SADC Tribunal. SADC has also endorsed the results of every election and congratulated Zimbabwe's government despite gross allegations of electoral fraud that has led to electoral disputes. Nevertheless, some regional leaders have issued strong public condemnations of violence and human rights abuses in Zimbabwe, with the leaders who make such statements being vilified by their peers. Botswana openly broke ranks with SADC when it condemned Zimbabwe, causing divisions among member states. Ian Khama, the former President of Botswana, described Mugabe as repressive and called for international supervision of its elections.

The Ministry of Foreign Affairs and International Cooperation later issued a statement in which it stated: "Botswana does not accept the results of the June 27th [2008] run-off election in Zimbabwe, as they violate the core principles of SADC, the African Union and the United Nations. The legal process of producing a Government in Zimbabwe has failed, leading to the ongoing talks to form a government. Under the present circumstances, the authorities in Harare should not be represented at the political level at any SADC Summit as that would be equal to giving them legitimacy." Botswana's decision to boycott the SADC summit that year was a powerful statement, demonstrating its commitment to democratic norms and its unwillingness to provide Mugabe with undeserved legitimacy. Suspending Zimbabwe's political representation at the Summit could have deprived Mugabe of the international legitimacy he sought from his peers. In response to this standstill, unfounded allegations were made against Botswana, accusing the country of conspiring with the United States and the United Kingdom to launch a military attack on Zimbabwe.

Tanzania and Zambia have also criticized Zimbabwean policy to a lesser degree, albeit more subduedly. However, the strategy of continuing support for the oppressive ZANU-PF government and disregard for human rights violations has weakened the democratic ideals in the country. SADC has demonstrated its limitation and its inability to provide a coherent response to regional issues. Due to the Zimbabwe crisis, the regional body has exposed some of its structural weaknesses, which include:

(i) Inability effectively respond to conflicts driven by a political crisis that has damaged the socio-economic prospects of a once vibrant African economy;

(ii) The divisions among member states on the nature of the response to the Zimbabwe crisis have exposed the consensus-driven decision-making process's challenges.

(iii) The personal relations between some leaders, primarily those from the liberation movements, have undermined any efforts for SADC to adopt a democratic path and enforce the democratic principles already adopted through regional agreements and protocols.

As can be seen, Zimbabwe has remained unchecked without risking negative repercussions because enforcement instruments do not exist to deal with non-compliant states. The Zimbabwe crisis has led to economic deterioration and has now become a regional and global concern. The health system in Zimbabwe was once one of the best in Africa, but it is almost non-existent today. An influx of Zimbabweans has sought refuge in countries like South Africa, Botswana and Europe due to Zimbabwe's catastrophic situation. The political and economic challenges in Zimbabwe characterises a nation at war with itself. Under the disguise of the liberation struggle, the political elites have deployed the state's security instruments on ordinary citizens, calling for a leadership change. Zimbabwe is run by a liberation party that has failed to improve the conditions for ordinary citizens; hence, leading to the government's loss of legitimacy. For ZANU-PF, unleashing violence on its people seems the only way of keeping hold of power.

As expected, SADC has failed to defend Zimbabweans' human rights and civil liberties while hiding behind the principle of solidarity and non-interference. The question that remains unanswered is solidarity with whom? It is a distorted form of pan-Africanism and sovereignty that protects old wartime friendships at the expense of people-centred humanitarian needs. As a result of this crisis, the SADC structures have proven ineffective in mitigating intra-state conflicts, and as a consequence, this failure has impacted other areas of regional integration.

The country's regional neighbours must respond to Zimbabwe's political and economic crisis with urgency and effectiveness if lasting peace is to be achieved. Zimbabwe needs a sincere and honest search for a democratic consensus since continued blind support for the authoritarian regime complicates SADC human rights violations. In this case, SADC has failed to maintain democracy in Zimbabwe since SADC leaders care more about Zimbabwean government elites' lavish travels worldwide than the misery Zimbabweans face due to the elites' unjust policies. SADC is technically endorsing continued electoral fraud and Zimbabwe's suffering by ignoring ordinary citizens' needs.

Zimbabwe cannot overcome its current situation if SADC member states do not commit to restoring democracy and the rule of law in that country. The only way out of this situation lies in developing an urgent and concerted effort to overcome the liberation party's authoritarian, violent, and intolerant attitude. Even though the liberation movement contributed to Zimbabwe's independence, it is now necessary for them to change their mentality about being the only custodians of political leadership. In the context of human security, SADC member states must adopt a new understanding of independence and prosperity that is people-driven. This situation in Zimbabwe demonstrates how urgent it is for SADC to enforce a minimum set of standards for good governance, press freedoms, and freedom of association, which are standards already enshrined in the SADC Treaty. In addition to the enforcement of minimum set standards, sanctions against member states that do not comply must be taken. NEPAD already has the African Peer Review Mechanism (APRM) established in 2003 for member states to systematically assess and review governance performance to promote political stability, accelerated regional integration, and economic growth. The APRM (2003) requires member states to measure their compliance to international governance commitments in four areas:

(i) Democracy and political governance;

(ii) Economic governance and management;

(iii) Corporate governance; and

(iv) Socio-economic development.

APRM's sole disadvantage is the lack of enforcement mechanisms since it is a voluntary assessment. As a condition of joining the APRM, a country must sign up to the NEPAD Declaration on Democracy, Political, Economic and Corporate Governance and agree to submit periodic peer reviews. There is a need for more coercive structures in Africa to enforce the normative frameworks on democracy and good governance. Due to the reluctance of African states to develop good governance and rule enforcement systems, APRM's framework is problematic.

Since electoral disputes have been a leading cause of conflict in Zimbabwe, the SADC Principles and Guidelines Governing Democratic Elections offer the country the opportunity to organize elections that represent democratic elections. However, as is the case with much of the Southern African leaders' protocol and agreement signings, the SADC Principles and Guidelines Governing Democratic Elections remain a paper tiger. Dzimba (2001) contends that most security threats in SADC come from within rather than from outside, which plays to SADC's advantage since it places the region's future in its own hands. Therefore, it is disappointing that SADC leaders ignore member states' failure to comply with democratic and governance norms that have contributed to a conflict-riddled environment.

Currently, the current crisis in Zimbabwe requires a broader range of response mechanisms. First, preventive diplomacy must be implemented, in which member states must act to prevent potential conflicts and address human rights concerns and abuses. Simply acknowledging that there is a political conflict, as has been the case in Zimbabwe, is insufficient. At the very least, preventive diplomacy should be implemented to prevent human suffering and violence. SADC needs to devise diplomatic strategies capable of averting crises, defusing tensions, and building consensus on crucial issues. Second, member states of SADC should consider the use of diplomats and high-level delegations, such as UN envoys or retired heads of state, in an effort to initiate dialogue and facilitate a non-violent resolution of the crisis. Such channels of communication may facilitate communication to assist in the resolution of the crisis.

One possible solution might be to utilize power-sharing initiatives to ensure all parties' interests are met. It is worth noting that this measure was unsuccessfully employed after the disputed elections in 2008, which led to the formation of a government of national unity (GNU) in February of 2009. After the disputed elections in 2008, South Africa used its influence to facilitate a power-sharing agreement between ZANU-PF and the Movement for Democratic Change (MDC). Mugabe remained president, and Morgan Tsvangirai became prime minister. This was a missed opportunity for SADC as there should have been a clause concerning SADC's involvement in the 2013 election management in the agreement. With new measures designed to conduct the 2013 elections, SADC should have instituted constitutional reforms in parliament. However, despite losing the elections and having a minority in parliament, Mugabe was allowed do whatever he wanted by SADC without facing any consequences.

Despite SADC's demands that all reforms agreed to during Government of National Unity negotiations be implemented, the Zimbabwean government ultimately failed to implement reforms. In failing to hold the Zimbabwean government accountable, SADC demonstrated a lack of seriousness. Following the signing of the Global Political Agreement (GPA), the two political parties that had signed the agreement with ZANU-PF complained to SADC about Mugabe's deliberate efforts that violated the agreement and his unwillingness to implement the majority of the critical clauses. Despite the concerns raised, SADC failed to act, resulting in the failure of the power-sharing agreement.

Mugabe showed no interest in respecting the details of the agreement. It was stipulated in Article 20 of the GPA that the three major political parties would share cabinet positions as prescribed by the agreement. The cabinet was to consist of 31 ministers and 15 deputy ministers, according to Chigora and Guzura (2011). Mugabe's party, the ZANU-PF, was allocated fifteen ministers, Tsvangirai's MDC-T was allocated thirteen, and MDC-M was allocated three. Instead of fifteen key ministries, ZANU-PF secured twenty-two. For the ministries left to MDC-T, major portfolio powers were transferred to ministries under Mugabe's party. Following the cabinet debacle, Mugabe created fifteen new cabinet positions, bringing the total to sixty-one. The new posts in the cabinet lacked any absolute authority. Even though Mugabe demonstrated open defiance towards the agreement, SADC failed to enforce the GPA. SADC's inability to rein in member states that defy its rule is evident by the ongoing political challenges in the country after Mugabe's ouster by the military.

It is not incorrect to argue that SADC missed an excellent opportunity to transform Zimbabwe's political fortunes when South Africa negotiated the Government of Nation Unity (GNU). In Zimbabwe, SADC's failure to monitor and evaluate the delicate political situation allowed the regime to flout the terms of the agreement without facing any consequences. Sibanda (2014) argues that the Joint Monitoring and Implementation Committee (JOMIC) as a monitoring arrangement was flawed since it was based on the assumption of good faith. SADC's missed opportunity to initiate lasting democratic reforms and improved governance illustrates the limited institutional capacity of the institution, resulting in its failure to take the initiative in the process. Creating a new constitution should have been conducted transparently with the continued support and guidance of SADC. SADC's failure to establish uniform political systems across the region has made it very difficult for member states to agree on a collective course of action, according to Sibanda (2014).

The SADC governments need to send a strong message to the Zimbabwean government by exerting more sustained political pressure and clarifying that more decisive action could be taken if necessary. SADC should protect the interests of all parties in any potential agreement, unlike the GPA, where Robert Mugabe decided the outcome. In the event that an agreement partner violates the agreement's conditions, SADC must prescribe further penalties. Whenever diplomatic negotiations fail, it is necessary to use more coercive measures, and these may include economic measures such as sanctions to influence Zimbabwe's behaviour. By using these measures, other potential offenders could learn from the example set by the regional body. Sanctions could also be used as part of a broader influence strategy that puts maximum political and economic pressure on those responsible for the crisis.

It is also unfortunate that the agreement purely focused on sharing government spoils by political elites in both camps by expanding the executive branch. SADC hoped that Zimbabwe's underlying political issues would be solved by offering positions in government to opposition members. Unfortunately, the agreement only helped the regime tighten its grip on power. SADC already has the Organ on Politics, Defence and Security Cooperation (SIPO) which provides a framework for advancing democracy, good governance and promoting peace and security across the SADC area. Likewise, the regional body has the Principles and Guidelines Governing Democratic Elections, aiming to institutionalize democratic credible elections that can produce legitimate governments.

In advance of any future agreements, regional member states must work within the framework of SIPO, and elections must follow SADC's electoral guidelines. The first line of SADC (2004) SIPO reads: "peace, security and political stability are the linchpins for socio-economic development." The principal objective of SADC (2004) SIPO is to "create a peaceful and stable political and security environment through which the region will endeavour to realize its socio-economic objectives. SADC's Principles and Guidelines Governing Democratic Elections commit member states to follow best practices in election management to ensure high quality, transparent, and credible elections that guarantee the following:

(i) Full participation of citizens in the political process;
(ii) Freedom of association;
(iii) Political tolerance;
(iv) Elections held at regular intervals, as provided for by the respective national constitutions;
(v) Equal opportunity for all political parties to access the state media;
(vi) Equal opportunity to exercise the right to vote and be voted for;
(vii) Independence of the judiciary and impartiality of the electoral institutions;
(viii) Voter education;
(ix) Acceptance and respect by political parties for election results proclaimed to have been free and fair by competent

national authorities in accordance with the law of the land; and

(x) Challenges to the election results, as provided for in the law of the land.

SADC must ensure that the existing two instruments are not voluntary but rather binding and enforceable. Any constitutional amendment adopted by SADC must incorporate these governance and electoral principles. By overcoming the challenges associated with democracy and governance, the country will overcome its socio-economic difficulties. These prerequisites are recognized by the SADC treaty and its supporting protocols, including the SIPO and electoral guidelines.

Combined with Zimbabwe's political, economic, and social instabilities, the region has been adversely affected in general. In addition to undermining regional stability, peace, and integration, the Zimbabwean government and its development prospects have also been negatively affected. Ideally, SADC should take the lead in resolving the governance crisis, which is likely to set the tone for the recovery and reconstruction of the economy. SADC should also acknowledge that it has failed to fulfil its essential role in addressing Zimbabwe's political and socio-economic crisis. There is now a need to take a more aggressive stance against Zimbabwe's regime, including economic and political sanctions.

Rather than targeting the entire population of Zimbabwe, maximum economic sanctions should be directed against the ruling party, specifically political leaders and their immediate families. It is possible to prevent undesirable effects and minimize suffering for innocent civilians through surgical sanctions imposed in the past. The FLS member states took similar measures during the liberation struggle against Ian Smith's Rhodesian regime. Cawthra (2010) asserted that "if Zimbabwe's neighbours closed their borders and cut off supplies, the Zimbabwean regime would crumble." Sanctions can play an essential role in supporting the preventive measures that have already been discussed. During sanctions, it is fundamental that diplomatic and political communication continues. Communication should be clear about the behaviour required for sanctions to be lifted and, if possible, include incentives. For sanctions to be effective, loopholes for violations must be minimized. As a result of these drastic actions, a clear message will be sent throughout the region that any unacceptable behaviour will be met with severe consequences. There are already penalties spelt out in AU (2007) Article 25 (1) for countries that violate its normative framework. The AU Peace and Security Council may suspend a state from participation in the institution's activities in cases where diplomatic efforts to restore constitutional order have failed. Further, consistent with AU (2007) Article 25 (2), these sanctions are enforced in pursuit of restoring democracy through diplomatic means.

Figure 6.5: Zimbabwean Security Forces captured mistreating a civilian during xprotests in the country's capital, Harare.

Source: Report Focus News

In general, however, structural preventive measures should also be employed and implemented in the region due to the persistent political instability that some member states experience. Mechanisms such as dispute resolution and cooperative arrangements are necessary to meet people's basic economic, social, and cultural needs. Humanitarian needs, such as security, wellbeing, and justice, must also be met so that citizens can engage in non-violent efforts to make their lives better. It is important to note that political legitimacy and national security are factors that cannot be separated. Open civil society and credible elections can strengthen the legitimacy of a government, both of which are essential to resolving conflict and political unrest. An elaborate democratic space could help the region address persistent security challenges; however, a lack of political will and political space has made this extremely difficult. The instabilities in Zimbabwe and the SADC region have inhibited developing a mature democratic culture based on a competition of ideas and policies instead of personal relationships and patronage. Having no legitimate governing authority, the Zimbabwean regime has felt compelled to suppress democracy through coercion. Changing this pattern requires Zimbabwe's leadership and its counterparts in the region to demonstrate courage and leadership to create an environment conducive to meaningful conversations. SADC now has an opportunity to help Zimbabwe take meaningful steps towards sustainable, positive change that the population so desperately needs.

The regional and international communities must recognize Zimbabwe as a complex country with many historical and identity challenges. Nevertheless, if SADC is committed to guiding Zimbabwe's governance reforms, the country's situation may be redeemed. The principle of non-interference and solidarity with the regime failed the Zimbabwean people, as did the 'quiet diplomacy' promoted by South Africa. As a matter of principle, the SADC should stand up for the people of Zimbabwe and not for its political elite.

It should be noted that the Zimbabwean regime has politicized the use of security instruments. Zimbabwe has become a security state because the military and police are extensions of the ruling party. In addition to its aggressive structure, ZANU-PF does not appear to be making any efforts to transform itself into a democratic party. Zimbabwe's military has become synonymous with the ruling party, which is not surprising given the country's history between the military commanders and politicians. The current crop of military leaders was involved in the liberation struggle alongside ZANU-PF politicians. According to a report published by the International Crisis Group (2017), Zimbabwe's politics has been militarized, and military force has become the currency of politics. As part of Operation Tsuro, the state has been using military means to achieve political goals since March 2000, with the security apparatus thus becoming the principal source of power. The military has become synonymous with the ruling party only serving the governing political parties. According to the Human Rights Watch Report (2005), the former Commander of Zimbabwe's Defense Force, General Vitalis Zvinavashe, once declared that he would never serve under the leadership of someone who had not been part of the liberation struggle. The military chiefs also play an important role in policy-making, often overshadowing the cabinet in important decisions. There is no surprise that General Constantino Chiwenga, who led the coup that removed

Mugabe, was appointed Vice President, further blurring the lines between the military and civilian government.

For Zimbabwe to overcome the existing challenges, SADC must support significant changes within the country's political, security and economic sectors. This can only be done if SADC takes the political crisis seriously and demands fundamental change. Furthermore, the nation's challenges go beyond the spheres of politics and economics, as the issue of reforming the security sector has also become more pressing.

It is important to mention that some SADC member states have argued that the international uproar and condemnation against the Zimbabwean government results from white people being the victims of the Zimbabwe crisis. Due to previous human rights abuses in Zimbabwe ignored by the international community, this argument may not be misplaced. According to a study published by Phimister (2008), Western countries cynically ignored the gross human rights violations committed in Zimbabwe in the 1980s, despite sufficient evidence that the Zimbabwean security forces had murdered thousands of Ndebeles in Matebeleland. Most of the SADC member states believe that Western countries' hostility toward the Zimbabwean government primarily results from land reforms that disadvantaged white farmers. Nonetheless, despite the differences SADC member states may have with Western powers, the political and economic crisis is real and urgent regional intervention is necessary.

During the 2003 SADC Summit, Tanzania's former President Benjamin Mkapa eloquently said in his statement as incoming chairman, "We must also take a keener interest in the affairs and well-being of neighbouring member countries. If your neighbour is not stable, you cannot be stable for too long. If your neighbour prospers, that prosperity will soon rub off on you. If your neighbour collapses, the fallout will not respect the boundary between you." Unfortunately, this discourse of "keener interest" failed to lead to an interventionist agenda under the SADC chairmanship of Tanzania. With a lack of action, two decades later, we are still talking about the Zimbabwe crisis. This time around, SADC can choose whether to become a relevant conflict resolution component or remain an enabler of Zimbabwe's authoritarian regime.

On a positive note, there have been occasions when SADC member states have worked together when dealing with the regime in Zimbabwe. A notable example occurred in 2008, a few months before the elections in Zimbabwe, when the Mugabe regime had been awaiting a shipment of arms from the People's Republic of China. This shipment had 77 tonnes of arms, including mortar bombs, grenades, bullets, and assault rifles. In collaboration with the Congress for South African Trade Union (COSATU), the Transport and Allied Workers Union refused to unload the shipment on South Africa soil. Consequently, the Chinese vessel was refused to dock and turned away by the South African authorities. COSATU extended its influence by lobbying other SADC member states to adopt a similar stance. A lobbying effort won the backing of SADC leaders, with former Zambian President Levy Mwanawasa urging SADC leaders not to allow the shipment to be offloaded in their ports. As a result, Angola, Mozambique, and Namibia refused to allow the vessel to unload the arms from their ports for fear that the weapons would exacerbate the conflict. Because of this situation, the Zimbabwean government had to use a port outside of SADC, demonstrating that SADC leaders can unite for a common purpose when they choose to do so. The shipment was offloaded in the Port of Pointe Noire in Congo, a country outside the SADC, and airlifted to Zimbabwe by charter flight.

Mugabe's removal from power by the military in 2017 and the post-election violence that followed in February 2018 demonstrates that Zimbabwe's political crisis is far from over. As a result of SADC's incapacity to initiate sustainable peace efforts, the integrated peace and security regime has come under international scrutiny. The SADC's failure in the Zimbabwe crisis illustrates its failure to institutionalise good governance and democracy, which are already enshrined in the SADC Treaty. Leaders of the region need to realize that progress in politics, economics, and social welfare can only be achieved if SADC can secure peace and incorporate it into the regional discourse. Regional leaders need to come together with open hearts and minds to confront the existing challenges successfully, even if it means confronting or sanctioning neighbouring states.

10

Supranationality: Towards Regional Cooperation and Convergence

Southern African countries have sought regional integration arrangements to accelerate economic development and stability over the past three decades. A structural framework analysis which informs expectations about their effectiveness is necessary to understand what such arrangements realistically accomplish. This chapter shows how regional integration can help in Southern Africa-and how to get there. An overview of the various types of regional integration arrangements is presented, along with evidence about their benefits and their actualization, as well as the impact of regional integration on the challenges facing Southern African countries and the current status of regional integration on the region.

The significance of regional institutions as instruments for overcoming political, economic, social, and security challenges cannot be over-emphasized. There is widespread recognition among scholars and policymakers that institutional quality has a significant impact on shaping prosperity across different regional economic communities.

Buzan (2004) argues that members of the regional community enjoy a sense of "we-ness or a shared identity. As such, they are able to adopt "regulative and constitutive norms which combine to give the regional community a distinctive social character and help extend predictability and expectations of pragmatic cooperation." Buzan continues to argue that "with the blurring of self/other distinctions, interests come to be defined conjointly rather than individually."

An organization with a strong regional influence is critical to maintaining high economic growth in the short term and to achieving socio-economic development in the long term. Nevertheless, Africa's experience with regional integration institutions has been a disappointment and failure. Often, it is argued that Africa is a lost continent because of its enduring political and economic failures. Both European integration, which began in 1957 and African integration, which began in 1963, had set similar aspirations toward prosperity, peace, and socioeconomic development for their people. Yet, six decades later, the results of integration have been different. Why have African countries failed to achieve a harmonious integration agenda like their peers in Europe? From the onset of the EU's creation, a narrative of a community of shared values of democracy, human rights, and a liberal market economy was created. The narrative was designed to counter a history of nationalism in Europe that had led to two calamitous World Wars. According to Buzan (2004), as the European states merged, the EU became the "most highly evolved form of stable peace." Buzan argues that the states eliminated their sovereignties and minimized the geopolitical significance of their territorial borders. Essentially, they could participate in a legitimate supra-state realm of political life, in which relationships between member states are jointly managed. Contrary to Europe, Africa's difficulties arise from an overzealous interpretation of sovereignty. In many African countries, political elites have faced challenges related to their collective identity, which has hindered integration due to their unwillingness to transfer their state powers to an independent regional institution.

As the Cold War ended, the desire to create new forms of association was growing in Africa. Within Southern Africa, the international political economy and global politics made the need for integration of the Southern African states more urgent. An interconnected economic and political environment provided the necessary conditions for the integration of Southern Africa. Despite all the rhetoric about African unity and integration, the complexity of the integration process has proven to be a barrier to integration efforts, which has, in turn, undermined the momentum for integration. According to Johnson (1995), the integration results in Southern Africa have been less than satisfactory. Economic and political integration can take on many different forms, depending on the level of commitment to the integration agenda among the member states. Building national commitment and making regional integration benefits visible have proven challenging. Having structural and political differences among states within the same region is problematic, as it is with the SADC region.

Further, one should consider that few African states have adequate domestic capacity or political commitment to RECs, which usually reflects the weakness of the African Union and its RECs. The challenges highlighted here emphasize the importance of building national commitment and highlighting the clear benefits of regional integration. AfDB (2014) identifies country commitment and ownership, implementation and governance arrangements, and a conducive policy environment as key factors of regional institutions' effectiveness. It is critical to comprehend that creating incentives for national collaboration and national ownership is integral to ensuring regional cooperation's sustainability. In many cases, RECs can take a broad range of forms and facilitate collective action through different mechanisms; however, RECs that do not integrate themselves into national agendas often cannot survive and are unlikely to succeed, which is a problem for African RECs.

Despite the unsatisfactory performance of regional integration schemes in Africa, governments have continued to pursue the continent's agenda for regional integration by enhancing institutional capacity and effectiveness. The adoption of modest reforms by member states and the implementation of new approaches can change the current situation if they are domesticated into national policies. Regional prosperity must rest on the commitment to collective survival rather than competition. African governments must recognize the limitations of their small and fragmented markets to take advantage of economies of scale and take the regional integration agenda seriously.

For instance, on 9 July 2002, African leaders gathered in Durban, South Africa, to bid farewell to the Organization of African Unity (OAU) and welcome the African Union (AU), an institution heralded as a new dawn for Africa and its people. Thabo Mbeki, the South African president, declared that the new Union would liberate the African people. AU was also seen as a vehicle for enhancing intra-African trade, resolving conflicts, and enhancing Africa's global profile. The creation of the AU was governed by a more progressive Constitutive Act that promoted democracy and human rights protection and gave the continental body the right to intervene in intra-state conflicts to prevent gross violations of human rights. The UN Secretary-General Kofi Annan gave African states a timely reminder to warn the leaders "not to confuse hope with achievement." Kofi Annan's warning was significant since the OAU had similarly been launched with much pomp, only to be replaced after failing to deliver.

RECs in Africa have also been undergoing some form of restructuring to respond to the evolving challenges. Nevertheless, some limitations have been encountered in efforts to enhance the effectiveness of the RECs in Africa. Soldatos (1989) argues that the choice of institutional structure and mechanisms must bear "a direct and proportional relationship to the nature, breadth and scope of what is to be integrated." As a result, the concept of new regionalism has gained increasing prominence. Bach (2009) asserts that the concept of new regionalism represents a new way of thinking about previously unconsidered issues.

Throughout the 1980s, there was a sudden and largely an unanticipated revival of regionalism. It is indisputable that the dynamism of non-state actors like regional institutions played a significant role in the de facto convergence of trade and investment flows around the world. As the EU's Single European Market agenda (1986-1992) was being implemented in North America, negotiations towards NAFTA (1991-1994) were in full swing. As this momentum coincided with the launch of the WTO in 1994, it stimulated debates on how regionalism can serve or master multilateralism, according to Hveem (1999). Regionalism in Africa has paradoxically coincided with the endorsement of European-style integration institutional models as the most efficient. The construction of Europe can be described as the result of a process of convergence of national states' governance, regulatory, and legislative structures. Along with the correlation between successive rounds of EU enlargement and the development of trade and investment relationships between old and new members, one can also see the 'magnetism' the EU has over its non-aligned neighbours. It has also been argued by Landau (1999) and Fawcett (1995) that this was accompanied by significant policy shifts in the agendas and mandates of established regional intergovernmental organizations.

The revival of regional integration in Southern Africa, and in Africa generally, was asymptomatic in that it led to ambitious plans for consolidated integration and mutualization of sovereignty, which had been evident as soon as countries gained independence in Africa. However, these ambitious regional integration projects were short-lived as sacrificing national sovereignty threatened some regimes in fragile states. Considering the state-centric agendas driving regional agendas in Africa, such a notion of robust regional institutions cannot be assumed. The result is dysfunctional institutionalism since neither ambitious institutionalization processes prescribed nor transfer of sovereignty have been employed. A dysfunctional process of this sort cannot be ignored considering current conditions within the region.

Both the RECs and the AU have been pursuing deeper institutional agendas since the 1990s. Both have been striving to build an economic and monetary union on the continent and mutualize sovereignties. However, the dysfunctional integration agendas have been counterproductive to implementing the Abuja Plan of Action, which was designed to contribute to African countries' political and economic integration, adopted in 1991. The continental blueprint calls for the creation of regional economic communities (RECs) that are to function as "building blocks" towards integration into the African Economic Community (AEC) by 2028. There is an expectation that the AEC will involve free movement of people and factors of production, a single African market, an economic and monetary union with a single African currency, and an African central bank.

Institutional arrangements supporting integration agendas, in this case, must be based on a robust institutional framework compatible with the goals being pursued. SADC's primary weakness has been its lack of supranational status, similar to the European Union, which has centralized systems for enforcing compliance and dealing with infringements by member states. The Merriam-Webster dictionary defines supranationalism as “the state or condition of transcending national boundaries, authority, or interests.” The Economic and Social Commission for Western Asia (ESCWA) defines a supranational organization as a "union, whereby member states transcend national boundaries or interests to share in the decision-making and vote on issues pertaining to the wider grouping."

A supranational organization is a system in which member states cede power to the regional body in certain areas. In Barnett and Finnermore (2004) view, supranational bodies are bureaucracies with institutional resources, operational guidelines, and mandates capable of setting norms and values. In essence, supranationalism implies the existence of an institution that has the authority and capacity to oversee its members. As such, decisions made by the regional body are legally binding and must be followed by all member states. To ensure that all member states adhere to the rules, there are courts and other enforcement mechanisms. There is now growing recognition in Africa that the narrowly defined sovereignty has hampered economic growth and stability.

With the SADC region facing many challenges on the economic, political, and security fronts, there have been calls for SADC to adopt an interventionist approach similar to that of the European Union (EU). Clearly, the success of the European political and economic integration has resulted in a reduction of national control over various policy areas and a realignment of political power as the EU adopted what is commonly referred to as supranational integration. In 1992, the European Union adopted the Maastricht Treaty, which promotes economic and political integration. Sinn (1994) defined the Maastricht Treaty as a set of social standards intended to harmonize social security systems, health conditions, and other policy areas. In the context of SADC, the Treaty was primarily a manifesto for collective prosperity and regional stability due to regional market liberalization and sound governance. Yet, regional integration in Southern Africa results in complicated and often conflicting interactions with regional leaders who are reluctant to support policies that might compromise their sovereignty.

Chapter 5 and 6 provide a detailed analysis of SADC's experience, its institutional structure, and the constraints that have hindered its efficiency and operational effectiveness. This part proposes a new institutional framework that would enable SADC to reinvent its fortunes and lead the region towards sustainable economic growth and stability. Throughout the analysis and discussions in Chapters 5, 6, and 6, 7 and 8, the book demonstrated how states and their national interests have interfered with achieving collective goals. Due to the intergovernmental arrangement, SADC member states have retained their full sovereign rights to advance their agendas and obstruct regional agreements' implementation. This obstructionist behaviour has often hampered or slowed the progress of the regional integration agenda. To implement unity of objectives and ensure that states do not renege on Community goals, it suffices to say that the success of regional integration in Southern

Africa will be dependent on redefining the mandate and institutional framework of SADC. An institution with supranational powers and supporting instruments must allow the regional integration agenda to move beyond state-centric influences and speed up the integration process.

The complex organisational structures required by contemporary regions stem from their multitude of crosscutting objectives across multiple sectors. With this multipurpose structure, they can build links between diverse sectors, including economics, politics, and security. Economic integration as such is considered a potential means of improving regional peace and security. This chapter examines how SADC can bring about changes that lead to sustainable economic growth and peace in the region. The deepening poverty and instability of southern Africa result from weak states and the structural weakness of the regional organization. The previous chapters acknowledged that the current SADC institutional framework had given too many powers to the states, allowing them to undermine regional agreements and priorities. Despite the abundance of natural resources in the region, the natural resources have been insufficient to stimulate economic growth. Likewise, the SADC Treaty, protocols, and agreements have failed to promote economic integration and regional stability. Nonetheless, SADC can contribute to regional stability and economic growth if there is a paradigm shift in the way SADC operates and is conceived by member states. The signing of the SADC Treaty implied a loss of national sovereignty; however, the power granted to the SADC Summit of Heads of State has institutionalized the privileged position of SADC member states.

Consequently, the regional body remains weak due to the weakening of the institutional framework. In order to lay the foundation for lasting peace and sustainable economic growth in SADC, there must be broad regional cooperation and the total commitment of regional leaders. The greatest challenge facing the SADC has been moving beyond mere rhetoric and declarations. SADC has the necessary ingredients for building a prosperous community with shared historical experiences and a vision to create a shared future for socio-economic development and stability. An effective and coherent regional structure is lacking to guide the regional integration process.

The demand for creating regional bodies with supranational powers has grown in Africa in recent years because regional norms are heavily burdened by inadequate implementation mechanisms. To overcome the continent's persistent challenges requires solid and transformative leadership that could provide the vision and the effective direction it requires. However, not all countries are motivated to pursue regional integration in the same way. It is for this reason that a supranational body is called upon to coax and persuade lagging states. A strong economic and political cooperation among Southern Africa's countries has enormous and obvious benefits. The benefits of this cooperation are so significant and could benefit each SADC member state. With the region's persistent challenges, it is difficult to understand why leaders have not prioritized finding solutions to its problems.

Chapter 10 discusses SADC's potential new regional institutional framework that will attempt to address the noted limitations. According to Hammerstad (2003), the protocols that make up the basic policy guidelines of the SADC provide an image of a comprehensive and in-depth project of regional integration. There is, however, a significant and growing gap between the protocols signed and the implementation in reality. Consequently, the chapter seeks to provide an in-depth analysis of the SADC institutional framework by examining the underlying factors that impact its effectiveness. An examination of the existing instruments, protocols, and institutional structures, which create the political and economic environment for Southern Africa, should be undertaken in the wake of an overview of the economic, political, and security challenges the region is currently facing.

The Quest For A Supranational Institution

Prior to the early 1990s, the African integration agenda failed to incorporate concepts of good governance, laws, human rights, democracy and human security, with economic cooperation serving as the primary rationale. While economic integration dominated the dialogue on cooperation, very little integration occurred. As is the case with the European states, the central assumption of regional integration is that some form of sovereignty is transferred from the state to a regional institution. In contrast, the prospect of an overarching supranational institution in Africa would pose a serious threat to the majority authoritarian regimes in that region. Most African countries followed a policy of non-interference, allowing autocrats to remain unaccountable to supranational entities. Due to Africa's profound economic, social, political, and security challenges, this debate has been re-energised, presenting a paradigm shift in the integration discourse. Clapham (1999) observe that: The model of inter-state integration through formal institutional frameworks, which has hitherto dominated the analysis of integration in Africa and elsewhere, has increasingly been challenged by the declining control of states over their own territories, the proliferation of informal networks, and the incorporation of Africa (on a highly subordinate basis) into the emerging global order.

Globalization poses a challenge to all levels of political and social institutions. Traditional government structures have been disrupted or even eroded at the domestic level due to the loss of sovereignty of national governments. In contrast to some other continents, regionalism in Europe has unique characteristics. First, the EU is in charge of many aspects that are a fundamental part of national sovereignty in other parts of the world. Furthermore, we need to note that Western European integration has progressed much more quickly than any other region. In general, the deeper the integration, the lesser countries can obstruct the process.

As well as enhancing investment returns, facilitating larger investments, and encouraging industries to relocate, integration can also lead to increased cost savings. By integrating, governments can improve security, strengthen their bargaining power, increase cooperation, and commit to reforms. The benefits of regional integration, however, are not automatic or necessarily large. In order to improve welfare in participating countries, regional integration arrangements must be viewed as a means rather than an end in themselves.

In light of Southern Africa's many weaknesses in resources and the inadequacies of its economic capabilities, revitalized regional integration offers one of the most feasible solutions to the region's development challenges. The daunting challenges can be overcome through collective efforts, coupled with a dynamic political commitment to integration. This is not the case with other regional institutions, where there are no appropriate structures to manage integration. In the context of SADC, the lack of inter-state political will, despite the numerous advantages presented by enhanced regional trade, is primarily attributable to divergent national priorities, historical differences, and concerns about some countries becoming more dominant than others. Dealing with the growing differences among SADC countries goes beyond discussing regional integration. Its institutional framework itself poses a risk for disagreements. Despite these concerns, they can be overcome if there is a genuine commitment and recognition that member states can only become stronger economically and politically by working together.

Without effective regional institutions, the governments' precarious behaviours cannot be managed—two fundamental aspects of government behaviour impacts business performance and growth. One aspect of uncertainty is the inadequacy of government policy (such as taxation and tariffs) and the unpredictability of government and judicial actions, both of which can result in business decision postponement and shorter-term investments. Furthermore, operating in a highly discretionary manner by the state (government, bureaucracy, and judiciary) creates inefficiencies by seeking and granting special privileges and suppressing investments. There is a stifling of growth in both cases because existing investments are curtailed, new firms can't enter and grow, and foreign investment is discouraged.

We cannot go back on regional integration; it is here to stay. The debate should be, how can we make it work? And if we can make it work, there have to be robust supporting instruments to help set the rules. It is important to note that regional institutions' conceptualisation is constituted by diverse constituencies who make competing knowledge claims regarding values, methodologies, politics, and the ideals of autonomy and regional institutions' independence. The differences in integration models have led to increased debates on how regional integration schemes must be pursued in the last six decades. Proponents of nationalism and internationalism have played a fundamental role in shaping these divisions. Various regional integration schemes in different parts of the world have used different models for pursuing and implementing their collective objectives. While some scholars have advocated ad hoc integration similar to intergovernmentalism, as is the case in Asia with the ASEAN, others have advocated political integration, which requires establishing a supranational authority that is autonomous in its operations.

Proponents of nationalism have promoted an inter-governmentalist ideology that retains the nation-state as a primary actor in regional integration. For example, Biswaro (2013) argues against regional bodies' supranational nature by stressing that regional institutions do not operate in a vacuum but rather depend on cooperation between member states. Two conflicting governance systems underlie the contraposition of intergovernmental and supranational discourse. The participating state actors are the key players in adopting, implementing, and enforcing the integration agenda in an intergovernmental system. This system is characterized by the predominance of national interests in interstate relations. Decisions are made by consensus, with the regional body's secretariat having a limited scope or no authority as all. In this case, national interests determine the modus operandi, with the states maintaining their sovereign rights. There has been concern that SADC member states might lose their sovereignty to a supranational SADC. However, Ferrari and Pollicino (2011) argue that SADC came into existence due to a freely negotiated agreement among member states. Therefore, this concern is somewhat misplaced.

Whenever SADC reforms are proposed, the institution's governance and decision-making structures must be taken into consideration. Therefore, it is imperative that the SADC Secretariat, as the principal institution, adopt a legal identity consistent with the vision and character of the SADC Treaty. Any effort to create a supranational institution should establish the legal framework of the institution and clearly define its mandate to give direction on its core functions. As part of any legal framework supporting a supranational entity, it is necessary to address the following questions: What are the consequences of non-compliance with treaty obligations? How do regional policies affect domestic policies and to what extent? How does the treaty affect the member states and their citizens?

The ideology of pan-Africanism continues to impart strong rhetorical support for ambitious regional integration agendas that translate into regional and continental agendas, partly because most African leaders recognize the rationale of pan-Africanism. This ideology echoes the aspirations of the OAU, and its predecessor, the AU, regional integration in Africa draws its ideological foundation. The AU's Agenda 2063: The Africa We Want provides a blueprint for transforming Africa into a global powerhouse. It is a strategic plan that calls for the African countries to unite to realize its Renaissance, with aspirations for "an integrated continent based on African ideals and the vision of Africa's Renaissance". Common experiences of decolonization and liberation struggle have likewise fostered a sense of identity and solidarity, which continues to influence regional cooperation and integration today. The AU also attributes its roots to its support for liberation movements in former African colonies during colonialism and Apartheid. African states also join regional organisations out of a sense of solidarity and avoid breaking ranks because of this background. The legitimacy and political capital gained from membership in these organisations are invaluable for ruling elites in member states.

As such, the question is not whether African countries should pursue regional integration; these countries are politically committed to it. For deep integration to occur, agreed policies must be effectively implemented, and conditions are created to maximize the benefits and provide concrete results for the African people. The importance of African economic integration cannot be overstated. According to the SADC Treaty, the overarching objective is to promote peace, sustainable development, freedom, and social justice for the people of Southern Africa and to eradicate poverty by creating the enabling environment for deep regional integration and cooperation. These objectives are specific, progressive, and well defined. Yet, SADC continues to face challenges that have impeded its objectives, and there are now calls to address these issues to speed up progress. For SADC countries to achieve peace and stability, policies promoting economic growth must be carefully calibrated to help them overcome poverty.

Figure 7.1: Tools of regional integration (intergovernmental framework)

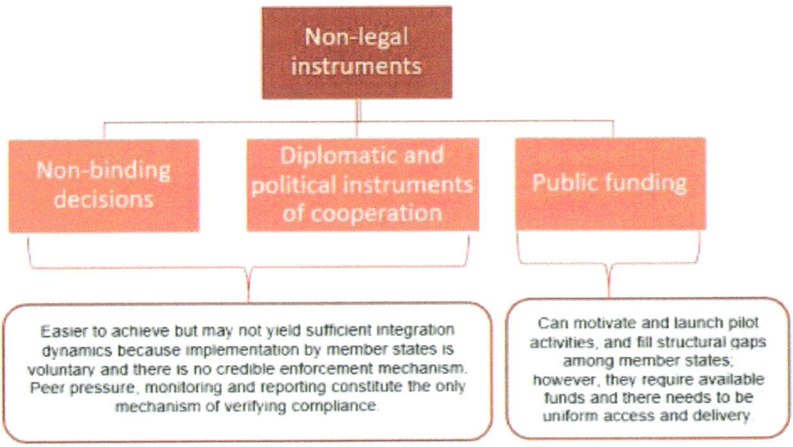

Source: ITC elaboration

Packer and Rukare (2002) point out that African leaders, particularly those in Southern Africa, showed their willingness to utilize regional integration-based institutions to strengthen regional cooperation from the onset of independence. African leaders were best positioned to coordinate and intensify their collaborative efforts to improve the African population's welfare and end all forms of colonialism and white supremacy. Packer and Rukare, however, acknowledge that the African regional institutions are unable to meet the persistent challenges facing the continent. Thus, African leaders have continued to deepen integration, and the African Union has been an excellent example. The new-look African body was created to encourage unity and closer cooperation among African states. The institution also has a robust peace and security architecture since stability has been recognized as essential for achieving collective prosperity. Despite the strong appeal for integration for several decades, perspectives on pursuing and being conceived are different today. Deeper integration, however, is dependent on the institutional structures that the regional institutions in Africa adopt.

In contrast, proponents of supranationalism like Adetula (2014) argue that: "the process involves shifting loyalties, expectations and political activities towards a new and larger centre whose institutions and processes demand some jurisdiction over those of the national states." A supranational model provides for the creation of regional institutions that can bind member states and limit the influence of member states on the agenda of regional integration. The supranational institutions are guided by majority decision-making procedures that enable the integration agenda to proceed without significant obstacles. The regional body may curtail the behaviour of any member state in areas that the supranational institution has been mandated to manage. Using a majority voting system limits the influence of reluctant member states that may undermine or obstruct the integration agenda.

The importance of regional cooperation and regional integration for addressing specific development challenges cannot be overstated. The African continent faces many challenges, affecting people in various areas, such as human security, governance, trade, infrastructure, and others. It has been argued by Erasmus (2011) that: "the more comprehensive the trade agreements and the more advanced the integration process, the stronger the need for appropriate institutions with supranational powers." A major objective of African countries, regions, and regional organizations has long been to improve regional cooperation and integration. As a result of the expansion of regional organizations' ambitions and mandates, a multitude of commitments, plans, and policy documents have been developed. In this case, any effort for a more robust integration agenda must be accompanied by equally sound supporting instruments. The instruments may be used only to harmonise the member states' economic, governance, and regulatory structures in accordance with the mandate contained within the treaty.

On the other hand, weak regional institutions have structures that are based upon non-binding decisions. No legal instruments support it, and the interaction takes place mainly on an ad hoc basis. Integration under this format cannot withstand the intricate dynamics of divergent national interests reflected in the political elites' consolidated sovereignty definition. It is the perception and pursuit of interests of ruling elites that shape what is presented as 'national interest', which then determines regional policies, so to speak. The disparity between institutional form and function, or rhetoric and action, is sometimes caused by the internal political calculations of the political elites. Accordingly, the political elites define the national interests, and the relationship between these interests and regional priorities is determined. Depending on the political regime in a country, national interests are expressed differently. Among SADC's member countries are a variety of repressive regimes that are widely regarded as authoritarian. Swaziland and Angola are among them, while Zimbabwe, a semi-authoritarian country that has democratic trappings, has been undermined by patronage, violence, and repression for the sole purpose of keeping the ruling elite in power.

As an example of a full-fledged democracy, South Africa presents a political bargaining environment that can threaten regional agreements. South Africa, for example, supports the regional industrialisation strategy of SADC in theory. However, in reality, the ANC in South Africa is currently grappling with balancing labour union support while implementing labour market reforms to reduce high levels of unemployment, a move that will likely anger these same unions. Due to these challenges facing ruling coalitions and political elites, and vested interests, leaders are under political pressure from particular industrial sectors and trade union leaders to protect markets, making it unlikely to implement a regional industrialization strategy. Robert Mugabe is believed to have tabled the industrialization strategy when he chaired SADC to draw attention away from the slipping trade agenda, as South Africa has been benefiting from their economic dominance in regional markets at their expense.

Different examples illustrate how political processes on the national level can influence and determine how countries engage in regional processes. Furthermore, national mechanisms of accountability, compliance and enforcement tend to be inadequate. When nations enter into regional agreements, they soon learn that the more restrictions they remove on goods and services movement, the less control they have over their economy. Further, if the process continues, the less control they have over domestic politics. Economic integration is usually done in stages, so the first preferential agreements present less danger to domestic control than later ones. As part of regional integration, the main goal is to eliminate discrimination between local and regional products, services, and factors of production and maintain protection from third parties.

Supranational systems have centralized governance structures established at the regional level, which have jurisdictional obligations and exclusive responsibilities. The EU is an excellent example of a supranational regional institution with supporting instruments like the European Commission, the European Court of Justice (ECJ), and the European Parliament. The citizens independently elect the European Parliament, and the European Commission is also independently appointed. In light of the fact that European legislation enacted by the European Parliament and policies implemented by the European Commission supersede national legislation, member states are not permitted to contradict European agreements or legislation. The European Court of Justice can impose sanctions or penalties on member states violating European laws.

AU and SADC drew inspiration from the EU experience of integrating norms, legal provisions, and institutions. The very act of SADC member states signing the SADC Treaty implied some loss of national sovereignty. As such, the institution attempted to mimic the ECJ when the SADC Tribunal was established. As a precursor to creating a SADC Parliament similar to the European Parliament, the SADC Parliamentary Forum was created. Besides the desire to mimic the EU, the level of integration among SADC member states has affected the institution's effectiveness.

For Africans, regional integration is governed by a sophisticated-looking structure of formal institutions. The problem with these forms of institutional organization, which are often similar to other best-practice models like those of the EU, is that they are not always effective in meeting their stated purposes. They also have formal organizational structures, primary decision-making bodies, regional parliaments, courts, and budgeting and accountability processes. One could easily misconstrue these instruments as carrying out institutional functions such as accountability, transparency, conflict mediation and arbitration, or the provision of regional public goods or services. Basically, what you see in these institutions is not always what you get. In part, this explains the wide gap between policy planning and implementation.

In addition to established institutions and programs, African RECs also have established arbitrators, tribunals, and courts-related compliance institutions. Few practices undermine free trade policies, including slow or insufficient translations of regional commitments into national legislation or regulations, uneven or inadequate execution of regional agreements, and (legitimate or illegitimate) non-tariff measures that hinder market integration. In most cases, rhetoric among SADC leaders has prevailed over genuine political commitment. According to Bilal (2007), "economic, political, and geostrategic conditions have not contributed to implementing ambitious integration goals. In SADC, the Treaty enables subsidiary legal instruments, such as protocols granting specific functions and mandates to various SADC institutions. A total of 23 protocols have been formulated to date." In practice, free trade areas typically exist in African RECs, but Bial et al. (2015) argue that non-tariff barriers (NTBs), internal taxes, and lists of 'sensitive goods' restrict trade between members. Despite efforts to improve some of them, existing norms prevent official dispute resolution procedures against other African states. Those institutions established to ensure compliance with regional agreements, such as SADC Tribunal, are underutilized and fail to perform their functions effectively. The importance of improving trade-related infrastructure cannot be overstated. Improved trade facilitation and logistics services performance, removal of non-tariff barriers, and effective transit regimes are equally urgent and vital. A lot of what is needed in regional trade agreements in Southern Africa has already been agreed upon; what remains is implementation. Resources are needed to accomplish this agenda, but more importantly, policymakers must engage in and commit to the agenda, as well as improving the capacity of national and regional authorities to remove regional trade barriers and track progress.

Thus, it is evident that SADC instruments' success or failure is not determined by their formal legal characteristics but rather by their operationalization. Some of the SADC instruments appear superficially similar to those of the EU; however, they differ significantly in detail and efficacy. As a result, a hybrid political and economic institution has been created that is supranational in character but intergovernmental in practice.

Why are we talking about a new regional institutional framework and structure? To answer this question, we must look at the current status and structure of SADC. The SADC has been in existence for more than three decades since its establishment in 1992, with its integration agenda shaped by the domestic politics of its member states. Chapters 5 and 6 identified institutional challenges that have prevented SADC from being effective. The majority of the identified constraints were related to the lack of supranational SADC instruments, which has exposed the institution to power struggles among member states. Thus, looking at the institution's performance, the SADC has encountered difficulties implementing its treaty agreements and protocols. Currently, these challenges are widespread and are presenting obstacles to the regional integration process. Different factors have contributed to SADC failing to meet its founding fathers' expectations, and the majority of them can be attributed to SADC's organizational structure. To understand the challenges SADC is facing, it is important to answer two important questions.

Figure 7.2: Tools of regional integration (supranational framework)

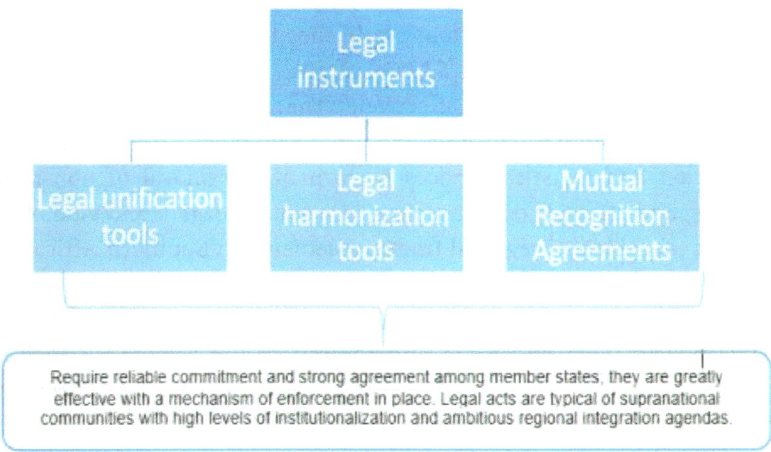

Source: ITC elaboration

To begin with, who or what other actors and factors impact the regional integration in the SADC area and its policy agenda? In what ways does implementation of the integration agenda get stymied? Our path forward will be determined by answering these questions.

Clapham (1999) states that: "The model of inter-state integration through formal institutional frameworks, which has hitherto dominated the analysis of integration in Africa and elsewhere, has increasingly been challenged by the declining control of states over their own territories, the proliferation of informal networks, and the incorporation of Africa (on a highly subordinate basis) into the emerging global order." Though the OAU was transformed into the AU, and efforts to increase SADC's effectiveness have been made, there is doubt among some observers that SADC will attain a well-integrated structural entity - like the EU - with attendant economic and political integration. Africa's central government-led regional experiments, such as SADC and AU, have largely failed to live up to expectations, contributing to a general lack of faith in formal state-led regionalism.

Vale, Swatuk and Odén (2001) contend that the liberal, foundational approach for integration emphasises interstate institutions and frameworks. The European Union serves as a comparative marker, model, or mentor. Those who adhere to this line of thinking believe that European experience has shown the power of regionalism and that regional integration in Africa is an important means of achieving peace, security, and development. The initial results of regional integration in Africa have been modest so far, and their implementation has been hindered by fragile African governments that are incapable of transferring sovereignty, taking meaningful collective action, and building the capacities of regional institutions and organizations.

It is not that strange that RECs in Africa borrowed the idea that the deepening of economic integration would proceed through transfers of sovereignty to a supranational entity, especially given Europe's extensive assistance and expertise. The EU has established itself as an important partner for African regional organisations because of its own experiences and political ties to Africa. It has assumed a unique responsibility that has added a significant value to the integration agenda for Africa. Economic growth, along with efficient regional public goods management, remains integral to the stability of Africa's political system. The EU's political-institutional structure influences a large portion of the revised AU treaty, although the organization in practice operates strictly in an intergovernmental arrangement. The EU and the AU have also developed a relationship where the EU has become a mentor, as their interactions have become more formalized, which also applies to SADC and other African RECs.

The SADC Treaty reflected the objectives of the founding member states to safeguard the prosperity and stability of the region that previous white-minority regimes had threatened in the region. Due to the intergovernmental nature of the SADC's institutional framework, it lacks the necessary instruments to enhance its effectiveness. The lack of legislative scrutiny, the ambiguity of the institution's mandate, and obstructionist decision-making procedures have resulted in incoherences and contradictions in the institution's objectives and practices. Vanheukelom et al. (2016) observe that African regional institutions adopt institutional forms to foster regional integration but often fail to achieve their intended goal. Since the supreme decision-making authority rests with the heads of states, the SADC Secretariat does not have discretionary powers to develop regional integration agendas or a parliament to create regional laws and hold Heads of State accountable.

Another obstacle has been the degree of state commitment to the common objectives enshrined in the SADC Treaty protocols and agreements. In light of the delays in protocol ratification and the SADC Tribunal incident, it is clear that government leaders can adopt different progressive decisions and only renege on their commitments and obligations after seeing the consequences. Sometimes, such decisions are regarded as threats to national sovereignty. Lack of commitment and political will to the regional integration agenda has weakened SADC, as the organization does not have the authority to enforce compliance. Instead, SADC member states operate under the *rebus sic stantibus* or *'à la carte'* cooperation, where states can implement or ignore anything they want without being penalized. By design, the current institutional framework creates institutions that mimic supranational institutions while remaining susceptible to influence from member states. From this perspective, any efforts to reform SADC should begin by focusing on its primary functions.

Treaties cannot be implemented without protocols. However, many SADC member states have been slow to sign and ratify regional economic community protocols, which are often contradictory. SADC should employ a more expeditious ratification process. It is possible to replace ratifications with "acts," "decisions," or "directives" that are effective immediately. In modernizing the number and content of protocols across regional economic communities, the African Union could help align these guidelines with continental objectives to secure convergence of subregional objectives.

Supranationalism refers to decision-making procedures in a system of integrated decision-making that entails transferring decision-making power to an authority that transcends its members' governments. The supranational process penetrates through the fabric of the Westphalian absolute sovereignty while also introducing a non-state actor responsible for guiding the processes of the regional institution. As a result of the pressures of globalization and the state's failure, this additional layer of governance is necessary to provide binding decisions for all member states. Hansohm (2005) argues that establishing a regional integration arrangement requires the development of regional institutions to which important aspects of national economic and political decision-making will be subordinated. Its successful establishment requires a significant transition, which can easily trip participating countries up. This may explain why active participation by member states do not match regional integration agreements in integration exercises. In the context of SADC, member states have resisted supranational judicial oversight, which invariably affects their sovereignty. Nathan (2012) asserts that SADC suffers from the residual influence of Frontline States ideas and a historical debt lingering in the collective political spirit that African states should be independent and free from foreign influence. Additionally, the absence of shared values exacerbates the failure of SADC due to reluctance of individual member states to delegate sovereignty to an external agency. Most leaders in the SADC area are preoccupied with preserving their monopoly of power and have been reluctant to make the sacrifices and commitments necessary to pursue a robust regional integration project.

The remarkable achievement of the EU in deepening and broadening European integration was undoubtedly enabled by regional economic structures and institutions put in place to facilitate intraregional trade and governance cohesion. The fact is, all of this was made possible by political efforts to unite Europe. It is unlikely that European unity would have become a reality without such an effort. Using the European integration as an example, citizens, policymakers, and business leaders in Africa must critically evaluate Europe's regional integration experiences. They can then evaluate the successes, failures, and issues of the European experience.

Generally, more developed and advanced countries are more likely to develop progressive political, economic, and social institutions than developing nations. However, other factors also affect the drive for institutional change that can translate to economic growth and development. It has been suggested by Lora and Oliviera (2004) that institutional reforms may likely take place during adverse cyclical conditions, such as those experienced in SADC countries. The transformation of SADCC to SADC in 1992 was a response to the destabilization efforts of the Apartheid regime. Southern African leaders agreed to move away from the ad hoc arrangement of SADCC to a more structured arrangement of SADC inspired by the EU. As SADC transformed from SADCC to SADC, there were many expectations. The aftermath of Apartheid provided an environment where member states could pursue a more ambitious integration agenda to consolidate the benefits of political liberation and accelerate human development across the region. However, nearly three decades later, there has been little progress in human development and political stability.

An integration scheme's success or failure is measured by the collective objectives it sets and the economic, political and institutional environment in which it operates. The Southern African integration experience within the SADC context demonstrates a history of failure due to the inefficient execution of regional objectives. There have been limitations resulting from the arbitrary character of the SADC institutional structure, which cannot respond to globalisation pressures. This weak institutional framework is considered to be the critical factor and probably the major obstacle to a more integrated Southern African Community.

In 1992, there was optimism, but that optimism has dissipated, and political harmony in the region has been replaced by political discord. The Southern African Community has lost its momentum of the Community existing to find solutions for shared problems. Although the SADC Community faces several common challenges, it cannot devise and pursue common solutions as it undergoes negative integration. In SADC, domestic political and economic conditions force governments to become more protective and guard their sovereignty with greater vigilance. The political context for integration has now changed, with regimes increasingly concerned with retaining power. This political paralysis has coincided with the growing popularity of populist politics on the African continent. The extent SADC objectives are adopted and implemented will depend on member states' political commitment to provide the SADC Secretariat with the necessary mandate and authority to enforce those agreed-upon objectives. A necessary outcome of this basic need is creating coherent community objectives under the direction of an effective regional institution that is pragmatic and capable of promoting regional integration. It has been suggested by Olaosebikan (2011) that African governments have failed to surrender their sovereignty, which has hindered successful regional and continental integration. There is an apparent lack of commitment among SADC member states to implement agreed-upon objectives, contrasting with their public pronouncements.

Throughout history, all integration efforts have been undermined by disputes over state sovereignty and supranational power, and overcoming these disputes has determined the success or failure of integration. According to De Melo and Tsikata (2014), African leaders are concerned that supranational institutions may restrict their ability to make their own decisions on domestic and international policies if decision-making power is centralized within the supranational institution. As part of the SADC Treaty, political integration has already been recognized as an essential component as it promotes the establishment of shared political values and norms. The shared values and norms enshrined in SADC Treaty protocols, agreements, and declarations govern regional affairs. Kingsolver (2011) defines political integration as the surrender of national sovereignty to a supranational sovereign entity. An important aspect of political integration is the promotion of shared political values and governance systems, democratic institutions, peace, security and stability. In simple terms, political integration consists of establishing the values and norms of a supranational entity.

The political integration process is the consolidation of political systems and the allocation of decision making power to a single institution, according to Ansah (2013). Rodrik (2000) identified non-market instruments that enable markets to function effectively. These institutions carry out regulatory, stabilizing, and legitimizing functions that are complementary and supporting elements to a well-functioning market economy. Their absence explains the divergence of growth paths among economies. Rodrik proposes five types of market-supporting governance institutions:

(i) Property rights institutions;

(ii) Regulatory institutions;

(iii) Macroeconomic stabilization institutions;
(iv) Social insurance institutions; and
(v) Institutions for conflict management

In the past three decades, the Southern African Development Community has attempted to establish an institutional structure and policy instruments to promote regional integration, including the amendment of the SADC Treaty in 2001. The new SADC institutional framework established a regional secretariat responsible for strategic planning, management, coordination, and regional policy development. However, Tjønneland (2005) analyzed the SADC institution structure and concluded that member states' reluctance to establish a supranational institution was a major deterrent to regional integration. According to Tjønneland, "SADC has ascended rapidly at the level of formal policies and agreements; however, the organization's institutions are still weak, and it has not made significant progress in implementing protocols and regional decisions." As a result, there is a significant gap between what SADC wants to achieve and what actually happens on the ground. In its Treaty (1992), SADC recognized the importance of the "evolution of common political values, systems, and institutions" as a fundamental aspect of regional integration. Non-compliance with regional decisions and agreements does not result in much or any costs for member states. Enforcement is reported as a challenge in all African RECs, according to GIZ (2014). As was the case with the SADC Tribunal, the institutions created to ensure that member states comply with regional agreements have been underused or undermined. This is partly due to existing principles of solidarity among state leaders that prevent African nations from enforcing conflict resolution and governance processes. Due to non-compliance by member states with the treaty, agreements, and protocols, the regional scheme has reached its present state.

SADC lacks the institutional framework and mandate to enforce the countries to fulfil their obligations. The SADC is not independent enough to carry out the integration agenda and operates according to the self-interests of its leaders. Leaders of SADC have remained resolute only in rhetoric that has failed to be matched by reality. Whenever progress has been made towards broader integration and common policies, those efforts have struggled to sustain themselves because such initiatives have been left to the whims of SADC leaders. A consensus exists among scholars that without credible governance structures supported by political will, democratic norms of free and fair elections, transparency, accountability, and respect for the rule of law, the SADC region cannot achieve socio-economic development and stability. The success of any regional integration scheme depends upon the compliance and commitment of the member states to protocols and agreements that guide the integration agenda.

The regional body must be given a new mandate with legal structures that support a unified economic, political, and security order to deepen integration. A good model for structuring regional political unions with powers to set norms on governance and markets is the European Union (EU). Over the past six decades, the EU has successfully transformed Europe into one of the most effective and competent actors globally. Southern African states can learn from what has worked in Europe and adapt the EU framework to their settings, which they have already attempted to do. What is missing is the operationalization of the agreed frameworks. The concept of shared sovereignty, unique to the EU, has allowed deeper integration; however, this shared identity is not readily apparent on the African continent.

Restructuring SADC is only the first step toward allowing the regional body to establish a vision, enumerate community goals, and guide the peace, security, and governance initiative. SADC member states should drastically alter the regional organization's functions and give it new powers to impose sanctions on states that violate the agreed obligations. Nevertheless, this is impossible if member states are reluctant to marshal the internal political will necessary to make the vision a reality and ensure their priorities are aligned with current economic, political, and security challenges. Member states must balance the partial loss of sovereignty and autonomy with regional prosperity to maximise economic gains. By doing so, SADC member states can harmonize their interests and stabilize the region simultaneously. Jabara et al. (1996) noted that SADC member states are sometimes slow or unwilling to ratify regional protocols because national interests are prioritized over regional interests. SADC (2012) acknowledges that, if member states are successful in overcoming challenges impeding the consolidation of regional integration, the following would be achieved:

(i) Contribute to increase in member states market development;
(ii) Increase regional trade and investment flow;

(iii) Promote the transfer of technology and expertise;

(iv) Create and sustain employment;

(v) Improve the standard of living; and

(vi) Increase cooperation on issues of common threat.

The biggest challenge in Southern Africa has been the inability to consolidate democracy, harmonize economic policies, enhance accountability, and adhere to the SADC treaty's agreements and protocols. The lack of an effective regional body in Southern Africa has resulted in contradictions and conflicting goals among the SADC member states. Nathan (2013) argues that these contradictions are inherent in the political systems of member states due to their differences in governance and democratic environments. Nathan claims that the absence of shared values among the SADC countries, combined with their unwillingness to cede part of their sovereignty to an independent regional institution, impedes creating a regional community based on regional governance and democratic norms. SADC member states are currently caught between the ideals of collective regional prosperity and the notion of popular national sovereignty. While countries like Botswana, Mauritius, South Africa, and Seychelles are among the highest-ranked in African on global governance indices, Angola, Swaziland, and Zimbabwe occupy the bottom spots. In failing to intervene in political crises in the region, SADC has undermined its ambition to build an economic, political, and security community.

A great deal of attention has been paid to the literature on regional integration and the need for policy coordination and harmonization despite the polar relationship in an integration arrangement. Lack of effective regional coordination can lead to contradictory policy positions in one member state, negating the expected outcome in another. A more integrated policy approach, including trade liberalization, is of utmost importance. The European Union (EU) provides an excellent model for structuring regional political and economic unions with sovereign powers to set market and governance norms. It is well established that a similar institutional framework, such as that of the EU, is the only instrument that can harmonize the political, social, and economic objectives of Southern Africa.

As there is no effective regional organization in Southern Africa, member states have contradictions and conflicting goals. Economically and politically diverse states have, however, characterized SADC. As a result, implementing regional agreements and protocols at the national level has proved challenging. Erasmus (2011) contends that the more comprehensive the trade arrangements and the further along the integration process, the stronger the need for appropriate supranational institutions. Specifically, Murithi (2003) argues that regional bodies with supranational powers are norm entrepreneurs, while peace and security tools are viewed as "interventionist" instruments. Murithi stated that "ensuring peace and order is a prerequisite for promoting peace, development, and improving African livelihoods."

Even though the causes of the political and security challenges in the SADC region are diverse, they are all related to the internal dynamics of the states, primarily the governance system. The inherent character of states has been a significant factor in many of these conflicts. With SADC member states blindly adopting the non-interference principle in member states' internal affairs for over three decades, SADC has seldom criticized the conduct of its members, even when their actions are flagrantly contradicting the SADC treaty provisions. According to Schiff and Winters (2003), countries may pursue far-reaching economic unions by ceding sovereignty to a supranational institution that develops and enforces rules. With SADC's ability to act above member states regarding specific areas of common interest, the integration agenda is firmly placed in neutral hands protected from the self-interest of regional leaders.

Moreover, this could ensure that the integration agenda proceeds efficiently since consensus would no longer be required to make decisions. As such, it is essential to reconsider the conceptual basis upon which such commitments are based. The most dominant states have been South Africa, Botswana, and Zimbabwe in terms of governance, peace, and security. However, the three countries have had different influences, and, in many cases, they have been at odds with each other. It has been a priority for Zimbabwe to preserve the liberation movement's legacy and its leaders. Known for championing democratic governance and accountability, Botswana challenges the status quo. South Africa's role has been more about occupying the middle ground than anything else. The South African government has championed democratic governance, but it has also shielded the legacy liberation leaders. According to Nathan (2016), the underlying factor is the absence of shared values among the SADC Member States, where two significant rifts arise from the conflict between democratic and autocratic tendencies.

Divided along democratic and authoritarian lines, SADC's member states' divergent governance systems have made it difficult for the regional body to attain its economic integration goals, poverty alleviation, regional stability, and uniformity of shared political values and governance institutions. Rarely do countries appear to be willing to partially relinquish their sovereignty, which is critical for the success of regional integration projects. Only the SADC members can transform the organization and give it the mandate and authority to develop into a supranational organization. African leaders are generally more inclined to launch new initiatives that deliver results, and SADC is no exception.

From a structural perspective, both the AU and its affiliate SADC were created to mimic the European Union (EU). Unfortunately, both institutions have not achieved their goals due to the lack of supranational instruments that ensure their effectiveness. Ultimately, it would be the responsibility of the supranational institution to formulate specific policies and ensure compliance among member states in order to achieve the aspired goals. The EU, for instance, has the European Parliament and the European Court of Justice (ECJ). The EU parliament formulates the laws, regulations, and policies that apply to all EU member states. At the same time, the Court of Justice enforces these EU laws, regulations, and policies. An EU member state that fails to implement or adhere to EU laws may be subject to legal action by the European Commission in accordance with EU treaties. In addition, the Court of Justice may impose financial penalties on member states responsible for the infringement.

African states adopted the Constitutive Act, which codified their behaviour to promote unity, solidarity, cohesion, and cooperation among member states. Furthermore, the Act reinforced the AU's commitment and legal framework for intervention, good governance, human rights protection, respect of human rights, and international humanitarian law. Although the AU had adopted Article 4 (h) of the Constitutive Act, which included the AU's right to intervene in the member state regarding the grave circumstance, the provision was amended quietly in 2003 by watering down the conditions for intervention. Regarding SADC, Article 5 of the SADC Treaty, one of SADC's fundamental objectives was to "evolve common political values, systems, and institutions." The SADC Treaty (1992) defines SADC as an international organization with a legal personality. This definition is identical to Article I-6 of the EU constitution, which means SADC and the EU are equal in their legal status. The only difference is in their enforcement and supporting instruments. Southern African states have laid the groundwork for transforming the region over the past three decades by creating catalyst instruments to provide a solid foundation for achieving sustainability and stability. The objective of these instruments is to define the region's future in the current economic and political system. In its efforts to enhance regional instruments to address some of the challenges that persist in the SADC region, the region has reached a critical turning point. Overcoming these challenges may seem overwhelming, but it is not impossible.

In a stable political climate, an institution with a supranational status would effectively exert its influence and control. SADC's integration process is undermined by the continued instability in some of its member states caused by election disputes, armed conflicts, and political and economic marginalization of some citizens. In this regard, the centrality of democracy and good governance in the integration agenda cannot be overstated. According to Ndlovu-Gatsheni (2011), governments in the region have repeatedly dismissed calls for greater accountability, better governance, and more effective institutional capacity despite the benefits that a more robust institution would bring to all members.

Over the years, progressive SADC instruments have been developed, but the elites have displayed little political commitment. An important contributing factor to the problem has been the dominance of the Heads of State in the decision-making process. In order to meet the regional objectives and aspirations, it is important to develop practical rules that govern political and economic interactions. With the lessons learned from the past, the region is now better positioned to move forward into the future. A more vibrant regional institution is desperately needed for the states of Southern Africa, which are capable of intervening in any potential governance lapses or conflict situations and imposing relevant sanctions to member states that fail to adhere to the prescribed normative values. Habib et al. (2006) contend that "these norms are critical to further deepening integration... Africa will unite faster if Africans embark on democratisation drives and create democratic institutions based on the logic of the self-empowerment of the people on the foundation of an effective and engaged state civil society nexus."

Even though there has been limited success with regional integration in Africa, the basic principles of regional integration suggest that regional integration schemes can still be effective if robust supporting institutions back them. The European market has grown into the most significant trading bloc globally after creating a prosperous and stable European Union. There is an important question that remains puzzling in the context of SADC. How can an institution with many brilliant ideas and talented bureaucrats continue on this trajectory of failure? The typical answer to this question is the dissonance between the supposed regional objective and the interests of the individual heads of state and government. Due to this dissonance, SADC has been unable to pursue critical issues of shared interest coherently and consistently.

SADC has been remarkably slow in learning from its past mistakes, in part because of the solid ideological sense of brotherhood and solidarity present among the Heads of State and Government, regardless of changing circumstances. Underneath the rhetoric of solidarity, some fundamental issues need to be urgently dealt with. As expected, SADC leaders continually seek to distance themselves from those problems and their own mistakes. Due to this, they do everything within their power to thwart any reform proposals that would interfere with their ability to control the regional integration agenda. The same Heads of State have dominated any reform debates that have failed to move the institution in the right direction. Having the same people responsible for the failed regional integration agenda debating SADC reforms has turned the process into a charade in which politicians pretend to address problems while their fundamental objective is to preserve the status quo.

It is essential to ensure that RECs respond to the needs of the poor and broader political and social concerns by ensuring transparency and holding leaders accountable. Despite being elected, most African political leaders are not directly accountable to the people once they are in office, and in many instances, electoral success is obtained through bogus elections. Lack of transparency and accountability harms the way regional institutions operate. In the absence of open discourse, summit deliberations and agreements are not subject to timely criticism or a conventional democratic process. To achieve regional economic success and stability, contemporary economies require a legal and democratic framework. In the context of SADC, one way of achieving such convergence was creating the SADC Tribunal in its original form.

Effective governance structures in the region could provide an enabling environment for FDI. The Southern African region desperately requires substantial FDI inflows to stimulate economic growth and enhance its production and infrastructure development. However, it is apparent from Chapter 7 discussion that the SADC region may only attract such investment if it is politically stable, secure, economically viable, and governed by rules that protect the interests of investors. Most multinational corporations (MNCs) with renowned brand names are susceptible to public perception and criticism, making them hesitant to do business with governments implicated in human rights violations. The SADC area is depicted as a region in economic, political, and security turmoil. Its challenges can be attributed to the lack of effective governance and weak regional integration schemes guided by regional leaders' whims. Individual personalities within the SADC leadership have shaped the implementation of the regional integration agenda.

An excellent example of the differences among SADC member states that impede regional integration is the delays encountered during the adoption and implementation of the SADC Trade Protocol. Berries (2000) reports that the Protocol was drafted and signed in 1996, but only five countries had ratified it by 1999. Similarly, it can also be said of other agreements and protocols, which are often ignored at will, as was the case with the SADC Tribunal's ruling.

It has also been noted that the current challenges that have led to Africa's political instability, economic decline, and social discontent reflect the leadership crisis on the continent. Assuming that the assumption is valid at the national level, the same can be said about the leadership of regional institutions. On a normative level, fundamental progress has been made in adopting protocols and agreements to address the SADC region's persistent challenges. However, this normative progress has failed to contribute to the effectiveness of the SADC. This has inevitably led to a decline in governance, socio-economic standards, and stability across the region.

Notwithstanding the required legal framework, there is an implementation gap that denies SADC a legal personality. A legal framework is not an end in itself, as is evidenced by the failure of SADC to resolve the persistent problems in the region. There are several reasons for this situation. Primary among those reasons is that the states' implementation powers have been retained, which has made the regional body defunct. Therefore, there are no instruments to ensure that all member states respect the protocols and agreements.

In establishing regional political unions with a single identity and the authority to set governance and market norms, the EU provides a viable model. In SADC, member states have a unique opportunity to revive their historical desire for a prosperous Southern Africa. This desire was inspired by the need to achieve socio-economic development and regional stability. The region can only achieve these objectives if past pitfalls of integration efforts are not repeated. The future should be inspired by the desire to achieve socio-economic objectives, democratic governance, and economic development that resonate with citizens' wishes. According to Kaplan (2008), strengthening regional organizations may be one of the best ways to conquer the problems that plague fragile states worldwide. Kaplan suggests that making changes to the business environment can significantly improve development prospects. Regional organisations can change societal dynamics by empowering people, unshackling them from the restrictions imposed by ineffectual governments. Kaplan (2008) asserts that development can only succeed when societal dynamics generate a momentum that promotes positive change. Under a supranational framework, intergroup rivalries can be lessened in intensity as all groups compete on equal terms.

SADC's experience so far indicates that the integration project has been ineffective. With member states characterised by high levels of corruption, bad governance, and authoritarianism, the regional integration schemes have nourished such governments. In general, scholars agree that SADC cannot function effectively within the existing structures. SADC Barometer (2005) observes that "weak institutional capacity presents some challenges" to SADC's institutional capacity. In addition, Tjønneland (2005) asserts that SADC's failures include its inability to advance a development agenda beyond infrastructure. SADC Secretariat functions primarily as an administrative instrument without any formal political powers. Implementing changes to SADC is only the beginning of the process as the institution, acting on behalf of member states, should have the capacity to lay out a vision and objectives for the region. Although member states' commitment to SADC on paper has been firm, there is a lack of political will within the region to transform the organization's vision and objectives into national priorities, thereby weakening its effectiveness.

Due to the lack of an effective regional body in Southern Africa, contradictions and competing objectives have arisen among the SADC member states. Even though the causes of the political and security challenges in the SADC region are diverse, the challenges are attributed primarily to the state's internal dynamics, particularly its governance system. Due to the blind adoption of the non-interference principle, the SADC has rarely criticized the conduct of its member states over the past three decades, even when the state's actions are directly in violation of their treaty obligations. Generally speaking, SADC has adhered to the principle of quiet diplomacy while publicly criticizing the international sanctions imposed on its member states. SADC's posturing has provided legitimacy and cover to authoritarian regimes in the region, such as DRC and Zimbabwe.

The notion of regime-boosting regionalism is discussed by Süderbaum in his book.....Süderbaum (2007) writes that this occurs when states seek to reinforce the status, legitimacy and general interests of the political 'regime' (not the nation-state per se), both internationally and domestically. Most African governments and political leaders engage in symbolic activities, such as praising the benefits of regional cooperation, signing cooperation agreements, and participating in summitry regionalism, without taking responsibility for implementing policies or being willing to bear the costs involved. One must consider the nature of statehood in Africa to understand how certain African regimes use regionalism to bolster their power. The majority of African states are considered to be weak. Perhaps this weakness explains why there has been no progress. Clapham (1996) contends there is persuasive evidence in the literature that weak African states tend to place a huge emphasis on formal and absolute sovereignty in their international relations, for example, the maintenance of existing borders and the principle of non-intervention in domestic affairs since it enhances the power of the ruling political elite and allows it to remain in power.

With a lack of democratic governance and regulatory convergence that creates disparities in the economic environment, harmonizing macroeconomic policies, economic and political integration cannot be overemphasized. According to Dinka and Kennes (2007), regional integration's viability and effectiveness are ultimately determined by the member countries' internal strengths and weaknesses and the degree to which they are willing to fulfil their obligations. Oghogho (2007) suggests that: "When a sub-regional group reaches a point where its set-up no longer allows it to meet the aspirations of its founding fathers or even the simplest of integration tasks, then it must be at dangerous crossroads and could be in dire need of reinvention." Due to the region's continued political and economic decline, the time has come to start an honest and dispassionate conversation about the immense political and economic tragedy the region is experiencing. Leaders in the region must recognize the immensity of the crisis. Many of the region members have suffered reversals in democracy, industrialization, and economic development, along with criticisms of institutional failures. Leaders of SADC have a steep and wide task at hand since they must reflect on and challenge the national interests of some of the regimes that have been tolerated for decades.

The discussion in Chapters 5 and 6 examined the factors that hinder regional integration and identifies growing concerns about the current institutional framework. A discrepancy between regional objectives and domestic policies is also noted. In combining national and regional interests, we can better understand subjective conditions that have prevented regional integration. There is a gap in this regard because there is no supranational institution charged with implementing and enforcing compliance with the decisions adopted. Currently, the SADC institutional framework does not give the regional body discretionary power to make decisions because it lacks legislative authority.

It is evident from the evidence that on some occasions, SADC member states have shown a desire to pursue supranationalism. The challenge lies in the disconnection between the commitment of nation-states to supranationalism and the conditions necessary for a supranational institution to flourish. Amidst commitments, agreements, protocols, and calls to adhere to shared norms and values, these demands have been undermined by the weakened institutional structure of SADC. Having the Summit of Heads of Government as the highest decision-making body, SADC operates at the whims of the political elite. Whether the integration agenda is exclusively focused on economic or market integration, democracy and good governance cannot be removed from the integration processes. Even though some policymakers may argue that human rights and other democratic norms should not be considered in economic debates, the absence of the rule of law may impact investors' willingness to commit their capital to an economy with democratic and governance challenges. Until the member states of SADC are fully committed to good governance and democratic ethos, the regional integration agenda in Southern Africa will remain a failure. They will fall far short of their potential.

SADC and South African Hegemony

The question of regional hegemony, such as South Africa for the SADC region, has also been raised when considering norm-setting on a regional platform and adopting a regional institutional framework with supranational powers. The political and economic dominance of South

Africa puts the country in a position of advantage to influence the creation of a regional community in which human security is indispensable and guaranteed to every citizen. Even though the post-Apartheid South African government embraced its leadership responsibilities within the Southern African community, South Africa has become less assertive in its leadership role over the years and, at times, has become complicit in driving regional disintegration. The lack of a reliable champion has been identified as a barrier to regional development and stability in Southern Africa.

A country's influence can be exerted in different areas according to its diplomatic, economic, military, and political resources and its ability to resolve stalemates, compensate losers, and coordinate regional collective actions. Bringing about deeper integration will require the considerable weight and leadership that certain states like South Africa can exert. The South African government is in a strong position to set the regional agenda and become a champion of regional policies. Hasenclever et al. (1997) argue that the hegemonic stability theory integrates a realist concept of power and security with cooperative elements contributing to establishing an international regime. Gilpin (2000) contributes to the discussions of the hegemonic stability debate by stating that a hegemon is necessary to maintain adherence to liberal international economic regimes and, by extension, liberal peace by subsidizing the costs of maintaining the security regime. At the same time, Adler and Barnett (1998) argue that common external threats facilitate cooperation and influence the dominant power to project shared norms. From this perspective, a major regional power such as South Africa can use its economic and political strength to enforce compliance among member states to ensure adherence to the rules, norms, and principles.

The role of South Africa in the African context is extremely significant both at the regional and continental levels. Having regional hegemons in charge of regional integration is beneficial, as lead countries can act as catalysts to help solve stalemates or resolve coordination failures. In their respective regional organisations, South Africa and Nigeria do so for a variety of reasons. Although hegemons can play a significant role in fostering regional agendas, they can also undermine them or abuse regional institutions for their advantage.

Historically, the dynamics of regional relations in Southern Africa were driven by the desire to support the South African liberation movement. Hanlon (1989) argues that Southern African states created a platform to mobilize international political and material support against Apartheid South Africa. With the ANC benefiting from the support it received from South African states, there was an expectation throughout the region that South Africa's economic might would help ease economic inequality. After Apartheid in South Africa ended and the first majority government came to power, SADC member states expected South Africa to play a leading role in the region's transformation. Several SADC member states had sacrificed everything to fight against Apartheid and had hoped that a new government in South Africa would help to improve the region's economy. However, this expectation was short-lived, as the enthusiasm did not translate into results. South Africa is the region's economic hub and can make or break the integration process in Southern Africa. As stated by Bertil Odén (1999), for South Africa to occupy a hegemonic position in the region, two conditions need to be met:

(i) South Africa must have the capacity and the will to create and maintain a mutually beneficial hegemonic regime
(ii) The other countries in the region must be willing to let South Africa play the benign hegemon's role and have sufficient capacity to participate within such a regime.

As a regional power, South Africa has been unable to effectively lead and transform the region's political, economic, and social fortunes. Despite its economic and military wealth, South Africa does not effectively leverage its soft power to gain consent for its ideas and values and assume leadership based on those values, as described by Adolfo (2009). Before taking office, the first democratically elected president of South Africa, Nelson Mandela, was well aware of Southern Africa's challenges and South Africa's future role in the region. In an article published in *Foreign Affairs* in 1993, Mandela (1993) stressed the priority of Southern Africa in South Africa's foreign policy and the relationship between South Africa and Southern Africa's future. In the article, Mandela stated: "The regional economy that emerged under colonialism entrenched the domination of one country (South Africa) and incorporated other countries in subsidiary and dependent roles as labour reserves, markets for South African commodities, suppliers of certain services (such as transport) or providers of cheap and convenient resources (like water, electricity and some raw materials). As a result, South Africa's visible exports to the rest of the region outnumber its imports from the region by more than five to one. That is a reflection of not just the stronger productive base of the South African economy, but of barriers of various kinds that have kept goods produced in regional states out of the South African market." A concern is that Mandela's description reflects both the past and the present as trade between South Africa and the rest of the region is highly imbalanced.

Meyns (2000) argues that while Mandela stated publicly that his country would pursue a "co-operative regionalist" strategy, the government's economic policies were moulded by the neo-mercantilist orientation of the Apartheid regime. Nelson Mandela's commitment to political and economic equality among all Africans can be traced back to his early years in politics. While testifying at the Rivonia Trial,following which he was sentenced to jail, Nelson Mandela ended his testimony with the following words: "During my lifetime, I have dedicated myself to the struggle of the African people. I have fought against white domination, and I have fought against black domination. I have cherished the ideals of a democratic and free society in which all persons live together in harmony and with equal opportunities. It is an ideal that I hope to live for and to achieve. But if needs be, it is an ideal for which I am prepared to die." Mandela's view of Africa shaped the foreign policy of the South African government primarily in rhetoric.

As a result of the ANC's successive governments, they have maintained the same trade policies as the Apartheid regime, protecting its markets and using its diversified economy to exploit its neighbours. Gibson (1998) states: "Despite calls for balanced growth, the creation of regional markets based upon trade liberalization and free-market principles does not tackle the problem of size disparities or the threat of de-industrialization in, for example, Malawi, Zimbabwe, and Zambia." South Africa's export drive to the region has led to South African companies buying breweries in Zambia, Zimbabwe and Malawi. In most of these acquisitions, South African companies have replaced local production with South African exports. In addition, South African retailers like Shoprite, Pep, Game and others have opened supermarkets and consumer goods retail outlets across the SADC region to take advantage of the region's lacklustre manufacturing and retail base. As most products are sourced directly from South Africa, the local supply chain industry has been destroyed. In this context, South Africa's hegemon also presents challenges to the regional project.

A thriving regional integration scheme in Southern Africa requires South Africa to play the role of a benign hegemon rather than a malign superpower. Mandela's successor Thabo Mbeki's foreign policy, was motivated in part by his vision of the African Renaissance, in which South Africa had to embrace its African identity. His view was that the fate of South Africa was directly related to the fate of the continent as a whole. The well-being of South Africans was dependent upon the politico-economic development and stability on the continent. Though South African leaders have demonstrated brotherhood on regional, continental, and international platforms, South Africa's hostile attitude toward other SADC members has resulted in citizens' increased xenophobic perceptions, which have resulted in more xenophobic incidents. Bischoff (1998) writes that "South Africa's preoccupation with halting the influx of immigrants, their treatment and deportation to many are indicative of xenophobic attitudes." However, South Africa can still redeem itself and play a more constructive role in the region despite all these failures. To demonstrate its commitment to leadership, South Africa must win the trust of its regional partners. South Africa must address the region's inequalities by taking tangible actions to address the trade imbalances and treating its neighbours as equal partners.

As a regional powerhouse, South Africa plays a unique and crucial role within the SADC structures in the social, political, and economic spheres. South Africa and its neighbours must acknowledge that the Southern African countries' problems transcend national borders and that all SADC members have a common interest in their collective survival. Due to concerns that South Africa may impose its will on the regional body, member states have been reluctant to grant more sovereignty to the regional organization. SADC member states are concerned that South Africa could use its power to influence regional agendas at other countries' expense due to its proximity to weaker states with smaller economies. Considering South Africa's trade diplomacy, which has been exploitative, these concerns are understandable. The success of the integration scheme in Southern Africa will be dependent on South Africa's policies and attitude regarding regional integration. Mandela (1993) acknowledged these challenges before he took office when he stated: "We are sensitive to the fact that any program that promotes greater cooperation and integration in Southern Africa must be sensitive to the acute imbalances in existing regional economic relations after Apartheid is carefully calibrated to avoid exacerbating inequities." Averting some of these challenges requires South Africa to stop lip service and take action. Considering the current situation and trends in Southern Africa, it can be argued that South Africa's fault is that its self-seeking economic strategies continue to exploit its comparative advantage while paying little attention to the consequences of its actions.

Even so, South Africa's position within the SADC bloc remains significant, and the country possesses the ability to provide direction for regional integration that benefits all member states. Van Nieuwkerk (2012) argues that after Apartheid, South Africa's foreign policy demonstrated to its citizens the importance of engaging the rest of Africa. Besides playing an active role in diplomatic interventions to resolve disputes, South Africa can also use its soft power to influence the region's governance culture and political values. However, South Africa has failed to effectively use its soft power to support its democratic ideals and values. With South Africa's limited influence in the region, authoritarian regimes have thrived unchecked, and in most cases, the South African government has emboldened authoritarian regimes.

On the peace and security front, the South African government has also failed to take the initiative. South Africa, for instance, failed to influence a coordinated SADC response to the DRC conflict after Uganda and Rwanda invaded a SADC member state in 1998, resulting in massive resource exploitation and loss of life. As a result of the absence of South African leadership, SADC's response was disjointed, with three SADC member states (Zimbabwe, Angola and Angola) intervening at Laurent-Desire Kabila's request. On the other hand, another SADC member, Tanzania, facilitated the Ugandan arms' movement for fighting in the DRC. In addition, South Africa's efforts to influence the Zimbabwe regime through quiet diplomacy have failed, with Zimbabwe remaining in a state of economic and political crisis for two decades.

After overcoming Apartheid and embracing a multiracial society, South Africa's liberal democratic values and international reputation provide a moral basis for the country to become a role model and cheerleader for democratic values and good governance. With a strong hegemony like South Africa in the region, its government can play a significant role in pushing for a political, economic, and security and governance regime. It is no secret that South Africa has the necessary capabilities to position itself as an unquestionable regional leader in the same manner that Nigeria has done in West Africa. Paul (2012) alludes that hegemonic stability theory implies "order in the function of a powerful state within the region, a state that can impose peace and command both respect and power." As discussed earlier in Chapter 9, with the rise of Ansar al-Sunna in Cabo Delgado, Mozambique's security crisis has become a priority for the SADC region. South Africa holds tremendous responsibility for leading a regional response, although, at the moment, Mozambique is insisting that it leads the regional military response despite its inherent weakness. South Africa and its neighbours should draw lessons from the rise of Boko Haram in Nigeria and Al Shabaab in Somalia. Both groups began as small Islamic militant groups operating in their region. As a result of the lack of a decisive counter-insurgency response, both groups became significant regional threats. Ansar al-Sunna continues to wage terror attacks primarily against targets in the Carbo Delgado region, in Tanzania with Mtwara, and they can spread mayhem across the region. As expected, South Africa did not take advantage of the urgent need to coordinate a timely regional military response to the Islamic insurgency, resulting in Mozambique seeking assistance elsewhere. Rwandan troops (non-SADC country) were the first to arrive in Cabo Delgado, which brings SADC's failure into the international spotlight once again.

As a regional hegemon, South Africa can play a fundamental role by projecting its military and economic power to bring about economic prosperity and stability. The early optimism over South Africa's role in the region was also echoed by scholars like Asante (1997), who observes: "South Africa can look forward to the close integration of the subcontinent's dominant economy into the economic and political structures of the region." Azam (1995) goes further to suggest that "South Africa's regional role could propel growth in Southern Africa in pretty much the same way that the Asian tigers (Hong Kong, South Korea, Singapore, and Taiwan) led the way for Malaysia and Southern China."

Whether or not these expectations were too optimistic, they were inspired by ANC's idealistic view on the region in which the organization viewed South Africa as the pillar of South Africa's foreign policy before ANC came to power. The ANC believed South Africa's destiny was intertwined with its neighbours, and South Africa's foreign policy also reflected this view when the ANC came into power. For example, the 2004 Department of Foreign Affairs (DFA) Strategic Plan emphasized South Africa's commitment to economic development through regional integration and development within the Southern African Development Community and the Southern African Customs Union. Further, it stressed interaction with African partners as equals. However, South Africa's pronouncements before the ANC came into power and the early years of the ANC have been in contradiction to contemporary pronouncements.

The Windhoek Declaration highlighted the importance of foreign direct investment into the region, passing through South Africa as the primary economic hub. That issue has also been addressed in the Protocol of Trade from 1996 and, most recently, in the Protocol on Finance and Investment from 2006. Mahembe and Odhiambo (2013) mention the objectives for promoting intra-regional trade liberalization, industrialization, and FDIs. As a means of increasing foreign direct investments, member states are encouraged to achieve political stability and economic cooperation. Amos (2010) and Lederman et al. (2013) argue that a stable political environment, whether intra - or inter-state, is conducive for attracting foreign investment. Te Velde and Bezemer (2006) suggest that belonging to a regional grouping is vital for attracting FDI. Hence, South Africa has an interest in ensuring economic growth and stability in the region.

South Africa's history of destabilizing its neighbours under the Apartheid regime leads Nathan (2013) to argue that the current ANC government has a moral obligation to contribute to its neighbours' stability and economic prosperity. South Africa has shown little interest in taking a leadership role in driving regional integration in the SADC region despite being the most powerful state in terms of economy, development, and governance structures. Instead, South Africa has shown more interest in cooperating with states outside of the region and the continent in general. The BRICS, an acronym for the combined emerging economies of Brazil, Russia, India, China, and South Africa, is a bloc developed to compete against Western blocs led by the United States and governed by the Bretton Woods Institutions. Additionally, South Africa unilaterally negotiated and signed free trade agreements (FTAs) with the European Union (EU) without consulting other SADC member states. As the region's largest economy, South Africa has considerable influence on international markets and can protect the interests of SADC members. By isolating itself in its trade agreements with the EU and the BRICS, it negatively impacts other SADC countries' perceptions of the country.

Considering South Africa's stature, the rest of the region could be persuaded if the country took a leadership role on critical regional issues such as good governance, democracy, human rights and security. The challenge is that smaller members are reluctant to adopt a position that contradicts South Africa's official position. Sadly, South Africa lacks the political will to take such drastic measures. South Africa is well-positioned to play a leadership role in establishing rules that can enhance regional integration. By virtue of its effective democratic and governance structures, South Africa can generate credibility for the entire region. However, this is only possible if South Africa takes the initiative to steer the SADC in the right direction. Germany has taken a leadership role in holding member states accountable for non-compliance, and South Africa can do the same.

South Africa must utilise its economic and political clout to finance the infrastructure development projects within the SADC through the Regional Development Fund. Such funds can be released if member states adhere to all SADC protocols on democratic governance, human security, transparency, accountability, and acceptance of monitoring and evaluation mechanisms. The objective of this fund must go beyond supporting regional infrastructure projects; South Africa should take the initiative to provide technical support for the implementation of peace making and peace keeping initiatives in the region. In the past, South Africa has been accused of failing to utilise its economic and political power to bring about a settlement in Zimbabwe. Although South Africa has one of the most developed democratic and governance structures, the country's failure to promote good governance across the region has been somewhat puzzling. The institutional weakness of the regional body makes it even more surprising that South Africa refuses to hold any of the SADC member states accountable for any violations of human rights, democratic values, and governance. The argument Nathan (2012) makes is that SADC "member states are bound by a common commitment to state solidarity and regime protection" rather than by a commitment to human rights and the rule of law seems more reasonable in this context.

Building Effective Governance And Security Apparatus

As a result of globalization's profound effects on the interdependence between nations, the concepts of governance and security have become unavoidable components of regional integration discourse. Regional integration agendas have to transcend state-centrism, primarily concerned with power structures at the national level. The African Union's Agenda 2063 lists good governance, democracy, respect for human rights, justice, and the rule of law as key to Africa's political and economic transformation. Over the last three decades, regional institutions have been engaged in reforms to combat poverty and enhance human development. The African Community has recognized that good governance and security are prerequisites for economic growth; however, many African countries have been unable to institute the reforms required to prevent authoritarian regimes, corruption, and socioeconomic decline. As a result of weak and ineffective leadership, political violence, and the lack of political will in the SADC region, countries like Zimbabwe, the Democratic Republic of Congo, and Mozambique face instability that impedes progress in promoting economic growth and human development. Many parts of Southern Africa suffer from conflict and democratic decline, despite progress in consolidating democratic values. It is unlikely that SADC will achieve Agenda 2063 unless competent institutions enforce good governance and safeguard security in the region.

As Schiff and Winters (2003) note, regional economic communities are formed for economic integration and non-economic purposes such as national security, peace, and assistance in developing political institutions. As discussed in Chapter 7, these political objectives have overwhelming economic implications for RECs as they create an environment conducive to successful economic integration. With the end of the Apartheid regime in South Africa, the SADC region has had an opportunity to enhance economic, political, and security integration with new structures established under the regional body. Nonetheless, SADC's integration and development efforts have been hampered by peace and security concerns. Achieving peace and security is critical to creating an environment conducive to fostering regional integration. In the meantime, several SADC member states continue to experience armed conflict and political instability. The destructive nature of these conflicts has had devastating consequences for the region and has led to constant insecurity. Developing a thriving regional integration project requires a secure and stable environment that creates viable markets and attracts foreign direct investment to stimulate economic growth and infrastructure development.

Khadiagala (2018) argues that "regional approaches are strongly needed in Africa to overcome economic fragmentation and political vulnerability. However, nationalistic tendencies impede the ability of African institutions to become loci of meaningful integration." In Khadiagala's view, "resolving these weaknesses requires African initiatives to strengthen the normative foundations of regional institutions and strengthen their capacity to achieve results." Furthermore, establishing a consensus that democratization is essential to the management of conflict is crucial." However, African institutions currently suffer from weakened structures that cannot achieve desired results. Organizations such as SADC are meant to serve as norm-setters and agents of democratization and good governance. Contrary to this, the SADC may be defined as an institution unable to enforce democratic norms and values while simultaneously providing cover for authoritarian regimes.

However, the end of Apartheid did not reduce conflict in Southern Africa as anticipated. Complex conflicts are still raging in the region. Conflicts in the region have exacerbated the notion that the region's conflicts are internal rather than external, necessitating the development of remedies that address the root causes of those conflicts. New conflict resolution measures are needed in light of the changing dynamics of the Southern African conflict. In recent decades, there have been calls for the SADC member states to transform themselves from a SADC of heads of state into a SADC of the people. The regional body originally established to enhance member states' economic cooperation has now recognized that economic success cannot be achieved without regional stability. The SADC has adopted the AU Constitutive Act by establishing regional security and governance instruments to address the persistent political and security threats unique to the Southern African region. Almost all of these instruments recognize that good governance is a prerequisite to economic growth and human development.

Despite a catastrophic political, economic, social, and humanitarian crisis raging across the region, the book's preceding chapters placed the responsibility for these challenges squarely on the SADC leadership and the lack of effective governance. As the principles of sovereignty and non-interference have guided the current interaction between regional member states, calls for urgent changes in the way SADC operates have been deafening in recent years. Nevertheless, due to the downward trajectory experienced by some member states, some problems have begun to spread to neighbouring countries. There are many adverse economic, social, and humanitarian challenges that continue to drain the region's resources and hinder economic growth, affecting investors' perception, and the regional body needs to make changes immediately.

Having proclaimed the promotion of peace, stability, security, and human rights as the primary objective of the AU and its sub-regional bodies, the AU's Constitutive Act enshrines the principle of humanitarian intervention and commits member states to fight impunity. For the existing instruments to be more effective against the challenges of the SADC region, we must consider two factors. Firstly, SADC member states have a significant role in realizing SADC's vision of a shared future, ensuring economic well-being, improving living standards and quality of life, freedom, social justice, peace, and security of Southern Africa. Secondly, the SADC region's susceptibility to conflicts remains a pre-existing factor and one that demonstrates the need for SADC to stay more robust and effective. The objectives for regional integration should be reinvested from being state-centred towards a human-centric character.

Englebert (2000) argues that "African states suffer on average from greater legitimacy deficits than other regions." Civil society should be included in constructing a new regional community where citizens' interests are placed at the forefront. Involving the civil society could also broaden the legitimacy of government, strengthening regional democratic instruments. Bringing civil society organizations closer to the integration process is crucial. As long as they emphasize the interests of the people they represent, private industry actors and civil society groups can affect regional agreements and initiatives. At the regional level, formal mechanisms must be established for consulting with apex private sector organizations and civil society groups. For instance, SADC would benefit significantly from a stable and lasting relationship with the region's universities. First, universities could research key aspects of regional cooperation and integration, which secretariats and governments often cannot deliver on time or thoroughly enough.

Similarly, labour organizations should maintain dialogue with regional integration mechanisms. Regional integration agendas might be enriched by engaging workers in discussions on labour mobility, the portability of pension rights, employment rights, certification of technical skill, health and safety procedures, training needs, and other topics of a more sector-specific nature. The public would also be made aware of integration schemes and the free movement of people, which would reduce xenophobic attacks.

As part of regional integration schemes, the private sector needs to be involved as well. Usually, the private sector does not participate in policy and program development, formulation, and implementation in most African countries. In many regional economic communities, private sector participation is not specifically addressed in agreements. Nevertheless, the private sector can play an important role in regional integration by providing financial and human resources to support the regional agenda. It can also influence government policy and push them to ratify and implement protocols, stabilize macro-economic conditions, produce high-performing institutions, and maintain legal standards. The rationalization of rules of operation across borders is also beneficial for companies operating across borders.

Currently, there is little connection between the decisions made by regional corporations and the decisions made by regional institutions at the moment. There are two sides to this, and both must play their part: both business organizations and integration schemes must set specific goals and create specific tasks to improve the dialogue. For regional value chains to succeed, business and labour, which are key players, must establish a dynamic dialogue. As a result of more informed and modernized dialogue, foreign trade and investment policies, innovation, and competitiveness policies would gain momentum, resulting in more remarkable value chain contributions in the region.

Aspirations of SADC member states for a peaceful and prosperous region should go beyond solidarity rhetoric and signing of agreements; aspirations should pursue a practical regional agenda. This is a regional agenda in which member states are committed to addressing obstacles hindering regional integration, resulting in stagnant economic growth and persistent political instability. SADC member states must adopt a unified approach to eliminate corruption, weak governments, and unaccountable governments. By promoting transparency and accountability on the domestic and regional levels, member states should embrace democratic norms and good governance ethos. In addition to promoting confidence in government, this transformation would help decrease conflict while also enhancing stability. There have always been underlying social-economic grievances at the root of resource-related conflicts; addressing these grievances through socio-economic interventions and negotiations may assist in averting these conflicts.

The geopolitical risks that threaten Southern African security and its economic prosperity are immense. Most SADC member states have experienced failed governance systems that have lost their political viability and legitimacy. As a result of these conditions, economic growth has been slowed due to high levels of corruption and rent-seeking. SADC's failure to intervene in the DRC and Zimbabwe may have only had a limited impact on regional stability. Yet, the failure to intervene in Mozambique may have far-reaching implications for regional security. Having a common external enemy like the Islamic group Ansar al-Sunna provides the member states of SADC a material incentive to cooperate rather than compete, as has been the case in the past. First and foremost, the SADC member states' leaders must recognize the challenges in their respective government structures that have contributed to these conflicts and embrace changes that could alleviate those challenges.

Furthermore, the failure of the Mozambican government to contain the insurgency has led to the country becoming a fertile breeding ground for terrorists and international criminal networks. To date, Mozambique has also become Africa's leading narco-state. Due to its porous borders, long coastline, and relative instability, illicit drugs from Afghanistan, India, and Eastern Pakistan are often smuggled into the country through its ports, often arriving in shipping containers hidden among legitimate goods. A multifaceted strategy is required to address the diverse security challenges in the region. Long-term commitments and efforts are necessary for the region's political, security, and governance cultures to be transformed. Regional instability has had security implications, and conversely, regional security threats have affected economic growth, development, and integration. Inaction in the region has had very high costs, as demonstrated by its poor human development outcomes and the continued fragility of its member states. The intensity of this fragility is characterized by the worst forms of human deprivation, violations of human rights, and interminable conflicts. It is now clear that the conflicts in the region have adverse effects far beyond the borders of the countries involved.

Southern African states have, to some extent, demonstrated their commitment to a collaborative approach to regional peace and stability through the adoption of some resolutions and instruments. However, with SADC lacking the character of what Murithi (2003) refers to as "norm entrepreneur," the presence of the peace and security instruments alone cannot resolve the persistent regional conflicts. Peace and security initiatives continue to be impeded by the absence of shared values and a fear of surrendering sovereignty to the regional organization. This has resulted in a security gap between what SADC wants to accomplish and what the two institutions can realistically achieve. The obstacles have been exacerbated by the division between democratic and authoritarian inclinations among the member states, preventing the body from addressing the political and security challenges propagated by authoritarian and repressive regimes throughout the region. As a result of the legitimacy deficit in SADC member states, establishing collective security regimes that incorporate human security has been complex. To achieve these values, there must be uniformity in democratic governance throughout the region. That is why it is imperative that the AU and SADC orient African political leadership and ensure that decisive actions are taken to ensure peace and security initiatives are successful.

SADC leaders appear to be deliberately working to weaken the institution's ability to safeguard the rights of people, despite protocols meant to guide processes that could ensure democratic governance, respect for human rights, and adherence to the rule of law. While the SADC countries have refused to enforce their treaty obligations on democratic governance and human rights, the ECOWAS has endorsed a Joint Protocol on Democracy and Good Governance in December 2001, elaborating a set of shared "constitutional convergence principles." Some of these principles include:

(i) The separation of powers;
(ii) Independence of the judiciary;
(iii) Free, fair, and transparent elections;
(iv) Zero tolerance for power obtained by unconstitutional means;
(v) Popular participation in decision-making;
(vi) Adherence to democratic principles and decentralization of power at all levels of governance;
(vii) Freedom from ethnic, religious, regional, or racial discrimination; and
(viii) Freedom of association and the press.

The ECOWAS protocol authorizes sanctions in the event of member states violating a principle, which may include suspension from the institution's decision-making bodies. The ECOWAS Security and Democracy Protocol has given ECOWAS a unique mandate to become a guarantor of peace and a guardian of effective democracy and human rights. SADC's Treaty (1992) established protocols oriented towards promoting "common values, political systems, and other shared values that are transmitted through democratic, legitimate, and effective institutions." Yet, one significant difference has been insufficient enforcement of these protocols, which has rendered them ineffective. In addition, these protocols have failed to reflect the operational environment on the ground. The SADC Treaty does not obligate its member states to adhere to the protocols, as is the case with ECOWAS. Therefore, SADC member states must rethink and restructure the regional body's institutional framework by strengthening its mandate and authority. The institution's chairmanship has been awarded to authoritarian leaders like Robert Mugabe, Edson Mnangagwa, and King Mswati, hence undermining its credibility.

There have also been instances in which dictators have been in charge of the Organ of Politics, Defence, and Security despite their distaste for democracy. SADC's position has been of decisive philosophical importance in determining how harshly the international community will judge it. The track record of these leaders with regard to adhering to democratic norms in their own countries is not very impressive. Being the face of SADC on democracy and governance issues has become more like an endorsement and a badge of honour for autocrats. In turn, this has weakened the credibility of SADC and the regional bloc's ability to deal with its governance problems.

The European Union has the Charter of Fundamental Rights, which guarantees the rights of its citizens. Since the EU has jurisdiction over all member states, governments cannot infringe on these rights. SADC member states should make it a practical goal to shift priorities if the region addresses the long-running humanitarian catastrophes by sanctioning human rights abusers, removing dictators who steal election results and working towards regional integration.

Nevertheless, SADC's regional integration agenda will continue to face challenges due to its implications for national sovereignty, which remains a contentious issue among political elites in the region for two reasons. In the first place, member states tend not to entrust security and sovereignty to anyone other than themselves. In the region, most leaders place their political survival above their responsibilities towards human and socio-economic development. Due to the region's continued economic and security decline, creating a regional security and governance regime has become more of a necessity than a luxury. As the threat of terrorism and criminal networks increases in the region due to governance deficiencies in some countries, most SADC member states face the same enemy, and SADC must develop mechanisms to address these challenges. By creating a united front, SADC member states will overcome the international arena's anarchic nature by retaining its relevance.

SADC is a region characterized by relatively weak countries, both economically and politically. Most states are facing economic challenges, which limit their ability to invest in regional peace initiatives. States tend to view issues through an inward lens and are often overwhelmed by their internal political challenges. On top of this, political leaders are also fighting for their regimes' survival, making regional objectives a lesser priority. For these states, the prospect of transferring security responsibilities to a supranational body has become increasingly difficult to accept. Poor political and economic policies have contributed to the region's security challenges, negatively affecting economic growth, employment, and the delivery of public services, among other issues.

Poor governance practices have led to governments taking steps to prevent citizens from protesting and seeking to change government policies through legitimate channels, such as elections and other organized forms of political activity. SADC member states should recognize SADC as an organization that supports national efforts to achieve national and regional political harmony. Per the SADC Treaty, this order should be based on democracy and human rights and all the institutions, rights, and obligations of a liberal democratic system. Nation-states in the region continue to articulate democratic governance and human security norms, but these norms have not yet been accepted and incorporated into national governance structures. These norms and shared values have been burdened by insufficient interest and the absence of confident and strong leadership in the member states.

Post-independence debates and the liberation movement legacy continue to shape regional relations in Southern Africa. At the expense of citizens, the ruling elite has hijacked the liberation legacy. The ruling elites have utilized their participation in the liberation struggle to consolidate their power, as noted in Chapters 3, 4, 6 and 9 of the book. Most of the regimes in the region have failed to deliver on economic and political promises that won them support from the people, resulting in loss of their legitimacy to govern. The legitimacy of their rule now derives from the liberation legacy, with the liberation parties becoming the self-anointed people's representatives. Now, the liberation parties are the only legitimate institution with the power to govern. Mbeki (2005) argues that liberation parties have adopted repressive government systems to control citizens who demand a better life and freedoms.

Against this background, the SADC bloc is characterized by tension and a lack of cooperation in regional conflict resolution. Most regional leaders have ties to the liberation struggle, so challenging or appearing to challenge regimes that violate SADC protocols and agreements remains difficult. The regional body struggles to confront these challenges from the conflict in DRC, Zimbabwe, Lesotho, Madagascar, and now Mozambique. Member states should clarify and improve their working principles and iron out disagreements that have hindered peacemaking initiatives in the region. According to Makinda et al. (2016), governance, security, and peace are all interrelated, and a failure to achieve one of them may hamper the achievement of the others. Galtung (1996) went so far as to claim that peace is the primary prerequisite for humanity's survival.

Table 7.1: Governance Indicator (GI) and GDP

	GI	Rank		GDP pc (US $)	Rank
Botswana	0.68	1.	Seychelles	18 700	1.
Mauritius	0.66	2.	Botswana	15 800	2.
South Africa	0.43	3.	Mauritius	12 400	3.
Namibia	0.33	4.	South Africa	10 400	4.
Seychelles	0.09	5.	Angola	9 100	5.
Madagascar	-0.18	6.	Namibia	5 500	6.
Lesotho	-0.25	7.	Swaziland	5 100	7.
Mozambique	-0.31	8.	Lesotho	1 600	8.
Tanzania	-0.32	9.	Zambia	1 500	9.
Zambia	-0.39	10.	Tanzania	1 400	10.
Malawi	-0.42	11.	Madagascar	1 100	11.
Swaziland	-0.60	12.	Mozambique	900	12.
Angola	-1.03	13.	Malawi	800	13.
D. R. of Congo	-1.38	14.	D. R.of Congo	300	14.
Zimbabwe	-1.58	15.	Zimbabwe	200	15.

Sources: World Governance Indicators VII, CIA World Book 2008

Several economic studies have also analysed the relationship between economic performance and the quality of governance. According to Kaufmann et al. (2000), this relationship pertains to market-enhancing governance, and the results indicated a positive causal relationship between good governance and economic growth. Khan (2004) argues that reforms of economic structures and governance systems are the initial steps to improving economic performance. The second step is allowing economic growth to enhance good governance. An excellent political and governance structure is assumed to be a precondition for good economic performance.

As shown in Table 7.1, the governance environment (GI) is measured in relation to the GDP per capita of SADC member states. According to the figure, three of the four countries with the highest GDP per capita also had the best governance environment. It is noteworthy that Angola recorded the fifth largest GDP despite ranking third lowest on governance indicators. Angola has benefitted from short term economic policies that have benefited from the oil wealth.

To date, integration and trade have been discussed from an economic perspective. Peace and security, or, to put it more generally, stability, are prerequisites to a success of a regional integration scheme. An investment-friendly environment is critical to attracting and retaining foreign capital. A stable regional environment is vital for investment in infrastructure, which holds the key to industrialization in an era of linked markets and borders. Africa has been facing internal conflicts that have caused severe cross-border spillovers for years, if not decades. When a region is riddled with conflicts, foreign direct investment will not flow to it. For Africa's trade and growth to flourish, stability needs to return. In general, economic factors and political factors affect regional integration. As part of this challenge, African integration arrangements must be adapted to lead to dynamic gains, facilitate and sustain reforms, and promote stability among member states.

The region has a great deal of mineral wealth and other natural resources that could make it a geopolitical powerhouse if tough decisions are taken to stabilize the region and improve its governance framework. Since its inception, the SADC has maintained a fundamental non-interventionist stance and has prioritized non-interference in internal affairs. For the SADC region to achieve its objectives and aspirations, this stance must be changed. Because regional institutions are familiar with the region and possess a deeper understanding of cultural, historical, and social dynamics, they can resolve regional conflicts. This should make them more competent and effective. It is in SADC's best interest to resolve conflicts in the DRC, Mozambique, and Zimbabwe to avoid adverse effects of conflict on neighbouring countries.

The violence that has occurred on the African continent, where Africans have committed cruel acts against their fellow Africans, resulting in millions of deaths, has often been caused by despotic regimes; Southern Africa is no exception. In contrast to the rest of the world, the SADC region has remained in the dark ages with a few shining stars such as Botswana, Namibia, and South Africa. For decades, the regional bloc has cultivated a false sense of nationalism by acting like a self-righteous colonial victim to shield dictators from international condemnation of human rights abuses. As a result, SADC leaders have consistently maintained that the West does not have the moral authority to criticize the region's governance. Yoweri Museveni famously referred to the then OAU as a "trade union of dictators" back in 1986. The irony is that he is now an integral member and defender of the same trade union he denounced when he stood on high moral ground.

According to Aning and Lartey (2014), regional economic communities are tasked with developing regional security tools to address security challenges in their areas. Through its subsidiary principle, the AU has delegated responsibility for regional peace and security to the regional economic communities, in this case, SADC for Southern Africa. Furthermore, Jackson (2000) points out that the UN has also promoted the regionalization of peace and security to manage certain types of conflicts wherein the regional institutions would be responsible for resolving conflict on the ground, while the UN would serve as a coordinator. Malan (1999) describes this process as a 'peace pyramid'. The RECs respond to regional conflicts as the first responders and the UN play a significant role in post-conflict reconstruction efforts.

However, these progressive peace and security initiatives have also been met with opposition and pushbacks from African leaders at the regional and continental levels. Edwin (2018) argues that SADC has not been able to promote peace through the institution of democratic governance. In his study of security integration in SADC, Edwin questioned SADC's ability to establish a regional security community. Members of the SADC have failed to transform themselves from the old paradigm of state (regime) security to the new paradigm of human security. This new approach resonates with King and Murray's (2001) argument that 'territorial security does not necessarily ensure the security of citizens within a state." The reluctance of African leaders to grant absolute authority to RECs has undermined their ability to provide practical guidance on peace and security.

As a result of the limited capacity of the AU and RECs, the "Responsibility to Protect" (R2P) principle has also been challenging to implement. Under the R2P mandate, member states have the right to intervene in the domestic affairs of other members if there is evidence of gross human rights violations. There is evidence that African leaders began to withdraw from this commitment by amending Article 4(h), which extended the Union's right to intervene in member states under severe threats to legitimate order to restore peace and stability. In this Article, the AU appears to have been authorized to intervene in electoral disputes and situations in which a regime has been illegitimately trying to maintain power. That fear influenced the adoption of the Ezulwini Consensus, which stressed that: "It is important to reiterate the obligation of states to protect their citizens, but this should not be used as a pretext to undermine the sovereignty, independence, and territorial integrity of states."

This amendment shows that African leaders were wary of the R2P principle, resulting in their reluctance to internalize it. In light of some of the regimes in the SADC region and Africa in general experiencing legitimacy issues, Article 4 (h) was perceived as intrusive and threatening. In Africa, regional bodies are governed according to the whims of leaders, who in some cases are dictators. Therefore, the desire to establish regional organizations that transcend the self-serving interests of dictators is unpopular. The adoption of the Ezulwini Consensus demonstrates the degree to which member states are willing to limit foreign intervention in intra-state affairs.

Changing the regional, ideological outlook can alter how RECs in Africa approach the region's peace and security challenges. As earlier discussed, one of the vital features of supranationalism is the character of the policies, agreements, and protocols that bind all member states. Furthermore, supranational institutions can only function effectively if all members are stable. As regional integration projects require uniform implementation and adherence, the instability in the SADC region, which is attributed to electoral disputes, high levels of corruption, human rights abuses, and marginalization of some demographic groups, has weakened their pursuit of uniform standards. In Zimbabwe, Mozambique, the Democratic Republic of the Congo, Lesotho, Swaziland and other countries, governments have undermined the ethos of good governance and democracy, leading to persistent intra-state conflict that has adversely affected the economic prosperity of the people.

SADC has set up protocols for security cooperation as well as safeguards regarding democracy and security. However, these protocols have proven to be insignificant as SADC continues to adhere to Hammerstad's (2005) principles of absolute sovereignty and solidarity. Some SADC member states have argued that the SADC Secretariat has intentionally been kept weak to avoid creating an interventionist supranational body. Nathan (2010b) argues that "for intra-regional peacemaking to be successful, states must share an internal logic with a normative consensus that allows them to operate with close political cooperation on a set of shared and enforceable norms." These norms and values are essential for states to overcome their differences, build trust and act with a common purpose. SADC's disjointed military intervention in DRC in 1999 was widely criticized as an example of the lack of unity within the organization that has often complicated or, at times, extended some aspects of conflicts in the region.

To promote human security and democracy in the region, the SADC leadership needs to develop a unified policy vision and approach. As part of this unified vision, some level of national sovereignty should be sacrificed, and the SADC Secretariat should be strengthened with a supranational mandate. Furthermore, leaders are required to break away from the existing approach that promotes state sovereignty and non-interference in pursuit of human security, civil liberties, and democratic principles in the region.

It has also been identified as one of the significant challenges impeding regional integration in Southern Africa that the regional organization is not sufficiently independent to implement integration efforts. The current setup allows the regional body to operate on regional leaders' whims, whose interests sometimes get in the way of regional objectives without facing any consequences or being held accountable. There is a strong correlation between the effective implementation of regional integration initiatives and the independence of the regional institutions. The ability of SADC to act above its member states in specific areas of shared interest would insulate regional objectives from domestic political influences. Additionally, it enables the implementation of policies more quickly since there is no consensus because the treaties and protocols bind all member states.

Nonetheless, member states' reluctance to cede some control to the regional body has enabled them to escape accountability for human rights violations. It appears that the development of a political solidarity culture among member states, fostered by the liberation struggles shared history, has failed to steer SADC in the right direction. In some cases, it has enhanced the legitimacy of authoritarian leaders. It is ironic that SADC, which promotes democratic ideals, has served as a safe haven for authoritarian leaders. SADC has continued to use what can be described as a 'false sense of nationalism' where member states have acted as self-righteous victims of neocolonialism while defending tyrants.

Additionally, we need to consider several factors that have made relationships between member states more complex. The historical circumstances have dictated the nature of the relationship among member states of SADC in this instance. There is a direct connection between these factors and the current crop leadership in the SADC area, which has created the context and perspectives of the actors involved in the integration process. In this way, we can better appreciate the prospects, tensions, and constraints that affect any regional cooperation agenda. Nevertheless, some ways in which SADC member states may resolve these historical differences continue to influence regional relations three decades after Apartheid ended. Liberation leaders who continue to perpetuate themselves as custodians of the region still find it challenging to overcome their arrogance. As expected, the regional leadership associated with the liberation era is expected to gradually decline from the political arena and make way for a new generation of leaders who have little or no connection to the liberation struggle. In disposing of this generation of politicians, we have the opportunity to break down some of the barriers preventing regional integration. Currently, Malawi, Zambia, and Botswana have all been able to replace the old generation of liberation struggle leaders.

The book adopts the view that the existing SADC decision-making process is problematic and has to be dismantled. The absence of legislative oversight and the reduced powers of the Tribunal have encouraged impunity tolerance with states violating agreed political values and the SADC treaty without facing any repercussions. Powell (2005) argues that SADC governments use the argument of national sovereignty to limit "interference" whenever they violate the regional agreements. This excuse contradicts the African Union's Constitutive Act, which "places important limitations on state sovereignty. It is based on the premise that sovereignty is conditional and is defined in terms of a state's willingness and capacity to protect its citizens."`

By conferring the supranational body's mandate on the regional body, the SADC will coordinate regional security, economic, and governance strategies and ensure that all member states adhere to regional agreements. If SADC promotes effective implementation plans critical to the regional integration scheme, there is a need to rethink the decision-making process. The existing decision-making processes give more powers to individual states to torpedo regional objectives. Several ambiguities exist in the decision-making mechanisms and powers of SADC. There are no provisions for breaking an impasse in the treaty where member states have failed to reach a consensus. Since all decisions are made by consensus, a member state can veto any policy to protect its interests. A gap in the institutional framework of SADC enabled countries like Zimbabwe to undermine decisions made by the SADC Tribunal.

Governments with weak governance systems can currently influence the policy direction of the regional body under the existing decision-making framework. Moreover, Saurombe (2012) argues that the consensus decision-making process has prevented the SADC Summit from making decisions that could be perceived as unfavourable by some member countries. In replacing the existing consensus-based decision-making process with the majority-based decision-making process, SADC will impose compliance measures and ensure uniformity of regional political and economic policies adopted throughout the region.

For the AU's highest decision-making body, the Assembly, to act, a consensus is necessary. Whenever consensus is not possible, Article 7 of the Constitutive Act provides that a two-thirds majority is adopted without veto powers accorded to any individual state. In the opinion of Landsberg (2004), the AU was created to promote democracy, accountability, good governance, and political openness. A key provision of the SADC Treaty, Article 5, mandates that member states promote "common political values, political systems, and other values which are transmitted through democratic, legitimate, and effective institutions." Sadly, this mandate is merely a form of lip service and not a reality since SADC member states are motivated to preserve the status quo. The book's previous chapters discussed how SADC's implicit and explicit organizational norms have allowed authoritarian regimes to dictate democratic and governance norms, undermining agreed democratic and good governance protocols and agreements. Although SADC has established protocols that promote democracy and good governance, it is not surprising that SADC has been undermined by the lack of implementation and non-compliance by member states, despite the existing institutional framework. According to Erasmus (2011), "the question marks are not about the formal legal dimension: it is mostly about poor implementation and insufficient monitoring of compliance."

Even with beautifully crafted protocols and agreements, the current institutional structure of the SADC has been unable to disentangle itself from the individual interests of member states since it lacks supranational authority. Most of the time, progress in the regional integration scheme is inimical to the individual interests of member states. Sako (2006) suggests that regional institutions can only overcome challenges impeding regional integration with the help of well-designed and effectively implemented regional integration instruments, which mandate adherence and compliance with all regional protocols and agreements.

In order to overcome SADC's perceived institutional weakness, member states must strengthen the regional body's capacities and mandates to address the persistent and complex challenges that the region is currently experiencing. To strengthen the SADC Secretariat's executive power, SADC should advocate for institutional and practical reforms. To ensure that SADC decisions are implemented by all member states and not conveniently ignored by some nations, the SADC Secretariat must be given both the mandate and the capability to enforce compliance to all agreements and protocols. SADC should also be tasked with developing a catalogue of possible sanctions in the event of violations of SADC rules or rulings.

SADC already possesses the instruments necessary to mitigate some of the challenges that impacted regional stability and impeded economic growth. With the Organ for Politics, Defense, and Security adoption, which encourages member states to develop democratic institutions and encourage universal human rights, SADC is on the right path. This instrument is complemented by the Principles and Guidelines Governing Democratic Elections, which was established to foster credibility and legitimacy of electoral processes. These existing peace, security, and democratization mechanisms demand that member states abide by democratic principles, social justice, and human rights standards. SADC should operationalize these instruments to overcome some persistent regional political and security challenges and promote democracy and stability in Southern Africa. SADC needs to re-evaluate its failures, as Zimbabwe's political crisis symbolizes SADC's ineffectiveness to advance democracy in the region. Though member states have made commitments on paper to meet regional objectives, progress has, for the most part, been excruciatingly slow, if not regressive. SADC adopted these instruments primarily to address persistent regional challenges. However, these instruments did not address the political and security challenges due to the inadequacies of the institutional framework and misplaced priorities of the political elite.

Currently, SADC remains an intergovernmental organization rather than a supranational institution. By making SADC a supranational organization, the organization would have the capability of creating laws, regulations, and rules binding on all member states, effectively ceding part of their sovereignty to the collective. In contrast, the intergovernmental body functions through member states' willingness to accept common norms, regulations, and rules. Due to SADC functioning as an intergovernmental body, its member states have the flexibility to cooperate on a range of agreements and protocols while retaining sovereignty on other issues. That leaves the discretion of adhering to agreements at the hands of the member states. This has become a challenge for regional cohesion due to differences in political and governance systems across the region, ranging from authoritarian to democratic. The implementation of protocols and agreements has also hampered progress on the regional integration project. With SADC's failure to address the governance deficit across the region, compliance with the mechanisms put in place has been affected by the non-binding nature of the regional protocols and agreements. Since implementing any SADC agreements is voluntary, states' cooperation and compliance will remain a challenge if the institutional framework remains unchanged.

Scholars have consensus regarding the importance of regional bodies' legislative powers, similar to those of the European Parliament. Terlinden (2004) argues that although regional legislative bodies are intended to assume regional institutions' legislative and democratic oversight functions, they remain in an infant stage of organizational development and remain far from being as effective as national parliaments. Article 9 of the SADC constitution provides for the establishment of a Parliamentary Forum. While the 1997 SADC Summit communique, which established the Parliamentary Forum, conferred the Forum with the primary objective "to establish a regional parliamentary framework for dialogue on issues of regional interest and concern." The Parliamentary Forum, however, has failed to establish a legislative oversight body until today. It seems that the SADC Summit has resisted the creation of a useful legislative instrument. The idea of a SADC parliament was omitted from the 1992 SADC Treaty and the 2002 amendments to that Treaty, which created the SADC Tribunal as the regional body's judicial body. The treaty provisions suggest that SADC strives to pursue a rule-based system, and deliberate efforts must ensure that this remains the case. The only challenge facing the institution is the excessive authority vested in the Summit of Heads of State. To prevent any possibility of SADC Heads of State undermining the treaty provisions, the powers of the SADC Summit should be limited, and an effective SADC Parliament would enable that to be achieved.

So far, no protocols have been spelt out to create a SADC Parliament. Having a competent legislative instrument with powers to hold the SADC Summit of Heads of State accountable would be desirable for the region. Like the Tribunal was modelled on the European Court of Justice (ECJ), creating the Parliamentary Forum was a prelude for creating a regional legislative body inspired by the European Parliament. Currently, SADC operates as an association of national parliaments from its member states, with no oversight authority. A fully functioning legislative body to operate as a supranational instrument with oversight powers on all member states could play an essential role in strengthening the regional bloc's oversight capabilities. There is an overwhelming consensus on the significance of a collective oversight forum that can respond to socio-economic and political challenges. SADC has been prevented from making decisions binding on all member states in the absence of a regional legislative arm. The current Parliamentary Forum is not part of the regional policy-making forum. An effective SADC parliament can also promote political, economic, and social development in the region.

The EU parliament can make laws, rules, and regulations binding on all its member states as a legislative body. As such, domestic laws are enacted in accordance with EU laws. Under Article 8(2)(b) of the SADC Parliamentary Forum, "upon the Forum becoming a Parliamentary structure, the Parliamentary Assembly would be the legislative body in full consultation with the SADC authorities and without interfering with the legislative functions of the national parliaments."

In view of this, any potential SADC Parliamentary Assembly would remain subordinate to the SADC Summit, thereby rendering it ineffective. An effective regional legislative body should be viewed as a vehicle that enhances regional integration efforts while at the same time spreading the culture of good governance, transparency, accountability throughout the SADC area. That could help SADC develop yet another supranational feature in its decision-making framework. SADC should adopt a structure that eases the challenges associated with compliance and adherence to regional protocols and agreements. There is a need to redesign the SADC Secretariat as a quasi-independent commission similar to the EU Commission. It would be appropriate for the SADC Secretariat to complement a legislative body capable of enacting laws, regulations, directives, recommendations, opinions, and decisions' binding on all member states, as with the European Union.

In the region integration scholarship, there is broad agreement that political and governance transformation is necessary for sustained poverty reduction, infrastructure development, and political stability if the regional project succeeds. From a trade reform-centred regionalism to a progressive response to regional conflicts, SADC needs to take a bold move in confronting the governance challenges impeding progress. Member states must start viewing regional integration as an instrument that can promote development only when all the necessary preconditions have been satisfied. A rules-based mechanism needs to be introduced to enhance regional protocols and agreements with possible score-card tracking compliance of member states. SADC member states must harmonize their domestic laws, regulations, and procedures to ensure economic, political, governance, and social convergence, which could help accelerate the integration agenda. This includes ensuring that all governments in the region maintain their legitimacy to govern. This disconnection between the leaders and the people they represent has led to governments' failure to support people-oriented programs.

The emergence of such regional structures, says Clapham (2001), is essential for the emergence of a good governance agenda that will enable economic growth. In order to establish these structures, he asserts that the member states must share a similar definition of what a "state" is. The liberal foundations of the European experience can thus be understood as ideological congruence. If a small core of predominantly democratic 'liberal' states can form a viable REC, this could potentially spread to include other states; the expansion of the EU to include former communist states from Central Europe and dictatorships from the Southern European countries offers some hope in this regard. A context-sensitive analysis must consider the impacts of African states on the development of their countries and the agenda for better governance within these countries. As one of the aims of the SADC Treaty, Member States are required to harmonize their political and socio-economic policies. It is the responsibility of each state to ensure that this Treaty is applied uniformly.

However, several SADC member states have experienced severe threats to their ability to hold credible elections when security forces have been used in political affairs to violate citizens' right to vote and their civil liberties. Considering these circumstances, the SADC Secretariat should establish an election support unit to coordinate and support the work of the SADC Election Advisory Council and other essential election-related activities. The election support unit should be embedded within the national election bodies to ensure that elections in all SADC member states meet the standards prescribed by the SADC Principles and Guidelines Governing Democratic Elections. Since SADC continues to experience electoral disputes, its mediation unit needs to be adequately staffed with impartial leadership and experts.

The SADC Tribunal was another regional instrument established to ensure adherence to and proper interpretation of the SADC Treaty provisions and decision-making on disputes referred to the Tribunal. The Tribunal demonstrated independence at the early stage, which made some of the member states uncomfortable. The fall-out that followed led to the member states changing the Tribunal's mandate rendering the Tribunal powerless in adjudicating cases related to human rights abuses by member states. Therefore, SADC member states must return to the drawing board and appreciate the SADC Treaty provision's objectives. Quashgad (1997) argues that a "human rights regulating mechanism that lacks the force of compulsion to ensure compliance with the decisions of the adjudicatory authorities is of little value to the aggrieved individual." Hence, the SADC Summit must reinstate the human and people's rights mandate to the SADC Tribunal to provide citizens with the appropriate recourse to justice and remedial options when individual governments fail to respect human rights and uphold the rule of law.

To contribute towards lasting peace, stability, and the capacity to deal with ordinary people's real needs, the leadership needs to vigorously implement regional and international human rights standards that protect all citizens across the region. Ever since SADC removed the human and people's rights mandate, the region has experienced many human rights violations that have remained unchecked by an independent adjudicator, and national law enforcement has appeared unwilling to investigate. For instance, in May 2016, 15 unidentified bodies were found under a bridge in Mozambique, with local enforcement showing reluctance to investigate the cause of death. Other governments like Zimbabwe, Swaziland, and Angola have also committed grave human rights violations against opposition figures. After the SADC Tribunal's failure, the regional body must introduce another regional institution with a multifaceted scope to address intra-state governance and democratic failures. For example, an Office of a Regional Ombudsman could act as the first instance of dispute resolution in intra-state political disputes.

According to Article 16 (5) of the SADC Treaty (1992), the Tribunal was "constituted to ensure adherence to and proper interpretation of the provisions of the SADC Treaty and subsidiary instruments and to adjudicate upon such disputes as may be referred to it" and its decisions were supposed to be binding. Article 16(5) of the SADC Treaty already has a provision stating that the SADC Tribunal decisions shall bind the parties involved in the dispute's parties. In this case, if the Tribunal's decisions were not binding and enforceable by the states, the whole purpose of the Tribunal would be defeated. Based on the well-rooted principle of international law principle of Pacta Sunt Servanda, there is an assumption that regional treaties and conventions are honoured in good faith by member states party to the conventions. In theory, the SADC Tribunal's decisions may be enforced in accordance with *Pacta Sunt Servanda* since it is stated in Article 32 of the Tribunal's Protocol that member states are expected to take measures necessary to execute the Tribunal's decisions. In a scenario that a state fails to comply with a decision, the failure must be reported to the SADC Summit, whose decisions are consensus-based. These provisions are inadequate and ineffective since states refusing to comply with the Tribunal's decisions are expected to decide on any further action taken against them.

The Tribunal was created to mimic the European Court of Justice during the consultation period. Several study tours were made to the European court to develop jurisprudence based on the European framework. While the European court has enforcement mechanisms, the SADC Tribunal had enforcement mechanisms left at the mercy of the SADC Summit as expected. This framework has allowed the perpetrators to influence the future of the instrument. Despite having South Africa as one of the most developed democracies in the region, the country failed to defend the Tribunal leading to its suspension and restructuring that led to a new watered-down version of the Tribunal, which was against the recommendations of SADC's justice ministers. The Tribunal debacle exposed in plain view what Dirar (2014) refers to as "consensus of non-enforcement" in Southern Africa. Why do Southern African leaders spend so much time formulating treaties if there is no will to enforce the negotiated agreements? The current consensus decision-making process and lack of enforcement have made adherence to treaty obligations almost non-existent in Southern Africa. Internal politics among SADC member states have allowed a culture of non-commitment to regional obligations. The culture is rooted in the entrenched justification of resistance against neo-colonial domination. Any external influence or even enforcement of negotiated regional treaty agreements is not entertained.

SADC member states need to revise the treaty to introduce provisions that are similar to Article 3 of the African Economic Commission (AEC) Treaty, which states: "Any Member State which persistently fails to honour its general undertakings under this Treaty or fails to abide by the decisions or regulations of the Community may be subjected to sanctions by the Assembly upon the recommendation of the Council. Such sanctions may include the suspension of the rights and privileges of membership and may be lifted by the Assembly upon the recommendation of the Council." The possibility of sanctions in the SADC Treaty would make it possible for the regional body to compel regional leaders into respecting fundamental human rights or face diplomatic and economic boycotts or suspension of their rights and privileges of membership to the regional body. The Tribunal as a regional court must be structured to allow its judgments to be enforced. SADC must introduce a list of coercive measures that can be used by the court to impose penalties or force member states to comply with the Tribunals decisions, and powers to sanction a member state must be left with the Tribunal.

In many parts of Southern Africa, political and armed conflicts continue to be a tragic reality or constant threat, largely because democratic institutions are weak, have poor economic performance, and have insufficient civil rights. As a result, conflict and political instability undermine institutional effectiveness and result in poor economic performance. (Schiff and Winters, 1998) says that regional integration reduces conflict in two ways. First, conflict becomes more costly when members are interdependent. In turn, economic integration may contribute to reducing the likelihood of internal conflict. The second benefit of regular political contact is that it can promote trust between members and facilitate cooperation, including security issues. In some cases, regional integration arrangements include security arrangements and mechanisms for resolving conflicts.

SADC needs to address the region's security concerns and political crisis by building a community of states and a functional body that moves beyond mere declarations. According to Vale (2003), the regional body's current status, SADC hardly exhibits any sense of community at all when he argues that "there is very little real sense of community between Southern Africa's states. That may again sound...well, mischievous: after all, the region's states claim to be joined in the SADC, and a treaty, protocols, a sense of renewal and even a few buildings attest to their commitment." This characterization of SADC suggests that member states need to continue developing and implementing common security policies that align national security institutions towards a common security regime. A common security structure could provide national security agencies guidelines to ensure that all member states have shared values and a framework for implementing the shared values.

ECOWAS is generally seen as a regional body in Africa that has made the most progress in peace and security, focusing on the human security agenda. The body has partnered with civil society organizations to investigate pre-election complaints, conduct fact-finding and monitoring missions, and reduce election-related violence in the region. Unlike SADC, ECOWAS, according to the body's Conflict Prevention Framework, has recognized that its member states "bear the primary responsibility for peace and security" and has worked to transform the regional body from an ECOWAS of the state; into an ECOWAS of the people." SADC can learn from this holistic approach and move beyond rhetoric by initiating its peacemaking and peacekeeping efforts. SADC should learn from ECOWAS, especially the clarity with which the regional boy conceptualizes peace and security. ECOWAS recognizes human security as the main component of peace and security, while SADC is still stuck on solidarity and non-interference.

As demonstrated in Zimbabwe during the power-sharing agreement negotiations, SADC member states have already utilized conflict management initiatives. In the long run, however, the Zimbabwe outcome proved unsuccessful due to inadequacies in the safeguards adopted. Although SADC continues to articulate democratic governance and human security norms, these norms are far from being accepted and implemented across the SADC region. There has been a demand for regional member states to make behavioural alterations and reduce the gap on governance deficit in countries still lagging and classified as dictatorships on different international governance indices. Diamond (2005) argues that African states have failed to realize their potential since they gained independence due to a governance deficit. With high levels of corruption, patrimonialism, and bad governance, these vices have damaged Africa as resources meant for health, education, and other public services have been abused by those in power, leading to social inequalities and injustices. In the SADC region, the challenging economic conditions are the result of the looting of state resources.

To establish a foundation for long-term political stability and security in the SADC region, member states must work together to address the causes of conflict and instability. Reshaping international bodies like SADC is a fundamental step where member states lay out a vision and goals for the regional body that must be implemented and enforced. The regional body needs a perspective that underscores the region's multiple opportunities to intervene in intra-state conflicts, as has been with ECOWAS in West Africa. Western African regional body adopted what Akindele (2003) refers to as a limited doctrine of intervention in states' internal affairs supporting democratic entitlement and response to a humanitarian disaster. All institutional organs for conflict resolution have been set up and have become operational. ECOWAS initiated reconciliation and stability in Liberia and Sierra Leone at the beginning of the millennium. Most recently, ECOWAS was also able to ensure stability in Ivory Coast and the Gambia after electoral disputes had brought the two countries on the verge of civil war. Soremeku (2006) has noted that the ECOWAS has adopted a three-stage conflict management strategy: at the onset of conflicts, during conflicts, and after ending conflicts. Post-conflict peacekeeping activities include disarmament, demobilization, and reintegration of belligerents, reconstruction and rehabilitation of government and social institutions, and monitoring the organization and conduct of elections if not involved. Against the backdrop of ECOWAS's success, there is a lot SADC needs to learn from the Western African regional bloc for SADC to overcome some of the persistent political and security challenges it is facing.

SADC's past failures must be used as a guide to deal with contemporary political and security challenges. The current ad hoc arrangement has suited authoritarian regimes that resist accountability, transparency, checks, and balances. With democracy and human rights becoming an integral part of the security agenda, there is now demand for a human-centred security component, commonly known as human security. Nkrumah (1972) was one of the first people in Africa to appreciate security in terms of people's freedoms when he argued that freedom for the African people was meaningful only to the extent that the whole world enjoyed peace and security. Kwame Nkrumah's philosophy indicates that security should be concerned with the dignity and protection of individuals. SADC needs to develop regional expertise in the area of democratic governance and conflict resolution. A regionally-based institute should be established to focus on researching and forecasting issues of concern in security and publishing early warnings. SADC already has an early warning system (EWS) that was established in 2010. EWS collects and analyses any potential crisis to inform response strategies, as stated by the Forum for Early Warning and Early Response (FEWER). During its launch, it was indicated that the EWS would operate in-country centres that would feed a central system in Gaborone, but how these signals are utilized is unknown. However, the slow establishment of in-country centres has impeded the effective implementation of a vibrant regional EWS.

Currently, the SADC EWS has only incorporated government intelligence systems across the region, which in most cases, are compromised to provide credible information. Most of the intelligence agencies in the SADC area are extensions of ruling parties, which, in turn, undermine their credibility in portraying the accurate picture of events on the ground. Most of the time, intelligence agencies amplify the narrative of those in power. Regional integration projects can only be achieved if mutual trust governs the relations between member states, and through these joint institutions, member states can rebuild confidence. The significant gap between the existing EWS and its effective utilization at the SADC level may impede its success. The early warning mechanisms have failed to detect the governance problems and the full extent of Mozambique's fragility that resulted in the Cabo Delgado crisis. SADC needs quality of information analyzed and reliably interpreted with no ambiguities. Truthful and verified information is what is needed with complete and up-to-date contingencies already in place. SADC can deploy these mechanisms through preventive diplomacy, economic measures, sanctions, inducements, conditionality, force measures, and conflict resolution.

SADC must broaden the regional EWS by establishing robust early warning centres in all member states that incorporate input from civil society organisations to improve the instrument. ECOWAS has an Early Warning System (ECOWARN) that operates under the Early Warning Directorate in the ECOWAS Commission, a system SADC must emulate. ECOWARN has field monitors (collecting information but does not have a role in alerting) and focal points in each Member State (usually two state representatives and one civil society representative separately) to obtain and feed the system with relevant information providing information to ECOWAS. Analysts at the headquarters then complement this information with open sources and provide weekly reports and reports on specific incidents. Once the ECOWAS Early Warning Directorate processes the information, it is then passed to the internal ECOWAS hierarchy for determining further action.

The factors that often lead to violent conflicts are usually predictable, such as the genocide in Rwanda in 1994, where early warning of deteriorating conditions was available through open-source media. In the months preceding the genocide in Rwanda, members negotiating the Arusha Accord were repeatedly warned that Hutu extremists were planning to unleash violence against the minority Tutsi. Unfortunately, no immediate steps were taken to implement preventative measures. The genocide still took place because the international community was slow to react to the rising violence each day at an alarming rate. Therefore, the existing early warning infrastructure needs to be enhanced and utilized by SADC to address potential violence risks.

SADC already has a Standby Force with a comprehensive mandate. According to the MOU on the SADC Brigade, the objective of the Standby Force is to "unite regional efforts towards collective self-defence and security and the preservation of peace and stability". The SADC Brigade has demonstrated readiness for deployment, successfully conducting joint military exercises like Exercise Umodzi conducted in October 2018. "Umodzi", which translates to "solidarity, partnership, and oneness" in the indigenous Malawian language, was designed to prepare the military, police, and civilians components for the performance of peacekeeping missions throughout the region. SADC must continue to strengthen the cohesion and capability of the Stand-by Force by conducting joint exercises on a more regular basis.

Financial constraints in Africa limit regional standby forces such as SADBRIG to conduct peacekeeping and security operations. As SADBRIG is primarily dependent on the political will of member states to approve a mission, the approval process is primarily determined by their willingness to commit financial resources. The majority of preliminary training exercises have been conducted with limited donor support, according to Ratala (2008). As evidenced by the challenges faced during the deployment of the SADC troops to Cabo Delgado, the deployment of SADC troops across the region for military intervention will require significant financial resources. This mission presents an opportunity for South Africa to stand out and be counted. South Africa has some military arsenal and military capabilities that other member states do not have. The country has sophisticated airpower and engineering capabilities, coastal patrol boats, signal capabilities, divers, naval support and intelligence apparatus, which other SADC member states lack. According to Nathan (2004), South Africa can shape peace and security interventions in the SADC region and Africa as a whole.

Nevertheless, the mechanisms for funding the actual operation are promising due to the existence of the AU Peace Fund and the potential for UN funding that is still being discussed between the AU and UN Security Council. As a partner to the AU, the EU's support of peace and security in Africa enhances its security due to the risk of terrorism and migration originating from the continent. Moreover, the EU has a seat on the Board of Trustees for the AU Peace Fund, making the likelihood of financial support of peace and security initiatives very high through the EU's European Peace Facility.

Among the main obstacles to regional integration is lack of political will to create effective and dynamic supranational institutions; failure to implement agreed treaties and protocols; and ineffective enforcement mechanisms against non-compliance with the fundamental ideals enshrined in the founding treaty. It is not uncommon for a member state to violate provisions of international agreements, such as the rule of law and good governance norms that are enshrined within a regional treaty or protocol. It is also difficult for members to speak up when a member state commits gross violations. As a result of significant membership overlap and economic hardships, RECs in Africa often lack sufficient funding, which adversely affects the ability of RECs to implement programs that will promote regional integration, including effective management of sometimes conflicting interests.

Individual countries may become members of several smaller blocs or separate groups within larger blocs to maximize benefits and minimize integration risks. Considering the confusion this causes, it seems justified to criticize the current integration arrangements. Only a very limited number of countries are members of one REC. However, the plethora of communities decreases the government ability to deal with diverse agendas and emergencies, complicates continental integration, and draws hundreds of communities into the integration process, all of which depletes the government's limited resources. Therefore, regional economic communities must be rationalized as soon as possible.

Table 7.2: African Standby Force (ASF) membership

FORCE MULTINATIONALE DE L'AFRIQUE CENTRALE (FOMAC)	SOUTHERN AFRICA STANDBY BRIGADE (SADCBRIG)	EASTERN AFRICA STANDBY FORCE (EASF)	NORTHER AFRICA REGIONAL STANDBY BRIGADE (NASBRIG)	ECOWAS STANDBY BRIGADE (ESF)
Angola		Burundi	Algeria	Benin
Burundi	Botswana	Comoros	Egypt	Burkina Faso
Cameroon	Lesotho	Djibouti	Libya	Cape Verde
Central Africa Republic	Madagascar	Ethiopia	Mauritania	Côte d'Ivoire
Congo (Brazzaville)	Malawi	Kenya	Tunisia	Gambia
Chad	Mauritius	Rwanda	Western Sahara	Ghana
Democratic Republic of Congo	Mozambique	Seychelles		Guinea
Equatorial Guinea	Namibia	Somalia		Guinea Bissau
Gabon	Zambia	Sudan		Liberia
São Tomé et Principe	Zimbabwe	Uganda		Mali
	Swaziland			Niger
	South Africa			Nigeria
	Tanzania			Senegal
				Sierra Leone
				Togo

Source: Ricardo Sousa

Table 7.2 illustrates that the crowded landscape of RECs in Africa is a perfect example of states' failure to commit to a single regional policy. The table indicates that Angola is a member of both ECCAS and SADC. Because both institutions maintain regional standby forces, Angola is expected to contribute troops to ECCAS Standby Force (FOMAC) and SADC Standby Force (SADCBRIG). As long as regional integration in Southern Africa continues to be defined by the "Spaghetti Bowl" integration, integration aspirations will remain distant. Abuja Treaty (1991) already acknowledged the feasibility of limiting African states to one economic community and reducing RECs to five.

A logical outcome of the multiplicity of membership to different RECs is that harmonization and coordination of regional policies become problematic to realize. The SADC member states belonging to multiple regional institutions may be restricted from fully participating in the SADC regional agenda and becoming a critical barrier to a more comprehensive regional integration process. These institutions' competing and sometimes conflicting objectives have created situations in which states have failed to fully adhere to the integration agenda. The overlapping and duplicated memberships of these regional bodies have, at times, resulted in them pulling in different directions, as discussed in Chapter 5. Lack of coordination and coherence has created opportunities for noncommitment to regional objectives. All SADC member states except Mozambique are members of other regional economic communities, which has resulted in overlapping trade and economic agreements. It presents challenges if those regional bodies have Standby Forces if they are members of multiple regional economic communities.

The Spaghetti Bowl integration system and the conflict between the RECs make the success of integration less feasible. Rationalising the integration process and establishing a framework that could consolidate limited RECs into larger RECs could remedy overlapping memberships. In this regard, SADC and COMESA could come together to create one regional bloc since almost every SADC member is also a COMESA member. Streamlining the RECs will eliminate duplicity of policies that sometimes contradict each other and pave the way for harmonized policies and activities.

However, over the past ten years, there have been calls for a merger between SADC, EAC and COMESA. With almost all SADC and EAC member states being members of COMESA, this merger makes much sense. In June 2011, leaders of EAC, SADC and COMESA signed a declaration to begin negotiations to create a Free Trade Area (FTA) comprising 26 countries with a market of 600 million consumers. Even though the merger of these regional bodies has been delayed, any suggestion to bring them together is welcome. Southern Africa countries are fully aware of the importance of addressing the challenges isolated African economies are facing. A more prominent, deeply integrated regional economic bloc could help the member states improve their economic performance.

Another challenge for the regional bloc has been the inclusiveness principle, where member states are admitted into the regional body based on their geographic location. There is a problem with that because member states with different political systems are expected to adhere to similar democratic norms while having veto power to undermine those norms. Efforts to promote human rights and respect for the rule of law have been deemed an intrusion on state sovereignty, affecting the organisation's effectiveness. The organization has been unable to reach a consensus on matters related to human rights violations under both authoritarian and democratic regimes. The issue of geography has influenced countries to join different regional bodies with different values and logic motivating their objectives. SADC's membership needs to be driven by shared values and objectives. The countries should take advantage of these mutual interests while defining cross-cutting challenges and working closely together. Working with divergent national interests has made it hard for SADC to reconcile all member states' interests. That can be overcome if SADC worked within a coalition of willing partners, and the integration process could move forward effectively. That is the case with the EU, where some fundamental governance conditions are non-negotiable, and reforms are met before a state is admitted into the European body.

Schiff and Winter (2003) observed that regional integration institutions could only be effective when imposing "club rules" such as democracy and human rights, which is currently lacking in Southern Africa. Such club rules can be identified in the EU and MERCOSUR in Latin America. According to Schiff and Winters (2003), the leadership of MERCOSUR signed a declaration on democratic commitment, which made democracy a pre-condition for membership. Regional integration in Southern Africa can only be successful if efforts are made for economic and political convergence. These changes could help enhance fundamental human development needs like economic well-being, human rights, peace, justice, and the rule of law. All these factors improve the chances of the member states becoming more democratic and secure. Regional integration in Southern Africa cannot be pursued in isolation without a broader consideration of all the factors that impact integration processes. As observed throughout the book's preceding chapters, all the factors affecting Southern Africa's regional integration make regional integration succeed or fail. SADC member states need to work closely together to achieve its core functions enshrined in the SADC treaty and support SADC protocols and agreements. Closer cooperation must be fostered by an absolute commitment and mutual trust among member states for the region to realize its potential.

11

Globalisation, Regional Integration and Regional Economic Governance

Having already mentioned the need for a stronger regional governance system to sustain a globalized economy in Chapter 10, we would also add that regional production, trade, and markets should be harmonised to ensure sustainability. Firstly, regionalization is a real phenomenon. The notion of globalisation is sometimes viewed as being driven by market forces, while policies drive regionalisation. However, in many ways, regionalisation is also driven by market forces and technological developments. Growth of commerce within regions outpaces that of commerce between them, and relocation of production is principally a regional phenomenon. According to various studies, physical proximity between firms and customers and suppliers has become even more important than before. Thus, regional integration follows logically from these market developments. However, regional integration has a broader purpose than free trade and investment.

For this book, the narrative of Africa as a promising new frontier and emerging market (Ladd, 2012) is rooted in the hypothesis that the continent is poised to experience a wave of region-building that will overcome the present fragmentation of markets. As we discussed earlier, regionalism has to do with the evolving position of states. In the modern international political economy, countries cannot regulate purely on the basis of their national jurisdictions. Consequently, regional integration preserves the prospect of citizens and their nations influencing events, which enhances deeper integration in some areas. Deeper integration is one in which infrastructure development, investment, economic policies, and even the free movement of people is taken into account. Regional integration has other political motives as well. Deeper integration helps smaller countries can increase their bargaining power in multilateral economic negotiations. Nevertheless, non-economic policy goals often have just as much importance as those discussed in the preceding chapters.

This Chapter focuses on the economic policies accompanying non-economic policies that can enhance economic growth and development in the SADC region. The discussion dwells around infrastructure development, trade-driven policies, harnessing resources and relationships with global powers, especially China. Governments need mechanisms to develop coherent, institution-spanning approaches to these policy issues and many other situations. We need a new bureaucracy that provides a forum for economic, social, and diplomatic discussion.

Regionalism And Socio-Economic Integration

Aside from cheap labour and raw natural resources, investors seek macroeconomic stability and a strong potential for market expansion generated by regional economic integration of small economies, rapid urbanization, and a growing middle class. Overcoming such fragmented markets is unquestionably required in both the regulatory and governance spheres. The notable feature of Southern Africa's economic landscape is the small and fragmented economies with limited production and trade capacities. The region is endowed with tremendous natural resources despite being one of the poorest regions in the world. According to SADC (2019), the region has an average gross domestic product (GDP) per capita of $2100, a combined GDP of $727 billion. A regional indicative strategic development plan (RISDP) outlines the necessary benchmarks for regional economic integration; however, several generic concerns have hindered efforts to enhance intra-regional trade and market integration. With a low manufacturing base, a heavy reliance on raw material exports, poor regional infrastructure, and a reluctance to liberalize regional trade, the region have been unable to stimulate economic growth and benefit from economies of scale.

Together with infrastructure and connectivity barriers, regulatory policies can play a key role in increasing markets. Depending on the situation, policies can be specified to maximize the benefits of favourable geographical features or to mitigate their disadvantages. While SADC has the most enabling policy environment, like the free trade area in this regard, lacklustre outward-oriented policies in Southern African countries have hindered significant integration outcomes. It is important to adjust and enhance regional economic cooperation and integration to lift the vast majority of 350 million people from extreme poverty. The promotion of trade and investment, supported by infrastructure development, can lead to job creation and income growth. This increase in income would, in turn, boost tax revenue, which will be used to fund social and developmental policies that will advance the Sustainable Development Goals.

As with the Industrial Revolution, the rapid expansion of trade and capital flows, the advancement of technology, and the exponential growth of information flow transform the international political economy. Cooperation and integration in the regional economy are being anchored by expanding value chains, and cross-border investment flows achieved by bringing down barriers and collaborating with financial institutions-both of which are important in accelerating economic growth across the globe. The global market has enabled states to become increasingly interdependent, a trend previously seen but now gaining momentum. Millions of people have stepped out of extreme poverty thanks to globalisation. The benefits of an open trade system are no longer contested.

In short, integration reduces fragmentation in markets for goods, services, capital, labour, knowledge, and information to conduct business transactions more efficiently. It facilitates the free flow of capital and labour across borders, as well as goods and services. By improving investment flow efficiency, trade and industry, as well as promoting innovation and diffusion of technologies, there is less room for asymmetries in information.

Regional integration seeks to meet the demands of the international economic environment, which, as previously mentioned, is increasingly characterized by integrated macroregions with enlarged markets and common trade and investment policies. Value chains are playing an increasingly important role in organizing global production, which explains this phenomenon. SADC member states can take advantage of the potential for regional integration by carefully exploiting regional opportunities through deeper economic integration. Southern Africa has small economies and, with very few exceptions, trade is oriented toward European markets rather than neighbouring countries, and basic comparative advantages drive specialization. Due to its small economy, Southern Africa cannot engage in meaningful exchange and complex specialisation, which is crucial to the success of RECs.

Southern Africa's fragmented markets must be integrated if the region is to become a desirable destination for the needed foreign direct investment to help build a competitive and more diversified economy. According to Onimade (1989), "regional and subregional initiatives are likely to be relevant when a domestic market is too small, and national capital and technology are insufficient to develop capital goods." In other words, the advocacy of economic integration is partly motivated by using it to pool the small capital, low technology, and limited markets of several small countries and use them to manufacture capital goods. In this sense, many see collective self-reliance as a foundation for practical self-reliance. Regional institutions such as SADC need to fulfil the requirements that could help shape regional integration policies. The integration agenda should have an institutionalized framework that enables the operationalization of agreed norms and values that can stand the test of time. Through a more vigorous regional integration agenda, resource allocations could be improved across the region by utilizing comparative advantages, resulting in productivity growth and solid economic fundamentals. Access to regional markets and integration of regional value chains can enhance the manufacturing capacity of regional producers to prepare them for global exports.

Global economic trends indicate SADC countries' best option is to move forward on their regional integration and collaboration efforts, jointly tackling some of their main challenges as a regional region. Therefore, the region would increase its business appeal, create business and production partnerships, open new business opportunities for international companies, and enlarge the scope of international partnerships. Taking concrete steps at the regional level would help SADC member states to be heard. The best way to take advantage of externalities associated with the production of regional public goods is to create broad, unified economic spaces. The convergence of a limited and critical set of public goods (for example, logistics, power, ICTs and trade facilitation) is crucial to realising socio-economic development.

In line with other ambitious protocols SADC has adopted, the SADC Treaty and Protocol on Trade seeks to establish an institutional framework for integrating member states' markets and economies. Throughout the book, it has been observed that most of these protocols have only been attractive on paper; in practice, SADC has a poor track record when it comes to implementation. To enhance trade-led growth, trade barriers must be reduced. However, the benefits of market liberalization may be restricted if factors of production are not rebalanced between or within sectors to maximise the comparative advantages of each member state.

Trade liberalization should be paced and sequenced concerning regional economic disparities and the circumstances of the individual states. Furthermore, the disparities between the regional economies are accompanied by capacity gaps. In addition, there may be structural inhibitors such as human capital and infrastructure. Since SADC is an intergovernmental organization with limited powers, it lacks legal structures to achieve its stated objectives of shared economic prosperity. In practice, SADC member states compete with one another rather than complementing one another.

SADC member states' geographic proximity is an essential factor that can facilitate intraregional trade. By strengthening the existing SADC institutional framework, the region can become a more united trading bloc. This would enable SADC to adopt regional value chains or component manufacturing of products with components for one product being manufactured in different member states, providing an opportunity for job market growth and comprehensive utilization of human resources. This could also assist the region in producing items recognized as SADC products, as is the case with most EU products.

There is now an increasing need to address the challenges associated with an intra-SADC trade deficit, primarily due to inadequate infrastructure development, governance deficits, conflicts, and security concerns. There are some challenges associated with mixed political systems, a lack of institutional coherence, and the difficulty of ensuring that all agreements and protocols are ratified. Within SADC, economic and political convergence is achieved through the implementation of protocols and agreements. Generally, convergence refers to the gradual reduction of differences among several countries among various economic and political indicators. Ben-David (1993) provides convincing evidence that increasing mutual trade among participating regional member states can lead to an upward convergence of GDP per capita. The study found that increased trade in Europe due to integration coincided with decreased per capita income disparities among the EU member states. While Linder (1961) contends that real convergence promotes integration across countries, countries with comparable living standards are more likely to engage in international trade than countries with different living standards. The convergence of democratic governance, institutional framework, security, and economic policies provides sufficient economic growth and regional stability, along with a favourable environment for foreign direct investment.

Figure 7.3: Impact of regional integration

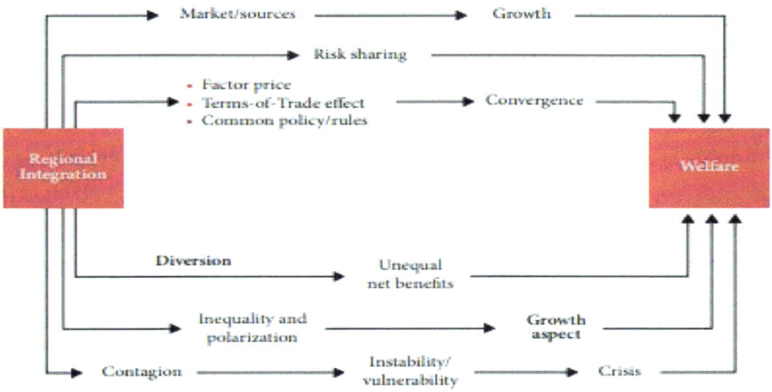

Source: Office Region Economic Integration, Asian Development Bank

Figure 7.3 shows how integration, economic growth, and instabilities are related. Regional integration allows for uniform adoption and implementation of common policies and trade environments to achieve governance convergence. According to the World Trade Organization

(2011), weak states may pose a significant obstacle to developing robust rules-based regional agreements since they cannot develop, manage, and implement them. According to Manirov (2015), divergent macroeconomic policies, along with a lack of coordination among member states, can undermine the potential gains of integration, particularly concerning interregional trade.

Historically, SADC member states have assumed that all of their challenges result from underdevelopment and weak economies. SADC member states can alleviate these problems by promoting closer economic cooperation. Nonetheless, what needs to be emphasized is that successful regional integration can only be achieved if regional leaders adopt good governance practices. As a result, an independent judicial system, strong governance, accountability institutions, and vibrant civil society would be established to promote citizens' interests. All of these attributes can be safeguarded if compliance mechanisms are in place within the regional body. Mutharika (1972) argues that economic integration requires the delegation of power to the regional body tasked with safeguarding both the interests of the supranational entity and those of the individual member states.

The SADC region requires a regional integration agenda resulting in deeper market integration that allows individual states to become part of a single extended SADC market. SADC member states should remove artificial barriers that impede trade and improve production efficiency to overcome their demographic challenges. A lack of linkages between the production industries and the creation of complementary industries has resulted in trade imbalances across the SADC region. In the absence of regional trade and production policies, conflicting interests and contradictory practices have resulted in SADC member states competing for market share. A structural change that could harmonize trade and production could offer SADC an advantage in identifying the industries that need further development and those that should be scaled down to maximize profitability.

According to Senbet (1997), Sub-Saharan Africa is increasingly perceived to attract more private capital if only it put its house in order. Global investors are looking for new frontier markets, and with progressive financial and market reforms, good governance initiatives, improved infrastructure and enhanced political stability, there is room to increase capital flows in the region. SADC member states should put their differences aside and work together to establish an institutional framework that will guide foreign direct investment before the contracting process is completed. Local labour laws, foreign currency restrictions, procurement restrictions, and foreign investment restrictions must be clarified and agreed upon. In any SADC member state's policymaking process, stability is vital for risk analysis for any inbound foreign investors.

As a result of removing trade barriers in the SADC region, employment opportunities and poverty reduction will be enhanced. As Baldwin (2003) notes, nations with few trade restrictions have the best chance of achieving rapid economic growth. From a neo-functionalism perspective, it is also possible that the formation of a regional bloc based on geographical proximity has also led to challenges in the regional integration project in the global south due to the diversity of domestic political and economic systems. Due to the overprotection of sovereignty and territoriality in SADC member states, integration has been slowed down despite the collective desire to create an integrated regional community. Addressing macro-economic convergence challenges would guarantee compliance of SADC member states to macro-economic protocols and macroeconomic targets. In addition, new cooperation frameworks need to be adopted to address supply constraints where the regional body takes the lead in distributing responsibilities across the region.

According to Gibb (2006), a study on economic integration by the (AfDB) carried out in 2003 concluded that "so serious are the challenges facing Southern Africa that governments cannot ignore...the limitations which national boundaries impose on the prospects for economic recovery and growth." Therefore, there is now demand for a legally binding arrangement that informed by what Article 1.2.2 of the RISDP refers to as "a developmental integration approach, which recognizes the political and economic diversities of regionally integrating countries including their diverse production structures, trade patterns, resource endowments, development priorities, institutional affiliations, and resource allocation mechanisms."

RISDP recognizes that one country's economic instability has a significant negative spillover effect on the rest of the region, with Zimbabwe posing the biggest challenge. However, RISDP has faced constraints in human resource capacity, financial deficit, and appropriate institutional framework. These challenges have harmed domestic implementation and adherence to the strategies in place. SADC member states have also lacked political will and commitment to drive regional initiatives, with most countries being driven by short-term state-centric objectives. That has led to limited cohesion of member states' domestic policies, e.g., national budgets and medium-term expenditure frameworks (MTEFs) and their broad macroeconomic targets not being in tandem with the overall regional economic objectives.

This failure of regional macroeconomic cohesion can also be attributed to a lack of a functioning institutional framework that enforces adherence to set strategies. Providing an institutional framework with authority to enforce and supervise macroeconomic convergence compliance by all member states would enhance shared economic objectives. The experience in Africa and the SADC region, in particular, has shown that cooperation among countries requires supranational institutions that are beyond the influence of any member state to act as a catalyst and stimulate the process of integration.

Strengthening intra- and inter-state legal systems and governance institutions is another crucial aspect facilitating enhanced regional economic integration. Any private sector's involvement in regional projects will involve engagement with the country's local legal system when the investment occurs. In the SADC region, the legal system, as well as culture, is strikingly pronounced. SADC member states need to build the institutional capacity that may lead to transparency, a precise and predictable policymaking process, and effective oversight mechanisms. The region needs to embark on reforms of the legal and regulatory environment in the whole region to promote cohesion of policies and regulations implemented. The business environment needs to be predictable and facilitative and where there are protective legal instruments and a judicial system that is free, fair, and sustainable. As illustrated during the discussion of political risk factors, investors are always looking for a business environment that protects the investment interests and is free from governments' interference.

Economic integration projects are always manifested and practised within a political vision and the leadership's ideological inclinations. In Southern Africa, it has become a concern since a change of government and leadership has predictably led to the cancellation of some contracts, the introduction of new policies, and new tax regimes. A predictable and stable policymaking process would enable a favourable environment for the private sector participation in the regional integration process. Businesses operating in the SADC region have faced complex and often volatile political risk environments, limiting new investment and some existing businesses scaling down their operations. NEPAD appreciates the significance of political will in meeting the objectives of closer regional cooperation. The organization has encouraged African leaders to resolve conflicts, promote good governance, establish an independent and transparent legal system, and provide a regulatory framework for regional trade. However, the effectiveness of these frameworks and governance institutions has been questionable, to say the list. Except for Botswana and Mauritius, SADC member states perform poorly on different international indices like corruption levels, doing business, and the justice system's independence.

The SADC region continues to face growing poverty and high unemployment, and income disparity continues to widen. These socio-economic challenges have fueled socio-economic discontent that led to the armed insurgency in Cabo Delgado, xenophobic attacks in South Africa, and countries like Malawi and Swaziland experienced riots and civil unrest over the last decade. The economic disparities between South Africa and the rest of the region have led to an influx of migrants to South Africa, which has amplified xenophobic reactions in South Africa. Zimbabwe's sanctions have led to the economy shrinking with very high inflation rates and high unemployment over the past two decades.

Considering the high levels of political risk in the SADC region, which has impacted the region's attractiveness to foreign direct investment, the region has been losing potential capital investments that could help transform the region. SADC member states' unwillingness to sacrifice part of their sovereignty and implement SADC protocols has made integration practically impossible. The member states have been reluctant to allow SADC to become a dominant supranational body as this is viewed as an intrusion into the domestic political and social sphere. The understanding of non-interference has been enshrined in SADC's silent rules of engagement. Without closer cooperation in the region, the member states remain politically and economically fragile and vulnerable to external manipulation. In turn, this has rendered the majority of the treaties and protocols already in place insignificant. Failure to implement these protocols and treaties has limited the possibility of harmonizing political, economic, and social practices, which would have created a better environment for regional integration and coordination on issues of democratic governance, conflict resolution, and economic cooperation. It is only through establishing SADC as a supranational entity that can enhance SADC member states' credibility.

In trade negotiations, member countries can increase their bargaining power by forming regional integration arrangements (Fernandez and Portes 1998; Schiff and Winters 1998). Nevertheless, members must negotiate collectively-an approach that isn't always taken due to divergent national interests. Raising the profile of members is also an objective of regional integration arrangements. Regional integration arrangements can, however, have serious drawbacks. Tax concessions are among the incentives used by developing countries, especially those that are small and low-income. Arrangements that give foreign firms in one member country free access to markets in all members could induce a "race to the bottom" as members compete to attract FDI through tax concessions. The only way to avoid this outcome is to regulate concessions through regional integration.

As a collective institution of restraint, a more robust regional integration facilitates economic and political reforms in member countries and provides a framework for coordinating policies and regulations in member countries (Fernandez & Portes 1998; World Bank 2000b). In terms of commitments, regional integration arrangements work best if their provisions and their enforceability are strong. Agreements are more effective when it is costly to break their rules, leave the agreement or be expelled. The ability to punish violations of rules and stronger economic ties between members lead to more effective agreements.

The supranational institution mechanisms allow member states to strengthen their credibility with domestic and foreign investors by demonstrating that their political leaders will not be swayed by populist sentiments that may harm the private sector. It is in this context that SADC can play a crucial role in enforcing government commitments. SADC relies heavily on regional economic integration as a strategy for survival, and through integration initiatives, it can bring its resources together and overcome its market marginalization. Unless SADC adopts measures to ensure rapid market integration and ensure all member states comply with regional agreements, it will not overcome these structural deficiencies and challenges.

In order to create a favourable investment climate for businesses, SADC member states must also focus on infrastructure development and regulatory conditions at home. Capital investment is the only means for new industries to be created, and existing industries can be improved. Improving manufacturing capacity and introducing complementary products through regional production cooperation is an important strategy for addressing supply constraints. Trade liberalization is critical for economic growth, but such an outcome can only be maximized if an enabling environment and policies are in place to mitigate the adverse effects of such initiatives. Until SADC member states to reform and transform the manufacturing sector and develop the SADC market, it will be challenging to negotiate Free Trade Agreements with other regional bodies. The Commonwealth (2017) report finds that regional institutions are better able to provide 'hard' infrastructure such as roads and energy networks and 'soft' infrastructure such as institutions facilitating and governing regional trade. According to Shams (2003), even if all prerequisites for establishing a trade agreement among developing countries are met, the divergence of macroeconomic policies and the lack of coordination among member states may hinder the potential benefits of integration. Potential benefits include an increase in trade integration. Regional integration is perceived as a critical tool supporting development and economic growth through the related benefits to trade and welfare. According to Marinov (2015), economic integration's welfare benefits include the positive impact on employment, productivity, income level, specialization, and competitiveness.

Due to the current conditions of SADC, political changes may be adopted by the organization. Some member states are more motivated to serve the interests of the regimes in power rather than the regional community's interests. There is now demand for a regional body that shifts its interests from regime security to human security. It is indisputable that an effective SADC is a fundamental institution that can stimulate economic growth, development, and stability only if there is unity among member states' character of governance across the region.

The idea of regional integration in Africa is not controversial since it is recognized as an essential strategy for economic development. However, the limited success of regional integration in Africa raises more questions about what is going wrong. As discussed in Chapter 5, trade and economic integration are fundamental to regional integration; however, intra-regional trade flows in the SADC area have been very low compared to other regional economic communities. The intra-SADC trade growth has been low principally due to poor infrastructures, instabilities, and ineffective macroeconomic and microeconomic policies. To maximize the benefits of the extended regional market, SADC member states should consider measures that address the constraints on the supply side. Among these measures are macroeconomic reforms and the strengthening of governance instruments.

There are some far-reaching goals shared by governments throughout the SADC region, regardless of political affiliation. Transforming the production structure, including social inclusion, integrating and cooperating at the regional level, and battling violent conflict with its consequences are among these. Even though integration is an aim in itself, it contributes to accomplishing other objectives in practice. In any case, the aim of transforming production is becoming increasingly tied to countries complementing each other in production. Therefore, regional integration efforts must be centred around achieving these goals over the next few years. In the context described, the integration agenda should build support, focusing on the areas of the integration agenda where there is most agreement and where the benefits are most evident. Moreover, regardless of the policy orientation of the integration mechanisms in the region, specific basic requirements should be met. Fulfilling these obligations involves preserving democracy, upholding good governance, and strengthening relations with other member states.

Regional Integration and COLLECTIVE Infrastructure Development

For a SADC's economic and territorial system to function, logistics infrastructure and services are critical. Infrastructure makes transactions within a particular geographic and economic space possible; by making trade flows and value chains physically possible over these networks, national economies can be linked to the rest of the world. African enterprises are faced with severe constraints due to poor infrastructure connectivity (transport and communications infrastructure), as well as expensive and unreliable power. Lack of trade facilitation, ill-defined non-tariff barriers, restrictive origin rules and inadequate regulatory frameworks impose additional physical limitations, delays and costs on private business and trade. Therefore, the integration of infrastructure is a vital aspect of developing and integrating production in the region. In the SADC region, a key milestone in the regional infrastructure integration process was the creation Regional Infrastructure Development Master Plan (RIDMP). In this case, integration projects in the transportation, energy, and communication infrastructure are being promoted within a shared regional approach. The forum has become an essential forum for infrastructure planning in the region. As with national infrastructure, regional infrastructure faces many of the same challenges. Other factors, however, such as the governance of institutions and the financing of infrastructure projects and the multiple perspectives relating to conception, implementation, and oversight of economic infrastructure and its services, create significant challenges with significant consequences for the economic and social development of economic infrastructure the region.

Evidence suggests that regional infrastructure projects create economies of scale, drive economic growth, and provide opportunities to strengthen Africa's unity and resilience. Among the factors that have impeded regional integration efforts in SADC is the lack of adequate infrastructure. Improving the regional infrastructure for transport, communication, and energy is essential for successful regional integration and economic growth. Like blood vessels of the human body, infrastructure is vital to the functioning of any economy, as it provides the basic foundation and connectivity for economic activities. For the SADC region to achieve prosperity, infrastructure development must be initiated.

Like most of Africa, the SADC region lags the rest of the world in strategic infrastructure classes. The region has a vast unmet infrastructure demand, reflecting a long history of limited infrastructure investment in the colonial era. Closing the infrastructure gap is very important for the region's economic development, improving citizens' quality of life, and for the manufacturing industry to succeed. The SADC region lags in road networks, border crossings, energy, and ICT infrastructure, which are all infrastructure required to facilitate economic activity and improve development outcomes. During colonial times, the colonial infrastructure of communication and transportation was heavily influenced by European interests in resource extraction. The post-colonial era has been shaped by attempts to reverse economic circumstances through regional infrastructure development initiatives.

Due to the increasing interdependence in the current international political economy, creating regional infrastructure synergies is the most effective means of resolving infrastructure-related challenges in the SADC region. Several sectors within the SADC have demonstrated potential for further integration within the existing regional framework. In SADC, untapped energy sources and industrial production can be enhanced through increased cooperation between regional policymakers and the manufacturing industry and harmonising logistical processes that could speed up the movement of goods and services. To promote trade mainstreaming, SADC must accelerate its liberalization programs and harmonize all trade procedures. To accomplish this, it is essential to develop a shared long-term vision and develop and implement an investment plan that makes infrastructure development a critical competitive advantage for the countries in the region.

A macroeconomic and microeconomic environment that addresses basic infrastructure needs, such as good roads, energy infrastructure, and improved ICT systems, is needed for trade mainstreaming to succeed. Africa has the smallest infrastructure stock globally, especially in the energy and transportation sectors. According to a study undertaken by NEPAD and the African Development Bank in 2011, access to roads (the number of people within two kilometres of all-season roads) in Africa is 34%, compared with 50% in other developing countries, causing transport costs to rise by 100%. According to Estache (2006), Africa's gap between the demand for and supply of essential infrastructure sectors (including electricity generation and distribution, water and sanitation, telecommunications, and transport) is widening. It has been estimated that \$130-\$170 billion must be invested each year in Africa's infrastructure, despite the \$108 billion funding gap. As a result of the funding shortfall, many infrastructure projects in Africa either fail to materialize or are poorly executed.

It is also generally recognized that inadequate financing is one of the main barriers to Africa's integration, and SADC is not an exception. Assessed contributions provide the major resources for supporting regional economic communities, however, paid contributions remain very low compared to budgeted needs and assessments. In order to mobilize resources, both internal and external resources should be mobilized. CEMAC exercises its right to self-finance the regional institution through the system of community levies, airport taxes, and dividends from debt relief, among other means. The SADC region needs sufficient resources to finance projects as the road and rail networks and can learn from the CEMAC self-financing mechanisms. Furthermore, the region must also agree on standard specifications such as axle load limits, design and construction specifications, and operational specifications for the rail infrastructure development.

An investment in regional infrastructure should not only focus on complex infrastructures such as railways, ports, and roads but also on improving soft infrastructures and developing sophisticated and effective regulatory policies that address coordination failures in logistical processes. For Masuch et al. (2018), high-quality regional institutions prerequisite to implementing reforms in other areas lead to convergence. Reforms in policy and regulatory measures are necessary to support infrastructure development plans. Investing in the transport system must be accompanied by reforms in border control procedures that cause delays in the movement of goods and people. Reforms of this nature can result in the removal of unnecessary roadblocks and weighbridges. Improving the IT infrastructure may also be necessary, leading to one-stop clearance of goods and enhanced transnational integration. SADC member states must have well-functioning institutions to restrain rent-seeking behaviour and socially unfair privileges of interest groups.

Having an inadequate infrastructure for logistics has been cited as a significant obstacle to trade, investment, and cross-border mobility of workers. Africa's road freight cost is about four times more than other regions in the world. That, in turn, has made Southern African exports less competitive and less attractive on the world market because of the extra mark-up charges due to high transport costs. That has also contributed to low-level productivity, low intra-regional trade, and low output of export commodities, resulting in the SADC region experiencing slow economic growth and the lowest productivity levels. Maripe et al. (2017), in their study Infrastructure and Economic Growth in the Southern African Development Community, observe that infrastructure development positively affects economic growth. Their analysis also concluded that the energy and transport sector accumulates the most considerable portion of the factor loading, hence SADC member states' necessity to invest in these two sectors.

Nevertheless, as already noted, SADC member states will only be able to attract foreign capital investment if there is a reduction in political risk to investors if the region is to cover the infrastructure gaps that have held back economic growth and development. As a result, new innovative approaches to infrastructure financing are needed. Infrastructure projects in Africa have often been unsuccessful due to a high level of corruption, security concerns, and political instability posing a threat to infrastructure development.

To meet the financial needs of infrastructure construction, significant capital investment is required, often greater than many SADC countries' capacity. With most African countries facing rising debts that may burden spending in infrastructure, for instance, in sub-Saharan Africa, the median debt-to-GDP ratio is at more than 50%, going up from 31% in 2012. As a result of these financing constraints, regional infrastructure development efforts hinder the competitiveness of the region's economy.

However, international investors have an appetite for financing infrastructure projects in Africa if an environment is suitable for foreign direct investment. McKinsey (2018) reports that Africa's current pipeline of infrastructure development projects is estimated at $2.5 trillion to be completed by 2025. Although much infrastructure-focused investment is coming into Africa, this investment is not enough to cover the infrastructure gap. One of the challenges investors in sub-Saharan African countries face is political instability which inhibits long-term development plans that can transcend political cycles. Diverse sources of uncertainty associated with large infrastructure projects in developing counties deter the entry of investors. The political volatility forces investors to focus on short-term projects. McKisey (2018) also points at concerns concerning delays in obtaining licences, approvals and permits for infrastructure development.

The SADC region needs the proper intervention to unlock the enormous capital still waiting for investment opportunities. The first step for SADC countries is to consider how member states can improve the private sector and foreign direct investment flow. As already mentioned, enormous capital is readily available for investment; what is lacking is a favourable investment environment and viable projects. Through deeper integration, SADC countries can take decisive action in mitigating economic, regulatory and political risks that investors are exposed to.

Private finance is essential for financing infrastructure investments in Africa, as are public-private partnerships. As a result of public-private collaboration, Africa's infrastructure can be built faster than it otherwise could. Due to the globalized economy, a variety of financing mechanisms can be utilized to finance infrastructure projects in the SADC region. According to the AfDB (2019), 100 trillion dollars are managed by institutional investors and commercial banks globally, allowing African countries to access liquid capital to develop profitable infrastructure. The developed countries have abundant capital savings that can be utilized to fill the infrastructure investment deficit in Africa. Excess savings in developed countries are primarily caused by low interest rates, which dampens economic growth prospects. Ben Bernanke, former Chairman of the US Federal Reserve Board, called this phenomenon "global savings glut" or "investment dearth" during the Sandridge Lecture, Virginia Association of Economists, cited by the U.S. Federal Reserve (2006). To maximize investment returns, investors should match their excess capital with investment opportunities available in Africa at the moment. A global arrangement to finance infrastructure in developing regions like the SADC would create a win-win scenario for developed and developing economies while positively impacting the global economy. However, such investment can only be available if the perceived political risks are reduced or mitigated. Reduced risk for investors provides the best environment for investors, allowing them to seize opportunities while avoiding risk. Investors need assurance before they can commit to back any complex projects. Deeper integration will help SADC countries create a bigger market and encourage harmonising norms and values that will create a good investment climate guided by the rule of law and good governance. Investors will benefit from the protections that deeper regional integration brings. With national governments failing investors for so long, investors are now demanding an extra layer of protection from regional institutions like SADC.

Rapid infrastructure investment is necessary, which requires a bold and drastic response from SADC member states. Lin and Wang (2014) proposed creating the Global Structural Transformation Fund to mobilise excess savings from advanced economies and institutional investors such as sovereign wealth funds and pension funds to finance infrastructure projects worldwide. This fund would help increase demand in the short term and accelerate economic growth in the long term. Developed economies would experience this growth due to an increased demand for sophisticated construction technology and equipment manufactured in the developed countries. For developing countries, infrastructure development would generate jobs and enhance human development.

For instance, the SADC region is rich in mineral and natural resources, which are burdened by poor infrastructure to facilitate trade and logistics. By ensuring that SADC member states can make the most of their natural resources, citizen welfare will significantly improve. Increasing infrastructure development becomes urgent for the resource extraction sector since it requires infrastructure development to extract and transport commodities. Sadly, the public infrastructure financing in Southern Africa falls far short of what is needed. As far as investors are concerned, Southern Africa's relative lack of infrastructure points to an untapped development potential that can be unlocked through more significant investment in the sector. According to the African Development Bank Group's Economic Brief of September 2010, commodity-linked bonds have not yet been explored as a source of funding infrastructure projects in Southern Africa. That occurs when regional export commodities traded on the futures market are used to boost infrastructure investments. SADC member states could issue debt contracts tied to those main exports, thereby reducing the debt burden. The commodity-linked bonds could help shield the debt from market fluctuations for commodities export earnings while at the same time reducing the risk of debt when commodity prices fall.

International bond markets are also a valuable source of infrastructure funding, with Ghana entering the Eurobond market in 2007 as a great example due to the low-interest rates. According to AfDB (2019), African countries have borrowed on the Eurobond market at rates below some countries within the Eurozone. For example, Zambia's borrowing rates were lower than Spain's, and Nigeria's borrowing rates were lower than the Republic of Ireland's. The Zambian government subscribed to a 10-year Eurobond worth $750 million with a yield of 5.6%, lower than the rates others can offer. Among the other countries active on the Eurobond market are Rwanda, Mozambique, and Gabon.

Institutional and governance issues remain obstacles to attracting readily available investments, and foreign direct investment will remain small if no action is taken on policy, regulatory, and governance issues among SADC members. The existing infrastructure deficit has resulted in high trade costs, which have hindered the full realization of trade benefits. As a result of these high costs, the SADC region in particular and Africa, in general, have difficulty gaining a larger share of the global market. A pragmatic approach to strategic infrastructure priorities is necessary to lower trade costs and facilitates trade across the region. Infrastructure investment projects in Africa are increasingly financed with blended finance and development funds. One of the largest financial sources of infrastructure funding in SADC is China which provides funding to SADC using natural resources and strategic infrastructure as collateral.

Such initiatives have already been used in DRC, with China stepping up its investment drive in pursuing infrastructure projects in Africa. According to Curtis (2008), the Chinese government and the DRC government signed a mineral-backed loan agreement in 2007 that involves about $8 billion in infrastructure development in the DRC.

Western countries were stunned by the sheer amount of the loan, which helped cement China's role as Africa's top development partner. A $3 billion loan was made for mining infrastructure development. The loan was obtained to restore the strategically important copper and cobalt mining sector to facilitate copper and cobalt concessions. Transport routes between extractive industries in the DRC are one purpose of the loan. Another $5 billion loan was paid to a Chinese engineering company to build 3,200 railway lines, 3,200 road networks, a power plant, and a power line. In addition, 30 hospitals and 20,000 housing units were to be constructed as part of the deal to allow China to gain access to the strategic metals.

According to the agreement, China would receive rights to mine up to 10 million tons of copper and 420 000 tons of cobalt (proven deposits) over 15 years, starting in 2013. In return, the DRC Government and the Chinese created a joint venture company called Sino-Congo Mining SARL or Socomin, which was given mining concessions to mine the region's abundant iron and other commodities. The company is 68% Chinese-owned and 32% owned by the DRC government. Following the agreement, profits from the project's first phase were earmarked to repay the $3 billion loan, and profits from the second phase were to be used to repay the $5 billion infrastructure loan. The mining concessions China obtained in Cobalt and Copper guaranteed Chinese industrial companies a reliable supply of strategic mineral resources that could meet the demand of the fast-growing Chinese economy. With Cobalt and Copper prices on the global market, China could have guaranteed supplies of these precious commodities at fixed prices. As of 2003, China surpassed the United States in global copper consumption and set up strategic mineral reserves for uranium, copper, aluminium, iron ore, and other minerals. For China, the reserves play a crucial role in adapting to market fluctuations, managing crises, and ensuring the security of its resource supply.

The Socomin Agreement provides an important model for African resource-driven infrastructure development. The terms of the agreement also ensured that Chinese workers were limited to 20%, which is one issue that has led to resentment of Chinese investments. The infrastructure development deal stirred fears among Western powers that China's hunger for precious mineral commodities would diminish their influence in the DRC.

Another area that needs to be explored and encouraged is the participation of the private sector in major infrastructure projects. In this context, foreign direct investment is intended to develop infrastructure. The private sector may also participate through Public-Private Partnerships (PPP) or solo ventures within the Build-Operate-Transfer (BOT) framework. Following a successful return on their investment, the investor can transfer the infrastructure's assets and management back to the state. A state may sometimes purchase the equity of the infrastructure, as was the case with the Cabora Bassa dam in Mozambique. Participation by the private sector is, however, dependent upon an enabling environment. The provision of incentives, the reduction of political risk, and the improvement of corporate governance standards may encourage private investors to finance and develop infrastructure. A legal policy and regulatory environment that permits private sector participation could positively signal to the private sector, demonstrating that SADC is ready to do business and embrace the private sector in developing regional infrastructure. Infrastructure is responsible for establishing physical connections between nations, constituting a significant part of trade costs. Infrastructure development in SADC is already attracting foreign investment, allowing some of the Southern African railway networks to be revamped, including those with regional dimensions.

For instance, the cross-border railway development project between Malawi, Mozambique and Zambia stands out. An international rail network linking the three countries - the Nacala logistics corridor - is being reconstructed by a consortium of investors working under the Central East African Railways (CEAR) brand name. It is operated by a consortium with Vale Logistics and Mitsui as shareholders and connects Moatize, Mozambique, with Chipata, Zambia via Lilongwe, Malawi. This initiative provides a cost-effective and more efficient method for transporting goods from the seaport in Mozambique to Malawi and Zambia. Besides the Tanzania-Zambia Railway Authority (TAZARA), another cross-border railway arrangement exists between Tanzania and Zambia, which is owned by the Tanzanian and Zambian governments and links the seaport of Dar es Salaam with Lusaka, Zambia's capital city.

The Mtwara transport corridor is another integrated road, rail, and water infrastructure project that will provide an alternative route for trade in the SADC region. The project initiated by the Tanzanian government will benefit Malawi, Mozambique, Tanzania, and Zambia through the construction of a road and rail link from Mtwara, on the coast of the Indian Ocean, to Mbamba Bay, on the shores of Lake Malawi. In Mbamba Bay, freight ships could ferry goods to the Malawian ports of

Chipoka and Nkhatabay for other rail or road connections to Malawian cities or Chipata, Zambia, thereby reducing transport costs. In addition, it has also been suggested that an oil pipeline should be built along the same route to augment petroleum supplies. The corridor also has tourism potential connecting the Indian Ocean beaches in Tanzania to the shores of Lake Malawi.

Some infrastructure projects have also been financed with private funds in the SADC region, including the Beitbridge Border Post (between South Africa and Zimbabwe), the Mozambique-South Africa Gas Pipeline and the N4 Toll Road linking those countries.

Figure 7.4: Distribution of population without access to electricity by region

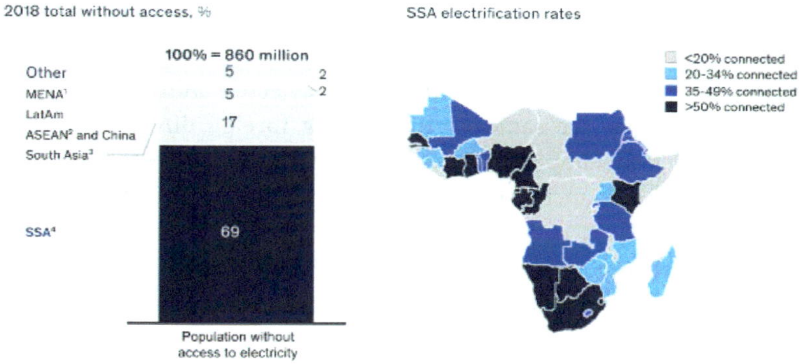

Source: McKinsey & Company (2018)

Figure 7.4 illustrate the power infrastructure gap in sub-Saharan Africa. It is also critical to pay close attention to the management of energy resources. According to a McKinsey (2020) report, it costs them three to six times what grid consumers pay in other parts of the world for both households and businesses in sub-Saharan Africa. The sub-Saharan African region also accounts for two-thirds of the world population without power. McKinsey forecasts that the continent's demand for electricity will quadruple by the year 2040.

There are abundant energy resources within the SADC region that are not distributed evenly among the countries. Consequently, many benefits can be derived from full energy integration. It has been shown by many studies that energy demand and supply are strategically complementary because of their scale and structures. According to the World Development Indicators (2013), SADC member states with "high energy potential have under-invested to the point that even domestic consumers lack reliable energy access: in 2009, the percentage of the population with access to electricity in Zambia, Tanzania, and Mozambique was respectively 12%, 14% and 19% against 31% on average in Sub-Saharan Africa." While access to electricity is limited, hydropower resources remain largely untapped in the SADC area. According to Kalenga (2012), the hydroelectric potential of the SADC region is estimated at over 142,000 megawatts per year. In fact, the SADC member states are currently only exploiting 7% of this energy potential at present. The lack of technical capacity and financial investment in the abundant energy resources has resulted in underutilization. According to the World Bank, the electricity demand is expected to grow by 40% over the next ten years, making cooperation and investment in electricity a regional priority. Due to erratic blackouts, SADC member states must invest in regional power plants to ensure reliable electricity within the region. Overcoming the power challenges could help SADC member states improve industrial capacity while at the same time attracting foreign direct investment hindered by frequent power disruptions. New power projects are needed to reduce the ever-increasing power deficit and growing demand in the SADC area.

SADC should continue to promote the development of low-cost energy generation and power trading mechanisms. At present, SADC has made significant progress in this area by interconnecting national grids through the Southern African Power Pool (SAPP). Developing a regional electricity market based on gradualism and reciprocity all falls under the goal of creating a competitive energy industry. This arrangement has allowed countries with vast energy reserves to export energy surpluses to neighbouring countries experiencing power shortages. To date, nine power utilities have been interconnected on the Southern Africa mainland, except for Tanzania and Angola. While substantial progress has been made in interconnecting the region, and several projects are slated to be implemented in the coming years, energy exchanges remain modest.

The region has seen an explosion of liquefied natural gas (LNG) projects that promise to establish solutions for securing the supply of energy, which will benefit the regional integration of power. The availability of new energy forms and natural gas discovery in Cabo Delgado can lead to a more plentiful and more convenient electricity supply throughout the region. The African Development Bank (AfDB) says LNG investment in Mozambique could drive industrial development in the country and the SADC region. In addition to creating new high-paying jobs, the projects in Cabo Delgado are expected to cover the large energy deficit. Furthermore, SADC member states have the opportunity to explore gas-fired power generation in addition to the business side of LNG reserves. Currently, the SADC is developing a Regional Gas Master Plan to promote the integration of gas into the regional energy mix to facilitate and enhance universal access to energy and industrial development.

In most SADC states, power generation has been dominated by hydroelectricity and diesel generators, except for South Africa and Angola. Mozambique's natural gas could become an essential asset for the whole region to extend its energy sources and boost economic development. For the region, natural gas may present a cleaner and more affordable option. SADC member states could emulate the Soyo combined-cycle natural gas turbine concept in Angola, a 750 megawatts natural gas-fired thermal power plant. With support from the International Finance Corporation (IFC), Zambia is also attracting significant investor interest in developing the country's first solar power plant.

Oil and natural gas have contributed to the economic development and the actions of human society throughout history. In the 20th century, fossil fuels led to dramatic economic growth in oil-producing countries. Natural gas and oil are vital commodities for most countries, and their production is a continuous activity. As energy demand increases and concerns about other fossil fuels grow, SADC member states have an opportunity to pursue cleaner energy sources available in the region. The member states should initiate sustainable energy projects that use the readily available resources in the region. This can be achieved by investing in LNG pipelines that would carry natural gas from Mozambique's shores to other SADC countries. So far, South Africa has begun construction of a pipeline spanning 2,450 kilometres. A pipeline that runs from Cabo Delgado to Richard's Bay in South Africa will provide the country with easy access to Mozambican natural gas. Compared with diesel generators and other sources of power, LNG is an inexpensive source of electricity. Besides being cost-effective, LNG is also a low-carbon fossil fuel due to its low carbon emissions. Besides being the direct energy source, LNG may also fuel renewable sources such as wind turbines when the latter cannot generate enough electricity due to wind loss. LNG energy provides a short-term solution to all of this as it occurs unexpectedly and can cover the loss of renewable energy.

Figure 7.5 illustrates the difference in electricity cost of production between oil, gas, and coal, with LNG-powered electricity being less than half the price of diesel-powered electricity. The recent discovery of natural gas reserves in Mozambique and Tanzania presents a new opportunity for the region to overcome its power shortages. Through regional power pools and interconnected grids, SADC seeks to minimize energy costs by exploiting economies of scale in addition to developing environmentally friendly sources of power. From that perspective, SADC has made significant progress. A power pool mechanism exists in the SADC region, which allows the interconnection of power between member states. Southern African Power Pool (SAPP) provides a mechanism for power-sharing and cross-border transmission. LNG can be a low-cost energy option for SADC members and alleviate the electricity generation's present deficit. The challenge is for regional leaders and policy-makers to determine the most effective strategy for taking advantage of the opportunities presented.

Figure 7.5: Gas, Oil and Coal Prices (US$ per gigajoule heat value)

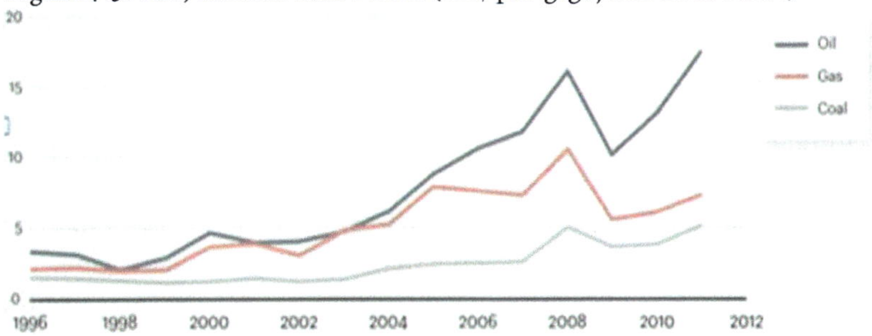

Source: BP Statistical Review of World Energy

From the perspective of energy security, SADC's oil and natural gas reserves also have geopolitical implications. The region has sufficient, affordable, and reliable energy supplies to meet domestic, industrial, transportation, and strategic requirements. The resource-rich region can also secure incomes that are often crucial to economic development and gain control over prices and market shares of difficult commodities to find elsewhere. Second, the availability of these precious resources and the revenue generated from these resources can contribute to instability in the region, as is the case currently. Due to the power deficit in the SADC region, there are frequent power outages that have impacted production time and costs. A reduction in the power deficit would result in productivity gains as a result of increased production levels.

While the number of households and businesses connected to the grid continues to grow, the electricity service they receive is inefficient and unreliable, marked by unforeseen and unplanned power outages that sometimes last for hours or days. In some cases, these outages are due to technical challenges. However, in most cases, they result from controlled shutdowns, also known as load shedding, where energy generation is rationed to prevent the system from collapsing. There are enormous economic costs associated with these power interruptions, adversely affecting the region's attractiveness to foreign direct investment.

Figure 7.6: Working hours lost due to power outages, 2009

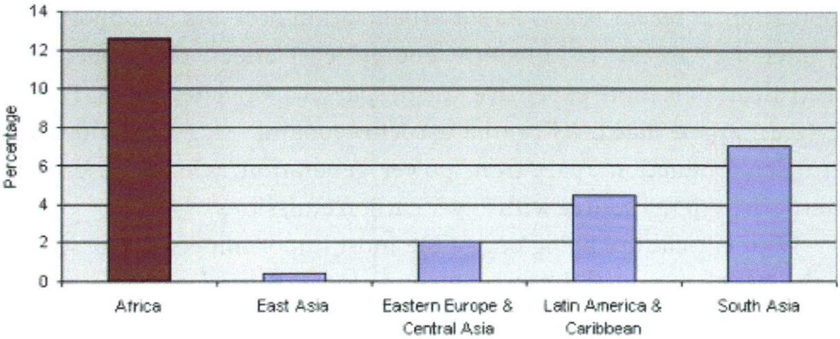

Source: AICD, 2009

Figure 7.6 demonstrates Africa’s crippling electricity problem and how this has impacted the percentage of working hours lost. Energy is viewed as an important factor that affects the economic performance of a country. Thus, an efficient power supply in terms of cost and quality has an impact on business performance. If the region is to attract the FDI required to stimulate the economies, much investment must be made in power generation. The growing energy resources incentivise investors to take advantage of the ever-increasing energy market and power supply gap. As illustrated in the above figure, businesses have lost many production hours due to power outages, and the available cheap labour has failed to compensate. The number of working hours lost in Africa is more significant than in any other developing region. With businesses receiving limited power supply from the national grid, businesses are adversely affected by unreliable electricity and are forced to use alternative but more expensive methods of generating power.

When businesses and households rely on backup diesel generators to supplement the erratic power supply, electricity can cost up to three times the regular rate. According to the World Bank, sub-Saharan countries experience power outages ranging from 50 to 4,600 hours per year. In a year with 8,760 hours, some areas of sub-Saharan Africa are without power for more than half the time. The high costs of electricity accumulate over time and become a burden for businesses. A significant amount of grid capacity is supplemented by diesel-driven backup generators in Malawi, Zambia, Zimbabwe, Tanzania, the Democratic Republic of Congo, Angola, and Mozambique.

Although most of the SADC member states population lives in rural areas, representing one of the world's highest rural populations, according to the UN (2012), there has been a rapid growth in the urban population in recent years. Rapid urbanization presents an opportunity to increase access to modern energy cost-effectively since rural electrification is more expensive due to sparsely populated areas. Foell et al. (2011) argue that LNG can be used for cooking, transportation, and fertiliser production apart from power generation, which presents an alternative energy source with lower carbon emissions.

With agriculture being one of the most important economic sectors in the SADC region and Africa in general, the natural gas discovery in Mozambique presents more opportunities beyond energy. The role natural gas plays as a feedstock for other industries is often overlooked. In its October 2014 article titled *"Everyone Wants to Dance with Shale Gas,"* the Wall Street Daily emphasized this point. Gas is not only important for the energy sector; it is also used in petrochemicals and has a huge value for agriculture since it is used as a fertiliser ingredient. Mozambique's ability to produce natural gas at a competitive price provides the SADC region with a competitive advantage in attracting fertilisers companies.

The hydrogen in natural gas is combined with nitrogen to make ammonia, used as a nitrogen fertilizer. With the revolution in natural gas, this ingredient has become more affordable, and the SADC region can take advantage of this. Jobs in the oil and gas industry are only the beginning, and we should not overlook the role fertilizer prices play in the SADC region's agriculture. The Malawian government, for example, spends 10% of its GDP on fertiliser imports. The fertiliser price doubled between 2020 and 2021, which might lead to an increase in food prices. By producing fertilisers in the SADC region, foreign exchange reserves of

SADC countries could be saved, and food prices for consumers would also be lower due to reduced input costs.

In the truest sense of the word, globalisation represents a revolution that has irreversibly and profoundly transformed our societies. In this digital age, technology is driving globalisation and speeding up the flow of information and communication. As a result of global communications and information technology (ICT), economic interdependence is intensifying. The revolution adds a considerable amount of power to human intelligence, and it enables us to change the way we do business and how we live. In essence, the development and widespread use of technology are prerequisites for globalization. Having access to it is also a necessary prerequisite to joining the global economy. As such, ICT is an important area requiring increased investment in Africa.

The development and spread of ICTs have transformed economic and social processes as never before in recent decades. The ICT industry has developed into one of the critical drivers of economic growth. More than 54.8% of the world's population are now internet users. According to the Statistical Research Department (2020) report, we now have more than 4.32 billion subscribers to mobile broadband fueled by mobile technologies. Over 90% of the population of the internet uses a mobile device for browsing the internet. The use of mobile devices is a routine part of life for billions of people worldwide.

The SADC region has among the world's youngest populations. The region represents a large portion of the world's population capable of leveraging technology to stimulate business growth, improve quality of life, and advance scientific research. In a 2017 report from the International Telecommunication Union (ITU), it is reported that 70% of the world's youth use the internet. Internet access is prevalent in 94% of the young population aged 15-24; however, in the Least Developed Countries (LDCs), only 30% have access. Specifically, nine out of ten young people without internet connectivity live in Africa. Africa is expected to be a major consumption market for ICT, given its emerging digital ecosystem.

Enhanced access has been accompanied by remarkable advances in processing power, allowing a wide range of electronic applications to be developed for every economic sector. The advancements in biotechnology, agrotechnology, nanotechnology, neurosciences, and artificial intelligence (AI) have all combined to accelerate scientific innovation and technological change. There has been extensive research on the relationship between ICT investment and productivity growth, with the results indicating that ICT investments drive productivity and economic growth. Draca et al. (2007) and Cardona et al. (2013) investigated the relationship between ICT investments and economic growth using different methods. In both studies, it was concluded that ICT investment had an impact on economic growth. In another study, Niebel (2014) examined the relationship between ICT and economic growth in developing, emerging, and developed countries. The results of the study confirmed that ICT has a positive impact on economic development. As per the World Bank Report (2012), "Information and communication technologies (ICTs) have the potential to reduce poverty, boost productivity, and increase income." While a UNCTAD (2015) report on digital development proclaims that "ICTs are essential tools to channel millennial potential into sustainable development processes."

Figure 7.7: Mobile broadband prices as a %age of GNI per capita

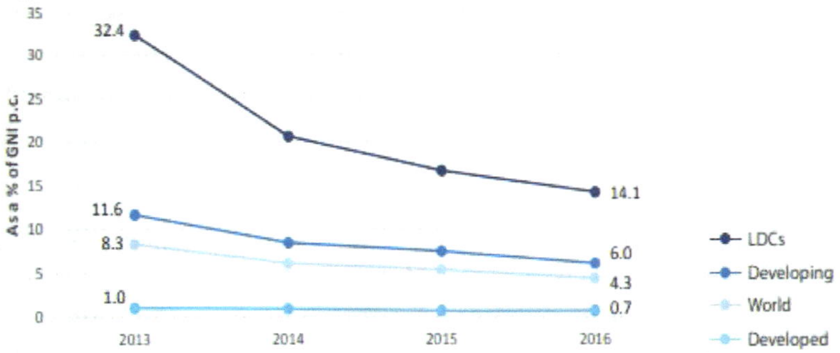

Source: International Telecommunications Union (2016)

A future for economic development depends on information and communication technologies, and the SADC region should strive to become an information-based society. UNESCO (2005) describes knowledge societies as the "capabilities to identify, produce, process, transform, disseminate and use the information to build and apply knowledge for human development." Africans are excluded from digital and information age participation due to the high costs of data. SADC countries have some of the highest data tariffs globally, despite being one of the poorest regions in the world. Even though mobile broadband is more affordable than fixed broadband in LDCs, mobile broadband prices represent 14.1% of the Gross National Income (GNI) per capita, compared to 0.7% in developed countries. Malawi, for example, has the highest mobile internet prices in Africa, with Malawian consumers paying 87% of their gross national income per capita for one gigabyte, compared with Rwandans paying only 2%.

With increased investment in ICT, data costs will be lowered, and connectivity will be enhanced. Africa's large market and youthful population present tremendous investment opportunities, but the poor infrastructure, including information and communications technologies, is one factor limiting foreign direct investment. However, deficiencies in ICT infrastructure also present opportunities for investment in ICT.

As Africa transitions into a knowledge society, Holmner and Britz (2013) argue that the region will participate as equal partners in innovation and the global information economy. Holmner and Britz propose investing in ICT projects to address the connectivity deficit in the internet and other global communication networks. African governments have made significant investments in ICT projects, but the demand is too great for governments alone to meet. There is still a gap between African governments and other countries in the ICT sector, and more effort needs to be put in by African countries to remain in the digital age and possibly close the gap. In the ICT Development Index (IDI), 2011, most African countries are ranked low or medium, with the best ranking African country ranking 70th overall (out of 155). Touré (2013) provides an excellent perspective of ICT's potential in Africa when he states: "ICTs are truly transformational. With the power of technology, we can educate every African citizen right across the continent. With the power of technology, we can open new opportunities and create new well-paid jobs for our people. With the power of technology, we can deliver healthcare services to every African citizen, even in the remotest villages. And with the power of technology, we can empower African women and leverage the fantastic energy and passion of young Africans. This is not just a pipe-dream: this is real."

As noted by Song (2015), the interaction between supply and demand has stimulated investment in ICT infrastructure in Africa due to the higher rate of return for investors. Africa's entrepreneurs have tapped into this gap in ICT infrastructure, including Zimbabwean-born businessman Strive Masiyiwa, Chairman of Pan-African telecommunications group Econet Group. Masiyiwa identified a niche market in Africa's ICT industry as early as 1993 and built one of the country's largest telecommunications companies with annual revenue of over $3 billion. Masiyiwa is quoted in a Brookings report (2019), stating that: "Africa has extraordinary problems and we must not wait for governments to solve them. If you see a problem, think of the ways you can solve a part of it."

Liquid Intelligent Technologies, a subsidiary of Econet Global, has raised billions of dollars for ICT investments across the African continent, including mobile services and broadband infrastructure. The company has installed the most extensive fibre networks in Africa, creating new digital corridors. Having built a fibre network in 14 countries and providing wholesale services to mobile network operators, the company is now a leading communications services provider in sub-Saharan Africa.

In addition to providing ICT access to the African population, we should also emphasize ICT training. It is clear from UNCTAD (2015) that capabilities must drive ICT capacity building. Thus, more investments should be made in programs that foster technical proficiency. Oracle Academy is a noteworthy investor in Africa's technology industry, offering free software and curriculum resources to students and educational institutions in Africa, with Kenya, South Africa, and Nigeria already benefiting. Investments in ICT education can transform the SADC region, considering the direct relationship between economic growth and ICT expertise.

Countries at the forefront of digital technology, innovation, and advanced technologies will likely gain a competitive advantage. Huawei and Oxford Economics (2017) estimated an $11.5 trillion digital economy globally, accounting for 15.5% of global GDP over the past 15 years. According to Barefoot et al. (2018), the US digital market has grown by 6.5% a year between 2006 and 2016. Generally, the most prominent companies are technology companies, with Amazon, Alibaba, Alphabet, Apple, Facebook, Microsoft and in the top ten.

We should not be surprised by the fact that the world's leading economies invest heavily in Research and Development (R&D). Between 2000 and 2015, the US's total scientific research spending went from $268.6 billion to $496.6 billion. China has seen a tenfold increase in its R&D spending within the same period, as have other leading economies. ICT plays a vital role in economic development, as evidenced by this sort of investment.

In addition to these radical shifts occurring, the most fantastic novelty resides in the accelerating pace at which new knowledge is being applied to production, thus reducing the time involved in developing products aligned with corporate strategies. As a result, the processes affect production and logistics, transportation systems, security innovation, goods tracking, and international trade. Advances in technology, liberalization of financial movements, as well as the opening up of markets to trade and investment have facilitated innovation, globalization, and standardization of processes. The international political economy is characterized by an increasing reliance on ICT assets such as computer hardware, software, and broadband internet infrastructure to enhance GDP and international competitiveness, according to Spiezia (2013). Africa cannot be left behind in the digital information age, where innovation, entrepreneurial dynamism, and IT-enabled industries have become critical economic indicators for developed nations.

Furthermore, Spiezia argues that ICT investments have significantly increased workers' productivity throughout the world and contributed to GDP growth. Today, most of the world's trade and production are part of what is known as value chains, including multinational enterprises. According to UNCTAD (2013b), over 80% of worldwide exports involve trade within value chains. ICT has facilitated global value chains or networks, making production processes fragmented geographically across different countries. ICT has also facilitated the digitalization of many activities and the internationalization of services, thus decreasing transport costs.

There is ongoing coordination about initiatives to improve the ICT infrastructure across the region at the SADC level, which is not surprising. Among the components of SADC's Regional Infrastructure Development Master Plan (RIDMP) is the ICT Sector Plan. The initiative aims at making ICT available and affordable for everyone within SADC. Increasingly, it is recognized that information and communication technologies can better integrate rural and isolated populations into regional integration efforts. Despite this regional effort, the plan remains just on paper, as regional aspirations of universal access to ICT remain largely unfulfilled. SADC should invest more in ICT infrastructure to participate in the digital age and enable economic transformation in the region. In Africa's agricultural sector, especially in SADC, ICT can connect farmers with buyers. Due to the existing information asymmetry between farmers and the market, ICT expansion in sub-Saharan Africa must be used to provide farmers with information about current market prices that could help them negotiate competitive prices. The digital economy can spur structural change in the SADC region combined with long-term investment, diversification of production structures, and convergence of productivity levels.

By creating seamless infrastructure, economic diversification can be supported, while trade barriers can be dismantled. This initiative needs to be incorporated into a broader strategy that incorporates other regional efforts and addresses "soft" connectivity issues, such as facilitating trade and investment, reducing non-tariff barriers, and working with investors for sustainable infrastructure development.

THE DYNAMICS OF TRADE-DRIVEN INTEGRATION

The United Nations Economic and Social Commission for Asia and the Pacific (2017) report indicates that contiguous borders, historical roots, and common languages are traditional drivers of cooperation and integration. Nevertheless, economic cooperation and integration depend on a much broader set of factors than these. Globalisation and foreign direct investment are influential drivers of advancement. Combined with appropriate regional trade and economic policies, these measures can effectively help countries in the region overcome geographical or domestic market limitations that limit their economic potential. From an economic perspective, the benefits of regional integration are largely attributed to the need for larger markets to encourage exchange and specialization that increases outputs and productivity. The argument goes mostly unchallenged despite structural constraints that limit African exports' complementarity.

Africa is a continent of contradictions with a great deal of economic value derived from its rich natural resources. African countries, however, score poorly on almost all global indicators of human development. It is reasonable to expect African countries to aggressively pursue resource-driven industrialization that takes advantage of their comparative advantage. The reality is that African countries continue to export raw materials to countries outside Africa, relying on the little revenue they raise to purchase manufactured goods for consumption. These are the same economic arrangements colonial authorities left behind. Due to the sheer size of the SADC market and the low level of trade complementarity between its economies, greater integration is needed. As a result of their small size and macroeconomic vulnerability, limited production capabilities and dependence on foreign markets, the SADC economies need to enhance their cooperation.

In the SADC region, progress toward harmonized and integrated markets has been slow. As a condition of integration and development, SADC has set macroeconomic convergence criteria to help its members focus on economic stability. However, owing to differences in economic conditions and political systems, in addition to conflicts, convergence has been difficult. In many cases, policy reversals have occurred after some progress had been made.

According to the classical trade theory developed in the first half of the twentieth century, countries should specialize in producing and exporting commodities in which they have a comparative advantage. Works by Heckscher (1919), Ohlin (1933), and Samuelson (1948) laid out the groundwork for the development of international trade theory and its importance on economic growth and development. As a general rule, the Heckscher-Ohlin-Samuelson theory holds that countries will export those commodities that depend on high levels of local production factors. From this classical perspective, African countries would export primary products and import manufactured goods. The importance of export diversification has been emphasized in recent theoretical and empirical research.

As part of all formal regional integration agreements, trade barriers (like tariffs) are reduced among member countries. Since free trade, according to economic theory, leads to a higher standard of living since consumers can get goods and services at the cheapest price, thereby reallocating resources according to comparative advantage, there is a temptation to conclude that regional integration arrangements will lead to improvement in people's welfare. Yet, because regional integration arrangements reduce trade barriers preferentially, they tend to create as well as divert trade. By creating trade, lower-cost production from partner countries can displace higher-cost domestic production due to lower barriers within regional integration arrangements, resulting in greater welfare. However, trade diversion, a phenomenon whereby more expensive goods from partners substitute inexpensive goods from nonmembers because barriers have been lowered, decreases it. The benefits of regional integration depend on trade creation rather than trade diversion, which cannot be predicted in advance.

In terms of export performance, the region presents some weaknesses reflected in its fundamental structural deficiencies. Due to their open economies, SADC countries are prone to adverse external shocks, such as fluctuations in commodity prices. Additionally, a notable feature of the intraregional trade structure includes the low proportion of total exports going to SADC countries. Thus, the importance of intra-regional trade to economic growth has also been extensively discussed; in conjunction with good market policies, regionalism has the potential of enhancing intra-regional trade. One of the striking characteristics of Southern Africa's economic life is its drive toward economic integration, with the FTA being a good example. The FTA was implemented to open up the regional market to businesses and trade. The FTA does not, however, constitute a sufficient stimulant for promoting trade and rapid industrialization. Based on UNECA (2002), the following objectives motivate African countries towards integration:

(i) To boost the transformation of growth of African economies;

(ii) To unleash industry and business, to become part of the world economy;

(iii) Promote multilateralism; and

(iv) To address common political problems.

Though the SADC region has been optimistic about removing trade barriers, intra-regional trade between member states is still problematic. The colonial legacy of African trade means that SADC countries have experienced limited market integration since the member states are net exporters of primary role materials targeted for the European markets. The continuous efforts for integration have also failed to bear fruit since the region is neither politically nor economically integrated. In terms of economic growth and rapid industrialization, integration has so far not been a reliable tool. It is not surprising that calls have been made for more innovative measures to accelerate economic integration without political integration which is an explanation of why economic integration failed. The sole focus on eliminating tariffs has not increased regional trade or production. One of the reasons for the slowdown of export growth is a lack of export diversification. Currently, regional trade exhibits narrow patterns of arrangements since most SADC countries export similar raw materials. As Geda (2002) points out, the pattern of African exports has been heavily influenced by Africa's historical links with the outside world, with over 50% of Africa's total trade coming from Europe and America. A free trade agreement alone will not suffice to facilitate trade within the SADC region, given the present level of intra-regional trade. It is crucial to provide a more comprehensive understanding of the market structures through a holistic approach.

Considering the unsatisfactory results on intra-regional trade, questions have been raised about the potential for intra-African trade and the role RECs like SADC can play in this regard. Due to the limitations associated with intra-regional trade, SADC member states need to take new measures to encourage more diversification. Are there ways SADC can improve its trade performance? To foster greater trade inclusivity in the SADC region, member states must accelerate export diversification. Due to market fluctuations in commodity prices, export diversification is crucial for countries to build resilience. The majority of African countries rely on fossil fuel and mineral rent as their primary sources of income.

To mitigate the problems caused by premature deindustrialization in some SADC countries, SADC must adopt a more pragmatic approach in mapping out short-, medium- and long-term strategies. A different conceptual perspective is necessary to understand the dynamics of the SADC region. Strengthening the regional institution seems to be the only feasible option for member states. This encompasses enhanced economic cooperation that could take the regional integration initiative to a higher level. New regional policies that can trigger large-scale industrial transformation are increasingly needed as regional industrial development expands. Collective learning is one of the crucial roles played by regional institutions. As they seek to evaluate the institution's effectiveness, SADC states have the opportunity to learn from their peers and other regions.

Member states must foster diversification for the SADC FTA to achieve its full potential. This requires private sector participation, as well as FDI. First, governments can use export subsidies to promote exports by providing direct monetary payments, cheap loans, and tax rebates to support domestic exporters. In that way, the domestic industry could gain a competitive edge in the international market. The measure, however, can have a heavy burden on government budgets and may be unsustainable in the long run since member states depend on tax revenues to survive. A second policy area is upgrading high-productivity sectors, such as manufacturing and other high-end sectors within SADC member states. Increasing the value of the product and entering new markets can be accomplished through technological advances. Thirdly,

SADC member states can establish export processing zones with duty waivers to promote export diversification. A Bole Lemi Industrial Zone, for example, was inaugurated by the Ethiopian government in 2013. As of 2015, the zone hosted 12 international shoe, textile, and garment companies, creating thousands of jobs. By opening up the trade market, a country's income can be enhanced, and resources can be transferred from low productivity usage to high productivity usage; while taking advantage of the country's comparative advantage.

Having a guaranteed market of over 350 million people, sound regional macroeconomic policies could promote economic activities for investors. By substituting regional products for imports, the manufacturing industry can prosper. Regulatory burdens could also be reduced by harmonizing regional policies, resulting in increased trade flow. For this reason, member states' intra-product specialization would help reduce the market concentration of similar products, as has been the case so far. Ndongko (1985) argues that "economic cooperation at the regional level in Africa leads to the efficient allocation of industrial activity, production capacity encourages the effective use of local raw materials and it will reduce dependence on foreign intermediate capital and even consumer goods." In broad terms, the production and trade-driven integration would allow SADC member states according to Toyo (1993) engage in "a joint production of what they can produce by joint efforts." Arndt and Kierzkowski (2001) pointed out that production sharing and fragmentation of the manufacturing process (production sharing) could also help develop manufacturing capacity across the region.

Production sharing occurs when production phases are divided into different production blocks, into different regions and locations. Nevertheless, production links such as transportation, communications, insurance, quality control, and managerial coordination need to be in place for this to work. Arndt and Kierzkowski (2001) went further to suggest that intra-product specialization "broadens the choice of development strategies and generally reduces the hurdles in the quest of industrialization." In this case, production sharing offers opportunities to higher-wage production centres like South Africa to give up local production of labour-intensive industry components to countries that can produce the same components with lower labour costs. Some developing country industries, such as Malawi, Zambia, and Mozambique, can establish their manufacturing bases by concentrating on labour-intensive manufacturing due to lower wages and low-technology demands. At the same time, they will gradually develop capacity in labour- and capital-intensive manufacturing. Thus, the region's economies would be able to move towards more technologically advanced forms of specialization as industrialization.

Overprotection of national markets and lack of priority given to creating useful links between natural resources, manufacturers, and markets contributed significantly to creating an industrial development heavily dependent on importing primary commodities materials to European markets. The shift in production matrix would help member states deal with the classic external constraint that has characterized the region's development by increasing and diversifying the supply of foreign direct investment and reducing dependence on an export structure overly dependent on raw materials. A complementary trade procedure should be integrated into national development strategies to coordinate exports and export policies coherent and mainstreamed. For example, the regional member states could use trade promotion strategies like bonded manufacturing zones or export processing zones. Mainstreaming should lead to a more integrated approach that enhances the region's competitiveness and supply capabilities. There is a need for SADC to identify and promote exports and diversification that are best suited to the regional member states. Individual countries should be assessed based on their strengths and the primary products they produce to tailor diversification efforts.

A coherent, predictable, and consistent regional market environment could result in a smoother, more efficient, and streamlined production and trading environment that could boost intraregional trade. Due to the inability to harmonise and coordinate macroeconomic reforms in the SADC region, transaction costs have increased. It is argued by Arndt and Kierzkowski (2001) that small fragmented economies in SADC make a compelling case for member states to form close cooperation if they are to reap efficiency gains, benefit from economies of scale, and reduce inefficiencies at the borders. The fragmented production allows intra-product specialization, where the intensity of the component rather than the final product is crucial. Ruane and Görg (2001) argue that intra-product specialization facilitates rapid participation in global industries. Because of the reduced cost of production and improved reliability of international service links required to coordinate production blocks, intra-product specialization may also become a catalyst for FDI flows across the region, including smaller economies. As trade costs are reduced, and production is fragmented, productivity could grow and help reduce unemployment.

Over the past three decades, South Africa's share of global trade has declined. Global exports from Africa have decreased by almost two-thirds in the past three decades, according to Portugal-Perez and Wilson (2009). Africa's export revenue has also declined, with the revenue in the 1970s ten times greater than the current value. When compared to other regional bodies, SADC's intra-regional trade has also experienced limited growth. As South Africa is one of the most significant sources of imports for SADC countries, smaller economies have seen little growth in exports to other region members. Despite the regional body removing more than 90% of the tariffs for regional imports, trade volume and balance have barely changed due to the absence of complementary products. A complex set of impeding regional trade stimulation issues are rooted in colonial economies that promoted the production and export of a limited number of primary commodities with minimal manufacturing value and intended only for export to European factories. Therefore, despite the countries gaining independence, the exportation and production structures haven't changed significantly.

If strategic interventionist policies are not adopted in the SADC region, SADC's ambition to increase its share of world trade will remain a fantasy. An increase in cooperation among member states is urgently needed with the SADC Secretariat and the relevant sector bodies deepening economic interaction and exploiting the potential of adding value to exports. Nevertheless, these initiatives won't succeed unless the region has the development infrastructure to support them.

Despite Southern Africa's efforts to remove trade restrictions and establish a common market, weak infrastructure and poor institutional policies have hindered trade growth. Liberalizing trade in the SADC region is an important initiative, but we should also recognize its limitations. By liberalizing regional trade, SADC can realize substantial economies of scale with larger regional markets, increase domestic competitiveness, increase investment returns, and subsequently attract foreign direct investment. This environment may lead to economic growth and technology transfer. However, SADC member states must diversify their exports to reap the financial benefits of intra-regional trade. Capannelli et al. (2009) claim that one unique feature of Asian economic growth is spreading the development process from more advanced to less advanced countries using market forces and government policies.

Consequently, a nexus of trade and investment flows developed, eventually leading to a robust regional economy and production network. This is similar to what Akamatsu (1961) refers to as a "flying goose" development pattern. According to Akamatsu, the flying geese (FG) model, latecomer economies could catch up with advanced economies through three channels:

(i) The intra-industry aspect is the development of products within a single industry within a particular developing country over three-time series curves: imports (M), production (P), and exports (E);

(ii) Industry-to-industry interaction: the sequential emergence and development of industries in a specific developing country with the industries becoming diverse and more sophisticated from consumer to capital goods; and

(iii) As a result of the catching-up process of developing countries, industries were relocated from advanced with the development process.

Kasahara (2004) argues that the flying geese paradigm of dynamic comparative advantage has accurately described the East Asian economic catching-up process through a regional hierarchy. First-tier countries include Japan, South Korea, Singapore and Hong Kong. The second-tier includes Malaysia, Thailand, Indonesia, China, and other countries in the region. As among East Asian countries, the paradigm remains an arguably common conceptual framework for explaining economic catching-up.

Based on the modern flying goose paradigm, regional development is hierarchical, with a dominant economy acting as the growth centre, followed by other developing economies. An increased sense of interdependence among Southern African regions has been interpreted as a sign of integration. Regional integration has emerged as another element of the modern paradigm flying goose. The SADC Secretariat has suggested a "flying goose" model in which a leading manufacturing country like South Africa could constantly introduce new manufacturing industries. If the country loses its competitive advantage in a particular product due to high wages, that product may be passed on to a regional partner with lower labour costs. Von Kirchbach and Roelfson (1998) study confirmed the validity of the "flying goose" model. They found promising similarities between Asian and Southern African countries, where some products' production shifted from Japan to other Asian countries. According to Von Kirchbach and Roelfson's study, the South African economy is sophisticated enough to carry entire regions. Several countries in the region operate at different economic levels, resulting in varying wages. Von Kirchbach and Roelfson analyzed SADC's trade patterns (between SACU and the rest of SADC, referred to as SADC 7) to identify potential shifts between South Africa and the other SADC members. This model could also attract foreign direct investment. SADC member states implementing the flying geese model could easily allow the investment to spread to other SADC member states. The FTA could also persuade South African companies to invest in other SADC countries.

It should be a priority for the SADC to identify specialized industries in each member state where duplication of products is eliminated and regional markets are protected. Member states of the SADC cannot continue to sell primary raw materials at low prices while paying very high prices for the finished products. The SADC member states must turn the regional market into a domestic market and stimulate a new industrial revolution. Commodity diversification requires structural transformation strategies, and these strategies must be actionable at the regional level. It is crucial to building deeper regional trade networks so that SADC countries can trade more products simultaneously as governments provide cushions to protect the regional market and regional manufacturing industries. Members of the SADC can enhance export performance by implementing a range of trade policies. Rodrik (2001) identifies three types of trade-related mainstreaming that have been tried in other countries in the past:

(i) Import-substituting industrialization (ISI)
(ii) Outward-oriented industrialization (OOI), and
(iii) Dual-track strategy (2-TS)

Import substitution industrialization (ISI) can be initiated by identifying import items that could be manufactured within the SADC region. Viner (1950) argues that integration in some cases may seem like a step towards free trade but more protection in others. Scholars agree that protectionist trade regimes can be beneficial for emerging economies if they are appropriately managed. According to Cooper and Massell (1965), the primary aim of integration agreements among developing countries is to support their industrial development. ISI policies can therefore contribute to growth by creating protected and profitable regional markets on which investors can channel their capital. Under the Abuja Treaty, safeguard measures may be imposed in the form of quantitative or similar restrictions or prohibitions in three scenarios: first, to resolve balance of payment difficulties. A second purpose is to protect an infant or strategic industry, while a third interest is to ensure that the importing country does not incur serious economic losses by importing certain products. There are also provisions regarding the application of safeguard measures in Article 20 of the SADC Protocol on Trade. The use of safeguard measures will only be permitted where it can be demonstrated that the product is causing or is likely to cause serious harm to the domestic industry producing comparable or directly competitive goods. WTO regulations determine the maximum time for the application of safeguards. Under the WTO Safeguards Agreement, the enforcement period is capped at four years, with an overall application period not exceeding eight years.

There is an opportunity to promote regional trade by implementing complementary products, as each country would need products that are not available locally. Malawi might be able to produce tobacco and value-add it before exporting it. In this case, the tobacco buyers could only purchase the commodity from Malawi, thereby adjusting their prices. Similar arguments can be made for Mozambique's cashew nut production and Zimbabwe's cotton production.

In industrialization in light manufacturing offers growing economies growth solutions thanks to low factor costs, cheap raw materials, and low-skilled labour. Most countries in Southern Africa have an advantage in these areas. The SADC member states must implement policies that secure the regional market for SADC-produced items to increase job opportunities and lift citizens from poverty. Despite SADC's market integration, there are challenges to implementing agreements at the national level. Member states have previously refused to accept suggestions to set up a monitoring framework to enforce these protocols. There are no consequences or punishments for countries that choose not to implement these protocols. In this context, conferring supranational status on the SADC Secretariat could facilitate integration.

Private sector involvement in intra-regional trade could encourage the private sector to diversify its products to satisfy SADC consumers while at the same time avoiding the production of items that are already manufactured in other member states. The private sector could also promote innovation by focusing on manufacturing products that are not available in the regional market. Winters and Martins (2004) study aggregated data on business costs in 92 economies drawn from four unique sources. The study results showed that private costs of manufacturing activity are much higher in small economies than in larger ones. According to Winters (2005), the challenge for small economies is to address their governance problem so special interests cannot influence them. This case illustrates how deeper integration built upon good governance and democratic principles can address governance challenges. Winters (2005) contends that establishing regional institutions does not imply establishing local capabilities to influence them. Ceding policy responsibilities, including economic, social and security policies, entails a genuine pooling of sovereignty. Winters views this system as one involving "mutual trust in sound regional institutions that adequately address local imperatives."

It is well documented that small, fragmented economies face difficulty achieving manufacturing efficiency. Export diversification is restricted in developing countries due to their small economies. Southern Africa's economies, as a result, are too small and fragmented to support industrialization. The countries should come together to secure certain scale economies and export market activities such as production, trade, and other economic activities. According to the Economic Commission for Africa (ECA), in its 1987 report, bringing together small economies into regional settings would increase trade among participating partners and boost the manufacturing sector.

Nevertheless, to accelerate regional integration and maximize the potential for trade, these efforts need to be balanced with a people-centred agenda of social, political, and institutional integration. By harmonising policies across the region, all regulatory, governance, trade, and investment arrangements will also be aligned. The SADC has all the necessary conditions to become the factory of the world, similar to China. All that is lacking are the right integration policies supported by a political commitment from the regional leaders.

Sakamoto (1969) argues that integration is equivalent to import substitution, which supports industrial development. Klochkovsky (1984) describes Import-substitution as: "striving at any cost, no matter what price, to achieve cuts in imports of the less sophisticated industrial goods by expanding their local production to ease the balance of trade problems, payments and reduce currency outlays on purchases abroad. The policy of import substitute production is based on substituting products that are already enjoying market success and have a guaranteed market. This process could protect SADC member states' already depleted foreign exchange reserves by avoiding imports that can be readily made in the region. This is the only way intra-regional trade within SADC can help member states expand their export markets while at the same time attracting foreign direct investment.

As the SADC markets become more integrated and enlarged, labour-intensive light manufacturing sectors can be identified and exploited. For instance, the toothpick market is extremely small in Malawi, making a potential investment in toothpick manufacturing not economically viable. The same is true for any other country in the region. Consequently, all SADC member states import toothpicks from a third-party supplier, in this case, China. However, SADC can ensure that the Malawian toothpick manufacturer has a regional market to ensure that none of the member states imports toothpicks from China. A toothpick manufacturer that has developed the industry in SADC will look to expand internationally by exploring markets beyond the region.

Having exploited the labour-intensive industry, the region in the future may pivot toward higher-value manufacturing to compete with other industrialised economies. This is a trajectory China took. The SADC economies can boost their manufacturing sectors by taking advantage of cheap labour and raw materials and targeting regional markets before pursuing international markets. Gaining a foothold in labour-intensive manufacturing industries could also help expand technology-intensive manufacturing.

According to AfDB's Regional Integration Policy and Strategy 2014-23 (2015), China is projected to graduate from labour-intensive industries due to rising wages. Lin (2011) argues that more than 85 million jobs are expected to be shifted to low-cost regions as labour dynamics change, and labour costs rise in China. Labour-intensive jobs in China are being replaced by fast-growing capital-intensive industries producing high-value items such as consumer electronics, information and communication technology, electrical machinery, transport equipment, and medical supplies. Through the rapid advancement of its technological capacity, China has been transformed into one of the world's leading manufacturers of sophisticated products. These are more profitable industries in the world economy, and according to Pecht (2006), China is now the world's largest producer and consumer of electronic products. Owing to the Chinese production dynamics and changes in employment structures, this presents an opportunity for Southern Africa to fill the vacuum created by the Chinese manufacturing capacity. However, that opportunity can be utilized if continuous investments are made in human capital and production infrastructure. To accomplish this, economic reforms and good governance must be implemented to attract FDI. The AfDB's Africa's Economic Outlook (2019) predicts that the working population in Africa will grow from 705 million in 2018 to almost 1 billion by 2030. There is increasing pressure to provide quality jobs with millions of young people entering the labour market. In Africa, the ever-growing population is either a boon to development or a hindrance if ignored.

While East Asian countries and other emerging markets like India and Brazil have transformed their economies through globalization, according to Burgis (2015), African economies have remained at the bottom of the industrial supply chain. The African continent accounts for 30% of the global reserves of hydrocarbons and minerals. Despite having 14% of the global population, Africa's share of exports is as low as 2%, while manufacturing accounts for only 1% and represent 3% of the global GDP.

Figure 7.9: Industrialisation framework

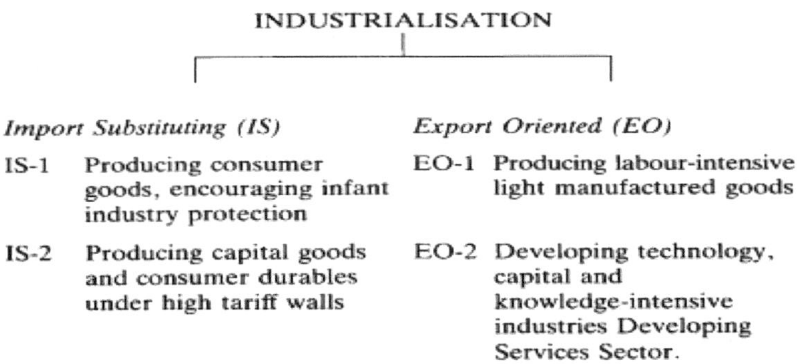

Source: Das (1992)

Rodrik (2001) identifies outward-oriented industrialization (OOI) as the second type of trade mainstreaming. It is an export-driven growth initiative to boost national or regional exports of goods and services, where the country has a comparative advantage. Basically, this strategy is based on the Korean export development strategy South Korea used to guide the pace and direction of its industrialization. According to Das

(1992), the strategy allowed South Korea to experience annual growth rates of 40.1% in the 1960s, 36% in the 1970s, and 47.5% in the 1980s. The average growth rates were the highest globally and transformed the country from a low-income country in the 1960s to a high income-country in the 1980s. Furthermore, South Korea exploited the market gap in the international market, which began with import substitution, to develop its local market and develop its manufacturing industry to the point where they could be competitive and exploit the global market gap. In this case, the improved performance of domestic manufacturing brought about significant improvement in output and productivity growth.

Horsny (2013) argues that developing countries need to view economic integration as a tool for improving their competitive edge in global markets. In this regard, SADC may identify a niche in the world economy for a specific export product and take advantage of its comparative advantage in low-cost labour to ensure that its products compete globally. Manufacturers of this product may receive government subsidies and incentives to make the product more competitive on the global market. The World Trade Organization (WTO) allows government subsidies in countries with GDP per capita below $1000, and half of SADC member states have GDPs below $1000. Export-led growth stimulated industrial diversification and technological advancement in East Asian tigers like China, Thailand, Sri Lanka, and Vietnam.

The key to this strategy is an improvement of domestic manufacturing and investment liberalization performance. Then, foreign capital can be funnelled into labour-intensive and low-technology manufacturing industries such as textiles, apparel, and footwear. According to UNIDO (2017), this strategy helped shift economic activities away from low-productivity subsistence farming to high-productivity growth activities. That helped Asia grow its global market share of manufactured exports as manufactured products became the principal exports of the Asian economies. In response to Asia's growing competitiveness as exporters, the countries began exporting more than they imported, helping to widen their trade surpluses.

A prime example of the dual-track strategy (2-TS) was the minimal reforms initiated by the Chinese government in the 1970s. The reform package combined an inward-looking approach to import substitution while simultaneously focusing on export processing. Ang (2016) describes China before it opened its markets in 1978 as a country governed by a Maoist bureaucracy with an impoverished planned economy transformed into a global economic superpower in three decades. Ang labels this a "franchised decentralization" and "directed improvisation." Under the leadership of Deng Xiaoping, China kicked off a series of economic reforms in 1978. Deng promoted Zhao Ziyang, who had a more liberal attitude, to serve as Prime Minister between 1980 and 1987. Zhao is credited with opening up the Chinese economy and transforming China. Zhao started by reaching out to Western economists seeking advice and putting their ideas into practice. Reforms began with a relaxation of the communal farming system. The Chinese government allowed farmers to sell their agricultural products on the free market once they had fulfilled their quota obligations to the state. This led to the creation of special economic zones that attracted foreign investment. As a result of these pragmatic economic measures, both farming and light industry production increased.

What is unique about these reforms is that both market track and state track co-existed. The market economy and socialist economy gradually converged as a result. China's entry into the World Trade Organisation in 2001 helped it enhance its status as the world's factory. China's export share increased from 1.8% in 1990 to 3.9% in 2000 to 11.2% in 2012. According to some observers, China's export share will reach 15% by 2030.

According to UNCTAD (2014), the main feature of the dual-track system was protecting strategic parts of the domestic economy from processing trade regime outputs and imported inputs. In SADC, Mauritius is another country that adopted the dual-track strategy over the post-independence period. Mauritius implemented institutional reforms in its economic sector following the collapse of import substitution strategies in the 1960s. In Mauritius, an Export Processing Zone (EPZ) was created under free-trade principles, which led to a boom in textile exports to Europe while simultaneously adopting a highly protected domestic economy until the 1980s. In addition, the EPZ created new employment opportunities while preventing the expansion of the EPZ from driving wages up in the domestic economy. The dual-track strategy allowed the economy to benefit from globalization while protecting the domestic economy from its adverse effects.

According to Rodrik (2001), these three broad categories have been used previously to mainstream trade and have had positive economic growth outcomes. The SADC member states have already eliminated import controls and reduced tariffs, creating a very open market for intra-regional trade. However, intra-regional trade has stalled due to limited supply capacity and low demand for regional products. Rodrik (2001) identified that SADC could adopt three categories of trade mainstreaming to increase supply capacity, enhance diversification, improve international competitiveness, and increase access to external markets. Africa is the only continent that has significantly lost the global market share of its imports. In contrast, other regions have experienced astronomical growth, as is the case with the Asian countries. It is time for SADC member states to adopt strategies that have proved successful in other regions.

There are various market-based incentives, microeconomic and macroeconomic approaches that can be adopted to promote economic development. That does not mean every approach works. The strategies that can jumpstart the regional economy may take different forms, and different countries or regions may adopt a mixture of approaches and regulations. Democracies and non-democracies may adopt different approaches due to differences in acceptable or unacceptable norms. For instance, some of China's limited labour rights and environmental protections approaches would not pass the prima facie test. The conditions acceptable in China might have provided commercial advantages for Chinese businesses, while businesses from democratic countries may have faced more scrutiny.

Njinkeu and Fosso (2006) argue that African markets are small, so they cannot generate an adequate quantity and quality of competitive exports or attract significant foreign direct investment. By forming a regional institution, member states can increase their bargaining power. Adopting a unified regional position on these issues will be critical to this process. For the negotiation of trade and commodity agreements with third parties, this is especially important. SADC members should know the importance of connecting and coherence when extracting natural resources and producing agricultural commodities. A number of Southern African countries have struggled to eliminate the legacy of colonial economics, which relied on natural resource extraction and exporting basic commodities. The trade profiles of most countries are similar, but they do not complement one another: Malawi does not need to import Tobacco from Mozambique, nor does Zimbabwe need to import groundnuts from Zambia, except for re-export. However, according to Sommer and Luke (2017), this lack of economic complementarity drives a lot of the political support for the FTA: African leaders seek to change the status quo and understand the FTA as a way to promote industrialization. Economic conditions do not need to be predetermined.

Another possible option for SADC to overcome the small market challenge is to create a single selling platform for some of its commodities. Regional integration calls for complementary economic policies and production structures. Policies addressing production and supply constraints should be implemented, including diversification of products and identifying commodities manufactured within the region to replace unnecessary imports. At present, the economies of SADC member states are not complementary, resulting in SADC member states competing for European, Asian, and American markets. For instance, SADC member states such as Malawi, Mozambique, Zambia, Zimbabwe, and Tanzania are among the top 15 tobacco producing nations. In this context, the similarity of exports undermines the bargaining process for better prices.

As a result of SADC's large share of the world tobacco market, the bloc can negotiate better prices if it acts as one bloc, considering that tobacco prices fluctuate internationally. Member states can develop consensus on production and trade policy issues by integrating regional agriculture production. This could help boost the bargaining power of the region in international trade negotiations. In addition, a coordinated approach could enhance the global position of SADC agricultural producers.

The fragmented tobacco market in the SADC region has allowed tobacco companies to exploit farmers. Evidence suggests that tobacco leaf buying companies control the tobacco market in the region, and dismantling this power monopoly is possible only if SADC member states work together. In past studies conducted by the World Bank, there is evidence of collusion between tobacco purchasing companies, resulting in low prices in different regions. The evidence suggests that tobacco companies have in the past smuggled raw tobacco from Zambia and Mozambique, intending to depress the tobacco market in Malawi. Companies that buy tobacco influence policymaking by ensuring that their corporate lawyers join tobacco policymaking institutions. In doing so, they ensure that tobacco buying companies benefit from government policies. Due to this corrupt syndicate, tobacco farmers have resorted to smuggling tobacco into neighbouring countries to get better prices. As stated in Article 4 of the Abuja Treaty, among the steps necessary to fulfil the Community's objectives are the harmonisation of agricultural policies at the national and regional level and the development of appropriate trading systems. In this sense, establishing a common market for agricultural products adheres to the underlying principles established in the Abuja Treaty.

The development of super platforms for the digital market of African agricultural products has also been suggested. Internet access and reliability are essential for this to happen, as discussed earlier. Mercy Corps AgriFin Accelerate (AFA) analyzed agricultural market models and smallholder farmers worldwide to comprehend this marketing framework better. In the study, eleven digital marketplaces were examined, including Taobao and Twiga Foods. Study results revealed that digital platforms are a viable means of linking smallholder farmers to expanding markets. A lower transaction cost and better prices were achieved by eliminating intermediaries. In order to succeed as an e-commerce platform, loyalty and trust are critical factors; therefore, farmers would need a compelling customer experience in order to join online marketplaces. Creating safe payment methods and improving quality checks can help meet this goal.

While there is a consensus on the significance of regional integration in promoting socio-economic development, the integration scheme's outcome is determined by the type of integration adopted. Cooperation in production must also go beyond manufacturing; cooperation must also extend to agriculture, mining, and other natural resources. Apart from conducting training and networking between regional actors in the sectors mentioned, SADC has no agriculture policy to improve agricultural production and market penetration. The same applies to a region-specific mining policy and other natural resources where no efforts have been made to harmonize the industries. Empirical evidence suggests that regional integration can only promote socio-economic development if sufficient pro-development-focused conditions are implemented. The natural and mineral resource endowment and the shared history of member states alone will continue to fail the region for socio-economic development if there is no pro-development approach to support production and trade. The prospect of diversifying the region's export and production structures depends closely on the success of the integration process. Thus, it is essential to link regional integration with national strategies to achieve uniformity in structural change for equality.

In order to make regional value chains competitive, it is essential to develop industrial policies that support productivity and innovation. In this case, the need to link national integration policies to national policies cannot be overstated. To promote regional production, a national approach is not enough. Specific industrial policy instruments, including training, quality certification, and generally all means for promoting the internationalization of manufacturing companies, including small firms, must have multinational or regional components. The coordination of industrial policies among nations presents numerous political, technical, and even budgetary challenges, which means initiatives should be gradually implemented, advancing by trial and error on critical areas that could impact regional value chains and intra-industry trade.

Indeed, trade may considerably widen or even aggravate productivity disparities between nations. However, the fact is that some nations have lower productivity rates and others have higher productivity rates means that developing the capacity of the least developed nations is a critical challenge for regional integration. South African manufacturers have taken advantage of their high productivity to their advantage in the SADC region, which has killed manufacturing industries in the least developed countries. For the least advanced economies to enter the competitive market, ensuring they have access to external support is crucial. Therefore, less developed countries should reform their particular and differential treatment to build their productive and technological capacity.

CHINESE TRADE, INVESTMENT AND DEBT PARADOX

The rapid rise of China as the world's second-largest economy, a leading exporter of goods, and a rising technological force cannot be ignored. China is demonstrating that rapid income convergence with industrialized economies is possible. By increasing the density of their production and technology bases, China has been able to play a more significant role as an exporter of certain manufactured goods and services with greater technological complexity. One of the defining issues of the decade will be the region's approach to China and other emerging economies. For Africa's economies, especially those in sub-Saharan Africa, the trade link with China has become a significant factor in their potential for growth, employment and macroeconomic stability. However, if poorly managed, relationships with China could also be detrimental to African economies.

The China-Africa Cooperation (FOCAC) forum was established to facilitate economic and development cooperation between China and

Africa as a semi-singular entity. This forum has been described by scholars like Gazibo and Mbabia (2012) as an 'imperfect multilateralism'. These commitments to cooperation implemented to a high degree failed to bring about the structural transformation needed in Africa. However, the commitments have merely increased the trade imbalances between African countries and China, causing it to specialize in primary commodities. The Chinese relationship with African countries has been perceived with suspicion as an unequal relationship that China manipulates. SADC cannot discuss import substations without discussing China and its impact on international trade. China's rapid economic growth has also led to its increased presence in developing nations, particularly in Africa.

Figure 7.10: The Chinese share of imports to SADC countries

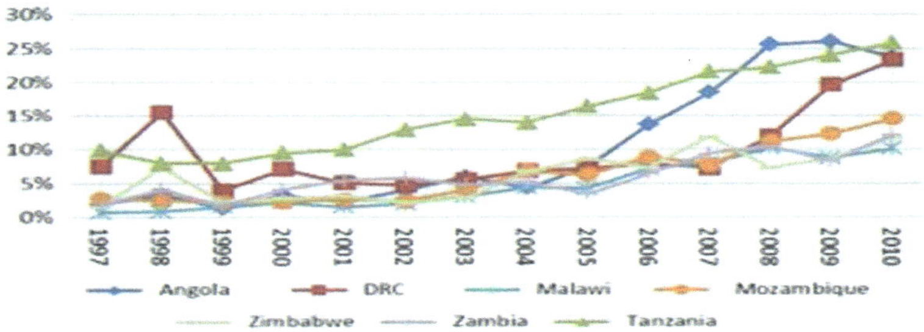

Since joining the WTO in 2001, China's global trade share in goods and services has grown considerably, while African countries have stagnated or declined. The trade relationship between China and Africa is perceived as predatory, primarily due to China's economic power advantage. Several Chinese manufacturers have been accused of using illegal trade tactics to dump cheap goods on the African market, harming domestic manufacturing. Under international law, dumping occurs when a country sells a product overseas at a lower price than domestically, sometimes even below its production price. China is accused of deliberately providing illegal subsidies to its manufacturers to mass-produce items to stifle manufacturing industries in other countries. Chinese goods are lowered in price to appeal to the importing market. These actions are sometimes taken to get rid of surplus goods in trade zones. While the WTO generally opposes trade restrictions, adverse consequences due to cheap products have affected Africa's economic development and industrialization prospects. Since 2000, Africa-China trade has grown around 20% annually, according to a Mckinsey report. The growth is, unfortunately, only one-sided. The SADC Protocol on Trade Article 18 allows member states to apply anti-dumping measures, provided such measures adhere to WTO provisions.

Over the past two decades, Chinese imports into SADC member countries have increased significantly, as illustrated in figure 7.10. Chinese goods accounted for 26% of Malawi's imports in 2008, up from 3% in 2003. Additionally, SADC member states have also experienced exponential growth, suggesting a strong appetite for low-priced Chinese goods. As a result of the fragmented SADC market, Chinese products have also replaced products manufactured within the region. Therefore, the SADC manufacturing industry losing its market share within the SADC area is regrettable due to the negative impact on employment opportunities and the pressure this places on the already depleted foreign exchange reserves.

The evidence of crowding out of SADC's products has also extended to crowding out of SADC's exports to other regions. Exports from SADC to China do not follow a similar growth trajectory, explaining the trade deficit between the two trading blocs. China only imports commodities from the SADC region that are not available in China. Instead of buying Chinese goods from outside, SADC member states can produce most of them by creating an enabling environment. In addition, most Chinese imports require limited technology and sophistication to manufacture, and African countries benefit from cheap labour. SADC members must identify products imported from third-party countries, such as China, and develop manufacturing substitutes within the region

China currently pursues a growth-oriented strategy in which several African countries, specifically those with natural resources, are seen by the Chinese government as potential sources of raw materials to fuel the growth of its economy. Others argue that Chinese initiatives are becoming a new form of colonialism as they exploit other economic sectors on the African continent. Kalu and Aniche (2020) argue that Sino-African economic relations can be compared to neo-dependence, which discourages intra-African trade by causing the continent to suffer substantial trade deficits with China. Africa also faces a deepening economic and development crisis, causing regional integration to be complicated. In 2007, former Zambian President Michael Sata wrote a paper on Chinese exploitation in Africa and presented it at Harvard

University, where he expressed concerns about Chinese investment tactics in Africa. Sata (2007) argues: "European colonial exploitation in comparison to Chinese exploitation appears benign because even though the commercial exploitation was just as bad, the colonial agents also invested in social and economic infrastructure services Chinese investment, on the other hand, is focused on taking out of Africa as much as can be taken out, without any regard to the welfare of the local people."Africa has become China's convenient target, being burdened with unmanageable Chinese debts in exchange for the continent's raw materials. In the absence of transparency and accountability norms, governments in Africa have chosen Chinese loans rather than comply with Western lending standards. China holds African governments hostage to its strategic interests using bribes, secret agreements, and strategic debt. Easy access to unsustainable loans has created debt traps, as African countries have signed lease agreements with China to operate strategic infrastructure financed by unserviceable Chinese debt.

Africa is facing a growing and unsustainable debt burden. Africa's gross public debt-to-GDP ratio reached 53% in 2017, according to AFD's Africa Economic Outlook (2019). Africa has sixteen countries with a debt to GDP ratio below 40% (including Algeria, Botswana, Burkina Faso, and Mali). Six nations (Cabo Verde, Congo, Egypt, Eritrea, Mozambique, and Sudan) have ratios exceeding 100%. In these settings, vulnerability to debt has worsened in some African countries, which requires urgent intervention to ensure that funds are not diverted away from growth-promoting projects. Chinese loans with high interest rates exacerbate the debt problems with limited prospects for debt cancellation. IMF (2014) believes these loans impose macroeconomic risks and make African countries vulnerable to debt distress.

China's lack of transparency in its loans to Africa has sparked concern and suspicion in the international community about its interests in Africa and the impacts of Chinese loans on African nations. In all standard Chinese loan agreements, sovereign immunity clauses are also incorporated. In the event of default, these clauses compel African states to surrender their economic sovereignty. Many people believe that these clauses have hidden intentions to undermine the sovereignty of African states by requiring them to hand over their strategic assets. Zambia's Kenneth Kaunda International Airport was forfeited to China in 2018 because Zambia failed to repay its loan. In the wake of the event, many Chinese employees at the airport were promoted to top positions, and

Chinese flags are displayed in offices. The state utility company and Zambian National Broadcasting Corporation are also talking with Chinese investors, which has raised concerns that the Chinese could control Zambia's critical infrastructure components. In light of China's involvement with Zambia, the issue has become politically charged

Besides China, countries such as Russia and India are also strengthening their ties with Africa. There is a growing mistrust of Chinese and Russian intentions in Africa, and SADC member states need to pay attention to what is happening. Despite Chinese and Russian predatory efforts on the continent being undesirable, Western governments are becoming more aware of the growing influence of China and Russia, which may be to Africa's benefit. Recently, the U.S. has become aware that China's presence in Africa has transformed its physical and diplomatic landscape. In December 2018, John Bolton, a former US National Security Advisor, accused China of holding African states hostage with bribes, opaque agreements, and strategic debt.

There is an urgency in US foreign policy to strategize a new working agreement with African countries that will create business opportunities for US companies and enhance development finance while respecting African sovereignty. In light of some developing countries' unsustainable debt, the US is reportedly concerned that China will acquire strategic assets in Africa. The U.S. strategy for Africa released in December 2018 reaffirmed commitment to forming strong partnerships with African states. It expressed its desire to promote trade and investment between African states, positioning itself as an alternative to Chinese and Russian interests in Africa, which the US views as predatory.

In the process, Africa's leaders have become mere pawns in the global chess match between the superpowers. African nations, however, are uniquely positioned to benefit from the increased tensions between the U.S. and China on trade. The escalating trade tensions between China and the U.S. have created supply gaps in both markets, resulting in both countries looking for cheaper sources of goods. A regional economic community like SADC can step in and take advantage of new business opportunities in China and the US. The African Growth and Opportunity Act (AGOA) is a free trade agreement between African countries and the United States that runs until 2025. Due to the duty-free access for African products, there is an opportunity to take advantage of the market gap in the US. The SADC can help fill the gap created by the US-China trade war by identifying the available market gap and increasing the production of the desired commodities.

Even though this opportunity is readily apparent, its realization is hindered by a lack of diversification and a weak competitive position of potential regional export suppliers. Therefore, it is vital to address the existing constraints in the region by assessing the underlying causes of supply constraints, low competitiveness, and low diversification. Some of these restrictions are:

(i) The nature of African economies and lack of progress in regional integration;

(ii) The absence or poor condition of trade-related infrastructure (including trade logistics); Macro-policy-related problems, such as the lack of macroeconomic coordination, including the multiplicity and inconvertibility of currencies; and

(iii) Supply-side measures: Export promotion, inefficient customs administration, international payment mechanism, and related trade facilities.

Today, African governments seem helpless and desperate, with some of the expensive Chinese projects having no economic impact but instead serving the populist interests of political leaders. The Chinese are aware of this desperation on the part of African leaders, and they strategically use economic coercion to advance their mercantilist economic practices. The Chinese "Made in China 2025" strategy clarifies that they intend to dominate critical industries globally, including those of Africa.

According to Large (2008), Chinese-African relations predate the start of the second half of the 20th century when African countries gained independence. To pursue its interests, the government of China uses the pillars of its foreign policy, specifically unconditional respect for state sovereignty and its corollary, non-interference. China is prepared to defend autocratic regimes that commit abuses of human rights and prevent democratic reforms to achieve its economic goals. Chinese loans are not tied to democracy or governance requirements, which has made them appealing to African leaders. China describes its policy as an entirely new and positive model of external engagement with Africa instead of the Western model of good governance and democracy.

As such, the Chinese model is accused of legitimising African authoritarian governments. The Chinese have used African rhetoric of brotherhood, non-interference in politics, and win-win engagement, which is potentially misleading, to win the trust of African leaders. In reality, the Chinese interests are self-serving. SADC should show interest in these foreign efforts and have a better understanding of these investments.

Furthermore, more economic integration can help vulnerable countries avoid falling into these debt traps. Intra-regional trade can be a potent stimulator of economic growth if managed carefully. Taking advantage of SADC member states' geographic proximity, economic size, and cultural affinity, intra-SADC trade can be increased. Southern Africa becomes better positioned to compete on global and regional stages as it rethinks its trade practices and develops its infrastructure. To compete globally, Africa countries must enact reforms that encourage foreign investment and boost infrastructure development. As global players remain uneasy about the global economy, superpowers are now turning their attention to Southern Africa. Amid the uncertainty and economic unpredictability of the global economy, there may be a new opportunity for the African continent. The trade war between China and the US is only one example of opportunities arising from uncertainty.

The complicated nature of China's engagement has raised speculation about its intentions, both long- and short-term. While China remains characterized by suspicion and cynicism, it is difficult to ignore its significant influence. Along with providing loans in an opaque and confidential manner, procuring them is also opaque. African countries are experiencing acrimonious debates over bribery and kickback allegations, fueled by political chaos and acrimony. For instance, the sovereign immunity clauses would require African countries to surrender economic sovereignty in the case of default. This situation becomes problematic due to confidentiality clauses protecting the loans from public view.

Africa cannot continue to accumulate debt without a long-term strategy. The United States government, among others, describes it as predatory lending, insisting that the Chinese government intentionally lends billions to African countries in exchange for natural resources, concessions, and political power. In accumulating debt, they systematically put Africa in a position where it is difficult to repay the money. Such loans are said to be collateralized by strategic national assets. The Chinese government seems unconcerned with reducing debt for Africa to help poorer nations cope with the impacts of the Covid-19 pandemic.

The easy access to Chinese loans has led many African countries to replace the arrangements with Western-backed institutions like the IMF and World Bank with the Chinese loans, but those unmanageable loans have placed more strain on Africa's fiscal management affairs. Consequently, some African governments have turned to the IMF and the Western development partners for support. The same Western partners that African governments sought to avoid when they turned to Chinese loans. Kenya, for example, announced its intention to use IMF reserves in Special Drawing Rights (SDR) assets in September 2021. As one measure of plugging the money hole resulting from the Kenyan government's fiscal deficit due to the country's large debt burden as it struggles to service the Chinese loans, these assets could be converted into government-backed money. Kenya will benefit from the SDR facility as it will prevent the Kenyan government from defaulting on a loan, which might have made its national strategic assets vulnerable to the sovereign immunity clauses attached to the Chinese, which could result in the Kenyan government surrendering the assets to the Chinese.

The Kenyan government had sought an extension on loan repayments from Chinese lenders, but this request was refused. In the end, the Kenyan government gave up because it had not been able to obtain the loan repayment holiday extension. The IMF has shown interest in assisting Kenya, although the assistance may include fiscal conditions that require fiscal discipline in government policy implementation, conditions that were avoided when Kenyan authorities chose to take out Chinese loans in the first place.

Kenya's efforts to seek Western assistance as it struggles to service Chinese loans is not unique among African nations. The Zambian government has also applied for debt treatment under the G-20 (Group of Twenty) common framework, which aims to give poorer nations a level playing field in restructuring or reducing unsustainable debt obligations. Due to the Covid- 19 pandemic has caused severe problems for many sub-Saharan African countries who have heavily borrowed from China for funding infrastructure projects due to economic growth slowdown. In an effort to access market access or resources, China funds unsound projects, which leave countries vulnerable to Chinese influence. In 2019, Chinese loans to African governments declined by nearly a third, a fall that is likely to continue as default risks continue to rise and African governments become more aware of the predatory nature of these loans. China's lending for African countries dropped below $9 billion for the first time in nearly a decade in 2019, according to a study conducted by the China-Africa Research Initiative at Johns Hopkins University.

China is heavily dependent on African minerals for its economic growth. Most of the country's cobalt imports come from sub-Saharan Africa, and significant amounts of manganese are imported from the region. Besides timber and chromium, sub-Saharan Africa has many other vital natural resources. The Chinese are now investing substantially in the Southern African mining belt, especially in the Democratic Republic of Congo, Mozambique, Tanzania, and Zambia. Metals such as gold, copper, iron and manganese are abundant in this region. By accepting sovereign immunity clauses included in Chinese loans, African countries set themselves up for debt traps. The Institute for Developing Economies Japan External Trade Organisation reports that Chinese metal imports amount to US$100 billion a year, taking up more than 25% of the world's supply. African countries should consider Chinese strategic interests in sub-Saharan Africa when negotiating trade or investment deals with Beijing.

Figure 7.11: Sub-Saharan African share of China's imports of selected natural resources (2001-2008)

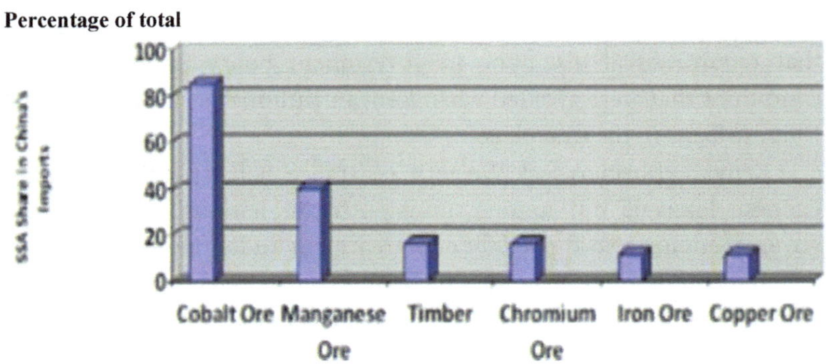

Source: Comtrade Database UNSD

Regional Integration and Harnessing the Extractive Industries

In general, investors and recipient communities of mining investment hope that the extraction industry can benefit both. Mining companies gain access to exportable resources, whereas communities benefit from increased development expenditures, employment, and land rental revenues. Considering the high capital intensity of commercial mining, many African states and communities cannot fully utilize their natural resource wealth. When foreign companies are allowed in, economic activity is generated that otherwise wouldn't happen, thus creating a win-win scenario on paper if not in reality. Collier and Laroche (2015) argue that "natural resources can support sustainable and inclusive growth in sub-Saharan Africa if key policy-areas in the natural resource management chain are tackled, and strong institutions are put in place."

Whether FDI leads to economic growth and development has been up for debate. Farole and Winkler (2014), on the one hand, argue "that investment matters for economic growth. Gains from FDI can materialize through increases in investment, employment, foreign exchange, and tax revenues." In contrast, other scholars have raised concerns about the resource curse hypothesis. Ross (2015) raises concerns about how heavy reliance on extractive industries is detrimental to manufacturing and export-oriented sectors, undermines political accountability, and encourages civil conflict. The outcome of investment in the extractive industry depends on the governance policies initiated.

The region has not successfully created governance mechanisms to channel non-renewable natural resources into the improvement of well-being and equality for citizens as well as generate new employment and economic development sources. With the SADC region experiencing a resource boom, harnessing these resources for sustainable development can maximize its potential. However, the presence of natural resources is known to bring risks and opportunities across the globe. In the past, the SADC region has experienced a natural resource curse with discoveries of natural resources leading to conflicts, or at the least, the proceeds benefiting political leaders' pockets more than the general population. Chapter 7 discussed how Botswana has successfully harnessed its diamond assets to sustain economic growth and development. The resource curse must be understood as a choice.

In most cases, natural resources are regarded as strategic national capital under the control of the sovereign state. Any illegal access to the resources by a foreign power is perceived as a direct attack on the sovereign. This assumption is supported by international law resolution 1803 (1962) that provides: "The right of peoples and nations to permanent sovereignty over their natural wealth and resources must be exercised in the interest of their national development and of the well-being of the people of the State concerned." When it comes to managing natural resources, states often act with a single set of objectives and a homogeneous voice. Despite this perspective's legality, smart reformers can craft broad coalitions to create social norms, and a multilateral framework aimed at optimising the management, exploitation and production of natural resources remains the primary objective of any regional integration scheme due to the complexities related to the industry.

The international governance of the extractive industry provides a policy arena for enhancing economic integration. In an increasingly interdependent world, the laws governing the extractive resources do not only rest of the domestic legal system; the responsibility also lies on the international governance systems to guarantee the protection of tradable property rights of investors and national interests. These composite legal regimes present a coherent and sustainable benevolent process for global or regional resource governance.

Mismanagement of the extractive industries, mainly in developing countries, has increased the necessity of international governance of natural resources. Natural resources have transformed Gulf States economies, where oil and gas have transformed Saudi Arabia, Qatar, Kuwait, and others. But Africa has demonstrated that natural resources do not always guarantee socioeconomic success. In Southern Africa, the combination of mineral wealth, political instability, and devastating poverty is not a coincidence. Burgis (2015), in his book *The Looting Machine: Warlords, Oligarchs, Corporations, Smugglers, and the Theft of Africa's Wealth,* investigates the paradox of Africa "the continent that is at once the world's poorest and, arguably, its richest." In the book, Burgis uses case studies and incidents to advance his argument of external actors manipulating political relations to gain access to Africa's natural resources at a minimal cost. Burgis observes that politicians seeking to cling to power sell national resources at a low price to raise funds for political campaigns. As Chabal and Daloz (1999) famously argued: "the aim of political elites is not only to gather power. It is more fundamental to use that power and the resources which it can generate, to purchase, as it were, the 'affection' of their people." Power is a winner-takes-all struggle for African politicians to control state resources, thus becoming a zero-sum struggle. For the politician, maintaining power is not necessarily driven by the desire to pursue positive development for the people but by meeting the needs of those in power and their immediate families.

As a result, African politics employ informal patron-client networks to distribute state resources and generate political power. It has adversely affected social and economic development in the continent's cash-poor, resource-rich states. DRC, for example, belongs to the top ten countries with significant natural resources but is also among the top ten poorest. As a result, collective resource governance must be enhanced with a compelling state administrative apparatus to allocate natural resources and viable commercial arrangements that benefit all citizens.

The International Monetary Fund defines a "resource-rich" country as a country at risk of succumbing to the resource curse and usually depends on natural resources for more than a quarter of its exports. In terms of natural resources, the SADC region falls into the "resource-rich" category. In geopolitical terms, the SADC region has a solid natural resource base. Some of the minerals found in the region can only be found in the SADC region. Among the SADC region's wealthiest mineral and natural resource areas are the DRC, South Africa, Mozambique, Tanzania, Namibia, Botswana, Zambia, Angola, and Zimbabwe. Due to the rarity of some of its resources used in industries worldwide, SADC has enough resources to secure a prominent position of influence. Natural resource management at the regional level allows for efficient production and exploitation and provides a more robust avenue for regional integration. For example, the DRC has 64% of coltan, a rare mineral used to manufacture modern electronics like mobile phones, laptops, jet engines, and other sophisticated equipment. The DRC is also a major producer of cobalt, a mineral used in aerospace and military hardware. Since these minerals are rare and have no alternative sources, the SADC bloc enjoys a geopolitical advantage if the countries were integrated.

Sustainable legal regimes must support a solid and transparent governance framework to manage natural resources effectively. According to the Revenue Watch Institute rankings, which measure transparency and accountability on natural resource management

Angola, the DRC, Mozambique, and Zimbabwe were either ranked poor or catastrophic in their natural resource management.

Nevertheless, Bassou (2017) points out that this lack of effective cooperation tools and complementary mechanisms gives the region the image of nation-states wanting to go beyond its dispersed order and reach for more effective forms of cooperation and integration. Unfortunately, instead of bringing economic prosperity to the SADC region, some natural resources have fueled conflicts.

Pourtier (2012) writes that: "The world history of conflicts teaches us that they are always multidimensional; although there is no unambiguous determination, the question of the links between resources and conflicts nevertheless remains." The international media and NGOs have adopted expressions like 'oil curse' and 'blood diamonds' to express this causal link, which should nevertheless be relativized. The centrality of resource extraction and conflict nexus informs Richard Auty's (1993) 'resource curse' theory with prominently MNCs in the mineral exploitation discourse.

Conflicts and mismanagement of Africa's natural resources have resulted in absolute poverty and suffering. In the context of SADC, most people in the region live in poverty because governments have failed to implement policies and institutions that would allow them to achieve economic growth. As observed in Cabo Delgado and the DRC, the economic decline in SADC member states has created vulnerabilities that reinforce Collier's conflict trap theory. Collapsed states and corrupt government officials have sustained the illegal extraction of natural resources, with the citizens having limited benefits from the natural wealth. While the international media has focused on the rebel groups and mass atrocities committed, limited coverage has been made on who is funding and arming these rebel groups.

The impact of natural resources on socio-economic development in Africa varies based on the mechanisms adopted for natural resource governance and distribution. Addison and Roe (2018) argue that the extractive industry has shaped economies, societies, and the politics of states for good and for bad. Some of the wealthiest nations owe their prosperity or at least part of it to the extractive industries. Meanwhile, some of the world's poorest and most unstable countries are also endowed with precious minerals and natural resources. Kaime (2004) suggests that Southern Africa's economic challenges are caused by resource mismanagement, encouraging countries to pursue regional integration to break the poverty cycle. Thus, it is crucial to create robust regional institutions to manage the extractive industry. Taking the SADC area as a whole, the region is rich, and the available natural resources are complementary. However, the absence of enhancing regional cooperation instruments and robust policies give the region a negative image. A multilateral framework for managing regional natural resources can enhance the region's comparative advantage because of the wealth of natural resources located within the region.

Since the Berlin Conference in 1884-85, the natural resource wealth on the African continent has attracted global powers' strategic attention. The Cold War brought competition over African resources even after independence. Emerging countries such as China, Russia and India have joined the race for African resources with the classical global powers. Global powers exploit Africa's fragmented economies and self-inflicted instability to dominate and exploit its resources, thereby eroding Africa's geopolitical potential. Because African countries have failed to unite under an integrated economic framework, some foreign investors have exploited the continent's natural resources because of governance deficits and political instability.

Given the sensitivity associated with the extractive industry, there is an increased demand for SADC member states to strengthen the raw materials policy framework to ensure cross-sectoral policy coordination across the region. SADC must develop a toolkit that is applicable across all member states to manage the extractive industry. SADC member states' responsibility is to transform the integration trajectory if economic growth and political stability are achieved. A unifying foreign policy, trade diversification, democratic governance, integrated natural resource management, and cohesive conflict intervention are critical factors for transforming the SADC region's economic fortunes.

The SADC region's political instability and other related problems result from its leadership problems and convenience to exploitative foreign interests. As Tutu (2004) points out, African governments differ in many ways from the Western countries they are modelled after. Despite being resource-rich, these natural resources have been a source of conflict in the region. Natural resources are being exploited aggressively by foreign MNCs taking advantage of the conflict and corruption, with no chance for citizens to benefit. MNCs continue to engage in corruption at an alarming rate throughout Africa. By ignoring corporate social responsibility and customary ethics, these corporations have aligned themselves with corrupt government officials and are detrimental to socio-economic development. Hawley (2000) argues that these conditions have "reinforced the systematization of corruption and graft that is prevalent in the region, as ruling elites take advantage of their incumbency to loot the public domain."

In response to the growing global demand for effective management of extractive industries, the United Nations and the African Union have developed a comprehensive international framework for managing natural resources. Robust management can significantly impact economic growth and stability on the African continent. Good governance is essential for countries to maximize the economic benefits of the extractive industry. Failure to manage resources effectively may also lead to conflict and severe human rights violations, as witnessed in the DRC and elsewhere in the SADC region. Regional integration in Southern Africa can also play a critical role in diversifying the economies solely relying on depleting resources. As regional integration continues to deepen, there is a potential for sound management of extractive resources. In this section, we look at how regional integration can overcome regulatory and institutional challenges.

The regional standard toolkit for managing natural resources in Southern Africa appears to be lacking, unlike other policies requiring international guidance. Because no enforceable policies are governing regional resource usage, conflicts result. The management of natural resources has also had contradictory outcomes in Africa. For instance, Botswana and Sierra Leone were both low-income countries with large diamond reserves in the 1970s. In just 30 years, diamonds sparked Sierra Leone's economic collapse and civil war. By the turn of the new millennium, the per capita income of Sierra Leone was lower than it was in 1970.

In contrast, diamonds transformed Botswana from a poor desert country to a middle-income economy. As a result of effective governance, the country has become one of the leaders on various governance indicators on the continent. Botswana and Sierra Leone only differed in their approach to natural resource management. As Africa seeks to diversify its sources of development funding, a greater share of resource rent is significant to increasing government revenue that can be used to address poverty, inequality and overcome the challenges associated with infrastructure development. As extractive revenue accounts for a third of tax revenue in Africa, harnessing extractive industries would boost revenue.

Figure 7.12: Events in the natural resource discovery and harnessing process

Source: ICG Growth brief

Discovering

The discovering processes of the extractive resources involve determining the contractual arrangements to establish a special legal regime for managing future exploitation of the natural resources. The scope of clauses in the legal regime depends on the host government's investment in the prospection process. African countries are known for underinvesting in the prospecting and exploration processes, leading to increased Production Sharing Agreements (PSA). A PSA is a contract involving host nations and foreign companies in the extractive industry that establishes the legal framework for exploring and exploiting natural resources. In the event there is suspected mineral wealth or hydrocarbon deposits, a government decides whether to explore these resources using its domestic resources or engage foreign commercial entities. To make the exploration possible, the African governments almost inevitably invite foreign involvement. PSAs are then created to determine how foreign participation will be achieved. Upon confirmation that the extractive resource is available, the agreement includes a licensing and taxation plan. These agreements are prevalent in low-income countries and reflect investors' risk perceptions and imbalances in negotiating processes between investors and host governments.

There are many challenges associated with PSA inherent in their arrangement. Kaime (2004) argues that foreign investors take advantage of sub-Saharan countries "owing to the unequal bargaining power," leading to a vicious circle where poor economic conditions impact the quality of FDI. Furthermore, investors have benefited from the better quality of information available about the resources they seek. The information is used to underreport the value and amount of the resources that will likely be exploited. Governments are forced to grant PSAs since they lack financial resources and expertise in this area.

Profit-sharing agreements are the core of PSAs, which designate the host country and investor as co-beneficiaries of exploration and mining concessions. Mineral exploration licenses are awarded to foreign companies in these agreements because the companies are bearing all upfront expenses for exploring and extracting. Afterwards, a formula is worked out with the companies having a certain share of extracted resources. Simply put, it aims to manage risks for investors and raise funds for host countries by creating a business structure. The agreements create a partnership between the investor and the host government where profits are shared. This is the most crucial part of the agreement since it affects how much revenue the host government receives. Certain agreements allow investors to postpone sharing profits until the investment has been recovered. Other PSAs allow profits generated to be shared from the very beginning. As a result, the state is granted equity in the company formed to extract the resource. The exploration costs are borne by the foreign company if there are no minerals or hydrocarbons found. This arrangement entails a high degree of risk for the foreign companies, explaining why they expect a relatively high return on their investment.

For African governments to counter this underevaluation challenge of natural resources, more investment is needed in public mineral resources and hydrocarbon surveys. In some cases, independent consultants not involved in the extraction process may be hired to do the prospecting. The information can then be utilized to attract prospective companies to partner with the government and investors benefiting from the same geological data. Consultants are commonly used by the Gulf States, such as Saudi Arabia and Kuwait, to conduct resource surveys. Unfortunately, in Africa, the investors have geological information, which gives them an upper hand in deciding the terms of any agreement. After the agreement, they inflate the costs of exploration while deflating the value of the assets.

Exploiting

The exploiting process requires enormous infrastructure such as transport links and reliable public facilities. A government in Africa typically sells concessions to private firms to avoid paying these extra costs. These relatively low upfront costs now amount to untold billions of dollars for foreign companies, causing significant losses for African nations. Unlike in Saudi Arabia, where state-owned oil companies like Aramco enjoy monopoly positions in exploration, production, and distribution, African governments seek private partnerships under exploitative arrangements. The problem is that these partnerships are vulnerable to bribery and corruption during capital raising and monitoring, and evaluation.

Unfortunately, the process is usually manipulated by corrupt officials negotiating the terms of any potential agreements. The government officials colluded with foreign companies to undervalue assets in exchange for bribes. In 2021, French-Israeli mining tycoon Beny Steinmetz appeared in a Swiss court over alleged corruption related to Guinea's major mining deal. Steinmetz is accused of paying bribes of millions of dollars to government officials in Guinea to obtain mining concessions for iron ore in the Simandou Mountains for $160 million in 2008. A Brazilian mining company, Vale, purchased the concessions 18 months later for $2.5 billion.

Guinea could have made billions of dollars if it had floated the mining concession on the open market. Instead, a few individuals pocketed $10 million and sold one of the most important iron ore deposits, denying the people significant revenue. These incidents aren't unique to Guinea; such incidents are common in Africa. Extraction concessions are sold below market value only to be resold for a higher price by the companies buying concessions a short time later. In the DRC, the Africa Progress Panel (2013) identified five deals undervalued by $1.4 billion over five years.

Taxing

Revenues from extractives come in different forms, and it is always in the government's interest to maximize revenue. Revenue is raised through sales of extraction concessions, royalties and taxes paid by companies extracting natural resources. An agreement between the government and companies carrying out the extraction determines the amount of revenue raised. Nevertheless, it is difficult to impose taxes on extracted resources because investors are notorious for inflating extraction costs and inflating their losses. All that is on top of negotiating substantial tax breaks. Most investors take advantage of government ties and use bribes to obtain tax exemptions and negotiate better royalties.

Zambian miners, it turned out, were paying higher tax rates than their employers. Resource extraction monitoring is also prone to bribery and corruption. The people who monitor resources receive bribes to ensure that investors keep the larger share. These problems stem from the secrecy that surrounds these negotiations. Transparency is essential during the negotiation process and at the time of contract signing.

In addition to negotiating tax exemptions, investors are also known to take advantage of international tax rules and tax havens to reduce their tax liabilities in African countries. According to the Panama Papers, many companies deliberately manipulated the value of goods to reduce their tax liabilities. An investigation of a diamond mining company in Sierra Leone revealed considerable discrepancies between the prices per carat of diamonds valued in-country and the prices they are sold overseas. These tactics are widely used throughout Africa, leading to the illicit outflow of billions of dollars in government revenue. This is why African governments and regional bodies must be transparent and forward-looking to protect these revenues.

Investing in Investing

The chronic lack of capital has been identified as an obstacle to governments realizing the full benefits of natural resources. To develop the capacity of the domestic private sector, governments must invest in productivity infrastructure and local skills. Despite Africa's abundance of minerals and natural resources, exploration expenditure remains below $5 per square meter, in contrast to $65 per square meter in Canada, Latin America, and Canada. An increase in investment in the extraction industry could help African countries unlock their production potential.

It is well-documented that some resource-rich African countries have only remotely benefited from their resource wealth because of the smaller shares of rents generated by the extractive sector. The governments can realize reasonable returns by investing in the domestic technical capacity to reduce the utilization of PSAs. Resource wealth could contribute to sustainable economic development, as most African resource-rich countries perform poorly on a host of development indicators.

For the continent's industrialization scheme to succeed, deliberate government efforts are needed. In countries with low industrialization, most natural resources are exported as unprocessed raw materials, so more investment would enable raw materials to be processed and the commodities to be valued. Adding value to exports could generate additional revenue to invest in public services. In addition, linkages could be established through regional integration to enhance extraction sophistication and industrialization. The supranational regional body could adopt new regulations, such as new rules on taxes and royalties and a contract negotiating framework, some of which the AU has already adopted.

Investing

In other words, revenues from the extraction industry should be invested in sustainable development areas that benefit the population. In light of the fact that most extractive assets are depleting, the investment must target areas that can sustain revenues to support long-term economic growth. Norway is a shining example of a country that harnesses natural resources successfully. Norway's resource income has been used to build massive sovereign wealth funds invested in various profitable businesses worldwide.

EXISTING REGULATORY INSTRUMENTS FOR THE EXTRACTION INDUSTRY

In 2009, the African Union adopted the Africa Mining Vision (AVM), which aims to guide African countries to achieve the Millennium Development Goals (MDAs) through the extraction industry. In it, the issue of generating value-added activities along regional mineral value chains is stressed as a means to forming an integrated, diversified, and inclusive economy in Africa that leverages natural resources responsibly, following dramatic falls in prices and returns. Ultimately, a mineral-based institutional arrangement is needed. With the African Mining Vision, regional cooperation is key to overcoming the limitations of unilateral economic policymaking, contract negotiation, infrastructure development, and other burdensome tasks without coordination. Rather than pooling their markets and negotiating contracts more effectively, mineral producers compete in a race to the bottom. AMV's objectives can be categorized into nine clusters:

(i) Cluster 1: Mining revenues and mineral rents management;
(ii) Cluster 2: Geological and mining information systems;
(iii) Cluster 3: Building human and institutional capacities;
(iv) Cluster 4: Artisanal and small scale mining (ASM);
(v) Cluster 5: Mineral sector governance;
(vi) Cluster 6: Research and development;
(vii) Cluster 7: Environmental and social issues;
(viii) Cluster 8: Linkages and diversification; and
(ix) Cluster 9: Mobilizing mining and infrastructure investment.

The African Mineral Governance Framework (AMGF)

The African Mineral Governance Framework is another policy implementation tool for AMV. The AMV monitoring indicator is a way to assess African countries' progress towards full implementation of the AMV. The AMGF also serves as a broad governance mechanism for the extraction industry. In addition to covering the AMV principles, it also loosely supports the nine clusters. The pillars include:

(i) Pillar 1: Fiscal Regime and Revenue Management;
(ii) Pillar 2: Geological and Mineral Information Systems;
(iii) Pillar 3: Artisanal and Small-Scale Mining;
(iv) Pillar 4: Legal and Institutional Environment;
(v) Pillar 5: Linkages, Investment and Diversification; and
(vi) Pillar 6: Environmental and Social Issues.

The Africa Mining Vision Compact with the Private Sector

The AMV Compact with the Private Sector is the third primary tool adopted by the AU in February 2016. The instrument is modelled on the UN Global compact for global business, in which 162 countries and more than 8,000 companies have adopted. The tool aims to create a public-private sector partnership that creates a sustainable and responsible extraction industry. Using the AMV Action Plan's nine clusters, the tool establishes principles that corporate actors should adhere to. Even though the AMV Compact is modelled after the UN Global Compact, it does not follow the UN guiding principles of human rights and other guiding principles. By developing an African Minerals Governance Framework and policy and regulatory reviews, the African mining sector can address a range of development issues while preventing the sector from exacerbating existing imbalances and inequalities. In the future, mining policy should also reflect the needs of mining workers in the informal sector.

Figure 7.31: The African Mining Vision Implementation Architecture

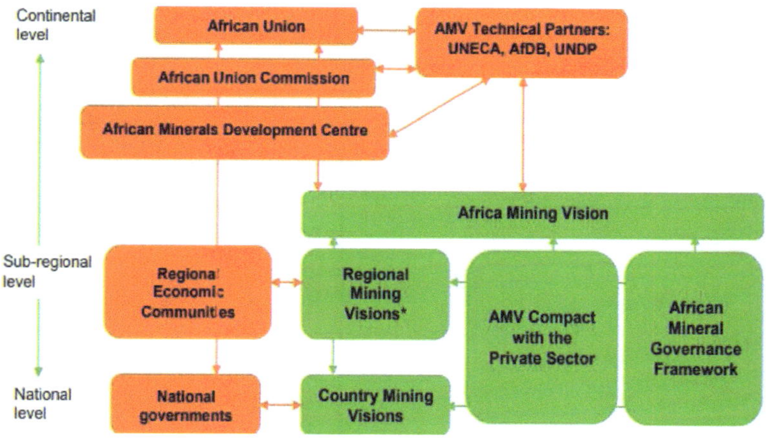

Source: Oxfam.org

Implementing mineral policies and governance has become the most challenging aspect; well-written and developed policies exist, but enforcement is weak, especially for regional and transnational policies. The AMV, AMGF, and the AMV Compact with the Private Sector are voluntary instruments to which states must opt-in. There is a need for a supranational institution in Southern Africa to ensure that all member states domesticate these instruments. In addition, a supranational SADC could take the initiative to ensure that member states follow the regulatory protocols prescribed in the instruments. The AMV is focused on extraction industry structural transformation. The AMV was created to ensure that African countries could strategically use their extraction resources for inclusive social and economic development as well as infrastructure investment.

12

THE SOUTHERN AFRICAN COMMUNITY AND THE FUTURE OF THE INTEGRATION AGENDA

Regional integration has benefitted global economies through enhanced trade, reduced political instability and economic disparities among participating states. The book's introductory chapter described how regional integration had become part of the modern international system employed by states to navigate what the realist school describes as an anarchical international arena. This is an international environment whose default equilibrium is one of pervasive geopolitical competition between nation-states. As the global political economy becomes unfavourable for any single country to succeed in trade without being part of a robust regional economic bloc, demand for integration becomes even more urgent for small isolated economies in Southern Africa.

As Europe's economies have flourished, economic and political pressure has increased on other regions to rethink their regional integration strategies. Europe's success was due to regional integration, especially the opportunities provided by globalization. The problem in Southern Africa is not with regional integration or globalisation but with how these concepts have been managed. The institutional structure of

SADC, which sets the rules of the game, contributes to the problem. The greatest challenge for SADC is not just in the institution itself but in the mindsets of regional leaders: making sure that democracy is promoted across all member states and the interests of the citizens are served. SADC in its current form has been problematic because it has served the interests of individual member states, especially leaders. While it reflects the views of those in power, its interests do not necessarily reflect the interests of its citizens. Historically, SADC has served more than just the interests of those in power - it has often adopted an incredibly narrow view of regional integration.

The demand for SADC reform is palpable. To comprehend the position of SADC, one needs to understand the conditions the regional integration agenda has been pursuing since 1992. This, in turn, is affected by one's view of regional integration. It was not my objective to examine the various theoretical debates within the study of regional integration. Instead, two major contradictory conceptualizations of regional integration explain the role of regional institutions, namely, the power approach and the liberal institutionalist approach. The two approaches present different perspectives on the past and current role of regional institutions in Southern Africa and their varying significance. However, power not only neglects the massive changes in the international system that have affected the centrality of sovereignty; it also ignores today's interdependence in international politics.

This book takes the liberal institutionalist approach and calls for the SADC to be reformed from merely a relationship between member states based on their relative power to one that is more focused on creating a regional community with accepted standards and rules. Southern Africa can be refashioned into a progressive, integrated community to realize its potential for a more prosperous future. The deep integration of SADC countries has become a guiding principle in their foreign policy as they seek to improve their bargaining power, access to the global market, productivity, and consumer welfare. Having close to 350 million inhabitants united by historical, cultural, and linguistic ties, SADC countries have a more substantial hand in pursuing a robust integration agenda. Globalization and the international political economy, which are currently characterized by integrated economies with enlarged markets and shared economic policies, drive regional integration. In other words, the creation of RECs like SADC responds to the market pressures resulting from globalization. All REC member states are determined to accelerate policy and regulatory convergence on their integrated market, as unified markets and trade spaces have become necessary, not a luxury.

However, regional integration efforts on the African continent have not yielded any tangible results. There has been too little consideration of the history and institutional framework of the SADC in regional integration discussions. Yet, the history and institutional structure have more centrality to the regional integration debate. This book provides an answer explaining that we must explicitly recognise the different ways member states act and their commitment to regional integration. Some countries in the SADC region already have strong democratic and governance institutions that can help deliver national and regional benefits. Others, on the other hand, suffer from fragile institutional structures that have challenged regional integration efforts. Top-down regional policies are likely to fail if we fail to assess, recognize, and factor in the political and social disparities in the region. Likewise, it is important to avoid imposing one-size-fits-all solutions on failing states without considering their interests' sensitivity.

Following a review of Southern Africa's regional integration from a historical, theoretical, and structural perspective, the book turns to this concluding chapter. A historical analysis discussed in Chapters 3 and 4 reveals the adverse dynamic cooperation environment that continues to drive regional integration. The post-Apartheid polity needs reconfiguration of Southern African states and their conceptualisation of sovereignty. Members of the Southern African Community have the dilemma of having common regional objectives and minimizing domestic and political pressures. Fear of losing control of state sovereignty has led many SADC member states to consolidate their power further. A consensus exists on the need for a political reorganization of SADC, but there are disagreements about its form. According to its founding treaty, SADC is committed to undertaking political and economic reforms to enhance integration and human development.

The realist school recognizes the state of anarchy in which small and fragile economies in Africa operate. SADC member states should, of course, focus on issues where regional collective action is necessary or desirable. In the past 30 years, there has been increased awareness of the region's challenges and the necessity of a regional governance system. SADC member states recognize that they can overcome economic, social, political, security, and development challenges through more profound integration.

As states' interdependence has increased, the need for regional collective action has grown in various spheres. The regional institution created in response to regional challenges has not worked flawlessly; the challenges are complex, and collective action is difficult if the institution functions on an ad hoc basis. Throughout Chapters 5, 6, 7, 8 and 9, we examined the failures that have adversely affected regional efforts to achieve prosperity and stability. In most cases, SADC has pursued an agenda that contradicts the institution's objectives. Several member states have regressed on democracy, security, human rights, and good governance. This has stalled the transition and transformation of SADC into a supranational organization that can provide for a democratic, rule-of-law-respecting community with respect for shared values and norms. Neofunctionalists view the future as requiring regional institutions to protect the human security of all citizens throughout the region. The demand for regional ingenuity to create a robust and effective regional institution is unprecedented. This prescription depends on the notion of sovereignty being resolved, which remains a contentious issue. Having an agreement on that issue would have broader implications on the type of regional institution that might exist, its roles, and its functions. The SADC Treaty and supporting protocols sought to weaken the sovereignty of member states; it is clear that the Summit of Heads of State has fought back to undermine those early attempts.

There will, however, be constraints on the speed of change in the region as member states will find it difficult to break their tradition of preserving national sovereignty, wherein the majority of cases, it is the only form of legitimacy left for some regimes. Rather than rely on a nation-centric model of regional cooperation, the new vision would be to eliminate it altogether. A more progressive agenda is needed for a regional body to be more effective, which calls for member states to relinquish some decision-making power to the regional body.

However, there is a democratic deficit in some of the SADC Community members. As a means of beating this challenge, the SADC Secretariat, with all the supporting instruments central to SADC's economic sustainability and stability, must be more potent and more effective. To combat these SADC obstructionists, the institution must enforce compliance with set norms and objectives. The robustness of the SADC Tribunal and the effectiveness of the SADC Parliament will help keep SADC governments in check and ensure that sanctions and penalties will be applied to rule-breakers whenever necessary. For the SADC region to experience meaningful change, member states must make sound commitments. The purpose of this book is to demonstrate why a serious regional integration scholar or professional cannot overlook the need to create a stronger regional institution to address persistent problems in the region. As a result, these challenges have become much more critical to the region's economic, political, and social stability. Even though regional integration has grown only modestly, the significance of SADC cannot be underestimated.

Potential institutional reforms must take into account factors that have hindered progress on the regional integration agenda. The book analyzes in detail the factors that have led to the derailment of regional integration. In many respects, one can argue what an excellent regional integration strategy looks like, and we need to pursue innovative methods to foster prosperity and stability in the SADC area. The book suggests reinventing the existing structures to deal with political, social, and economic problems with specialized support instruments. A critical point to recognize is that many regional and national initiatives have been ineffective over the past three decades regarding economic transformation and regional stability, and some reversals have occurred. In the SADC region, a growing number of challenges are being met by inefficient bureaucracy and more interference from member states.

Historical and contemporary factors have converged in different proportions to create an environment marked by political conflicts, corruption, weak economies, weak governance systems, insecurity, and poverty. The book traces the history of regional cooperation in Southern Africa, which led to the Frontline States (FLS) creation in 1975, later replaced by the Southern African Development Coordination Conference (SADCC). After the FLS and SADCC were established to counter the Apartheid regime in South Africa that destabilised the region, the period of peace after Apartheid was seen as an opportunity for the region to achieve sustainable economic growth and stability. During the early 1990s, the Southern African Community evolved a framework to accommodate the new relationship with post-Apartheid South Africa. In 1992, the Southern African Development Community (SADC) was created to promote regional development, believing that peace and security were crucial factors that could enable economic development. SADC, however, is now facing new obstacles that are hampering its progress toward realizing its aspirations. It is often argued that historical circumstances shape contemporary events, and SADC is no exception. SADC's response to regional challenges has been influenced by historical circumstances, which have hindered regional integration. The analysis identified historical factors that influenced social, political, and economic forces that shaped the progress of regional integration. The historical factors include:

(i) Colonial legacy;
(ii) Apartheid and white nationalist regimes;
(iii) Liberation movements;
(iv) Historical relations between member states; and
(v) Changes in the international political economy driven by the end of the Cold War and globalization.

We have examined the history of regionalism in Southern Africa and highlighted how the principle of solidarity shaped the relationship between states and liberation movements throughout the book. While the principle of solidarity successfully challenged and ended the oppressive, racist minority regimes in the region, this book has revealed how non-interference and solidarity have contributed to developing a stable and prosperous regional economy. Historical trends in economic, social, and political interaction point to a politicised bureaucracy that is less effective. In the past, SADC has only been good at defining problems and establishing rules without enforcing the obligations of the member states. While the regional socio-political development continues to decline, SADC leaders are still quarrelling over which state should guide the integration agenda. This disjointed cooperation has failed to produce a sound foundation for creating a more sound and robust regional integration scheme. Regional integration can only stimulate economic growth if more profound regional integration scheme opportunities are carefully nurtured.

It would be remiss to end this book without acknowledging and appreciating the role of the liberation movements and the Southern African states during the liberation struggle. The majority of Southern African states were the staunchest supporters of the liberation movements, which is commendable. The liberation movements were given a platform to build structures that transformed them into ruling parties after independence. The conception of solidarity by Southern African states allowed them to sustain their support to the liberation movements while enduring relentless destabilization efforts from the white minority regimes. However, since the early 1990s, Southern African states have failed to shift their priorities. There has been a continued focus on preserving the regimes of liberation leaders and preserving the liberation legacy. Despite SADC having all the necessary agreements and protocols promoting democracy and good governance, regional member states have ignored the international outcry to hold the Zimbabwean government accountable for human rights violations.

There have been debates about whether the ties formed during the liberation movement are still relevant to regional stability, economic growth, and trade challenges. Through the convergence of different sectors, and as observed throughout the book, the pursuit of an integrated regional political, economic, and security regime is highly desirable although complex politically. Political will is critical due to the differences in political, economic, social, and governance systems, which have become a major obstacle to more coordinated action and effective integration schemes.

Although these obstacles may exist, they shouldn't be allowed to become a permanent threat to the integration of the regions. Rather, the SADC region needs to work on reducing these differences to achieve a more substantial convergence. To succeed in regional integration, building trust and an institutional framework capable of addressing challenges are fundamental.

A diverse governance system has also made it difficult for regional convergence to occur. The SADC Treaty (1992) commits members states to respect human rights, democracy, and the rule of law. However, SADC governments have regressed in recent years and undermined fundamental rights protection mechanisms. As an example, in August 2014, SADC leaders agreed to strip the SADC Tribunal of its mandate to hear complaints from individuals or organizations, limiting the tribunal's ability to adjudicate disputes between member states only. As a result, its human rights protection mandate was removed. SADC must respond to the needs of ordinary citizens by implementing and enforcing policies centred on human security to contribute to lasting stability and safeguard democracy throughout the region. As this book illustrates, one way to help resolve the ongoing conflicts in the region and overcome governance and governance challenges is through regional collaboration in enhancing human rights, good governance, democracy, and security by using potent regional instruments. The debate over regional integration in everyday discourse should adopt a more optimistic viewpoint that focuses on past accomplishments and attempts to overcome its challenges. The history of Southern Africa is rich with a history of interdependence during the liberation struggle. Promoting a shared past could help improve attitudes towards regional integration and mobilize public support for a prosperous shared future.

The book's central premise is that the regional aspirations of SADC member states must be translated into practice. The importance of integration in Southern Africa cannot be understated, with regional integration discourse playing a central role in transforming the region's political, economic, security, and governance landscape. Southern African states have been inspired to pursue a broader and more ambitious regional integration agenda to deal with regional challenges. However, Southern Africa's unique regional integration experiment through SADC has had limited success.

Balancing two parallel processes of globalization, one that demands deeper integration and focuses exclusively on protecting national sovereignty, requires many compromises. To achieve these ambitions, member states will have to compromise and move toward political integration. SADC's original aim was to build a regional body that could promote good governance, harmony, stability, and democracy among member states. As discussed in Chapters 4 and 5, however, these ambitions have been hampered by many obstacles. To promote the regional integration agenda, there must be political will at the national level. Despite the limitations of its institutional framework, the SADC has failed to meet its collective objectives.

This book aims to shed light on the actors and factors that have affected regional integration in Southern Africa. Based on the analysis in this book, there are significant differences in regional objectives and practices. Members of SADC have had a difficult time adhering to regional norms despite the adoption of national norms. In light of current domestic political factors affecting the integration process, a more outstanding political commitment and public support of the integration agenda would facilitate harmonising national and regional objectives and policies. The basis of sustained economic growth and stability in any region is an effective and efficient regional integration institution.

A strong case is made for a supranational approach to regional integration in this book, which focuses on transforming the SADC institutional framework. The book's focus on SADC's potential role in international trade and global politics contributes to the debates on creating a fully integrated region. A more robust coordinated approach to the regional agenda is the key to building a more progressive regional institution with clear responsibilities. Indeed, fundamental questions remain as to why SADC's integration efforts are causing such controversy. To such a question, the most considered answer is that SADC has existed for three decades, but internal factors and actors have undermined its integration efforts. SADC is seen as an institution with great potential, considering its vast wealth of natural resources and young population. Natural and mineral resources provide opportunities for economic growth and prosperity throughout the SADC region if harnessed.

The book attempts to analyze the factors that hinder regional integration in Southern Africa and the actors who hinder it from being more comprehensive. Examining the limitations and constraints impeding progress on the regional integration agenda was undertaken by drawing attention to critical questions highlighting the existing limitations. The book reflects on the following questions: What are the existing obstacles to regional integration? What underlying issues have led to the current situation Southern Africa is in? Who is responsible for the current failures of the regional body? The answers to these questions are essential for understanding where SADC stands today and its potential moving forward.

If regional integration efforts are seriously focused on the existing challenges undermining efforts to operationalize regional agreements and protocols, regional integration can succeed. For political, economic and security integration to succeed, SADC member states need to overcome historical, structural, and institutional factors within and between their countries.

By focusing on the impact of a more significant regional bloc on industrial development and political stability in the region, this book seeks to enhance integration ideas in a broader sense. The insights provided in the book are similar to those of other regional bodies across Africa, even though it focuses on Southern Africa. The institutional framework and capacity of most regional bodies in Africa prevent them from serving the purpose they were created. The importance of regional integration to Southern Africa's political stability and economic development is largely agreed upon. Integration can only succeed if the states participating in the scheme create a conducive environment. Additionally, that requires member states to embrace a new conceptualization of regional integration that transcends economic cooperation. An integration process based on political integration recognizes security, human rights, and liberal democratic values.

Schiff and Winters (2013) argue that RECs can be helpful tools for strengthening political and governance institutions. Schiff and Winters contend that regional institutions with strict club rules can help initiate democratic reforms in member countries. Furthermore, these institutions increase the likelihood of realizing and sustaining democracy, especially in RECs with hegemony that has developed democracies. Magistretti and Tabellini (2019) agree with Schiff and Winters by suggesting that regional economic integration promotes democracy from more to less democratic countries. More advanced democracies like Botswana, Mauritius and South Africa provide a blueprint for democracy and good governance. Thus, this provides an impetus for SADC member states to continue making progress in democratic development, good governance, human rights, and transparency.

SADC must also initiate well-planned and coordinated activities to resolve the region's armed conflicts and political disputes. It is only possible to achieve stability in the region if democracy and good governance are incorporated into the integration agenda, which is possible only if the participating states overcome the anti-democratic trends that characterize the majority of SADC states.

There is a profound conflict between the ambitions of SADC to consolidate democracy, good governance, and human rights and the interests of some governments with authoritarian tendencies. Norms promoting democracy, good governance, and human rights have been adopted at the regional level, but this book shows that the dynamics on the ground are quite different. Questions are now being raised on whether SADC member states are genuinely committed to the cause. As a result of protracted political and security crises in Zimbabwe, Mozambique, and the DRC, the SADC's failure to promote human security as part of its normative integration agenda has been amplified.

In the previous Chapter, the vital link between regional stability and economic growth was highlighted. SADC has undergone an institutional transformation by establishing protocols, agreements, and instruments that could enhance economic and political convergence since it was established in 1992. Its importance has been explicitly enshrined in the SADC Protocol for Politics, Defense and Security, and the SADC Elections Protocol, which can go a long way toward addressing the region's security and political challenges.

Taking advantage of the operationalization of the existing peace and security architecture allows the region to capitalize on Africa's security responsibility delegated to regional organizations like SADC. Currently, Southern Africa faces persistent circumstances that require collective regional intervention. To improve SADC's effectiveness against the region's challenges, we need to consider two crucial factors. As a first step, SADC was formed in response to Southern Africa's vision for a prosperous, peaceful, and developed region. The susceptibility of Southern Africa to intra-state conflicts remains a constant constraint; hence, it is essential for a more potent and effective regional body. Among the fundamental aspects of the Organ for Politics, Defence, and Security is the need for SADC to take adequate measures to prevent conflicts in the region. The SADC Standby Force provides the region with a rapid deployment military capability that can be activated in conflict hot spots under the AU Constitutive Act's Article 4 (h) provision. While creating an environment conducive to foreign investment is a primary objective, trade remains a powerful tool for economic growth and development in the region.

It is argued in the book that SADC should do more to create an environment that encourages economic growth and political stability. There is an extent to which the success of SADC operations cannot be de-linked from political convergence. Mozambique, the DRC, and Zimbabwe demonstrate that a measure of stability and peace is needed in the SADC region to attain socio-economic development. In SADC, member states have a vital role in shaping the discourse on human security and must take responsibility for conflict mitigation. Peace and development initiatives will only succeed if the AU and sub-regional groups like SADC adopt effective institutional frameworks and structures. Member states can build governance institutions that address regional challenges through the existing institutional framework, consisting of mechanisms and instruments supporting democracy. It remains to be seen whether such support will persist.

Due to the disproportionate amount of time spent on conflict-related issues that have been unresolved for decades, a new regional framework could reverse the current political and economic climate. It is often the case that circumstances dictate events, as has been the case during the Zimbabwe crisis. Member states have demonstrated restraint in responding to the crisis, a seemingly straightforward action condemning the authoritarian Zimbabwean regime. The book offers several approaches to dealing with the complex conflicts in Zimbabwe,

Mozambique, and the DRC. For the mechanisms to be successful, functional cooperation and coordination between member states are required. Collaboration in this area must recognize the relative advantage of ending persistent conflicts in the region. SADC member states' interest in the region's conflicts is noteworthy due to the spillover effects of these conflicts on their neighbouring countries.

Of course, there is a significant correlation between poverty and conflicts. In keeping with SADC's socio-economic goals, there is a strong argument for a new SADC idea where security discourse involves human security elements already outlined in the treaty. SADC must become a supranational institution that enforces these values and norms rather than remaining an intergovernmental association. The SADC organ's elaborately outlined frameworks already provide a well thought-out structure of the regional security architecture that can be utilized if the regional body is determined to overcome the persistent security and political challenges. In light of SADC's lacklustre performance, efforts will need to be made to increase its capacity to initiate its operations effectively as soon as possible and on a long-term basis. Despite having the necessary instruments for managing political and armed conflicts, SADC has been slow to respond to crises in fast-changing regional conflicts and is instead stuck in outdated frameworks and approaches. SADC needs to adopt a more progressive regional agenda that identifies and removes integration barriers while harnessing transformation agents. Regional instability, governance deficit and declining democratic values should be a priority to overcome some of the persistent conflicts that have fuelled instability across the region.

Though the process of establishing these instruments has been unquestionable, the operationalization of these instruments has been uneven. Firstly, there is no consensus among SADC member states on how the instruments should be operationalized. Secondly, a lack of political will has prevented SADC from becoming a regional political community. The book has demonstrated how SADC's enthusiasm for regional integration has not been matched by the same enthusiasm and commitment to promote and implement regional agreements and enforce those agreements. Thirdly, member states' ideological differences over governance systems have slowed down regional initiatives. SADC needs to enter the terrain of addressing democracy, good governance, and human rights from a human security perspective, which are enshrined in the SADC Treaty. Finally, the region has had an unimpressive track record when it comes to creating norms, creating a competent institutional framework, and implementing agreements and protocols.

SADC member states must strengthen their governance institutions by adopting good governance practices, respect for the rule of law, and an effective judicial system. SADC should create enforcement mechanisms in which sanctions are imposed on member states who violate SADC values and objectives. The SADC region's future success depends on how each member state's political situation develops and whether there is momentum towards de-escalation of conflicts that could lead to regional stability. The regional body needs to take stock of interventions undertaken to promote peace and stability in the past and learn from its failures. Zimbabwe's silent diplomacy and solidarity approach has failed miserably, and new measures need to be adopted, including renegotiating Zimbabwe's governance terms. SADC must also adopt good governance as a pre-condition for regional membership and possibly adopt basic standards for measuring good governance in all member states.

Addressing the internal capacity of SADC and focusing on factors that can stimulate intra-regional trade is a fundamental starting point. Unfortunately, these efforts cannot bear fruitful results if the regional body cannot resolve conflict-related issues. These challenges may be resolved through cohesive and determined regional response efforts. Enhanced integration in the region could inevitably lead to increased political and economic stability if SADC member states can integrate into a security community. The restoration of a degree of stability in large key countries like Zimbabwe, Mozambique, and DRC can reverse the region's characteristic as a region that is slowly disintegrating at an alarming rate. Fundamental norms like human rights, democracy, and good governance can only be promoted by establishing and maintaining ethical instruments like the SADC Tribunal that provide citizens with external recourse to justice and mechanisms to hold their governments accountable. With a clearer understanding of past failures, SADC should assume the role of promoting human rights and fundamental liberties as part of their agreements' collective values. The countries failing to adhere to these values should be pressured by their regional peers to do so. Regional courts like the SADC Tribunal should be revamped into their original form so that the instrument becomes an external guarantor for human rights.

The book recognizes that safeguarding peace and security through regional mechanisms provides opportunities for resolving the armed conflict and political conflicts in the DRC, Mozambique, and Zimbabwe. Stability in the region remains a vital prerequisite for realizing sustainable stability and economic growth in the SADC area. This book's discussions acknowledge that human security and state security are increasingly becoming complementary and symbiotic. The book suggests that the starting point to sustain stability must be the process of initiating and safeguarding democratic governance across the region. Holding elections alone is insufficient to sustain democracy, as observed in Zimbabwe and other member states experiencing a decline in democracy. SADC can also play an essential role in strengthening national public institutions across the region that could necessitate effective public services delivery.

The absence of effective early warning systems and risk assessment capabilities has exposed the inadequacies and weaknesses in regional conflict prevention mechanisms. SADC needs to develop the national and regional capacity for responses that would lead to sustainable conflict resolution strategies to address these challenges. The region already has requisite structures that require political will from regional leaders to become effective. SADC member states require a real commitment from the commonly used philosophy of non-interference towards the principle of non-indifference, which the AU has already adopted. The principle of non-indifference demands states to recognize that intervention in an intra-state conflict is justified when gross human rights violations and abuses occur. The existing political and security architecture agreed upon by all member states was created to deal with the current security and political challenges. Mwanasali (2008) describes this shift to the principle of non-indifference as an interventionist phase in the AU's and sub-regional bodies' management of peace and security. Operationalizing the existing collective security apparatus is the only thing that is left. The success of collective security depends on the member states' willingness and ability to enforce the agreed norms and collective security objectives. While some response mechanisms may have long-term objectives, several armed conflicts and political crises require an urgent response. The implementation of the response options will vary according to the different contexts within which the various conflicts occur and the root causes of the conflicts. Despite SADC's apparent shortcomings, the regional body still represents existing fundamental instruments for security and conflict management that can be utilized in Southern Africa. As the UN and AU have explicitly approved SADC in managing regional conflicts, it is also crystal clear to SADC members that they must develop the capacity to deal with their problems.

Some scholars have argued that regional institutions can only play a limited role, and even if they do, it is in their interest to protect strategic national interests. That philosophy is gradually challenged by contemporary demands for interventionist philosophy that protects individuals against grave human rights violations by state and non-state actors. The increase of catastrophic conflicts in Africa has led to the growing demand for expanding regional bodies' mandate into areas of human rights, good governance, and democratization. The book considers that regional institutions like SADC provide a viable framework for maintaining regional peace and security. This perspective is consistent with Chapter VIII of the UN Charter, which recognizes the regional institutions' role in preventing, managing, and resolving disputes. SADC must address the region's security and political challenges since there is a symbiotic relationship between regional political instability and economic growth. Political unrest leads to slow economic growth, thereby impacting political stability. The numerous persistent threats to regional security have continued to impact regional security and stability, consequently inhibiting economic growth, development, and democracy.

In general terms, SADC member states have had little interest in ceding some of their power to the regional body. According to Nathan (2002), the states are susceptible to limiting their sovereignty. Nathan (2002) further argues that "SADC states do not want to be governed by an independent forum whose decisions are binding on them." The argument advanced here is that despite the move towards regional integration, the individual member states still have an essential role in providing that enabling environment. That is why more attention must be paid to building the institutional capacity and structure that regional integration requires. The current SADC institutional structure best illustrates the limitations regional bodies have when it comes to conflict management. The lack of political will and consensus among SADC member states on the instruments' operationalization has undermined these instruments' objectives despite having the requisite instruments for promoting human rights and advancing democracy.

Moreover, the ideological differences among member states have made it difficult for countries to respond to regional conflict hotspots and help the regional body evolve into a regional security community. Thus, there is an urgent need to reform and restructure the SADC institutional framework. SADC is a brilliant institution that is currently being hampered by a cumbersome bureaucratic system driven by some leaders' self-interests and agendas. These diverse self-interests have rendered the institution ineffectiveness.

Infrastructural development and Foreign Direct Investment have been impeded by regional instability; most of these conflicts are attributed to the consistently weak governance in the SADC region. To achieve deeper integration, member states must demonstrate a significant commitment to addressing the political and security challenges of the region. A significant failure of SADC is its inability to ensure compliance with treaty obligations like democratic norms, human rights, accountability, transparency, and good governance. Conflict, instability, and economic development have been negatively affected by failed attempts at democratic governance. To improve access to all state resources and adequately distribute state resources among all citizens, patronage systems that have crippled regional economies need to be dismantled.

SADC presents a potentially untapped market for regionally diversified commodities produced from locally obtained raw materials from an economic standpoint. Thus far, the potential of the regional bloc has been overwhelmed by the convergence of external and internal social, political, and economic forces that have conspired against any chance of prosperity. Colonial legacy and post-independence Capitalist economy characterized by globalization constitute external forces. Internal forces, such as authoritarian systems, weak economies, and corrupt and patronage systems, have undermined the region's capabilities to improve welfare and human development. All these factors have converged in many proportions to fuel intra-state conflicts and poverty. As seen in Mozambique, the region is now a potential breeding ground for terrorism, narcotraffickers, and other criminal networks.

Previously, we discussed how Africa's share of world trade declined from 6% to about 2% in the last three decades. For Africa to overcome its persistent challenges, it is unwelcome to continue down this path. Even more concerning is the low intra-regional trade in Southern Africa, which is still under 16% compared to 60% in Western Europe, where trade occurs with other European countries. Low intra-regional trade has had far-reaching consequences since production and export structures have focused on primary commodities that are less competitive within the SADC region. Integrating the region's fragmented markets is critical to attracting substantial capital investments from within the region and the rest of the world to help build competitive and diversified economies. The high trade costs in the region prevent maximizing the potential gains from trade expansion; therefore, the region is also disadvantaged.

Southern Africa's survival depends on regional economic and political integration. By integrating regionally, SADC would be able to pool its valuable resources to create a healthy, unified, and diversified market with the potential to grow its global share of trade. New strategies are needed to address supply and production constraints for market integration to be deepened. A coherent trade policy can enhance trade and market integration when identified and incorporated into domestic strategies. Several policies have been suggested to address supply constraints and competitiveness of exports and create a cooperative framework at the macro and micro levels that effectively assigns responsibilities across countries and regions. To make the most of larger markets, SADC member nations should avoid duplicating export goods. The book encourages further initiatives to promote industrialization and diversification of imports for regional and international markets. Fundamentally, this is critical since the manufacturing sector is critical to SADC's sustainable economic growth.

SADC's comparative advantage in terms of labour and resource availability, resulting in low production costs, needs to be exploited to grow its manufacturing base. It is also critical that SADC member states capitalize on low-tech manufacturing to expand their manufacturing sector before turning to technology-intensive production methods. It is vital that the private sector coordinates and thinks strategically when identifying import replacements for regional markets. The private sector in the region has a critical role in achieving structural diversification and maximizing regional trade potential. Making the manufacturing and processing industry more efficient and competitive globally should be the driving force behind any regional agreement. Member states of SADC should utilize existing regional political and economic arrangements to utilize the benefits of a regional market while reducing external dependence on exports that can be produced within the region.

In addition to poor design and planning, regional integration efforts have also been hampered by a focus on trade liberalization and market integration, while complimentary efforts have not been taken to increase and coordinate regional production to sustain market integration and export diversification. In addition, trade within SADC has been impeded by fundamental logistical challenges such as infrastructure (transport, energy, and ICT), making trade physically tricky. Due to a lack of foreign investment and self-financing resources, limited investments have been made in regional infrastructure and manufacturing. The improvement of this infrastructure could result in a significant boost to exports. Poor manufacturing and logistics have hindered intra-regional trade, with poor transport infrastructure hampering the movement of goods, services, and people between SADC member states. To ease delays in regional trade, it is necessary to develop transport and communication infrastructure. In a region with colossal energy potential ranging from hydropower to natural gas, investments in energy production should become a priority as this could boost the manufacturing base and people's access to electricity. Aside from investments in manufacturing and infrastructure, incentives should be provided for skill development and productivity enhancement for better results. A lack of a skilled workforce, lack of industrial and technological sophistication, and inadequate infrastructure have left most SADC economies at a systematic disadvantage, forcing them to export unprocessed raw materials at low prices.

Members must address all obstacles known to hinder regional trade. As member states develop their production capability and industrial sophistication, they can use their raw material endowments and make them more valuable. Within the SADC region, new opportunities need to be explored for diversified products, and changes in the direction of trade need to be made. Since the regional trade is still below 16%, the regional body will need to explore other trade products to expand the export base. By looking at the regional market as a domestic market, the private sector should broaden and exploit its economic market space. Besides processing commodities, SADC member states should diversify their export bases to include other essential manufactured goods. Presently, export products receive minimal value addition, which reduces the benefits of the regional FTA.

Regional integration requires a new perspective that transcends narrow nationalistic considerations, along with a sense of urgency. A second crucial question is what South Africa's future is in the Community. The country already has the most robust economy and the best governance and democratic institutions in the region. As the core state in the region, South Africa needs to demonstrate leadership in shaping the direction of regional integration. Due to South Africa's presence in the region, SADC can also strengthen its position in international economic and governance debates. Integration efforts in the region are successful only if regional hegemons, such as South Africa, play a crucial role. SADC will have to grapple with practical challenges and put in place mechanisms capable of addressing the region's economic, development, human rights, and security issues with South Africa at the helm.

Small and isolated economies in Southern Africa need regional integration to escape marginalization in the global economy. Unless SADC's institutional framework is changed, structural impediments to regional integration will remain difficult to overcome in the region. The EU has presented a clear rationale for a fully functional and successful regional body. Based on credible evidence, SADC can achieve regional stability and economic growth if the integration process adopts a new structural framework. It implies that member states sacrifice part of their sovereignty to the supranational body, and all members speak with one voice. States don't establish supranational institutions when they join forces to create a global governing body under their control; rather, they establish supranational institutions when states freely and willingly surrender some of their tightly guarded sovereignty to control the institution within their agreed mandates. In some areas, these mandates give this institution overriding powers to hold the states accountable.

Although regional leaders have avoided expressing their insecurities in the open, their actions speak louder. Their argument about sovereignty merely serves to protect their monopoly on political power. Today's competitive international political economy requires integrated political, security, and economic structures, and even the most advanced economies continue to enhance integration. This underscores the need for SADC member states to begin working together urgently. Closer cooperation among member states becomes valuable in the SADC area because of the current economic, political, social, and security conditions. SADC as a whole must deal with challenges related to improved governance, economic productivity, strengthened cooperation, and closer political and security ties. Ladan (1994) argues that African governments must minimize their differences to achieve a more unified and cohesive front.

Creating a supranational body in the SADC area outweighs any argument on sovereignty promoted by nationalists. The regional body is currently faced with the practical implications of the conflict between supranationalism and national (regime) interests. There has been reluctance from SADC member states to strengthen the regional body's decision-making process because they don't want the organization to rule against their interests. Additionally, the regional bodies' weaknesses have prevented them from enforcing some of the existing agreements and protocols. SADC states need to convert from "hard" to "soft" sovereignty, which is part of any good governance agenda. SADC must have the legal foundation to achieve political, economic, security, and social convergence as a supranational organization by eliminating disagreements over sovereignty. SADC member states can overcome the narrow-minded economic nationalist and sovereignty burdens by riding the wave of brotherhood generated at the launch of the regional body. Despite the heavy burden of political, security, economic and social disorder, this brotherhood has sustained the support given to liberation movements across the region. Through the same resilience displayed during the struggle against Apartheid and white minority regimes, integration can also be enhanced in the region. At present, SADC leaders are firmly ensconced in their fiefdom, as an integration strategy would require them to relax their grip on sovereignty. SADC is hampered by the clique's political elites' desire to preserve and protect their self-interests rather than the citizens' interests. The result is a regional bureaucracy that is inefficient and ineffective. As evidenced by the SADC's inability to resolve Zimbabwe's political and economic crisis, this failure is evident.

One way to restructure SADC is to abandon consensus-based decision-making and adopt a majority-based approach. SADC member states have used consensus as a means of escaping external oversight and escaping accountability for human rights violations for many years. Members have had equal veto powers over any joint decisions that are deemed unfavourable. In the case of the SADC Tribunal, there was a ruling against the Zimbabwean Government's illegal land occupation, which led to the Tribunal's demise. Furthermore, decision-making based on majority agreements can allow states to profit from a few actors' visionary perspectives and refocus collective interests, avoiding stalemates. However, the lack of common values, mutual trust, and a shared vision among SADC member states has made it challenging to align authoritarian with democratic perspectives.

Regional integration means more than just liberalizing markets and signing protocols that are not worth the paper they're written on, as SADC's inability to integrate has demonstrated over the last three decades. An effective and deeper regional scheme requires direct intervention on factors interfering with prosperity and stability in the region, such as production and diversification challenges, instability, marginalization of some communities, corruption, human rights concerns, and governance issues. It is argued in the book that attempts to analyze integrationist projects of economic, political, and market integration in Southern Africa should be conducted from a cross-sectional perspective while considering both macro-and micro-level factors. SADC leaders must be willing to treat SADC challenges as national priorities and envision building an integrated, prosperous, and peaceful Southern Africa with a human security and development agenda.

SADC has progressive institutional frameworks, but most states have regressive and oppressive structures at the national level. Convergence of democratic and governance norms among member states can only be achieved by creating a SADC with a supranational identity. However, Southern African governments have resisted any efforts to entrust international bodies with meaningful responsibilities without the supervision of the member states. Considering the member states' contradicting political and economic characteristics, the regional statesmen have loathed any attempts to cede any sovereignty aspects to a supranational authority. Nevertheless, there is consensus that regional integration is critical to tackling challenges that individual states cannot solve.

There are disparities between countries regarding their democracy and economic development, which challenge the regional integration project, resulting in slow economic growth and a lack of market integration. There is a profound structural problem parallel with the institution's political, social, and economic conditions. SADC members need to take a proactive role in regional stability and economic development in the current regional economic and political environment. The region will need to revisit its regional integration treaty more rigorously to address persistent challenges as part of this process. In the short term, the SADC must first continue its efforts to resolve conflict through existing institutional mechanisms. Due to the lacklustre performance of the regional integration project so far, efforts must be geared towards creating an organization that can effectively handle future challenges. In Southern Africa, the only option for member states to maintain peace and improve the socio-economic status of their citizens is an effective regional body. It is almost impossible to prescribe a set of solutions for the region's challenges that have hampered peace, political stability, and economic growth without reshaping SADC's institutional framework. In addition to antagonistic relations, low intra-regional trade levels, and inadequate infrastructure, the regional body continues to face challenges. In contrast, lessons from the EU demonstrate that regional integration benefits justify establishing institutions that could require a neo-liberal political economy and institutions of governance to ensure democratic and good governance in the region.

The SADC area benefits from history from a policy perspective as it provides great lessons about what has worked and what hasn't. Unfortunately, history is characterized mainly by failure, and the mentality of doing business as usual has not proven successful. Southern Africa must have a regional institution capable of initiating positive changes in regional politics and economics. If these drastic measures are not taken, the structural obstacles will persist, and SADC will not become a stable political and economic bloc. In order to explain why things are the way they are in Southern Africa, one can use a political-economy lens to explain why effective regional blocs need to empower talented and professional bureaucracies to accomplish these goals.

Globalization conditions mean that sovereignty is slowly losing its meaning, and countries must therefore come together as a community. Tilman (1995) asserts: "This sovereignty is now being emptied of its previous meaning on the smaller and the larger scale by the rapid course taken by the interlinked societies. The dialectic relationship between the rapid globalization of the economy, communications, and culture and the simultaneous more and more complex and subtle formation of different social spheres makes the idea of a central decision-making body seem an anachronism, although nobody doubts that the nation-state as an important level of action, perhaps the most important, will continue to exist for a long time to come. It is, however, losing its claim to exclusivity."

The conventional implementation of SADC protocols, agreements, and decisions within a supranational framework has also been argued as an opportunity to diminish the state behaviours that have previously impeded regional integration. Rather than allowing national interests to dominate regional integration discourse, SADC should play a role in neutralizing them. Member states of SADC must allow SADC to operate exclusively according to its institutional mandates and strengthen its capacity where it is weak. To minimize its weaknesses and prevent erosion of credibility, all of these factors should be considered when designing a new regional institutional framework. Countries in the region must be adaptable to the experiences of other regions regarding cooperation and integration. In particular, the European Union should be cited as an example of the pragmatism that characterized European countries, which prevented significant political differences from becoming an insurmountable obstacle to the design and implementation of regional integration and cooperation initiatives.

Southern Africa's reality is reminiscent of what Machiavelli wrote in Chapter XXVI of The Prince relating to the period when Italy was in a more dire situation: "And if, as I said, the Israelites had to be enslaved in Egypt for Moses to emerge as their leader; if the Persians had to be oppressed by the Medes so that the greatness of Cyrus could be recognized; if the Athenians had to be scattered to demonstrate the excellence of Theseus: then, at present, in order to discover the worth of an Italian spirit, Italy had to be brought to her present extremity. She had to be more enslaved than the Hebrews, more oppressed than the Persians, more widely scattered than the Athenians; leaderless, lawless, crushed, despoiled, torn, overrun; she had to have endured every kind of desolation." Southern Africa is currently at the bottom of every socio-economic and development category. The leaders of Southern Africa should take inspiration from Machiavelli, gather courage, and work together to face the persistent challenges by building a united region.

Some scholars have taken a more pessimistic view of Southern Africa, arguing that an ad hoc form of regional cooperation is justified due to underdevelopment in the region and a lack of political will for integration. Several theories are presented in the book to help overcome the challenges presented by small economies, instability, and lack of cohesion in governance and political approaches. These factors have pushed the region far behind in the development race. Without a more robust regional integration plan, current economic, political, security, and governance challenges will continue to threaten the stability of Southern Africa. Efficacious regional integration can lead to accelerated socio-economic development via the collective exploitation of Southern Africa's potential. A primary focus of this book is to highlight opportunities for growth within the SADC and the need to strengthen regional integration mechanisms. An unfavourable business climate and instability in the region have previously hampered the potential.

SADC needs a new generation of visionary leaders who will recognize the region's challenges and pursue democratic consolidation while promoting other aspects of good governance such as transparency, accountability, and responsiveness. Good governance and democracy can only be achieved if governments can promote human security in their countries while at the same time allowing the regional body to monitor and enforce democratic norms and good governance. SADC member states must implement democratic and governance policies with a sincere commitment to achieving this goal. Investing in a supranational structure with far-reaching decision-making capabilities is imperative for a successful SADC. SADC has failed to realize the objectives aspired by its members at its inception. The current regional body gives the benefit of the doubt to authoritarian leaders who have found comfort in the organization and remain protected from international condemnation and economic sanctions. A re-examination of SADC's realities is required by reconsidering the existing approaches that have not yielded the desired results for the past three decades; else, the shared targets will remain a dream. We need to adopt new measures, including sanctions, to discourage noncompliance with regional agreements and protocols.

From its inception, SADC set out to promote economic development, democracy and human rights, enhance interstate relations, establish collective security mechanisms, and enhance regional stability. Meanwhile, the region continues to experience underdevelopment, political instability, and poor governance. Pfaff (1995) argues that a "Cooperative Euro-African trust organization" should be created, and African countries should be assigned "a defined authority" to govern them. However, political commitment is the only currency that can play a significant role in any integration scheme's success. Granting requisite powers to a regional institution is a fundamental requirement that forms a robust regional cooperation foundation. The success of a supranational SADC could be enhanced by learning from the experiences of other regional bodies like the EU. The EU experience testifies to several advantages of robust regional integration schemes. SADC should become an institution concerned about improving people's conditions from the standpoint of economic standards, human rights, security, and everyone's general well-being. The member states already made commitments to direct their policies towards creating favourable conditions for realizing the SADC treaty's aspirations

By looking at the enormous powers granted to the SADC Summit, we can see the SADC Treaty's weaknesses. As a result of the character of some regimes in the region, the dominance of individual authoritarian leaders in decision-making has undermined the efforts and objectives of the regional body. SADC must continue to strive for success despite all of its challenges. A vision and leadership are necessary for developing policies that move the SADC region away from its heavy reliance on primary commodity exports. It will largely depend on leadership quality in the region and the political will to initiate changes. Having strong leadership is crucial for preventing deterministic political economy forces. In order to achieve better outcomes, leaders need to drive scenarios that break with the status quo. The operationalization of all mechanisms and instruments adopted to mitigate the challenges must be guided by lessons learned from past experiences. SADC has now entered a new terrain to address the constraints that have inhibited regional integration, and these challenges are enormous.

The preceding discussion has also shown that regional integration can help move SADC member states from deplorable conditions towards development and stability. However, as the analysis has shown, replicating the EU's structural framework without creating a supranational mechanism will not make SADC a success. This book's arguments revolve around the idea that SADC can be made a supranational body to address structural challenges. The regional institution becomes a more efficient and effective organization better positioned to achieve the region's goals. With the Southern African states failing to uplift the citizens from the evils of corruption, authoritarianism, human rights violations, political instability, and absolute poverty, the book adopts the view that creating a supranational institution like the EU in Southern Africa could improve the welfare of the citizens and restore hope for the region's peoples.

RECs in Africa will continue to fail as long as the regional political elite remains the sole custodian of decision-making processes. As SADC consists of 16 countries characterized by poverty, fragility, and diverse political systems, reaching a consensus on governance issues would be difficult. A glimmer of hope can be seen in adopting instruments such as the SADC Tribunal, peace and security architecture, and the governance framework, including the SADC Principles and Guidelines Governing

Democratic Elections. For these institutions to succeed, they must adhere to the provisions that established them. The SADC member states must enhance these institutions to play a leading role in initiating, formulation, implementation, and adjudication of policy without any obstruction from member states.

Based on evidence from the EU, where the regional framework has allowed the European institution to establish instruments that have successfully managed the regional integration project while ensuring cohesion in implementing the agreements and protocols across the two regions. With respect to SADC, it is clear that the regional organization has not delivered results. SADC's member states have shown a limited willingness to part with some of their sovereignty, which is essential to the success of regional integration. As a result of inadequate enforcement and compliance mechanisms, most protocols, agreements, and decisions have been worthless. For the agreements that have been implemented, national states have taken extra measures to sidestep the agreements. That is what happened with the SADC Tribunal and the non-tariff measures to limit imports into the region. SADC is currently an intergovernmental organization, which limits its ability to grow into a fully integrated community.

In Southern Africa, regional integration has been limited to areas where member states can command consensus, according to the analysis. Despite the compelling evidence regarding the importance of a more profound regional integration, mainly since weak states characterize most Southern Africa due to economic and political factors, these conditions have persuaded member states to embrace an intergovernmental approach to regional integration. SADC has mainly played a political role rather than an economic one. To ensure greater convergence of regional aspirations, SADC leaders now need to engage in dialogue. At the very least, convergence should focus on a minimum set of standards that must be enforceable across the region, with those who don't comply face penalties and even suspension.

Despite being highly desirable, the current political climate makes it challenging to integrate numerous existing agreements into one inter-regional framework. In essence, the biggest challenge is to build bridges between member states and to bind member states to the treaties so that their future convergence is easier. Keeping the region from fragmenting further, whether in terms of political allegiances or integration goals, is paramount. Currently, trade policy, development strategies, and governance systems differ between SADC countries, making coordination tricky. Nevertheless, these circumstances should not be allowed to become permanent. As such, efforts must be made to reduce these differences while leaving the door open for the day when there is greater convergence. A precaution should also be taken to prevent extra-regional trade negotiations or initiatives obstructing future convergence. The trade agreement between South Africa and the EU is an excellent example.

Although regional integration has been pursued in Southern Africa for more than three decades, market integration is still lagging due to different factors, including duplication in regional memberships. Duplicating regional memberships demonstrates a lack of commitment among member states, which undermines regional cohesion. A majority of Southern African states are members of multiple regional institutions without any economic basis for membership. Despite the risk of economic convergence being undermined, these regional political institutions have helped enhance their legitimacy through their membership to multiple regional institutions. It is now becoming more evident that there has been discussion relating to the merger of SADC, EAC, and COMESA, eliminating this duplication and building a regional institution that makes more economic sense.

In summary, because the SADC area is experiencing armed conflicts, economic decline, and the disintegration of democratic institutions, realizing a fully functioning regional body that can make binding decisions for all states is crucial. Due to integration's primary objective of achieving political and economic convergence, SADC requires a political and economic system that integrates a supranational unit with unified policies and objectives. It is essential to develop a unified narrative encompassing a region's role in the international system and identify its diagnostic analysis and vision for its future. In terms of narrative, regional integration should undoubtedly be assigned a substantive role; otherwise, unresolved issues within SADC will continue to hinder the region's ability to cooperate on regional integration objectives. An integrated SADC region could help provide a degree of order at manageable levels.

A comprehensive historical account is provided in the analysis, highlighting the obstacles to regional integration and development in the SADC region and highlighting the need for a change in the strategy adopted and embraced by SADC in the last three decades. Overcoming these existing obstacles for regional integration presents SADC with a picture of hope for stability and human development success. However, the state and actions of the political elites are critical to the project's success or failure. We have seen that policymakers in Southern Africa cannot ignore the importance of a strong regional institution. Growing demand for collective responsibility for responding to security, social and economic pressures is likely further to increase economic and political significance in emerging economies. The experience of regional integration in Southern Africa stands in stark contrast to that of Europe. Reviving SADC's potential belongs to Southern Africans, the very people trapped in a deep ditch of political, economic, social, and security challenges.There is much work still to be done in integrating Southern Africa, as observed throughout the book. The structural problems of SADC have shaped the challenges faced by regional integration in Southern Africa. These problems have led to SADC member states remaining at the cooperation level with limited practical integration. Southern African states need a more competent regional institution with supranational powers to survive the anarchy in the international arena.

INDEX

REFERENCE

Abadie, A. (2004) Poverty, Political Freedom, and the Roots of Terrorism, National Bureau of Economic Research, Inc., NBER Working Papers: No. 10859.

Abbot, K.W. & Snidal, D. (2000) "Hard and Soft Law in International Governance", International Organization 54, No. 3

Abraham, K. (2000) The Challenges of Regional Integration for Development in Africa: Problems and Prospects Pan-African Economic Integration. Paper presented at the Conference on Economic Integration and Transboundary Resources Organised by the Ethiopian International Institute for Peace and Development (EIIPD), June, Addis Ababa.

Acemoglu, D. & Robinson J.A. (2012) Why Nations Fail: The Origins of Power, Prosperity, and Poverty", New York: Crown Business.

Acemoglu, D., Naidu, S., Restrepo, P., & Robinson, J.A., (2019) "Democracy Does Cause Growth", Journal of Political Economy, Vol. 127 (1)

[6] Adar, K. G.,(2005). „New Regionalism and Regional Reconstruction: The Case of the East African Community, in Politeia, Vol. 24 (1), Calgary: City of Calgary.

ADB (2013) Regional Cooperation and Integration in a Changing World, Manila: Asian Development Bank

Adedeji, A. (2002) History and prospects for Regional Integration in Africa, paper presented at The Third Meeting of the African Development Forum, on the theme of 'Defining Priorities for Regional Integration', Addis Ababa

Adelmann, M. (2003) Regionale Kooperation im Südlichen Afrika, Karlsruhe: Ernst Grässer

Adeniyi, O. Omisakin, O. Egwaikhide, F. and Oyinlola, A. (2012), "Foreign Direct Investment, Economic Growth, and Financial Sector Development in Small Open Developing Economies," Economic Analysis and Policy, vol. 42, No. 1, Amsterdam, Elsevier.

Adetula, V. (2004) Regional Integration in Africa: Prospects for Closer Cooperation between West, East and Southern Africa, Paper

presented at the meeting of IDASA/FREDSKORPSET Research Exchange Programme –Governance and Democracy.
Adetula, V. (2014) The Regional Integration and Quest for Peace and Stability in Africa, Evolutions, Vol 2, Issue 1.
Addison, T & Roe, A. (2018) Extractive Industries: The Management of Resources as a Driver of Sustainable Development, Oxford University Press, Oxford
Adler, E. and Barnett, M. (Eds.) (1998) Security Communities, Cambridge Studies in International Relations, Cambridge, Cambridge University Press.
Adler, E. (2000). Security Communities, Cambridge: Cambridge Univ. Press.
Adolfo, E. (2009) The Collision of Liberation and Post-Liberation Politics within SADC, A Study on SADC and the Zimbabwean Crisis, FOI, Swedish Defence Agency Research.
Adotevi, S. (1997) Cultural Dimensions of Economic and Political Integration in Real Lavergne (ed) Africa in Regional Integration and Cooperation in West Africa: A Multidimensional Perspective" IDRC, Canada
Aeby, M. (2018) Peace and Security Challenges in Southern Africa: Governance Deficits and Lacklustre Regional Conflict Management. Policy Note No 4. Geneva: The Nordic Africa Institute (NAI).
AfDB (2019) Financing Africa's Infrastructure: new Strategies, Mechanisms, and Instruments, African Development Bank Publication.
Africa Progress Panel (2013) Equity in Extractives: Stewarding Africa's Natural Resources for All.
African Center for Strategic Studies, (2016) The Role of Civil Society in Averting Instability in the DRC November 15, The Role of Civil Society in Averting Instability in the DRC
African Economic Community, (1991) International Legal Materials 1241
African Economic Outlook. (2012) Promoting Youth Employment in Africa, Geneva: International Labor Organization.
African Union (AU) Constitutive Act (2001)
African Union, (2003) Protocol on Amendments to the Constitutive Act of the African Union, Addis Ababa: Addis Ababa
African Union, (2004) Strategic Plan of the African Union Commission, Vol. 1: Vision and Mission of the African Union, Addis Ababa.

Available at http://www.africa-union.org/root/au/AboutAu/Vision/Volume1.pdf (accessed 10 December 2020).

Ahmad, M.H. & Ahmed, Q.M. (2014) Does the Institutional Quality Matter to Attract the Foreign Direct Investment? An empirical investigation for Pakistan: South Asia Economic Journal, Vol. 15 No. 1

Ahlquist, J.S. (2006) Economic Policy, Institutions, and Capital Flows: Portfolio and Direct Investment Flows in Developing Countries. International Studies Quarterly

Ahwireng-Obeng F & McGowan, P.J.(1998) Partner or hegemon? South Africa in Africa Journal of Contemporary, African Studies, 16 (1)

Akamatsu K (1961). A Theory of Unbalanced Growth in the World Economy. Review of World Economics, 86:

Akindele, R.A. (2003) ECOWAS: Good Governance and Sub-Regional Security in West Africa, in Akindele, R.A. (ed) Civil Society, Good Governance and The Challenges of Regional Security in West Africa AFSTRAG and Vantage Publishers, Ibadan

Aldolfo, A. (2009) The Collision between Liberation and Post-Liberation Politics within SADC, Swedish Defence Research Agency

Alesina, A. Ozler, S. Roubini, N. & Swagel, P. (1996) Political instability and economic growth, Journal of Economic Growth, 1 (2)

Alexander, J. S. (2014) The Rule of Law and Foreign Direct Investment in the Developing World. UC Irvine.

Alkire, S. (2002) Conceptual Framework for Human Security, Oxford, UK: Centre for Research on Inequality, Human Security and Ethnicity (CRISE Working Paper)

Allison, G. & Zelikow, P. (1971) Essence of Decision: Explaining the Cuban Missile Crisis.

Ametoglo, M.E., Guo, P. Wonyra, K.O. (2018) Regional Integration and Income Inequality in ECOWAS Zone, Journal of Economic Integration, Vol.33 No.3

Amos, S. (2010) Role of South Africa in SADC Regional Integration: The Making or Breaking of the Organization, The Journal of International Commercial Law and Technology, 5(3)

Annan, N (2014), Violent Conflicts and Civil Strife in West Africa: Causes, Challenges and Prospects. Stability: International Journal of Security & Development, 3(1)

Andresen, H. et al. (2001) Promoting Regional Integration in SADC, Reports and Working Papers No. 5/2001: German Development Institute (GDI), Bonn.

Ang, Y.Y. (2016) How China Escaped the Poverty Trap, Cornell University Press

Anglin, D. (1988) Southern Africa under Siege: Options for the Frontline States, the Journal of Modern African Studies, 26(4)

Aning, K. & Lartey, E.A. (2014) The Role of RECs in Peacebuilding in Africa: Past Experiences and the Way Forward. Cairo Policy Briefs,

Ansah, J. W. (2013) The political dynamics of regional integration in Africa: The Subjective Side. Global Advanced Research Journal of Social Science (GARJSS), 2(9)

Arndt, S.W. (2001) Offshore Sourcing and Production Sharing in Preference Areas, In Arndt, S.W. and Kierzkowski, H. (Eds), Fragmentation: New Production Patterns in the World Economy. Oxford: Oxford University Press.

Article 1.1.2, From SADCC to SADC, SADC Regional Indicative Strategic Development Plan

Arusha Declaration, 1967

Aryeetey, E (2000) Regional Integration in West Africa' (Paper Presented at A Policy Workshop organized by the OECD Development Center at the Graduate Institute of International Studies, Geneva 13 October 2000)

Asante, S.K.B. (1997) Regionalism and Africa's Development, Macmillan: London

Asiedu, E. (2002) On the determinants of foreign direct investment to developing countries: is Africa different? World Development, 30(1)

Asmus, Ronald. (2008) Europe's eastern promise: rethinking NATO and EU enlargement, Foreign Affairs

Aspinall, E. (2007) The Construction of Grievance, Journal of Conflict Resolution 51 (6)

AUC Chairperson, Report on current challenges (2011)

Auty, Richard. (1993) Sustaining Development in Mineral Economies: The Resource Curse Thesis, London, Routledge

Axline, A. (1994) The Political Economy of Regional Cooperation. Comparative Case Studies, London, Pinter Publisher.

Axelrod, R. & Keohane, R.O. (1985) Achieving Cooperation under Anarchy: Strategies and Institutions, World Politics, Cambridge University Press, Vol. 38(1)

Ayuk, E.T & Kabore, S.T. (2013) Wealth Through Integration: Regional Integration and Poverty-Reduction Strategies in West Africa Edited by International Development Research Centre Ottawa, Ontario, Canada

Azam, P. (1995) Development Policy for Africa: A Research Agenda, in Barthelemy J (ed.), Wither African Economies? Paris: OECD

Bach, D. (2009), Régionalismes, Régionalisation et Globalisation, in Mamoudou, Gazibo & Céline, Thiriot (eds.), Le Politique en Afrique: étatdes débats et pistes de recherche , Paris: Karthala

Bach, D. (2013) Thick Institutionalism vs Lean Integration: New Regionalism in Africa, Moore, C, (ed) in Integration and Social Cohesion: Perspectives from the Developing World

Baker, C. (2001). Revolt of the Ministers: The Malawi Cabinet Crisis, 1964-1965 London: I. B. Tauris

Baker, C. (2006) Chipembere: The Missing Years, Kachere, Zomba.

Baker, D.P. (2007) The AU Standby Force and the Challenges of Somalia, African Security Review. 16(2)

Balassa, B. and Stoutjesdyk, A. (1975) Economic Integration Among Developing Countries, Journal of Common Market Studies 14

Baldwin, R. (2003) Openness and growth: What is the Empirical Relationship? NBER Working Paper 9578

Baldwin, R. (2016) The World Trade Organization and the Future of Multilateralism, Journal of Economic Perspective

Ballentine, K., & Haufler, V. (2009) Enabling economies of peace: Public policy for conflict-sensitive business. New York: United Nations Global Compact.

Baptista, I. (2018a) Space and Energy Transitions in Sub-Saharan Africa: Understated Historical Connections. Energy Research & Social Science 36

Baptista, I. (2018b) Electricity Services Always in the Making: Informality and the Work of Infrastructure Maintenance and Repair in an African City. Urban Studies

Barefoot, D., Curtis, W. J., Nicholson, J. R., & Omohundro, R. (2018) Defining and Measuring the Digital Economy. Retrieved from https://www.bea.gov/system/files/papers/WP2018-4.pdf

Barnett, M. and Finnemore, M. (2004) Rules of the World: International Organisations in World Politics, Ithaca, USA, Cornell University Press

Barta, G., Kaufmann, D. & Stone, A. (2003) Investment Climate around the World: Voices of the Firms from the World Business Environment Survey. Washington, DC: World Bank.

Barwani, K., (2005) Regional Integration of the Gulf Cooperation Council Countries, Paper presented at Claremont: KIEP Conference on Political Economy of Regional Integration, 18 – 19 November

Bassou, A. (2017) Africa's Natural Resources and Geopolitical Realities, OCP Policy Center, Policy Brief 17/19

Basu, A. and Srinivisan, K. (2002) "Foreign direct investment in Africa: Some case studies" IMF Working Paper WP/02/61. International Monetary Fund, Washington, D.C

Bayart, J.F. (1993/1989) The State in Africa: the Politics of the Belly, Paris: Fayard.

Baylis, J. (2001) International and Global Security in the Post-Cold war era: In John Baylis and Steve Smith 2nd Ed. The Globalisation of World Politics an Introduction to International relations, Oxford University Press

Beckfield, J. (2006) European integration and income inequality. LIS Working Paper Series No. 447

Ben-David, D. (1993). Equalizing Exchange: Trade Liberalization and Economic Convergence. Quarterly Journal of Economics 108 (3)

Benassy-Quere, A. Coupet, M. and Mayer, T. (2007) Institutional Determinants of Foreign Direct Investment, The World Economy, 30 (5)

Bhagwati, J (1995) U.S. Trade Policy: The Infatuation With Free Trade Areas, in The Dangerous Drift to Preferential Trade Agreements (Jagdish Bhagwati & Anne O. Krueger eds., Aei Press

Bidwell, C. (1993) Maastricht and the UK, Public Affairs Consultants Europe Ltd

Bilal, S. (2007) Is the EU a Model of Regional Integration? European Centre for Development Policy Management (ECDPM)

Bilal, S. Byiers, B. & Vanheukelom, J. (2015) Political Economy Dynamics Matter most to Africa's Regional Integration, International Trade Forum 8 (2)

Bilder, R.B. (1992) International law in the new world orders: some preliminary reflections. Florida State University Journal of Transnational Law and Policy, 1 (1)

Bilder, R.B. (1997) Adjudication: International Arbitral Tribunals and Courts' in I. William Zartman and J. Lewis Rasmussen (eds.),

Peacemaking in International Conflicts: Methods and Techniques, Washington, D.C., United States Institute of Peace Press.
Bischoff, P. (2012) What has been Built in Twenty Years? SADC and Southern Africa's political and regional security structure, Strategic Review for Southern Africa. XXXIV, 2
Bischoff, P.H., Southall, R. (1999). The Early Foreign Policy of Democratic South Africa, in S. Wright (ed.), African Foreign Policies, Boulder, Colo.: Westview Press
Bischoff, P.H. (1998). Between general perceptions and aggregating identity: South Africa's advance of an African Renaissance. Paper presented at the Third Pan_European International Relations Conference, Vienna, 16 to 19 September
Biswaro, J.M. (2013). The Role of Regional Integration in Conflict Prevention, Management, and Resolution in Africa: The Case of African Union, FUNAG
Blizkovsky P., Grega L., Verter N. (2018): Towards a Common Agricultural Policy in Africa? Agriculture Economics, Mendel University, Czech Republic
Blomström, M. & Kokko, A. (1997) Regional Integration and Foreign Direct Investment: A Conceptual Framework and Three Cases. PolicyResearchWorking Paper 1750, World Bank, Washington, D.C
Blomström, M. and Kokko, A. (1998) Foreign Investment as a Vehicle for International Technology Transfer" in Giorgio Barba Navaretti, Partha Dasgupta, Karl G. Maler, and Domenico Siniscalco, eds., Creation and Transfer of Knowledge: Institutions and Incentives. Heidelberg and Berlin: Springer Verlag.
Bloom, N. (2009) The Impact of Uncertainty Shocks" Econometrica, 77 (3)
Bøås, M (2001) Regions and regionalization: A heretic's view in Regionalism and Regional Integration in Africa: A Debate of Current Aspects and Issues, Nordiska Afrikainstitutet, Uppsala
Bogland, K. Egnell, R. & Lagerstrom, M. (2008) The African Union-A Study Focusing on Conflict Management, Swedish Defence Agency
Boix, C. (2008) "Economic Roots of Civil Wars and Revolutions in the Contemporary World" World Politics 60:390–437.
Bollen, K.A. & Jackman, R. (1985) Economic and Noneconomic Determinants of Political Democracy in the 1960s." Research in Political Sociology
Braithwaite, K. & Greenidge, K. (2005), "Foreign direct investment and growth in Barbados", Bridgetown, Central Bank of Barbados

Brands, H. & Suri, J. (2016) History and Foreign Policy: Making the Relationship Work, in The Power of the Past: History and State Craft, Foreign Policy Research Institute

Brenton, P. Di Mauro, F. & Lücke, M., (1999) "Economic Integration and FDI: An Empirical Analysis of Foreign Investment in the EU and Central and Eastern Europe." Empirica 26 (2)

Breuning, M. (2007) Foreign Policy Analysis: A Comparative Introduction (New York: Palgrave Macmillan, 3.

Brock, L. (2004): Der erweiterte Sicherheitsbegriff: Keine Zauberformel für die Begründung ziviler Konfliktbearbeitung, in: Die Friedens-Warte 79 (3–4)

Brouthers, K. (2002) Institutional, Cultural and Transaction Cost Influences on Entry Mode Choice and Performance. Journal of International Business Studies, 33 (2)

Brown, C. & Ainley, K. (2005) Understanding International Relations, 3rc Edition, Palgrave Macmillan, Basingstoke

Bruno, R., et al. (2017) Economic Integration, Foreign Direct Investment and International Trade: The Effects of Membership of the European Union, Centre for Economic Performance, London School of Economics, London

Bryson, J.M. and Crosby, B. (1992) Leadership for the Common Good: Tackling Public Problems in a Shared Power World. San Francisco, Jossey-Bass

Buchanan, J. M., (1990). An American Perspective on Europe's Constitutional Opportunity, Cato Journal, 10(3)

Buhaug, H. & Gleditsch, K. (2008) Contagion or Confusion? Why Conflicts Cluster in Space. International Studies Quarterly 52

Burgess, R., Stern, N. (1993) Taxation and development, Journal of Economic Literature, 31(2)

Burgis, T. (2015) The Looting Machine: Warlords, Oligarchs, Corporations, Smugglers, and the Theft of Africa's Wealth, Public Affairs, New York

Busse, M. (2003) Democracy and FDI, HWWA discussion paper no. 216, HWWA, Hamburg

Busse, M. (2004) Transnational Corporations and Repression of Political Rights and Civil Liberties: An Empirical Analysis" Kyklos, 57 (1)

Busse, M. & Hefeker, C. (2007) Political Risk, Institutions and Foreign Direct Investment, European Journal of Political Economy, 23 (2)

Buzan, B. (2004) From International Anarchy to International Society? English School Theory and the Social Structure of Globalisation, Cambridge, Cambridge University Press

Cabrita, J. (1983) A South Africa Department of Foreign Affairs Document

Cabrita J.M. (2000) The Conflict with Malawi and Rhodesia. In: Mozambique. Palgrave Macmillan, London

Cadestin, C. & Fall, F. (2017), Effectiveness of Trade Policies in SADC Compared to other Regional Communities, OECD Economics Department Working Paper

Campos, N. Coricelli, F. & Moretti, L. (2015) "Norwegian Rhapsody: The Political Benefits of Regional Integration" CEPR Discussion Paper 10653

Candland, T. Finck, A. Ingram, H. and Poole, L. (2021) The Islamic State in Congo, Program of Extremism, George Washington University

Cardona, M., T. Kretschmer, and T. Strobel (2013) "ICT and Productivity: Conclusions from the Empirical Literature". Information Economics and Policy 25(3)

Carlsnaes, Walter (2002) Foreign Policy, in Walter Carlsnaes, Thomas Risse-Kappen, and Beth A. Simmons, Eds., Handbook of International Relations Thousand Oaks: Sage

Castel-Branco, C.N. (2014) Growth, Capital Accumulation and Economic Porosity in Mozambique: Social Losses, Private Gains. Review of African Political Economy 41(sup1)

Cawthra, G. (2008) Southern Africa: Threats and Capabilities, Africa Program Working Paper Series

Cawthra, G. (2010). The Role of SADC in Managing Political Crisis: The case of Madagascar and Zimbabwe. Published by Friedrich-Ebert-Stiftung Mozambique

Cederman, L.E. et al. (2011) "Horizontal Inequalities and Ethnonationalist Civil War: A Global Comparison." American Political Science Review 105(3)

Centre for Conflict Resolution (2012) Governance and Security Challenges in Post-Apartheid Southern Africa" CCR November Report

Cervenl, Z. (1977) The Unfinished Quest for Unity, London, Julian Friedmann Publishers Ltd

Chabal, P. & Daloz, J.P. (1999) Africa Works: Disorder as Political Instrument. James Curry, Oxford.

Charalambides, N. (2010). Addressing NTBs in regional goods trade in Southern African countries", Sustainable Commerce Consulting, Gaborone

Cheeseman, N. & Fisher, J. (2019) Authoritarian Africa: Repression, Resistance, and the Power of Ideas, African World Histories Oxford University Press.

Chigora, P. & Guzura, T. (2011) The Politics of the Government of National Unity (GNU) and Power-Sharing in Zimbabwe: Challenges and Prospects for Democracy, African Journal of History and Culture 3

Chingono, M. & Nakana, S. (2009) The Challenges of Regional Integration in Southern Africa". African Journal of Political Science and International Relations.3 (10)

Chiume, K. (1975) Kwacha: An Autobiography, East African Publication, Nairobi

Chowdhury, A., and Mavrotas, G., (2005). FDI and Growth: A Causal Relationship, United Nations University, WIDER, Research Paper No: 2005/25.

Cilliers, J. (1999) Building Security in Southern Africa, An Update on the Evolving Architecture, ISS Monograph Series No. 43 Nov.

Cilliers, J. (2004). Human Security in Africa – A Conceptual Framework for Review: Monograph for the African Security Initiative

Clapham, C (2001) The Changing World of Regional Integration in Africa. in C Clapham, G Mills, A Morner, and E Sidiropoulos, Regional Integration in Southern Africa: Comparative International Perspectives, South African Institute of International Affairs.

Clapham, C. (1998). African Guerrillas, Oxford: James Currey.

Cleaves, P. (1974) Bureaucratic Politics and Administration in Chile Berkeley: UC Press

Cockram G.M. (1970). Vorster's Foreign Policy, Pretoria and Cape Town Academia

Cohen, H.J. (1996) Conflict Management in Africa, CSIS Africa Notes 181

Collier, P. (1999) On the Economic Consequences of Civil War. Oxford Economic Papers, 51(1)

Clapham, C. (1996) Africa and the International System. The Politics of StateSurvival, Cambridge: Cambridge University Press.

Clapham, C. (1999) 'Boundaries and States in the New African Order', inDaniel C. Bach (ed.) Regionalization in Africa: Integration and Disintegration, Oxford: James Currey.

Clapham, C. (2001) ‚The Changing World of Regional Integration in Africa‘ in Clapham, C; Mills, G; Morner, A; and Sidiropoulos, E. Regional Integration in Southern Africa: Comparative International Perspectives, South African Institute of International Affairs, Johannesburg.

Cliffe, L & Rock, J. (1997) 'Identity Livelihoods and Post Conflict Recovery in Ethiopia and Eritrea' in Frederickson B and Wilson, F (eds), Livelihood, Identity and Instability Centre for Development Research, Copenhagen, Denmark

Collier, P (2000) Doing Well out of War: An Economic Perspective' in Berdal and Malone (eds) Greed & Grievances: Economic Agendas in Civil Wars, International Development Research Centre, Lynne Rienner

Collier, P. et al. (2003). Breaking the Conflict Trap: Civil War and Development Policy, Washington, DC, Oxford: World Bank and Oxford University Press UK

Collier, P. & Hoeffler, A. (2002) Greed and Grievance in Civil War, World Bank, Washington

Collier, P. (2007) The Bottom Billion: Why the Poorest Countries Are Failing and What Can Be Done About It, Oxford University Press, Oxford.

Collier, P. Hoeffler, A. & Söderbom, M. (2008) Post-conflict Risks, Journal of Peace Research, 45(4)

Collier, P. & Venables, A.J. (2008) Managing Resource Revenues: Lessons for Low-income Countries.

Collier, P. & Venables, A.J. (2008) Trade and Economic Performance: does Africa's fragmentation matter? ‘ Annual World Bank Conference on Development Economics, Cape Town, South Africa, June

Comte, P. (1962). Portuguese Africa and the Rule of Law: A Study of the Political, Economic and Social Situation of the African Population in the Portuguese Territories of Continental Africa. Commission of International Jurists

Constitution of the Republic of Ghana, 1992

Constitutive Act of the African Union

Cooper, C. A. & Massell, B.F. (1965) Toward a General Theory of Customs Union for Developing Countries, The Journal of Political Economy 73 (5)

Cooper, N. (2002). State Collapse as Business: The Role of Conflict Trade and the Emerging Control Agenda. Development and Change, 33(5)

Coser, L. (1967) Continuities in the Study of Conflict, New York Free Press
Cox, R. (1981) "Social Forces, States and World Orders: Beyond International Relations Theory". Millennium, Vol 10 (2)
Crocker, C. (2019) African Governance: Challenges and Their Implications, Hoover Institution, Winter Series, Issue 119
Dar-Hsin, C. Feng-Shun, B. & Chun-Da, C. (2005) The Impact of Political Events on Foreign Institutional Investors and Stock Returns: Emerging Market Evidence from Taiwan. International Journal of Business, 10 (2)
Darwin, C. (1845) Voyage of the Beagle, Journal of Researches into the Natural History and Geology of the Countries, 2nd edition, London: John Murray, Albemarle Street
Das, D.K. (1992) Outward-Oriented Industrialisation Strategy. In: Korean Economic Dynamism. Palgrave Macmillan, London.
Daude, C, & Stein, E. (2007) The quality of Institutions and Foreign Direct Investment. Economics & Politics
Davies, R. (1999) 'Building a new relationship in Southern Africa: The challenge facing South Africa's Government of National Unity', in Hettne B, Inotai A, & O Sunkel (eds), Globalism and The New Regionalism. Macmillan: London,
Davies, James C. (1962) Towards a Theory of Revolution. American Sociological Review 27(1)
DBSA (Development Bank of Southern Africa), (2015) 'DBSA infrastructure financing investment in SA', Presentation, Gallagher Estate, Midrand, 1 October
De Melo, J. and Tsikata, Y. (2014) Regional integration in Africa: Challenges and prospects. A contribution to the Handbook of Africa and Economics
De Mesquita, B.B. & Smith, A. (2010) Leader survival, revolutions, and the nature of government finance. American Journal of Political Science, 54(4)
De Waal, A. (2002) What is new in the New Partnership for Africa's Development? International Affairs, 78(3)
De Wilde, P., & Zürn, M. (2012) Can the Politicization of European Integration be Reversed? Journal of Common Market Studies
Decalo, S. (1992) The process, prospects and constraints of democratization in Africa. African Affairs 91 (10)
Dent, M.J. (1994) John Ngwiri, Head of the Civil Service: Servant of Malawi, 1930-92, Keele

Department of Foreign Affairs Strategic Plan (2004) Pretoria: Department of Foreign Affairs

DeRoche, A. (2016) Kenneth Kaunda, the United States and Southern Africa, Bloomsbury Publishing, London

Deutsch, K.W. Burrel, S. et al. (1957) Political Community and the North Atlantic Area: International Organization in the Light of Historical Experience, Princeton, Princeton University Press

Devlin, R. & Ffrench-Davis, R. (1999) Towards an Evaluation of Regional Integration in Latin America in the 1990s, The World Economy 22 (2)

Diamond, L. (1999) Developing Democracy: Toward Consolidation. Baltimore: Johns Hopkins University Press

Dieter H. (1997) 'Regionalisation in the Age of Globalisation: What Limits are there to Economic Integration in Southern Africa?" in Heribert Dieter (ed.) The Regionalisation of the World Economy and Its Consequences for Southern Africa, Africa?," Marisburg, Metropolis

Dieter, H. & Higgott, R. (2003) Exploring Alternative Theories of Economic Regionalism: From Trade to Finance in Asian Co-operation? Review of International Political Economy

Dinan, D. (ed.) (2000) Encyclopedia of the European Union, Boulder/London: Lynne Rienner

Dinka, T. & Kennes, W. (2007) Africa's Regional Integration Arrangements History and Challenges Africa's Regional Integration Arrangements: History and Challenges -ECDPM

Dirar, L.D. (2014) Rethinking and Theorizing Regional Integration in Southern Africa, 28 EMORY INT'L L. REV. 123

Dixit, A. & Pindyck, R. (1994) Investment under Uncertainty, Princeton University Press, Princeton, New Jersey

Dolan, C. and Schafer, J., (1997). Reintegration of Ex-Combatants in Mozambique: Manica and Zambezia Provinces, Refugee Studies Programme, University of Oxford.

Draca, M., R. Sadun, and J. Van Reenen (2007) "Productivity and ICT: A Review of the Evidence" The Oxford Handbook of Information and Communication Technologies, Mansell, R. (ed). Oxford University Press

Dreher, A. Gould, M., Rablen, M.D. et al. (2014) The Determinants of Election to the United Nations Security Council. Public Choice, 158 (1-2)

Du Toit, A. (1994) The Construction of Afrikaner Chosenness, in Hutchison, W.R. & Lehmann, H (eds). Many are Chosen: Divine Election and Western Nationalism. Minneapolis: Fortress Press.

Duffield, M. (2006) Human Security: Linking Development and Security in an Age of Terror, in S. Klingebiel (ed.) (2006): New Interfaces between security and development: Changing concepts and approaches, Bonn: German Development Institute (Studies 13)

Dunne, T. (2008) "Liberalism" in Baylis, J., Smith, S., Owens, P. (eds) The Globalization of World Politics – An introduction to International Relations. Oxford University Press, Oxford

Dunne, T. & Schimdt, B.C. (2008) "Realism" in Baylis, J. Smith, S. Owens, P. (Eds) 2008 The Globalization of World Politics – An introduction to International Relations. Oxford University Press, Oxford

Dzimba, J. (2001) A common sub-regional agenda for peace, human security and conflict prevention: A view from SADC, in Peace, Human Security and Conflict Prevention in Africa, Proceedings of the UNESCO-ISS Expert Meeting held in Pretoria, 23 - 24 July 2001.

Economic Commission for Africa, (1987) "Survey and Outlook for Industrial Growth in Africa" (mimeo) cited in Allison A. Ayida, Reflections on Nigerian Development Malthouse Press/Reinmann

Economic Commission for Africa (2010) Assessing Regional Integration in Africa IV: Enhancing Intra-African Trade

Economic Community of West African States (ECOWAS),(2001) Protocol A/SPI/12/01 on Democracy and Good Governance Supplementary to the Protocol Relating to the Mechanism for Conflict Prevention, Management, Resolution, Peacekeeping and Security, Dakar: ECOWAS Executive Secretariat

Edwin, Y., (2018), When Bullets Replace Ballots: The Role of SADC in Promoting Peace through Democratic Governance in Zimbabwe, Journal of African Union Studies, Vol. 7

Eilstrup-Sangiovanni, M. (2006) Debates on European Integration, Palgrave Macmillan: Basingstoke

Elbadawi, I. (1997) 'The Impact of Regional Trade and Monetary Scheme on Intra-Sub-Saharan African Trade' in A.Oyejide, I. Elbadawi and P.Collier (eds). Regional Integration and Trade Liberalization in Sub-Saharan Africa, Volume I: Framework, Issues and Methodological Perspectives. London: Macmillan.

Engel, U. and Porto, J.G. (2011) "The African Union's New Peace and Security Architecture: Towards an Evolving Security Regime?", in

Söderbaum, F, and R Tavares (eds), Regional Organizations in African Security. London: Routledge
Englebert, P. (2000) State Legitimacy and Development in Africa, Boulder, CO: Lynne Rienner
Englebert, P. Tarango, S. & Carter, M. (2002) Dismemberment and Suffocation: A Contribution to the Debate on African Boundaries, Comparative Political Studies 35
Erasmus, G. (2011) Is the SADC Trade Regime a Rules-based System? SADC Law Journal
Erasmus, G. (2012) What has Happened to the Protection of Rights in SADC? (TRALAC) Stellenbosch
Ernst H "International Integration: The European and the universal process," (1961)
Estache, A. (2006) Africa's infrastructure: challenges and opportunities. Paper presented at the high-level seminar organized by the IMF Institute and the Joint Africa Institute, Tunis, February 28 – March 1.
Eustace, A., and Fay, M. (2007) "Current Debates on Infrastructure Policy. "World Bank Policy Research Working Paper 4410, November.
Evans, M. (1984), The Frontline States, South Africa and Southern African Security: Military Prospects and Perspectives, Zambezi, XII
Ewusi S.K & Nelson C. 2015. "Traditional Justice System in National Recovery and Peacebuilding: The Case of Gacaca in Rwanda." In Ewusi SK (ed) Peacebuilding in Sub-Saharan Africa: African Perspectives. University for Peace, Africa Programme. Addis Ababa, Ethiopia.
Farole, T. & Winkle, D. (2014) Making Foreign Direct Investment Work for Sub-Saharan Africa: Local Spillovers and Competitiveness in Global Value Chains. The World Bank.
Fauvet, P. (1984) Roots of Counter-Revolution: The Mozambique National Resistance, Review of African Political Economy No. 29
Fawcett, L. (1995), "Regionalism in Historical Perspective" in Fawcett, Louise and Andrew Hurrell (eds.) (1995), Regionalism in World Politics: Regional Organization and International Order, Oxford: Oxford University Press
Fearon, J. & Laitin, D. (2003) Ethnicity, Insurgency, and Civil War, The American Political Science Review, 97(1)
Fernandez, R. (1997). Returns to Regionalism: An Evolution of Non-Traditional Gains from RTAs. NBER 5979

Fielding, D. (1996) Asymmetries in the Behaviour of Members of a Monetary Union: A Game-theoretic Model with an Application to West Africa, Journal of African Economies, 5(3)

Foell, W.S. et al. (2011) Household Cooking Fuels and Technologies in Developing Economies. Energy Policy 39, No 12

Foroutan, Faezeh and Lant Pritchett (1993) 'Intra-Sub-Saharan African Trade: is it too Little?', Journal of African Economies, 2(1)

Forum for Early Warning and Early Response (FEWER) (1999) Conflict and Peace Analysis Response Manual 2nd edition

Foster V & Briceño-Garmendia, C. (2015) 'Africa's Infrastructure: A Time for Transformation'. Washington DC: World Bank, 2010; Gutman J, Sy A & S Chattopadhyay, 'Financing African Infrastructure: Can the World Deliver?'. Washington DC: Global Economy and Development at Brookings, March.

Fourie, F.C. & Burger, P. (2017) How to think and reason in macroeconomics, 4th ed. Cape Town: Juta and Company Ltd.

Francis M. and Deng, et al. (eds) (1996) Sovereignty as Responsibility: Conflict Management in Africa, Washington, D.C: The Brookings Institution

Frankel, J.A. (1997) Regional Trading Blocs in the World Economic System. Washington, D.C.: Institute for International Economics

Fredrickson, G.M. (1981) White Supremacy: A Comparative Study in American and South African History. New York: Oxford University Press.

Freud, S. (1950) Beyond the Pleasure Principle, New York: Liveright.

Frey, B. & Eichenberger, R. (2001) Economic incentives transform psychological FREY, Bruno and Reiner EICHENBERGER, 2001. Economic Incentives Transform Psychological Anomalies, in Frey, B & Elgar (eds) Inspiring Economics, Cheltenham

Fusu, Kwasi (1990) Export Composition and the Impact of Exports on Economic Growth of Developing Economies, Economics Letters, Vol. 34

Galtung, J. (1996). Peace and Conflict Research in the Age of the Cholera: Ten Pointers to the Future of Peace Studies. International Journal of Peace Studies, 1(1)

Gambari, I. A. (1991) "Political and Comparative Dimensions of Regional Integration: the Case of ECOWAS". Atlantic Highlands: Humanities Press International.

Gani, A. (2007) Governance and Foreign Direct Investment Links: Evidence from Panel Data Estimations. Applied Economics Letters

Gathii, J. (2009) African Regional Trade Agreements as Flexible Legal Regimes, 35 N.C. Journal of International Law

Gazibo, M. & Mbabia, O. (2012), Reordering International Affairs: The Forum On China-Africa, Brazilian Journal of Strategy & International Relations

Cooperation, 1 Brazilian Journal of Strategy & International Relations

Gyandoh, S.O. (1990) Human Rights and the Acquisition of National Sovereignty, in Berting, J. et al. (ed.). Human Rights in a Pluralist World, Greenwood, Westport, CT, USA

Geddes, A. (2004) The European Union and British Politics Basingstoke: Palgrave Macmillan

Genest, M.A. (1996) Conflict and Cooperation: Evolving Theories of International Relations Belmont, CA: Thomson & Wadsworth.

Genna, G. & Hiroi, T. (2015) Regional Integration and Democratic Conditionality: How Democracy Clauses Help Democratic Consolidation and Deepening, Routledge

Gevisser, M. (2007) Thabo Mbeki: The Dream Deferred, Cape Town: Jonathan Ball

Ghana Constitution (1960) - University of Alberta

Gibb, R. (1998) "Southern Africa in Transition: Prospects and Problems Facing Regional Integration". In Journal of Modern Africa Studies, vol. 36 (2)

Gibb, R. (2006) Rationalisation or Redundancy: Making Eastern and Southern Africa's Regional Trade Units Relevant. Brenthurst Discussion Papers

Gibb, R. (2009).Regional Integration and Development Trajectory: Meta-theories, expectations and reality. Third World Quarterly Vol. 30, Number 4 (21), pp. 701-721. Development Studies, Vol. 43 (2)

Giliomee, H and Mbenga, B (2007) New History of South Africa, Cape Town: Tafelberg Publishers

Gilpin, R. (1987) The Political Economy of International Relations. New Jersey: Princeton University Press

Gilpin, R. (2001) Global Political Economy: Understanding the International Economic Order. Princeton: Princeton University Press

Gilson, J. (2005) New Regionalism? The EU and East Asia, in Regional Integration, Vol 27(3)

Ginkel, H.V. Court, J. & Van Langenhove, L (2003) Integrating Africa: Perspectives on Regional Integration and Development, ed. Ginkel, Hans van, Court, Julius and Van Langenhove, Luk (Tokyo: UNU/HQ
Gohou, G. & Soumare, I. (2012) Does Foreign Direct Investment Reduce Poverty in Africa, and are there regional differences? World Development, 40(1)
Goodhand, J. (2001) Violent Conflict, Poverty, and Chronic Poverty, CPRC CPRC, Working Paper 6
Görg, H. & Greenaway, D. (2004) Much Ado About Nothing? Do Domestic Firms Really Benefit from Foreign Direct Investment? in The World Bank Research Observer
Gray, J. (2013) Can Foreign Aid Buy Cooperation? External Funding and International Organisational Adaptation, University of Pennsylvania
Green, R and Seidman, A., (1967) Unity or Poverty?: The Economics of Pan-Africanism Penguin Books
Green, S. (2007) Crime, Victimisation and Vulnerability. In Walklate, S. (ed) Handbook on Victims and Victimology. London, Routledge
Grieco, J. (1995): The Maastricht Treaty, Economic and Monetary Union and the Neo-Realist Research Programme. Review of International Studies, Vol 21, No 1
Grindle, M. S. 2004. Good enough governance: poverty reduction and reform in developing countries. Governance, 17(4)
Grossmann, J. (2006) "EU Membership as a Tool for Democratization." Conference on Democracy-Promotion and International Cooperation, Denver
Haas, E.B. (1958) The Uniting of Europe, Stanford, Stanford University Press
Haas, E. B. (1958) The Century of Europe. Stanford: Stanford University Press.
Haas, E. B. (1968). The Uniting of Europe, Political, Social, and Economic Forces 1950- 1957, Stanford: Stanford University Press
Haas, E.B. (1970) The Study of Regional Integration: Reactions on the Joy and Anguish of Theorising. International Organisation, 24(4)
Habib, A. Muchie, M. & Padayachee, P. (2006) "African Integration and Civil Society: The Case of the African Union" Institut for Historie, Internationale Studier og Samfundsforhold, Aalborg Universitet.
Haftel, Y.Z. (2007) "Designing for Peace: Regional Integration Arrangements, Institutional Variation, and Militarized Interstate Disputes." International Organization 61(1)

Halpern, J. (1965) South Africa's Hostages: Basutoland, Bechuanaland and Swaziland, Baltimore, Penguin Books.

Hamada J. Haugerudbraaten, H. Hickman, A. and Khaykin, I. (2004) Country and Political Risk, Practical Insights for Global Finance, Sam Wilkin, Risk Books

Hammerstad, A. (2003) Defending the State or Protecting the People: SADC Security Integration at a Crossroads, SAIIA Report No. 39

Hammerstad, Anne (2005) Conclusion, in Hammerstad, A. (ed) People, states and regions, Building a collaborative security regime in Southern Africa, Johannesburg South African Institute of International Affairs

Hancock, K.J. (2010) 'What Role for the EU in the Southern African Customs Union (SACU): Advocate, Cajoler, or Bully?' Prepared for the Conference on the Diffusion of Regional Integration, Kellog-Forschergruppe, Transformative Power of Europe, Berlin

Hanggi, H. (2003) Regionalism through Interregionalism: East Asia and ASEM, in Regionalism in East Asia: Paradigm Shifting?, Liu, Fu-Kuo. and Regnier, Phillipe (eds), London, Routledge

Hanlon, J. (2004) Do donors promote corruption? The case of Mozambique, Third World Quarterly 25(4)

Hanlon, J. (2010) Mozambique: 'The War Ended 17 Years Ago, But We Are Still Poor', Conflict, Security & Development

Hanlon, J. ((1989) SADCC in the 1990s: Development on the Frontline, London: The Economist Intelligence Unit

Hansohm, D. et al. (2005) 'Conclusion: Progress towards integration in Southern Africa in 2004-2005', in Hansohm, D et al. Monitoring regional integration in Southern Africa Yearbook, vol 5, Windhoek: NEPRU.

Hasenclever, A., Mayer, M., & Rittberger, V. (1997) Theories of International Regimes, Cambridge University Press, Cambridge

Haskel, J. et al. (2007), "Does Inward Foreign Direct Investment Boost the Productivity of Domestic Firms?" Review of Economics and Statistics

Hausmann, R. Hwang, J. and Rodrik, D. (2007) What You Export Matters, Journal of Economic Growth, Vol. 12

Hawley, S. (2000) 'Exporting Corruption: Privatisation, Multinationals and Bribery' The Corner House June, Briefing No 19.

Heckscher, E. 1919. The effect of foreign trade on the distribution of income. Ekonomisk Tidskriff, 497–512. Translated as chapter 13 in

American Economic Association, Readings in the Theory of International Trade, Philadelphia: Blakiston, 1949
Hedges, D. (1989) Notes on Malawi-Mozambique Relations, 1961-1987, Journal of Southern African Studies, Vol. 15, No. 4 October
Hedges, D. (1999) História de Moçambique Volume Dois: Moçambique no Auge do Colonialismo, 1930-1961. Maputo: Livraria Universitária Universidade Eduardo Mondlane.
Hegre, H. (2003) Disentangling Democracy and Development as Determinants of Armed Conflict, Working Paper 24637, the World Bank
Heleta, S. (2019) Xenophobia and Party Politics in South Africa, Mail & Guardian, Sept 3
Helliwell, J.F. (1994) Empirical Linkages between Democracy and Economic Growth, British Journal of Political Science, 24 (2)
Hamerton-Kelly, R. (1993) Biblical Justification of Apartheid in Afrikaner Civil Religion, in Keulman, Kenneth (ed). Critical Moments in Religious History. Macon, Georgia: Mercer University Press.
Henderson, R. (1977) Relations of Neighbourliness - Malawi and Portugal, 1964-74 The Journal of Modern African StudiesVol. 15, No. 3
Hendrickson, D. et al. (Eds.). (2013). African Peace Facility Evaluation - Part 2: Reviewing the Overall Implementation of APF as an Instrument for African Efforts to Manage Conflicts on the Continent. EU, ADE & IBF Final Report.
Herbst, J. (2000) States and Power in Africa: Comparative Lessons in Authority and Control, Princeton and Oxford: Princeton University Press.
Hettne B, Inotai, A. Sunkel, O. (1999). Globalism and the New Regionalism, London: MacMillan Press Ltd.
Hettne, Björn (2005), 'Beyond the "New" Regionalism', New Political Economy, Vol. 10, No. 4
Hettne, B. & Söderbaum, F. (2000) Theorizing the Rise of Regionness, New Political Economy, Vol 5, No 3
Hettne, B. & Söderbaum, F. (2000) Regional Security in a Global Perspective, in Ulf Engel, João Gomes Porto and Doug Bond (eds.) Africa's New Peace and Security Architecture. Promoting Norms and Institutionalizing Solutions, Ashgate Vol. 1
Hettne, B. Inotai, A. & Sunkel, O. (eds) (1999) Globalism and the New Regionalism (Basingstoke: Macmillan).

Hexham, I. (1981) The Irony of Apartheid: The Struggle for National Independence of Afrikaner Calvinism against British Imperialism. New York and Toronto: Edwin Mellen Press.
Heywood, A. (1997) Politics. London: Macmillan
Hinsley, F. H. (1966) Sovereignty (London: Hutchinson).
Hirschman, A. (1971) A Bias for Hope: Essays on Development and Latin America. Yale University Press, New Haven and London
Hochschild, A. (1999) King Leopold's Ghost: A Story of Greed, Terror, and Heroism in Colonial Africa, Houghton Mifflin Harcourt, Boston, USA.
Hoeksma, J. (2021) The European Union: From Organisation 'Sui Generis' to Democratic Regional Organization, The Federal Trust for Education and Research
Hoffmann, B. (1999) Inside Terrorism, London: Victor Gollancz.
Hoffmann, S. (1966) Obstinate or Obsolete: The Fate of the National-State and the Case of Western Europe, Daedlus, 95(3)
Hoffmann, S. (1964) The European Process at Atlantic Cross Purposes. Journal of Common Market Studies 3, No. 1
Hoffmann, S. (1982) "Reflections on the Nation-State in Western Europe Today," Journal of Common Market Studies 20 (1-2)
Hoffmann, S. (1997) Significant Books of the Last 75 Years: Western Europe, FOREIGN AFF.
Holbraad (2003) Internationalism and Nationalism in European Political Thought, Palgrave Macmillan, USA
Holger, G. and Greenaway, D. (2004) On whether Domestic Firms Benefit from Foreign Direct Investment, The World Bank Research Observer, 19(2)
Holmner, M., & Britz, J. J. (2013) When the Last Mile becomes the Longest Mile: A Critical Reflection on Africa's Ability to Transform itself to become part of the Global Knowledge Society. Innovation: Journal of Appropriate Librarianship and Information Work in Southern Africa, 46
Horst, S. (1986) Why the Commonwealth mission to South Africa failed, The Christian Science Monitor
Horvath, R. (1972) A Definition of Colonialism, Current Anthropology, Vol. 13(1)
Hosny, A.S. (2013) Theories of Economic Integration: A Survey of the Economic and Political Literature. International Journal of Economy, Management and Social Sciences 2 (5)

Houston, G. (2013) Oliver Tambo and the Challenges of the ANC's Military Camps, Human Sciences Research Council (HSRC)
Huawei & Oxford Economics (2017) Digital Spillover: Measuring the True Impact of the Digital Economy, Retrieved from https://www.huawei.com/minisite/gci/en/digital-spillover/files/gci_digital_spillover.pdf
Hummels, D. (2007). 'Transportation Costs and International Trade over Time', Journal of Economic Perspectives, 21 (3)
Hurrell, A. (1995) Regionalism in Theoretical Perspective, in Fawcett, Louise and Hurrell, Andrew, Regionalism in World Politics, Regional Organization and International Order
Hveem, H. (1999), Political Regionalism: Master or Servant of EconomicInternationalization?, in Björn, Hettne; Andras, Inotai & Osvaldo, Sunkel(eds.), Globalism and the New Regionalism, London: Macmillan
Hyden, G. (11983) No Shortcuts to Progress, African Development Management in Perspective, Surrey, Biddles Ltd.
Ibrahim, M.O. (2008), Challenges of Regional Collective Security: Economic Community of West African States (ECOWAS) Standby Force: A Case Study. A Thesis Presented to the Faculty of the U.S. Army Command and General Staff College.
Iglesias, C.A. (2009). European Internal Market and Foreign Direct Investment, The Determinants of FDI, Regional and Sectoral Economic Studies
Ihonvbere, J.O (1981) Integration in a Dependent Regional Economy: Goals and Problems of the Economic Community of West African States (ECOWAS)," M.A Thesis, The Norman Paterson School of International Affairs, Carleton University, Ottawa.
Iqbal, Z. & Khan, M. eds., (1997), Trade Reform and Regional Integration in Africa Washington: International Monetary Fund.
International Crisis Group (ICG). (2007). 'Zimbabwe: A Regional Solution'. Africa Report 132, 18 September.
International Crisis Group (ICG). (2008) Negotiating Zimbabwe's Transition, Africa Briefing No 51, Pretoria/ Brussels, 21 May
Jabara, C. Harman, J. Corey, R., Gash, A., Pogany, P. & Brown, L. (1996) US Africa Trade Flows and Effects of the Uruguay Round Agreements. United States Trade Commission, Washington DC

Jackobeit C (2008) 'Overlapping Membership in COMESA, EAC, SACU and SADC: Trade Policy Options for the Region and the EPA Negotiations

Jackson, R. & Rosberg, C. (1982) 'Why Africa's Weak States Persist: The Empirical and Judicial Statehood', World Politics, 35 (1)

Jackson, R., & Rosberg, C. (1986) Sovereignty and Underdevelopment: Juridical Statehood in the African Crisis. The Journal of Modern African Studies, 24(1)

Janeba, E. (2002), Attracting FDI in a Politically Risky World. International Economic Review 43(4)

Jackson, R. (2000). The Dangers of Regionalising International Conflict Management: The African Experience. Political Science, 52 (1)

Jaster, R.S. (1983) A Regional Security Role for Africa's Front-line States: Experience and Prospects (London, The International Institute for Strategic Studies, Adelphi Paper

Jaumotte, F. (2004) Foreign Direct Investment and Regional Trade Agreements: The market Size effect revisited International Monetary Fund, Working Paper, Middle East and Central Asia Department

Jeffery, K. (1999) The Second World War, in The Oxford History of the British Empire, Volume IV: The Twentieth Century, edited by Judith Brown and Wm. Roger Louis Oxford, Oxford University Press

Jenkins, S. (1980) The Great Evasion; South Africa: A Survey, The Economist

Jenkins, S. (1981) The Survival Ethics: South Africa: A Survey, The Economist

Jenkins, S. (1983) 'Destabilisation in Southern Africa, The Economist

Jensen, N.M. (2003) Democratic Governance and Multinational Corporations: Political Regimes and Inflows of Foreign Direct Investment, International Organization

Jensen, N.M. (2008) Political Risk, Democratic Institutions, and Foreign Direct Investment. The Journal of Politics, 70(4)

Jinadu, L.A. (2009) Nkrumah, Pan-Africanism and the Future of Africa, in The African Union and the New Strategies for Development in Africa, eds. S. Adejumobi and A. Olukoshi (Dakar: CODESRIA

Johnsom, O.E.G., (1995) Regional integration in Sub-Saharan Africa, Journal of European Integration, 18(2-3)

Johnson, S. Ostry, J. & Subramanian, A. (2007) The Prospects for Sustained Growth in Africa: Benchmarking the Constraints, IMF

Working Paper WP/07/52, International Monetary Fund, Washington, DC.
Jundanian, B. (1974) 'Counterinsurgency in Mozambique', World Politics
Kacowicz, A. Bar-Siman-Tov, Y. Elgstrom, O. and Jerneck, M. (1998) Stable Peace among Nations, Rowman & Littlefield Publishers, New York
Kahnert, F. Richards, P. Stoutjesdijk, E and Thomopoulos, P. (1969) Economic Integration among Developing Countries. Paris: Development Center of the Organization for Economic Co-operation and Development (OECD)
Kaime K (2004) "SADC and Human Security: Fitting Human Rights into the Trade Matrix." Africa Security Review 13(1)
Kaldor, M. (2012) New and Old Wars Organised Violence in a Global Era, Third Edition Polity Press.
Kalenga (2012), Regional Integration in SADC: Retreating or forging ahead? Trade Law Centre (TRALAC), South Africa Isaacman and C. Sneddon, "Toward a Social and Environmental History of the Building of Cahora Bassa Dam," Journal for African Studies
Kalu, K. & Aniche, E.T., (2020) China-African Economic Relations: A Double-edged Sword for Africa. African Journal of Economic and Sustainable Development, 7(4)
Kaplan, R.D. (1994) The Coming Anarchy: How Scarcity, Crime, Overpopulation, Tribalism, and Disease are Rapidly Destroying the Social Fabric of our Planet, The Atlantic Available at: https://www.theatlantic.com/magazine/archive/1994/02/the-coming anarchy/304670/ (Accessed: 27 May 2021)
Kaplan, S. (2008) Fixing Fragile States: A New Paradigm for Development, Praeger Security International, West Port
Kastler, M. and Liepert, K. (eds.) (2008) Security and Development in Africa-Strengthening Conflict Prevention, Resolution and Management. Munich: Hanns Seidel Stiftung.
Kaufmann, D. Kraay, A. & Zoido-Lobaton, P. (1999) Aggregating Governance Indicators, World Bank Policy Research, Working Paper 2196.
Kaufmann, D. & Kraay, A. (2003) "Governance and Growth: Causality which way? Evidence for the World", brief World Bank, working paper

Kayuni, H, Banik, D. & Chunga, J. (2019) Malawi's Dream of a Waterway to the Indian Ocean May Yet Come True, The Conversation, November 5.

Keane, J., Massimiliano, C. & Kennan, J. (2010).Impediments to Intra-Regional

Keen, D. (2009) Economic initiatives to tackle conflict: Bringing politics back in (Occasional Paper 9). London: Crisis States Research Centre.

Keen, D. (2012) Greed and Grievance in Civil War, International Affairs, Volume 88 (4)

Keohane, R.O. & Nye, J.S.J. (1977) Power and Interdependence: World Politics in Transition, Boston: Little Brown

Keohane, R.O. (1984), After Hegemony: Cooperation and Discord in the World Political Economy. New Jersey: Princeton University Press.

Keohane, R.O. (1989) International Institutions and State Power, West View Press. Colorado.

Kesternich, I. & Schnitzer, M. (2010) Who is Afraid of Political Risk: Multinational Firms and their Choice of Capital Structure, Journal of International Economics, 82 (2)

Khadiagala, G. (1994) Allies in Adversity: The Frontline States in Southern African Security, 1973-1993. By Athens, OH: Ohio University Press

Khan M. (2004) State Failure in developing countries and strategies of institutional reform, working paper

Kida, N.M. (2014) Foreign Direct Investment Environment and Economic Growth, Acta Universitatis Danubius. Economica, Vol. 10 (4)

Kim, K. Et al. (2020) Benefits and Spillover Effects of Infrastructure: A Spatial Economic Approach, in Susanton, Bambang. & Park, Cyn-Young (eds) Future of Regional Cooperation in Asia and the Pacific, Asian Development Bank (ADB)

King, G. Keohane, R, Verba, S. (1994) Designing Social Inquiry: Scientific Inference in Qualitative Research, Princeton: Princeton University Press

King, G. & Murray, C. (2001) Rethinking human security, Political Science Quarterly 116(4) (Winter 2001–2002)

Kingsolver, J. (2011). Prospects for continued European political integration: A case study analysis of the United States and its implications for Europe. Bloomington: Indiana University.

Kisangani, E. (2012). Civil Wars in the Democratic Republic of Congo, 1960–2010, Boulder: Lynne Rienner Publishers.

Klingebiel, S. et al. (2008) Donor Contributions to the Strengthening of the African Peace and Security Architecture, German Development Institute / Deutsches Institut für Entwicklungspolitik (DIE), Bonn

Klochkovsky, L.L. (1984) The Economics of the Countries of Latin America, Moscow, Progress Publishers

Koponen, J. (1993). The Partition of Africa: A scramble for a mirage? Nordic Journal of African Studies, Vol. 2(1)

Kouassi, R. (July 2002) "The Itinerary of the African Integration Process: An Overview of the Historical Landmarks". African Integration Review Vol. 1(2)

Krapohl, S. (2010) Asymmetries and Regional Integration, University of Bamberg Working Paper.

Krapohl, S. (2019) Games Regional Actors Play: Dependency, Regionalism, and Integration theory for the Global South, Journal of International Relations and Development, 23 (4)

Krugman, P. R. (1991). The Move toward Free Trade Zones, Economic Review, 76 (6)

Kuziemko, I., & Werker, E. (2006) How Much Is a Seat on the Security Council Worth? Foreign Aid and Bribery at the United Nations, Journal of Political Economy, 114(5)

Kweka, J. & Mboya, F. (2004) Regional Integration and Poverty: The case of Tanzania. Report. Economic and Social Research Foundation

Kwok, C.C.Y & Tadesse, S. (2006). The MNC as an agent of change for host-country institutions: FDI and corruption. Journal of International Business Studies

Ladd, S. (2012), Emerging Africa Expected to See Rise in Investment, IMF Survey, 12 January.

Ladan, M. T., (1994). Introduction to ECOWAS Community Law and Practice: Integration, Migration, Human Rights, Access to Justice and Security, Zaria: Ahmadu Bello University Press.

Landsberg, C. (2004) "The Fifth Wave of Pan-Africanism", in Adekeye Adebajo and Ishmail Rashid (eds), West Africa's Security Challenges-Building Peace in a Troubled Region, Boulder: Lynne Rienner

Lamb, G. (2001) Putting Belligerents in Context, The Cases of Namibia and Angola, in Simon Chesterman (ed.) Civilians in War. Boulder: Lynne Rienner

Lamb, G. (2002) Debasing Democracy: Security Forces and Human Rights Abuses in PostLiberation Namibia and South Africa, in Yul Derek Davids/Christiaan Keulder/Guy Lamb/Joao Perreira/Dirk Spilker,

Measuring Democracy and Human Rights in Southern Africa. Uppsala: The Nordic Africa Institute (NAI Discussion Paper; no. 18)

Landau, Alice (1999), Multilateralism & Regionalism in International Economic Relations, in Daniel C., Bach (ed.), Regionalisation in Africa: Integration and Disintegration, Oxford: James Currey

Langhammer, R. J. Hiemenz, U. (1990). Regional Integration among Developing Countries, Opportunities, Obstacles and Options, Kiel Studies 232, Tübingen

Laporte, G. (1995). Regional Cooperation and Integration in Africa: An Agenda for Action at the National Level

Diamond, L. (2005) Building a System of Comprehensive Accountability to Corruption Control, The Center on Democracy, Development and the Rule of Law, Stanford University August

Leão, A. (2007) Different Opportunities, Different Outcomes – Civil War and Rebel Groups in Angola and Mozambique, Bonn, pp. 1.

Lebale. N. et al. (2009) Economic Development in Africa Report: Strengthening Regional Economic Integration for Africa"s Development, UNCTAD, Geneva

Lebow, R.N. (2007) "Classical Realism", in Dunne, T., Kurki, M. & Smith, S., International Relations Theories: Discipline and Diversity, Oxford University Press, Oxford.

Lederman, D. Mengistae, T. and Xu, L. C. (2013) Microeconomic Consequences and Macroeconomic Causes of Foreign Direct Investment in Southern African Economies, Applied Economics, 45(25), 3637-3649.

Lee, M. (2002) Regionalism in Africa: A Part of Problem or a Part of Solution, Numero Special, Vol. 9

Lee, M. (2003) The Political Economy of Regionalism in Southern Africa. Cape Town: University of Cape Town (UCT) Press

Lehmann, A. (1999) Country Risks and the Investment Activity of U.S. Multinationals in Developing Countries, IMF working paper, PP.133

Levine, R. 2005). Finance and growth: theory and evidence. Handbook of Economic Growth

Lewis, A. (1954) Economic Development with Unlimited Supplies of Labour, The Manchester School, Vol 22, Issue 2, pp. 139-191

Lewis, J. (2001). Reform and Opportunity: The Changing Role and Patterns of Trade in South Africa and SADC (p.22). World Bank, Washington

Lewis, P. (1996) From Prebendalism to Predation: the Political Economy of Decline in Nigeria, The Journal of Modern African Studies, 34 (1)
Li, Q. & Resnick, A. (2003) "Reversal of fortunes: Democracy, property rights and foreign direct investment inflows in developing countries" International Organization
Limão, N. & Venables, A. (2001) Infrastructure, Geographical Disadvantage, Transport Costs, and Trade, World Bank Economic Review 15 (3)
Lin, Justin (2011) Flying Geese, leading dragons and Africa's potential. The World Bank Blog.
Lin, J. Y. & Wang, Y. (2014) China-Africa Co-operation in Structural Transformation: Ideas, Opportunities, and Finances. WIDER Working Paper Series 046, World Institute for Development Economics Research (UNU-WIDER), Helsinki, Finland.
Lindberg, L. (1963) The Political Dynamics of European Integration. Stanford: Stanford University Press.
Linder, S. (1961) An Essay on Trade and Transformation. Uppsala: Almqvist and Wiksells.
Lodge, J. (1989c) European Political Cooperation: Towards the 1990s, in Lodge (ed), The European Community and the Challenge of the Future, London: Francis Pinter.
Longmire, P. (1990) "Land and Labour in the Namibian Economy" IN Konczacki, ZA, Parpart, JL, Shaw, TM (eds) Studies in the Economic History of Southern Africa, Vol 1; The Front Line states, Frank Cass Publishers.
Longo, R. & Sekkat, K. (2001) Obstacles to Expanding Intra-African Trade, OECD Technical Paper No. 169, Paris: OECD.
Ludo de Witte, (2001). The Assassination of Lumumba, London: Version, 2001, xvi.
Luo, Y. (2008). Political Risk and Country Risk in International Business: Concepts and Measures, in Oxford Handbook of International Business (2nd edition), ed. Rugman, A. M. 740- 764. Oxford: Oxford University Press
Mabey, N. & McNally, R. (1998) Foreign Direct Investment and the Environment: From Pollution Havens to Sustainable Development, A WWF-UK report, World Wildlife Fund, UK, July
Conchiglia, Augusta, (2017) Mysterious Death of Samora Machel, November, Le Monde Diplomatique, Translated by George Miller
Machiavelli, N. (1981) [1513] The Prince. Penguin, New York, USA.

Machlup, F. (1977) A History of Thought on Economic Integration, New York: Columbia University Press.
MacLean, S. (1999) Peacebuilding and the New Regionalism in Southern Africa, Third World Quarterly, 20(5)
MacQueen, N. (2002) United Nations Peacekeeping in Africa since 1960, 22.
Machlup, F., (1976) A History of Thought on Economic Integration, in Economic Integration Worldwide, Regional Sectoral, F. Machlup (ed.) Macmillan Press
Macuane, J.J. Buur, L. and Monjane, C.M. (2018) Power, conflict and natural resources: The Mozambican crisis revisited. African Affairs 117(468)
Madichie, N. (2011) Assessment of Middle East investments in Sub-Saharan Africa: Insights from the mobile telecom sector. Thunderbird International Business Review, 53 (1)
Magistretti, G. & Tabellini, M. (2019) Economic Integration and Democracy: An Empirical Investigation, Harvard Business School, HBS Working Paper Series
Mahembe, E. & Odhiambo, N. M. (2013) The dynamics of foreign direct investment in SADC countries: experiences from five middle-income economies. Problems and Perspectives in Management, 11(4), 35-45.
Makinda, S. M. (2002) Terrorism, Counter-terrorism and Norms in Africa. African Security Review, 15(3)
Malamud, A. (2003). Presidentialism and Mercosur: A hidden cause for a successful experience. In Finn Laursen (ed.) Comparative Regional Integration: Theoretical perspectives. London: Ashgate
Malamud, A. (2013). Overlapping Regionalism, No Integration: Conceptual Issues and the Latin American Experiences (EUI Working Papers RSCAS 2013/20).
Malan, M. (1999) The OAU and African Sub-regional Organisations: A Closer Look at the 'Peace Pyramid'. Institute for Security Studies, Occasional Paper
Mallampally, P. and Sauvant, K. P. (1999) Foreign Direct Investment in Developing Countries. Finance and Development, 36(1)
Mamdani, M. (2001) When Victims Become Killers: Colonialism, Nativism and the Genocide in Rwanda. Kampala: Princeton University Press.
Mandela, N. (1993). South Africa's Future Foreign Policy. In Foreign Affairs, vol. 72 (5)

Mandela, N. (1994) Long Walk to Freedom. London, Abacus

Mansfield, E. D. & Solingen, E. (2010) Regionalism. Annual Review of Political Science, 13 (1): 145-63.

Mansfield, E. D. & Reinhardt, E. (2003) Multilateral Determinants of Regionalism: The effects of GATT/WTO on the formation of preferential trading arrangements. International Organization, 57 (4)

Mansfield, E.D. & Reinhardt, E. (2003) Multilateral Determinants of Regionalism: The Effects of GATT/WTO on the Formation of Preferential Trading Arrangements. International Organization

Mapuva, J. (2013). Unpacking Regional Economic Integration Challenges Bedevilling the Sadc Regional Grouping: A Synopsis, Developing Country Studies Vol.3 (13)

Marinov, E. (2015). Economic Determinants of Regional Integration in Developing Countries, International Journal of Business and Management 3(3)

Martin, P. Mayer, T. and Thoenig, M. (2012) The Geography of Conflicts and Regional Trade Agreements, American Journal: Macroeconomics, 4(4)

Marx, K. and Engels, F. (2010/1848) Manifesto of the Communist Party, Marxists Internet Archive

Masuch, K. Moshammer, E. and Pierluigi, B. (2016) Institutions, Public Debt and Growth in Europe, European Central Bank, Frankfurt am Main (ECB Working Paper Series

Mattli, W. (1999) The Logic of Regional Integration: Europe and Beyond (Cambridge: Cambridge University Press).

Maurice & Hoekman (2002) Benefiting from Regional Integration, in Development, Trade and the WTO, Washington DC, The World Bank

Mauro, P. (1995). Corruption and Growth, Quarterly Journal of Economics, 110 (3)

Mayall, J. (1970). Malawi's Foreign Policy, The World Today, vol. 26 (10)

Mazower, M. (1998) Dark Continent: Europe's Twentieth Century, Bantam Books, New York

Mbeki, M. (2005) Perpetuating Poverty in Sub-Saharan Africa: How African Political Elites Undermine Entrepreneurship and Economic Development, London: International Policy Press

McCarthy, C. (1999). Polarised Development in a SADC Free Trade Area, South African Journal of Economics, 67(4)

McCarthy, C. (2007). Is African Economic Integration in Need of a Paradigm Change? Thinking out of the Box on African Integration, in

Bsl, A.et al. (eds), Monitoring Regional Integration in Southern Africa Yearbook Volume 7. Stellenbosch: tralac, Konrad-Adenauer-Stiftung and NEPRU.
McKinsey & Company (2020) Solving Africa's Infrastructure Paradox
Mearsheimer, J. (1995). The False Promise of International Institutions," in International Security, 19 (3)
Mearsheimer, J. (2007). Structural Realism", in Dunne, T., Kurki, M. and Smith, S., International Relations Theories: Discipline and Diversity, Oxford University Press, Oxford
Melber, H. (2004) Challenges to regional integration: The Case of SADC, News From the Nordic Africa Institute
Meyns, P. (2000). Conflict and Development in Southern Africa-Series: Basic Knowledge Politics Vol 27
Michel, S. (2012) European Integration Theories and African Integration Realities. Leiden University.
Mistry, P.S. (2000) Africa's Record of Regional Cooperation and Integration, African Affairs
Mitrany, D. (1966). A Working Peace System" Chicago: Quadrangle Books
Mitrany, D. (1975). "Prospects of Integration: Federal or Functional" in Groom, A.J.R and P. Taylor (eds). Functionalism: Theory and Practice in International Relations. London: University of London Press.
Mittelman, J. (1994). The Globalization Challenge: Surviving at the Margins. Third World Quarterly, Vol 15 (3)
Mittelman J, Falk R (2000) Global hegemony and regionalism. In Regionalism in the Post-Cold War World, S Calleya (Ed), Burlington: Ashgate.
Mlambo, A. S. (2000). Zimbabwe Migration up to 1990: A Historical Overview, in Crush, J & Tevera, D (eds). Zimbabwean Migration
Moravcsik, A. (1991): Negotiating the Single European Act. In Keohane and Hoffmann (eds.) The New European Community. Decision Making and Institutional Change, Westview Press, Boulder.
Moravcsik, A. (1993) Introduction: Integrating International and Domestic Theories of International Bargaining, in Jacobson, E.H.K. and Putman, R.D. [eds.], DoubleEdged Diplomacy. Berkeley: University of California Press
Moravcsik, A. (1993) Preferences and Power in the European Community: A Liberal Intergovernmentalist Approach, Volume 31, No. 4.
Moravcsik, A. (1998) The Choice for Europe: Social Purpose and State Power from Messina to Maastricht. Cornell University Press

Morgenthau, H (1993). Politics among Nations McGraw Hill, Boston MA

Morris, M. (1974) Armed Conflict in Southern Africa: A Survey of Regional Terrorism from their Beginning to the Present with a Comprehensive Examination of the Portuguese Position. Cape Town: Jeremy Spence.

Morrison, D.G, Stevenson, H. (1971). Political instability in independent black Africa: More Dimensions of Conflict Behavior within Nations, Journal of conflict resolutions, Sage Journals

Morrison, D.G et al. (1989) Black Africa: A Comparative Handbook, London, MacMillan Press

Müller, J. A. (2012). The Inevitable Pipeline Into Exile. Botswana's Role in the Namibian Liberation Struggle, Basel, Switzerland: Basler Afrika Bibliographien Namibia Resource Center and Southern Africa Library.

Muller, R. (2004) War, Religion, and White Supremacy in Comparative Perspective: South Africa and the American South. Verbum Et Ecclesia, Vol 25

Murdoch, J. & Todd, S. (2002). Economic Growth, Civil Wars and Spatial Spillovers, Journal of Conflict Resolution 46(1)

Murithi, T. (2005) The African Union: Pan-Africanism, Peacebuilding and Development, London: Ashgate Publishers

Murithi, T. (2013) Conclusion, in K. Aning & H. Lulie, eds. The African Union Peace and Security Council: A Five-year Appraisal. ISS Monograph no. 187. Pretoria: Institute for Security Studies.

Mutambara, T.E. (2001) The Nature of Economic Integration and Co-operation within the Southern African Region and a Survey of Economic Benefits to the Member States. Unpublished Master of Arts dissertation, Rhodes University, Grahamstown

Mutharika, B. (1972) Towards Multinational Economic Cooperation in Africa, Praeger, New York

Mwanasali, M. (2008) From Non-interference to Non-indifference: The Emerging Doctrine of Conflict Prevention in Africa, in Akokpari, A et al. (eds), The African Union and its Institutions. Auckland Park: Fanele.

Moyane, D. (2015). Mystery Still Surrounds Samora Machel's Death, City Press

Nagar, D. (2020). Politics and Pan-Africanism: Diplomacy, Regional Economies and Peace-building in Contemporary Africa, Bloomsbury Publishing, London

Narsey, W. (2004) 'PICTA, PACER, and EPAs: Weaknesses in Pacific Island Countries' Trade Policies', Pacific Economic Bulletin, 19(3)

Nathan, L. (2002). Organ Failure: A Review of the SADC Organ on Politics, Defence and Security. In Laakso (ed.) Regional Integration for Conflict Prevention and Peace Building in Africa, Ministry for Foreign Affairs, Department for International Development Cooperation

Nathan, L. (2004). The Absence of Common Values and Failure of Common Security in Southern Africa, 1992-2003. Working Paper No. 50, London: Crisis States Programme/London School of Economics.

Nathan, L. (2012). Community of Insecurity: SADC's struggle for peace and security in Southern Africa. London, United Kingdom: Ashgate: Ashgate Publishing Limited.

Nathan, L. (2013). African Solutions to African Problems: South Africa's foreign policy. SAFPI Policy Brief No 51.

Nathan, L. (2013) Synopsis of Community of Insecurity: SADC's struggle for peace and security in southern Africa, African Security Review, vol.22 (3)

Nathan, L. (2013) How should the Peace and Security Performance of SADC be Evaluated? African Security Review, 22(3):201-209.

Nathan, L. (2016). Community of Insecurity: SADC's Struggle for Peace and Security in Southern Africa, Routledge

Nathan, L. (2010b) The Peacemaking Effectiveness of Regional Organisations, Crisis States Research Centre, Working Paper no. 81, October

Ndomo, A. (2009) Regional Economic Communities in Africa - A Progress Overview, Study Commissioned by GTZ, Nairobi

Ndongko, W.A. (1995) Introduction. In W .A. Ndongko (ed.) Economic Cooperation and Integration in Africa, CODESRIA Book Series

Ndikumana, L. & Verick, S. (2008) The Linkages between FDI and domestic Investment: Unravelling the developmental impact of foreign investment in Sub-Saharan Africa. Development Paper series[1]Institute for the Study of Labor (IZA). No 3296.

Newitt, M. (1981) Portugal in Africa: The Last Hundred Years, London: C. Hurst & Co

Newitt, M. (1995) A History of Mozambique, London: C. Hurst & Co.

Newman, C. et al. (2016) Made in Africa: Learning to Compete. Brooking Institution Press, Washington, DC

Niebel, T. (2014) ICT and Economic Growth - Comparing Developing, Emerging and Developed Countries, Centre for European Economic Research, Discussion Paper No. 14-117

Niemann, M. (1993) Diamonds Are a State's Best Friend: Botswana's Foreign Policy in Southern Africa. Africa Today, Vol. 40, No. 1, Botswana: Achievements and Challenges. 1st Qtr

Nkrumah, K. (1972). Axioms (London: Panaf).

North, D.C. (1991) Institutions, Institutional Change and Economic Performance; Cambridge University Press: Cambridge, UK.

Ntloedibe, E.L., (1981) "The Position of South Africa" in The Decolonization of Africa: Southern Africa and the Horn of Africa, The UNESCO Press, France

Nujoma, S (2001) Where Others Wavered, Panaf Books, Bedford

Nye, J.S. (1970) Comparing Common Markets: A Revised Neo-Functionalist Model' International Organization, Volume 24 (4)

Nzewi, O. (2011) Africa's Regional Integration: a Reflection on Grand Theory, Department of Public Administration, University Fort Hare

Nzongola-Ntalaja, G. (2002) The Congo from Leopold to Kabila: A People's History, Zed Books, London

O'Connell, S. (1997). Macroeconomic Harmonization, Trade Reform and Regional Trade in Sub-Saharan Africa, in Ademola, Ibrahim Elbadawi and Paul Collier (eds) (1997). Regional Integration and Trade Liberalization in Sub-Saran Africa, London: Macmillan Ltd.

OECD. (2012) Attracting Foreign Direct Investment for Development, Paper presented at the Global Forum on International Investment, Shanghai, China

O'Gorman, E. (2011) Conflict and Development, London and New York: Zed Books.

O"Neill, M. (1996) The Politics of European Integration, A Reader. London: Routledge

Odén, B. (1996a) Regionalization in Southern Africa. World Development Studies 10, WIDER. The United Nations University, Helsinki

Oghogbo, O. (2007). 'Dressing ECOWAS in a new garb' The Guardian (Nig) 4 April 16

Ohlin, B. (1933) Interregional and International Trade. Harvard Economic Studies. Vol. XXXIX. Harvard University Press; London: Humphrey Milford.

Ohmae, K. (1990) The Borderless World, London: Collins

Okafor, C. Ujah, N. Elkassabgi, A. and Ajalie, W. (2011) Democracy and FDI Inflow: Evidence of discordance in Sub-Saharan Africa, International Research Journal of Finance and Economics, 63

Okem, A. & Asuelime, L. (2015) An Insight into South Africa's Xenophobia: Impacting on Africa's Integration. Journal of African Union Studies, 4(2/3)

Okoyo, M. (1977 Africa and Political Stability, Africa, No. 74

Olaosebikan, A. J. (2011) Kwame Nkrumah and the proposed African Common Government, African Journal of Political Science and International Relations, 5(4)

Olney, W. (2010) A Race to the Bottom? Employment Protection and Foreign Direct Investment, Journal of International Economics, Elsevier, vol. 91(2)

Olson, M. (1982) The Rise and Decline of Nations, New Haven, Yale University Press.

Omeje, K. (2005), Youths, Conflicts and Perpetual Instability in Nigeria; African Renaissance

Open Society Initiative for Africa (OSISA) (n.d) Inequality in Southern Africa: Options for Redress, Policy Brief.

Oppenheimer, J. (2012) Principles of Politics: A Rational Choice Theory Guide to Politics and Social Justice, Cambridge: Cambridge University Press, 15.

Organisation of African Unity (1963) OAU Charter, Addis Ababa: African Union

Organization for Economic Co-operation and Development (OECD) (2005)

Osakwe, P. (2015) Exports, Diversification and Employment in Africa, Presentation at the DESA/ILO Expert Meeting on the Implementation of the Second United Nations Decade for the Eradication of Poverty Addis Ababa

Ostergaard, T. (2003) SADC: A Political and Economic Survey, Ministry of Foreign Affairs, Denmark, 1990, p.51; Lee MC, The Political Economy of Regionalism in Southern Africa, Boulder CO: Lynne Rienner

Oxfam, IANSA and Saferworld (2007) Africa's Missing Billions [date of use 27 Sep 2020]

Packer, C.; Rukare, D. (2002) The New African Union and Its Constitutive Act, The American Journal of International Law, Vol 96 (2)

Pain, R. (2003) Old Age and Victimisation, in Davies, P., Francis, P. & Jupp, V. (eds) Victimisation Theory and Policy. London, Palgrave

Paiva, P. & Gazel, R. (2003) Mercosur: past, present and future. Nova Economica, Belo Horizonte, 13 (2)

Pakenham, T. (1992). The Scramble for Africa: White Man's Conquest of the Dark Continent from 1876 to 1912, Avon Books, New York

Palley, T. (2011). The Rise and Fall of Export-led Growth, New York: New America Foundation

Palmer, N. (1991) The New Regionalism in Asia and the Pacific. Lexington, MA, Lexington Books

Panusheff, E. (2003) Economic Integration in the European Union, Nekst PH, Sofia

Paterson, M. (2012) The African Union at Ten: Problems, Progress and Prospects, International Colloquium Report (August 30 -31) The Centre for Conflict Resolution, Cape Town/ Friedrich Ebert Stiftung, Berlin.

Paus, E. & Gallagher, K. (2008) Missing Links: Foreign Investment and Industrial Development in Costa Rica and Mexico." Studies of Comparative International Development 43 (1)

Peng, M.W. Wang, D.Y.L. & Jiang, Y. (2008) An Institution-based View of International Business Strategy: A Focus on Emerging Economies. Journal of International Business Studies, 39

Pentland, C. (1976) International Organisations, in Rosenau, J.N. Thompson, K.W. & Boyd, G. (eds), World Politics: An Introduction, New York, The Free Press

Peter-Berries, C. (2000). Regionale Integration und Kooperation in Afrika südlich der Sahara, Fallstudie Southern Africa Development Community (SADC), Harare

Peters-Berries, C. (2010). Regional Integration in Southern Africa: A Guidebook. Bonn: Invent

Petersson, L. (2003). Production Fragmentation and Specialisation with Special Reference to SADC Textile and Clothing Industry, South African Journal of Economics, 71(5)

Pevehouse, J.C. (2005) Democracy from Above: Regional Organisations and Democratisation, University of Wisconsin, Madison

Pfaff, W. (1995) A New Colonialism: Europe must go into Africa, Foreign Affairs 2-6

Phimister, I. (2008) The Making and Meanings of the Massacres in Matabeleland", Development Dialogue, no. 50, December

Phiri, K. M., (2000) A case of revolutionary change in contemporary Malawi: The Malawi Army and the Disarming of the Malawi Young Pioneers, Journal of Peace, Conflict and Military Studies

Pointing, S. & Whyte D, (2012) Counterterrorism and State Political Violence, Routledge

Polachek, S. Seigle, C. & Xiang, J. (2012) Globalization and international conflict: Can FDI increase peace? Background Paper, Washington, DC, World Bank

Posner, D. & Young, D. (2007) The Institutionalization of Political Power in Africa, in Journal of Democracy, 18 3

Pourtier, R. (2012) Natural Resources and Conflicts in Sub-Saharan Africa) Bulletin de l'Association de Geographes

Powell, K. (2005) The African Union's Emerging Peace and Security Regime: Opportunities and Challenges for Delivering on The Responsibility to Protect", The North-South Institute

Pecht, M. (2006) China's Electronics Industry: The Definitive Guide for Companies and Policy Makers with Interests in China, New York: William Andrew Publishing

Press release issued by the Botswana Ministry of Foreign Affairs, Gaborone, 8 August 2003.

Protocol on Politics, Defence and Security Co-operation

Przeworski, A. (1999). Minimalist Conception of Democracy: A Defense. In Ian Shapiro and Casiano Hacker-Cordon (eds). Democracy's Value. Great Britain: Cambridge University Press

Quashgab, E.K. (1997). Human Rights and Integration in Real Lavergne ed Regional Integration in West Africa: A Multidimensional Perspective, Africa World Press/International Development Research Centre

Ratala, E. (2008) Interview with Rear. Adm Head of Joint Operations Division, 21 February, Thamba Tswane

Ravenhill, J. (1985). Collective Clientelism: The Lome Conventions and North-South Relations, Columbia University Press, New York

Record of SADC Summit held in Blantyre, Republic of Malawi 8 September 1997.

Rehn, E. (2003) Excessive Reliance on the Use of Force does not Stop Terrorism, In T. Hoeksema and J. ter Laak (eds) Human Right and Terrorism. Holland NHC/OSCE

Reiterer, M. (2006) Interregionalism as a New Diplomatic Tool: The EU and East Asia, European Foreign Affairs Review, vol. 11

Ricardo, D. (1971). Principles of Political Economy and Taxation (Harmondsworth: Penguin).

Robinson, D. (2006) Curse on the Land: A History of the Mozambican Civil War, PhD thesis presented at University of Western Australia

Robinson, P. (1996) 'Potential Gains from Infrastructural and Natural Resource Investment Coordination in Africa', in J. J. Teunissen (ed). Regionalism and the Global Economy: The Case of Africa. The Hague: FONDAD.

Rodney, W. (1972) How Europe Underdeveloped Africa, London: Bogle-L'Ouverture and Dar es Salaam, Tanzania Publishing House.

Rodrik, D. (2000) Institutions for High-Quality Growth: What They Are and How to Acquire Them." Studies in Comparative International Development 35(3)

Rodrik, D. (2001) The Global Governance of Trade as if Development Really Mattered, United Nations Development Programme.

Rodrik, D. (2011): The Globalization Paradox: Democracy and the Future of the World Economy. New York - London: W. W. Norton and Company.

Rodrik, D. (2016) Premature Deindustrialisation," Journal of Economic Growth, Vol. 21 (1)

Rogoff, K. & Reinhart, C. (2003) FDI to Africa: The role of price stability and currency instability, IMF Working Paper WP/03/10. International Monetary Fund, Washington, D.C

Rosamond, B. (2000). Theories of European Integration, New York: St. Martin's Press. Palgrave

Rosamond, B. (2005). The uniting of Europe and the foundation of EU studies: revisiting the neo-functionalism of Ernst B. Haas, in Journal of European Public Policy, Vol. 12 (2)

Ross, M. L. (2004). What do we know about natural resources and civil war? Journal of Peace Research, 41(3), 337-356.

Ross, M.L. (2015) What Have We Learned About the Resource Curse? Annual Review of Political Science, Vol. 18

Rotich, J. (2012) Overview of the Process toward the EAC Political Federation, Arusha, EAC

Ruane, F. & Görg, H. (2001) Globalization and Fragmentation: Evidence for the Electronics Industry in Ireland, in Arndt, S.W. and Kierzkowski, H. (eds), Fragmentation: New Production Patterns in the World Economy. Oxford: Oxford University Press. pp. 144-164.

Ruggie, J. (1992) Multilateralism: The Anatomy of an Institution. International Organization, no. 3, The World Trade Organization (WTO)

Rugumamu, S. (2004) Africa's Search for Regional Cooperation and Integration in the 21st Century. ACBF Working Paper ACBFWP/03/2004, The African Capacity Building Programme.

Rupiya, M. (2005) The Odd Man Out: A History of the Malawi Army Since July 1964. In Rupiya, M. (ed.), Evolutions & Revolutions: A Contemporary History of Militaries in Southern Africa, Pretoria: Institute for Security Studies.

Ruprah, I.J. and Sierra, R. (2016) Engine of Growth? The Caribbean Private Sector Needs More than an Oil Change, Washington, DC: Inter- American Development Bank.

Sachs, J.D. and Warner, A.M. (1995) Natural Resource Abundance and Economic Growth, National Bureau of Economic Research, NBER Working Paper No. 5398

SADC Mutual Defence Pact, Articles 7 and 8

SADC Parliamentary Forum, (2000) SADC Parliamentary Forum Strategic Plan (2000–2005). Windhoek: SADC Parliamentary Forum.

SADC Parliamentary Forum (2004) SADC Parliamentary Forum Constitution, Windhoek: SADC Parliamentary Forum,

SADC Barometer (2005), Evaluation Progress, March (Issue 8), Braamfontein: South African Institute of International Affairs

SADC, (2001), Protocol on Politics, Defence and Security Co-operation Gaborone: Botswana.

SADC Secretariat, 'Terms of Reference for the SADC Sector on Political Cooperation, Democracy, Peace and Security: Meeting of SADC Ministers Responsible for Foreign Affairs, Defence and SADC Affairs'

SADC's Uncommon Approach to Common Security, 1992-2003, September 2006. Journal of Southern African Studies 32 (3)

SADC Parliamentary Forum Strategic Plan, (2006) www.sadcpf.org

Sako, S. (2006) Challenges Facing Africa's Regional Economic Communities in Capacity Building. The African Capacity Building Foundation, Paper No. 5

Salehyan, I. & Gleditsch, K. (2006) Refugees and the Spread of Civil War, International Organization 60(2)

Samuelson, P.A. (1948) Economics: An Introductory Analysis, New York: McGraw-Hill Company

Saul, J. & Leys, C. (2003) Truth, Reconciliation, Amnesia, The 'ex-Detainees' Fight for Justice, in Henning Melber (ed.), Re-examining Liberation in Namibia, Political Culture since Independence, Uppsala: The Nordic Africa Institute

Saurombe, A. (2010) The role of South Africa in SADC regional integration: the making or breaking of the organization, Journal of International Commercial Law and Technology, Vol. 5 Issue 3. 2010

Saurombe, A. (2012) The Role of SADC Institutions in Implementing SADC Treaty Provisions Dealing with Regional Integration, Potchefstroom Electronic Law Journal, Vol. 15 (2)

Schiff, M. & Winters L. A. (2003) Regional integration and development, Washington DC: World Bank and Oxford University Press.

Schmitter, P. (1971) A Revised Theory of Regional Integration, in Lindberg and Scheingold (eds.) Regional Integration Theory and Research, Harvard University Press, Cambridge

Schneider, F. & Frey, B. (1985) Economic and Political Determinants of Foreign Direct Investment, World Development, vol. 13, No. 2, Amsterdam, Elsevier

Schraeder, P.J. (1994) United States Foreign Policy Toward Africa: Incrementalism, Crisis and Change (Cambridge: Cambridge University Press

Schwelb, E. (1960) Republican Constitution of Ghana

Scott, W. (1995) Institutions and organizations, Thousand Oaks, CA: Sage

Senbet, L.W. (1997), The Development of Capital Markets in Africa: Constraints and Prospects, Paper Presented at the Meeting of the Expert Group on Capital Markets Development, UNECA, March 26.

Shams, R. (1998) Natural Integration": A New Approach to Integration Policy in Developing Countries, HWWA-Discussion Paper No. 61, Hamburg

Shams, R. (2003) Regional Integration in Developing Countries: Some Lessons based on Case Studies. HWWA Discussion Paper no. 251, Hamburg, Germany: Hamburg Institute of International Economics.

Short, P. (1974) Banda, Routledge, and Kegan Paul, London

Shleifer, A. & Vishny, R.W. (1993) Corruption. Quarterly Journal of Economics, Vol. 109

Sibanda (2014), SADC Mediation in Zimbabwe's Global Political Agreement (GPA): A Reflection on Opportunities and Complexities, Africa's Public Service Delivery and Performance Review

Signe, L. (2019). Africa's Emerging Economies to Take the Lead in Consumer Market Growth. Washington DC: Brookings Institute, Africa in Focus. April 3

Simon, D. (1998) Reflections: Writing (on) the Region. In Simon (ed) South Africa in Southern Africa. Reconfiguring the Region, James Curry, Oxford

Sinn, H.W. (1994) How much Europe? Subsidiarity, Centralization, and Fiscal Competition, Scottish Journal of Political Economy 41 (1)

Smith, A. 1976 [1776] An inquiry into the Nature and Causes of the Wealth of Nations. In The Glasgow edition of the works and correspondence of Adam Smith, Vol. 2, eds. R. H. Campbell, and A. S. Skinner. Oxford: Oxford University Press.

Söderbaum, F, StÅlgren, P. & Van Langenhove, L. (2005) The EU as a Global Actor and the Dynamics of Interregionalism: a Comparative Analysis, Journal of European Integration, 27 (3)

Söderbaum, F. (2007) Regionalism in Africa and EU-African Interregionalism in Mario Telo (ed) European Union and New Regionalism. Regional actors and global governance in a post-hegemonic era, Aldershot: Ashgate, 2nd edition

Söderbaum, F, & Rodrigo, T. (2009) Problematizing Regional Organizations in African Security, African Security 2(2-3)

Soldatos, P. (1989). The Institutional and Political System of the European Communities in a Changing World: Theory and Practice.

Sommer, L. & Luke, D. (2017) Smart Industrialization. Addis Ababa: ECA.

Song, S. (2015) Africa Telecoms Infrastructure in 2014. Africa Telecoms in Review, Many Possibilities, Bruylant, Brussels, Belgium

Söderbaum, F. (2015) Early, Old, New and Comparative Regionalism: The Scholarly Development of the Field, KFG Working Paper Series No. 64, Kolleg-Forschergruppe (KFG) The Transformative Power of Europe, KFG Working Paper

Sousa, R. & Real, P. (2017) United Nations Security Council primacy over military interventions in Africa and the African Peace and Security Architecture (APSA), in Moita, Luís and Pinto, Luís Valença (Coord.) Espaços económicos espaços de segurança, Lisboa, UAL; OBSERVARE

South Africa, DIRCO (Department of International Relations and Cooperation), 'Communiqué of the 37th Summit SADC of Heads of State and Government OR Tambo Building, Department of International Relations and Cooperation (DIRCO) Pretoria, South

Africa, 19th–20th August 2017', 20 August 2017, http://www.dirco.gov.za/docs/2017/sadc0821.htm, accessed 15 September 2020.
Southern African Development Community (2003) Regional Indicative Strategic Development Plan (RISDP). Gaborone: SADC
Southern African Development Community (SADC), Consolidated Text of the Treaty of the Southern African Development Community (Gaborone: SADC, 2011), 6; and SADC, SADC Principles and Guidelines Governing Democratic Elections (Gaborone: SADC, 2000, revised 2015).
Southall, R. & Melber, H. (eds) (2006) Legacies of power: Leadership change and former presidents in African Politics. Cape Town: HSRC Press and Uppsala: The Nordic Africa Institute
Spiezia, V. (2013) ICT investments and productivity, OECD Journal: Economic Studies, (1), 199-211. Retrieved from https://www.oecd-ilibrary.org/economics/ict-investments-and-productivity_eco_studies-2012-5k8xdhj4tv0
Srinivasan, T.N. & Bhagwati, J. (1999) Outward Orientation and Development: Are the Revisionists right? Economic Growth Center Discussion Paper No. 806, Yale University, New Haven.
Starr, M. (2006) Growth and Conflict in the Developing World: Neo-liberal Narratives and Social-Economy Alternatives, Review of Social Economy, The Association for Social Economics, Vol, LXIV, No. 2, Routledge
Statement issued by the South African Department of International Relations and Cooperation https://www.sajbd.org/media/statement-issued-by-the-south-african-department-of-international-relations-and-cooperation-dirco
Steven, R. (1972). The History of the Anglo-South African Conflict over the Proposed Incorporation of the High Commission Territories, in Potholm, C. & Dale, R., (eds). Southern Africa in Perspective: Essays in Regional Politics. New York, The Free Press
Stewart, F. (2002) Horizontal Inequalities: A Neglected Dimension of Development, QEH Working Paper Number 81, Queen Elizabeth House, University of Oxford
Stiglitz, J. (2002) Globalisation and its Discontents, Columbia University
Strachan, A.L. (2018). Relationship between Regional Cooperation and Political Stability and Prosperity, K4D Helpdesk Report, Brighton, UK: Institute of Development Studies

Stremlau, J. (2016). Africa's Democracies: Promises, Progress and Prospects, Electoral Institute for Sustainable Democracy in Africa. Johannesburg, South Africa

Sustainable Development Network,(2014) Potential for regional use of East Africa's Natural Gas briefing paper, May, in Piano and A. Puddington (eds). Freedom House in the World 2004: The Annual Survey of Political Rights and Civil Liberties (Lanham, MD, Rowman and Littlefield, 2004).

Sundaram, A. (2006). Making Order Out of Chaos for the 2006 Election, Inter Press Service News Agency, Monday, August 28, 2006.

Sutherland, P. et al. (2005). The future of the WTO: Addressing institutional challenges in the new millennium, Geneva: WTO Consultative Board.

Sweeney, M. (2008) Private Sector Development in Post-Conflict Countries: A Review of Current Literature and Practice, the Donor Committee for Enterprise and Development, Cambridge, UK

Szentes, T. (2003): World Economics The Political Economy of Development Globalization and System Transformation. Budapest: Akadémiai Kiadó.

Tallberg, J. (2002) Paths to Compliance: Enforcement, Management and the European Union. International Organization, 56(3)

Tallberg, J. (2002) Delegation to Supranational Institutions: Why, How, and With What Consequences? West European Politics 23-46

Tanyanyiwa, V. and Hakuna (2014) Challenges and Opportunities for Regional Integration in Africa: A Case Study of SADC, Journal of Humanities and Social Science (IOSR-JHSS) Volume 19, Issue 12, Ver. IV (Dec. 2014)

Tanter, R. (1972). International System and Foreign Policy Approaches: Implications for Conflict Modelling and Management. World Politics, 24

Te Velde, D. W. & Bezemer, D. (2006) Regional Integration and Foreign Direct Investment in Developing Countries, Transnational Corporations, 15(2)

Teravaninthorn, S. & Raballand, G. (2008) Transport Prices and Costs in Africa: A Review of the Main International Corridors. The World Bank, Washington.

Terlinden, U. (2004) African Regional Parliaments: Engines of Integration and Democratization? Bonn: Friedrich Ebert Stiftung.

Terlinden, U. (2005). African Regional Parliaments/Parliamentary Bodies as Engines of Integration: Current State and Challenges". Paper presented to the Roundtable on the Interface between Regional Parliamentary Bodies and the Pan-African Parliament, Lusaka, Zambia, 8-9 August 2005.

The Commonwealth (2017) A Handbook on Regional Integration in Africa: Towards Agenda

The Historical Evolution of SADC(C) and Regionalism in Southern Africa Kyu Deug Hwang 2007 10: 55International Area Studies Review

The New York Times, Nov 7, 1986, Pretoria Accuses Neighbour of Plot

Thomsen, S. (1994) Regional Integration and Multinational Production, in Vincent Cable and David Henderson, (eds) Trade Blocs? The Future of Regional Integration, London: The Royal Institute of International Affairs

Thomson, A. (2004) An Introduction to African Politics. Routledge

Thonke, O. and Spliid, A. (2012) 'What to expect from regional integration in Africa', African Security Review, 21 (1)

Tieku, T.K. (2013). Theoretical Approaches to Africa's International Relations A Handbook of Africa's International Relations

Tilman (1995) Law and State 32-33.

Timmermans, C.W.A. (2008) Genesis and Development of the European Communities, in Kapteyn & VerLoren van Themaat, The Law of the European Union and the European Communities, Alphen aan den Rijn

Tjønneland, E.N. (2005). Making SADC Work? Revisiting Institutional Reform, In Monitoring Regional Integration in Southern Africa Yearbook (Vol. 5), (Ed, Dirk Hansohm, W.B., Trudi Hartzenberg, Colin McCarthy)

Touré, H.I. (2013). The Role of ICTS in Africa's Development.

Toyo, E. (1993). The International Politics of Capital Drain (Nigerian Society of International Affairs Annual Lecture Series 3. PP. 45

Treaty Establishing the African Economic Community (AEC Treaty) (1991)

Tschirgi, N. (2006): Security and Development Policies.: Untangling the Relationship, in Stephan Klingebiel (ed.) (2006): New interfaces between security and development, Bonn: German Development Institute (Studies 13)

U.S. Department of State (2007) Office of the Coordinator for Counterterrorism, Country Reports

UN Department of Economic and Social Affairs, Population Division (2012) World Urbanization Prospects
UN, (2012) World Economic Situation and Prospects 2012: Update as of mid-2012.
UNCTAD (1971) Trade Expansion and Economic Integration among Developing Countries, TD/B/85/Rev. 1, New York, PP. 6-10.
UNCTAD (2000) World investment report: Cross-border Mergers and Acquisitions and Development, United Nations: New York and Geneva
UNCTAD. (2013a) Foreign Direct Investment to Africa Increases, Defying Global Trend for 2012.
UNCTAD (2018) World Investment Report 2018: Investment and New Industrial Policies. New York and Geneva: UNCTAD.
UNDP (2011) Regional Integration and Human Development: A Pathway for Africa, United Nations Development Programme, New York
UNECA (2010) Economic Report of Africa, Addis Ababa
UNESCO (2005) Towards knowledge societies. Paris, Unesco Publishing.
UNICTAD (2011) Economics Development in Africa Report 2011-Fostering Industrial Development in Africa in the New Global Environment, New York, United Nations Conference on Trade and Development
United Nations (2000b) Report of the Panel of Experts on Violations of Security Council Sanctions against UNITA, S/2000/203, New York: United Nations Secretariat
United Nations Economic Commission for Africa (2008) Annual Report, Addis Ababa, Ethiopia
United Nations Economic Commission for Africa (2016) Innovation, Competitiveness and Regional Integration, Addis Ababa: United Nations Economic Commission for Africa
US Federal Reserve Board (2005) Remarks of Governor Ben Bernanke At the Sandridge Lecture, Virginia Association of Economists, Richmond, Virginia.
Vale, P. Swatuk, L. & Odén, B. (eds.) (2001). Theory, Change and
Southern Africa's Future. New York: St. Martin's Press/Macmillan.
Vale, P. (2003) (manuscript). The First Amongst Unequal
Van Nieuwkerk, A. (2011). Security Co-Operation in the Southern African Development Community: Insights from the New Institutionalism. Scientia Militaria, South African Journal of Military Studies, Vol 34, Nr 2

Van Nieuwkerk, A. (2014). The Strategic Culture of Foreign and Security Policymaking: Examining the Southern African Development Community. African Security, 7(1)

Van Nieuwkerk, A. (2012) A review of South Africa's peace diplomacy since 1994 In C. Landsberg et al., eds. South African Foreign Policy Review: Vol. I. Pretoria: AISA & IGD.

Van Nieuwkerk, A. (2011). The Regional Roots of the African Peace and Security Architecture: Exploring Centre–Periphery Relations. South African Journal of International Affairs, 18(2)

Van Nieuwkerk, A. (2006). Security co-operation in the Southern African Development Community: Insights from the new institutionalism. South African Journal for Military Studies, 34 (2)

Van Niekerk, L. K. & Moreira, E. P. (2002) Regional integration in Southern Africa: Overview of recent developments. Regional Integration and Cooperation Africa Region Discussion Paper, World Bank

Vanheukelom, J. Byiers, B. Bilal, S. & Woolfrey, S. (2016) The political economy of regional integration in Africa: What drives and constrains regional organisations? Synthesis Report, ECDPM.

Vankovska, B. (2007) The Human Security Doctrine for Europe: A View from below. International Peacekeeping 14 (2)

Vickers, B. (2011) Between a Rock and a Hard Place: Small States in the EU-SADC EPA Negotiations 187 The Round Table: The Commonwealth Journal of International Affairs

Vickers, J. and Yarrow, G. (1991) Economic Perspectives on Privatization, Journal of Economic Perspectives, 5

Viljoen, F. (2007) International Human Rights Law in Africa. Oxford: Oxford University Press

Viner, J. (1950) The Customs Union Issue. New York: Carnegie Endowment for International Peace.

Vines, A. (1996) Renamo: From Terrorism to Democracy in Mozambique? London: James Currey.

Von Kirchbach, F. & Roelfson, H. (1998) Trade in the Southern African Development Community: What is the Potential for Increasing Exports to the Republic of South Africa? African Development in a Comparative Perspective, Study no 11. United Nations, Geneva.

Walklate, S. (2011) Reframing Criminal Victimisation: Finding a Place for Vulnerability and Resilience, Theoretical Criminology, 15(2)

Wallerstein, I. (1976): "Semi-Peripheral Countries and the Contemporary World Crisis". Theory and Society, 3(4)

Wallesteen, P. (1998) Preventive Security, Direct and Structural Prevention of Violent Conflicts. Uppsala University

Waltz, K. (1979) Theory of International Politics, Addison-Wesley, New York

Waltz, K. (1992) Realist Thought and Neorealist Theory (Chapter 2 in The Evolution of Theory in International Relations Rothstein, Robert (ed.) University of South Carolina Press

Weber, M. (1947) From Max Weber: Essays in Sociology. Lowe & Brydone, London

Weerakoon, D. (2004) Globalisation and South Asia: the role of foreign direct investment in economic development. South Asian Survey, 11(1)

Wei, S. (2000) How Taxing is Corruption on Internal Investors? Review of Economics and Statistics, 82 (1)

Weinberg, L. (2005). Global terrorism: Beginners guide. England: One world Publications.

Welensky, R. (1964) Welensky's 4000 days: The life and death of the Federation of Rhodesia and Nyasaland, Collins, London

Welz, M. (2013) Integrating Africa: Decolonization's Legacies, Sovereignty and the African Union. Routledge.

Wendt, A. (1999) Social Theory of International Politics. Cambridge: Cambridge University Press

Wentworth L, (2013) 'PERSIA Case Study 2: Financing 2 Wentworth L, 'PERSIA Case Study 2: Financing for Development Policy Management), August

Whalley, J. & Peroni, C. (1994) The New Regionalism: Trade Liberalisation or Insurance, National Bureau of Economic Research, Working Paper No. 4626, January

White, L. and Larmer, M. (2014) Introduction: Mobile Soldiers and Un-National Liberation of Southern Africa, Journal of Southern African Studies, 40 (6)

Wilkin, S. & Minor, J. (2001) Managing Today's Political Risks, AON Trade Credit

Williams, C. (2015) Liberation Movement Camps and the Past of the Present in Southern Africa, in National Liberation in Postcolonial Southern Africa: A Historical Ethnography of SWAPO's Exile Camps (African Studies, Cambridge: Cambridge University Press.

Winters, L.A. (1997) What Can European Experience Teach Developing Countries about Integration?' World Economy 20 (5): 889-912

Winters, L.A & Martins, P.M.G. (2004) When Comparative Advantage is not enough: Business Costs in Small Remote Economies', World Trade Review, 3(3)

Winters, L.A. McCulloch, N. & McKay, A. (2004) Trade liberalization and poverty: The evidence so far, Journal of Economic Literature

Winters, L.A. (2005) Policy Challenges for Small Economies in a Globalising World, in Chand, S. (ed) Pacific Islands Regional Integration and Governance, Asia Pacific Press

World Bank, (2005) Global Economic Prospects: Trade, Regionalism, and Development, The World Bank, Washington, D.C.

World Bank (2013) World Development Indicators, Database

Yannopoulos, G.N. (1990). Foreign Direct Investment and European Integration: The Evidence from the Formative Years of the European Community. Journal of Common Market Studies, Vol. 28

Yeats (1998) What can be Expected from African Trade Arrangements: International Trade Division, The World Bank.

Zantsi, L. (2019). Mkatashinga: Narratives of the Mutiny in ANC Camps in Angola (1983/84). Journal of Global Faultlines,